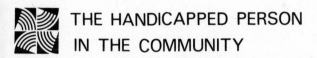

THE HANDICAPPED PERSON
IN THE COMMUNITY

The handicapped person in the community

A reader and sourcebook

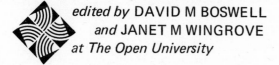 *edited by* DAVID M BOSWELL
and JANET M WINGROVE
at The Open University

Published by Tavistock Publications
in association with The Open University Press

First published in 1974 by
Tavistock Publications Ltd,
11 New Fetter Lane, London EC4
Typeset by Preface Limited, Salisbury and
printed in Great Britain by
Butler & Tanner Ltd, Frome and London

Selection and editorial material
copyright © The Open University 1974
ISBN 0 422 74750 5 (hardback)
     0 422 74760 2 (paperback)

IN MEMORIAM

R. M. Titmuss 1907-1973

R. H. S. Crossman 1907-1974

Who strove for social justice

Acknowledgements

SVEN-OLAF BRATTGAARD, Social and psychological aspects of the situation of the disabled
Lecture given in Australia.

KARL GRUNEWALD, The guiding environment: the dynamic of residential living
Victoria Shennan (ed.) 1972. *Action for the Retarded*. London, NSMHC.

PETER TOWNSEND, The disabled in society
Peter Townsend 1973. *The Social Minority*. London, Pelican Original, Penguin Books. © Peter Townsend.

MICHAEL RUTTER, JACK TIZARD, AND KINGSLEY WHITMORE, The epidemiology of handicap: Summary of findings
Michael Rutter, Jack Tizard, and Kingsley Whitmore (eds.) 1970. *Education, Health, and Behaviour*. London, Longmans.

TONY LYNES, Disabled income
This article first appeared in *New Society*, London. The weekly review of the social sciences.

Care with dignity, an analysis of costs of care for the disabled
The Economist Intelligence Unit Ltd.

ANN SHEARER, Housing to fit the handicapped
The Guardian 26 June 1973.

PETER LARGE, Outdoor mobility: the situation today
Physiotherapy Vol (8); 264—7.

ERVING GOFFMAN, Stigma and social identity
Erving Goffman © 1963. *Stigma: Notes on the management of a spoiled identity* pp. 1—40. Reprinted by permission of Prentice-Hall, Inc., Englewood Cliffs, New Jersey, USA.

LOUIS BATTYE, The Chatterley syndrome
Paul Hunt (ed.) 1966. *Stigma: The experience of disability*. London, Geoffrey Chapman.

RONALD J. COMER AND JANE ALLYN PILIAVIN, The effects of physical deviance upon face-to-face interaction: the other side
Journal of Personality and Social Psychology 1973. 23 (1): 33—9. © 1973 by the American Psychological Association. Reprinted by permission.

ROBERT A. SCOTT, The constructions of conceptions of stigma by professional experts
Jack D. Douglas (ed.) 1970. *Deviance and Respectability: The social construction of moral meanings*. New York, Basic Books.

RONALD MACKEITH, The feelings and behaviour of parents of handicapped children
Developmental Medicine and Child Neurology 1973. **15** (5): 24—7.

ARNOLD BENTOVIM, Handicapped pre-school children and their families: effects on child's early emotional development
British Medical Journal 1972. 3: 634—7.

A. I. ROTH, The myth of parental attitudes
The British Journal of Mental Subnormality 1963. **9** (17): 51—4.

The stress of having a sub-normal child
Stress in Families with a Mentally Handicapped Child (Report of a Working Party). 1967. London, NSMHC.

SHEILA HEWETT, Who will help? The family and the social services, statutory, and voluntary
Sheila Hewett 1970. *The Family and the Handicapped Child*. London, George Allen and Unwin.

Robert
Liz Cooper and Roberta Henderson (eds.) 1973. *Something Wrong?* London, Arrow Books.

SYLVIA KING, In memoriam
DIG Occasional Paper No 11. 1971

ROSALIND CHALMERS, Victim invicta
Paul Hunt (ed.) 1966. *Stigma: The experience of disability*. London, Geoffrey Chapman.

R. S. ILLINGWORTH, The development of the infant and young child, normal and abnormal: interpretation
R. S. Illingworth 1972. *The Development of the Infant*. 5th edition. Edinburgh, Churchill Livingstone.

PETER MITTLER, Purposes and principles of assessment
Peter Mittler (ed.) 1973. *Assessment for Learning in the Mentally Handicapped*. Edinburgh, Churchill Livingstone.

STEPHEN A. RICHARDSON, ALBERT H. HASTORF, AND SANFORD DORNBUSCH, Effects of physical disability on a child's description of himself
Child Development 35: 893—907. © Society for Research in Child Development, Inc., 1964.

JOHN D. KERSHAW, Handicapped children in the ordinary school
V. Varma (ed.) 1973. *Stresses in Children*. London, University of London Press.

ESTER COTTON, Integration of treatment and education in cerebral palsy
Physiotherapy **56** (4): 143—7.

MARGARET M. MORGAN, Like other school-leavers?
Paper read at the thirty-first National Biennial Conference/Course of the Association of Special Education (now the National Council for Special Education) held at Cardiff on 24—7 July 1972.

ANN SHEARER, Sex and handicap
This article first appeared in *New Society*, London. The weekly review of the social sciences.

JOHN DENMARK, The education of deaf children
Hearing **28** (9): 3—12

R. CONRAD, The effect of vocalising on comprehension in the profoundly deaf
British Journal of Psychology **62** (2): 147—50

R. CONRAD, Short-term memory in the deaf: a test for speech coding
British Journal of Psychology **63** (2): 173—80.

GILL RIMMER, The hard of hearing in Britain: are their needs being met?
© Polytechnic of London.

Organisation of Schools for the visually handicapped (*The Vernon Report*)
The Education of the Visually Handicapped 1972. Report of the Committee of Enquiry appointed by

the Secretary of State for Education and Science in October 1968, chapter 5, Department of Education and Science. London, HMSO. Permission of the Controller of HMSO obtained.

Educational provision for the visually handicapped, comments on *The Vernon Report*
  Jointly submitted to the Secretary of State for Education and Science by the National Federation of the Blind of the United Kingdom and the Association of Blind and Partially Sighted Teachers and Students, October 1973.

ROY G. FITZGERALD, Reactions to blindness: an exploratory study of adults with recent loss of sight
  Archives of General Psychiatry 22 (4): 370–9. © 1970, American Medical Association.

LEWIS ANTHONY DEXTER, A social theory of mental deficiency
  American Journal of Mental Deficiency 1958. 63: 920–8.

NORMA V. RAYNES AND ROY D. KING, Residential care for the mentally retarded
  First International Congress for the Scientific Study of Mental Deficiency, Montpellier. *Report* 637–49.

ALBERT KUSHLICK, The need for residential care
  Victoria Shennan (ed.) 1972. *Action for the Retarded*. London, NSMHC.

ALISON C. ROSEN, Residential provision for mentally handicapped adults
  G. McLachlan (ed.) 1972. *Approaches to Action: A symposium on services for the mentally ill and handicapped*. London, Oxford University Press for the Nuffield Provincial Hospitals Trust.

ROBERT B. EDGERTON, Passing and denial: the problem of seeming to be normal
  Robert D. Edgerton 1967. *The Cloak of Competence: Stigma in the lives of the mentally retarded*. Originally published by the University of California Press, reprinted by permission of The Regents of the University of California.

Concepts of rehabilitation and reasons for the failure of the present provision
  Rehabilitation Report of a Sub-Committee of the Standing Medical Advisory Committee. (The Tunbridge Report). 1972. Parts of chapters 3 and 4. Department of Health and Social Security, Welsh Office, Central Health Services Council. London, HMSO. Permission of the Controller of HMSO obtained.

J. G. SOMERVILLE, The rehabilitation of the hemiplegic patient
  The British Council for the Rehabilitation of the Disabled.

GILLIAN S. JOHNSON AND RALPH H. JOHNSON, Paraplegics in Scotland: a survey of employment and facilities
  British Journal of Social Work 3 (1): 19–38.

P. J. R. NICHOLS, Assessment of the severely disabled
  P. J. R. Nichols 1971. *Rehabilitation of the Severely Disabled*. Part II *Management*. London, Butterworths.

LEE MYERSON, NANCY KERR, AND JACK L. MICHAEL, Behaviour modification in rehabilitation
  Sidney W. Bijou and Donald M. Baer (eds.) © 1967. *Child Development: Readings in experimental analysis*. Reprinted by permission of Prentice-Hall, Inc., Englewood Cliffs, New Jersey, USA.

OGDEN R. LINDSLEY, Geriatric behavioural prosthetics
  Abridged from Ogden R. Lindsley, Geriatric Behavioural Prosthetics. In R. Kastenbaum (ed.) *New Thoughts on Old Age* pp. 41–60. © 1964 by Springer Publishing Company, Inc., 200 Park Avenue South, New York. Used with permission.

J. L. GEDYE, The 'university contribution' to the definition of objectives for the disabled
  Paper presented at a symposium on 'Defining Objectives in the Field of Handicap', British Psychological Society Annual Conference, pp. 5–9, April 1973.

IRENE H. BERMINGHAM, Organisation and development: systems analysis and planning for the intellectually handicapped
  Rehabilitation International 1972. Report of a conference held in Australia 27 August–1 September 1968.

ANTHONY FORDER, T. RETI, AND J. R. SILVER, Communication in the health service: a case study of the rehabilitation of paraplegic patients
  Social and Economic Administration 3: 3—16

ISABEL E. P. MENZIES, Nurses under stress: a social system functioning as a defence against anxiety
  International Nursing Review 7 (6): 9—16.

PETER TOWNSEND, The political sociology of mental handicap: a case study of policy failure
  Peter Townsend 1973. *The Social Minority*. London, Pelican Original, Penguin Books. © Peter Townsend.

WALTER JAEHNIG, Seeking out the disabled
  Kathleen Jones (ed.) 1972. *Year Book of Social Policy in Britain*. London, Routledge and Kegan Paul.

ROSALIND BROOKE, Civic rights and social services
  William·A. Robson and Bernard Crick (eds.) 1970. *The Future of the Social Services*. London, Penguin. © *The Political Quarterly*.

GERALDINE M. AVES, The volunteer
  Geraldine M. Aves 1969. *The Voluntary Worker in the Social Services*. London, George Allen and Unwin.

JONATHAN BUTLIN, Aid for the disabled
  School Technology 1971. 2: 78—82.

DOROTHY E. S. HODGES, Handicapped adventure
  Social Work Today 13 (10): 7—10.

Setting up a good neighbour scheme
  National Council of Social Service, 1972. *Time to Care: A handbook on good neighbour schemes*. London, National Council of Social Services.

Contents

PART NINE
Policy, practice and community involvement in the social services

Introduction

DAVID M. BOSWELL
Lecturer in Sociology at
The Open University

This reader has been designed to meet a demand for information, on the situation, services and needs of handicapped people, required in training courses that are generic in either or both of the following ways: (a) across the range of various forms of handicap experienced by the population of Britain, (b) across the range of different professions, agencies and persons involved with handicapped people. It is specifically intended as a sourcebook for the first of the Open University's post-experience courses in this field. A wide range of material is drawn together to play a useful educational function in this and similar courses. We have, where possible, selected items that relate to the situation of and services for handicapped people in Britain but we do not claim that these items all attain the same level of conceptual sophistication, research expertise, efficiency and right-mindedness, if such goals are conceivable! Taken together these items represent something useful to work on.

The contents are best understood in the light of the objectives and content of the course. *The Handicapped Person in the Community* offers a new approach to in-service training in a field where changing public attitudes and new legislation have produced an urgent need for more professional skills. It is intended primarily for people whose professional activities bring them into contact with handicapped people — social workers, teachers, therapists, health visitors, nurses, doctors and members of other supportive professions. It will also interest some administrators, personnel officers, those engaged in vocational guidance and rehabilitative training and people involved in a variety of types of voluntary work.

Our main objective is to improve professional and social skills in order to assist handicapped people to achieve maximum autonomy. This basic principle is well illustrated by short papers by two of the leading advocates of rehabilitation and environmental modification in Sweden, Brattgard and Grunewald, with which the book begins. We assume that most readers will be familiar with some of the problems faced by handicapped people, but expect that this knowledge may be limited to a particular professional approach or to one specific form of handicap. What is required is an examination of professional roles and ideologies that will encourage an inter-professional approach to problems. We hope that this book will enlarge their capacity for informed cooperation with other workers, with disabled people and with the wider community and also provide a basis for those who may take a lead in involving their local community in action for the improvement and expansion of the sorts of service that handicapped people require.

Although we have given particular consideration to readers who will be working through this book according to the recommendations of their Open University course, we have grouped the individual items in ways suitable for other readers. We have not, therefore, directly followed the structure of the Open University course because the related correspondence texts, activities and supplementary material may not be readily available to general readers. In particular, we have brought together items relating to the prevalence and special needs of handicapped people living and moving in the community in Part Two immediately following the statement of basic principles.

These items indicate the difficulties in investigating the existing aims and state of services for handicapped people in Britain. Prevalence of handicap, incomes, access and accommodation require immediate attention if handicapped people are going to have the chance of ordering their own lives. Without the easing of current constraints, prevailing professional and societal priorities will determine how handicapped people may be dealt with most conveniently and the present choice between domestic abandonment and institutional dumping will remain the dominant one facing the disabled and their families.

Parts Three, Four and Five, on perceptions and conceptions of impairment, families with handicapped members, and the education and development of handicapped children, may be seen as interlocking because, broadly speaking, they represent different viewpoints of what it means to be cared for or to grow up handicapped. We have drawn on a wide range of different professional and academic accounts and recommendations as well as the personal experiences of handicapped people and their families. In addition to studying the self-conceptions of those with some serious impairment it is important to examine the ways in which they become labelled. Some labelling processes, i.e. modes of assessment, can be used positively to identify the functions that are jeopardized by an impairment and the programmes of action that may be instituted to counteract a loss of function and its impact on people. The themes of rehabilitation, initial habilitation and education run through the book and readers with particular interests will find cross-references to relevant items in the introduction to each part.

The three parts devoted to sensory impairment, incompetence and residential care, rehabilitation and behaviour modification refer to the situation of and services for those whose mental, sensory and motor functions have been impaired. These parts of the book should be seen as attempts to consider some of the particular needs of people with these disabilities, and as such carry implications for some of the relevant services: e.g. residential care, the establishment of objectives and appropriate caring regimes, educational methods and organization, individual assessments and programmes of rehabilitation and training. Although each set of needs and each service may be considered in relation to one form of disability,

they contribute to a general review of the range of services potentially required by each person. Similarly, the particular characteristics of each impairment contribute to an understanding of the general pattern of disablement as well as what, incidentally, is assumed to be normal. Because the fields of mental illness and geriatric care are so large we have decided they require separate treatment, with the result that both are considered in this book only in so far as they have a general bearing on the situation of other handicapped people with whom they share problems and services.

The final part on organizational analysis, policy and practice in the social services, and community and voluntary work, should be assessed in conjunction with the first two parts of the book. We live in what are, hopefully, exciting times for the disabled in Britain but it is too early to chart exactly what is going on and, more particularly, what long-term achievements are being established. We have no doubt that the greatest achievements will be those that permit handicapped people and their families to decide what they will do, where they will go and what they will work at. It is only by attaining this position of autonomy that they will be able to go their own way like other citizens, without being largely dependent on the attitudes, resources and prejudices of those fortunate enough to be able-bodied and supposedly mentally alert, whose services are discretionary with many strings attached to them. The battle that disabled people are now waging for themselves is one that has been waged in the past for employment, income maintenance, health and education. Its target is the 'public burden model of welfare' that Richard Titmuss exposed in his essay on the 'Welfare State and Welfare Society'. What they seek are their civic rights and the provision of the necessary infrastructure upon which they may build their own lives, and thus be able to contribute to what may then be considered their society on equal terms with other citizens. This aim is exemplified by the legislative measures in the Appendix.

Several items in the book indicate something of this hope, but Part Nine stresses it. Apart from the discussion of objectives and preferred types of service provision, most investigations have demonstrated the inadequacy of existing policies and practices rather than the implementation of new ones. But the aim of the course to which this book relates is to further a consideration of new policies and practices. We have therefore drawn together material enquiring into the objectives of rehabilitation, contributions to the systematic organization of services and their deficiencies, and the reasons why legislation and policy directives are circumvented and appear stillborn. We have also illustrated some very different modes of voluntary action that may be provided with the assistance of professional skills by neighbours, parental groups and school children.

But we do not see anything like the Child Poverty Action Group coming over the horizon until after the adoption of a generic approach to the status of handicapped people and their services, although the Disabled Income Group and various joint committees have made significant advances in the fields of pensions and mobility. We should heed the observation of Belknap, writing of the mental hospital situation in the USA in 1956, 'The cycle has repeated itself too often to be fortuitous. The sequence of exposé, reform, progress, indifference, apathy and decline has been repeated with variations in a dozen states of the Union in the past twenty years.' With the reorganization of local government and the national health service and the creation of the social service departments, an opportunity has been presented which must be taken, with proper central funding to establish what is required. We should like to have devoted more space to considering these administrative and structural changes as well as to the whole process of planning in the social services, but this has proved too difficult at this stage. Most of the discussion is at a high level of generality, or is concerned with larger categories of the general population than the minority who are disabled. This is particularly the case where the subject is the role of social scientists in planning (e.g. as in Rossi 1972, Donnison 1972 and Platt 1972). Nevertheless we hope that many of the problems and issues arising from attempts to define needs and plan services for handicapped people in the community will be apparent in various items in different parts of this book, which are specifically concerned with particular age categories, types of disability, for forms of service.

In selecting, collating, editing and introducing this reader, we have been considerably assisted by many of those contributing to the course whom we should like to acknowledge:
Members of the Open University course team: Richard Argent, Vida Carver, John Chapman, Sheila Dale, Judith Fage, Nick Farnes, Jean Jordan, Keith Livingstone, Caroline Pick, Geoffrey Tudor, and the chairman, Phillip Williams.
Consultants: Martin Bax, John Gill, Peggy Jay, Walter Jaehnig, Albert Kushlick, Peter Large, Eric Miller, Peter Mittler, Fred Reid, Michael Rodda, Rae Walker and James Woodward.
The final stages of preparation have been facilitated by Margaret Johnson and Roger Lubbock of the OU publishing division, Diane Goldrei, Brenda Madden and Marion Latimer.

This reader is but one component of a multimedia course which also includes personal tuition, correspondence instructional texts, BBC radio and television programmes and other prescribed books, including the following specific monographs as set books dealing with particular situations of handicapped children and adults:

ANDERSON, E. (1973) *The disabled Schoolchild*, London, Methuen.
MILLER, E. J. and GWYNNE, G. V. (1971) *A Life Apart: a pilot study of residential institutions for the physically handicapped and the young chronic sick*, London, Tavistock Publications.
JAY, P. (1974) *Coping with Disablement*, London, Consumers' Association.

and one highly recommended general text:
YOUNGHUSBAND, E., BIRCHALL, D., DAVIE, R. and KELLMER PRINGLE, M. L. (eds) (1970) *Living with Handicap: the report of a working party on children with special needs*. London, National Children's Bureau.

Items for this reader have therefore not been selected from these books, which are complementary to it.

REFERENCES

BELKNAP, I. (1956) *Human Problems of a State Mental Hospital*, New York, McGraw-Hill, p. vii.

Department of the Environment (1971) *Local Government in England* (Chairman: Lord Redcliffe-Maud), Cmnd 4585, London, HMSO.

Department of Health and Social Security (1971) *National Health Service Reorganization: Consultative Document*, London.

Department of Health and Social Security (1972) *Management Arrangements for the Reorganized Health Service*, London, HMSO.

DONNISON, D. (1972) 'Research for policy' *Minerva*, 10, pp 519—36.

Home Department, Department of Education and Science, Ministry of Housing and Local Government, Ministry of Health (1968), *Report of the Committee on Local Authority and Allied Personal Services* (Chairman: Sir Frederick Seebohm), Cmnd. 3703, London, HMSO.

PLATT, J. (1972) 'Survey data and social policy' *British Journal of Sociology*, 23, pp 77—92.

ROSSI, P. H. (1972) 'Testing for success and failure in social action' in Rossi, P. H. and Williams, (eds) (1972) *Evaluating Social Programs*, New York, Seminar Press.

TITMUSS, R. M. (1968) 'Welfare State and Welfare Society' in *Commitment to Welfare*, London, Allen & Unwin, pp 124—37.

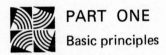

PART ONE

Basic principles

1. Social and psychological aspects of the situation of the disabled*

SVEN-OLAF BRATTGARD
Professor, Department of Handicap Research, University of Gothenburg, and Chairman of the Fokus Society.

When basic social services are discussed the starting point is very often technical aids and arrangements, planning of buildings and surroundings or financial resources. All these questions are very important. I will start the discussion from another point — the social and psychological problems which must be solved by the social services so that we can give the disabled the chance of a real life. In order to secure a basis for such a discussion the social and psychological division of the Department for Handicap Research has made a series of investigations. Some of these investigations deal with the social and psychological problems of parents with disabled children or young people, other investigations have been concentrated on the problems of young severely physically disabled people or of middle-aged people with disabilities.

A disabled person runs the risk of isolation in the community and segregation from other people. All psychological and sociological investigations show the impossibility of improving the individual resources of a person if he lacks stimulating contacts with other human beings. One of the most important things for the disabled is to receive full support so that he can live as normal a life as possible in the community and in co-operation with others.

The disabled who wishes to have a real life must accept his mode of life, his abilities and the people around him.

It is very important that the disabled does not look upon his situation as a static one. He must also give more interest to his abilities than to his disabilities. He is a man with other abilities than those of the non-disabled, but he is not without abilities. The social and psychological situation of the disabled will be a better one if those who meet him do not fix their interest on his disabilities but on his abilities. In our medical nursing system the rule is to concentrate interest on those functions which have been diminished or lost. It is important that the nurse at the maternity clinic, the teacher in the school, the doctor at the hospital and the social assistant heed, not only their words, but also their reactions when they meet a child or an adult with disabilities. The only way of achieving the right attitude to the disabled is to accept him as a collaborator and fellow member of the community; a man who can take full responsibility for his life and his actions.

Of importance to the disabled himself is his readiness to demonstrate that he has abilities. Many disabled people are anxious and ask for a social system with complete security. They have very often been persuaded that such a security is necessary for them. It is very interesting to note that this distrust of the disabled is shared by many of the disabled themselves. They distrust their fellows as well as themselves. Many therefore ask for some type of institution which takes care of them and are satisfied there. From sociological and psychological points of view these total institutions are not good. Our investigations show that it takes years of hard work to rehabilitate and resocialize a person who has spent several years in such an institution. The disabled must be taught to take full responsibility for his actions and choices. All general nursing systems in which the disabled person is sequestered must be avoided. The way to a free and independent life is not to be well cared

*From the Fokus Society, Sweden, pp. 1—4

for. The right way is to train the disabled to take care of himself.

In my country we have tried to help the disabled to find his own way by making it possible for him to live in integration with non-disabled people. This integration starts already in pre-school and goes on during further schooling. Integrated flats for disabled adults are also very important. More difficult but of equal importance is to find a way of integration during working hours and in leisure time activities. When we now follow up the results of such efforts we will find several of interest and importance to the subject.

The interest and readiness shown by doctors, politicians and many others to spend money and other resources on giving the disabled a real chance of a social life stand in glaring contrast to the interest shown in giving resources to advanced medical measures. Most of the money spent on medical treatment and medical rehabilitation will be of little value if we forget our duty to bring the disabled person back to a social life and give him the possibility of living such a life.

Another interesting result of our investigations was the discovery that most people look upon integration as being a question of technical problems. They believe that integration will be initiated automatically if only we give the disabled technical aids, adapted flats and remove the obstacles confronting him when taking his place in society. All these measures are of considerable importance, but the results of our investigations compel us to emphasize that integration is a psychological process and that most disabled people need psychological help as well as technical aids. Many attempts of integration have failed when this fundamental fact was forgotten.

Yet another valuable finding when organizing social activities is that people so easily forget that integration is a time consuming process. On leaving the sheltered environment of schools or rehabilitation clinics many disabled believe that their lives outside these institutions will automatically become easier and better than inside them. Very few have had a real chance of living independently and must therefore be trained gradually for such a way of life before they can take the final step out of institutions and into society.

In the systems of nursing and integration the disabled person has to play several different roles. In the customary institution he is a passive receiver of help and assistance. When living freely and independently, the disabled person—like all others—has to ask for service. Our investigations show that many disabled people starting their integrated lives find it difficult to exchange the passive role of a receiver for the active one of ordering service. We found that nurses and service assistants have the same problem although the direction is here reversed. A well-educated and well-trained nurse who is familiar with her role of thinking and acting for the disabled will have considerable psychological trouble when she has to take her place as a service assistant to the disabled. If we are unable to teach and train the disabled as well as the service staff for these new roles we will lose the possibility of a real integration. This training is therefore a very important part of the rehabilitation process.

If we wish to give the disabled the chance of a social life the most important thing is to give him a home of his own and not a room or a bed in an institution. In Sweden, during the last four or five years, we have made an interesting experiment. The Fokus Society has arranged well-adapted flats — altogether 280 flats in thirteen cities — for severely disabled people. The flats are integrated with those of the non-disabled and every disabled person has a flat of his own. Fifteen such flats for disabled people are located to one house in order to make the day and night service easier. All disabled tenants come from nursing homes or the homes of their parents. The psychological effect of getting a home of their own and living in the same apartment building as non-disabled people can never be under-estimated. I must point out, however, that many of these severely disabled persons encounter many difficulties during their first six to twelve months in this new environment. For the first time many of them have to take full responsibility for their own lives, plan their time, order their purchases, clean their clothes, and so on. None of the 300 young disabled persons in the thirteen cities, who have been involved in these experiments, wish to return to their earlier situation.

From this extensive experiment we find that nearly as important as the flat itself are the opportunities for the disabled to get out of it. In the above mentioned cities the transportation system was arranged in such a way that the disabled tenant can order a ride in special buses or call for a taxi when he wants to go out. When such transportation was unobtainable the disabled suffered considerable difficulties. Our investigations have proved how very important it is for the disabled — especially in integrated flats — to get out whenever they wish and go wherever they like. The feeling of independence thus obtained is of the greatest importance to their life as a whole.

For many disabled, and young people especially, the problems of love and sex cause difficulties. Many nursing or service members of rehabilitation teams hesitate to discuss this kind of problem with the disabled. They are afraid of what will happen if they really accept that the disabled has the same feelings and reactions as the non-disabled. In such a situation the easiest way is to avoid the questions. But this is impossible if we want to help the disabled to live a real life. From our investigations and experiences with housing and service for the severely disabled we found that many frustrations are reduced when the disabled have their own homes where they can have normal contacts with people of the other sex. The experience thus gained affords them a true knowledge of their capacities and may in its turn engender a valuable feeling of self-confidence. Many of them will also find that sexual activities are important but not necessary for their love of another person.

The problems confronting the disabled who has to go out and find a job are considerable. From the view-point of our findings I will focus interest on some special points. One of them is the habitual attitude to work itself. Most people must work for their livelihood. For many disabled this is not the situation. They have their pensions or are taken care of in institutions. Two other things are more important for them. At work they meet other people and learn to know them. The work itself — as well as the money they earn for it — contributes to their self-reliance and self-esteem. From these two aspects the sheltered workshop is not as good as the open market. A real integration in the working situation is of equal importance to integration in education, housing and leisure time activities. The sheltered workshops are often the easiest way to avoid solving the problems of the disabled and at the same time afford us the impression that we are doing something for them. We have here a situation analogous to the nursing system, where living in institutions removes the problems of housing and service without solving the real problem.

Many disabled have an abundance of leisure hours but few opportunities of doing anything during them. From a psychological point of view it is very important for them to share leisure activities with other people. Interest in and practice of sports or different cultural activities are specially useful. It is, however, necessary to train the disabled for such activities. In rehabilitation it is therefore important to afford the disabled this kind of stimulation at the same time as we give him training and exercise for the reduced abilities he may have in muscles or joints.

In my country we have a disability pension system which gives the disabled person a relatively good support. The disability pension, however, is not large enough to give the recipient a chance of paying for the total cost of living. We therefore have a subsidiary system for rent, transportation, personal assistance and technical aids. This system, necessary as it is today, is not good from a psychological point of view. A system of this kind reduces the possibilities for the disabled person to make his own choices. A larger pension and fewer subsidies are much better for him. He must then take full responsibility for the use of his money.

The basic social service must give the disabled a real chance of living a social life. This can only be done when the community is prepared to accept the disabled as a person with the same requirements and demands as other people; the same right to his own home with the necessary personal help and the possibilities of communicating with other people. The community and its doctors, social assistants, politicians and other such persons must give the disabled a possibility of choosing his own way and taking responsibility for this choice. We have to avoid every form of guardianship over him, but this does not mean that we should leave him alone with his problems. We must give him help and psychological support when he asks for it. The medical rehabilitation must go on side by side with the social rehabilitation process. Of great importance to the disabled is a home of his own. ADL-functions and transportation assistance are also important. These two types of service are necessary for a normal contact with other people. If we wish to give the disabled an independent existence and a chance of finding his own way in life, we must also give him psychological support. The basic social services afforded him by society must be organized in such a way that he can make his own decisions and be responsible for his own life.

2. The guiding environment: the dynamic of residential living*

KARL GRUNEWALD
Director, Mental Retardation Care Services,
Swedish Board of Health and Welfare.

All types of provisions for services to handicapped individuals can be said to pass through certain stages of development. The first stage — and in Scandinavia it started 100 years ago — features identification of the particular problems that a specific group of individuals have. The first stage might be called the *diagnostic stage* since it is then that diagnoses are made and plans are formulated to meet particular needs.

The second stage is one of *specialisation* as particular needs are met by special solutions specific for those needs. This leads to centralisation of the services; for example, a single institution might be decided upon for the whole country or for a certain part of the country. The second stage is dominated by specialists to whom the consumers of services must subordinate themselves and, thus, the other needs of the handicapped individuals become of secondary interest to the experts.

The third stage can be called the stage of *differentiation*. At this stage it is realised that a particular service cannot be standardised for all recipients. Factors affecting differentiation are, for instance, different age groups; need for interaction of medical, educational, and social specialists; and the degree of retardation itself. The Scandinavian countries are presently in the stage of differentiation while other countries close to Scandinavia are mainly in the specialisation stage.

Finally, provisions for services to individuals with different handicaps reach the fourth, and

*From Victoria Shennan (ed.), (1972) *Subnormality in the 70's: action for the retarded*, London, National Society for Mentally Handicapped and World Federation of Mental Health, pp. 27—33

what we think of today as the last, stage. It is a composite one characterised first by *decentralisation* of services, then provision for *integration* of services to the handicapped with those similar services which non-handicapped individuals receive from the community. This stage we have only started to formulate and tackle. In order to effect decentralisation and then integration in community services there must be enough trained personnel who can offer services in a given geographical area, a transportation system for the handicapped, and a general state of readiness and relative open-mindedness among the population.

Institutions and development

It is easy to generalise, as I have done here, and declare our existing institutions bankrupt. It takes at least two generations to build a system of institutions in a country; it takes one generation to formulate what's wrong in the system, and another generation before one can make real what one has succeeded in formulating. It is not enough to tear down our institutions however, we must build up a new type of service based upon the knowledge we have today of the mentally retarded person's potential to develop.

Mental retardation as a function of personal relations

We all agree that the only thing that mentally retarded individuals have in common is a hampering of the development of intelligence. It is not those who labour with intelligence structures, but rather those psychologists who theorise that intelligence is the effect of a system of processes who have contributed the most to our understanding of methods for creating therapeutic environments.

Compared to one with normal development, a person with slow development of intelligence has a greater number of failures and consequently is more dependent upon his environment. If the environment is a poor one or the individuals within it are unwilling to understand the handicapped child, then the latter's readiness for failure is increased and positive aspects of his behaviour are not reinforced.

Behaviour is formed in a constant process of interaction between the individual and his environment. All mentally retarded individuals can develop and learn something, only it takes them longer and puts greater demands upon the environment than it does with non-retarded persons. We must focus upon these facts when forming suitable environments for the mentally retarded.

Thus, in practice, we must always view mental retardation in relation to the person's environment. This means that the environment we create for the individual must always be evaluated according to the same principles and with the same accuracy we use in evaluating retardation itself. The more complicated the environment, the more retarded the handicapped will function or — as in developing countries — the less complicated the environment, the fewer the individuals who will function as retardates.

The principle of the small group

There is an old observation made by those who work in institutions that severely retarded individuals appreciate a 'small environment' where the number of interactions with other people is few. Many workers have observed the positive effect on a severely retarded individual when he was moved from a large ward of 20 to 30 persons to a small group of ten or less (five to eight would be preferable). Suddenly the retardate's reactions become predictable and one sees that he can recognise and grasp reality. Observations such as these have led psychologists to formulate the *Principle of the small group*.

From these observations we deduce that an influence for favourable development is to be found partly in the small number of interpersonal relations forced upon the retardate thus making them potentially stimulating rather than frustrating, and partly in the homelike atmosphere and

equipment of the room and of the unit to which the room is connected.

The homeliness — or homelikeness — may need to be modified when one considers certain more or less permanent medical needs, and such technical arrangements as necessary to provide a suitable environment for individuals with certain additional handicaps. What is important when planning for residential living is that the starting point be an environment, normal, homelike, and small.

When reviewing our provision for care in historical perspective we are astonished to learn that it is the size of the group cared for that constitutes the greatest failure in our provision for care. First, large inhumane collective wards were established having extremely poor physical facilities. These collectives were in no sense necessary, but they fitted well into the value pattern of many generations — that mentally retarded persons were regarded as subhuman persons with deprived sensory and aesthetic experiences. Actually the retarded became more so in the unorganised, complex environment and thus could neither express feelings nor have experiences in a manner that would be called human.

To summarise, we might very well say that we do not have any mentally retarded people, but we do have retarded environments or surroundings. Of course, this is particularly true in regard to our institutions. Being inside such a collective ward, one is sometimes tempted to ask which is the most retarded, the person living there or his environment!

Heterogeneous groups

In a guided environment interpersonal relations among residents play an outstanding role, perhaps even more so than relations between residents and staff. The prerequisite for the favourable environment is that the composition of the small group — those who live together in a unit (ward) — is carefully planned. Within the limits of the children's or adults' grouping, the small group has to be as heterogeneous as possible. This philosophy is in opposition to that of segregating those with physical handicaps, the blind, the deaf, etc., into special units. A distribution of these 'minorities' among all units limits the number of multi-handicapped persons in each unit and gives them an environment more active and rich in stimuli than otherwise. The prerequisites for this arrangement are that enough specialists and specialised services be available and that the ward be properly equipped to take care of the additional handicaps.

The one group with which one may have to break this fundamental principle is the group of deaf adults and school age children — but of this group we know too little as yet.

As to the degree of retardation within a group — the most hampered should always be in a minority within the group so that they may be 'drawn upwards' by the other group members. And the span of retardation should not be larger than the group activities permit for maximal benefits to the individual group member.

We have started a very careful mixing of the sexes in the mildly and moderately retarded groups and some of them are allowed to live as married.

Learning and application

Psychologists have taught us the importance of a clearly structured learning situation for the individual. Research shows us how much we can achieve with the gravest retarded persons by individualising and simplifying the influence techniques. Psychologists and educators are producing increasing amounts of carefully programmed and systematised learning sequences based upon exact pretraining analysis of the level each retardate has reached in his various capabilities. These clearly structured sequences must be realised in both individual and group situations. Applications of these structured influences must be made in a small group and in an environment very rich in stimuli as e.g. in a surrounding that contains all that is found in a normal home and which makes possible normal self and group activity. In these situations the child or the young persons should have the opportunity to experience what the psychologists call 'transfer' to related situations.

The point is that the pupil does not have to change his conceptual structure in order to apply what he has learned, as these must be basically the same in one situation as another. There must be slight concrete changes, however, in order to be transferable to increasingly different situations. This transfer ability determines the potential for development of intelligence and eventually for the integration of different abilities at increasingly higher levels. Thus one can say that good adapta-

tion requires transfer training; that transfer requires a small environment rich in stimuli; and that individualised, well-structured, and meaningful influence techniques are required in order for the handicapped individual to achieve the greatest benefit from the stimuli of a small environment.

I want to stress that the application milieu must be a socially real and concrete environment. It is not possible to build up substitute situations within institutions. The retarded individual needs training in a situation identical to that in which he is going to function, at his own pace however. This means that we must offer our severely retarded persons social environments and situations where they may apply freely and in a natural way that which they have learned in the specific instructional situation. This application concept is an important consideration when determining where in our community a hostel or residential home for retarded individuals is to be located.

Consequences for residential planning

Attempts to construct socially real applicational environments have already been made in Sweden. We have built a residential home for severely retarded children that is situated in a normal private residential area in a town. Streets, sidewalks, and traffic are part of the regular pattern in the community. The children can watch traffic from the windows or be taken outside on to the sidewalks to experience natural light and sounds, to play in the yard or exchange greetings with neighbours and passersby. They have the opportunity to visit shops along with the staff members as the latter go to buy magazines, etc. Thus the children have some of the opportunities a normal child experiences in a close community.

Another home, partly for severely retarded children less than seven years of age, consists of three houses in an ordinary block of row houses.

These examples of placing smaller residential units in the centres of our communities are only hints of how to give the most severely retarded children and adults a concrete and close educational environment.

The planning of comprehensive services

How are we to build up our services if we accept these fundamental principles of learning mentioned before? First, we cannot run systematic programmes of guidance without considering the emotional ties of the child or young person. Therefore it is quite evident that services of the future will support parents to a much greater extent than presently. These children who cannot stay at home continuously will at first be taken into residential units for short-term care and for observation or relief care. Educators will teach those children who cannot come to a group, in their homes, and the parents will be offered courses individually or in groups.

We must plan our services by starting from the normal community. The flow and development of increasingly comprehensive services should be moving from outside the institution inwards and not from within out towards society. This means that specialists who organise services and supervise staff must not be tied to institutions. All services for retarded persons must be regarded as of equal importance and the priority for serving residents in a residential home on a 24-hour-a-day basis must be broken. The development of care at home and other kinds of day care will benefit. This concept of serving the retardate in the community also means that we should put greater demands on all kinds of specialists whose skills we can use in our provision of services and buy such services as far as possible instead of building up a specialist service of our own. Personally, I think the time has passed when there are reasons for a particular speciality, categorising doctors who worked with retardates, some kind of oligophrenia doctors. We need exactly the same specialists for retarded persons as for other children and adults. What retarded individuals have in common — retardation in development of intelligence — is not in itself of medical interest.

The emphasis on provisions for services should be transferred to the community. The retarded individual should be regarded only as one among all others who needs some form of support or service. It is not enough to normalise the retarded person but we must also normalise our services and the entire organisation of services. In reality, the retarded persons are part of the total community and can help us in a process of de-intellectualisation that I think is necessary for the good of all.

When planning and forming future services for mentally retarded individuals two important factors must be considered: one is that we

apparently will have less severe retardates in the future. According to certain Swedish statistics we have a concentration of the most severely retarded in the age group 15 to 25 years old. In older groups there appears to have been a very high death rate. With the age groups below 15, we have been more active in habilitation and have given better prophylactic care. Possible contributory causes to the concentration of severely retarded in the 15 to 25 year age group are that these individuals did not benefit from recent improvements in premature care, which now save the lives of many children, and the widespread use of penicillin and other antibiotics. In the future I think we will have a decreasing number of additional severely retarded individuals each year. At the same time we can expect an improvement in the functioning level of the severely retarded individuals for whom we now provide.

The other factor is that we must be consistent when we build up services for retarded individuals in separating residential living, occupation, and leisure time. This applies also as much as possible to 24-hour institutions for the retarded. We want a geographical distance, for instance, between the school and the residential home as well as between all other types of living and the daily occupation. It also means that as far as possible we want to use the community's leisure-time and recreational facilities. Our goal is to have leisure time spent out in the community, preferably individually but otherwise in groups.

The dynamics of living

The dynamics of residential living are initiated and developed by our creation of small heterogeneous environments so rich in stimuli that the retarded individual assimilates the benefits of the environment and can advance to a new and even more normal setting. In the future we will need many relatively small units located in the middle of society, which are more or less specialised for the functional level and actual needs of the retardate. This means that the retarded individual, as he progresses, will have to move more often than he has had reason to so far. Movement is regarded as a disadvantage by many people who think it is good and a matter of security for the retarded person to live and stay in one place for his entire life. We ourselves, however, often experience economic or personal development and renewal when we change places of work and residence. So the experience should not be specifically restricted to the non-handicapped.

1. WITH CHILDREN

In the future children will not have to live in special residential homes but will live at home to a greater extent, or as an alternative. Today we have had good experience with group homes housing four to six children in each unit, located in ordinary flats in apartment buildings and private houses. In each service district at least one central unit is needed with seven-day homes relatively near a training school.

In this respect some of our educators have given guiding examples. They have proven that all children aged seven to seventeen can be instructed. This means that every child should receive some form of educational stimulus with the contents adapted to the needs of the child and the time limits set for what the child can manage. From this information I conclude that our architects must design future group homes so that even the most severely retarded children can live in them. There is no longer any reason to separate these children from the less-retarded. The special medical services they need can be given in one house as well as in another. Of course a certain age differentiation will be needed, but in principle one should strive towards heterogeneous family-like groups. That children should not live in the same area as adult retardates I see as self-evident.

Apart from these group homes, places (units) in hospitals are needed for those retarded children who also are ill. These hospital units should be used for short-time care for children who otherwise would live in group homes or in their own homes, and also for longer term care for the multihandicapped, especially those who are seriously physically disabled and epileptic. The care in these hospital units would be integrated with medical care for children in the community. If there is a demand for a whole unit then the unit should be attached to a facility for non-retarded physically disabled children.

2. WITH ADULTS

When it comes to dealing with adult retardates I think trends now developing in planning for them will prove that we shall be more and more able to manage with only two forms of collective living;

namely, group homes situated in ordinary apartment buildings, and local hostels. For back-up or supportive services, we need available places in hospitals for medical and psychiatric care — particularly short-time care. Presently there is the risk that we may be building residential homes that are too large which, because of their size, are segregated automatically from the community, and that we are building too many hospital units that tie the retarded individuals to a level of dependency that is much too high.

In Sweden we have a five-year plan for developing different living possibilities.[1] According to this plan the percentage of adult retardates living in hospitals for the retarded will comprise only 12 per cent (rather than the present 19 per cent) of all adult retarded individuals in need of residential care. Our special hospitals average at present 300 beds each and our central residential homes (generally one in each of our 25 counties) average 200 beds each. When the plan is fulfilled in five years about 35 per cent of the adults will live in this type of residential home.

The next step in the normalisation process is to live in a local hostel organised as an annex to a central residential home. There are a little over 100 of these in Sweden. Their number will increase in the next few years and they will house on the average 48 people each. In order to be economically stable these hostels cannot have less than approximately 25 residents each, which still means that they are relatively small homes, and — being community centred — will have a fairly good potential for promoting social relations. Thirty-eight per cent of all adults — the greater part of all of our adult retardates — will live in these local residences.

Our greatest achievement in collective living at present is with the group-type home. In only a few years the number of such homes has increased from a handful to some 90 homes. The average number of beds per home is approximately eight. Around 6 per cent of the adult retarded individuals live in these homes today, but in four years this will increase to 14 per cent. This means that we then will have 2,200 adult retardates living in such small group homes, most of which consist of regular flats in apartment buildings, rented by the county administration on the same conditions as for private tenants. Renting, by the way, contributes to quick availability of this type of home.

In the future there will be different types of group homes from those housing three to four persons and practically no staff to those with seven or eight retarded persons in each home. A larger number is not desirable. Small apartments should be concentrated in one residential area. Together they constitute a Group Home with a supervisor who assigns staff as needed. We want to avoid 'night personnel' in group homes for adults, and we make a clear distinction between group homes for adults and hostels.

Decentralisation and integration of residential living into the community result in a more flexible relation to other provisions for services, particularly different types of day care. In a community one could build up a Service Centre with a specialist staff who could provide comprehensive services for every retardate in that community. This would yield greater possibilities for adapting services to the individual needs and conditions. Such flexibility would provide more option and make it easier to rid oneself of a home or a form of service that no longer meets actual demands.

The creation of different normalised environments makes possible dynamic living where the retarded person is stimulated by being a member of a small group. Here the adult retardate will be able to develop simply by living.

In this manner, one may formulate new norms and organisational forms that tear down what earlier generations have built with much toil and economic hardship. With humanity, however, it is one of the rules of the game that rigid and sterile order is broken by creative unrest — just as upheaval follows upon rest — and that the establishment of a new order requires new means. Indeed, in our society, this is living itself.

NOTE

1. Sweden has eight million inhabitants of whom 0.37 per cent, as retardates, receive some form of services. 0.20 per cent live in 304 residential facilities of various kinds.

PART TWO
The prevalence and special needs of
handicapped people in the community

Introduction

Before any serious attempt can be made to provide relevant services for any category of the population, some estimate must be made of the prevalence of such people in the general population and their particular situation and special needs. In their study of those registered as disabled who were living at home in the community, Townsend and Sainsbury (1970, 1974) directed their attention to piloting a means of conducting a functional assessment of handicaps and to establishing the patterns of living and relative deprivation experienced by physically handicapped adults. Townsend emphasizes their great age, their lack of domestic amenities and their poverty which constitute their inferior status as different from normal people. The disabled have an impulse towards social integration but are confronted by the segregative practices of society, a characteristic to which several subsequent sections of this book devote attention. A later pilot study by the Bedford College Research Unit (1969) was used as the basis for the first major survey of handicapped and impaired adults in the community, conducted by Amelia Harris (1971, 1972).

These surveys draw a distinction between *impairment,* that is, 'lacking part or all of a limb, or having a defective limb, organ or mechanism of the body'; *disablement* as 'the loss or reduction of functional ability'; and *handicap* which refers to 'the disadvantage or restriction of activity caused by disability' (Harris 1971, Part 1 p.1). Their emphasis is on 'the activities which the individual is unable to perform rather than on the underlying impairment or deficiency itself' (Jefferys 1969 p.304).

This terminology and this mode of classification have become fairly general because of the use to which they have been put in local authority area surveys, but it is important to consider the much more exhaustive breakdown of functional disabilities itemized by Nichols, in Appendix 2 to Part Eight, as well as Agerholm's classification of intrinsic handicaps which the Association of Disabled Professionals (1973) has recommended using as a basis for the collection of statistics from which an effective Register of Disabled Persons could be compiled. These include locomotor, visceral, visual, communication, intellectual and emotional handicaps as well as a variety of superficially invisible and shockingly visible ones. There is very general agreement that this sort of classification and assessment is what is useful because it presents the problems requiring solution rather than a historical, medical or accidental account of why and how the person became impaired and hence disabled and handicapped.

No national survey of handicapped children has been conducted but much more routine information is obtained through the school health and psychological services, and there has been a series of reports by committees enquiring into the situation of specific categories of children. The epidemiological survey of children conducted by Rutter *et al.* in the Isle of Wight does, however, present a relatively complete picture of the situation in a comparatively affluent area. It is useful to consider what different kinds of handicap — intellectual, educational, psychological and physical — may mean to a child and the extent to which they overlap or are interrelated, e.g. reading-retardation and anti-social behaviour. Further attention is given to children's educational needs in Parts Five and Six.

The remaining items in Part Two are specifically concerned with some of the particular difficulties and disadvantages experienced by handicapped people and the ways in which their alleviation is being practically considered. In his presentation of the main issues underlying current negotiations for an assured income for disabled people, Lynes poses several questions. Should such a pension aim to compensate for restriction of activity or loss of earnings? Why should a distinction be drawn between those who have lost the ability to work and those who have never been able to do so? Why should the cause of the disability be an overriding consideration as it tends to be in Britain? He contrasts the aims of the Disablement Income Group to obtain an earnings-related pension and of Townsend and others to devise a pension related to degree of impairment, and the extent to which the former mode of provision has been made more difficult by the last Conservative government's abandonment of a single national pension scheme in favour of various occupational schemes backed by the life offices. At the time of writing active negotiations are under way and it appears that the Labour government is giving serious consideration to a disability income scheme that would include the criterion of income-relationship. A recent precedent is the 1972 Accident Compensation Act passed in New Zealand following a Royal Commission with a brief similar to Lord Justice Pearson's.

The Economist Intelligence Unit's study, *Care with Dignity*, which like Townsend's initial survey was carried out on behalf of one of the associations of disabled people, highlights three overriding obstacles to normal domestic living: the primary explanation of institutionalization is a lack of people to care at home for those who are admitted to residential institutions; the failure of local authorities and regional hospital boards to provide capital grants for the provision of appropriate domestic accommodation; and the tendency of social service departments to spread scarce resources thinly to prop up those less severely disabled, instead of diverting resources from costly 'homes' and Part III Accommodation to providing domiciliary services for those with more severe disabilities yet without any need for constant nursing and medical attention. The cost of even the most intensive form of care at home would be no more than that required for a modern local authority home and considerably less than the hospital service can provide.

Ann Shearer exemplifies some of the forms of sheltered housing schemes that are under way in Britain and the different continental models that could be adopted, particularly those in Sweden and Denmark. She also highlights the disastrous effects of dual means of governing and financing such services in Britain, which result in social problems being cast in the guise of particular services irrespective of the needs and expressed desires of their potential users. Special funds have been earmarked for removing chronically sick young people from geriatric hospital wards but, being provided through regional hospital boards, the funds are merely used to build yet more wards for this category of patient. The patients want to live in the community and should have a right to housing like any other citizen. How may these needs be met? In Part Two it may be seen just how acutely they are felt, and in Part Seven attention is given to the needs of one particular category, mentally handicapped children and adults.

Finally, the chairman of the Joint Committee on Mobility for the Disabled, Peter Large, considers some of the mobility barriers encountered by physically disabled people trying to use public transport and gain access to public buildings and facilities. He lays particular stress on the plethora of responsible bodies and interests in this public domain, the benefits to be obtained from a self-controlled means of personal mobility, i.e. the automobile, and the exclusion practices resulting from the current trend towards the separation of areas used by pedestrians and by vehicular traffic.

REFERENCES

Association of Disabled Professionals (1973) *Memorandum on the consultative document: The Quota Scheme for Disabled People, issued by the Department of Employment*, May 1973, Warlingham, Surrey.

Disablement Income Group (1972) *Creating a National Disability Income,* London.

HARRIS, A. I. *et al.* (1971, 1972) *Handicapped and Impaired in Great Britain* London, HMSO. Parts 1, 2 and 3 provide extensive general information as well as a specific onsideration of the impaired housewife; the leisure activities of impaired persons; work, education and qualifications; housing; income and entitlement to supplementary benefit.

HARRIS, A. I. and HEAD, E. (1971) *Sample Surveys in Local Authority Areas: with particular reference to the handicapped and elderly,* London, Office of Population Censuses and Surveys, Social Survey Division SS477.

JEFFERYS, M., MILLARD, J. B., HYMAN, M. and WARREN M. D. (1969) 'A set of tests for measuring motor improvement in prevalence studies', *Journal of Chronic Diseases,* 22, pp 303—19.

Royal Commission of Inquiry into Compensation for Personal Injury in New Zealand (1967) *Report* (Chairman Mr. Justice Woodhouse), Wellington, New Zealand.

SAINSBURY, S. (1970) *Registered as Disabled,* Occasional Papers on Social Administration, No. 35, London, Bell.

SAINSBURY, S. (1974) *Measuring Disability,* Occasional Papers on Social Administration No. 54, London, Bell.

3. The disabled in society[*][1]

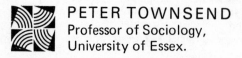

PETER TOWNSEND
Professor of Sociology,
University of Essex.

In Britain about 1½ million people, or 3 per cent of the population, are found in groups *officially* described as disabled or handicapped.[2] Over a million live at home. The Ministry of Labour lists 654,000 persons on the Disabled Persons Register.[3] There are approximately 450,000 disablement pensioners from the two world wars and nearly 200,000 industrial injury disablement pensioners.[4] The local authorities' registers contain the names of 110,000 blind, 30,000 partially-sighted and 205,000 other disabled and handicapped persons, the great majority of whom live at home.[5] There are many persons with long-term mental or physical handicaps, probably about 200,000 who reside in hospitals, particularly those for the chronic sick and mentally ill, or in residential homes or hostels.[6] They include 65,000 subnormal and severely subnormal patients in psychiatric hospitals. Altogether 90,000 subnormal and severely subnormal and another 71,000 mentally ill or psychopathic persons living at home have mental health services provided by local health authorities.[7] The Supplementary Benefits Commission (formerly the National Assistance Board) pays allowances to 138,000 incapacitated persons living at home who are not receiving sickness or other insurance benefits.[8] There are 76,000 handicapped children of whom about 32,000 are physically handicapped in special schools or units.[9] Other administratively defined categories might be added. There is considerable duplication in these figures. Their very fragmentation and the confessed inability of the Ministry of Health to give 'comprehensive national statistics'[10] forces us to ask whether we are doing all we should to develop our understanding of handicap and disability and whether the services to meet the needs of the disabled are adequate.

In this paper I shall describe the results of a survey carried out between 1964 and 1966 from the University of Essex. This was carried out in London, Essex and Middlesex by Sally Sainsbury, a research officer at the university, under my guidance. The Greater London Association for the Disabled generously commissioned the work in the belief that it would contribute to the task of re-thinking the roles that should be played respectively by local authority and voluntary organizations as a result of the reorganization of London government. Our data cover one group of the disabled in the three local authority areas — those registered in the 'general classes' of the physically handicapped — that is, excluding the special groups of blind, deaf and hard of hearing. A sample of men and women on the registers was visited and a total of 211 persons were interviewed, the majority being in London. Eight per cent of the original sample refused an interview and another 3 per cent were too ill to give information. The average interview took over two hours.

The survey was thus relatively modest in numbers of persons and of areas covered. This fact should be borne in mind throughout the following report. Moreover, registration with a local authority is voluntary and some kinds of disabled

*A lecture given at the Royal College of Surgeons on 5th May 1967 under the auspices of the Greater London Association for the Disabled and published by them in pamphlet form.
[1] Also published in P. Townsend (1973) *The Social Minority*, London, Allen Lane, Chapter 7, pp. 108—29.

persons do not see why they would benefit by registering. Other disabled persons are not advised by government and local authority departments and voluntary organizations to do so.

Our sample does not adequately represent certain kinds of handicaps such as blindness, deafness and mental illness or subnormality. Only 5 per cent were war or industrial disablement pensioners. Nonetheless, a wide range of people was included, some with multiple handicaps. As many as 45 different kinds of handicaps were represented. There were rather more women than men. Nearly half were married and another third widowed, separated or divorced. Some were in their teens, twenties and thirties but two fifths were middle-aged (45-64) and another two fifths elderly (65+). The main source of income for nearly a fifth was derived from employment; two fifths depended primarily on retirement pensions, nearly a fifth on sickness benefit and the rest on national assistance, disablement pensions and unemployment benefit.[11]

The chief conclusion of the study is that there is an imbalance between the impulses of the disabled towards integration into ordinary social and occupational life and the segregative practices of society. One wants what the other largely fails either to recognize or translate into real opportunity. Although a majority of the people registered with the local authorities are severely incapacitated and a majority middle-aged or elderly, most emphasize physical and economic independence and integration in work and society. They are usually realistic about their limitations but believe they could lead an approximately normal life if only they could obtain more help with physical aids, housing, transport and employment. In general they regard special clubs or residential Homes and special workshops as second-best, like other symbols of separate disability status. By contrast, society tends to give weak support to the principles of economic independence and social integration or participation and fairly strong support, some of it unwitting, to the enforced dependence and social segregation of the disabled.

This conclusion naturally requires qualification, for the supporting arguments are by no means entirely consistent. It depends on a wide variety of evidence about the actual situation of the disabled — their environment, work and income and their relationships with family and social services.

There is lamentably little factual knowledge. I shall endeavour to present some of the more important strands of evidence in this lecture. A necessary first step is to discuss the underlying concept of disability and explain why new definitions and measures are essential both for knowledge and policy.

The meaning of disability

What do we mean when we say that someone is disabled? First, there is anatomical, physiological or psychological abnormality or loss. Thus we think of the disabled as people who have lost a limb or part of the nervous system through surgery or in an accident, become blind or deaf or paralysed, or are physically damaged or abnormal in some particular, usually observable, respect.

Secondly, there are chronic clinical conditions altering or interrupting normal physiological or psychological processes, such as bronchitis, arthritis, tuberculosis, epilepsy, schizophrenia and manic depression. These two concepts of loss or abnormality and of chronic disease tend in fact to merge, for although a loss may be sustained without disease, disease long continued usually has some physiological or anatomical effect.[12] Among the people whom we interviewed a wide range of conditions were represented. About 31 per cent specified rheumatoid arthritis, osteo-arthritis or just arthritis and between 4 per cent and 13 per cent in each instance specified the after-effects of poliomyelitis, disseminated sclerosis, bronchitis, epilepsy, coronary thrombosis, or were amputees or hemiplegics. For both meanings of disability the clinical reference-object is the normal human body, of like sex and age.

A third meaning is functional limitation of ordinary activity, whether that activity is carried on alone or with others. The simplest example is incapacity for self-care and management, in the sense of being unable or finding it difficult to walk about, negotiate stairs, wash and dress, for example.[13] But this principle of limitation can be applied to other aspects of ordinary life. By reference to the average person of the same sex an estimate can be made of the individual's relative incapacity for household management and performance of both general social roles as husband, father or mother, neighbour or church member, say, and of specific occupational roles.

A fourth meaning is a pattern of behaviour

which has particular elements of a socially deviant kind.[14] This pattern of behaviour is in part directly attributable to an impairment or pathological condition – such as a regular physical tremor or limp, or an irregularly occurring fit. But it is also attributable to the individual's perception of his condition and his response to others' expectations of him. Thus, activity may not only be limited, but different. And it may be different as much depending on how it is perceived by the individual and others as on its physiological determination. Two people with an identical physical impairment may differ greatly in their behaviour, one acting up to the limit of his capacities and the other refraining from actions of which he is capable. Alternatively a man with little or no impairment may play the disabled role. Sociologists have recently paid increasing attention to the concepts of the sick role and of illness behaviour.[15] Society expects the blind or the deaf or the physically handicapped to behave in certain approved or stereotyped ways. We all know of instances of people assuming deafness or handicap. They may adopt whole patterns of behaviour. Individuals can be motivated towards such behaviour when their physical or neurological condition does not compel it. A family or a subculture can condition it. There are cultural differences in disability behaviour. People of different nationality or ethnic group vary in their stoicism in face of pain and handicap.[16] All this can be a fascinating focus for inquiry.

Finally, disability means a socially defined position or status. The actor does not just act differently. He occupies a status which attracts a mixture of deference, condescension, consideration and indifference. Irrespective of a disabled individual's *specific* behaviour or condition he attracts certain kinds of attention from the rest of the population by virtue of the 'position' that the disabled, when recognized as such, occupy in that particular society. There are countries and populations which do not recognize or identify mild forms of subnormality, schizophrenia or infirmity, for example. In working-class British society euphemisms for certain handicaps are used. Someone has 'nerves' or is 'hard of hearing' or is 'a bit simple'. So far this would mean that deviance simply is not recognized or clearly distinguished. But the technical, conclusive and stigmatizing labels are avoided. A place is not taken in a rank or a hierarchy. This can, of course, have its advantages. Some people can continue to be treated as ordinary members of the community. To identify or register them as disabled may entitle them to certain special benefits or professional treatment but it may also separate them from society and encourage people to look on them if not as a race apart, like lepers, then with aloof condescension. Disability can imply inferior as well as different status.[17] The extent to which an individual belongs to special groups or clubs, has special sets of relationships with doctors and nurses and social workers, relies on particular forms of income and sheltered forms of occupation and is patronized by voluntary organizations will all determine his particular position and status or the extent to which he is integrated into the social fabric. Of much of this doctors, social workers and administrative personnel may be unaware. While the sociologist would not pretend to be able to advance medical knowledge, casework and administration as such, it is his responsibility to develop this aspect of knowledge.

Operational measures of disability as a guide to action

It would be possible to assemble a large number of data on each of these interpretations of disability. All of them have implications both for our understanding of disability as well as the means with which to offer help and service. Clinical particularizations are essential if pathology is to be investigated or arrested but there can be unfortunate social and administrative consequences. The proliferation of specialist consultants for particular diseases or disabilities and of statutory and voluntary organizations gives emphasis to the separateness rather than the similarity of many disabled conditions with consequential confusion, fragmentation of effort and injustice. Some conditions receive favourable publicity and attention. Others, with worse effects, are neglected. The thalidomide children have attracted vastly more public sympathy than children suffering from subnormality or congenital syphilis. The Spastics Society has an income of around £2 million but the National Society for Mentally Handicapped Children only £40,000.[18]

One consequence is inconsistency of assessment. How do we assess *degree* of disability so as to determine level of pension or of other needs?

The McCorquodale Committee on the Assessment of Disablement repeatedly referred in its report to the principle that assessment should be determined by 'means of a comparison between the condition of the disabled person and that of a normal healthy person of the same age',[19] but took no steps to apply the principle empirically. The committee did not obtain information systematically about disabled persons and healthy persons of equivalent age. Nor did the committee try to examine the rationale of current medical assessment. They largely confined their attentions to amputations and loss of limb or eye and did not, even for these minority disabilities, seek empirical justification for percentage assessments. For example, they accepted the loss of four fingers and of a leg below the knee (leaving a stump of between 3½ and 5 inches) each as equivalent to 50 per cent disability. We might question the logic of both rate and equivalence. The loss of three fingers, the amputation of 'one foot resulting in end-bearing stump', the amputation 'through one foot proximal to the metatarpophalangeal joint' and the loss of vision in one eye were all regarded as equivalent to 30 per cent disability. In refraining from exploring the functional, psychological and social effects even of different kinds of limb amputation they failed to take advantage of the growing body of knowledge and research methods developed by the social sciences in the last twenty years. The same kind of criticisms might be made of the more general and rather different definitions of disability currently used by the Ministries of Social Security, Labour and Health.[20] Britain is still largely governed in its conduct towards the disabled by the *source* rather than the *effect* of disability. Too little effort has been made to develop *functional* indices, based on questions about individual capacities. Such indices are difficult to develop and have to be treated with caution. But they are implicit in nearly all official definitions and have been partly but unsystematically used in some medical and administrative procedures. For example, the information supplied by doctors on a form used by the Ministry of Labour includes the kind of conditions which doctors believe the disabled person should *avoid* in his employment. The information does not adequately reflect either the general or specific capacities of the disabled person although some 'functional' information is given.[21] Britain is not alone in having failed to size up to this problem.[22] If we did apply functional measures it is likely that we would identify between 3 per cent and 6 per cent of adults under pensionable age as physically or mentally handicapped. A recent Danish survey established that around 6 per cent of adults were physically handicapped. There was little difference between the rates for men and the rates for women but both rates increased sharply in the fifties. About 3 per cent in the twenties and thirties were disabled and 7 per cent in the forties, but by the late fifties the figure reached 17 per cent, topping 20 per cent in the early sizties.[23] In Sweden disability pensions reached 2½ per cent of the adult population. The rate also rises sharply in the fifties and early sixties. But some of the less disabled may not qualify for such pensions.

We developed a crude index of incapacity to manage personal and household activities which involved assessing twenty-three tasks and activities.[24] Each activity was scored two if it could not be done at all and one if it could be done only with difficulty. Altogether as many as 17 per cent of the disabled in the three counties were very severely incapacitated (scoring 23 and over). Another 36 per cent were severely incapacitated (scoring 15-22), making 53 per cent altogether. Only 11 per cent were slightly incapacitated (scoring 6 or less). Incapacity tended to increase with age. Only a third of those younger than 45 were severely or very severely incapacitated in our sense, compared with nearly half those aged 45-64 and nearly two thirds of those aged 65 and over.

This kind of approach allows us to compare persons with multiple disabilities. Nearly half the sample had at least two. It also allows us to begin comparing the effects of different disabilities and the ways in which the extent of incapacity changes over time. Very little work has been done on this. Nearly 20 per cent had disabilities which were quickly progressive and another 40 per cent slowly progressive. Many were prone to depression and feared increasing dependence on others. Some people found that their capacities fluctuated according to the nature of their condition and changes in the weather. Even those whose disabilities were quickly progressive found there were periods of recovery or restoration of capacity. In all this I am stressing the relativity of disability, like the relativity of intelligence. There are times, for example in illness or after accidents, when most of us cannot walk or cannot dress or cannot speak. Many of us have a 'permanent' limitation of some kind. It is appropriate therefore to ask to what degree the disabled are more incapacitated than ourselves as a way of asserting a common involvement and preparing the ground for a rational examination of their occupational and social opportunities.

Housing

The first major problem is that of housing. We found that the disabled live in housing which is in some respects worse in basic facilities than the rest of the community. Only a fifth of the sample were owner-occupiers compared with over two fifths of the total population.[25] Their incomes were usually small. Half were council tenants. Over time they had qualified for a council flat or house. But some had been recently placed in houses or flats erected between the wars rather than in the last twenty years and a number were in flats not on the ground floor. About a quarter were tenants in private housing and in general these had the worst facilities. Altogether 30 per cent had no hot water supply, 23 per cent no bath and as many as 21 per cent no W.C. indoors. We met people who had to get water from a well or a pump in the garden or a tap in the back yard; who had to share a miserable lavatory with other households or get to one across a yard or to the bottom of a garden along a broken path. Inability to use a W.C. was universally regarded as being the greatest personal indignity. As many as 20 per cent of the persons in the sample lived in homes which were deficient in three or more basic facilities.

Stairs pose a critical difficulty. Seventy-four per cent of the people in the sample had to climb or descend at least one flight of stairs to the entrance of their homes or inside from the W.C. or kitchen to the living room. Thirty-three per cent had to negotiate stairs both outside and inside. One partially-sighted woman who was an epileptic had to mount a flight of steps from her basement flat with no handrail and the fourth step missing. Five per cent had to use lifts to reach their council flats on the upper storeys. This minority all complained that the lifts frequently broke down with sometimes disastrous effects so far as they were concerned. Councils who place disabled and elderly persons on the higher storeys of blocks of flats under the assumption that lifts secure constant access seem to be mistaken.

Against basic structural deficiencies or difficulties such as these the efforts of welfare authorities to introduce adaptations inevitably seem puny. Adaptations had in fact been carried out in just under half the homes of the sample, some by individuals and hospital authorities and a few by voluntary organizations, but the majority by the welfare departments of local authorities. Most of these were of a simple kind: handrails on stairways and in passages and lavatories; ramps up single steps; lavatory seats raised; a few doorways widened and a few electric light switches lowered and electric points raised. There is no doubt that such alterations can make life a lot easier and there is scope for a massive expansion of activity.

Twenty-four per cent specified adaptations which they felt needed to be carried out by the local authority but many others had been told or believed they lived in accommodation which was unsuitable for satisfactory adaptation. We asked the disabled about a variety of facilities which they could not use *because* they were ill-placed or ill-designed. Seventy per cent could not open and shut windows; 42 per cent and 40 per cent respectively could not reach gas and electric meters; 22 per cent were unable to use a cooker and a similar proportion could not use taps, use a sink and reach any cupboards. These are disconcerting statistics.

The problem is partly one of standardizing certain kinds of units so that they can be introduced into homes quickly. But there is a limit to opportunities of standardization. Chairbound people need to have a low sink in the kitchen but an arthritic housewife who cannot stand or bend needs a high stool and a fairly high sink. Moreover, physiotherapists may prefer obstacles to remain for particular persons so that limbs and muscles are properly exercised. Individual solutions will always to some extent be necessary. The problem is also one of devising an effective administrative plan and implementing it quickly. In instances which were all too rare welfare officers had achieved just this. But do local authorities complete a detailed schedule of household deficiencies when a disabled person is newly registered? And can they organize a blitz on the dwelling so that improvements are introduced simultaneously over a very short period and not piecemeal over many months, with all the disruptive and depressing effects this can have on a household? I suspect we are going to need local authority work teams which are seconded to welfare departments by housing departments with the blessing of local trade unions.

Adaptations sometimes achieve much less than they are supposed to achieve. We met persons who used a handrail to help them along a passage and down a couple of steps into a kitchenette but who could not carry a tray of food back and felt obliged to eat meals off a draining board. Nearly all the ramps which had been installed or which could be laid across outside steps could not be used by the disabled individual without help. One woman said that when she tried to go in her wheelchair down a short ramp into her kitchen without help she could not control it and went headlong into the opposite wall. The main problem for wheelchairs, as much in new council flats as old private properties, was manoeuvrability. There was rarely sufficient space in kitchens and living rooms and lavatories to turn round or go easily through doorways and along passageways.

Here the question is how the disabled can be transferred to good housing which first has modern amenities and which secondly does not provide obstacles to persons with limited mobility. The question of special design or adaptation — for that is the real question — is secondary. Some of the people we interviewed wanted to transfer from council homes which were unsuitable structurally or in their siting. Others who rented privately owned homes had applied for council flats. Altogether 16 per cent were on council housing lists, more than half of them for at least two years and a few for over ten years. Half the owner-occupied homes needed major improvements, some of which would be possible to finance or subsidize under existing legislation if only local officials took the initiative to assist applications and organize builders and decorators. I suspect that new scales of priorities have to be drawn up by health and welfare departments on the one hand and housing departments on the other. The former should have responsibility for allocating and administering a high proportion of the accommodation for the disabled and elderly.

Community care services

The second major problem is personal and household help. Nearly a fifth of the disabled persons whom we interviewed were unmarried and many others were widowed, divorced or separated. We found that 15 per cent lived alone and the relatives in the vicinity could not provide all the services that were needed. Finally, around a third of the sample were people who lived with husbands and wives or relatives but who were not employed and were alone for substantial parts of the day. Some had to wait from 8 a.m. to 5 or 6 p.m. for a hot drink and meal. Others reported falls and other accidents which left them lying waiting for help until a relative returned in the evening.

For care in illness and regular care in the household substantially more people relied on family help than on all the health and welfare services put together. For example, during their last illness 66 per cent had been looked after by relatives while 10 per cent had gone into hospital (21 per cent looked after themselves, 2 per cent were looked after by neighbours and 1 per cent by friends). Again, 75 per cent had meals prepared for them by relatives and 9 per cent received them occasionally or often in the week from a meal delivery service. Friends and neighbours furnished valuable, usually supplementary, help to nearly half the sample, mainly by shopping, preparing a meal or cleaning.

The health and welfare services were nonetheless a major source of help. Thirty per cent had a home help, 9 per cent meals delivered to them, 13 per cent were visited regularly by district nurses, 10 per cent had chiropody services at home and another 25 per cent had chiropody elsewhere, and 2 per cent in each instance were helped by the home bathing and borough laundry services. Altogether nearly half the sample had at least one domiciliary service, of whom half had two or more services. In London rather more than a half and in Essex and Middlesex rather less than two fifths of the sample had one or more services. In addition people were in touch with welfare departments and voluntary agencies. Eighty-four per cent said they had been visited at least once, a quarter three or more times, by the welfare officer in the previous twelve months, the other 16 per cent claiming not to have been visited. Three quarters of the visits were said to be routine, lasting from 10 to 30 minutes, but 6 per cent were in connexion with holidays, 8 per cent alterations and 7 per cent aids or gadgets. The welfare departments maintain what is at present mainly a referral service. Thirty per cent were in touch with a voluntary agency of some kind. For two thirds of them this meant membership of a club. For a third or more it meant occasional or regular visits, some routine checks on present circumstances, some inquiries about means, aids, alterations, food parcels and so on. Proportionately more of those who were only slightly or moderately incapacitated were in touch with voluntary agencies.

Doctors and medical social workers in hospital played an important role in referring patients for welfare services. It was not our purpose to investigate medical and hospital care but a substantial number were in close contact with a G.P. Over half had seen one within the previous month and as many as a quarter said they were visited regularly. There was a fifth, however, who had not seen their G.P. in the previous year. A few very incapacitated persons would have liked regular consultations. Others spoke of the problems of getting to hospital out-patient departments.

Despite this range of services we found evidence of considerable need. A third as many disabled people again as were receiving a home help, meals delivered at home and a district nurse expressed a wish for such a service. The majority were very severely or severely incapacitated by the strict standards that were applied. There was a huge latent demand for home bathing, laundry, chiropody and optical and dental services and between 10 and 20 per cent of the entire sample in each instance expressed a desire for these services. Others did not express a desire for such services but by objective assessment seemed to require them. Thus a fifth of those who were severely incapacitated lived alone and did not have a home help. They did not always feel the need for such help. Among those getting the service as many as a fifth (or 6 per cent of the entire sample) received more than eight hours help per week but half received it for only between an hour and three hours and half of them felt the need for more frequent visits.

Some of those living alone did not ask for meals to be delivered because the service had a poor reputation. Only a third of the people having meals said they were hot when they arrived. Many warmed them up though a few could not use the cooker and ate them cold. A third said the meals were usually delivered before 11 a.m. Again, although some received meals five days a week

over half received them only twice a week. An inquiry into the diets of a sub-sample suggested that in a quarter to a fifth of instances they were unsatisfactory.

One function of the National Health Service, local authorities and other agencies is to provide aids for the handicapped. A large array of aids, from wheelchairs, tricycles, crutches, sticks and surgical corsets to special eating utensils, long-handled combs and 'permanent' collars and ties, were being used by persons in the sample. The lack of really satisfactory false legs and aids to mobility, despite the far greater numbers having difficulties with legs than with arms, was repeatedly drawn to our attention. Sixty-four per cent of the sample were affected by disability in the lower limbs only and another 28 per cent were affected in both lower and upper limbs. Only 3 per cent were affected in the upper limbs only.[26] As many as 65 per cent of the men and 70 per cent of the women in the sample used some aid to get about outdoors and nearly as many indoors. Most of the people with artificial legs who were interviewed had a great deal of trouble either because stumps were sore, or because they suffered from phantom pains. All found walking indoors and outdoors difficult. Leg supports or substitutes such as crutches and wheelchairs are remarkably cumbersome. The value of aids should not be minimised. We made various calculations which showed that average incapacity to undertake a range of tasks was reduced by over a quarter by aids already available. It became possible for people to do more tasks. Incapacity could be further reduced. But there is little doubt that by any rational assessment the top priorities are more good housing, better community services and more generous motorized transport. Ingenuity and research are important but even more important is the willingness to finance services and transport.

In 1956 the Piercy Committee pointed out that expenditure on the disabled by local authorities was not substantial. 'It is clear that only the fringes of the field have yet been touched. The Act gives local authorities very wide permissive powers to make provision for the welfare of disabled persons, and on the evidence received there is no doubt that there is a need for a fuller and better provision and scope for considerable development'.[27] The committee recommended an Exchequer grant for these services but this was not accepted. The Ministry of Health later spoke of steady progress and tried to reassure the public, although from the vantage point of history I believe the attitude adopted by the department will be seen as grudging. It did not even match the cautious and unimaginative approach to reform of the Piercy Committee. In 1963 the Ministry acknowledged that up to a year or so earlier 'the development of local authority welfare services (for the physically handicapped) had been very uneven and a number of authorities had not even made schemes for the deaf or dumb or for the general classes'.[28]

The fact that there are far more disabled persons requiring welfare services than are registered has been lamented officially for years. Yet between 1957 and 1965 the numbers of blind, deaf and physically handicapped persons registered with local authorities in England and Wales grew by only 74,000 to 288,000, or six per 1,000 population. The total includes nearly 148,000 physically handicapped other than the blind or deaf, or 3 per 1,000 population. Yet the variations between local authorities are inexplicably wide. The numbers of generally handicapped persons on the registers per 1,000 population range from 0.8 in Chester, 1.2 in Portsmouth, 1.3 in Oxford and Southport, 1.4 in the North Riding, Coventry and Leicestershire, 1.5 in Staffordshire and 1.7 in Kent, at the lower levels, to 6.9 in Lincolnshire (Holland), 7.1 in Glamorgan, 7.2 in Hastings, 7.9 in Bath, 8.2 in West Bromwich and 10.7 in Kingston-upon-Hull, at the higher levels.[29] If all authorities were to register proportionately as many as the top ten authorities another 150-200,000 would be added nationally to the registers. It is evident that the problem has scarcely begun to be identified, still less met.

Employment

The third major problem is occupation. Thirteen per cent of the total sample of 211 were in paid open employment and another 4 per cent were employed in a sheltered workshop or at home. More than a quarter of those below pensionable age were in paid employment, some of whom were severely incapacitated. Over half of the thirty-three persons below pension age who were employed were not registered on the Ministry of Labour's Disabled Persons Register. Some who were employed full-time had been told by Disablement Resettlement Officers at the employment exchange that they were unsuitable for work and found work for themselves.

There was an air of near-desperation in the attitudes of many persons below pensionable age to their need for a paid job. As many as 25 per cent expressed a wish for employment. At least half of these did not seem on the face of it to be too incapacitated to obtain a job. If our figures are broadly representative then there are 28,000 on the local authority registers seeking paid employment, 16,000 of them full-time employment. A number in the sample had difficulties in getting work because they could not obtain appropriate transport. The disabled still find it difficult to qualify for specially designed tricycles and adapted cars, especially if their disability is progressive and they have to convince Ministry officials that it is more difficult than it used to be to get to and from work. Some who do qualify find that by contrast with modern vehicles on the roads the tricycles and cars are inferior even in standards of comfort and possibly unsafe. Until recently they were not fitted with heaters, so many of the older vehicles are still grim to drive in winter.

It is difficult in some respects to understand why more of the disabled on the local authority registers who are not at work than who are at work are seeking it, for in status, pay and conditions it is often so unattractive. The disabled tend to be given light assembly work, packing, filing, cleaning and storekeeping. Some are in so-called designated employment, as car park attendants and lift attendants.[30] The average wage of the men on the sample in full-time employment in 1965 was £14 compared with £19 at that time in London and the south east.

A disproportionately large number of those in employment were in unskilled and semi-skilled jobs. Some who had accepted paid work at home, making up rosettes or flower-holders and packing toys by the gross, for example, had to work extremely long hours for very little money. In all the instances we came across the average earned was less than three shillings an hour. The local authorities play little role as protective or referral agents for the disabled and most home-work is contracted privately.

The true situation is disturbing: 9 per cent of those on the Ministry of Labour's Disabled Persons Register are unemployed, compared with 2 per cent nationally.[31] But this greatly underestimates the scale of the problem. The Ministry declares in effect that many of the long-term unemployed who are not on the Disabled Persons Register have personal handicaps because of age or physical or mental condition.[32] There are substantial numbers of disabled on the local authority registers seeking work who are not listed at the local employment exchanges. Some of them will presumably be assessed by the Disablement Resettlement Officers as unsuitable for admission to the Ministry's Disabled Persons Register.[33] And no doubt there are substantial numbers of other disabled persons on no official register who are in a similar position. It is time we recognized that this situation is absurd and unjust and should be remedied. The numbers of the genuinely unemployed are being under-represented.

Current activity on behalf of the disabled is not encouraging. Some of the people we interviewed spoke enthusiastically about the efforts made by Disablement Resettlement Officers. But more spoke of discouragement and many had made no use of the special services.[34] Training at Industrial Rehabilitation Units is difficult to secure and when secured is not always as up to date as it might be. Little or no help is given in particular to retrain women and older men. Sheltered workshops are few and far between and get too little subsidy and managerial investment to be successful. In any event disabled persons often feel that such employment is to be avoided at all costs. Work in the home would be welcomed by a large proportion of the disabled but depends on skilful organization. Local authorities have permissive powers to operate home-working schemes. Few do so. The disabled need work-finders and transport-organizers and work-flow teams more than occupational therapy as understood in the narrow sense of that term. Some occupational therapists spend a lot of time finding employment for handicapped persons and some uncertainty between them and the D.R.O.s about division of function might well be investigated.[35]

The quota of disabled persons is one of the most important instruments of policy. All employers with more than twenty employees must employ 3 per cent of disabled persons. Only 52 per cent of firms in fact satisfy the quota.[36] Recently it was also revealed that fewer than 3 per cent of Government employees are disabled. There is no doubt that there are many sympathetic employers who are prepared to go to considerable lengths to help a disabled person. We were given instances of people being given time off and having working hours and conditions adjusted. On the other hand there is no doubt that some employers abuse the provisions of the Disabled Persons (Employment) Acts by persuading some lightly handicapped persons applying to them for jobs to register as disabled persons so that they can meet their quota. Others in practice pay low wages and offer inferior working conditions to the disabled. Discrimination is perhaps practised unconsciously more often than consciously. Nonetheless, the quota is a more effective means of assuring employment than designated employment, Remploy and sheltered workshops. It also encourages ordinary forms of employment, which the disabled prefer.

It seems important to liberalize the conditions under which people can qualify for admission to the register. In broad principle official help should be given to all persons seeking employment, whatever their sex or age and whatever doubts may exist about their capacity to hold employment. This part of the Ministry of Labour's work needs to be imaginatively expanded. The ultimate aim would be the integration of all disabled persons wanting work into open employment. Various forms of subsidy and encouragement to employers might be tried. An immediate step could be the manipulation of Selective Employment Tax in favour of disabled employees.

Income

A fourth problem is low level of resources. We have seen that relatively few disabled persons on local authority registers owned their own homes and that those in paid employment had relatively low earnings. In general the disabled in the sample had low incomes. Altogether 60 per cent of households had a total income of less than £10 a week and another 26 per cent less than £20. (A third of the households, it should be remembered, contained three or more persons.) Three quarters had less than £50 savings. Nearly half depended partly or wholly on national assistance and about 5 per cent might have qualified for supplementary assistance had they applied for it. There is no doubt that a disproportionately large number of the disabled are in poverty or on its margins.

Social security benefits for the long-term disabled are not related to limitation of capacity except secondarily and there is no consistent system of extra allowances for constant attendance or personal support and help. There are anomalies as between different kinds of allowances.[37] A man with a wife and two children who is bedfast or chairbound because of multiple sclerosis, say, will receive £8 15s. a week if he is on sickness benefit (including family allowance) or under £10 a week, plus a rent allowance, if he is on national assistance. Yet a man in similar family circumstances who is incapacitated after an industrial injury may receive a pension of £6 15s. plus dependants' and other allowances making a total of £18 5s. Moreover, if this man was once awarded an industrial injury disablement pension of 100 per cent and is rehabilitated so that he can take paid employment again he continues to receive the pension of £6 15s. If he happens to fall sick he receives exactly the same as the first man, that is, £8 15s., plus his pension of £6 15s. A disabled housewife is in the worst plight. If her husband is in full-time work she will usually get nothing, not even national assistance. Thus disablement for her family can be a disaster, especially if her husband's earnings are small or barely cover the normal day-to-day needs of the household.

The Disablement Income Group is rightly calling for the introduction of a national system of disability pensions. I believe that a generous pension should be introduced for both men and women based on the principle of limitation of capacity as ascertained by the kind of functional assessment discussed earlier. This would be difficult to work out in practice but seems to be fairer and less arbitrary than any alternative, such as a pension based on the principle of limitation of earning power. The 100 per cent pension might be fixed initially at 30 per cent of average industrial earnings, which would be just over £6 at the present time. There would be additional allowances for dependent adults and children. The pension could be permanent or temporary according to the degree of certainty about the condition, as under the Swedish system.[38] These benefits would be supplemented by a system of allowances for constant attendance and personal help. This system of benefits would normally apply upon the termination of six months' earnings-related sickness or unemployment benefit or earlier in instances of undoubted long-term handicap. Earnings-related supplements would continue to be paid to disabled persons over retirement age, as to all other retired persons under the Labour Party's scheme for National Superannuation which is to be introduced before 1970. People disabled in middle or late-middle age would also receive earnings-related supplements to reflect extra contributions made in working life. I would hope that this system would largely overtake special war and industrial pension levels. Discrimination between people disabled in war, industry and civil life is distasteful as well as being an administrator's and a lawyer's nightmare.

The present Government's provisions must surely be regarded as makeshift, because earnings-related benefits cease after six months. The long-term sick will be worse off under the new scheme than the short-term sick. And there is a kind of hiatus implicit in present legislation, earnings-related supplements ceasing after six months of sickness and an unconditional flat-rate allowance of 9s. being awarded by the Supplementary Benefits Commission after two years of sickness. A man who has been unemployed though disabled is not entitled to this extra allowance.

The problems of integration

There are of course many other problems and I have touched only on what seem to be the major ones. How acute are they? Have I skirted those which matter even more to severely disabled persons? It is reasonable to suppose that personal relationships with members of the family and with friends and the physical struggle to participate in many activities concern the disabled much more than campaigning for more home help, motorized wheelchairs and even a modern council flat or house on the ground floor. But politics and the organization of professional services are not aspects of life which are unconnected with private relationships. The institutional fabric which we have created and within which we live shapes our behaviour and values. We would be unwise to discount it. However much we struggle to avoid allowing the wider social and political structure to influence our views, it causes us to treat some people, even in our own families, as inferiors or as redundant. And it causes the objects of our indifference or of our self-righteous pity to underestimate their rights. They need to complain and assert themselves, even more for our sake than their own.

I hope I have sketched sufficient evidence to show that as a society Britain has what amounts to an elaborate system of discrimination against the disabled. We do not ensure they have good housing, adequate community services, employment with dignity or an adequate income. We do not even think it necessary to count their numbers.[39] I venture to suggest these are facts, not opinions, which we must take into our reckoning.

What stood out in this largely depressing survey was the warmth and strength of many of the personal relationships of those who were disabled. Many of the people whom we interviewed had close friends or neighbours who were concerned about them. Nearly half were married, as I have said, and another third were widowed, separated or divorced. On the one hand, we found evidence of marital strain. Nearly a tenth of those with a husband or wife who was alive were now separated or divorced. The rate seems to be a little higher than in the general population of comparable age. Another tenth, particularly wives, had marital difficulties of one kind or another. On the other hand, the great majority seemed to be content or, indeed, richly rewarded in their marriages. They could count on devoted support and they contributed a great deal themselves. Much the same is true of relationships with other members of the family, though it does seem that disability reduces the scope and therefore the interchangeability of contacts with the extended family. Relationships are concentrated among a few people. What is disturbing is the lack of adequate relief for many wives and husbands and sons and daughters who give personal and household care. Community services are required to provide a temporary substitute or a permanent relief for relatives who are under excessive strain.

How can this principle of participation or involvement in family and other primary-group relationships be extended to employment, recreation and welfare? There is a gulf, in effect, between private and public life for the disabled. There must be no illusions. Major improvements in the circumstances of the disabled cannot ·be secured by modest increments in legislation or services. A gradual reconstruction of the attitudes and values of society is required which can proceed only in relation to the reduction or elimination of many forms of social prejudice and superiority — involving colour, old age and economically unproductive work, for example, as well as handicap or disability. The fundamental difficulty here for individuals and society is one of recognizing diversity without ordering groups of people in superior and inferior social ranks.

I have tried to argue the relatedness of disability to the human condition. There are features of disability such as pain, shyness, awkwardness, and abnormality which are known to us all. We have met some of them in our illnesses; we may carry some of them with us in our everyday lives and most of us can expect to encounter them in old age even if we are not thrust face to face with them by ill-luck in youth or middle age. We have to come to terms with the condition, to recognize it frankly and not to banish it from sight and mind. This involves recognizing that there are creative outcomes and original ways of looking at life as disabled persons as well as permanent limitations and idiosyncrasies. As one disabled person who has written sensitively about the problems has said, 'If those of us who are disabled live as fully as we can, while being completely conscious of the tragedy of our situation . . . then somehow we can communicate to others an awareness that the value of the human person transcends his social status, attributes and possessions or his lack of them'.[40]

This principle of relatedness, integration or participation has to be applied in various ways. The work of many different statutory and voluntary agencies has to be merged or coordinated if the universality of many of the problems of disability are to be recognized and met. Such emphasis as there is on separate organizations, separate services and separate institutions for the blind, the deaf, the epileptic and the subnormal may need to be reduced. Such emphasis as there is on separating the disabled from the non-disabled in sheltered workshops, residential institutions, housing and clubs may need also to be reduced. The possibility of rearranging and consolidating the work of the local authorities in a major new family service in which the disabled can participate, of inviting voluntary agencies to play a vital supplementary role, is one which the present Seebohm Committee could do much to make real. But there must be more central direction and strategy, beginning with a determined attempt to identify numbers and introduce new pensions, employment opportunities and access to good housing. In this, as in many other respects, we require imaginative leadership as well as popular good-will, interest and effort.

NOTES AND REFERENCES

1. This lecture owes much to Sally Sainsbury, who carried out the survey on which it is largely based. [See her book, *Registered as Disabled*, Bell, 1970.]
2. The figure is a conservative estimate which allows for double — or multiple — counting of the same persons in some of the categories listed in the rest of this paragraph. Judging from research in other countries, for example, Denmark and Sweden, a figure of 6 per cent of all adults aged 21-64 is likely to be reached when disability is defined broadly. Allowing for a smaller proportion of children but a much larger proportion of the elderly the figure for the whole population would probably be higher. See, for example, Anderson, B. R., *Fysisk Handicappede i Danmark*, Socialforskningsinstittutets Publikationer 16, Copenhagen, 1964, pp. 55-6. [On the basis of a major survey carried out by the Government in 1969, 1.1 million in Britain aged sixteen and over were estimated to be very seriously, severely or appreciably handicapped, and a further 1.9 million were impaired but needed little or no support for normal everyday living activities. Harris, A., *Handicapped and Impaired in Great Britain*, HMSO, 1971.]
3. *Ministry of Labour Gazette*, April 1967, p. 308.
4. *Report of the Ministry of Pensions and National Insurance for the Year 1965*, Cmnd. 3046, HMSO, 1966.
5. For England and Wales, *Report of the Ministry of Health for the Year 1965*, Cmnd. 3039, HMSO, 1966, pp. 127—30. Figures for Scotland were obtained from Home and Health Department and added.
6. About 48,000 of those living in council or supported voluntary Homes in England and Wales are described as 'handicapped'. See *Report of the Ministry of Health for 1965*, p. 124.
7. England and Wales, *Report of the Ministry of Health for 1965*, p. 119.
8. In March 1967 the total had reached 144,000 (private communication, Ministry of Social Security). Most of them 'are persons incapacitated since birth or early childhood and living with their parents'. *Report of the National Assistance Board for the Year ended 31 December 1965*, Cmnd. 3042, HMSO, 1966, p. 13.
9. *Education in 1966 — Report of the Department of Education and Science*, Cmnd. 3226, HMSO, 1967, p. 44.
10. *Health and Welfare: the Development of Community Care*, Cmnd. 1973, HMSO, 1963, p. 31.
11. Many of those receiving retirement pensions and unemployment or sickness benefits were also receiving supplementary national assistance. People receiving personal disablement benefits (war or industrial injury) were also eligible to receive national insurance benefits.
12. See also the analysis by Nagi, S. Z., 'Some Conceptual Issues in Disability and Rehabilitation', in Sussman, M. B. (ed.), *Sociology and Rehabilitation*, American Sociological Association, 1966, particularly pp. 100—103.
13. An attempt to develop a measure of this was made in 'Measuring Incapacity for Self-Care', in Townsend, P., *The Last Refuge*, Routledge, 1962, pp. 464—76.
14. Goffman, E., *Stigma: Notes on the Management of Spoiled Identity*, Spectrum Books, 1963; Friedson, E., 'Disability as Social Deviance' in Sussman, M. B., *Sociology and Rehabilitation*, American Sociological Association, 1966. More generally see Becker, H. S., *Outsiders: Studies in the Sociology of Deviance*, The Free Press, 1963, particularly Chapters 1 and 2.
15. See, for example, Mechanic, D., 'The Concept of Illness Behaviour', *Journal of Chronic Diseases*, vol. 15, 1962; Mechanic, D., 'Response Factors in Illness: The Study of Illness Behaviour', *Social Psychiatry*, vol. 1, August 1966.
16. See, for example, Zborowski, M., 'Cultural Components in Responses to Pain', *Journal of Social Issues*, vol. 8, 1952; Jaco, E. G. (ed.), Patients, Physicians and Illness, The Free Press, 1958.
17. The 'dependent and segregated status [of the disabled] is not an index merely of their physical condition; to an extent only beginning to be recognized it is the product of cultural definition — an

assumptive framework of myths, stereotypes, aversive responses, and outright prejudices, together with more rational and scientific evidence'. Ten Broek, J., and Matson, F. W., 'The Disabled and the Law of Welfare', *California Law Review*, vol. 54, no. 2, May 1966, p. 814.

18. According to the Charity Commissioners the Spastics Society received £1.8 million in 1962, and the National Society for Mentally Handicapped Children £39,000 in 1964.

19. *Report of the Committee on the Assessment of Disablement* (the McCorquodale Report), Cmnd. 2847, HMSO, December 1965.

20. In awarding war pensions and industrial injuries disablement pensions the Ministry of Pensions bases assessments on comparison between 'the condition of a disabled person and that of a normal healthy person of the same age. Assessment on this basis measures the general handicap imposed by loss of faculty. Loss of faculty may be defined as the loss of physical or mental capacity to lead a normally occupied life and does not depend on the way in which the disablement affects the particular circumstances of the individual. A normally occupied life includes work as well as household and social activities and leisure pursuits.' *Report of the Committee on the Assessment of Disablement*, p. 4. To be admitted to the Ministry of Labour's Register of Disabled Persons an applicant must (1) 'be substantially handicapped on account of injury, disease (including a physical or mental condition arising from imperfect development of any organ) or congenital deformity, in obtaining or keeping employment or work on his own account otherwise suited to his age, qualification and experience; the disablement being likely to last for twelve months or more; (2) desire to engage in some form of remunerative employment or work . . . and have a reasonable prospect of obtaining and keeping such employment or work . . .' Finally, local authorities are empowered by Section 29 of the National Assistance Act, 1948, to promote the welfare of persons who are blind, deaf or dumb, and others, 'who are substantially and permanently handicapped by illness, injury or congenital deformity or such other disabilities as may be prescribed by the Minister'. Registers are compiled on this basis from a variety of sources.

21. The Medical Report form includes a section which allows the doctor to indicate whether an individual can use upper limbs (shoulders, arms, hands, fingers and touch) and lower limbs (walking, standing, sitting only, hurrying, balancing, climbing stairs, climbing ladders), and can kneel, stoop, push and pull, and lift and carry. The extent of hearing and vision also can be noted. The need for better functional assessment was recognized by a Working Party of the British Council for Rehabilitation of the Disabled reporting in 1964: *The Handicapped School-Leaver*, British Council for Rehabilitation of the Disabled.

22. See, for example, Hess, A. E., 'Old Age, Survivors and Disability Insurance: Early Problems and Operations of the Disability Provisions', *Social Security Bulletin*, U.S. Department of Health, Education and Welfare, December 1957.

23. Andersen, B. R., *Fysisk Handicappede i Danmark, Bind II*, Socialforskningsinstittutets Publikationer 16, Copenhagen, 1964, pp. 55–6.

24. Including going up and down stairs, getting about the house, washing and bathing, dressing and putting on shoes, cutting toe nails, brushing and combing hair, going to toilet on own, cleaning floors, cooking a hot meal, seeing, speaking and hearing, and organizing thoughts in lucid speech.

25. For national figures of tenure see Donnison, D. V., *The Government of Housing*, Penguin Books, 1967, p. 186.

26. It is interesting to note that, in 1965, 17,163 artificial legs but only 2,736 artificial arms were supplied under the National Health Service. *Annual Report of the Ministry of Health for 1965*, p. 165.

27. *Report of the Committee of Enquiry on the Rehabilitation, Training and Re-Settlement of Disabled Persons*, Cmnd. 9883, HMSO, 1956, p. 26.

28. *Health and Welfare: The Development of Community Care*, p. 31.

29. Calculated on the basis of information kindly supplied by the Ministry of Health.

30. According to the Ministry of Labour's information on designated employment for August 1964, all but a small minority of the 2,769 lift attendants and 2,584 car park attendants were registered disabled.

31. *Ministry of Labour Gazette*, April 1967.

32. This was stated of 80,000 of the 104,000 men unemployed for six months or more in a special inquiry carried out in 1964, 'Second Inquiry into the Characteristics of the Unemployed', *Ministry of Labour Gazette*, April 1966. In a special study of the unemployed who were receiving assistance in

June 1956 the National Assistance Board found that a majority had some specific physical handicap. Moreover, they also found that only 72 per cent of the men and 50 per cent of the women with physical handicaps were registered as disabled persons with the employment exchange, *Report of the National Assistance Board for 1956*, Cmnd. 181, HMSO, 1957, p. 42.

33. The history of registration is puzzling. In 1950 the register reached a peak of 936,500 but then declined, in some years rather sharply (the figure for 1966 being 654,000). In 1957 the Ministry explained that only part of this decline was attributable to a falling off in the numbers of disabled servicemen. Many disabled persons did not renew their registration, either because they felt secure enough in their employment, or because the DROs, supported by the Disablement Advisory Committee Panels, were interpreting disability more strictly 'so as to exclude the lightly handicapped'. There is also the fact that soon after registration started employers persuaded some of their employees to register to help meet the 3 per cent quota. Even if persons who stay with one firm do not re-register they are still counted in the quota. This is plainly unsatisfactory, for some are no longer disabled or have remained no more than marginally disabled. See *Annual Reports of the Ministry of Labour* for 1949—60, particularly for 1949 (Cmnd. 8017), 1957 (Cmnd. 468), and 1960 (Cmnd. 1364).

34. Some have called for an independent review of the work. Members of staff of the Ministry fill the post of DRO by rotation, serving for five years. They then move on to other work. There is no established training course. Lady Hamilton, 'Integrating the Physically Handicapped', *New Society*, 5 May 1966.

35. Jeffreys, M., *An Anatomy of Social Welfare Services*, Michael Joseph, 1966, pp. 68 and 288.

36. The percentage varies from 67 per cent in Wales to 59 per cent in the north west to 49 per cent in the Midlands and 45 per cent in London and the south east. Information for 1 July 1966 kindly supplied in a private communication by the Ministry of Labour.

37. For a clear account of some of these see Willmott, P., 'Social Security in Disablement', in Hunt, P. (ed.), *Stigma: The Experience of Disability*, Geoffrey Chapman, 1966.

38. English translation of *National Insurance Act*, 25 May 1962, Swedish Ministry of Social Affairs, 1963.

39. [In 1968, partly as a consequence of pressure from the Disablement Income Group, the Child Poverty Action Group and other bodies, the Minister of Social Security, Mrs Judith Hart, announced the research which culminated in a survey of the handicapped and impaired in Britain by the Office of Population Censuses and Surveys: Social Survey Division. See Harris, A., *Handicapped and Impaired in Great Britain*, HMSO, 1971.]

40. Hunt, P., 'A Critical Condition', in Hunt, P. (ed.), op. cit., p. 148.

4. The epidemiology of handicap: summary of findings*

MICHAEL RUTTER
Professor of Child Psychology, Institute of Psychiatry, University of London.

JACK TIZARD
Professor of Child Development, Institute of Education, University of London.

KINGSLEY WHITMORE
Senior Medical Officer, Department of Education and Science.
et alia

The object of our research was not only to estimate and record the prevalence, background and nature of intellectual, educational, physical and psychiatric handicaps among the children we studied. We wished also to examine how far existing services were structured to deal with the problems which the handicaps posed for children and their families. This is an essential procedure preliminary to the planning of services, and the planning and evaluation of services to meet the special educational, social and to some extent medical needs of handicapped children was our ultimate objective. In this chapter, therefore, we summarise those of our findings that are relevant to this purpose.

The prevalence of handicap

In the 1964 survey we identified children born between 1 September 1953 and 31 August 1955 who had severe difficulty in reading and also those who were severely retarded in general intelligence. We used the Neale Analysis of Reading Ability Test to measure a child's reading difficulty, and identified two groups of children.[1]

(a) those *backward in reading*, i.e. with a reading accuracy or comprehension which was 28 months or more below the child's chronological age: 154 children.

(b) those *specifically retarded in reading*, i.e. with a reading accuracy or comprehension which was 28 months or more below the level predicted on the basis of a child's age and short WISC IQ: 85 children.

Seventy-five of the eighty-five children with a specific reading retardation were also *backward* in reading while the remaining ten were retarded but not backward. In addition, there were nine severely subnormal children who had been excluded from the reading groups by definition but who nevertheless presented an educational problem. Thus, the total number of children with an educational problem was 173, equivalent to 7.9 per cent of the child population of that age.

We used the WISC for measuring intelligence, and taking a scale score of two standard deviations or more below the mean (average) scale score of all children in the control group as our criterion, we

*From M. Rutter, J. Tizard and K. Whitmore (eds) *Education, health and behaviour*, (1970) London, Longman, Chapter 22 compiled by the Survey Team, pp. 347–57.

identified 58 children who were intellectually retarded: 2.6 per cent of the population.

In the second stage of the survey, we identified children in the same age cohort who had a psychiatric disorder and children born between 1 September 1952 and 31 August 1955 who had a physical handicap. We defined 'psychiatric disorder' as an abnormality of behaviour, emotions or relationships which was sufficiently marked and sufficiently prolonged to cause a handicap to the child himself and/or distress or disturbance in the family or community, which was continuing up to the time of assessment. This was present in 118 children (5.4 per cent of the population).

We classified as physically handicapped any child with a physical disorder which was chronic (lasting at least one year), present during the twelve months preceding assessment, and associated with persisting or recurrent handicap of some kind. Of the children in the three-year cohort whom we examined, 186 had such a disorder. Sixty-five of them were in the oldest of the three age groups and as this was not screened for educational problems or psychiatric disorders, we have omitted these children from subsequent calculations in this chapter. Thus, there were 121 children with a physical disorder (5.5 per cent of the population).

The number of handicapped children

In order to plan services it is necessary to know not only the prevalence of different disorders, but also the total number of children with disorders, either single or multiple. Because of the overlap between handicaps this figure will be less than the total sum of separate prevalence rates for each of the different disorders.

From this analysis a most striking finding emerges. Among 2199 children aged nine to eleven years living on the Isle of Wight, there were 354 with some form of handicap (Tables 4.1 and 4.3). Thus, considering only the four principal types of handicap studied, 161 children in every thousand, or approximately one child in every six, of those in the middle years of their schooling, were found to have a chronic or recurrent handicap.

The meaning of handicap

One child in every six with a chronic or recurrent handicap may seem a very high figure. However, in order to judge the implications for services of this figure it is also necessary to consider what 'handicap' means in this context. The definitions used in defining handicap have been given in previous chapters but here we are concerned with the meaning of handicap for the child.

Reading retardation was defined in terms of

Table 4.1 Numbers of children with one, two, three or four handicapping conditions in a population of 2199 children of whom 354 were handicapped (for definition, see text)

	Intellectual retardation	Educational backwardness	Psychiatric disorder	Physical handicap	Total handicap
One handicap only	6	98	75	86	265
Two handicaps					
Intellectual retardation +	—	27	1	2	67
Educational retardation +	27	—	22	7	
Psychiatric disorder +	1	22	—	8	
Physical handicap +	2	7	8	—	
Three handicaps					
Intellectual + educational + psychiatric	4	4	4	—	17
Intellectual + educational + physical	10	10	—	10	
Intellectual + psychiatric + physical	3	—	3	3	
Educational + psychiatric + physical	—	—	—	—	
Four handicaps	5	5	5	5	5
TOTAL WITH EACH HANDICAP	58	173	118	121	354

Table 4.2 Prevalence of four handicapping conditions among nine- to eleven-year-old children. Age specific rates per 1000 children, based on Isle of Wight population surveys (n = 2199)

	Intellectual retardation	Educational backwardness	Psychiatric disorder	Physical handicap	Rate per 1000*
One handicap only	2.7	44.7	34.2	39.2	120.8
Two handicaps					
Intellectual +	—	12.3	0.5	0.9 ⎫	
Educational +	12.3	—	10.0	3.2 ⎬	30.5
Psychiatric +	0.5	10.0	—	3.7 ⎭	
Physical +	0.9	3.2	3.7	—	
Three handicaps					
Intellectual + educational + psychiatric	1.8	1.8	1.8	—	
Intellectual + educational + physical	4.6	4.6	—	4.6 ⎫	
Intellectual + psychiatric + physical	1.4	—	1.4	1.4 ⎬	7.8
Educational + psychiatric + physical	—	—	—	— ⎭	
All four handicaps	2.3	2.3	2.3	2.3	2.3
Total* with each handicap	26.4	78.9	53.8	55.2	161.4

*Computed.

how much progress children had made in relation to the progress of the total group of children in that age and level of intelligence. In somewhat similar fashion, intellectual retardation was defined in terms of children's scores on an intelligence test as judged in relation to the scores of other children of the same age. Obviously, whenever a test of intelligence or educational attainment is given there must be some children whose scores are lower than those of other children, just as some children must always be bottom of the class in reading or arithmetic. This will remain true however successfully children learn to read or perform on intelligence tests in future generations, If all children can read fluently, the child who is worst in reading may not be handicapped at all. Thus, handicap must be judged in terms of what the child can and cannot do rather than in terms of his relative position in the class or on some test.

Put in these terms, it is evident that the retarded children are indeed profoundly handicapped. They are, in fact, on the borderline of illiteracy. Furthermore, their reading difficulties, as shown by our follow-up studies, are remarkably persistent so that not only do they fail to benefit fully from their schooling but also many will be limited in the life they can lead after leaving school. To the backward (or retarded) reader,

handicap means inability to follow instructions in a do-it-yourself kit, embarrassment when unable to read and complete official forms without assistance, ignorance where books and newspapers might provide information, and the lack of opportunity to experience the pleasure that reading may bring.

Intellectual retardation meant an IQ of 70 or less. Most of the brighter children in this group were unable, without special education, to benefit from their schooling and many were in schools for the educationally subnormal. On leaving school, most will need support and supervision during their early employment. The duller ones are likely to graduate from junior to senior training centres, and to need sheltered employment and supervision throughout their lives. The most handicapped require total care and are unable to undertake even the simplest job. [. . .]

Psychiatric handicap may mean suffering in the shape of anxiety and unhappiness or it may mean conflict between society and the child, bringing trouble to both. Some of the neurotic children were unable to do what they wanted because of incapacitating fears, many lay awake at nights worrying, and distress was a frequent experience for all. For the child with a conduct disorder conflict and discord at home and at school were characteristic, but also many were miserable, fearful or worried as well. Perhaps most striking of all was the high proportion of children with all types of psychiatric disorder who had serious difficulties in their relationships with people; for example, half were said to be not much liked by other children.

Of all the disorders studied, physical disorder is perhaps the type most generally associated with handicap. Paradoxically, some of the least affected children were included under this heading. A small number of asthmatic attacks during the previous year or the presence of a visible skin lesion was sufficient for inclusion in the group. Most, however, were a good deal more affected than this, either in terms of frequent absences from school through illness or in terms of restriction of physical activities or often both. For some children particularly those with brain disorders, handicap meant an inability to lead an ordinary life due to partial or even total dependence on others for feeding, dressing or getting around from place to place.

Thus, handicap for most of the children studied meant a considerable interference with their ability to lead a normal life.

The overlap between handicaps

In Table 4.3 the figures show more clearly the proportion of children with each type of handicap who also had other handicaps. Ninety per cent of the intellectually retarded children had other handicaps as did 43 per cent of the educationally retarded, 36 per cent of the children with psychiatric disorder and 29 per cent of those with a physical handicap. Altogether, a quarter of the handicapped children had at least two handicaps[2]. Put in population terms, 161 children per 1000 had a chronic recurrent handicap; 121 per 1000 had a single handicap, 30 per 1000 a dual handicap, 8 per 1000 a triple handicap and over 2 per 1000 had all four handicaps studied.

To understand the needs of the children it is necessary to know the nature as well as the extent of the overlap between handicaps. As would be expected, four-fifths of the intellectually retarded children also had an educational handicap. However, while most children with an intellectual handicap were also severely backward in reading, the converse was not true. Although a quarter of the educationally backward children were also intellectually retarded a substantial proportion had a normal level of intelligence. It was these children

Table 4.3 Percentage of children with intellectual, educational, psychiatric or physical handicaps who have additional handicaps

	Intellectual	Educational	Psychiatric	Physical	Per cent with different numbers of handicaps
One handicap only	10.3	56.6	63.6	71.1	75.0
Two handicaps					18.8
Intellectual +	—	15.6	0.8	1.7	
Educational +	46.6	—	18.7	5.8	
Psychiatric +	1.7	12.7	—	6.6	
Physical +	3.4	4.0	6.8	—	
Three handicaps					4.8
Intellectual + educational + psychiatric	6.9	2.3	3.4	—	
Intellectual + educational + physical	17.2	5.8	—	8.3	
Intellectual + psychiatric + physical	5.2	—	2.5	2.4	
Educational + psychiatric + physical	—	—	—	—	
Four handicaps					1.4
Intellectual + educational + psychiatric + physical	8.6	2.9	4.2	4.1	
Total number of cases	58	173	118	121	354

who were included in the category of specific reading retardation.

One-third of the intellectually retarded had a physical handicap (most often this was a neurological condition which was probably the primary cause of their retardation) and more than a fifth had a psychiatric disability. As only one in ten of the intellectually retarded had no other handicap, it is abundantly clear that most intellectually handicapped children present multiple problems, and that these are not merely ones related directly to their learning difficulties.

The children with an educational handicap also frequently (but less often than the intellectually retarded) had multiple handicaps. One in six had a psychiatric disorder (usually antisocial in type) and one in eight had a physical disorder.

Just over a third of the children with a psychiatric disorder had multiple handicaps. One in six had a physical disorder and over a quarter were educationally backward. Antisocial children tended to be backward educationally much more often than neurotic children; thus, 45 per cent of antisocial boys had a specific reading retardation of at least two years compared with only 6 per cent of neurotic boys. The association between reading retardation and antisocial behaviour is an important one with implications for services, although the nature of the association is still ill-understood. Both may develop on the basis of similar types of personality difficulties, but also it seems that delinquency may sometimes be *caused*, in part, by educational failure.

Most physically handicapped children did not have any other handicaps but an important and substantial minority (29 per cent) did. Nearly one in five had an educational handicap and one in six had a psychiatric disorder. One in six was intellectually retarded. Many children with chronic or recurrent physical disorders were also handicapped in other aspects of their development, a finding which has a bearing on the planning of services for this group of children. It is also relevant that in most cases the handicap involved the child's family as well as the child himself. In over half the children the disorder was associated with some disorganisation of family routine, in some there were impaired family relationships, and over half the parents expressed some dissatisfaction with present services.

Background of handicaps

The features of the child himself, his family and social circumstances which were associated with each handicap have already been discussed and summarised in previous chapters. Here only a few of the findings (other than those mentioned under the overlap between handicaps) which have particular importance for the planning of services will be noted.

Our studies, although limited in this respect, have shown important associations between children's sociofamilial background and the presence of handicap. Intellectually retarded children frequently came from large families in which the father had an unskilled or labouring job. The fathers of children with reading retardation more often did skilled manual work but again the families were mostly large. To a lesser extent, children with psychiatric disorder also came from large families, but there was no marked association with social class. On the other hand, a broken home and emotional difficulties in the parents were associated with psychiatric disorder in the children. There are many reasons for these associations but to some extent it is likely that adverse sociofamilial circumstances have played a part in the development of the children's handicaps. To this extent, there are opportunities for the identification of children at particular risk to develop handicaps, and also, potentially, for the prevention of some of these disorders.

In this context it is relevant that the Isle of Wight is a fairly prosperous community of people living in small towns and villages. There are very few children who are not of United Kingdom parentage, and the number of 'immigrants' (a current euphemism for coloured children whether or not they were born in this country) is tiny. The grossly adverse social circumstances present in city slums in which many children, and particularly those in minority groups, are brought up, are almost unknown on the Island.

Many of the children with an educational handicap were found to have language and speech problems, poor motor coordination and difficulties differentiating right from left. These are developmental functions, and histories obtained from parents concerning the ages at which their children started walking and talking suggested that many of the children had had these developmental difficulties from early childhood. Evidence from this and other studies suggested that these difficulties may have played a part in the causation of the later educational retardation. Again, this presents an opportunity for the earlier identification and treatment of children who are likely to have severe problems in learning to read.

The size of the problem

Our findings were based on total population studies of specific age groups. However, the rates must be regarded as 'minimal' prevalence estimates for the following reasons:

(*a*) Except where otherwise stated, the figures have been based on the numbers actually ascertained in our studies. Inevitably, some children with handicaps must have been missed, despite the efforts to make the case-finding as complete as possible. We have been able to obtain some estimate of the numbers of cases omitted. The numbers are not large but, as in any epidemiological study, there are some missed cases, which, if discovered, would increase the prevalence rates obtained.

(*b*) Not all handicaps were studied. Children with primary handicaps of a social nature and children with certain developmental disorders (such as speech problems and enuresis) were not included unless they also had one of the four main handicaps which we studied.

(*c*) Although social circumstances on the Island are fairly similar to those in England and Wales as a whole, the worst kinds of slum conditions and the problems of social disorganisation seen in parts of most major cities were not represented on the Isle of Wight.

(*d*) The prevalence rates of handicap in other age groups are unlikely to be much less, and may even be considerably higher than in the nine- to twelve-year-old children we studied. For example, developmental problems which have greatly diminished by the age of nine years are much commoner in children just starting school. More five-year-olds are severely retarded in their use of language and more wet their beds. Problems of severe overactivity are also more frequent in the young child. In the adolescent, on the other hand, delinquency is a much commoner problem than in the age group we studied. There is little point in making comparisons between studies of different age groups as different methods have been used

and as there are no satisfactory estimates of the rate of handicap in very young children or in children of an age to leave school. However, what evidence there is suggests that the rate of handicap in other age groups is not appreciably less than that which we found.

Existing services

Before considering the implications for services it is appropriate to end this brief summary of the epidemiology of handicap by noting the extent to which the handicapped children on the Isle of Wight were already receiving whatever treatment was needed.

The Island services existing at the time of the surveys in 1964/65 were for the most part better than or at least as good as those found in other parts of the country. The pupil—teacher ratio in the Island schools was somewhat better than in the country as a whole, and the rate of turnover of teachers was also slightly lower. The Island had an excellent modern purpose-built school for educationally subnormal children and the number of special school places per population was greater than in other parts of England and Wales. There was also a day centre for children with severe neurological handicaps. The amount of consultant paediatric time available was roughly the same as for other areas, although a part-time appointment was less satisfactory than it would be on the mainland in that travelling is more difficult when a sea journey is necessary. The Island's child guidance clinic was staffed by a consultant child psychiatrist attending two days per week, a full-time psychiatric social worker and an educational psychologist for half his time. This is a common pattern of staffing and the amount of professional time available for a school population of nearly 13,000 children compares quite favourably with what is available in other parts of the country.

The Island's Children's Department runs two children's homes, one for reception and short-term care and one for long-term care. Health visitors help with the social problems of children in their own homes, and there is an active school Welfare Department providing an important link between home and school on matters affecting welfare, including such material assistance as free dinners, clothing, uniform grants and maintenance allowances. Again, the provision compares favourably with other parts of the country.

There are certainly inadequacies in Island services, but these parallel inadequacies elsewhere and it is likely that the deficiencies to be noted in relation to the care of the handicapped children we studied are no greater, and probably appreciably less in many respects, than those to be found in most other parts of the United Kingdom (and doubtless other countries as well).

The diagnosis and care of handicapped children
The care provided for children with intellectual or educational retardation was as follows. A sixth were in special schools and a sixth were in 'progress' classes in ordinary schools. However, nearly two-thirds were in regular classes in ordinary day schools and for these children there was no special remedial help as, at that time, no trained remedial teacher was available for any of the Island's primary schools. It can hardly be doubted that this degree of special provision for educationally retarded children in ordinary schools (most of whom were quite properly placed there) falls well short of the needs of these children. The kinds of treatment which are needed will be discussed elsewhere. Suffice it to say here that the follow-up study of children with reading retardation showed that during a period of twenty-eight months (taking them up to about age twelve years) they made on average only ten months' progress in reading accuracy and so, relatively speaking, the severity of the retardation had actually increased. Whatever form of special educational treatment is most effective, these children were *not* getting what was needed.

Most of the children with physical handicap were under some form of medical care. For the most part, the strictly medical aspects of treatment appeared fairly adequate. The deficiencies here arose in relation to the other educational and psychiatric handicaps which were present in nearly 30 per cent of the group, and in relation to the social problems experienced by many of the families. Parents often said that they needed more guidance in the individual management of the handicapped child; more moral support and advice in coping with the disturbed family situation and relationships sometimes associated with handicap, especially when there was also a psychiatric disorder; and more tangible help to relieve them of the mental, physical and financial burden of caring for and living with severely handicapped children. The nature and extent of the medical services provided for these children were not studied in any detail but, as judged from the frequency of associated handicaps and from the family reactions, it seemed that sometimes medical treatment may have been too narrow in approach and sometimes links with social, educational, and psychiatric services fell short of what was required.

Of the children suffering from psychiatric disorder only one in ten was attending a child psychiatric·clinic. Nine-tenths of the Island children with psychiatric disorder had not been expertly diagnosed or assessed; furthermore, that, as an almost inevitable consequence, those dealing with these children in their daily lives at home and at school must have been acting in the light of incomplete information. Two-fifths of the children with antisocial disorder were severely retarded in their reading and like other children with reading difficulties they were receiving little special help for this.

It was not an aim of the research to assess the effectiveness of services on the Island and it would not be appropriate to comment further upon them. We have already mentioned that, from what evidence we have, in most respects Island facilities compared favourably with those found in other parts of the country. Nevertheless, many of the handicapped children we studied were not receiving adequate treatment.

NOTES

1. For this purpose and throughout this chapter, figures are given for children in local authority schools. Intellectual and educational difficulties in children attending private schools were also examined. However, children in the private sector of education were excluded from the survey of psychiatric and physical disorders. Thus, in order to facilitate examination of the overlap between handicaps the one child with reading retardation and the one child with intellectual retardation who attended a private school have been excluded in this chapter.

2. Readers may be puzzled to see in Table 4.3 that although, overall, 75 per cent of handicapped children had only one handicap, the proportions of children in each of the four groups with only one handicap were all smaller than 75.0 per cent. The reason is that the multiply handicapped children were included in each of the categories in which they were handicapped. A simplified example will show the consequence of this multiple counting. Suppose there were one hundred children in each of the four categories (intellectual, educational, psychiatric and physical) and that all of these 400 children had only *one* handicap. Suppose also that there were 100 additional children each of whom had all four handicaps. Then of the 500 handicapped children 400 (80 per cent) would have only one handicap. But in each handicapped group only 100 children (50 per cent) would have a single handicap and an additional hundred would have more than one handicap. The 'additional hundred' in each group would, of course, all be the same children.

5. Disabled income *

TONY LYNES
Formerly of the London School of Economics,
writer in Social Security

Few causes command so much public sympathy as that of the disabled. Of all the national pressure groups, DIG (the Disablement Income Group) has had least difficulty in attracting all-party support. If progress in translating pressure into action has been disappointingly slow, it is not through any lack of agreement on the basic proposition that disabled people, as a class, need higher incomes. The limiting factors, apart from the usual one of cost, have been of a more technical nature.

The diversity of circumstances and needs among the disabled, and the variety of sources from which they can be met, is indicated by the table opposite, which sets out some, but by no means all, of the more important variables. It is easy to criticise the fragmented nature of existing provisions, with their excessive preoccupation with the causes of disability, but no single scheme, however elaborate, can take account of all these variables. What is needed is a measure of agreement as to the relative importance to be attached to each of them.

Is compensation for restriction of activity to take precedence over compensation for loss of earnings? Is it justifiable to treat those whose working life is terminated prematurely more generously than those who have never been able to work? To what extent should the cause of disability determine the amount of benefit or compensation? Widely varying solutions are proposed, depending on the answers to such questions or, too often, on unstated assumptions as to what the answers ought to be.

*From *New Society* 3rd May (1973) *24* No. 552, pp. 23–5.

At present, two categories are accorded preferential treatment: those suffering from the effects of war injuries and of industrial accidents or diseases. They get higher benefits than those incapacitated through other causes; their benefits are not dependent on the number of contributions paid; they can continue to draw their disablement pensions after returning to work; and, while the amount of the pension depends mainly on loss of faculty, it can be increased to take account of individual circumstances such as attendance needs and reduced earning capacity.

Until 1971, the only benefits available without a means test to disabled people of working age, outside the industrial injury and war pension schemes, were the flat-rate national insurance sickness benefit (now £6.75 per week for a single person) and the earnings-related supplement payable after the first two weeks for up to six months. These, however, were payable only to those who had paid a minimum number of contributions, either as employees or (for flat-rate benefit only) as self-employed persons. and only during periods of total incapacity. As soon as the claimant was regarded by his doctor as fit for work, even if his earning capacity was substantially reduced, entitlement to sickness benefit ceased. Those disabled from childhood, who had never worked for long enough to satisfy the contribution conditions, were obliged to rely on help from their family and friends or on supplementary benefit.

The present government has improved the situation of the 'civilian' disabled in two respects. Sickness benefit is now replaced after 28 weeks (i.e., when the earnings-related supplement runs out) by a flat-rate invalidity pension payable at the same basic rate but augmented by a small invalidity pension payable at the same rate but augmented by a small invalidity allowance (at most £1.15, for those whose incapacity began before the age of 35). Invalidity pensioners also get the higher children's allowances previously paid only for widows' children. But total incapacity is still a condition for drawing benefit, and the congenitally disabled still do not qualify.

The second and more radical innovation is the attendance allowance, which extends to the civilian disabled the principle of compensation for the expenses of disability, already recognised in the industrial injury and war pension schemes. Taken over from the Crossman pensions bill which died with the Labour government, the £5.40 allowance already reaches 85,000 people, compared with the 50,000 expected claims — a salutary reminder of the inadequacy of our knowledge of the extent of disability, despite the efforts of Amelia Harris and her colleagues at the Office of Population Censuses and Surveys, whose survey of the disabled has now produced three volumes of statistics (*Handicapped and Impaired in Great Britain*, Parts I-III, HMSO). Payment of the attendance allowance at a lower rate (£3.60) to those needing assistance either by day or by night is expected to raise the number of recipients to 250,000 by December 1974.

Despite these improvements, our social security arrangements still fall far short of providing all disabled people with a standard of living reasonably comparable to that of the rest of the population. The main gaps that remain are:

The disabled and their income

1. Sources of disablement income

war pension	unemployment benefit
industrial injury disablement pension	retirement pension
national insurance invalidity pension	supplementary benefit
attendance allowance	civil damages
occupational pension	criminal injury compensation
private insurance	

2. Factors in income

a. Age
children
adults (working age)
old people

b. Effects of impairment
loss of faculty
restriction of activity
loss of earnings
pain and suffering
expense

c. Cause of disability	
congenital	industrial accident/disease
chronic sickness—stable	road accident
chronic sickness—progressive	other accident—due to others' negligence
war injury	other accident—not due to others' negligence

d. Previous employment status
never worked
employed
self-employed
unemployed
housewife
retired

1. Compensation for loss of earnings is limited in most cases to the flat-rate invalidity benefit — at most £7.90 for a single person.

2. Apart from the attendance allowance and means-tested supplementary benefit, there is still no provision for disabled children, adults disabled from childhood, and disabled housewives; and for wives and children even supplementary benefit is not normally available since they are regarded as the husband's dependants.

3. The attendance allowance recognises only one type of expense associated with disablement and is available only to those so severely handicapped that, in the words of the official leaflet, they 'need a lot of looking after.'

4. The legal obstacles facing those whose disability gives rise to a claim for damages against some other person produce uncertainty, lengthy delays, and often inadequate settlements, as the thalidomide affair has demonstrated.

DIG's proposals for filling the first three of these gaps were published in 1972 (*Creating a National Disability Income*, 25p from DIG). The main demands were for earnings-related invalidity benefits, a more adequate system of expense allowances, and flat-rate invalidity pensions for disabled housewives and those disabled from childhood. Other reforms suggested by DIG include the payment of invalidity benefits at a reduced rate if substantial loss of earning power persists after rehabilitation and a tax allowance for the extra working expenses incurred by disabled people; a major criticism of existing provisions being the disincentive effect of withdrawing the whole of the invalidity benefit as soon as the recipient's earning capacity is even partially restored.

Each of these proposals, considered in isolation, seems reasonable enough. What DIG has not said is at what rate the various benefits should be paid and how they would fit into a coherent and fair disablement income scheme. What, for instance, should be the relationship between earnings-related benefits for those who have worked and flat-rate benefits for those who have not? What proportion of earnings should invalidity benefit replace, and should this proportion be higher for the lower-paid? What kinds of expenses should be covered by the proposed expense allowances? Without at least approximate answers to these questions, it is impossible to cost DIG's proposals

or to establish an order of priority for their implementation.

One reason for the lack of precision is DIG's determination to preserve its non-party image by fitting its demands into the broad pattern of social security measures proposed by whichever party is in power. The Vicar of Bray approach is especially apparent in relation to the proposal for earnings-related invalidity benefits, by treating an employee who had been in receipt of sickness benefit for six months as prematurely retired. His pension would have been calculated on the basis of his individual earnings record, the missing years up to normal pension age being filled in by crediting earnings at half the national average.

The [Conservative] government's decision to leave the provision of earnings-related pensions as far as possible to occupational schemes made it far more difficult to legislate for invalidity pensions, which the Inland Revenue do not allow occupational schemes to provide unless the invalidity involves retirement from work, and which the life offices regard as 'uninsurable' in this form except with a very severe reduction in the accrued pension. Even if they could be included in an insurable form (for example, linked to the payment of a basic invalidity pension), the levels of benefit would be lower than in the Crossman scheme and would build up much more slowly, and the problems of preserving pension rights on a change of jobs would be increased. Despite these difficulties, DIG declared itself 'neither for nor against the government's policy of seeking to use occupational schemes to the greatest possible extent,' and limited its demands to the provision of invalidity pensions consistent with the pensions payable on retirement under the government's proposals.

Not surprisingly, there are differences of opinion even among DIG's membership as to whether this was the right approach. Even if the more generous benefit formula of the Crossman scheme were adopted, it would still be open to the objection that those already near retirement age would generally get bigger pensions than those forced to give up work in mid-career. Moreover, the most severely disabled would be likely to have had the poorest earnings record, while those disabled from childhood and unable to do any paid work would get, at best, a low flat-rate benefit plus an expense allowance. Similarly, an earnings-related scheme would not help those whose working life had come to an end before the scheme commenced (though they might benefit from the more recent proposals mooted by Labour spokesmen for crediting existing pensioners into a revived Crossman scheme).

These objections are summed up in a resolution submitted by the Westminster branch of DIG for discussion at DIG's annual general meeting this weekend:

'Having regard to the fact that a large majority of the disabled are retired, unemployed, or low wage-earners, and that therefore an earnings-related disability pension scheme would help only a minority, would leave many people still dependent on means-tested benefits and would introduce major new anomalies of the kind DIG was founded to abolish; this Annual General Meeting rejects all such earnings-related pension schemes and resolves to campaign for comprehensive disability benefits based not on contribution record but solely on degree of impairment.'

Influential support was given to the idea of disability benefits based solely on degree of handicap, irrespective of previous earnings (if any), in a recent 'round-robin' letter to the Prime Minister. The initiative for this came from Professor Peter Townsend, himself one of DIG's patrons, and the signatories included the group's recently retired honorary director, Mary Greaves. The Townsend letter calls for an 'equitable system of allowances and pensions' for all handicapped persons, children as well as adults, based on a functional (rather than medical) assessment of degree of handicap and subject to periodic review.

The advantage of a scheme of this sort is that it would avoid discriminating between different categories of the disabled on the basis of age, labour force participation or cause of disability. In compensating for handicap, it would automatically provide for part at least of the additional expense resulting from it, though the attendance allowance would still be needed. Not being based on loss of earnings, the pension could continue regardless of the recipient's subsequent earnings, thus avoiding any disincentive to resume work (though the threat of having the degree of handicap reassessed at a lower level might act as a disincentive to rehabilitation). Above all, given both the will and the resources, such a scheme could be introduced with no more delay than was necessary to carry out the assessments of handicap.

But there are snags in Townsend's approach, too. Like DIG, he does not say at what rates the proposed benefits should be paid or what the total cost might be. Nor does he explain how the disability pension would be coordinated with other benefits. Presumably sickness or invalidity benefit would still be payable to those able to satisfy the contribution conditions, but not to those who had never worked or whom despite their disability, were regarded as fit for work.

To remove these distinctions would require two other reforms: giving disabled school-leavers an immediate entitlement to invalidity benefit without contribution conditions; and, more controversially, making unemployment benefit payable (as invalidity benefit already is) without any limit of duration. Similarly, the Townsend solution does not remove the awkwardness of the transition from flat-rate disability benefits to earnings-related pension at normal pension age. Particularly for those disabled in the later years of working life, the DIG concept of an earnings-related invalidity pension anticipating the normal retirement pension is, from this point of view, more attractive.

There is something to be said for both the flat-rate (degree of handicap) and the earnings-related (premature retirement) approach to disablement benefits, and an acceptable solution may well be found in a combination of the two. To some extent, the Crossman pension scheme would have provided this. Those qualifying for an invalidity pension in the early years of their career would have received a pension based mainly on assumed earnings of half the national average, while those nearer retirement age would have got pensions reflecting more closely their individual earnings. It would not have been impossible to include the congenitally disabled by crediting them with an assumed level of earnings for the whole of their careers. Nor would it have been difficult to amend the pension formula to give a better deal to those qualifying for pension at an early age.

The [Conservative] government, on the other hand, has resisted pressure from DIG to incorporate earnings-related invalidity pensions in the conditions for recognition of occupational schemes under the Social Security Bill, or in the proposed state reserve pension scheme. It has concentrated instead, on extending the attendance allowance and improving marginally the flat-rate invalidity allowance. The latter, however, remains far below any conceivable definition of adequacy and is still payable only to those certified as totally unfit for work.

The concept of partial incapacity, or of payment of reduced invalidity pensions during and after rehabilitation, has not yet been included in the detailed proposals of either party, though *Labour's Programme for Britain*, published in 1972, promised that 'compensation will be paid for loss of earnings whether that loss is total or partial.' This may well be the most hopeful direction in which to look for progress in the short term, since there are indications that, in examining the experience of other countries in Europe, the government has been impressed by the emphasis placed on rehabilitation in providing benefits for the disabled.

Finally, there is the question of compensation through the legal system, which Lord Pearson's royal commission is now studying. Everybody agrees that the present situation, in which compensation depends on proof of fault, and payment is often delayed for many years, must be changed. But it would be tragic if the Pearson commission regarded this as a separate problem from that of providing, through the social security system, for the needs of the disabled as a whole. There is, in fact a strong case for broadening both the terms of reference and the membership of the commission, to cover the whole field of financial compensation for disability, however caused.

It is too much to hope that a unanimous recommendation for any single solution would result. But if the commission managed to produce a number of coherent options, this would be an invaluable contribution to what must ultimately be a political debate about the allocation of resources to the disabled.

6. Care with dignity: an analysis of costs of care for the disabled*

 Report by the

ECONOMIST INTELLIGENCE UNIT LTD.

1. The costs of care in different circumstances

INTRODUCTION

In this chapter we undertake a comparison of the costs of care of the disabled in different living circumstances. Our approach will be to analyse the costs of the various branches of care separately, and then bring together the results in a comparable way. We then go on to consider the implications of different rates of deterioration for the costs of care. We will discuss some of the snags inherent in a policy of greater reliance on community care. Finally we suggest some possible measures for increasing the volume of community care services.

THE NATURE OF THE MARGINAL POPULATION

In order to do this effectively, we need to be clear on the nature of the marginal population — those who medically might be in either home or hospital care. It is well established that the vast majority of disabled live at home, and many of the most severely disabled at home are at least as incapacitated as those in hospital or institutional care. The home dialysis and St. Thomas experiments show that with good, intensive care, even the most severely disabled people can be cared for at home. However, individual discharge decisions remain the responsibility of the hospital consultant, and he will partly be influenced by the knowledge of the situation to which the patient is

*Extracts from Action Research for the Crippled Child Monograph (1973) *Care with dignity: an analysis of costs of care for the disabled*, London, National Fund for Research into Crippling Diseases, Section 1 from chapter 4: section 2 from chapter 5, pp. 22—46

discharged. This knowledge probably explains why middle class patients are discharged earlier than working class ones — there is more often a wife or husband free to care for the patient and there are more likely to be adequate financial resources, for example, to pay for extra help.

Housing too, is crucial. Indeed, the marginal group may be a quite different, and on average a more severely handicapped group, when the alternative to hospital is modern purpose-built accommodation for the disabled, rather than unfit slum dwellings which are the only alternative for many disabled people.

The most critical element in marginality is the presence of relatives, or sometimes, friends, who can care for the disabled person for the bulk of the time. This lack is indeed the primary explanation of institutionalisation.

Marginality is thus as much a result of a person's social circumstances as his medical condition. For our purposes, we take the home alternative as modern accommodation, with or without family support. We also assume that the disabled person does not require continuous professional medical attention, but is moderately to severely disabled on the widely used functional scales.

THE COSTS OF HOSPITAL CARE

Hospital care is expensive. The weekly running cost for an in-patient at an acute London teaching hospital by early 1972 was close to £100 a week. To this must be added capital costs. However, the average length of stay in expensive acute hospitals is short, around ten days, and this is some two thirds of the figure for ten years ago.[1]

The type of patient who is the concern of this study, the chronic sick or disabled, is unlikely to stay long in an acute hospital or an acute ward. Insofar as there may be some chance of reducing the length of stay, or preventing it altogether, the proper basis of comparison is with the long stay or chronic sick hospital or wards. It is time spent there, not in acute beds, that will be avoided by better community and outpatient care. The cost per week in such hospitals varies from £25-30 a week, as shown in the following table:

level of professional care is needed, i.e. doctor's and nurse's time, then for the patient at home (or in a residential home) similar costs will be incurred, plus travelling time. Cost of drugs and dispensing will also be higher outside hospitals.[2] Offsets to this might be the substitution of (cheaper) GP's time for hospital consultants, and substitution of amateur for professional nursing care. However, if the marginal patients are typically moderately to severely disabled and lacking in relatives, then the scope for this switch must ordinarily be limited.

Table 6.1   Cost per in patient week, non-teaching hospitals in England, 1970/71*

	Average size	Cost per week (£)	Of which:	
			Nursing and Treatment (£)	Other 'hotel' costs (£)
Acute, over 100 beds	278	66.7	41.6	25.1
Convalescent	51	25.1	12.3	12.8
Long stay	193	29.7	16.6	13.1
Chronic	73	26.2	15.3	10.9

*1970—71 financial year.
   Source: Hospital costing returns, 1971.

For the purposes of comparison with home care, the costs need to be split between medical and 'hotel' costs. In general one would expect that the strictly medical costs would be unlikely to be any less as a result of home care. Outpatient, and GP services will replace hospital services. Transport costs will tend to make the total cost rather higher but the total cost of medical attention is low in both situations.

The costs of the 'hotel' element are likely to be less because the disabled may be able to do some housework themselves, but mainly because of wholesale substitution of amateur for professional time — neighbours, friends and relatives, and cheap home helps, for expensive trained nurses.

The following concordance shows how a split of costs might be made for the hospital-home comparison (the domestic-residential home comparison is similar except for the in-patient medical costs. Most homes employ some trained nursing staff).

Medical costs
Comparison of these cannot readily be made in a general way, because so much depends on the condition of the individual patient. If the same

Moreover, throwing the burden of nursing care on relatives does not make it any less real, however much less it may cost the state services. Some rough comparisons can be made as a check. The National Survey (Harris et al, 1971) shows that half the very severely disabled people consult their GP regularly, typically once a month.

The average cost of a GP's consultation is probably about £1.2 and for chronic patients most consultations are not likely to be unduly lengthy. If a home nurse calls twice a week, the cost will be £1.4.

If we also assume one out patient treatment a month at £2.4, we arrive at a total average medical and nursing cost of £5.0 per week. This is only a very rough estimate, and would vary enormously between patients. It can be compared to the weekly cost of medical time (nurses and doctors) of £11 — £12 a week in chronic and long stay hospitals, of which less than a tenth is doctor's time.

For long stay and chronically sick patients in hospitals, nurse's pay accounts for 80 per cent of all medical and nursing expenses. If hospital patients are to be effectively cared for, only a limited alleviation of this cost can be made by transferring them elsewhere. Care in the household means transfer of the work burden to the family or domiciliary services, and the volume of nurses and other workers needed in these services must necessarily be correspondingly increased.

The only major gain can be through use of unskilled rather than trained nurses' time and to a lesser extent, unpaid family time rather than paid time, where the family is able and willing to provide it. [Elsewhere] we suggest ways by which this might to some extent be accomplished in a family household context.

Comparison of non-medical costs
Apart from medical and treatment expenses, the 'hotel' costs are around £11 – 13 a week (see table below). There are some qualifications to this. Ward costs include some £1.90 per week of domestic labour, and not all the nursing costs represent strictly medical attention.

This basic figure has to be compared with the domestic care costs of a disabled person, (excluding rent). Quite obviously, the comparison is not such an overwhelmingly favourable one as might have seemed to be the case at first sight – although few disabled people have £13 a week to spend after rent!

A closer look at the cost of the 'domestic' element of care suggests that the hospital has some advantages in the costs of food and laundry, but this is offset by very high maintenance, cleaning and general administrative costs.

Table 6.2

Chronic Hospitals*, England Non Medical Costs in 1970 (£/in-patient week)

Catering	3.09
Laundry	0.81
Power, light and heat	1.24
Total	5.14
Building and Engineering maintenance	1.35
General administration	1.30
General portering and cleaning	0.90
Maintenance of grounds	0.30
Other	1.98
Total overhead	5.83
Grand total	10.97

*Long stay hospital costs are very similar in structure, but fractionally higher throughout.
Source: Hospital Costing Returns, 1970/71.

Further detail is available in the analysis of departmental unit costs. Catering costs divide between costs of provisions and preparation:

Table 6.3

Hospital

Cost of provisions	2.02
Other (excluding staff dining room service)	1.11
Total	3.13
Laundry operating cost/per 100 articles	1.85
per 100 lb dry weight	2.03

Conclusions on hospital 'hotel' costs
A meal on wheels at present costs around 27p. To provide the equivalent of two full meals a day at home and assuming a disabled person manages to make their own breakfast at 10p a time, gives a cost of £4.48. Clearly, both meal costs and prima facie, laundry costs when compared on a unit cost basis are low compared with care in the community. Heating costs are almost identical with expenditure by OAP's on heat and light, and hospitals would certainly maintain better standards of warmth than the £1.2 spent by pensioners living on their own.

However, the advantages on this front are greatly outweighed by the heavy costs of maintenance and general overheads, which more than doubles the basic running cost within hospitals.

THE COST OF CARE IN LOCAL AUTHORITY AND VOLUNTARY HOMES
Part III[3] of the National Assistance Act of 1948 obliges local authorities to provide accommodation for the elderly and disabled who are unable to continue to live at home. In England and Wales 116,000 people are accommodated under this Act. This accounts for 1.8 per cent of the population over 65. Most of the residents in these homes are very elderly or frail and most would be classed as mildly but not severely disabled. The homes also provide accommodation for some 8,300 disabled people under 65, most of whom are over 50. Generally accommodation is for those who are continent and of normal mind. Mostly they are single people, predominantly women, aged over 75. Extreme geriatric and psychiatric cases tend to be found in hospitals or specialised units such as that opened in Bedford.

Comparisons between the costs of care in modern Part III homes, and of people living at home, have already been made by Wager (1972). He concludes that it is marginally (about £3–4 a week) cheaper to care for people in this group at home than in Part III.

FINANCE AND ORGANISATION OF SPECIALISED HOMES FOR THE DISABLED

For the severely disabled, special facilities are required. Most local authorities board out their more severely disabled with voluntary societies, but some have their own specialised homes. The largest of the voluntary groups is the Cheshire homes, with some 1,500 spaces. Along with the Spastics Society and many others they account for the bulk of the 5,000 places occupied by the most handicapped. Some of the voluntary bodies also have patients from Regional Hospital Boards, and some RHB's have wards or units which specialise in caring for the severely handicapped.

The present administrative arrangements for support are rather haphazard. Local authorities contribute to the running cost of the disabled in voluntary homes, usually to the amount it would cost them in Part III or some two thirds of actual running costs. It is exceptional for any contribution to be made to capital costs.[4] The RHB's pay the full running costs of their patients, but also do not contribute to the capital costs of the voluntary homes.

These different methods of financial support do not directly affect the real cost of the resources required to care for the disabled, which is measured by the total of running costs plus capital costs – using 10 per cent of the current market cost or valuation of the property used.

However, these do make a practical difference to the standards of care and the effectiveness of the voluntary bodies. To a great extent, the local authorities support the voluntary bodies because doing so reduces the financial burden to them of caring for a small, expensive, and awkward group of people. The consequence has been that the voluntary homes are under-capitalised and are often located in cheap rural areas, with few single-bedded rooms – the 'country house' syndrome. Strenuous efforts are being made by some homes to rectify, especially, the latter difficulty. Nonetheless, the lack of loan finance in an inflationary era makes it very difficult for the voluntary bodies

to raise the capital required to improve conditions. Ironically, the Cheshire Homes as a group were net *lenders* to local authorities to the tune of £100,000 in 1969/70. (This is quite understandable – local authority bonds would usually be a convenient and high yielding instrument for fund treasurers to use.)

There is a marked contrast between this situation and that which prevails in sheltered housing for the aged where local authorities who support housing associations such as Help the Aged, Hanover etc. provide the *whole* of the capital cost as a 100 per cent mortgage, and the charity acts essentially as an executive agent and provides furnishings and minor amenities out of its own funds. Under such arrangements the 'muliplier' on charity finance is far greater than in the case of the voluntary associations for the disabled. More important perhaps, is the rate of development of modern accommodation that is possible. The Help the Aged Housing Association has built some 4,000 dwellings in 5 years.

We believe that it is quite wrong that local authorities or RHB's do not make a capital contribution to the cost of homes for the physically handicapped run by voluntary bodies.

THE RESULTS OF OUR SURVEY

In order to ascertain current capital and running costs of local authority homes, and also costs and rents of specially built flats and bungalows, we undertook our own survey of local authorities by mailed questionnaire. The selection of local authorities was based on those who had plans in The Plan for Community Care, to build special accommodation. The response was some 40 per cent, and included a fair balance of authorities from London, County Councils and County Boroughs. Inevitably, the data was patchy: many respondents gave us current estimates of costs of accommodation not yet built or still under construction. The following tables give the basic information:

Table 6.4   Homes for the physically handicapped

Capital Cost
Number of replies: 9
Range by size: 20–35
Capital cost per place: £4,140–£12,160
Average of replies: £6,660
Running cost: range £18–£20 week.

Table 6.5　　Housing for the disabled

Number of replies: 5
Number integrated with other housing: 4
Range of number of units: 8–51
Range of capital cost per unit: £4,000 (1 bed unit)
　　–£6,500 (3 bed unit)
Rent range: £3.4/week (1 bed) to £6.26 (2 bed)

These figures can be compared with information on the voluntary homes. Spastics Society homes running costs vary from £18/week to £35/week. Capital costs of a new home for the Spastics Society was £3,220 per place in 1967, excluding land (*Architects Journal* 1969).

A reasonable estimate of average costs in this type of accommodation, at 1970/71 prices, would be some £20 per week running costs. Capital costs at current prices are some £6,000 per space, so at 10 per cent, the figure we use throughout for the cost of capital, £11.50 must be added for the capital component.

COSTS OF CARE WITHIN THE COMMUNITY
There are considerable difficulties in estimating the cost of care within the community. For the elderly disabled, the Family Expenditure Survey gives detailed information on pensioners' spending patterns. This was Wager's source of information, (Wager 1972). The third volume of the National Survey (Harris *et al.* 1972) showed that one in three of all impaired people claim to have extra expenses due to that impairment. But whereas one in four of the general population living alone had incomes of £10 or more a week, only one in ten of the handicapped living alone had incomes of that amount. Spending patterns will, therefore, be considerably distorted by lack of sufficient resources to spend.

The most effective way of tackling this difficulty is to estimate the costs for someone who enjoys the highest normal level of social security benefit. This can be taken as a peak of expenditure by the individuals themselves. Rent must be estimated at resource cost using our standard of 10 per cent, as was the case with hospitals and homes. Domiciliary services vary enormously. What we can do is estimate the difference between the costs of home care, excluding domiciliary care and the alternatives: we can then consider the amount of domiciliary services that this margin could 'buy'.

Clearly, if an individual disabled person is consuming fewer home services than this margin buys then home care is cheaper: if more, then home care is more expensive.

Housing costs
If the disabled person lives alone, the whole of the cost of modern accommodation falls on that person. In a 1 bed purpose-built flat at £4,500, the economic cost at 10 per cent is £8.92 a week. The more common case is that of a disabled person living in a family house or flat. There, the cost is the difference between the economic cost of the modified flat and the economic cost of a conventional house or flat with one bedroom less which the family would otherwise be occupying. Another way of putting this is that the cost is that of the disabled person's extra bedroom, plus any increase in floor area to permit wheel-chair mobility, plus aids and adaptations. A figure of £2,000 would seem a likely maximum for this. The weekly cost of this is £4.12. In both cases, we assume perpetual life for the house, and depreciate aids and adaptations of £750 contained in the cost, over 20 years.

It is worth emphasising that rent charged by the local authority is not relevant to a resource cost comparison nor are rates, and the above figures are maximum estimates, since in some cases full modification will not be necessary.

Spare bedrooms may be available in the homes of relatives: the cost then reduces to the annual cost of aids and adaptations which is unlikely to run at more than £1.73 a week on £750 worth of work, depreciated over 20 years.

Subsistence costs
For disabled people under 65, an indication of the cost of basic necessities (excluding rent) can be taken to equal the Supplementary Benefit basic rate – in 1970/71 £5.20 per week, plus the long term allowance of 50p, plus 50p extra heating[5] giving a total of £6.20 per week. For those not living alone, other rates apply, but the rate at this date was so low (it has since been increased) that we have felt it not unrealistic to use it under both sets of conditions in the calculations which follow. Total costs thus amount to £8.92 plus £6.20 in separate dwellings – £15.12 – and £4.12 plus £6.20, or £10.32 in shared dwellings.

DOMICILIARY SERVICES

Many hospital patients, especially the sizeable number suffering from diseases of the central nervous system, have relatively intensive specialist care requirements. Others, suffering from common conditions such as arthritis and bronchitis, need relatively simple types of care which can often be readily provided within the family. The extent to which care outside hospital or institution requires some permanent attendance is critical to the costs incurred. Where, in the extreme case of responauts, two full time attendants are required, costs are clearly very high.

The distinctive feature of a hospital or other institution is the *continuity* of care provided, and ensuring this continuity absorbs a large part of the substantial administrative costs. The comparable element in home care is the burden of constant attendance. The allowance of £4.80[6] is not directly an opportunity cost, but is the government's own measure of compensation, in practice, essentially to the family, of meeting this need. Many, though by no means all, hospital patients would qualify for it. Even where they do not, the burden is still there, and we take this as the money measure of that burden of constant care. On top of this are the costs of domiciliary services, as such, and dispensed drugs. If the cost of these is greater than the gap between home care and hospital institutional care, then the latter is cheaper, and vice versa. Often provision is inadequate, but the relevant figures are those services provided which do represent an adequate volume of care. What we have done is to hypothesise two packages, one relevant to intensive care patients, the second to easier cases, and closer to what is usually provided.

Table 6.6 Intensive package (£ per week)

Home nurse,	7 visits at 71p	4.97
Home help	10 hrs. at 44p	4.40†
Meals on wheels,	5 at 27p	1.35†
Other*		1.50
GP + Outpatient + costs‡		1.12
		14.34

*Including physiotherapy, drugs at cost, etc.
†An alternative package might well include day centre attendance 5 days a week, and exclude those costs.
‡GP consultation 1 a month, OP once a month, at £1.50 and £3.00 respectively.

Table 6.7 Modest package (£ per week)

Home nurse	2 visits	1.42
Home help	4 hrs.	1.76
Meals on wheels	5 at 27p	1.35
GP + Outpatient*		0.37
Other		0.75
		5.65

*Once every 3 months.

Bringing all the costs together we have the following table (costs in £):

We can see from this table that the cost of care at home in modern accommodation varies from £16 to £30 a week, depending on the combination of circumstances, with the 'packages' of domiciliary services we have assumed. We can now compare this with the earlier results for hospitals and other institutions.

Table 6.8 Weekly costs of care — summary table (£)

		Housing	Subsistence	Constant attendance	Domiciliary services	Total
A.	Single dwelling, moderate package	8.92	6.20	—	5.65	20.77
B.	Shared dwelling, intensive package, constant attendance	4.12	6.20*	4.80	14.64	29.76
C.	Shared dwelling, moderate package, constant attendance	4.12	6.20*	4.80	5.65	20.77
D.	Shared dwelling, moderate package	4.12	6.20*	—	5.65	15.97

*See rates given in text.

Table 6.9 Weekly costs of care — summary table (£)

		Running	Capital	Other	Total
	Long stay hospital	29.70	10.00	1.00*	40.70
	Modern residential home	20.00	11.50	1.00*	32.50
	Home care				
A.	Single dwelling, moderate package	11.85	8.92	–	20.77
B.	Shared, intensive package, constant attendance	25.64	4.12	–	29.76
C.	Shared, moderate package, constant attendance	16.65	4.12	–	20.77
D.	Shared, moderate package	11.85	4.12	–	15.97

*Taking £1 a week for pocket money of institutional and hospital residents, included in supplementary benefit entitlement of person living at home.

Certain points stand out about the above table. Firstly, it is clearly normally cheaper to care for people at home than in institutions. Secondly, the difference, whilst varying between cases, is of the order of £10 a week, which is significant but certainly less than the figures sometimes quoted. Quite apart from the preferences of patients, the standard of home care assumed is higher than hospitals in that single bed rooms are assumed which is not the case for the hospital.

The reasons for the difference in cost are firstly that the capital cost of an *extra* bedroom in a family house or flat, and the full quota of special fittings, is certainly less than the capital cost of a place in a new institution. Secondly, the family can cope with constant attendance at less cost than an institution, even allowing for incidental expenses and some earnings losses. Finally, organising the logistics of constant attendance, which effectively cost a hospital £5 a week, costs the family nothing directly. Indirectly, it may be the main cause of the severe stress families caring for the disabled often suffer, but no simple financial cost can be attached to that burden. Where relatively generous 'packages' of domiciliary services are available as postulated here, it will be minimized. Organising care on the lines of the Danish 'collectivhaus' would still further reduce it (The Cripples Building Society).

We have presented here a 'photograph' of the costs of caring for disabled people at a point in time, in different circumstances. We now consider the more complex picture of costs over a period of time. Subsequently, we will discuss briefly the very considerable practical difficulties that attach to a policy of giving greater care within the community. Costs are by no means the only relevant factor to the balance of care.

THE DYNAMIC ASPECTS OF THE COSTS OF CARE
Introduction

The analysis of the costs of care in different types of accommodation given above is necessarily based on the assumption that the medical progress of the condition of the person is similar in each case, and that a person follows a progression from home, through specialised hostel or home to hospital in descending order of medical state, until death. Implicitly, comparing costs in this way assumes that this rate of deterioration is unchanged by the nature of care and conditions of living.

This is essentially unrealistic. Whilst nothing can ultimately be done to prevent physical and mental degeneration in extreme old age, the rate of medical deterioration of a disabled person is likely to be quite significantly affected by the level of care he or she receives, and the quality of the home environment *long before* any question of hospitalisation or institutionalisation arises.

The individual effects of adequate heating, good food, and good nursing — the basis of good physical care – and the encouragement of sound contact with relatives and friends, a basic psychological element of good care – cannot easily be disentangled. There is some statistical evidence that this may be significant in the shorter average length of stay in hospital of people in social classes I and II compared to the rest of the population.

Most crippling diseases entail some element of progressive deterioration. The Tower Hamlets study (Skinner, 1969) for example, found that over 60 per cent, were classified as quickly/slowly progressive, and this would broadly be typical of the rest of the population, since this is generally true of arthritis, bronchitis, and other classes of disability.

If the rate of deterioration could be slowed down, by better home care, then prolonged hospitalisation would be delayed, and perhaps reduced in average duration. This would constitute a major benefit from better standards of home care services, and one that would not be picked up by a direct comparison of costs at a particular stage.

Because the effects of different levels of care are cumulative and depend on many elements, direct experimental study using a large sample and a large control group is virtually impossible and would take many years. To our knowledge it has never been attempted. However, it is possible to study the implications of *assumptions* about different deterioration rates by constructing a model of the ageing-hospitalisation process, and feeding into it various rates of deterioration under various conditions.

In this way, we could at least explore the implications of different assumptions and weed out unlikely ones. We could discover what are the really sensitive elements in the situation – which are often not entirely obvious on first examination of the problem – and concentrate efforts on improvements of these points.

If the average duration of hospitalisation were doubled by an increase in the average deterioration rate, of say 2 per cent, then clearly it would be worth considering the expenditure of substantial resources to prevent this, even if we were not sure exactly what that rate was.

A computer model
A computer simulation model seemed the appropriate method for exploring further this problem

and accordingly we drew up an initial model, and gave considerable thought to an appropriate quantitative format to the problem. It became apparent that the time and resources needed to 'debug' the model, and to assemble a suitable data base, would far exceed that which could be allotted to it. Consequently, this section offers some general consideration of the problem which hopefully may be of value to future work.

Any model of the situation of a population of ageing people must abstract a great deal in order to create a manageable model, but at the same time retain the most important interactions. Our model consisted of a population of 1,000 adults aged 50. It was assumed further, that they were subject to a series of risks, year by year, of death, and of contracting a disabling disease, of deterioration in that condition, of change in family circumstances (isolation), and depending on family circumstances and degree of disability, of referral to an institution or hospital. All of these have differing costs. By assuming a reduction in the rate of deterioration, through e.g. a higher level of domiciliary support, the implications for hospital and other costs could be explored.

One feature of such a model is that it is logical to group diseases by their cost structure rather than by medical origin. Clearly, some diseases such as multiple sclerosis, impose very high costs: other fatal diseases such as fatal strokes and pneumonia have very low costs. In between is cancer, which typically kills quite swiftly but involves substantial medical and care costs.

On further examination, it became reasonably certain that to postpone the onset of institutionalisation is distinctly advantageous from an economic point of view:

(a) because an expense postponed, on a present value basis, costs society less:
(b) because any disabled person who avoids hospitalisation or institutionalisation for a time, is at risk of death from some other cause, including 'quick killers' such as pneumonia, and may therefore never become institutionalised.

This is perhaps a slightly gruesome way to put the matter, but it is an essential part of the logic of the argument.

Putting these two factors together, the total reduction in cost of institutional care from a year's postponement of institutionalisation might be as much as 15–20 per cent of the cost of a year's institutional care. This can only be a very approximate estimate indeed at this stage.

THE VARIABILITY OF LOCAL AUTHORITY SERVICES

It is well established that local authority social services of all kinds vary greatly between different areas. Some (but only a small part) of the variation reflects variation in need. These variations have been the subject of elaborate analysis by academic writers such as Bleddyn Davies and N. Boaden, and more succinctly, by Michael Meacher (1971). 'The Implementation of the Chronically Sick and Disabled Persons Act, 1970' provides an up-to-date examination of these variations as they relate to the 'specific provisions of this Act'. The straightforward statistical comparisons that can be made using IMTA statistics in fact *understate* the variability in availability of services to individuals, because local surveys, of which an increasing number are now available, show that available services vary widely *within* borough areas: some wards are notably better off than others. Services such as lunch clubs and day hospitals, or sheltered workshops often have a limited practical radius for most disabled would-be clients.

This variability is very important in the context of a policy of expanded community care for the disabled. It is not sufficient to show that the resource cost of community care is less than hospital or institutional care, if the domiciliary services do not exist to provide care to similar standards. Discharging institutional patients would, and sometimes does, lead to even lower costs – at the price of neglect and low standards. [. . .]

The psychological defects of institutions are well known [see Miller and Gwynne 1972]. Institutions do however generally provide an adequate basic standard of *physical* care. Patients in hospital may often be bored and regimented, but they do not freeze to death, they do not suffer from malnutrition, and their basic nursing needs are met. Hospital discharge studies, such as that of Butler and Pearson (1970), confirm that some hospital patients could be discharged earlier, having no vital medical reason for remaining. Others such as that of Skeet (1970) show that discharge from hospital is often to gruesome

conditions of poor housing and totally inadequate if not non-existent community support.

There is a real danger that community care will become a slogan concealing policies of neglect rather than positive, intensive care.

THE NATURE OF CONTROL IN HOSPITAL AND COMMUNITY

We believe that the differences between the relative *uniformity* of standards of care in institutions and the variability in the community, are an inevitable result of the nature of the organisations responsible. The patients of a hospital are visible and accessible, and responsibility for care standards is assignable. There is consequently strong pressure to maintain at least a minimum standard of physical care under all circumstances.

In the community however, the target population is unknown: the worst neglect is that of those people social service departments have never even heard of. Field workers concentrate on the immediate, visible problems, and others go by default.

The difference in administrative style that results is quite clear. A hospital desperately short of nursing staff will go to a nursing staff agency. How many local authorities supplement trained home help services with agency staff? In neither case is the agency solution very attractive, but on the one hand essential services are maintained, on the other the service is cut in hours or numbers of clients supplied, or both.

Similarly, the Hospital Advisory Service annual report provides trenchant criticism of the hospital services. No such independent and critical appraisal of the community services exists,[7] nor is it likely to so long as local authority 'independence' is used as justification for not enforcing uniform minimum standards of care.

THE PARADOX OF RESOURCE ALLOCATION

The previous section shows clearly that the cost of care at home in most circumstances is less than that for permanent institutional accommodation. This is not surprising: since relatives substitute for expensive nurses' time. However, this does not in itself lead to the automatic conclusion that severely disabled people should be cared for at home.

The difficulty is that as is well known, there is in most places a shortage of domiciliary services staff. Faced by this shortage, a social services director will keep the greatest possible number of people at home by allocating these home care resources first to those who need only a *small* amount to avoid institutionalisation. In general terms, this means the elderly at risk of entering Part III, rather than the younger but more severely handicapped.

Even though it *is* generally cheaper, and the savings per person may often be higher, the claim of the younger disabled goes unmet. This may be partly the result of administrative restrictions on access to the services. But even if these problems are swept away, the fundamental difficulty still remains. If one severely disabled person takes, say 10 hours a week of home help time, and 5 home nursing visits, then perhaps 5 old people could stay at home with each having one fifth of that amount.

It is at this difficult stage of decision that the rising tide of elderly is so important to the care of the younger disabled – they are unquestionably competitors for scarce services, and likely to remain so. Only by increasing the total supply and the uniformity of availability of services, will domiciliary care on a wider scale become practical.

THE ST. THOMAS'S EXPERIMENT

St. Thomas's hospital, which has cared for 'responauts' for some time, has undertaken a project on community care of 18 severely disabled responauts: 14 live at home (of whom 4 work), 3 others are in a Cheshire home, and one was in hospital, (Research team of the Department of Clinical Epidemiology and Social Medicine, St. Thomas's Hospital Medical School 1972).

This study found wide variations in the degree of support provided by local authorities. It also illustrates perfectly the dilemma we have just discussed. Patients financed by the hospital with no families were given two full time attendants, one of whom at least, was resident. Costs were not given, but must be £60–70 a week. On top of this of course, must be added other domiciliary costs. Prima facie, it seems unlikely that there are in this case any great savings in home care, although the reduction of overheads and capital costs may have reduced total costs by £10–15 week.[8] Equally, those two full-time attendants might have cared for as many as twenty much less handicapped people in their own homes.

A further point raised in the article is the need for an intermediate attendant, able to undertake some nursing duties, also able to do ordinary home chores such as the home help performs. Such people would be of great value of course, especially with stable intensive care clients such as the responauts. We are very pessimistic about the chance of recruiting people of such competence in any numbers at rates much below that paid to nurses. We would also note the limitations in their use in local authority service, for the key factor there is the *variability* of the needs of clients. It is the ability to cope with this variety of circumstances, (including emergency situations) which distinguishes the trained nurse from the competent but untrained lay assistant. Potential recruits of the calibre required would, we believe, in most cases be better used to 'board out' the disabled, thereby limiting any training to the needs of a single person. This is discussed further in the final section.

SUMMARY

A comparison of costs of care in different situations shows that home care is typically around £10 a week cheaper than in long stay hospitals or residential homes. The difference is due to the lower capital cost of additional rooms in private dwellings, even when aids and adaptations are fully fitted, compared to the capital cost of new institutional accommodation, and to the substitution of family labour for trained and paid nurses.

When the influence of differential rates of deterioration as between good and poor standards of home care is taken into account, then substantial further savings can be expected on delaying institutionalisation through improved domiciliary care.

Despite this, and the relatively greater economic savings on the more severely disabled as opposed to typical Part III references, a social services director with limited domiciliary services will minimize the number of people in residential care by dealing with those least handicapped first. This usually means the elderly rather than the younger physically handicapped. This paradox lies behind the comparative neglect of the younger handicapped, in the competition for the limited services available.

2. Increasing the volume of non-institutional accommodation available to the disabled

This section presents our suggestion for development of accommodation to enable the disabled to live in the community to the maximum feasible extent, and in reasonable conditions of care. We believe that this requires early action to meet the expanding numbers of disabled: over 6,000 dwellings a year suitable for the *increase* in the severe or very severely handicapped alone.

An effective policy requires flexibility and a variety of approaches. This is a cliche, but past policy has been unimaginative compared to that found overseas. In Denmark, over ten years ago, accommodation was built to house, especially, polio victims and their relatives *paid* to look after them by the state (Engberg, 1961). Also, there is the well known experiment of Het Dorp village for the disabled in Holland.

Existing waiting lists are a poor guide to potential demand. Many disabled people are reluctant to move to fresh surroundings even in modern accommodation. A great deal of this problem is due to the offer of new accommodation being made when the person is too old or immobile to make new social contacts. A person with arthritis, for example, should be offered modern accommodation before it becomes totally disabling. To be able to do this, a far bigger stock of suitable accommodation is required.

Existing 'purpose built' accommodation is not always of a very high standard, and we understand that the forthcoming Design Bulletin being prepared by the Department of Environment is likely to recommend higher standards than are used at present.[9] Many disabled people are placed in modern, but not purpose designed, council flats. These are often far from satisfactory. Accommodation built for the Spastics Society to a very high standard costs half as much again as the average local authority home.

The need for choice

We believe that a satisfactory housing situation for the disabled will not be achieved unless a wide choice is available to the disabled person, and his or her relatives if they are involved. Choice, as a matter of economic logic, requires the availability of some spare capacity: hence there is a need to expand rapidly all kinds of accommodation, including to some extent, modern types of residential care.

A PROGRAMME FOR IMPROVEMENT

Rapid expansion of purpose built (or occasionally, improved) accommodation requires as many channels of development as possible. These are complementary to each other.

What we present here is a series of proposals, each of which obviously requires more detailed examination. Each represents what we believe is the most practical and economical approach to improving living conditions for the disabled. All of them could be the subject of a large measure of private initiative with a view to ultimately procuring public sector support.

These proposals, in order, are as follows:

1. A group of financial institutions aimed at catering principally for the needs of the disabled – a housing association, a building society, house agency and finance house.

2. A development of boarding out using significant financial incentives.

3. A programme of heating installations and insulation in the homes of the elderly and disabled.

4. A programme of counselling services initially for those in residential care.

None of them, even if substantially developed, would require any major increase in public expenditure, other than some acknowledgement by local authorities of the obligation to provide a capital contribution to the cost of care of the physically handicapped.

NOTES

1. For England and Wales, the average stay in acute specialities was 16.5 days in 1959 and 11.7 days in 1969 (Digest of Health Statistics, 1971).
2. There are three good reasons for this: 1) bulk purchase of drugs by hospitals, 2) hospital pharmacists can substitute cheaper but equivalent non-branded drugs for branded drugs prescribed by the doctor,

3) the volume of work lowers overheads and partial mechanisation (e.g. use of such practices as pill counters) reduce the unit cost of prescription. Exact comparison would require a detailed study.

3. Hence the use of the term 'Part III accommodation' sometimes used in the literature.

4. There is one recent development in London in which the GLC is financing sheltered housing, with care facilities being provided by Cheshire homes in a nursing annex.

5. To produce a realistic figure we *added* these items, with a critical note that it was SBC practice to offset the long-term allowance in calculating heating allowances. Happily, the Budget proposals included the concession that the SBC should discontinue so doing, thus assisting an estimated 400,000 recipients.

6. The original rate, but not yet payable during 1970/71 financial year.

7. Although NHS reorganisation will lead to a local watchdog committee for NHS services.

8. Cost per week in London teaching hospitals averaged £96, of which some £17 was operating theatre and X ray costs, giving a net cost for non surgical cases of £80 a week.

9. *Housing for People who are Physically Handicapped* (1972).

REFERENCES

BOADEN, N. (1971) *Urban Policy-Making: influences on county boroughs in England and Wales*, London, Cambridge University Press.

BUTLER, J. R. and PEARSON, M. (1970) *Who goest home?: a study of long-stay patients in acute hospital care*, Occasional Papers on Social Administration, No. 34, London, G. Bell & Sons.

DAVIES, B. (1968) *Social Needs and Resources in Local Services: a study of variations in standards of provision of personal social services between local authority areas.* London, Michael Joseph.

Department of Employment and Productivity (Annual) *Family Expenditure Survey: Report*, London, HMSO.

Department of the Environment (1974) *Housing for People who are Physically Handicapped*, Circular 74/74, London, HMSO.

Department of Health (1966) *Health and Welfare: The Development of Community Care*, Cmnd. 3022 London, HMSO.

Department of Health and Social Security and Welsh Office (1972) *Hospital Costing Returns 1970/71*, London, HMSO.

Department of Health and Social Security (1972) *Digest of Health Statistics, 1971*, London, HMSO.

ENGBERG, E. (1968) 'Family flats with a nursing annexe' *Lancet 1*, 1106.

11 and 12, George VI Cap. 29 *National Assistance Act, 1948*, London, HMSO.

HARRIS, A. I. et alia (1971) *Handicapped and Impaired in Great Britain*,
    Part 1. Handicapped and Impaired; the Impaired Housewife; Leisure activities of impaired persons.
    Part 2. Work and Housing of Impaired Persons in Great Britain.
    Part 3. (1972) Income entitlement to supplementary benefit in Great Britain., London, HMSO.

'Homes for the physically handicapped', (1969), *Architects Journal 150*, 365.

Hospital Advisory Service (annual) *Reports*, London, HMSO.

MEACHER, M. (1971) 'Scrooge areas' *New Society*, December 2, London.

MILLER, E. J. & GWYNNE, G. V. (1972) *A Life Apart; a report of a pilot study of residential institutions for the physically handicapped and young chronic sick*, London, Tavistock Publications.

ORWELL, S. (1973) *'The implementation of the Chronically Sick and Disabled Persons' Act, 1970'*, London, National Fund for Research into Crippling Diseases.

Research team of Department of Clinical Epidemiology and Social Medicine, St. Thomas's Hospital Medical School (1972) 'Collaboration between health and social services; a study of the care of responauts' *Community Medicine 128*, No. 23, September 22.

SKEET, M. (1970) *Home from Hospital; A Study of the homecare needs of recently discharged hospital patients*, London, The Dan Mason Nursing Research Committee of the National Florence Nightingale Memorial Committee of Great Britain.

SKINNER, F. W. (ed) (1969) *Physical Disability and Community Care*, Tower Hamlets Council of Social Service, Bedford Square Press of the National Council of Social Service.

The Cripples' Building Society (De Vanføres Boligsekskab) n.d. Copenhagen, Thejls Bogtryk.

WAGER, R. (1972) *Care of the Elderly: an exercise in cost benefit analysis commissioned by Essex County Council*, London, Institute of Municipal Treasurers.

7. Housing to fit the handicapped *

ANN SHEARER
Social Services journalist and founding member of the
Campaign for the Mentally Handicapped.

The Habinteg housing scheme is offering physically disabled people their best chance in this country so far to live in the kind of housing they need, with the help that makes it possible, and still be part of the immediate community.

The Habinteg Housing Association is an independent offshoot of the Spastics Society, but caters for people with any sort of physical disability, whether single or married, with children or without. The first scheme, at Haringey, offers 17 homes for disabled people among its total of 58; the size of other schemes will vary between 100 in Milton Keynes and 10 in a Kent village.

The Habinteg philosophy goes further than others in special housing. It isn't enough, it reckons, to plonk down a 'special' block of housing for disabled people in an ordinary estate and call it 'integrated.' This marks the inhabitants out as 'special' from the start and so, society being what it often is, liable to find that their only friends are each other. No one yet knows the ideal mix, but Habinteg is at the moment providing about a quarter of its homes in any one scheme for disabled people. Because they are often single, this will work out at around a tenth of the scheme's whole population.

They will be able to summon a 'community assistant' when they need help. They will also be able to make their way around the rest of the scheme when they want to. For, unless it is all accessible to them, Habinteg thinks integration is going to remain a pretty empty idea. The other

tenants come off the local authority's housing list, chosen by the association. So far few disabled people have turned down the chance — though one person did because even a scheme as carefully 'unspecial' as this one seemed too different from the normal for him.

Rents will run between £7 and £14 a week all round, for housing for between one and seven people. This sort of flexibility should offer, for instance, the chance for an elderly mother to go on living with her middle-aged disabled son even when she is herself beyond coping with his physical needs. It should offer families the chance of staying together when one parent becomes disabled, amd give single disabled people their chance of independence. It has already meant that three spastic couples have been able to get married. For all such people too often at the moment the only alternative is an institution, with all the end to normal social expectations that this must bring.

Community care is something we talk about for severely physically disabled people no less than for the elderly, or people recovering from mental illnesses, or people who are mentally handicapped — one of the blanket Good Things of social provision over the last decade. The institutional provision for all these groups, and for others categorised as 'single-homeless,' is seen as a poor second best to living independently. The physically disabled can't complain, either, that we discriminate against them by letting the practicalities of their situation override our theories. We are for ever sending old people into residential care because it's simpler than providing the sheltered housing that could allow them to keep their dignity, just as we are for ever advising that

*From *The Guardian* 26th June (1973) p 16.

mentally handicapped people should go into hospitals for lack of an alternative in the community.

Nevertheless, some of the present official plans for severely physically disabled people provide a grotesque example of the gap between what we say and what we do. It is for severely disabled people that we have 'younger chronic sick units' in our hospitals.

This is not a happy way to designate a group of human beings; it is also misleading. Their inhabitants are not generally young, for most people come to these places in middle age, when families are no longer able to cope at home. They are not chronically sick, as someone who needs kidney dialysis could be said to be. Mostly, they are not 'sick' any more often than the rest of the population, but happen to be suffering from a series of diseases which bring physical disablement that is likely to get worse rather than better.

The Government has been urging an increase of younger chronic sick units on its hospital boards since 1968, when a survey found that half the 4,200 or so severely disabled people being catered for by the NHS were in geriatric wards, even though they had not reached the great divide of their 65th birthday. Seventy-four of them, indeed, were under 34. Another 1,300 were in general hospital wards, and only 500 in special units with others of their kind.

Crash programme
A couple of years later, the Chronically Sick and Disabled Persons Act made a special point of saying that younger disabled people should not live in geriatric wards. And so the Department of Health released £5 millions for a crash building programme to get them out. By 1975 another 1,800 beds are promised in special younger chronic sick units, and hospital architects are now drawing up the plans. 'The aim,' as the original Government memorandum on the subject said, 'should be to provide as relaxed and permissive an atmosphere as possible within a hospital setting.'

At Ashurst, in Hampshire, the Wessex Regional Hospital Board has had its pilot unit open now for something over four years. It is in the grounds of a geriatric hospital, with which it shares staff, and to some extent occupational therapists, who come in during the afternoon for basket-making and other diversions. There can be no doubt at all that this is a hospital, from the polished lino (carpet in the waiting-room only), to the four-bedded wards where some of its inhabitants are still in bed at 11 in the morning, because they are said to be more comfortable that way. It is very clean, very bright, and very clinical. There is, as one disabled visitor noticed, a very large bedpan steriliser and a very small dayroom. And this is where 16 people will live out their days, unless the housing situation outside improves or they go away to a general hospital to die. An able-bodied person would recoil from calling such an environment home. So do the 'younger chronic sick' themselves. The difference is that for most people the prospect is hypothetical.

At a recent seminar in London, run by Centre on Environment for the Handicapped, a group of the disabled made their reaction to such places perfectly clear. Paul Hunt, who has had his share of hospital living and is now married and living in an ordinary flat, said flatly that to talk of design for such places was irrelevant, for their whole concept was 20 years out of date. 'I do not think,' he said, 'that anyone can seriously imagine that if they were given a genuine choice, the disabled would actually *choose* to go into a younger chronic sick unit. But it seems to be quite clear that there has never been any intention of offering us a choice. So many thousands of people, whose only crime, is that they are disabled, are being sentenced without trial to imprisonment for life. These are harsh words; but anyone who has lived in a chronic sick ward will know that the analogy with prisons is not simply a figure of speech.'

Not one of the other disabled people at the seminar disagreed with him, and the regional architects and staff, and the men from the Department of Health, were duly flummoxed. It was bad enough to be confronted by consumer representatives — 'But they never leave their units, do they?' asked one perplexed delegate on being told who the consumers were going to be. But such determined and logical opposition, from a group who indeed had never once been consulted about their own preferences in the matter, was virtually impossible to resist.

The point about the particular disabled people who took part in this seminar is that, although none of them at this precise time live in a younger chronic sick unit, each and every one of them is a candidate for a place if their personal fortunes should change. And this to many people is the central fallacy about having such units at all. 'Younger chronic sick' people are not medically defined in any sense of that word.

The situation is not peculiar to people with this particular label. In the same way, some mentally handicapped people become overnight candidates for hospital places not because their handicap has suddenly worsened, but because a parent has died; some elderly people end up in back wards of psychiatric hospitals not because they have a mental illness or confusion, but because they cannot find the help they need to go on living outside.

For every one person in hospital in each of these categories, there is another, equally or more disabled, living at home. The dividing line is not illness, nor degree of disability, but the degree of choice they are offered. Half the people living in the Ashurst unit could go home tomorrow if they could be sure of proper help, according to Dr Douglas Lilley, who runs the place; one woman is kept in the unit by six steps between her and her flat. He confirms that some of the people who come into the unit for short stays to give their family a break are in fact more disabled than some of the permanent residents.

All these things are known, and behind each academic study that confirms them are people eking out their lives. Yet the Government puts £5 millions into a crash programme for younger chronic sick units which potential inhabitants contemplate with pain and despair.

At the CEH seminar, some people argued that these places are necessary because they provide the sort of skilled nursing that some severely disabled people need. But are they really vital, if families are caring for people as, if not more, handicapped? The care they get in such places can actually be inferior to what families can provide; one delegate told of the disabled son of a 78-year-old mother who never got bedsores except when he came into a specialist unit to give her a break. Even if disabled people do not live at their own home, there is no need for them to go into hospital. Local authority homes cater for exactly the same range of disability as hospital units, with only a few trained nurses on the staff. Le Court, the first and best-known Cheshire Home, spells this out even more clearly; it has people sponsored by both local authorities and hospital boards, and the two groups are indistinguishable in degree of disability.

Some people support such units for people in the last stages of their disease. Dr Lilley, at least, maintains that younger chronic sick units should not cater for anyone who is unconscious, as that is a job for the skills of a general hospital. Dying in hospital, in any event, is not something that everyone would choose; there can be dignity in death in a caravan, and there is dignity in death, so we were told, at Le Court.

Others argue for younger chronic sick units to cater specifically for people whose physical disability brings them psychiatrically definable mental distress. But at Ashurst, at least, local psychiatrists are not anxious to expend much therapeutic energy on the inhabitants, and, as the disabled delegates at the seminar said, a change of social environment and relationships works wonders on the psyche.

Poor compromise

In the end, there was no defence. The units were going up because there was £5 millions in the kitty, and people were going to live in them because the units were there. Better, argued their defenders, than living in a geriatric ward. And so it probably will be. But what measure of success is there in this administrative compromise?

The compromise is important to nail because it has bedevilled so much of our planning for so many people who need social help in their living arrangements. As long as these people end up under the wing of the NHS — whether in younger chronic sick units, psychiatric hospitals or geriatric wards — the real nature of their need is going to be obscured. Medicine, geared as it is to 'cure,' can do nothing to reverse their condition. It can treat occasional acute illnesses, as with any member of society; what it cannot do is 'cure' degenerative disease or mental handicap. The very term 'chronic sick,' as applied to any of the groups who bear it, means that medical knowledge, in its present state, has failed them.

It seems peculiar, then, to hand the severely disabled over at this point to the very people who admit, as they stick on the label, that they cannot cope. Peculiar in theoretical terms, that is; entirely comprehensible as a move to get local authorities off the hook of their own responsibility for people's social needs, to shift care on the rates to care from central coffers. As long as the NHS facilities are there, they will be used; and as long as they are there, they will from time to time be abused.

As important as relationships with the outside world are those within the residential community. There seems no doubt that the traditions and hierarchies of the hospital service are not, and cannot be, the best foundation for what is in effect home. Any kind of residential establishment for severely disabled people is bound not to be an easy place to live and work in; rejection by the outside world without hope of improvement in their condition is what, after all sent most of the inhabitants there in the first place. Eric Miller and Geraldine Gwynne recently turned a Tavistock eye on the nature of institutions of this kind in their book *A Life Apart*, and concluded that the first task of such places was to cater for the period between the social and physical death of the residents; not comfortable for the outsider, perhaps, but acceptable to realistic inhabitants.

Nevertheless, there are ways and means of dealing with this hiatus, and the hospital way is not the one the residents appreciate. *A Life Apart* identified two solutions: the warehousing and the horticultural. The first emphasises the prolonging of physical existence and the dependent side of the residents' lives; this is found mainly in hospital units, where medical diagnosis concentrates on what people cannot do and nurses are geared to caring for people who cannot, by their very presence in the unit, care for themselves. The second emphasises not what residents cannot do, but what they can, concentrating on personal growth and fulfilment, and is found mainly outside the hospital setting.

Put baldly like this, the thesis sounds too neat to be useful, and indeed its authors modify its outlines and the division between hospital and other types of care as they go along. But it remains uncanny how far the outlines jump to life in a couple of visits. The research was actually suggested by a group of residents at Le Court, and to compare life there with the Ashurst unit is to get an idea of the differences between warehousing and horticulture.

The first thing that hits you at Le Court is the activity. There is a constant coming and going of battery operated wheelchairs, huddling around in corridors to make every space a social one. It is untidy and noisy and everyone seems to be doing, which makes a sharp contrast to a morning in bed

or watching the television at Ashurst. Miller and Gwynne reckon that the staff attitudes to the use of battery-powered wheelchairs is one of the best indicators of the temper of the place. These, and other gadgets, can either be offered to give each resident maximum independence, or can be left in a corner, perhaps because the staff feel their own job more clearly defined if they are doing things for people. At Ashurst it's hard, they say, to get the nurses to use what's there to make the job lighter.

There are other differences that follow the thesis. At Ashurst, such work as there is is organised by the occupational therapists; at Le Court, the residents run their own workshop.

At Ashurst, there is no doubt about who is in charge and who dependent. At Le Court — though not without hassle — the residents have got themselves full voting places on the management committee, have a say in who is hired as staff and who not, and run the social life of the place. The one looks after people, because that is what nurses are trained to do — particularly, perhaps, those who spend much of their time in the geriatric hospital across the way. The other helps people as far as possible to run their own show. The difference is enormous.

This is not to say that the staff who run hospital units are wicked or wrong. It is just that they are geared to a completely different set of needs from those of people who aren't ill but happen to need a certain amount of physical help. The sad thing is that residents can start to fulfil their side of the contract, and become either suitable cases for warehousing or suitable plants for horticulture.

Not so sick

One resident of Le Court, for instance, reckons that the people in the wing for the supposedly 'sicker' group, although in fact indistinguishable from those on the other side, actually behave sicker because thay are encouraged to by the high concentration of staff and atmosphere there. It's not surprising that they should, just as it's not surprising that elderly people deteriorate in special homes for the mentally infirm, or that mentally handicapped people behave more handicapped in hospital than they do if they are able to leave it. You would have to be a tough character to withstand the expectation of the society around you, particularly when independence can be label-led 'troublemaking' and you haven't the option to wheel yourself out.

So is the answer for severely disabled people more horticultural homes? There are some 50 new local authority homes on the stocks just now, as the Department of Health points out when it defends its younger chronic sick units as part of a grander strategy for the disabled. But there is, of course, absolutely no guarantee that one local authority home will be any better or richer for the people living there than another hospital unit; indeed it could be worse in its quality of life. Habinteg, and the few other schemes that exist, hope to show that institutional living need not be necessary at all for many severely disabled people. Exactly the same distinctions as apply to younger chronic sick units in relation to local homes apply to local homes in relation to sheltered housing. Which, after all, would any of us choose of the three?

Other Europeans have gone about solving the housing shortage for severely disabled people in different ways. At one end of the scale is the Dutch experiment, Het Dorp, which a decade or so ago was reckoned about the most advanced pro-vision for this group of people in the world. This is a special village where around 400 severely dis-abled people have every opportunity and en-couragement to make the most independent life they can. Every architectural device has been used to simplify their living, and each can summon the assistance he needs to his own and individual apartment.

To build a Het Dorp is to recognise that all this talk of integration and participation in community life is bound to be an unrealistic attempt to gloss over the hard fact that physically disabled people are disabled, are not able to share in many of the activities common to the people around them and can only bring themselves frustration if they try. This kind of place will appeal to those who agree with these arguments, just as those who want to protect mentally handicapped people from the rigours of life in our urban communities will be attracted by the 'villages' that have been our main form of provision for them for 100 years, whether we call these 'colonies' or 'hospitals.' The essence of such communities is that they are segregated from the main streams of life as it is lived outside; at Het Dorp, the village hall, petrol station and supermarket were meant to be used by the surrounding community as a ploy for inte-gration – they are not.

Physically disabled people are now a lot less enthusiastic about the Het Dorp solution than they were – though in a situation of real choice, there could be some who would opt for it. The point is to establish a choice rather than impose one particular solution or another, and we are a very long way indeed from choice.

Sweden has gone about provision for several disabled people very differently and its Fokus housing is now the inspiration behind Habinteg and others edging towards community solutions. Since 1964, Fokus has built some 300 flats for disabled people, scattered through normal housing blocks all over the country. Staff are available at any time the residents want help, with housewives paid to come in at the 'peak' morning, evening and lunch-time hours.

When Fokus started, it was told by the pro-fessionals working in the field that it was im-possible to cater for people so disabled in ordinary domestic surroundings. Over three-quarters of its tenants are now in wheelchairs, nearly a quarter need help with eating, a third need turning and help during every night to go to the lavatory, some get their only independence through the near-miraculous response of electronic gadgets to their breathing. The professionals have had to pipe down.

Fokus is meticulous in relating research on disability and capability to what it provides for its tenants. All the fittings of its flats, for instance, are entirely flexible for height and position and it tests individual tenants' reactions to them for a year before making their positions final. As one measure of what Fokus means to its tenants, over a third of them are now either married or living together – before they came here, the proportion was under 10 per cent. Only a quarter of the population is housebound; the rest either work or are completing their studies. Before they lived here, a third were in their family home, and the rest in nursing homes and other institutions.

Fokus started as a voluntary body. Now it has been taken over, together with its philosophy, by the State. The aim is to have a block of its flats in every town in the country. Professor S. O. Brattgard, its president, himself responsible for much of the research into living solutions for disabled people at the University of Gothenburg, reckons that Sweden needs 2,000 Fokus flats if everyone who wants one is to get the chance. The institutional solution is completely rejected.

Fokus, as Professor Brattgård says, is not an architectural solution, it is a philosophy built on two very sensible assumptions, that the only people who know how the disabled want to live are disabled people themselves, and that the State has an obligation to do all it can to meet these demands. This is a very long way from the present British situation; when the disabled people at the CEH seminar tackled the men from the Department of Health about why they had not been consulted on younger chronic sick units, they got nothing more than the vaguest of assurances that they were perfectly free to drop in and see them any time for a chat. In view of the wheelchairs, this was, it's fair to say, amended to being perfectly free to drop the Department a line. But there was nothing at all in the way of concrete suggestions to join future working parties.

In Britain, some disabled people are beginning to work out their own solutions. If Fokus shows that even extremely disabled people can live in a way that respects their independence and offers them the opportunity to run their own lives as they want to, Margaret and Jack Wymer show that with enough determination you can play the system to go rather further than that. Both wheelchair-bound, they got married, and began working out what they needed; as they say, if they had waited for the provision to make it possible, they would never have got started at all. They got a council flat from Norwich — which is a progressive council in its approach to disabled people — and with 'special allowances' from social security, now find, hire and train part-time housewife staff to give them the 22 hours of physical help that they need in a week. It works — though not without anxiety about their helpers turning up and the arrangement has now been going on for three years. If they lived in Sweden, they would be guaranteed as of right four hours' help a day as well as a disability income.

Individual experiments like this knock right on the head the argument that severely physically disabled people can't be offered dispersed — that is, normal — housing because they need too much physical help to be catered for separately. Many, in fact, need around two-and-a-half hours a day,

and it shouldn't be beyond the wit of our social agencies to provide this outside a local authority home or hospital ward. Very slowly, the message is beginning to creep through to the official planners. Selwyn Goldsmith, an architect who knows more than any other in Britain about designing for disabled people, is now working part time with the sociological research branch of the Department of the Environment. His unit is trying to find local authorities who will build, say, six flats for disabled people into normal housing provision and work with social service departments to get the help the tenants need to cope with independent living.

The local authorities haven't been picked yet, but the experiment, though by now not new in its broad outlines, will be an important chink in official policy. One of the things that holds up experiment in community care for disabled groups — particularly when their members are single people — is the gap between local authority housing and social service departments. As things go at the moment, Housing builds houses for people and Social Services build homes for the disabled, and very different the two ways of life offered can turn out to be. Until housing authorities are obliged to turn over a proportion of their ordinary stock to the people who need sheltered housing, the gap is bound to persist; even though the right to a house may turn out to be the right to jostle on the waiting list, it's surely an overdue principle to be established.

The same cost

While the Department of the Environment experiments, the Department of Health could do worse than remember one or two items from its own history. During the last Labour Government, there was some concern about a group of people suffering from respiratory polio living out their time in an annex of St. Thomas's Hospital, even though each of them could have lived outside if they had had the funds. So, as an experiment, each of them got the cost of their hospital bed to spend as they would, and very satisfactory it has turned out to be. One, for instance, is in a residential home of her choice; another found a flat, a job, a resident helper and a part-time chauffeur and has been living thus ever since.

Hospital boards don't even have to go that far. There is positive power in the White Paper on mental handicap, for instance, for them to provide domestic housing as an alternative to wards, in residential areas instead of on hospital sites. Admittedly, the signs so far aren't hopeful; for a start, only two Boards have taken up the option in any large way and one of these has been doing it for some years, while the other is a Government experiment. Admittedly too, hospital board architects have a rather different idea of what constitutes a small domestic house from almost anyone else in Britain. Admittedly yet again, if the people who are to live in these houses are able to sustain this kind of life, they should be free of the atmosphere of the health service.

Yet in our present tangled situation, where local authorities appear to be so crushed with work that they have little time, money or inclination for new ventures, while the hospitals seem to have both cash and the ability to do something about it, the principle of extending health service provision could be seized on rather more energetically. If the reorganisation of our health service to unite hospital and community care more closely is to mean anything at all to the consumer, it is surely essential that experiments in community living aren't left entirely to social service departments.

Just think, as one disabled person said wistfully, what others like him could do with the £40 or so a week that it will cost to keep someone in a younger chronic sick unit. Just think too of using that £5 millions to acquire housing which could then be handed over to the local authority to support. This is not to say that some severely disabled people may not either need or choose residential alternatives to supported life in the open community. The sadness is that the residential provision is coming first and isn't at the moment an alternative to anything. When Paul Hunt and his colleagues dubbed younger chronic sick units a sentence to life imprisonment, they weren't joking.

REFERENCES

BRATTGARD, S. O. and Research Group (1969) *Principles of the Fokus housing units for the severely disabled*, Goteborg, Sweden, *Fokus* Society.

BRATTGARD, S. O. (1972), Sweden: *Fokus*: a way of life for living' in Lancaster-Gaye, D. (ed) pp 25–40.

Campaign for the Mentally Handicapped (1972) *Even Better Services for the Mentally Handicapped*, London, CMH.

Department of Health and Social Security (1971) *Better Services* for the Mentally Handicapped, Cmnd. 4683, London, HMSO.

FREDERICKSON, J. (1972) 'The Danish approach to residential care and community integration' in Lancaster-Gaye, D. (ed) pp 41–51.

GOLDSMITH, S. (1967) *Designing for the Disabled*, London, RIBA.

LAPWIG, A. and BIJLEVELD, W. P. (1072) 'Holland's approach to residential care' in Lancaster-Gaye, D. (ed) pp 52–73.

LANCASTER-GAYE, D. (1972) *Personal Relationships, the Handicapped and the Community: some European thoughts and Solutions*, London, Routledge and Kegan Paul.

MILLER E. J. and GWYNNE, G. V. (1971) *A Life Apart: a pilot study of residential institutions for the physically handicapped and young chronic sick*, London, Tavistock Publications.

Research team of Department of Clinical Epidemiology and Social Medicine St. Thomas's Hospital Medical School (1972) 'Collaboration between health and social services: a study of the care of responauts *Community Medicine*, 128 No. 23 Sept. 22.

(n.d.) '*The Cripples' Building Society*' (*De Vanføres Boligselskab*), Copenhagen, Denmark, Thejls Bogtryk.

8. Outdoor mobility: the situation today*

PETER LARGE

Chairman of the Joint Committee on Mobility for the Disabled, and of the Association of Disabled Professionals, committee member of the Central Council for the Disabled and parliamentary spokesman for the Disablement Income Group.

'Many of the nation's physically handicapped are unable to take advantage of the economic and social opportunities of their community, even though they possess valuable vocational skills, an ability to learn, and a full human capacity for enjoyment of social and personal relationships. For the nation as a whole, this is a waste of its most valuable resource: people. For the individual ... it can mean a life of loneliness, self-criticism and despair. Why?'. The question is posed and partially answered in *Travel Barriers*, a summary of a study of the outdoor mobility needs of handicapped travellers and how transport system design can help disabled people back into society.[1]

The ability to travel where, when and with whom one chooses is an essential element of civilised life. Leaving aside the pursuit of pleasure, people want to travel to earn a living, to transact other business and to fulfil social duties. Disabled people are no different. They too want to go to work, get to a bank, post office, shop or dentist, go to church, visit a friend or relative, attend evening classes, go to a restaurant, cinema or exhibition. These journeys, some more essential than others but typical of the normal life of even the unadventurous, can involve four modes of travel: pedestrian, bus, train and the underground. Holidays can involve two more – aircraft or ship – and there is also the private car, the importance of which merits separate attention.

Even a modest journey can involve several modes of travel – pedestrian, bus and train for instance – and each mode has its different travel barriers. There are different designs of bus and railway coach each requiring different activities of the traveller. The one-man bus presents different problems to that of the bus with a conductor. Getting in and out of a bus is not the same as getting in and out of a train. Mounting is not the same as dismounting. Getting to and from a platform and changing from one travel mode to another involves a series of travel barriers: escalators, travelators, kerbs and a variety of steps and stairs with different treads, risers and handrails. Travellers are required to be able to read, hear, talk, walk, climb, reach, hold, balance, stand and wait and carry suitcases or packages. Often they must function efficiently under stress in jostling crowds and in accelerating or decelerating vehicles.

Who are handicapped travellers?

Handicapped travellers are defined in the US report as 'those with an inability to perform one or more of the actions required by existing transport systems at a comfortable level of efficiency'. Considering the conditions and the activities required of the traveller, one can easily conclude that travel by public transport is only for athletes and that everyone else is a handicapped traveller to some extent or on some occasions. Few commuters would disagree.

Improvements in public transport would therefore help everyone but are particularly desirable

*From *Physiotherapy* (in press)

68

for the obviously handicapped traveller. These include many of those referred to as 'impaired' in the survey of the Office of Population Censuses and Surveys (see Harris and Smith 1971, and also Buckle 1971), (those 'lacking all or part of a limb or having a defective limb, organ or mechanism of the body', including those with defects of the heart, lungs or circulatory system, blind or deaf people, wheelchair-bound people and the ambulant disabled using crutches, walking frames or sticks); the temporarily disabled (someone with a strained wrist, a broken arm or a leg in plaster and even pregnant women); the voluntary handicapped (those carrying suitcases or packages); people handicapped by social roles including men and women accompanying young children or elderly relatives; and a host of others including young children on their own, oversized or undersized adults and the elderly and infirm who can do everything required of them on a transport system but with far less facility than younger people.

There has been no survey of the travelling needs of disabled people in the UK and no survey of how many handicapped travellers there might be. Surveys discover the requirements of existing travellers but not the desires and needs of those who are not travelling or cannot travel.

Amelia Harris's survey[2] revealed that there were about 3,071,000 'impaired' people above the age of 16 living at home in Great Britain and that of these about 1,128,000 were 'very severely, severely or appreciably handicapped' in relation to self-care ability in the sheltered environments of their homes. Most would obviously encounter great difficulty in the far more onerous conditions of public transport. The survey revealed the travelling difficulties of those who were not housebound (about 354,000 reported difficulty) but nobody knows how many of the 400,000 or so housebound impaired were housebound because they could not travel. Nor do we know how many of those who claimed they were not prevented from going anywhere they wished had been forced to give up wishing. Life is intolerable for people who pine to do things they cannot do. One adjusts and justifies the adjustment. In time the disabled person will insist to himself and to others that he really has no desire to do what he knows he cannot do in existing circumstances. The survey also indicated the impact of immobility on employment opportunities. About 16 per cent of the

554,000 impaired people in work stated that they encountered difficulty and about 10 per cent said that their disablement affected the distance they could travel to work. Presumably this affected their choice of work and their earnings. Difficulty in travelling was the reason given for not working at all by 2 in 5 of the 291,000 unemployed, impaired people under retirement age.[3]

Take the problems of these people and add the elderly and infirm and all the other categories of 'handicapped traveller' referred to and, clearly, the problem of access and convenience of use of public transport systems is considerable and seriously affects a substantial section of the population. Summing up the section on travelling difficulties of the impaired and chronically handicapped traveller, Harris commented: 'Perhaps the most needed developments are those that would enable the disabled to use public transport systems more easily'.

Public transport
There are several reasons why public transport will never be suitable for all even though engineers could construct such transport systems. One reason is cost. The less agile need not be forced through the same routes as the athletic. You can have signs for the deaf and hard of hearing and audio information and braille signs for blind or partially sighted people. You can have stanchions and handrails for the ambulant disabled and uncluttered entrances for the wheelchair-bound. You can have steps and ramps, and lifts and escalators. Such systems cost more to build but not that much more if the needs of handicapped travellers are considered at the design stage. Certainly the cost would be a fraction of that involved in adapting existing systems and often it is not technically feasible to alter existing systems to the extent required. The removal of one barrier within a transport system does not mean that everyone who encountered difficulty with that barrier would then be able to use the system. The US study revealed, for instance, that 16 per cent of the handicapped traveller sample could not walk long distances but that the elimination of this barrier would help less than 6 per cent of those people because many of them also encountered difficulty in climbing stairs, moving rapidly and standing or maintaining balance in an accelerating vehicle. Any campaign to remove one type of

barrier such as stairs is therefore bound to be less effective than one which eliminates all the barriers associated with a predominant set of disabilities (predominant in the sense of frequency of occurrence in a given population). For new and old systems alike there is therefore a trade-off between increasing the proportion of the total population that can be efficiently handled and increasing cost.

Operating costs are also increased. It costs money to operate lifts and escalators and the totally accessible bus illustrates another aspect of increased operating cost. Buses can be made accessible to the wheelchair-bound with hydraulic lifts that can function as folding steps making access also easier for the ambulant disabled. But buses already hunt in packs and delays in operating them for the less mobile would increase this tendency to the annoyance of the fit. More buses would then be required to serve the same number of passengers with the same frequency.

Another reason why public transport throughout the UK will probably never reach the ideal standards required is that there are a host of different authorities involved with different terms of reference. There are 4 Passenger Transport Executives, the London Transport Executive, British Rail, the National Bus Company and the Scottish Transport Group (with 60 different operators), about 68 municipal transport undertakings, and more than 120 independent undertakings each owning more than 24 vehicles.[4] Most of these authorities must run commercially profitable services and those that can avoid this constraint have to make good losses by subsidies from the ratepayer or taxpayer. There is no central advisory service on the needs of handicapped travellers and no central control over the day-to-day decisions of these authorities, decisions which cover the design of systems and selection of vehicles, and there are no central funds available to help them make their transport systems more accessible.

There are therefore practical, administrative and economic constraints limiting the percentage of the total population that can be comfortably (or uncomfortably) accommodated on public transport. Only nominal progress has been made in the UK in the face of these constraints since a clause to make public transport accessible to disabled people was rejected in the Lords during the passage of the Chronically Sick and Disabled

Persons Bill.[5] The Department of the Environment has issued a Circular drawing the attention of transport operators and manufacturers to the needs of disabled people.[6] The Department has also sponsored research through the Transport and Road Research Laboratory into improved bus designs. British Rail has at last acknowledged that their new carriage stock is or can be made accessible to wheelchair-bound people and have issued a useful statement of intent.[7] Improved bus designs may be tied to Exchequer grants, but accessibility will not be made a condition for all grants for public transport. Alfred Morris sought this but was told: 'No. Such a general rule would not be practicable'.[8] Radical improvements in public transport, which could make the car less popular and less essential are therefore unlikely in the forseeable future.

Private transport

The problems of many handicapped travellers would remain unsolved even if only ideal public transport systems were built from now on. New systems have to tie in with old unadaptable systems, inter-mode barriers remain and public transport, ideal or otherwise, can never provide a door-to-door service everywhere. There is only one travel mode that can provide a total geographical coverage on demand and that is the private road vehicle. Its popularity is assured by the inadequacies of public transport and for many of the most severely disabled the private car (or van) is and will remain their sole means of mobility outdoors. The importance of this mode of travel for these people is undeniable and the existence of the invalid vehicle service of the Department of Health and Social Security is evidence of this even though the service leaves much to be desired.

INVALID VEHICLE SERVICE

Just over three years ago it was stated in Parliament that the invalid tricycle was regarded as 'basically a kind of artificial limb'.[9] It has enabled many disabled drivers to get back to work and many other drivers to escape the confines of their homes and get back into society, but its single seat limits its value for any driver with a spouse or friend. It has also been explained that: 'The present Health Service arrangements for providing powered vehicles for disabled persons — or for giving some assistance in lieu — all depend on the disabled person being able to drive the vehicle, the concept is that of restoring as much personal physical mobility as it is possible to provide'.[10] In this context 'personal physical mobility' is strictly limited in meaning and implies total self-sufficiency. 'Personal' means 'without the help or intervention of others'. If the phrase were applied to other transport modes it would mean that you would have to be able to drive in order to travel by bus or taxi. Some minor changes in the service were announced in February 1972. Cars were given to a few more categories of disabled driver and help was extended to other disabled drivers. Drivers who could afford one or more cars were allowed to choose between an invalid tricycle as a spare and the £100 a year allowance for a car. Drivers who could not afford to buy a car still had to rely on invalid tricycles. The service was still hamstrung by the concept of 'personal physical mobility' (which neatly excludes the more severely disabled) and, as it was still very far from perfect, Lady Sharp was appointed in April 1972 to examine its defects and recommends improvement. Her inquiry was to be completed in 12 months but her report was not submitted to the Secretary of State until October 1973 and its publication is still awaited.[11]

The invalid vehicle service thus still offers help only to those who can drive. This service for the physically disabled is still based illogically on a physical ability — the ability to drive — and there is still no help for the more severely disabled who are too disabled to either walk or drive. The needs of these 'disabled passengers' must be met. It would obviously be absurd to insist that people cannot travel by air unless they can pilot an aircraft and even more absurd to offer financial help towards the cost of air travel only to disabled people who hold a valid pilot's licence. Unfortunately these absurdities still apply in the case of the invalid vehicle service. It can never be a service for the physically disabled until it is recognised that 'disabled passengers' have identical outdoor mobility needs to those of the more fortunate 'disabled drivers'. It will never be a true service until it meets the needs of all disabled people who cannot use public transport.

Constraints on cars

Disabled passengers and drivers who are fortunately mobile in a vehicle of their own choice would appear to have no problems. Unfortunately this is not so. Apart from steadily rising motoring costs their freedom to travel where and when they choose is threatened by other factors. The car has many opponents. Some would ban it and have everyone cycling or walking or using public transport. Many want further restrictions on its use in cities.

In most cities the number of on-street parking places (free and metered) are being reduced, and more kerbs are being decorated with yellow paint. Competition for on-street parking increases and more motorists are being forced onto off-street car parks. This does not reduce traffic congestion and some local authorities are now seeking control of off-street public car parks to impose swingeing charges and limit opening hours. Commuting motorists would be banned and others would be financially encouraged to use public transport. Similar measures are proposed in connection with existing off-street private car parks at offices, shops, factories and other buildings, and the amount of space that can be made available for parking in new developments has been reduced by some local authorities — planning permission is refused if there is too much. Parking close by the desired destination is the most valuable there is for disabled people who cannot walk far or have to travel in wheelchairs and reductions in off-street private parking space is just as serious for them as reductions in on-street parking. Other measures to restrict the use of cars in cities include supplementary licensing schemes and full road-pricing schemes. Both would impose financial penalties on people using cars in cities, either in specified areas or in certain areas and at certain times. The full panoply of measures have been contemplated by the GLC (1972)[12] and (1973)[13] and most cities are adopting at least two or three. All these measures are aimed at forcing people to use public transport and they are all indiscriminate. They are against the car; the fact that the car could contain a disabled commuter or shopper or visitor who cannot possibly be diverted to public transport is ignored. Those who would ban the car must remember this. The interests of people with locomotor disabilities are also threatened by two other measures to make cities more attractive to people in general. The first is the closure of some roads to cars at certain times and the second is the complete closure of streets to all traffic to form pedestrian areas. Buildings along these streets are inaccessible if parking in nearby side-streets is not made available to people with locomotor disabilities. Often the diversion of traffic increases congestion in nearby streets making it essential to prohibit parking in these streets as well. The affected area spreads and more buildings become unapproachable. Pedestrian areas are fine for fit pedestrians even perhaps in the rain, wind, sleet or snow, but they are no good at all, even in high summer, for those who cannot reach them. Brand new pedestrian precincts can incorporate covered walks for odd days when the weather is unsuitable for a leisurely coffee outdoors. Access along service roads and parking inside the areas for people with locomotor disabilities can be provided so that no part of a new pedestrian precinct is inaccessible even to those with the most limited mobility range. But new pedestrian precincts do not always incorporate all these essential features and streets converted into artificial pedestrian areas are generally devoid of any.

Solutions?

City planning, traffic planning, road management and parking are in the hands of thousands of individuals throughout the country. Most are totally unaware of the needs of disabled people and severely handicapped travellers. While many of their activities are prescribed by regulations laid down by various authorities, no authority insists that they take account of these needs. If tackled individually many would agree that the special needs of disabled people must be considered but the systems within which they work generally do not allow them to do this themselves. Their problems are traffic and people in general — the

human problems of a car's occupant and the needs of disabled people in particular are the concern of others.

Outdoor mobility for disabled people is therefore in the hands of thousands of people with different special interests, different authority and responsibility and different terms of reference. Leaving aside the three government Departments, a model of the influences affecting the outdoor mobility of disabled people and handicapped travellers would be a froth of thousands of inter-connecting, overlapping and intersecting bubbles. Each bubble would prescribe a volume of special interest, responsibility, influence, authority, demand and supply, technical and financial viability, administrative practice and practicability and profit and loss. The interests and needs of a variety of disabled people are concealed by this froth of systems and, considering handicapped travellers, it cannot be divided into 'them' bubbles and 'us' bubbles.

If the question posed at the beginning of this article remains unanswered it will be because we allow the froth to envelope us, allow the systems to run us. It is up to everyone with a special interest or knowledge of the needs of handicapped travellers and disabled people to ensure that we do not have inaccessible and inconvenient public transport *and* an invalid vehicle service that only helps the less severely disabled *and* traffic planning *and* parking *and* town developments that, in combination, ignore the interests and needs of a substantial section of the population. The solution to outdoor mobility problems are fairly obvious; their implementation requires everyone's efforts all the time.

NOTES and REFERENCES

1. US Department of Transportation (August 1969) *Transportation Needs of the Handicapped: Travel Barriers* (PB 187 327) Clearinghouse for Federal Scientific and Technological Information, Springfield, Virginia 22151. (The summary, *Travel Barriers*, May 1970 US Department of Transportation, Office of the Secretary, Washington DC 20390).
2. HARRIS, A. C., COX, E. and SMITH, C. R. W. (1971) *Handicapped and Impaired in Great Britain* (Part I), London, HMSO.
3. BUCKLE, JR. (1971) *Handicapped and Impaired in Great Britain* (Part II): *Work and Housing of Impaired Persons in Great Britain*, London, HMSO.

4. HIBBS, J. (1971) *Transport for Passengers,* London, Institute of Economic Affairs (Hobart Paper No 23).
5. HOUSE OF LORDS, *Hansard* (30 April 1970) (Committee Stage).
6. Department of the Environment (28 August 1973) *The Disabled Traveller on Public Transport*, Circular 102/73, HMSO.
7. British Railways Board (December 1973) *Facilities for the Disabled* (Memorandum to Central Transport Consultative Committee).
8. House of Commons, *Hansard* (20 July 1973) col 153.
9. House of Commons, *Hansard* (10 December 1970) col 813.
10. House of Commons, *Hansard* (16 April 1970) col 1709.
11. The Sharp Report was published soon after the new government came to power after five months spent passing around the Department.
    Department of Health and Social Security (1974) *Mobility of Physically Disabled People*, London, HMSO.
    Its recommendations included the phasing out of the special invalid tricycles; the provision of ordinary minicars adapted where necessary although they could be available for someone driving the handicapped person; and the control of expenditure by the operation of new social qualifications for eligibility additional to a person's inability to walk. Making a statement on the day of its publication, the Secretary of State, Mrs. Barbara Castle, indicated her rejection of any proposal to remove vehicles from those who had them at present because it would make them virtually housebound. It remains to be seen how the report is implemented.
12. Greater London Council (July 1972) *Traffic and the Environment: A Paper for discussion.*
13. Greater London Council (March 1973) *Transport in London: Living with Traffic.*

PART THREE
Perceptions and conceptions of impairment

Introduction

Introduction

In selecting useful and representative items for this book, we have of course been faced frequently with the difficulty of deciding what to cut out. In fact we have experienced the opposite only when searching for effective studies of existing services, especially ones exemplifying good practice. Nowhere has selection been more difficult than in this section, which is why some reference must be made in this introduction to other material. To have included more readings would have over-balanced the book, but to ignore the wide range of illuminating writing seems close to deception. There are many reasons why the analysis of stigma and social identity should have been relatively well considered. Handicapped people, however dependent, disadvantaged and socially or emotionally depressed, have spoken their mind. Those campaigning on their behalf within or outside bureaucratic organizations have had to justify their claim for resources and indicate objectives for projected services, and professionals have had to justify their jobs. In addition this analysis comes at the critical meeting-point of the sociological and psychological analyses of normality and the evaluation of different forms of service and community attitudes and involvement.

Goffman's work, like Townsend's, underlies many sections of this book. Its particular value at this point lies in the presentation of a coherent model of stigma as a general social process not peculiar to specific forms of deviance or impairment. Deviance may take the form of visible or only privately disclosable physical abnormality or character disreputability, or it may result from the unwisdom of being born to a discredited lineage, ethnic category or social class! The literature generated by handicapped people themselves, e.g. Paul Hunt's *Stigma*, Jack Ashley's *Journey into Silence*, and Henry Minton's *Blind Man's Buff*, is full of references to their experiences of being or becoming different, special and at least initially second-rate. Battye's essay on non-person-hood according to the stereotype of D. H. Lawrence, the apostle of blood and gut reactions, depicts the assumptions helping to formulate this sub-world to which handicapped people get relegated. Fitzgerald's report of research into the reactions of those who have become blind (in Part Six) is also of relevance here.

The most critical encounters are those between the handicapped and people who, at any rate in relation to the specific disability involved, pass as normal. Goffman is most concerned with this in analysing stigma, and as well as with the different types of relationship in which such people are involved. The demarcation line is well demonstrated by the following account of a spastic undergraduate's first experiences of friendship at a British university, after a lifetime of special schooling.

There are two types of marriage open to the handicapped: marriage between handicapped people and 'mixed-marriages'. I call them 'mixed' because I once got involved with a non-handicapped girl who rejected me. At the time she said something that made me think. She said 'Its not because you're spastic. I don't care whether my boyfriend is spastic, black or any other colour'. Does society equate my sexual relationship with a non-handicapped girl with that between black and white, and with the same fear and disgust?

The answer is, of course, that it does.

Considerable attention has been devoted to psychological studies of the adjustment, self-conception and interaction patterns of handicapped people in the United States. In this book these are exemplified by Comer and Piliavin's experimental testing of hypotheses derived from Goffman's analysis, and by the items by Richardson *et al.* in Part Five. Important research in this field was pioneered by Barker and Wright and continued by Kleck, to whom Comer and Piliavin frequently refer. The latter article has been selected as a methodological example of research as well as for the specific hypotheses the authors set out to test. It would have been particularly interesting to have seen the results of a similar experiment in which both sets of participants were naive to the testing situation.

Goffman draws a distinction between the *own*, i.e. similarly impaired people, and the *wise*, who are people especially privy to their disabilities, such as workers in relevant occupations and close friends and relatives (e.g. see Edgerton's item on the cloak of competence and the benevolent conspiracy in Part 8). It is important to view the demands of high-status handicapped people in relation to their difference from as well as their association with other people with similar disabilities. It is also essential to pay close attention to the particular societal and professional assumptions and ideologies of the wise who play so

significant a role in structuring the world of handicapped people. Scott indicates how greatly these may differ by presenting ideal types or models of services for the blind in the USA, Britain, Sweden, Catholic Europe and the USSR. His account tallies with Minton's recent description of rehabilitation by the Royal National Institute for the Blind: 'They mean to leave no stone unturned in trying to convince us that to be blind can be fun... I don't want to become a blind Peter-Pan. I want to get to grips with my situation' (p.85). Scott also suggests, although with less exemplification, how conceptions of stigma are created by professionals working according to different societal assumptions, financial objectives or professional ideologies. There is researched data but, with the exception of Miller and Gwynne's study of residential care establishments for chronically sick and disabled young adults, this has tended to be restricted to the fields of psychiatric care and the nursing profession e.g. Strauss *et al* (1964) and Menzies (1960). Raynes and King's report of their research into caring regimes for mentally handicapped children in Part Eight does, however, open the way for the application of some of these concepts and observations to the sorts of service discussed in this book. The value of such a comparative approach is, as Scott suggests, that it heightens one's ability to see assumed statements of fact as expressions of core values woven into the general culture or professional subculture of those expressing such statements. It will be instructive to bring this detached eye to bear on subsequent items in this book.

REFERENCES

ASHLEY, J. (1973) *Journey into Silence*, London, Bodley Head.

BARKER, R. G. (1948) 'The social psychology of physical disability' *Journal of Social Issues* 4 (4) pp. 28—38.

HUNT, P. (ed) (1966) *Stigma: the experience of disability*, London, Geoffrey Chapman.

KLECK, R. (1969) 'Physical Stigma and task oriented interactions' *Human Relations* 22 (1) pp. 53—60.

MENZIES, I. E. P. (1960) 'A case study in the functioning of social systems as a defence against anxiety: a report on a study of the nursing service of a general hospital', *Human Relations* 13 pp. 95—121.

MINTON, H. G. (1974) *Blind Man's Buff*, London, Elek.

STRAUSS, A. L., SCHATZMAN, L., BUCKER, R., EHRLICH, D. and SABSHIN, M. (1964) *Psychiatric institutions and ideologies*, London, Collier Macmillan.

WRIGHT, B. A. (1960) *Physical disability: a psychological approach*, New York, Harper and Row.

9. Stigma and social identity*

ERVING GOFFMAN
Professor of Sociology,
University of Pennsylvania, USA.

The Greeks, who were apparently strong on visual aids, originated the term stigma to refer to bodily signs designed to expose something unusual and bad about the moral status of the signifier. The signs were cut or burnt into the body and advertised that the bearer was a slave, a criminal, or a traitor – a blemished person, ritually polluted, to be avoided, especially in public places. Later, in Christian times, two layers of metaphor were added to the term: the first referred to bodily signs of holy grace that took the form of eruptive blossoms on the skin; the second, a medical allusion to this religious allusion, referred to bodily signs of physical disorder. Today the term is widely used in something like the original literal sense, but is applied more to the disgrace itself than to the bodily evidence of it. Furthermore, shifts have occurred in the kinds of disgrace that arouse concern. Students, however, have made little effort to describe the structural preconditions of stigma, or even to provide a definition of the concept itself. It seems necessary, therefore, to try at the beginning to sketch in some very general assumptions and definitions.

Preliminary conceptions

Society establishes the means of categorizing persons and the complement of attributes felt to be ordinary and natural for members of each of these categories. Social settings establish the cate-gories of persons likely to be encountered there. The routines of social intercourse in established settings allow us to deal with anticipated others without special attention or thought. When a stranger comes into our presence, then, first appearances are likely to enable us to anticipate his category and attributes, his 'social identity' – to use a term that is better than 'social status' because personal attributes such as 'honesty' are involved, as well as structural ones, like 'occupation'.

We lean on these anticipations that we have, transforming them into normative expectations, into righteously presented demands.

Typically, we do not become aware that we have made these demands or aware of what they are until an active question arises as to whether or not they will be fulfilled. It is then that we are likely to realize that all along we had been making certain assumptions as to what the individual before us ought to be. Thus, the demands we make might better be called demands made 'in effect,' and the character we impute to the individual might better be seen as an imputation made in potential retrospect – a characterization 'in effect,' a *virtual social identity*. The category and attributes he could in fact be proved to possess will be called his *actual social identity*.

While the stranger is present before us, evidence can arise of his possessing an attribute that makes him different from others in the category of persons available for him to be, and of a less desirable kind – in the extreme, a person who is quite thoroughly bad, or dangerous, or weak. He is thus reduced in our minds from a whole and usual person to a tainted, discounted one. Such an

*From Erving Goffman (1963) *Stigma: notes on the management of a spoiled identity*, New York, Prentice Hall; (reprinted 1968) London, Penguin Books, Chapter 1, pp. 1–40.

attribute is a stigma, especially when its discrediting effect is very extensive; sometimes it is also called a failing, a shortcoming, a handicap. It constitutes a special discrepancy between virtual and actual social identity. Note that there are other types of discrepancy between virtual and actual social identity, for example the kind that causes us to reclassify an individual from one socially anticipated category to a different but equally well-anticipated one, and the kind that causes us to alter our estimation of the individual upward. Note, too, that not all undesirable attributes are at issue, but only those which are incongruous with our stereotype of what a given type of individual should be.

The term stigma, then, will be used to refer to an attribute that is deeply discrediting, but it should be seen that a language of relationships, not attributes, is really needed. An attribute that stigmatizes one type of possessor can confirm the usualness of another, and therefore is neither creditable nor discreditable as a thing in itself. For example, some jobs in America cause holders without the expected college education to conceal this fact; other jobs, however, can lead the few of their holders who have a higher education to keep this a secret, lest they be marked as failures and outsiders. [. . .]

The term stigma and its synonyms conceal a double perspective: does the stigmatized individual assume his differentness is known about already or is evident on the spot, or does he assume it is neither known about by those present nor immediately perceivable by them? In the first case one deals with the plight of the *discredited*, in the second with that of the *discreditable*. This is an important difference, even though a particular stigmatized individual is likely to have experience with both situations. I will begin with the situation of the discredited and move on to the discreditable but not always separate the two.

Three grossly different types of stigma may be mentioned. First there are abominations of the body – the various physical deformities. Next there are blemishes of individual character perceived as weak will, domineering or unnatural passions, treacherous and rigid beliefs, and dishonesty, these being inferred from a known record of, for example, mental disorder, imprisonment, addiction, alcoholism, homosexuality, unemployment, suicidal attempts, and radical political be-

havior. Finally there are the tribal stigma of race, nation, and religion, these being stigma that can be transmitted through lineages and equally contaminate all members of a family.[1] In all of these various instances of stigma, however, including those the Greeks had in mind, the same sociological features are found: an individual who might have been received easily in ordinary social intercourse possesses a trait that can obtrude itself upon attention and turn those of us whom he meets away from him, breaking the claim that his other attributes have on us. He possesses a stigma, an undesired differentness from what we had anticipated. We and those who do not depart negatively from the particular expectations at issue I shall call the *normals*.

The attitudes we normals have toward a person with a stigma, and the actions we take in regard to him, are well known, since these responses are what benevolent social action is designed to soften and ameliorate. By definition, of course, we believe the person with a stigma is not quite human. On this assumption we exercise varieties of discrimination, through which we effectively, if often unthinkingly, reduce his life chances. We construct a stigma-theory, an ideology to explain his inferiority and account for the danger he represents, sometimes rationalizing an animosity based on other differences, such as those of social class.[2] We use specific stigma terms such as cripple, bastard, moron in our daily discourse as a source of metaphor and imagery, typically without giving thought to the original meaning.[3] We tend to impute a wide range of imperfections on the basis of the original one,[4] and at the same time to impute some desirable but undesired attributes, often of a supernatural cast, such as 'sixth sense,' or 'understanding'. [. . .]

Further, we may perceive his defensive response to his situation as a direct expression of his defect, and then see both defect and response as just retribution for something he or his parents or his tribe did, and hence a justification of the way we treat him.[5]

Now turn from the normal to the person he is normal against. It seems generally true that members of a social category may strongly support a standard of judgment that they and others agree does not directly apply to them. Thus it is that a businessman may demand womanly behavior from females or ascetic behavior from monks, and not construe himself as someone who ought to realize either of these styles of conduct. The distinction is between realizing a norm and merely supporting it. The issue of stigma does not arise here, but only where there is some expectation on all sides that those in a given category should not only support a particular norm but also realize it.

Also, it seems possible for an individual to fail to live up to what we effectively demand of him, and yet be relatively untouched by this failure; insulated by his alienation, protected by identity beliefs of his own, he feels that he is a full-fledged normal human being, and that we are the ones who are not quite human. He bears a stigma but does not seem to be impressed or repentant about doing so. This possibility is celebrated in exemplary tales about Mennonites, Gypsies, shameless scoundrels, and very orthodox Jews.

In America at present, however, separate systems of honor seem to be on the decline. The stigmatized individual tends to hold the same beliefs abou' identity that we do; this is a pivotal fact. His deepest feelings about what he is may be his sense of being a 'normal person,' a human being like anyone else, a person, therefore, who deserves a fair chance and a fair break. (Actually, however phrased, he bases his claims not on what he thinks is due *everyone*, but only everyone of a selected social category into which he unquestionably fits, for example, anyone of his age, sex, profession, and so forth.) Yet he may perceive, usually quite correctly, that whatever others profess, they do not really 'accept' him and are not ready to make contact with him on 'equal grounds.' Further, the standards he has incorporated from the wider society equip him to be intimately alive to what others see as his failing, inevitably causing him, if only for moments, to agree that he does indeed fall short of what he really ought to be. Shame becomes a central possibility, arising from the individual's perception of one of his own attributes as being a defiling thing to possess, and one he can readily see himself as not possessing.

The immediate presence of normals is likely to reinforce this split between self-demands and self, but in fact self-hate and self-derogation can also occur when only he and a mirror are about:

When I got up at last . . . and had learned to walk again, one day I took a hand glass and went to a long mirror to look at myself, and I went alone. I didn't want anyone . . . to know how I felt when I saw myself for the first time. But there was no noise, no outcry; I didn't scream with rage when I saw myself. I just felt numb. That person in the mirror *couldn't* be me. I felt inside like a healthy, ordinary, lucky person — oh, not like the one in the mirror! Yet when I turned my face to the mirror there were my own eyes looking back, hot with shame . . . when I did not cry or make any sound, it became impossible that I should speak of it to anyone, and the confusion and the panic of my discovery were locked inside me then and there, to be faced alone, for a very long time to come.[6] [. . .]

The central feature of the stigmatized individual's situation in life can now be stated. It is a question of what is often, if vaguely, called 'acceptance.' Those who have dealings with him fail to accord him the respect and regard which the uncontaminated aspects of his social identity have led them to anticipate extending, and have led him to anticipate resolving; he echoes this denial by finding that some of his own attributes warrant it.

How does the stigmatized person respond to his situation? In some cases it will be possible for him to make a direct attempt to correct what he sees as the objective basis of his failing, as when a physically deformed person undergoes plastic surgery, a blind person eye treatment, an illiterate remedial education, a homosexual psychotherapy. (Where such repair is possible, what often results is not the acquisition of fully normal status, but a transformation of self from someone with a particular blemish into someone with a record of having corrected a particular blemish.) Here proneness to 'victimization' is to be cited, a result of the stigmatized person's exposure to fraudulent servers selling speech correction, skin lighteners, body stretchers, youth restorers (as in rejuvenation through fertilized egg yolk treatment), cures through faith, and poise in conversation. Whether a practical technique or fraud is involved, the quest, often secret, that results provides a special indication of the extremes to which the stigmatized can be willing to go, and hence the painfulness of the situation that leads them to these extremes. [. . .]

The stigmatized individual can also attempt to correct his condition indirectly by devoting much private effort to the mastery of areas of activity ordinarily felt to be closed on incidental and physical grounds to one with his shortcoming. This is illustrated by the lame person who learns or re-learns to swim, ride, play tennis, or fly an airplane, or the blind person who becomes expert at skiing and mountain climbing.[7] Tortured learning may be associated, of course, with the tortured performance of what is learned, as when an individual, confined to a wheelchair, managed to take to the dance floor with a girl in some kind of mimicry of dancing.[8] Finally, the person with a shameful differentness can break with what is called reality, and obstinately attempt to employ an unconventional interpretation of the character of his social identity.

The stigmatized individual is likely to use his stigma for 'secondary gains,' as an excuse for ill success that has come his way for other reasons:

For years the scar, harelip or misshapen nose has been looked on as a handicap, and its importance in the social and emotional adjustment is unconsciously all embracing. It is the 'hook' on which the patient has hung all inadequacies, all dissatisfactions, all procrastinations and all unpleasant duties of social life, and he has come to depend on it not only as a reasonable escape from competition but as a protection from social responsibility.

When one removes this factor by surgical repair, the patient is cast adrift from the more or less acceptable emotional protection it has offered and soon he finds, to his surprise and discomfort, that life is not all smooth sailing even for those with unblemished, 'ordinary' faces. He is unprepared to cope with this situation without the support of a 'handicap,' and he may turn to the less simple, but similar, protection of the behavior patterns of neurasthenia, hysterical conversion, hypochondriasis or the acute anxiety states.[9]

He may also see the trials he has suffered as a blessing in disguise, especially because of what it is felt that suffering can teach one about life and people:

But now, far away from the hospital experience, I can evaluate what I have learned. [A mother permanently disabled by polio writes.] For it wasn't only suffering: it was also learning

through suffering. I know my awareness of people has deepened and increased, that those who are close to me can count on me to turn all my mind and heart and attention to their problems. I could not have learned *that* dashing all over a tennis court.[10]

Correspondingly, he can come to re-assess the limitations of normals, as a multiple sclerotic suggests:

Both healthy minds and healthy bodies may be crippled. The fact that 'normal' people can get around, can see, can hear, doesn't mean that they are seeing or hearing. They can be very blind to the things that spoil their happiness, very deaf to the pleas of others for kindness; when I think of them I do not feel any more crippled or disabled than they. Perhaps in some small way I can be the means of opening their eyes to the beauties around us: things like a warm handclasp, a voice that is anxious to cheer, a spring breeze, music to listen to, a friendly nod. These people are important to me, and I like to feel that I can help them.[11] [...]

The responses of the normal and of the stigmatized that have been considered so far are ones which can occur over protracted periods of time and in isolation from current contact between normals and stigmatized.[12] This book, however, is specifically concerned with the issue of 'mixed contacts' — the moments when stigmatized and normal are in the same 'social situation,' that is, in one another's immediate physical presence, whether in a conversation-like encounter or in the mere co-presence of an unfocused gathering.

The very anticipation of such contacts can of course lead normals and the stigmatized to arrange life so as to avoid them. Presumably this will have larger consequences for the stigmatized, since more arranging will usually be necessary on their part:

Before her disfigurement [amputation of the distal half of her nose] Mrs. Dover, who lived with one of her two married daughters, had been an independent, warm and friendly woman who enjoyed traveling, shopping, and visiting her many relatives. The disfigurement of her face, however, resulted in a definite alteration in her way of living. The first two or three years she seldom left her daughter's home, preferring to remain in her room or to sit in the backyard. "I was heartsick," she said; "the door had been shut on my life."[13]

Lacking the salutary feed-back of daily social intercourse with others, the self-isolate can become suspicious, depressed, hostile, anxious, and bewildered [. . .]

When normals and stigmatized do in fact enter one another's immediate presence, especially when they there attempt to sustain a joint conversational encounter, there occurs one of the primal scenes of sociology; for, in many cases, these moments will be the ones when the causes and effects of stigma must be directly confronted by both sides.

The stigmatized individual may find that he feels unsure of how we normals will identify him and receive him.[14] An illustration may be cited from a student of physical disability:

Uncertainty of status for the disabled person obtains over a wide range of social interactions in addition to that of employment. The blind, the ill, the deaf, the crippled can never be sure what the attitude of a new acquaintance will be, whether it will be rejective or accepting, until the contact has been made. This is exactly the position of the adolescent, the light-skinned Negro, the second generation immigrant, the socially mobile person and the woman who has entered a predominantly masculine occupation.[15]

This uncertainty arises not merely from the stigmatized individual's not knowing which of several categories he will be placed in, but also, where the placement is favorable, from his knowing that in their hearts the others may be defining him in terms of his stigma. [. . .]

Thus in the stigmatized arises the sense of not knowing what the others present are "really" thinking about him.

Further, during mixed contacts, the stigmatized individual is likely to feel that he is "on,"[16] having to be self-conscious and calculating about the impression he is making, to a degree and in areas of conduct which he assumes others are not.

Also, he is likely to feel that the usual scheme of interpretation for everyday events has been undermined. His minor accomplishments, he feels, may be assessed as signs of remarkable and noteworthy capacities in the circumstances [. . .]

A blind person provides an illustration:

His once most ordinary deeds — walking nonchalantly up the street, locating the peas on his plate, lighting a cigarette — are no longer ordinary. He becomes an unusual person. If he performs them with finesse and assurance they excite the same kind of wonderment inspired by a magician who pulls rabbits out of hats.[17]

At the same time, minor failings or incidental impropriety may, he feels, be interpreted as a direct expression of his stigmatized differentness. Ex-mental patients, for example, are sometimes afraid to engage in sharp interchanges with spouse or employer because of what a show of emotion might be taken as a sign of. [. . .]

A one-legged girl, recalling her experience with sports, provides other illustrations:

Whenever I fell, out swarmed the women in droves, clucking and fretting like a bunch of bereft mother hens. It was kind of them, and in retrospect I appreciate their solicitude, but at the time I resented and was greatly embarrassed by their interference. For they assumed that no routine hazard to skating — no stick or stone — upset my flying wheels. It was a foregone conclusion that *I* fell because I was a poor, helpless cripple.[18]

Not one of them shouted with outrage, 'That dangerous wild bronco threw her!' — which, God forgive, he did technically. It was like a horrible ghostly visitation of my old roller-skating days. All the good people lamented in chorus, 'That poor, poor girl fell off!'[19]

When the stigmatized person's failing can be perceived by our merely directing attention (typically, visual) to him — when, in short, he is a discredited, not discreditable, person — he is likely to feel that to be present among normals nakedly exposes him to invasions of privacy,[20] experienced most pointedly perhaps when children simply stare at him.[21] This displeasure in being exposed can be increased by the conversations strangers may feel free to strike up with him, conversations in which they express what he takes to be morbid curiosity about his condition, or in which they proffer help that he does not need or want.[22] One might add that there are certain classic formulae for these kinds of conversations: 'My dear girl, how did you get your quiggle'; 'My great uncle had a quiggle, so I feel I know all about your problem'; 'You know I've always said that Quiggles are good family men and look after their own poor'; 'Tell me, how do you manage to bathe with a quiggle?' The implication of these overtures is that the stigmatized individual is a person who can be approached by strangers at will, providing only that they are sympathetic to the plight of persons of his kind.

Given what the stigmatized individual may well face upon entering a mixed social situation, he may anticipatorily respond by defensive cowering. [. . .]

Instead of cowering, the stigmatized individual may attempt to approach mixed contacts with hostile bravado, but this can induce from others its own set of troublesome reciprocations. It may be added that the stigmatized person sometimes vacillates between cowering and bravado, racing from one to the other, thus demonstrating one central way in which ordinary face-to-face interaction can run wild.

I am suggesting, then, that the stigmatized individual — at least the 'visibly' stigmatized one — will have special reasons for feeling that mixed social situations make for anxious unanchored interaction. But if this is so, then it is to be suspected that we normals will find these situations shaky too. We will feel that the stigmatized individual is either too aggressive or too shamefaced, and in either case too ready to read unintended meanings into our actions. We ourselves may feel that if we show direct sympathetic concern for his condition, we may be overstepping ourselves, and yet if we actually forget that he has a failing we are likely to make impossible demands of him or unthinkingly slight his fellow-sufferers. Each potential source of discomfort for him when we are with him can become something we sense he is aware of, aware that we are aware of, and even aware of our state of awareness about his awareness; the stage is then set for the infinite regress of mutual consideration that Meadian social psychology tells us how to begin but not how to terminate.

Given what both the stigmatized and we normals introduce into mixed social situations, it is understandable that all will not go smoothly. We are likely to attempt to carry on as though in fact he wholly fitted one of the types of person naturally available to us in the situation, whether this means treating him as someone better than we feel he might be or someone worse than we feel he probably is. If neither of these tacks is possible, then we may try to act as if he were a 'non-person,' and not present at all as someone of whom ritual notice is to be taken. He, in turn, is likely to go along with these strategies, at least initially.

In consequence, attention is furtively withdrawn from its obligatory targets, and self-consciousness and 'other-consciousness' occurs, expressed in the pathology of interaction — uneasiness.[23] As described in the case of the physically handicapped:

> Whether the handicap is overtly and tactlessly responded to as such or, as is more commonly the case, no explicit reference is made to it, the underlying condition of heightened, narrowed, awareness causes the interaction to be articulated too exclusively in terms of it. This, as my informants described it, is usually accompanied by one or more of the familiar signs of discomfort and stickiness: the guarded references, the common everyday words suddenly made taboo, the fixed stare elsewhere, the artificial levity, the compulsive loquaciousness, the awkward solemnity.[24]

In social situations with an individual known or perceived to have a stigma, we are likely, then, to employ categorizations that do not fit, and we and he are likely to experience uneasiness. Of course, there is often significant movement from this starting point. And since the stigmatized person is likely to be more often faced with these situations than are we, he is likely to become the more adept at managing them.

The own and the wise

Earlier it was suggested that a discrepancy may exist between an individual's virtual and actual identity. This discrepancy, when known about or apparent, spoils his social identity; it has the effect of cutting him off from society and from himself so that he stands a discredited person facing an unaccepting world. In some cases, as with the individual who is born without a nose, he may continue through life to find that he is the only one of his kind and that all the world is against him. In most cases, however, he will find that there are sympathetic others who are ready to adopt his standpoint in the world and to share with him the feeling that he is human and 'essentially' normal in spite of appearances and in spite of his own self-doubts. Two such categories will be considered.

The first set of sympathetic others is of course those who share his stigma. Knowing from their own experience what it is like to have this particular stigma, some of them can provide the individual with instruction in the tricks of the trade and with a circle of lament to which he can withdraw for moral support and for the comfort of feeling at home, at ease, accepted as a person who really is like any other normal person. One example may be cited from a study of illiterates:

> The existence of a different value system among these persons is evinced by the communality of behavior which occurs when illiterates interact among themselves. Not only do they change from unexpressive and confused individuals, as they frequently appear in larger society, to expressive and understanding persons within their own group, but moreover they express themselves in institutional terms. Among themselves they have a universe of response. They form and recognize symbols of prestige and disgrace; evaluate relevant situations in terms of their own norms and in their own idiom: and in their interrelations with one another, the mask of accommodative adjustment drops.[25]

Another from the hard of hearing:

> I remembered how relaxing it was, at Nitchie School, to be with people who took impaired hearing for granted. Now I wanted to know some people who took hearing aids for granted. How restful it would be to adjust the volume control on my transmitter without caring whether or not anyone was looking. To stop thinking, for awhile, about whether the cord at the back of my neck was showing. What luxury to say out loud to someone, 'Ye gods, my battery's dead!'[26] [...],

In the sociological study of stigmatized persons, one is usually concerned with the kind of corporate life, if any, that is sustained by those of a particular category. Certainly here one finds a fairly full catalogue of types of group formation and types of group function. There are speech defectives whose peculiarity apparently discourages any group formation whatsoever.[27] On the boundaries of a willingness to unite are ex-mental patients — only a relatively small number are currently willing to support mental health clubs, in spite of innocuous club titles which allow members to come together under a plain wrapper.[28] Then there are the huddle-together self-help clubs formed by the divorced, the aged, the obese, the physically handicapped,[29] the ileostomied and colostomied.[30] There are residential clubs, voluntary to varying degrees, formed for the ex-alcoholic and the ex-addict. There are national associations such as AA which provide a full doctrine and almost a way of life for their members. Often these associations are the culmination of years of effort on the part of variously situated persons and groups, providing exemplary objects of study as social movements.[31] [...]

Finally, within the city, there are full-fledged residential communities, ethnic, racial, or religious, with a high concentration of tribally stigmatized persons and (in contradistinction to much other group formation among the stigmatized) the family, not the individual, as the basic unit of organization.

Here, of course, there is a common conceptual confusion. The term 'category' is perfectly abstract and can be applied to any aggregate, in this case persons with a particular stigma. A good portion of those who fall within a given stigma category may well refer to the total membership by the term 'group' or an equivalent, such as 'we,' or 'our people.' Those outside the category may similarly designate those within it in group terms. However, often in such cases the full membership will not be part of a single group, in the strictest sense; they will neither have a capacity for collective action, nor a stable and embracing pattern of mutual interaction. What one does find is that the members of a particular stigma category will have a tendency to come together into small social groups whose members all derive from the category, these groups themselves being subject to overarching organization to varying degrees. And one also finds that when one member of the category happens to come into contact with another, both may be disposed to modify their treatment of each other by virtue of believing that they each belong to the same 'group.' Further, in being a member of the category, an individual may have an increased probability of coming into contact with any other member, and even forming a relationship with him as a result. A category, then, can function to dispose its members to group-formation and relationships, but its total membership does not thereby constitute a group —a conceptual nicety that will hereafter not always be observed in this essay.

Whether or not those with a particular stigma provide the recruitment base for a community that is ecologically consolidated in some way, they are likely to support agents and agencies who represent them. (Interestingly, we have no word to designate accurately the constituents, following, fans, subjects, or supporters of such representatives.) Members may, for example, have an office or lobby to push their case with the Press or Government, differing here in terms of whether they can have a man of their own kind, a 'native' who really knows, as do the deaf, the blind, the alcoholic, and Jews, or someone from the other side, as do ex-cons and the mentally defective. (Action groups which serve the same category of stigmatized person may sometimes be in slight opposition to each other, and this opposition will often reflect a difference between management by natives and management by normals.) A characteristic task of these representatives is to convince the public to use a softer social label for the category in question:

> Acting on this conviction, the League [New York League for the Hard of Hearing] staff agreed to use only such terms as hard of hearing, impaired hearing, and hearing loss; to excise the word deaf from their conversation, their correspondence and other writings, their teaching, and their speeches in public. It worked. New York in general gradually began to use the new vocabulary. Straight thinking was on the way.[32]

Another of their usual tasks is to appear as 'speakers' before various audiences of normals and of the stigmatized; they present the case for the stigmatized and, when they themselves are natives

of the group, provide a living model of fully-normal achievement, being heroes of adjustment who are subject to public awards for proving that an individual of this kind can be a good person.

Often those with a particular stigma sponsor a publication of some kind which gives voice to shared feelings, consolidating and stabilizing for the reader his sense of the realness of 'his' group and his attachment to it. Here the ideology of the members is formulated — their complaints, their aspirations, their politics. The names of well-known friends and enemies of the 'group' are cited, along with information to confirm the goodness or the badness of these people. Success stories are printed, tales of heroes of assimilation who have penetrated new areas of normal acceptance. Atrocity tales are recorded, recent and historic, of extreme mistreatment by normals. Exemplary moral tales are provided in biographical and autobiographical form illustrating a desirable code of conduct for the stigmatized. The publication also serves as a forum for presenting some division of opinion as to how the situation of the stigmatized person ought best to be handled. Should the individual's failing require special equipment, it is here advertised and reviewed. The readership of these publications provides a market for books and pamphlets which present a similar line.[. . .]

An intellectually worked-up version of their point of view is thus available to most stigmatized persons.

A comment is here required about those who come to serve as representatives of a stigmatized category. Starting out as someone who is a little more vocal, a little better known, or a little better connected than his fellow-sufferers, a stigmatized person may find that the 'movement' has absorbed his whole day, and that he has become a professional.[. . .]

It might be added that once a person with a particular stigma attains high occupational, political, or financial position — how high depending on the stigmatized group in question — a new career is likely to be thrust upon him, that of representing his category. He finds himself too eminent to avoid being presented by his own as an instance of them. (The weakness of a stigma can thus be measured by how eminent a member of the category may be and yet manage to avoid these pressures.)

Two points are sometimes made about this kind of professionalization. First, in making a profession of their stigma, native leaders are obliged to have dealings with representatives of other categories, and so find themselves breaking out of the closed circle of their own kind. Instead of leaning on their crutch, they get to play golf with it, ceasing, in terms of social participation, to be representative of the people they represent.[33]

Secondly, those who professionally present the viewpoint of their category may introduce some systematic bias in this presentation simply because they are sufficiently involved in the problem to write about it. Although any particular stigma category is likely to have professionals who take different lines, and may even support publications which advocate different programs, there is uniform tacit agreement that the situation of the individual with this particular stigma is worth attention. Whether a writer takes a stigma very seriously or makes light of it, he must define it as something worth writing about. This minimal agreement, even when there are no others, helps to consolidate belief in the stigma as a basis for self-conception. Here again representatives are not representative, for representation can hardly come from those who give no attention to their stigma, or who are relatively unlettered.[. . .]

I have considered one set of individuals from whom the stigmatized person can expect some support: those who share his stigma and by virtue of this are defined and define themselves as his own kind. The second set are — to borrow a term once used by homosexuals — the 'wise,' namely, persons who are normal but whose special situation has made them intimately privy to the secret life of the stigmatized individual and sympathetic with it, and who find themselves accorded a measure of acceptance, a measure of courtesy membership in the clan. Wise persons are the marginal men before whom the individual with a fault need feel no shame nor exert self-control, knowing that in spite of his failing he will be seen as an ordinary other.[. . .]

Before taking the standpoint of those with a particular stigma, the normal person who is becoming wise may first have to pass through a heart-changing personal experience, of which there are many literary records.[34] And after the sympathetic normal makes himself available to the stigmatized, he often must wait their validation of him as a courtesy member. The self must not only be offered, it must be accepted.[. . .]

One type of wise person is he whose wiseness comes from working in an establishment which caters either to the wants of those with a particular stigma or to actions that society takes in regard to these persons. For example, nurses and physical therapists can be wise; they can come to know more about a given type of prosthetic equipment than the patient who must learn to use it so as to minimize his disfigurement. Gentile employees in delicatessens are often wise, as are straight bartenders in homosexual bars, and the maids of Mayfair prostitutes.[35] The police, in constantly having to deal with criminals, may become wise in regard to them, leading a professional to suggest that '. . .in fact the police are the only people apart from other criminals who accept you for what you are.'[36]

A second type of wise person is the individual who is related through the social structure to a stigmatized individual — a relationship that leads the wider society to treat both individuals in some respects as one. Thus the loyal spouse of the mental patient, the daughter of the ex-con, the parent of the cripple, the friend of the blind, the family of the hangman,[37] are all obliged to share some of the discredit of the stigmatized person to whom they are related. One response to this fate is to embrace it, and to live within the world of one's stigmatized connection. It should be added that persons who acquire a degree of stigma in this way can themselves have connections who acquire a little of the disease twice-removed. The problems faced by stigmatized persons spread out in waves, but of diminishing intensity.[. . .]

In general, the tendency for a stigma to spread from the stigmatized individual to his close connections provides a reason why such relations tend either to be avoided or to be terminated, where existing.

Persons with a courtesy stigma provide a model of 'normalization,'[38] showing how far normals could go in treating the stigmatized person as if he didn't have a stigma. (Normalization is to be distinguished from 'normification,' namely, the effort on the part of a stigmatized individual to present himself as an ordinary person, although not necessarily making a secret of his failing.) Further, a cult of the stigmatized can occur, the stigmaphobic response of the normal being countered by the stigmaphile response of the wise. The person with a courtesy stigma can in fact make both the stigmatized and the normal uncomfortable: by always being ready to carry a burden that is not 'really' theirs, they can confront everyone else with too much morality; by treating the stigma as neutral matter to be looked at in a direct, off-hand way, they open themselves and the stigmatized to misunderstanding by normals who may read offensiveness into this behavior.[39] [...]

Moral career

Persons who have a particular stigma tend to have similar learning experiences regarding their plight, and similar changes in conception of self — a similar 'moral career' that is both cause and effect of commitment to a similar sequence of personal adjustments. [...]

One phase of this socialization process is that through which the stigmatized person learns and incorporates the stand-point of the normal, acquiring thereby the identity beliefs of the wider society and a general idea of what it would be like to possess a particular stigma. Another phase is that through which he learns that he possesses a particular stigma and, this time in detail, the consequence of possessing it. The timing and interplay of these two initial phases of the moral career form important patterns, establishing the foundation for later development, and providing a means of distinguishing among the moral careers available to the stigmatized. Four such patterns may be mentioned.

One pattern involves those with an inborn stigma who become socialized into their disadvantageous situation even while they are learning and incorporating the standards against which they fall short.[40] For example, an orphan learns that children naturally and normally have parents, even while he is learning what it means not to have any. After spending the first sixteen years of his life in the institution he can later still feel that he naturally knows how to be a father to his son.

A second pattern derives from the capacity of a family, and to a much lesser extent a local neighborhood, to constitute itself a protective capsule for its young. Within such a capsule a congenitally stigmatized child can be carefully sustained by means of information control. Self-belittling definitions of him are prevented from entering the charmed circle, while broad access is given to other conceptions held in the wider society, ones that lead the encapsulated child to see himself as a fully qualified ordinary human being, of normal identity in terms of such basic matters as age and sex.

The point in the protected individual's life when the domestic circle can no longer protect him will vary by social class, place of residence, and type of stigma, but in each case will give rise to a moral experience when it occurs. Thus, public school entrance is often reported as the occasion of stigma learning, the experience sometimes coming very precipitously on the first day of school, with taunts, teasing, ostracism, and fights. Interestingly the more the child is 'handicapped' the more likely he is to be sent to a special school for persons of his kind, and the more abruptly he will have to face the view which the public at large takes of him. He will be told that he will have an easier time of it among 'his own,' and thus learn that the own he thought he possessed was the wrong one, and that this lesser own is really his. It should be added that where the infantilely stigmatized manages to get through his early school years with some illusions left, the onset of dating or job-getting will often introduce the moment of truth. In some cases, merely an increased likelihood of incidental disclosure is involved:

> I think the first realization of my situation, and the first intense grief resulting from this realization, came one day, very casually, when a group of us in our early teens had gone to the beach for the day. I was lying on the sand, and I guess the fellows and girls thought I was asleep. One of the fellows said, 'I like Domenica very much, but I would never go out with a blind girl.' I cannot think of any prejudice which so completely rejects you.[41]

A third pattern of socialization is illustrated by one who becomes stigmatized late in life, or learns late in life that he has always been discreditable — the first involving no radical reorganization of his view of his past, the second involving this factor. [...]

While there are certainly cases of individuals discovering only in adult life that they belong to a stigmatized tribal group or that their parents have a contagious moral blemish, the usual case here is that of physical handicaps that 'strike' late in life:

But suddenly I woke up one morning, and found that I could not stand. I had had polio, and polio was as simple as that. I was like a very young child who had been dropped into a big, black hole, and the only thing I was certain of was that I could not get out unless someone helped me. The education, the lectures, and the parental training which I had received for twenty-four years didn't seem to make me the person who could do anything for me now. I was like everyone else — normal, quarrelsome, gay, full of plans, and all of a sudden something happened! Something happened and I became a stranger. I was a greater stranger to myself than to anyone. Even my dreams did not know me. They did not know what they ought to let me do — and when I went to dances or to parties in them, there was always an odd provision or limitation — not spoken of or mentioned, but there just the same. I suddenly had the very confusing mental and emotional conflict of a lady leading a double life. It was unreal and it puzzled me, and I could not help dwelling on it.[42]

Here the medical profession is likely to have the special job of informing the infirm who he is going to have to be.

A fourth pattern is illustrated by those who are initially socialized in an alien community, whether inside or outside the geographical boundaries of the normal society, and who then must learn a second way of being that is felt by those around them to be the real and valid one.

It should be added that when an individual acquires a new stigmatized self late in life, the uneasiness he feels about new associates may slowly give way to uneasiness felt concerning old ones. Post-stigma acquaintances may see him simply as a faulted person; pre-stigma acquaintances, being attached to a conception of what he once was, may be unable to treat him either with formal tact or with familiar full acceptance:

My task [as a blind writer interviewing prospective clients for his literary product] was to put the men I'd come to see at their ease — the reverse of the usual situation. Curiously, I found it much easier to do with men I'd never met before. Perhaps this was because with strangers there was no body of reminiscences to cover before business could be gotten down to

and so there was no unpleasant contrast with the present.[43]

Regardless of which general pattern the moral career of the stigmatized individual illustrates, the phase of experience during which he learns that he possesses a stigma will be especially interesting, for at this time he is likely to be thrown into a new relationship to others who possess the stigma too.

In some cases, the only contact the individual will have with his own is a fleeting one, but sufficient nonetheless to show him that others like himself exist:

When Tommy came to the clinic the first time, there were two other little boys there, each with a congenital absence of an ear. When Tommy saw them, his right hand went slowly to his own defective ear, and he turned with wide eyes to his father and said, 'There's another boy with an ear like mine.'[44]

In the case of the individual who has recently become physically handicapped, fellow-sufferers more advanced than himself in dealing with the failing are likely to make him a special series of visits to welcome him to the club and to instruct him in how to manage himself physically and psychically.[...]

In the many cases where the individual's stigmatization is associated with his admission to a custodial institution such as a jail, sanatorium, or orphanage, much of what he learns about his stigma will be transmitted to him during prolonged intimate contact with those in the process of being transformed into his fellow-sufferers.

As already suggested, when the individual first learns who it is that he must now accept as his own, he is likely, at the very least, to feel some ambivalence; for these others will not only be patently stigmatized, and thus not like the normal person he knows himself to be, but may also have other attributes with which he finds it difficult to associate himself. What may end up as a free-masonry may begin with a shudder. A newly blind girl on a visit to The Lighthouse directly from leaving the hospital provides an illustration:

My questions about a guide dog were politely turned aside. Another sighted worker took me in tow to show me around. We visited the Braille library; the classrooms; the clubrooms where the blind members of the music and dramatic groups meet; the recreation hall where on festive occasion the blind dance with the blind; the bowling alleys where the blind play together; the cafeteria, where all the blind gather to eat together; the huge workshops where the blind earn a subsistence income by making mops and brooms, weaving rugs, caning chairs. As we moved from room to room, I could hear the shuffling of feet, the muted voices, the tap-tap-tapping of canes. Here was the safe, segregated world of the sightless — a completely different world, I was assured by the social worker, from the one I had just left. . . .

I was expected to join this world. To give up my profession and to earn my living making mops. The Lighthouse would be happy to teach me how to make mops. I was to spend the rest of my life making mops with other blind people, eating with other blind people, dancing with other blind people. I became nauseated with fear, as the picture grew in my mind. Never had I come upon such destructive segregation.[45]

Given the ambivalence built into the individual's attachment to his stigmatized category, it is understandable that oscillations may occur in his support of, identification with, and participation among his own. There will be 'affiliation cycles' through which he comes to accept the special opportunities for in-group participation or comes to reject them after having accepted them before.[46] There will be corresponding oscillations in belief about the nature of own group and the nature of normals. For example, adolescence (and the high school peer group) can bring a marked decline in own-group identification and a marked increase in identification with normals.[47] The later phases of the individual's moral career are to be found in these shifts of participation and belief.

The relationship of the stigmatized individual to the informal community and formal organizations of his own kind is, then, crucial. This relationship will, for example, mark a great difference between those whose differentness provides them very little of a new 'we,' and those,

such as minority group members, who find themselves a part of a well-organized community with longstanding traditions — a community that makes appreciable claims on loyalty and income, defining the member as someone who should take pride in his illness and not seek to get well. In any case, whether the stigmatized group is an established one or not, it is largely in relation to this own-group that it is possible to discuss the natural history and the moral career of the stigmatized individual.

In reviewing his own moral career, the stigmatized individual may single out and retrospectively elaborate experiences which serve for him to account for his coming to the beliefs and practices that he now has regarding his own kind and normals. A life event can thus have a double bearing on moral career, first as immediate objective grounds for an actual turning point, and later (and easier to demonstrate) as a means of accounting for a position currently taken. One experience often selected for this latter purpose is that through which the newly stigmatized individual learns that full-fledged members of the group are quite like ordinary human beings: [. . .]

If I had to choose one group of experiences that finally convinced me of the importance of this problem [of self-image] and that I had to fight my own battles of identification, it would be the incidents that made me realize with my heart that cripples could be identified with characteristics other than their physical handicap. I managed to see that cripples could be comely, charming, ugly, lovely, stupid, brilliant — just like all other people, and I discovered that I was able to hate or love a cripple in spite of his handicap.[48]

[. . .] Another turning point — retrospectively if not originally — is the isolating, incapacitating experience, often a period of hospitalization, which comes later to be seen as the time when the individual was able to think through his problem, learn about himself, sort out his situation, and arrive at a new understanding of what is important and worth seeking in life.. [. . .]

NOTES AND REFERENCES

1. In recent history, especially in Britain, low class status functioned as an important tribal stigma, the sins of the parents, or at least their milieu, being visited on the child, should the child rise improperly far above his initial station. The management of class stigma is of course a central theme in the English novel.
2. Riesman, D., 'Some Observations Concerning Marginality,' *Phylon*, Second Quarter, 1951, 122.
3. The case regarding mental patients is presented by T. J. Scheff in a forthcoming paper.
4. In regard to the blind, see Henrich E., and Kriegel, L., (eds), *Experiments in Survival*, Association for the Aid of Crippled Children, 1961, pp. 152 and 186; and Chevigny, H., *My Eyes Have a Cold Nose*, Yale University Press, paperbound, 1962, p. 201.
5. For examples, see Macgregor, F., *et al.*, *Facial Deformities and Plastic Surgery*, Charles C. Thomas, 1953.
6. Hathaway, K. B., *The Little Locksmith*, Coward-McCann, 1943, p. 41, in Wright, B., *Physical Disability: A Psychological Approach*, Harper and Row, 1960.
7. Keitlen, T., (with Lobsenz, N.), *Farewell to Fear*, Avon, 1962, Chapter 12, pp. 117—29 and Chapter 14, pp. 137—49. See also Chevigny, *op. cit.*, pp. 85—6.
8. Henrich and Kriegel, *op. cit.*, p. 49.
9. Baker, W. Y., and Smith, L. H., 'Facial Disfigurement and Personality,' *Journal of the American Medical Association*, CXII (1939), 303. Macgregor *et al.*, op. cit., p. 57 ff., provide an illustration of a man who used his big red nose for a crutch.
10. Henrich and Kriegel, *op. cit.*, p. 19.
11. *Ibid.*, p. 35.
12. For one review, see Allport, G. W., *The Nature of Prejudice*, Anchor Books, 1958.
13. Macgregor *et al.*, *op. cit.*, pp. 91—2.
14. Barker, R., 'The Social Psychology of Physical Disability,' *Journal of Social Issues*, IV (1948), 34, suggests that stigmatized persons 'live on a social-psychological frontier,' constantly facing new situations. See also Macgregor *et al.*, *op. cit.*, p. 87, where the suggestion is made that the grossly deformed need suffer less doubt about their reception in interaction than the less visibly deformed.
15. Barker, *op. cit.*, p. 33.
16. This special kind of self-consciousness is analyzed in Messinger, S., *et al.*, 'Life as Theater: Some Notes on the Dramaturgic Approach to Social Reality,' *Sociometry*, XXV, 1962, 98—110.
17. Chevigny, *op. cit.*, p. 140.
18. Baker, *Out on a Limb*, McGraw-Hill, n.d., p. 22.
19. *Ibid.*, p. 73.
20. This theme is well treated in White, R. K., Wright, B. A., and Dembo, T., 'Studies in Adjustment to Visible Injuries: Evaluation of Curiosity by the Injured,' *Journal of Abnormal and Social Psychology*, XLIII, 1948, pp. 13—28.
21. For example, Henrich and Kriegel, *op. cit.*, p. 184.
22. See Wright, *op. cit.*, 'The Problem of Sympathy,' pp. 233—37.
23. For a general treatment, see Goffman, E., 'Alienation from Interaction,' *Human Relations*, X, 1957, pp. 47—60.
24. Davis, F., 'Deviance Disavowal: The Management of Strained Interaction by the Visibly Handicapped,' *Social Problems*, IX, 1961, p. 123. See also White, Wright, and Dembo, *op. cit.*, pp. 26—7.
25. Freeman H., and Kasenbaum, G., 'The Illiterate in America,' *Social Forces*, XXXIV 1956, 374.
26. Warfield, F., *Keep Listening*, Viking Press, 1957, p. 60.
27. Lemert, E., *Social Pathology*, McGraw-Hill, 1951, p. 151.
28. A general survey is provided in Wechsler, H., 'The Expatient Organization: A Survey,' *Journal of Social Issues*, XVI, 1960, 47—53. Titles include: Recovery, Inc., Search, Club 103, Fountain House Foundation, San Francisco Fellowship Club, Center Club. For a study of one such club, see Landy, D., and Singer, S., 'The Social Organization and Culture of a Club for Former Mental Patients, *Human Relations*, XIV, 1961, pp. 31—41. See also Palmer, M. B., 'Social Rehabilitation for Mental Patients,' *Mental Hygiene*, XLII, 1958, 24—8.
29. See Baker, *op. cit.*, pp. 158—9.
30. White, D. R., 'I have an ileostomy . . . I wish I didn't. But I have learned to Accept it and Live a

Normal, Full Life,' *American Journal of Nursing*, LXI, 1961, 52: 'At this time, ileostomy and colostomy clubs exist in 16 states and the District of Columbia as well as in Australia, Canada, England, and South Africa.'.

31. Warfield, *op. cit.*, pp. 135—6, describes a 1950 celebration of the New York hard of hearing movement, with every successive generation of leadership present, as well as representatives of every originally separate organization. A complete recapitulation of the movement's history was thus available. For comments on the international history of the movement, see Hodgson, K. W., *The Deaf and their Problems*, Philosophical Library, 1954, p. 352.
32. Warfield, *op. cit.*, p. 78.
33. From the beginning such leaders may be recruited from those members of the category who are ambitious to leave the life of its members and relatively able to do so, giving rise to what Lewin, K., in *Resolving Social Conflicts*, Part III, Harper and Row, 1948, called 'Leadership from the Periphery.'
34. Mailer, N., 'The Homosexual Villain,' in *Advertisements for Myself*, Signet Books, 1960, pp. 200—5, provides a model confession detailing the basic cycle of bigotry, enlightening experience, and, finally, recantation of prejudice through public admission. See also Angus Wilson's introduction to Carling, F., *And Yet we Are Human*, Chatto & Windus, 1962, for a confessional record of Wilson's redefinition of cripples.
35. Rolph, C. H., (ed.), *Women of the Streets*, Secker and Warburg, 1955, pp. 78—9.
36. Parker, T., and Allerton R., *The Courage of his Convictions*, Hutchinson 1962, p. 150.
37. Atholl, J., *The Reluctant Hangman*, John Long, 1956, p. 61.
38. The idea derives from Schwartz, C. G., 'Perspectives on Deviance — Wives' Definitions of Their Husbands' Mental Illness,' *Psychiatry*, XX, 1957, 275—91.
39. For an example in regard to the blind, see A. Gowman, 'Blindness and the Role of the Companion,' *Social Problems*, IV, 1956, pp. 68—75.
40. Discussion of this pattern can be found in Lindesmith, A. R., and Strauss, A. L., *Social Psychology*, rev. ed., Holt, Rinehart & Winston, 1956, pp. 180—3.
41. Henrich and Kriegel, *op. cit.*, p. 186.
42. Linduska, N., *My Polio Past*, Pellegrini and Cudahy, 1947, p. 177.
43. Chevigny, *op. cit.*, p. 136.
44. Macgregor *et al.*, *op. cit.*, pp. 19—20.
45. Keitlen, *op. cit.*, pp. 37—8.
46. A general statement may be found in two of E. C. Hughes' papers, 'Social Change and Status Protest,' *Phylon*, First Quarter, 1949, 58—65, and 'Cycles and Turning Points,' in *Men and Their Work*, Free Press of Glencoe, 1958.
47. Yarrow, M., 'Personality Development and Minority Group Membership,' in Sklare, M., *The Jews*, Free Press of Glencoe, 1960, pp. 468—70.
48. Carling, *op. cit.*, p. 21.

10. The Chatterley syndrome*

LOUIS BATTYE

Author and novelist

I

'Having suffered so much, the capacity for suffering had to some extent left him. He remained strange and bright and cheerful, almost, one might say, chirpy, with his ruddy, healthy-looking face, and his pale-blue, challenging bright eyes. His shoulders were broad and strong, his hands were very strong. He was expensively dressed, and wore neckties from Bond Street. Yet still in his face one saw the watchful look, the slight vacancy of the cripple.'

It is in these rather carelessly chosen words that D. H. Lawrence first describes Sir Clifford, Lady Chatterley's paraplegic husband, on the second page of his notorious novel.[1] Out of all the flood of words that, since the famous trial of 1960, have lapped and gurgled round this book comparatively few have been devoted to the man whose war-smashed body and consequent impotence caused his fair wife to seek — and find — consolation in his game-keeper's earthy embrace; nevertheless, I feel a sharp though sympathetic look at Sir Clifford, and his creator's attitude towards him, might reveal several things of interest, especially to his fellow cripples. (I prefer the old, blunt but accurate word 'cripple' to clumsy euphemisms such as 'disabled person', and at the risk of causing offence I intend to use it throughout this essay. By it I mean an adult of normal intelligence who, through disease or injury, has been deprived in part or in full of the use of his limbs, particularly

his legs, and whose condition is static and incurable. I say 'adult of normal intelligence' because I do not wish here to discuss the quite separate problems of crippled children and the mentally affected.)

It will, I think, be generally agreed that the brief description of Sir Clifford which I have quoted is a reasonably fair and accurate sketch of a common type of paraplegic, the hitherto strong and healthy young man who as a result of cruel injury has been condemned to spend the rest of his life in a wheelchair, the only hint of criticism being in the phrase about 'the slight vacancy of the cripple'. In this passage Lawrence's bias against the crippled is well under control; indeed, one feels he is almost leaning over backwards to be fair, even sympathetic. For Lawrence's irrational 'philosophy' of the physical, the sensual and the intuitive deeply prejudiced him against the physically abnormal. This is not the place to speculate on the underlying psychological reasons for his adoption of his highly personal phallic mystique, though it is distinctly possible that, as in the case of Nietzsche, it was a form of compensation for his own physical inadequacy — he was a weedy neurotic consumptive.

The admirably detached attitude towards Sir Clifford which we have noted continues for several pages. On page 16 we read: 'But his very quiet, hesitating voice, and his eyes, at the same time bold and frightened, assured and uncertain, revealed his nature. His manner was often offensively supercilious, and then again modest and self-effacing, almost tremulous.' The portrait is beginning to take on depth. 'Offensively supercilious?' Well, he is after all a member of the

*From Paul Hunt (ed) (1966) *Stigma: the experience of disability*, London, Geoffrey Chapman, Chapter 1, pp. 2–16

English landed gentry, one of the many sub-divisions of the human race to arouse Lawrence's disapproval. But the note of comparatively sym-pathetic detachment is about to change. Very soon, after an account of how little contact Sir Clifford has with the miners who work down his colliery, we find: 'He was remotely interested; but like a man looking down a microscope, or up a telescope. He was not in touch. He was not in actual touch with anybody . . . Connie [his wife] felt that she herself didn't really, not really touch him; perhaps there was nothing to get at ulti-mately; just a negation of human contact.' Note how the sympathy is already beginning to shift from husband to wife, from the cripple himself to the woman whose sexual and emotional frustration he is responsible for.

Even Sir Clifford's attempt to fulfil himself by becoming a writer is neatly turned against him. 'He had taken to writing stories; curious, very personal stories about people he had known. Clever, rather spiteful, and yet, in some mysterious way, mean-ingless. The observation was extraordinary and peculiar. But there was no touch, no actual contact. It was as if the whole thing took place in a vacuum. And since the field of life is largely an artificially-lighted stage today, the stories were curiously true to modern life, to the modern psychology, that is.' It is pretty clear by now that he is going to have a struggle to do anything right. 'Clifford was almost morbidly sensitive about these stories. He wanted everyone to think them good, of the best, *ne plus ultra*. They appeared in the most modern magazines, and were praised and blamed as usual. But to Clifford the blame was torture, like knives goading him. It was as if the whole of his being were in his stories.' This is a very significant passage. It reveals simultaneously Lawrence's remarkable insight and his equally remarkable prejudice. As every cripple who has tried seriously to write knows only too well, the temptation – indeed, the necessity – to try to put 'the whole of his being' into his work is inevitable, in spite of the agony and struggle it costs him: one thinks of Denton Welch lying for years in a hospital bed, striving, by means of his beautiful, anguished books, to create art and meaning out of a shattered life.

But all this cuts no ice with Lawrence. The implication is that the whole of Sir Clifford's being is so insignificant it can be contained within a

handful of clever, superficial stories. Even the wretched Latin tag is a sneer, Sir Clifford's perfectly natural though perhaps somewhat pathe-tic craving for success being for his creator something childish and contemptible.

And so it goes on, this process of denigration. At first with relative moderation and subtlety, then with increasing crudeness and brutality, Sir Clifford is reduced from an intelligent, talented man to something almost sub-human. I could fill the entire space at my disposal with examples of this process, from the quotation marks when we are told that he is 'working' to Mellors's elegant statement that his employer has 'no balls' and the even more elegant assertion by Sir Malcolm Reid, Connie's father, that his son-in-law is a 'lily-livered hound with never a fuck in him.' Finally, after Connie has informed her husband that she is going to leave him, he becomes 'a hysterical child', and even the village nurse who has been engaged to look after him and to whom he turns emotionally after his wife's desertion, despises and hates him. 'He was to her the fallen beast, the squirming monster. . . . The merest tramp was better than he.' The work of demolition is complete.

My excuse for devoting so much space in what is supposed to be an essay on the problems of the physically handicapped to a consideration of a grotesque book by a remarkable but wildly over-estimated author is that, as I suggested earlier, it might reveal several interesting and relevant points for discussion. I hope to show that it has.

II

Although the general reaction of an intelligent cripple to a reading of *Lady Chatterley's Lover* might well be anything from boredom to ecstasy, it would be surprising if Lawrence's treatment of Sir Clifford failed to rouse in him a feeling of resentful indignation. But it would be far better to keep this natural indignation in check and to try to consider the matter carefully and dis-passionately. Let us begin by studying Sir Clifford in the context of the novel as a whole.

The theme of the healthy, attractive young wife who finds herself tied to an impotent invalid who she abandons for a healthy, virile lover is not only a perfectly allowable subject for literature, it is a situation of enormous personal interest for most cripples, and one that is actually happening every day. There must be hardly a chronic ward or residential home that hasn't a crippled patient who is there simply because his or her marriage partner has given up the physical and emotional struggle and walked out. This situation can, of course, be looked at from more than one angle, but it will be agreed that it is a sad one, even tragic. From the point of view of a novelist, either detached and Godlike towards his characters or involved almost to the point of total indentification with just one of them, and at the same time concerned to transmute his raw material into art, a reasonable attitude towards the Chatterley triangle might be: 'Here is a tragic situation. A well-to-do and hitherto healthy young man is badly crippled by war. His beautiful wife still loves him and does all she can for him, but his injuries have rendered him impotent, thus depriving her of any sexual life. In spite of her loyalty, her health and looks begin to suffer. The psychological after-effects of her husband's injuries now make him appear cooler towards her, which increases her suffering. In this state of mind she allows herself to be seduced by an employee and then falls in love with him and he with her, in spite of the class barrier between them. She is torn between her loyalty to her husband and her passion for her lover. After great agony of mind she eventually decides to leave her husband, who she considers no longer really needs her, and to go to live with her lover. Although her action is indefensible from the standpoint of conventional morality, she is also the victim of a situation she found intolerable, therefore she shouldn't be condemned. Indeed, compassion is called for towards all three chief characters, particularly the unfortunate husband.' The moral – if you must have one – might be an indictment of war, or simply 'Well, that's life. . . .'

But Lawrence's attitude is completely different. The whole book is, in effect, a pagan hymn to physical love, an illustration of his mystical belief in salvation through sex. Sex is good, a feeble broken body an insult to the dark gods. When Sir Clifford's body was smashed he automatically ceased to be a man. The essential sexual relationship between himself and his wife having been destroyed, he was from then on defrauding her of her birthright; his attempt to replace this lost physical relationship with an abstract tenderness being, in Lawrence's view, not only a vile insult, a supreme gesture of contempt, but a kind of blasphemy. Sir Clifford should have died from his wounds; he had no right to have survived in his repulsive condition. He richly deserved all he got.

We have arrived at last at the heart of the matter. For, disregarding his instinctual phallic mystique, what is Lawrence's attitude towards Sir Clifford but a highly idiosyncratic restatement of the age-old half-conscious fear and hatred of the cripple, the hunchback, the dwarf – the primitive belief that a weak, malformed and ugly body probably enshrines a weak, malformed and ugly soul? Literature and folklore are full of misshapen villains, from the wicked dwarfs of mythology to the modern thriller's sinister criminal mastermind, planning particularly nasty murders in his wheelchair. Even in serious history the physically abnormal are seldom given the benefit of the doubt: modern historians are divided as to whether Richard III really did murder the Princes in the Tower, but he was a hunchback, therefore it can be assumed that he was capable of such an atrocity. Although he didn't realize it, Lawrence was merely echoing a mindless superstition that is at least as old as civilization.

'So that's why Lady Chatterley took a lover,' the intelligent cripple might say with a wry grin at this point. 'We're archetypal villains – no wonder we receive the Chatterley treatment! But surely there has been enormous progress in medical and social thinking during the last hundred-and-fifty years. The attitude of society towards us has undergone a complete revolution. Lawrence may or may not have been a literary genius: he was certainly a reactionary thinker, a strange kind of intellectual Luddite. Surely what he wrote about a crippled character in an absurd erotic fantasy is of no relevance to the question of our position in modern society, or to the psychological and spiritual problems we each have to face as best we can.'

The answer, I'm afraid, is that it is of considerable relevance. For the harsh truth is that the basis of Lawrence's attitude towards Sir Clifford is not all irrational prejudice, the ancient popular attitude towards the physically abnormal, not all mindless superstition. Somewhere deep inside us is the almost unbearable knowledge that the way the able-bodied world regards us is as much as we have the right to expect. We are not full members of that world, and the vast majority of us can never hope to be. If we think otherwise we are deluding ourselves. Like children and the insane, we inhabit a special sub-world, a world with its own unique set of referents. Although it has correspondences and communications with that greater world within which it is encapsulated, it is not the same world nor even co-extensive with it: it is within — lesser, weaker, poorer. And at the same time dependent upon it. Let us, who inhabit this sub-world, try to see ourselves as clearly as possible.

III

'What a piece of work is man!' marvelled Hamlet, though perhaps he was being ironic. However one rates the human species, a man must be considered as a whole. His body is an incredibly wonderful piece of fully automated engineering, but in itself it is not a man. His mind, soul, spirit is an even more wonderful and complex thing, but in itself it still does not constitute a man. To make a man you must put the two together. He is more than the mere sum of these parts, but a deficiency in one means a deficiency in the whole. Lawrence's view that after Sir Clifford became a cripple he was no longer a man is extreme, but it contains more truth than we may like to admit. A cripple is still a man, but, as it were, on a smaller scale. His totality is diminished, his image distorted. He is not a whole.

It inevitably follows, then, that there must always be this barrier of difference and distortion between us and the inhabitants of the normal world. No matter how close our individual relationships with our able-bodied friends may seem, it is impossible for them to have the same *kinds* of relationship with us that they can have with others from their own world. This is perhaps the bitterest truth of all, the one that most of us find the hardest to accept — that we are forever barred from the deepest and most intimate levels of human intercourse. I can already hear the shocked cries of denial: 'He never thinks of me as being a cripple!' Not consciously, perhaps, but in his innermost heart he knows you are, and he always will. It is this fundamental unconscious knowledge, rather than sexual frustration or the sheer struggle of looking after a badly crippled partner, that breaks up so many marriages between the inhabitants of these two worlds. There are barriers that even love cannot penetrate — always assuming there can be complete love between a complete person and an incomplete one, which I doubt. (In

parenthesis, it might be objected that this gloomy theory appears to break down when one considers the blind. According to my argument, the blind, lacking one of the most important and valuable of faculties, are as incomplete as the crippled, and, like them, must be separated from the normal world; yet marriages between the blind and the sighted seem on the whole to be as happy and permanent as those between two sighted people. The answer would seem to be that a great many blind people never leave the normal world, which continues to accept them to a much greater extent than it accepts us. For some obscure Jungian reason, blindness hasn't the same sinister associations that physical abnormality has in the collective unconscious: indeed, it has strong associations with poetry and wisdom — blind poets and sages abound in history and legend.)

IV

We must now make an important distinction between the two great divisions of cripples: those who were normal until they reached adult age, perhaps being married and becoming parents, even achieving some measure of worldly success before their personal disaster occurred; and those who were 'born that way' or who became cripples during childhood. Normal people often speculate on which state is worse — never to have known the full richness and physical joys of normal life and so perhaps never really to miss them; or to be cruelly deprived of them while in one's prime, but having a rich store of memories to provide a degree of consolation during the long years of frustration and suffering that may lie ahead. This is one of those 'chicken-or-egg' questions which it is impossible to answer, though, as a congenital cripple, my personal guess is that those in the other group probably have the worse deal. What *is* certain is that each group's basic outlook on life is bound to differ.

An example of the 'disaster' group could again be Sir Clifford Chatterley, though in some ways he was luckier than many. He had studied at Cambridge and Bonn, and had enjoyed the usual pursuits of his age and class. We are told that he and Connie lived on 'a rather inadequate income' after his discharge from hospital; nevertheless he was the Squire of Wragby Hall and the owner of a colliery, even if the mining industry was then going through hard times. He was also the possessor of considerable literary talent with which he earned a fair amount of artistic and commercial success. He was, in fact, well enough off not only to be able to live comfortably without any real financial worries, but also able to afford all the gadgets and nursing assistance he might need. In spite of the National Health Service, rehabilitation schemes, Remploy, and Governmental provision of invalid cars, there must be many paraplegics today who would be quite willing to change places with him, gamekeeper or no.

The first reaction of an intelligent and spirited young adult, after he has recovered from the shock of his disaster, is a grim urge to fight back, to try to pick up the pieces of his broken life and rebuild it, either modelling the new structure as closely as possible on the old, or trying to design a completely fresh one better adapted to his new limitations. He wants to earn his own living, to resume supporting his dependents: if it is impossible for him to continue in his old job he must find another, perhaps being trained to acquire new skills. He wants to learn afresh how to cope with the physical details of everyday life, to get into and out of bed or on and off the lavatory seat, to wash, bathe, shave and dress himself without assistance — all those mundane but essential actions which, until his disaster, he had performed with scarcely a conscious thought, but which he now finds demand hitherto unimaginable physical and mental efforts. Above all he wants to resume his former social, sexual and emotional life, to return to his former status in society, to re-create the old image of himself. The fact that so many do manage to construct viable existences out of the wreckage of their lives is a vivid illustration of human adaptability and courage. But the cripple will never succeed in *fully* recovering the life he has lost; he will never *really* manage to recreate his former image. Even those who love him most will now regard him in a new way: love will inevitably be adulterated with pity. He has been transferred to the sub-world. 'Clifford looked at Connie, with his pale, slightly prominent blue eyes, in which a certain vagueness was coming. He seemed alert in the foreground, but the background was like the Midlands atmosphere, haze, smoky mist. And the haze seemed to be creeping forward. So when he stared at Connie in his peculiar way, giving her his peculiar, precise information, she felt all the background of his

mind filling up with mist, with nothingness. And it frightened her. It made him seem impersonal, almost to idiocy.' And a page or two later: 'When Clifford was roused, he could still talk brilliantly and, as it were, command the future . . . But the day after, all the brilliant words seemed like dead leaves, crumpling up and turning to powder, meaning really nothing, blown away on any gust of wind. They were not the leafy words of an effective life, young with energy and belonging to the tree. They were the hosts of fallen leaves of a life that is ineffectual.' Words like 'meaningless,' 'nothingness,' 'nonsense' are repeatedly used about him in his writing; and perhaps cruellest of all: 'Really, if you looked closely at Clifford, he was a buffoon, and a buffoon is more humiliating than a bounder.' The Master of Wragby has been banished to the sub-world with a vengeance!

In contrast, the congenital cripple or the one whose disaster occurs during childhood never suffers this painful expulsion from the normal adult world because he has never lived in it. He passes straight from the sub-world of childhood to the sub-world of the cripple. He will nowadays probably go to a special school where a more or less optimistic attempt will be made to 'fit him for life' by teaching him some vocational skill in addition to the usual school subjects. I have often wondered how many children trained in this way eventually do earn their own livings by practising the skills they were taught: not a large proportion, I suspect. Unlike the member of the other group, he has no really overwhelming incentive to be rehabilitated because essentially there is nothing to rehabilitate, no old life to rebuild, no former image to recreate. Of course, if he is intelligent he will have ambition, he will want to earn his own living and 'live a normal life' — he may even have hopes of marriage. But only the most determined and capable — and the luckiest — ever achieve anything approaching their ambitions: the going is too tough, the incentives are too theoretical. At the special boarding school where I was taught during the Thirties, we were often warned by the staff that in order to compete with normal people we would have to be *better* at our jobs than they, for faced with a choice between a crippled applicant and an able-bodied one of equal skill, a prospective employer would always choose the latter (in general this still holds good, even with current quota regulations, which many firms succeed in evading). We would nod soberly, but somehow the information never really seemed to enter our bones, to become an organic part of our ambitions: like our incentives, it was too theoretical, too abstract. I think we felt in our hearts that the world didn't *really* expect us to earn our own livings; that if we did it would be mildly pleased and say how clever we were, but that if we didn't it would be neither surprised nor disappointed, and would be quite willing to keep us alive in some fashion. Even in pre-welfare times the cripple was generally expected to beg rather than to work.

The least abstract and theoretical incentive the adolescent cripple possesses is the sexual one: his glands have undergone the normal disturbances, he suffers the normal torments and dreams the normal dreams. Unless he is particularly unattractive, he probably won't have much difficulty in acquiring a girl friend, her feelings towards him largely genuine enough but inevitably containing a certain amount of pity and curiosity. He may be deeply in love and think he has detected signs of a similar feeling in her, and the relationship may reach quite a high level of mutual affection as the girl's original curiosity is satisfied and she learns to appreciate him for his qualities as an individual; but pity will rarely be entirely eliminated. Eventually a climax will be reached, a crisis, after which the affair will either plane down to a lower, more realistic level, or — and this is much more likely — stop abruptly. He will console himself by thinking that this kind of thing happens to everybody, crippled or not, and that there are other fish in the sea. But although one or two more may swim into his net, the odds are overwhelming that they will swim out again, and bitterly he will begin to realize that he is in for the lonely, perverted life of the enforced celibate.

For the congenital cripple even more than for the member of the 'disaster' group, it is almost inevitable, unless he is as well off as Sir Clifford Chatterley, that sooner or later he will find himself a patient in the chronic ward of a long-stay hospital, surrounded by the old, the incontinent and the dying. Because he is still comparatively young, he will generally find that the staff are sympathetic and kind, perhaps even indulgent, towards him — they ,will quite often break the rules (which in any case are usually more flexible and human than in an acute hospital) to give him some small extra comfort or pleasure. But the atmosphere of the workhouse, like the smell of disease, defaecation and death, still tends to hang round these places, and if he remains there he will in time succumb to it and become dull and apathetic, his life circumscribed by the petty, tedious, sordid routine of a place designed for a quite different type of patient: he will become, in a word, institutionalized. And the longer he remains there, the more institutionalized he will become. It is not unknown for people to spend forty years in such prisons.

He may, however, be luckier and get a place in one of the small residential homes that in recent years have been opened for the care of the severely disabled. Here he will find on the surface a far different atmosphere, informal and homelike. The authorities and staff will be friendly and helpful, and treat him as an individual: he will receive greater freedom, eatable food and many small luxuries. But unless he fights a constant battle to retain his intellectual integrity and sense of purpose, as the years go by he will gradually feel the atmosphere of the place closing in on him, as it did in the chronic ward, shrinking his horizons to the limits of the house and grounds, a condition in which trivial details of the home's day-to-day routine assume a disproportionate importance. In spite of efforts to arouse or retain his interest in life, he will feel boredom and apathy creeping over him like a slow paralysis, eroding his will, dulling his critical wits, dousing his spirit, killing his independence. The temptation to sit day after day, year after year, with the same little clique in the same corner of the same room, doing the same things, thinking the same thoughts, making and listening to the same banal remarks, becomes almost irresistible. In a subtler, more civilized way than in the chronic ward, he will have become institutionalized. The difference between a residential home however comfortable, and a chronic ward is really only one of degree, not of kind: at the bottom they are both places where one simply whiles away the time until death — dead ends in an all too literal sense; and no amount of benevolent idealism, skilled care, homelike surroundings, good food, entertainments, outings, Christmas parties and occupational therapy can disguise this melancholy fact.

V

And so, however he came to be in it, the cripple, the physically underprivileged man, lives in his underprivileged sub-world, the world in which all his actions are strangely distorted and diminished in scale and significance, so that in some ways they seem like incompetent and slightly ridiculous parodies of the real thing. When doing something that is not normally attempted by the severely disabled, I have personally experienced the highly disturbing, almost Kafka-esque sensation that I am merely going through the motions of this particular act, that what I am doing does not in fact *mean* the same as when performed by a normal person. Hence Lawrence's implacable insistence on the essential meaninglessness of Sir Clifford Chatterley's life. If at this point I hear mutters of 'Inferiority complex!' I can only reply with the old chestnut about the man who was treated for months for this condition — until the psychiatrist discovered that his patient simply was inferior.

The cripple is an object of Christian charity, a socio-medical problem, a stumbling nuisance, and an embarrassment to the girls he falls in love with. He is a vocation for saints, a livelihood for the manufacturers of wheelchairs, a target for busy-bodies, and a means by which prosperous citizens assuage their consciences. He is at the mercy of overworked doctors and nurses and underworked bureaucrats and social investigators. He is pitied and ignored, helped and patronized, understood and stared at. But he is hardly ever taken seriously as a *man* — for reasons I have tried to indicate.

Lawrence saw us clearly. After we have allowed for the eccentric bias of his views, we are forced to admit that he knew our essential irrelevance to the real business of living, and, brutally though he expressed that terrible vision, we should be grateful to him, for he has helped us to see ourselves as we really are. The sight is not a comforting one, but somehow we must find the courage to face it squarely. It is neither masochism nor despair to dwell on our inadequacies, but the first step towards coming to terms with them and with life.

In spite of all I have written, a tiny minority of us *will* be taken seriously as men. The mightiest nation on earth was ruled for twelve years by a cripple; a legless man became a wartime legend. But for every Roosevelt and Bader there are a thousand Sir Cliffords. The man I am holding up as an example, however, is one I mentioned earlier — Denton Welch. He ruled no one but himself; the only war in which he fought was with himself. But *his* life was *not* meaningless; out of his helplessness and pain he created strength and beauty; his entrails nourished the world. Denton Welch never escaped from his sub-world — he did something better. He transcended it.

NOTE

1. Penguin 1960.

11. The effects of physical deviance upon face-to-face interaction: the other side *

RONALD J. COMER
Clark University, USA.

JANE ALLYN PILIAVIN
University of Wisconsin, USA.

Goffman (1963) has provided a beautifully written, provocative description of the stresses and strains of interactions between the 'stigmatized' and the 'unstigmatized.' Weaving his own conceptualizations with the theorizing of other professional writers on the subject and judiciously selected quotes from autobiographies of the blind, the lame, the deformed, and the ex-mental patient or criminal, he provides us with a rich set of hypotheses for systematic study. At the most basic level, his suggestion is that in such an interaction, both participants are far more concerned about the 'management' of the interaction than either of them would be if they were interacting with 'their own kind.' Referring to the perceptions of the normal, and quoting Davis (1961 p. 123), he says,

> The underlying condition of heightened, narrowed, awareness [of the stigma] . . . is usually accompanied by one or more of the familiar signs of the discomfort and stickiness: the guarded references, the common everyday words suddenly made taboo, the fixed stare elsewhere, the artificial levity, the compulsive loquaciousness, the awkward solemnity (Goffman 1963 p. 19).

That physically normal persons often report definite feelings of uncomfortableness and uncertainty when interacting with persons who have some physical handicap (one type of stigma) has been documented (Davis 1961; Kleck 1966; Richardson, Hastorf, Goodman, & Dornbusch

1961). This uncomfortable reaction has been shown to reveal itself in several ways. When Kleck, Ono, and Hastorf (1966) had able-bodied subjects interact with an apparently handicapped confederate, the behavioral output of the subjects was stereotyped, inhibited, and overcontrolled, as compared to other subjects interacting with the same confederate appearing physically normal. The subjects who talked to the handicapped individual terminated the interaction sooner, distorted their expressed opinions, and tended to demonstrate less variability in their behavior. Kleck (1968) also reported greater motoric inhibition by normal subjects in the presence of the handicapped confederate. Kleck, Buck, Goller, London, Pfeiffer, and Vukcevic (1968) also demonstrated that the ascription of epilepsy to a confederate interviewer resulted in less proximate interaction by physically normal subjects than in the case where epilepsy was not ascribed to the interviewer. In private correspondence, Kleck (personal communication 1969) noted that the smiling behavior of able-bodied subjects decreased during interactions with physically handicapped individuals.

These studies, however, ignore the other side of the handicapped — normal interaction, namely, the problems of the handicapped in dealing with the normal. Goffman (1963) clearly stated that 'We and he [the stigmatized other] are likely to experience uneasiness . . .' (p. 19) 'during mixed contacts, the stigmatized individual is likely to feel . . . self-conscious and calculating about the impression he is making . . .' (p. 14) 'since the stigmatized person is likely to be more often faced with these situations . . . he is likely to become the more adept at managing them' (p. 14). These

* From *Journal of personality and social psychology*, (1972) 23, No. 1, pp. 33–9.

100

statements clearly suggest that for a more complete understanding of the interaction between the handicapped and the normal (as between the black and the white), it is time that we looked at the contribution of the minority group member, rather than viewing him as Campbell (1967) has said we have done in the past, as 'a living inkblot.'

Goffman (1963 pp. 108–25) goes into a lengthy discussion of the delicate problems of self-presentation encountered by the stigmatized, taking many of his examples from the writings of the handicapped. In essence, he said that society places on such stigmatized individuals a very heavy burden: that of appearing to carry their lot lightly, being well adjusted, and yet not behaving inappropriately 'for a cripple.' That is, they should act out the role expected of them, not being either too depressing or too 'normal.' Only when with the similarly stigmatized or with close friends (called 'the wise' by Goffman) can they relax, as illustrated by a quote from Carling (1962).

> I also learned that the cripple must be careful not to act differently from what people expect him to do . . . I once knew a dwarf . . . In front of people . . . she played the part of the fool with the same mocking laughter and the same quick, funny movements that have been the characteristics of fools ever since the royal courts of the Middle Ages. Only when she was among friends, could she throw away her cap and bells and dare to be the woman she really was: intelligent, sad, and very lonely. (pp. 54–55).

Similarly, referring in this case to illiterates (educationally handicapped), Freeman and Kasenbaum (1956) stated that 'in their interrelations with one another, the mask of accommodative adjustment drops' (p. 374).

Thus, it would seem to be important for the understanding of the handicapped-normal dyad to perform an experiment in which the handicapped are subjects who interact with an interviewer, presented as either handicapped or normal. To the extent that the handicapped other *does* behave differently toward 'his own' and toward others, there are new dimensions of the interaction to be explored in the future. We already know, both from the writings of the handicapped and from the systematic work of Kleck, that the uneasiness of the physically normal comes out in stereotyped, tight, unnatural behavior, clearly perceptible to an observer who is sensitive to it. This presents a problem to the handicapped individual in the management of the interaction. If, in turn, he engages in similarly observable behavior, one might expect an interaction that rapidly becomes too uncomfortable for either participant to prolong beyond the length that is socially required.

In the present study, the following predictions were made concerning differences between handicapped subjects interacting with a confederate, presented as either physically normal or having a disability affecting his legs (like the subjects): Subjects in the handicapped – normal interaction would (a) terminate the interaction sooner, (b) show greater motoric inhibition, (c) demonstrate less variability in their verbal behavior during the interaction, (d) maintain a less proximate interaction, (e) exhibit less smiling behavior, and (f) admit later to feeling more uncomfortable during the interaction.

In addition to the above, it was hypothesized that the handicapped subjects interacting with a physically normal confederate would demonstrate less eye contact during the interaction than would handicapped subjects interacting with a handicapped confederate, in spite of the fact that Kleck (1968) was not able to demonstrate reduced eye contact by the normal subjects during his handicapped-normal interactions. Exline and Winters (1965) have demonstrated that eye contact is positively correlated with felt affect in a dyad. Also, Goffman (1963) has argued that eye contact may be negatively correlated with the degree of tension in a relationship. No prediction was made concerning the direction in which opinion distortion may take place, although the data were examined for any consistent tendencies.

Method

OVERVIEW

The interaction situation used was a highly structured one in which a confederate served as an interviewer and the subject answered questions presented by the confederate, generally concerning certain of the subject's attitudes. The format was a modified version of the one previously used by Kleck *et al.* (1966 Experiment I). Each subject met with the confederate for one interview session. The same person, a 22-year-old white male, was the confederate in all sessions. With half of the subjects, the confederate assumed the role of a handicapped person (handicapped condition) confined to a wheelchair and wearing a leg brace. With the remaining subjects, the confederate presented himself as the nondisabled individual he actually was (normal condition).

SUBJECTS

Thirty physically disabled male patients from the Piersol Rehabilitation Center and the Department of Physical Medicine of the Hospital of the University of Pennsylvania served as subjects in the study. All subjects had a disability that affected their legs; the group included 12 amputees, 10 paraplegics, and 8 hemiplegics. The subjects' ages ranged from 23 to 54, with a mean age of 45. Their mean level of completed education was 11.5 years, and their occupations (or previous occupations) were generally nonprofessional. Subjects were matched for age and type of disability for assignment to conditions. Each was paid $1 for his participation.

PROCEDURE

The experimenter (the first author) asked each subject to participate in an experiment in 'group dynamics,' investigating how a person interacts with a stranger on their first meeting.[2] It was emphasized that this was not a personality or psychological study of the subject. The subject was also told that the experimenter would observe the interaction. The setting was an 11 foot x 7 foot room in the Psychiatric Clinic of the Hospital of the University of Pennsylvania. A one-way mirror was on the wall, to the side of the interacting subject and confederate. The room was unfurnished with the exception of a small desk.

As the experimenter pushed the subject (in his wheelchair) to a predetermined position in the middle of the room, the experimenter pointed out the mirror through which the interaction was to be observed. He then explained that the stranger (confederate) would read a list of questions asking for information and opinions from the subject. The experimenter told the subject to feel free to answer and contribute, since the actual content of what he would say was not being focused on, but simply the nature of the new interaction. After giving the subject a minute to accustom himself to the experimental room, the experimenter returned

with the confederate and asked the subject to come out to meet him.

In the normal condition, the confederate was walking while carrying a light chair. In the handicapped condition, the confederate was in a wheelchair with a short brace on his left leg. After introducing the two, the experimenter took the confederate into the room to a predetermined spot (while the subject waited in the hall). The subject then wheeled himself into the room and stopped where he wished.

When the subject stopped his chair, the confederate began the interview by reading the following:

> On this first question, I am going to ask you to tell me when you are through speaking so that I know when to go to the next question on our list. It is: just tell me about yourself. Simply describe yourself starting from scratch. Take as long as you wish in answering the question, and remember to please tell me when you are through.

This open-ended question was previously used by Kleck *et al.* (1966).

After the first question, 10 more specific questions were read by the confederate in the following order:

(*a*) What is the importance of friends to a person?

(*b*) What is the importance of females in a man's life?

(*c*) What is the importance of sports in one's life?

(*d*) What is the importance of academic and intellectual achievement in one's life?

(*e*) What is the importance of physical appearance in judging others?

(*f*) What is the importance of being religious?

(*g*) What is the importance of money?

(*h*) What is the importance of good health in one's life?

(*i*) What is the importance of a good personality?

(*j*) What is the importance of being aggressive in the world today?

The entire interview was taped for later content analysis and coding.

After the final answer, the confederate informed the subject that they had finished. The experimenter then came and took the subject to a different room where he was asked for ratings of how much he liked the interviewer and his degree of discomfort, and asked for information about himself.

The experimenter then asked the subject whether he had any suspicions about the interview, asked what he thought was the purpose of the interview session, and explained the study in part to the subject, omitting the fact that the handicapped confederate was actually normal. He then asked him not to tell any other patients about the study or its purposes.

MEASURES

The following measures were obtained from the interaction:

(a) The answers to each of the specific interview questions were coded onto a 9-point scale of importance, with "1" always indicating relatively greater importance. These data were analyzed for opinion distortion and variability.

(b) Length of the interaction.

(c) The amount of 'eye contact' between the subject and the confederate – This measure was obtained by the confederate who was instructed to look at the subject's eyes throughout the interaction and record when the subject was looking at him on a stopwatch concealed in his jacket pocket.

(d) Interpersonal distance at the end of the interaction – This measure was taken by the experimenter from behind the one-way mirror.

(e) Motor activity throughout the interaction – One observer watched hand movements, giving the subject a score of 1 for each motion of 6 inches or more; a second observer watched head turns, giving each turn of 45 degrees or more a score of 1. These scores were spot checked by the experimenter at two points in the study with virtually complete agreement found between the experimenter and the observers.

(f) Smiling behavior – A third observer noted the total amount of time during which the subject was smiling, using a stopwatch. She also tallied the number of discrete smiles.[3]

Five practice sessions were run until the confederate's behavior seemed comfortable and uniform and the observers became relaxed and consistant. All three observers and the confederate were unaware of the hypotheses of the study. Only the observer of interpersonal distance, who

was the experimenter, could have been subject to bias on the basis of his expectations.

Results

EFFECTIVENESS OF EXPERIMENTAL MANIPULATIONS

The attempt to simulate a considerable physical disability was apparently quite effective. When the subjects were asked to state any suspicions that they had about the study, none questioned the genuineness of the confederate's disability.

The cover-up story was also apparently successful. When asked to state the purpose of the interaction at the conclusion of the experiment, the subjects all gave virtually the same explanation that had been given by the experimenter (i.e., a study of initial interactions with a stranger).

Although no measures were taken, the confederate's behavior appeared to the observers to be uniform in the two conditions. Since the subjects were themselves uniform (i.e., all physically handicapped) and since the confederate read the questions to them, it was not too difficult for the confederate to behave consistently. Also, the confederate was not informed of the experimental hypotheses until the conclusion of the study, and he saw none of the data, not even the eye-contact time that he was recording, so he should not have been subject to experimenter bias effects. At no time did he express any awareness of differences in the behavior of subjects in the two conditions or put forth any opinions concerning them.

LENGTH OF INTERACTION

As had been expected, the subjects interacting with the normal confederate terminated the interaction significantly sooner than the subjects interacting with the handicapped confederate. As is shown in Table 11.1, the mean length of the interaction between handicapped subjects and a normal confederate was 392.9 seconds (or 6.55 minutes); the mean length for the interaction between handicapped subjects and a handicapped confederate was 573.6 seconds (or 9.56 minutes). The difference between these means, almost a full 3 minutes, yields a t of 2.83 ($df = 28$, $p < .01$).[4] All other measures of the subjects' non-verbal behavior are corrected for length of interview.

MOTORIC INHIBITION

Kleck (1968), in his measurement of general motoric activity, gave each 6-inch movement of

Table 11.1 Mean scores of subjects' interactions with a normal and a handicapped confederate on several observational measures.

Confederate	Length of interaction (in minutes)	Motor score/ interaction length	Interpersonal distance (in inches)	Smiling time/ interaction length	No. smiles/ interaction length	% eye contact time
Normal	6.55	.093	67.5	.091	.028	13.2
Handicapped	9.56	.135	79.2	.098	.041	23.0
t	2.83	2.64	3.67	<1	2.36	2.36
p	<.01	<.02	<.01	ns	<.05	< .05

Note: $n = 15$ in each condition.

any body part a score of 1, and proceeded to compare the total scores of subjects. Although we did not have available in this study the apparatus and materials that Kleck used to achieve his precise measurement, we did have a measure of motor activity. Our observers' scores for hand and head movements were therefore added together to give each subject a crude approximation to Kleck's 'general motor activity' score. These scores were then divided by interaction length to give an index of movement per unit of time. As predicted, the subjects interacting with the normal confederate demonstrated greater motoric inhibition than did subjects interacting with the handicapped confederate. The respective mean scores of the two groups were .093 and .135, a difference significant at the .05 level of confidence ($t = 2.64$, $df = 28$).

DISTANCE BETWEEN THE SUBJECT AND THE CONFEDERATE

Subjects were expected to maintain a greater distance from the normal confederate than from the handicapped confederate. However, the subjects maintained a mean-distance of 67.5 inches from the normal confederate, as compared to a mean distance of 79.2 inches from the handicapped confederate, a difference significant ($t = 3.67$, $df = 28$) at less than the .01 level. One possible explanation might be that when the confederate was sitting in a wheelchair, he gave a 'larger' appearance than when sitting in the folding chair. Thus, it is possible that the subjects perceived a bigger confederate when he was handicapped and that they accordingly kept a greater distance.

SMILING BEHAVIOR

It was predicted that the handicapped subjects would demonstrate less smiling behavior when interacting with the normal confederate. Two smiling scores were calculated for each subject: a total smiling time score adjusted for interview length and a score for the number of smiles adjusted for interview length. As Table 1 indicates, the subject did, as expected, demonstrate more smiling behavior when interacting with the handicapped confederate; however, this difference only reached an acceptable level of significance on the number of smiles score ($t = 2.36$, $df = 28$, $p < .05$).

EYE CONTACT

The subjects maintained significantly less eye contact with the normal confederate than with the handicapped confederate. This result was again as predicted. Their mean scores, analyzed in terms of percentage of total interview length on which the subject had eye contact with the confederate, were 13.2% by subjects with a normal confederate and 23% by subjects with a handicapped confederate. The difference was significant ($t = 2.36$, $df = 28$, $p < .05$).

QUESTIONNAIRE RESPONSES

On the questionnaire that the subjects filled out after the interaction, giving their reactions to the interview and the confederate, the mean comfort score of subjects in the normal condition was lower than the score of the subjects in the handicapped condition (see Table 11.2), although the difference was significant at only the .10 level ($t = 1.99$, $df = 28$). On both questions about the interviewer — how much they liked him and the likelihood that he was the type of person with whom they could be friends — the subjects in the handicapped condition gave significantly more favorable responses.

Table 11.2 Subjects' mean responses on questionnaire items to normal and handicapped confederate

Confederate	Comfort during interaction*	Liking for Confederate†	Friendship possibility†
Normal	5.00	2.33	2.27
Handicapped	6.33	1.60	1.53
t	1.99	2.31	2.87
p	<.10	<.05	<.01

*High scores indicate greater comfort.
†Low scores indicate greater liking, higher likelihood.

OPINION VARIABILITY AND DISTORTION

It was expected that subjects interacting with a normal confederate would demonstrate more stereotyped behavior as a group, thus leading to decreased variance across subjects in the normal condition as compared to the handicapped condition. The variance of each group in response to each of the 10 interview questions about importance was therefore calculated. Means and variances for the two conditions on the 10 questions are reported in Table 11.3.

The differences in variance are generally not very large; however, on 8 of the 10 questions, the variance is larger in the normal condition rather than in the handicapped condition ($p = .11$ by applying the binomial expansion to the signs of the differences). Furthermore, the differences between the variances on two critical questions are significant or nearly so (sports: $F = 11.00$, $p < .001$; academic achievement: $F = 2.31$, $p < .10$). It is clear that the variability of the subjects' behavior is not decreased in the normal condition; on the contrary, there is some evidence that it is increased.

For the analysis of opinion distortion, one must assume that if differences exist in what handicapped persons say to a normal interviewer and to a handicapped interviewer, those talking to the normal interviewer are the ones who are distorting their expressed opinions. Using this assumption, there is strong evidence for distortion on two items: sports, on which subjects talking to the normal interviewer say that sports are *less* important; and religion, on which they say it is *more* important; and some evidence for distortion on a third item, physical appearance, on which they say it is *less* important. The pattern on these items

Table 11.3 Means and variances of responses to 10 interview questions for handicapped condition, normal condition, and comfortable and not-comfortable subgroups of normal condition

Interview item	Handicapped condition (n = 15)	Normal condition (n = 15)	Comfortable—normal (n = 7)	Not-comfortable—normal (n = 8)
Friends				
$\bar{X}$	2.2	2.67	2.57	2.75
σ^2	.44	.49	.53	.44
Females				
$\bar{X}$	2.2	2.00	2.29	1.75
σ^2	.57	.80	.78	.69
Sports				
$\bar{X}$	3.40	4.60†	4.14	5.00‡
σ^2	.24	2.64‡	1.96‡	2.75‡
Academic achievement				
$\bar{X}$	3.40	3.10	3.14	3.13
σ^2	.51	1.18*	1.84†	.61
Physical appearance				
$\bar{X}$	6.53	7.66*	7.43	7.88
σ^2	2.10	1.16	1.10	1.11
Religion				
$\bar{X}$	3.20	2.50†	2.57	2.50
σ^2	.43	.52	.82	.25
Money				
$\bar{X}$	4.00	4.00	3.50	3.73
σ^2	.93	1.26	1.14	1.25
Health				
$\bar{X}$	2.10	1.86	1.57	2.00
σ^2	.38	.56	.24	.75
Personality				
$\bar{X}$	2.60	2.50	2.86	2.13
σ^2	.37	.38	.12	.36
Aggressiveness				
$\bar{X}$	3.30	3.00	3.00	3.00
σ^2	.60	.29	.75	.53

Note: Lower means indicate that higher importance is attributed to the category.
　* $p < .15$.
　† $p < .05$.
　‡ $p < .01$.

taken together seems to suggest that at least some of the handicapped subjects in the normal group are trying to 'manage' the interaction so as to present to the interviewer a picture that they think he expects — one that is consistent with the stereotype of the handicapped held by normals. Comer (1969) found that normal subjects rated a handicapped person shown in a photograph as significantly more religious ($p < .05$) than a normal. Kleck *et al.* (1966) found that normals talking to a handicapped interviewer, as compared to a normal interviewer, said they thought that sports, dancing, physical appearance, and dating were less important (Experiment I), and that sports and physical appearance were less important and achievement and religion were more important (Experiment II).

In the Kleck *et al.* (1966) study (Experiment II), the subjects who said that they were uncomfortable displayed this tendency most strongly. For this reason, the seven subjects in the normal condition of the present study who said that they were comfortable have been separated from the eight who checked 'neutral' or 'uncomfortable.' The data for these two groups are also shown in Table 11.3. Evidence that the non-comfortable – normal-condition subjects were the ones who were doing most of the distorting comes from the fact that in eight of nine possible comparisons, the mean of the comfortable–normal group is closer to the mean of the handicapped group than is the mean of the not-comfortable–normal group (p = .039, two-tailed, by applying the binomial expansion to the sign of the differences). The two groups did not differ significantly on any of the nonverbal measures of discomfort, although the comfortable group gave longer interviews, more and longer smiles, and more eye contact. The results of this study are thus consistent with the Kleck *et al.* (1966) study in that it is the uncomfortable subjects who appear to be distorting their opinions, but inconsistent in that distortion seems to go with greater rather than less variability in the present study.

Discussions and conclusions

The results of this study conclusively demonstrate the significant contribution of the handicapped individual to the 'pathology' of the interaction between the handicapped and the physically normal. Thus, the major goal of the research has been realized. A large number of questions still remain to be answered, or have been raised by the results of the present research. Possibly the most fascinating question raised by this study seems to be whether the physically normal individual perceives the discomfort of the handicapped and is himself made more uncomfortable by it (as is apparently the case for the handicapped, to judge by their autobiographical writings) or whether the self-presentation that the handicapped engage in has its intended effect, namely, that of making the normal individual feel more comfortable. A study of the interactions between naive individuals, one handicapped and one physically normal, whose 'normal' behavior with one of 'their own' has already been assessed, should provide the answer.

It is of course unfortunate that it was not possible in this limited, largely unsupported study to perform the complete four-celled design: both handicapped and normal subjects, with the same interviewer playing both handicapped and normal roles, in order to be able to draw some conclusion concerning the relative degree of behavioral alteration that is contributed by each participant. Clearly, the next steps in research should be to perform that study and the one outlined above. After that, we should be well on our way to a better theoretical understanding of both the causes of the pathology and the techniques used in attempting the management of interactions between the normal and those with 'spoiled identities.' At that point we should also have a better ability to counsel and assist those on whose shoulders the major burden for the management falls: the stigmatized themselves.

NOTES

1. The study reported in this paper was taken from a portion of an honors thesis done by the first author as part of his honors program at the University of Pennsylvania. The authors express their thanks to the Department of Psychology for funds with which the confederate and the subjects were paid.
2. Most of the subjects were well acquainted with the experimenter before the study, since the experimenter was employed as a group social worker at the Hospital. We would also like to thank Ronald Rosillo, Psychiatrist at the Piersol Rehabilitation Center, for his advice and assistance.
3. We would like profusely to thank David Slotkin (hand movements), Hadaso Slotkin (head movements),

and Marlene Slotkin Comer (smiling behavior and coder), who served, without remuneration, as the observers and raters in the study.
4. All p values reported are two-tailed.

REFERENCES

CAMPBELL, D. T., 'Stereotypes and the perception of group differences', *American Psychologist*, 1967, 22, pp. 817–29.
CARLING, F., *And yet we are human*, Chatto & Windus, 1962.
COMER, R. J. 'The physically disabled: A study of attitudes and social interaction'. Unpublished senior honors thesis, University of Pennsylvania, 1969.
DAVIS, F. 'Deviance disavowal: The management of strained interaction by the visibly handicapped', *Social Problems*, 1961, 9, pp. 120–32.
EXLINE, R. V., & WINTERS, L. C. 'Affective relations and mutual glances in dyads', in Tomkins, S. S., & Izard, C. E., (eds.), *Cognition and personality*, Springer, 1965.
FREEMAN, H., & KASENBAUM, G. 'The illiterate in America', *Social Forces*, 1956, 34, pp. 371–5.
GOFFMAN, E. *Stigma: Notes on the management of spoiled identity*, Prentice-Hall, 1963.
KLECK, R. 'Emotional arousal in interactions with stigmatized persons', *Psychological Reports*, 1966, 19, p. 1226.
KLECK, R. 'Physical stigma and nonverbal cues emitted in face-to-face interactions', *Human Relations*, 1968, 21, pp. 19–28.
KLECK, R., BUCK, P. L., GOLLER, W. L., LONDON, R. W., PFEIFFER, J. R., & VUKCEVIC, D. P. 'Effect of stigmatizing conditions on the use of personal space', *Psychological Reports*, 1968, 23, pp. 111–18.
KLECK, R., ONO, H., & HASTORF, A. H. 'The effects of physical deviance upon face-to-face interaction', *Human Relations*, 1966, 19, pp. 425–36.
RICHARDSON, S. A., HASTORF, A. H., GOODMAN, N., & DORNBUSCH, S. M. 'Cultural uniformity in reaction to physical disabilities', *American Sociological Review*, 1961, 26, pp 241–7.

12. The construction of conceptions of stigma by professional experts *

ROBERT A. SCOTT
Assistant Professor of Sociology,
Princeton University, U.S.A.

Throughout history, the mentally ill, the crippled, the mentally retarded, the maimed, the poor, and others who were similarly stigmatized as morally inferior have occupied an unenviable status in most societies of the world. Traditionally, such persons have been viewed as helpless dependents, incapable of mastering the elementary skills essential for engaging in productive social and economic activities. Mingled with these ideas were certain imputations about moral culpability. The mere possession of a stigmatizing condition or attribute was often viewed as prima facie evidence of God's punishment for one's sins. Those who were stigmatized usually were not allowed to mingle freely in the community nor were they ordinarily accorded the rights and benefits that were extended to average citizens. Many of these people were placed in asylums, where they were treated in punitive and degrading ways; others were at the mercy of their families or acquaintances, who were obliged by the community to provide for them but seldom felt compelled to treat them in the same way that ordinary persons were treated.

In the last hundred years or so in industrialized societies of the Western world, a notable departure from this traditional pattern has occurred.[1] Among the enlightened in these societies, the view has emerged that helplessness and dependency are not inherent in conditions that are stigmatizing, so that many such people are able to engage in productive social and economic activities if given

help and training. Moreover, the existence of traits or qualities that stigmatize is no longer explained by recourse to notions of moral culpability; rather, the deficiencies are seen as the product of ordinary genetic, psychological, social, and economic processes that operate in all societies. Along with these changes in the connotations associated with stigma there has been a corresponding shift in the locus of responsibility for the education, rehabilitation, and care of people affiliated with them. This responsibility has been moving from the family to professionally trained people who claim to have a special expertise which uniquely qualifies them to understand and treat the problems associated with stigmatizing conditions.[2] Many of these experts have trained in social work, rehabilitation counseling, work with the deaf, work with the blind, psychiatry and the various mental health professions. Moreover, a majority of them work in specialized helping organizations, most of which have become large, complex bureaucratic structures. These trends toward professionalization and bureaucratization are having an enormous impact both on stigmatized individuals and on the conceptions and reactions that laymen have to them. [...]

These professional and bureaucratic trends have also affected the socialization of stigmatized persons into the social role of deviant. The claim of expertise in treating problems associated with stigmatizing conditions implies that the claimants possess a specialized body of knowledge which has been acquired through careful professional training and/or years of clinical experiences. As a rule, this knowledge is codified into theories about particular conditions such as mental illness, blindness,

*From Jack D. Douglas (ed.) (1970) *Deviance and respectability: the social construction of moral meanings,* New York, Basic Books, Chapter 9, pp. 255–90.

deafness, poverty, and so on. These theories contain general assertions about the nature of human behavior, its causes, and how to change it; and specific assertions about the nature of the particular stigmatizing condition in question. Specific assertions describe the experts' beliefs about such things as the causes of the condition, the basic problems and crises which people who have it will experience, the ways in which these problems might be solved, the self-attitudes and patterns of behavior that they should develop if they are to make a successful adjustment to it, and the relationships between the condition and normalcy. In these theories, then, are found the meaning which a stigma has to the expert. They embody a kind of putative identity that the expert has constructed for the person who comes to him for help. This putative identity is manifested as the expert's expectations for the clients' self-attitudes and behavior. Some clients internalize these expectations into their self-concepts; others simply play the part that their counselor expects them to play, if only because they want to matriculate through the program as quickly and effortlessly as possible. In either case, this putative identity contained in an expert's theory about a stigma is a potent factor in the client's socialization into the role of deviant.

More and more the character of stigma in industrialized societies is changed to fit professional experts' conceptions. This chapter is about these theories of stigmata that experts have constructed. In it, I will present illustrations of expert conceptions about stigma and attempt to show how these conceptions reflect aspects of the social, cultural, and economic environments of which the experts are a part. I will try to assess the kind of impact that expert conceptions of stigmata have on the individuals on whom they are imposed, and I will comment on the process by which these meanings are constructed.

There are two terminological clarifications I want to make. First, I use terms like 'professional ideologies about stigma,' 'constructed meanings of stigma,' 'theories of stigma,' and 'expert conceptions of stigma' to refer to the experts' beliefs, assumptions, and definitions about conditions that are stigmatizing. The experts whose conceptions interest me are not those who are removed from social control agencies, but the ones who are, so to speak, on the firing line. It is the people who

design and administer programs and engage in education, care, and rehabilitation at the clinical level whose conceptions and definitions have the greatest impact for change.

Second, I use the term 'stigma' to refer to any physical condition, personality trait, or attribute of behavior which marks an individual as being morally inferior.[3] Throughout I will refer to many forms of stigma, including mental illness, crime, delinquency, poverty, blindness, mental retardation, and alcoholism. It is the fact of moral deviation which is common to all of them — the sense of moral inferiority, culpability, and depravity — that allows me to regard them as comparable phenomena.

Variations in expert conceptions of stigma

It is common knowledge among social scientists that stigmatizing conditions that are formally the same can have different meanings to 'natives' or laymen who are from different cultures of the world. A part of the evidence for this generalization is drawn from studies of attitudes toward stigma in different periods of history. Haffter, for example, has traced the attitudes found in European folklore toward handicapped children from the Middle Ages to the late nineteenth century.[4] He reports that at the beginning of the Middle Ages, abnormal children were viewed as potential harbingers of good fortune, but that by the late nineteenth century they were seen as evil creatures who had been punished by a vengeful God. Hes and Wollstein report that the attitudes toward mental illness expressed in ancient Hebrew texts were basically empathetic and optimistic ones.[5] There was little evidence of the ostracism and intolerance of mental illness that are characteristically found in contemporary societies. Similarly, Davis reports that prostitution has not always been as demeaning as it is in the contemporary Western world.[6] In ancient Roman society, certain prostitutes were accorded a special, esteemed status, a fact which is also true for certain classes of prostitutes in contemporary Japanese society.

Other evidence in support of this generalization comes from anthropological studies of contemporary cultures of the world. From the Human Relations Area Files we learn of societies such as Tibet, Burma, and Turkey where the crippled and maimed are cast aside as lesser human beings; and of other societies, such as Korea and Afghanistan, where people with these same conditions are believed to possess unusual, culturally valued abilities for which they are accorded a special and superior status. [. . .]

These illustrations are quite striking; it is not difficult to understand why the generalizations that they support have become common knowledge to the social scientist so quickly. What is not so apparent in the social science literature on stigma is that there are equally striking differences in the meanings of stigma that are found in experts' theories about them. Perhaps one reason why this fact has not been clearly seen is that these differences in meanings are masked by a common, highly vocal commitment on the part of experts to the basic ideal of assisting those who have such conditions to achieve some semblance of a normal life. It is only when one begins to study how expert theories about stigma are actually implemented that these differences in meanings become apparent. I want to present a number of examples to illustrate this point; I will begin with some from a study of blindness.

The significance of these examples from work for the blind will be more apparent to the reader if he is aware of a basic fact about the condition of blindness. It is that the only restriction which the condition itself imposes on an individual results from the fact that the absence of vision prevents him from relating directly to his distant environment.[7] It therefore follows that people who cannot see will be unable to navigate in unfamiliar environments without mechanical aids or assistance from others. If they are totally blind, they will not have direct access to the printed word, nor can they directly experience such things as distant scenery, paintings, or objects such as buildings, that are too large to be apprehended by touch. One can infer from these facts that blind people will not be able to engage in certain types of activities such as reading ink print, flying airplanes, playing tennis, and so on. There is little else, however, that can be predicted about blind people from the nature of the condition alone. With this fact in mind, I want to begin my discussion of blindness by examining some of the theories about it that have been developed by professional experts in a number of different countries.

In the United States, workers for the blind espouse many different theories about blindness. Most of these theories are cast in psychological terms. In them, the focus is on the impact which blindness is thought to have on personality and psychological adjustment.[8] Many experts believe that the loss of vision is a basic blow to self and personality so that deep shock inevitably follows the onset of this condition. Grief and depression also occur; the former because of the loss of basic skills for coping with everyday life, and the latter because of the resulting disorganization of the total personality. A basic goal of rehabilitation is adjustment to blindness. In most expert theories, a blind person is viewed as adjusted when he has faced and fully accepted the fact that he is blind; only then can he be ready to learn the skills and attitudes that enable him to compensate for the losses he has suffered. The final product of rehabilitation is the birth and evolution of a new self: that of a blind man who accepts his condition, having learned to live with it.

Workers for the blind in other countries have defined the meaning of blindness differently. Leading experts in Sweden, for example, regard blindness as little more than the loss of one sense modality. These workers say, 'Blindness does not mean that their [blind persons'] other senses are blunted, that their personality has been blotted out or that the structure of the abilities that the individual has been equipped with has undergone a change.'[9] Rather, 'Blindness is a technical handicap. It can be compensated by the mastery of new techniques and by the use of technical aids.'[10] It is recognized that learning to use technical aids correctly implies an acceptance of blindness; however, the 'real way back to a normal life [requires the] acquisition of a new technique . . . and the use of technical aids.'[11] Great reliance is placed on the development and mastery of technical equipment such as travel guides, special devices for the home and for personal grooming, reading devices, and the like. Rehabilitation is viewed as a process of 'learning how to use techniques and technical aids most effectively, and where necessary, of developing new devices and techniques to aid the particular needs of specific individuals.'[12] The psychiatric counseling, clinical therapy, and adjustment training that are a standard part of most rehabilitation programs for the blind in America are played down or omitted in virtually all Swedish programs.

Professional ideologies about blindness among leading workers for the blind in England are cast in terms of 'mood states.' These workers feel that the blind are especially vulnerable to the doldrums; they are constantly in danger of becoming depressed and filled with despair about their plight. One of the chief goals of work with the blind is to buoy their spirits. To this end, rehabilitation centers have been established to which many blind people return for a few weeks each year. These centers are usually found in surroundings near the sea. There is a distinctive air of cheerfulness about them which is particularly noticeable when staff members interact with clients. Music is everywhere, and much of the day is spent in diversionary social and recreational activities. Training in mechanical aids such as Braille or the 'white cane' is undertaken primarily because it provides the worker with opportunities to 'cheer up' his client. In some countries, such as our own and Sweden, the ability to be independent in mobility and other activities of everyday life is a quality which many experts feel a blind man should have. In England, however, many of the blind to whom their leading experts point with the greatest pride and admiration are unable to walk about at all unless they are guided by someone who can see. The meaning of blindness which these workers for the blind in England have constructed centers around good-naturedness and cheerfulness in the face of adversity.

In Italy, and to a lesser extent France, provisions for the blind have been traditionally linked with the Catholic Church. In these countries, some expert meanings of blindness have been formulated in theological terms. According to these theories, blindness is regarded as a kind of spiritual or religious problem, carrying with it the imputation either that those who are blind have had a serious 'falling out' with God, or, alternatively, that the blind are a special 'chosen' group who are able to enjoy spiritual experiences ordinarily denied to those who can see. The experts who embrace the former meaning think of rehabilitation as a process of prayer and meditation aimed at achieving a new communion with God; those who advocate the latter meaning seek to cultivate and deepen the blind person's special spirituality.

These conceptions of blindness are the ones espoused by some leading workers for the blind in each country. They should not be interpreted as full statements of the 'English' or 'American' or 'Swedish' view of blindness. Indeed, the disagreements among workers for the blind in some of these countries are so great that it would be misleading to suppose that there is a single conception of this disability. The point of the examples is to draw our attention to the fact that professional experts may impute different meanings to stigmatizing conditions which are formally the same. We see these differences especially from a cross-cultural perspective; but, once sensitized to them, we can begin to make finer discriminations in the meanings of stigma among experts who are from the same culture. I can illustrate this point with some examples from work for the blind in America.

I have stated that psychological adjustment is a major theme in many practice theories of blindness in work for the blind in America. There are, however, substantial differences among workers for the blind in different kinds of rehabilitation centers regarding the kinds of behavior patterns that constitute evidence of adjustment.[. . .]

For example, all rehabilitation centers and related agencies for the blind in the United States are committed to the goal of helping blind people to become independent and self-sufficient. At the concrete, operational level, there are some important differences of interpretation of this principle. Some centers interpret this goal to mean that many disabled people have the capacity to function independently in the everyday life of the community. To this end, they provide a variety of services aimed at giving the disabled person the skills that enable him to do this. Other agencies take the view that the level of independence and self-sufficiency possible for most disabled people is very slight. It is unrealistic to expect the average client to go back into the community and to live on his own. In turn, one is limited as to how much he can hope to accomplish in the way of training the client for independence; the safest course it to alter the social and physical environment of the center itself in order to accommodate it to him. In centers which take this approach, the independence and self-sufficiency are achieved by lowering demands to a minimal level, by performing for the individual many of the elementary tasks of everyday life, and by contriving and simplifying the physical environment in other ways.[13] These two approaches to rehabilitation signify differing assumptions about the impact that blindness has on individuals and their capacity to recover from it, which in turn implies that workers for the blind are attaching different meanings to this condition.

The case of blindness is not a unique one; there are equally wide variations in the meanings that experts have constructed for other stigmata as well. Mental illness is a good example. In their study of two mental hospitals in Chicago, Strauss and his colleagues found that there were three different practice theories of mental illness: the psychotherapeutic, the somatotherapeutic, and the sociotherapeutic.[14] According to these investigators, the psychotherapeutic theory of mental disorders is cast entirely in psychological terms. Their etiology lies in psychological processes, and 'the impact of intrapsychic systems by either internal or external psychological trauma constitutes the necessary and sufficient condition for the development of mental illness.' (ibid. p. 56). Treatment involves specific forms of psychotherapy for specific types of illnesses. According to the somatotherapeutic ideology, mental illness involves 'malfunctioning of the central nervous system, whether it results from physiological, neurophysiological, biochemical, or physical-chemical dysfunctions.' (ibid.). Genetic processes are prominently featured in this ideology; they are seen as 'interacting with biological systems to produce aberrations or propensities toward mental abnormality.' (Ibid.). Therapy is individualized and tends to involve drugs, shock treatment, surgical operations on the brain, and similar medical procedures. The sociotherapeutic ideology of mental illness proceeds from the assumption that the mind is a *tabula rasa* on which mental illness is imprinted. Social factors are clearly preemptive, including early deprivation (in social terms) or later processes in which the external environment impinges stressfully on the organism. (Ibid.). The treatment that is utilized by advocates of this ideology is nonspecific; the basic notion is to mobilize a large number of therapeutic resources in a setting that is conducive to recovery and rehabilitation.[...]

These examples indicate that there are important differences in the meanings which experts have constructed for stigmatizing conditions which are formally the same. Moreover, even a superficial analysis of these examples indicates that these meanings do not vary randomly; they seem to be related to such things as core cultural values, the experts' professional training, and the institutional settings in which they are practiced. A satisfactory understanding and explanation of the theories of stigma that experts construct will not be possible until we have explicitly spelled out what these relationships are. I want to take a step in this direction by identifying some of these relationships.

Some determinants of conceptions of stigma that experts construct

[...] There are four sets of forces that I want to consider. They relate to aspects of experts' cultures, the professions in which they are trained, the organizations for which they work, and the clientele on whom their meanings are being imposed. These particular sets of forces do not exhaust the range of factors that affect the experts' conceptions of stigma.

CULTURAL VALUES

Expert conceptions of stigma reflect prevailing cultural values, attitudes, and beliefs. In a sense, this is inevitable. Experts must use the 'native tongue' in order to communicate their constructed meanings to laymen, and the modes of expression that a language affords are grounded in the core values of a culture. Moreover, it is laymen who usually grant legitimacy to experts' claims to special knowledge about stigma; any constructed meanings that are dissonant with lay values, beliefs, and attitudes will probably be rejected as nonsensical. Thus, whatever its other merits may be, a purely mechanical conception of a physical handicap is not likely to 'make sense' to people who live in a culture in which religious values are the central ones, just as a religious conception of disability will probably be rejected as old-fashioned in a materialistic culture such as our own. This point is simple enough. However, the connections between expert conceptions of stigma and core values, beliefs, and attitudes of a culture go much deeper than this.

Financial resources are the lifeblood of any organized intervention program. Without money a program simply cannot operate. In all industrialized societies that support such programs these resources are controlled by laymen, a fact that has enormous ramifications for the kind and amount of intervention experts can ever hope to initiate. Their core beliefs, values, and attitudes have a tremendously important bearing on this matter. For one thing, there are certain categories of the stigmatized in all societies who are regarded as undeserving because their past or present actions, or even their personal characteristics, violate some major cultural value.[. . .]

There is another way in which cultural values bear on the question of support for intervention programs and therefore bear indirectly on the meanings of stigma that experts construct. It is recognized by many people that effective rehabilitation programs must deal with more than just the stigmatized person; they must also involve the groups of normals whose attitudes and reactions to the stigmatized person control that person's participation in the community. This implies that collective action may be necessary to achieve the objectives of full rehabilitation. However, cultural values may operate to limit the possibilities of collective actions. As Zald notes, 'If cultural traditions place a strong emphasis on individual responsibility and action, then collective solutions are likely to be resisted. On the other hand, a group can have values which stress the importance of collective actions as a general rule and, consequently, welfare problems, too, will call forth a collective response.'[15] [. . .]

Some of the core beliefs and values in our culture are grounded in the assumption that man can control nature and his own fate. However, these are societies in which more fatalistic views prevail; in them, the responsibility for man's fate is thought to reside in external forces of nature that are beyond his control. Where such beliefs prevail, there is much less possibility for mobilizing collective actions than in societies which believe in man's capacity to master nature. Such a view prevailed among the ruling elite of England during much of the nineteenth century. Steven Marcus, in an essay on British responses to the Irish famine of the 1840's, shows how these beliefs, which were firmly grounded in Malthusian theory, worked to prevent the British government from taking collective action to save the Irish from starvation.[16] [. . .]

Marcus illustrates once again the basic principle of sociology that a society's core values are deeply rooted in its economic system; they reflect the system, and they change in response to change in it. The core values of societies with one type of economic system will therefore be different from core values of societies with a different type of system. In view of the fact that experts' concep-

tions of stigma reflect a society's core values, we are led to expect that the meanings of stigma that experts construct will systematically vary according to the form of the society's economic system. While there is no conclusive evidence on this point, it is interesting to note that expert conceptions of stigma in societies that have a capitalistic system tend to stress individual responsibility, whereas expert meanings of stigma in societies which have a socialistic economic system tend to stress collective responsibility. Clearly, this is a question that deserves serious and extensive study.

[. . .] There is still another, more direct way in which laymen exert an impact on the meanings of deviance that experts construct. This impact can be described as follows. The existence of stigma poses at least two sets of problems: one is for the person to whom the stigma belongs, and the other is for the community in which that person lives. For each set of problems, there are corresponding needs. For stigmatized persons, the problems and the needs revolve around such things as social acceptance, a desire to become invisible in the same way that normal people are invisible, and a wish for others to interact with them on terms other than those based on stigma.[17] The problems which stigma poses for the community are different ones, and the corresponding needs may not coincide with the ones which the victim has. Stigma threatens the community and presents it with unpleasant problems it would rather not confront or think about. Old people, poor people, people who are blind or crippled, and those who are crazy make us uneasy; they threaten our sense of mastery of nature, and they are disruptive of routines of daily life. A community's needs relating to stigmata may be to hide them from public view, or at least to dress them up in a way that makes them more palatable to laymen or at least less offensive to them. In writing about mental hospitals, Goffman has stated the point as follows: 'Part of the official mandate of the public mental hospital is to protect the community from the dangers and nuisances of certain kinds of misconduct.'[18] Orlans has described public mental institutions as 'American death camps.'[19] He writes, 'The aged, insane paupers of the American asylum are surely the most pitiful members of American society; but no one will give them more than pity, and they also evoke feelings of abhorrence and fear. Asylums are institutions which have been created to remove this sight from our eyes.' (ibid. p. 167). Such institutions, then, are places to which the unwanted of the community can be sent and where they can be 'taken care of.'

We can see these community needs regarding stigma reflected in the conceptions of stigma that experts have constructed. For example, in our society, these conceptions focus attention primarily on the individual to whom the stigma belongs. He is treated as though he is in some way responsible for having acquired his condition, as though the solutions to his problems are in his own control. This almost exclusive emphasis on treating the victims of stigma without involving members of the community reflects a conception of such conditions that is more attuned to the community's needs than it is to the needs of those who are afflicted. Or again, in the last section I described two different approaches to rehabilitating the blind. One was a restorative approach, aimed at teaching the client the kinds of skills required to function independently in everyday life; the other was a custodial approach aimed at creating a special, protected environment in an organization which specifically catered to the client's disability. Blind people who have been clients in agencies following the restorative approach are often able to move back into the community and function independently in it; those who are the clients of agencies adopting the custodial approach are often only able to function in the environment which the agency has created. Indeed, in many cases they come to depend on it quite heavily. There is reflected in the restorative approach to rehabilitation a conception of blindness which is more attuned to the needs and problems of the blind person; on the other hand, the custodial approach is more attuned to the desires of the community for the stigmatized person. It is significant that there are so few rehabilitation centers in America that follow the restorative approach and that those which do are often in serious fiscal difficulty. Custodial agencies, on the other hand, have endured for many years and in most cases are fiscally sound.

The organized intervention programs that experts manage, therefore, have two different constituencies whose 'needs' are not only different but may actually be contradictory. As a rule, the constituency consisting of people in the community is a much more powerful one than the

constituency consisting of stigmatized people. The reasons for this are that laymen, and not clients, control an institution's financial resources, so that lay control and power are built directly into the fabric of the program.

In summary, the meanings of stigma that experts construct are deeply influenced by values, attitudes, and beliefs that are central to the society. These values affect the expert in several ways; they are a part of the language he uses to express his meanings; they are an integral part of the assumptive world of the culture against which the meanings of his conceptions of stigma are judged; and they are critical elements in decisions concerning the willingness of laymen to give financial support for programs.

PROFESSIONALISM AND THE CONSTRUCTION OF EXPERT MEANINGS OF STIGMA

The development of organized intervention programs for the stigmatized has been accompanied by the emergence of various professions which claim special expertise with the problems that people with stigma have. The processes of professionalizing that began some years ago have had, and continue to have, an important impact on the meanings of stigma that experts have constructed. The most obvious impact is related to the way in which university and college-based training programs have developed. One of the core problems confronting training programs has been that of gaining enough legitimacy in the academic community and in the world of practice to permit persons trained in them to make their claims to expertise viable. One of the ways this has been done is by borrowing the concepts, procedures, and approaches that have already been proven and accepted in other, more established professions. [. . .]

There is another way in which the process of professionalization has had its impact on the construction of expert meanings of stigma. In the various fields of practice such as mental health, work for the blind, or work for the deaf, there is not just one profession or group of experts; there are many. It is generally assumed that if any effort at helping the physically disabled or mentally ill is to be truly effective, it must involve the skills and the knowledge of professional educators, clinical psychologists, social workers, physicians, rehabilitation counselors, lawyers, professional admini-strators, psychiatrists, and so on. It is also gener-ally assumed that one's own particular profession ought to play the central role, with other profes-sions subordinated to it. Conflicts and disputes about this point inevitably arise wherever ques-tions are raised about the distribution of financial resources, the allocation of time with clients to various professionals, the kinds of new staff members to hire, the assignment of physical space, and other related policy decisions. Strauss and his colleagues found that the various professionals that work in mental hospitals must continually attempt to 'stake out claims in treatment pro-cess'[20] and then protect these claims against infringement from other disciplines. In these con-flicts, it is rare for any one profession ever to gain full control over all resources. As a result, the meaning of a stigma such as mental illness that is contained in the ideology of a single profession is seldom put into practice in its entirety. The meanings that are practiced are 'hybrids' that emerge out of these negotiations among the professionals who are involved in treating the mentally ill.

There is one final point I want to make about professional ideologies. It is that the process of professionalization is not complete in any of these fields. All of them include many people whose expertise is acquired through experience alone and not through formal training of any kind. The opportunity structure and the career patterns open to the expert who has been professionally trained are quite different from those available to person-nel whose expertise has been acquired only through practical experience. The essential differ-ence between them is that the expertise of the former is usually generic in character, whereas the expertise of the latter is highly specific. A person who has been trained in a college-based program learns a set of generic skills and approaches to practice as well as the techniques for tailoring then to different circumstances and problems. This generic approach affords the trained professional a tremendous amount of flexibility in pursuing a career. If he is unhappy with the practice of one agency, he can easily move to another; and if he becomes disenchanted in working with the pro-blems of one group of stigmatized people, his skills and training give him the option of transferring into another field. Moreover, one of the most

important elements in his career is his colleagues, whose esteem and praise are at the core of his professional self-image.

In contrast to this, the situation of the indivi-dual who has not had any professional training is quite different. Typically, such persons have en-tered helping organizations at low-level jobs, often as clerical workers, secretaries, or administrative assistants. Over time, they are able to gain prac-tical experience with one or a few of the methods and techniques that go into rehabilitation. For example, some learn how to read and record in Braille; others become proficient in the use of particular types of audiometric equipment; and still others learn how to teach the disabled to use particular kinds of prosthetic devices. The exper-tise which is thus acquired is limited in two ways. One is that it is technique-specific. By this I mean that the person may know how to teach a blind man to use a 'white cane,' but in all likelihood he will not know much about the more general problem of physical mobility. The other limitation is that his expertise is often organization-specific. Until recently, and even today, there has been little uniformity in the techniques used by organi-zations that specialize in helping people with the same type of stigma. For example, most blindness agencies teach their clients mobility, but the methods that are used are quite different, particu-larly if the mobility expert has gained his expertise through practical experience rather than through generic professional training. This dual limita-tion — that acquired expertise tends to be tech-nique-specific and organization-specific — has enormous ramifications for the career lines of the experts involved. For one thing, if a program were to change so that the specific technique that the expert has mastered were to be abolished, it would be difficult for him to move on to other activities that are only related in a generic way. As a result, the person whose expertise is acquired is often resistant to any change that might diminish the significance of his specific skills. For another thing, he does not have the same freedom that trained people have to move from one organiza-tion to another. His status, income, and influence usually depend on the continued existence of the specific organization in which they have been built. He will therefore tend to resist any policy that jeopardizes 'his' organization. The implication of this for the meanings of stigma that are constructed are that untrained experts will evolve meanings that give primary emphasis to specific techniques and will guarantee the survival of the organization for which they work. An example of this point is found in the distinction between custodial agencies and agencies that attempt to restore blind people to the community. In work for the blind, professionally trained experts have been the most vocal advocates of the restorative approach, while persons whose expertise is acquired have been the most vocal advocates of the custodial approach. It is particularly significant that organizations following the restorative approach encounter the greatest fiscal risks and those following the custodial approach seem to enjoy the greatest economic security.

BUREAUCRATIC PROCESS AND THE CONTENT OF EXPERT MEANINGS OF STIGMA

Most intervention programs of services for people with stigmatizing conditions are housed in bureaucratic structures, many of which are large and complex. These bureaucratic structures and the processes to which they give rise are reflected in the content of expert ideologies about stigma in several ways. For example, the services that are provided in the context of bureaucratic structures must often be programed and routinized. The individual client as the unit of rehabilitation is often replaced by collectivities such as the class, the ward, or the therapy group. Moreover, the same efficiency and formalization that enable the expert to implement certain kinds of service programs to large numbers of people may also become constraining in the sense that they preclude him from engaging in major innovations. Even the physical plant which a bureaucracy requires may impose serious constraints on the kinds of programs and services that are possible and realistic to carry out.[21] Numerous other examples of this point could be given. However, rather than try to develop a comprehensive list of them, I want to select one in particular and explain it in some detail. The example I have selected is the phenomenon of official or 'legal' definitions of conditions that are stigmatizing.

When organized intervention programs first began, informal criteria were used in deciding whether or not an impaired person was eligible for an organization's services. As a rule, the early organizations focused their primary efforts on extreme and obvious cases of disability; because these organizations were local and often private, it was an easy thing to make exceptions in order to help people whose needs were great, but whose impairments may not have been extreme. As the state and federal governments began to support these service programs, the problem of whom to consider blind or deaf or mentally retarded or mentally ill became a serious one. It was no longer possible to decide about eligibility for such services as cash payments, comprehensive rehabilitation, or special tax benefits on an ad hoc or common-sense basis. Uniform guidelines had to be developed for deciding who among the hard of hearing was deaf, or who among those with seeing problems was blind, or who among the intellectually impaired was retarded, and so on. These bureaucratic problems gave rise to the construction of 'legal' or 'administrative' definitions for various kinds of stigmatizing conditions.

In constructing these definitions there was an important factor that had to be taken into account. Conditions such as total blindness, total deafness, or severe retardation are rare ones in our population. It is difficult to justify national or state programs for people with these impairments when the programs are limited only to those who are the most severely impaired. Moreover, such programs can hope to expand only so long as the populations in need are large ones. It seemed desirable to offer services not only to those who were totally impaired but to the severely impaired as well. These considerations had to be taken into account in constructing legal definitions of stigmatizing conditions. The essential question was, how far toward 'normal' should one go? In order to answer, it was necessary to develop highly technical definitions of impairment. The legal definition of deafness that was adopted specified the precise level of decibel discrimination that an individual had to be unable to make before he would be considered deaf. The definition of mental retardation adopted by the American Association of Mental Deficiency defined that condition as 'intellectual functioning which originates during the development period and is associated with impairment in adaptive behavior.'[22] In practice, a mental retardate may be classified in one of five different levels, the criterion being his test score on standardized measures of intelligence. Legal blindness was defined as 'Central visual acuity of 20/200 or less in the better eye with correcting lenses; or central visual acuity of more than 20/200 if there is a field defect in which the peripheral field has contracted to such an extent that the widest diameter of visual field subtends an angle distance no greater than 20 degrees.'[23]

One feature of these definitions is that there is not a direct correspondence between them and the ones that a layman would use in labeling others as physically or mentally impaired. In order to determine if an individual who has a severe problem seeing is 'legally blind,' it is necessary to give him a careful, clinically controlled test of visual acuity. This test requires not only an exact determination of maximum levels of vision discrimination; it also requires that his discrimination levels be ascertained after he has been fitted with glasses that correct his vision to its best possible level. Even so, disagreements about 'best corrected vision' are common among people who are experts at measuring visual acuity. Another feature is that the closer one is to the point where the experts' demarcation lines are drawn between normalcy and impairment as it is legally defined, the less correspondence there is likely to be between expert definitions of these conditions as stigmas and the lay person's subjective experiences and reactions to them. This point is extremely important for the following reason. The distribution of visual acuity, intelligence, hearing acuity, and related conditions in the general population all approximate the normal or bell-shaped curve. Thus, the number of people who are totally blind, totally deaf, or severely retarded is quite small, and these numbers increase as we move away from the extremes and toward the normal. The legal definition which demarcates the line between the 'legally' impaired and the normal creates a population of impaired people, the largest segment of which falls exactly at or very close to this arbitrary demarcation line. A majority of people who are therefore 'legally' blind are, in fact, seeing people with visual acuity of exactly 20/200. Similarly, a majority of those who are mentally retarded according to the current 'legal' definition are either borderline or mildly retarded. As one expert on this subject has observed, 'Most people who are defined as mentally retarded are not profoundly, severely, or even moderately retarded. Quite the contrary, fully 85% of all mental retardates are only mildly retarded.'[24]

It was bureaucratic necessity that led to the creation of legal definitions of impairments. However, once they were constructed, they became sacred and were reified. The 'legally deaf' were perceived as deaf, the 'legally blind' as blind, and the 'legally retarded' as retarded. There often resulted some major discrepancies between the definitions that experts imposed on a person who was impaired and that person's own subjective reactions to his condition. According to the definition used by the expert, a person with a tenth of normal vision is blind; from the perspective of the client, however, a blind man is someone who cannot see. It is difficult for him to understand why experts believe he is 'denying reality' when he is looking his counselor squarely in the eye. As for the expert, he has been specially trained to give professional help to impaired people. He cannot use his expertise if those who are sent to him for assistance do not regard themselves as being impaired. Given this fact, it is not surprising that the doctrine has emerged among experts that truly effective rehabilitation and adjustment can occur only after the client has squarely faced and accepted the 'fact' that he is, indeed, impaired.

In the case of legal definitions of conditions that are stigmatizing, then, we have an example of the impact that bureaucratic structures have on conceptions of stigma that experts construct.

CLIENTELE

A final factor affecting experts' conceptions of stigmatizing conditions is the people whom the expert is attempting to educate, care for, and rehabilitate. This factor can be described in the following way. The organizations in which experts work have many different constituents to whom they must respond. Among them are clients, benefactors, the general community, various professional groups, and the like. As we have seen in the section on cultural values, the problems which a stigma poses for clients and the ones which it poses for an organization's other constituents are often quite different and even contradictory. The issue is whether or not the client has the same 'muscle' with experts as other constituents of an organization have; is he able to force experts to take his needs, wishes, and desires as seriously as they must the needs, wishes, and desires of these other constituents? The answer that has been given to this question by several leading students of social welfare is that he does not. This answer is based on several different facts about clients.

For one thing, most clients do not buy the services they receive. This is in part because most of them cannot afford to and in part because many agencies prohibit them from doing so. The consequence of this, according to Zald, is that 'the agency personnel may be less intent on satisfying the client and meeting his needs.'[25] For another thing, the general societal status of a person with stigma is very low. 'Clients in welfare organizations,' writes Zald, 'are often not full participants in the society; they frequently come to the agency as supplicants without full rights or means. Not only are they legally without full rights but, psychologically, they are not full participants; they are the downtrodden and the vanquished.' (ibid.). Social welfare organizations have a greater legal control over clients than most other organizations have; they are authorized to act on the client's behalf in many areas of his personal life over which ordinary citizens retain full control. A client's access to the resources of the community as well as the degree of his participation in it are largely governed by the agency. Genuine alternatives for the client are essentially nonexistent; the client is free to leave an agency and go to another one, but the chances are very great that he will encounter these same problems of powerlessness and overcontrol wherever he goes.[...]

The implications of these facts are as follows. Most important policy decisions that have to be made affect the interests of every one of the agency's constituents. Those who make these decisions cannot afford to ignore the interests of benefactors, professional groups, or the community at large, if they are to remain in business. They can, however, ignore the clients' interests without seriously jeopardizing either the fiscal integrity or the social reputation that the agency enjoys. This fact suggests in turn that experts have a considerable amount of freedom to define and conceptualize stigmatizing conditions. By this, I mean that they are free to emphasize any one of a great many themes in the life experiences of the stigmatized in order to tailor the conception of stigma to the political and economic realities confronting experts and helping organizations. We

have seen that experts in different cultures and even in the same culture have defined the real problems of stigma in different ways that are sometimes even contradictory. The freedom to do this is afforded the expert because his client is basically powerless to resist it. It is important to recognize that one reason why this can be done is that the experts' definitions can become real simply by creating a general consensus and conviction that they are real. The problem of blindness can be defined in a great many ways, any one of which has the potential to become in reality the real problem of blindness simply by persuading others that it is so.[26]

There are only a few cases in which clients have been able to become a truly powerful constituent of an organization. One such case is in services for the blind in Sweden. There, blind people organized themselves and literally took over the major blindness organizations. In fact, bylaws were passed which specifically provided that no seeing person could hold executive office in any blindness organization. All people who are detected as blind are invited to join, and for those who do, the organization acts as the intermediary between the individual blind person and all public programs.[...] What is distinctive about the Swedish program is the absence of an ideology that requires the blind person to undergo intensive personality restructuring or basic changes in self. One reason for this may be that the experts who construct special meanings of blindness are clients themselves.

The effects of professional ideologies on the stigmatized

[...] One way to gauge the impact that expert meanings of stigma are having on the stigmatized of a society is to examine the extent of development of the organized intervention programs in which these meanings are constructed and enforced. The data relating to this topic suggest that a clear demarcation can be made between highly industrialized nations (especially those in the Western world) and preindustrial and developing nations. In all but the most highly industrialized societies, organized intervention efforts for the stigmatized have been developing only on a small scale, and in some societies these efforts are virtually nonexistent[27] There are only a few developing countries that have any national program, and even they receive only modest financial backing from the government. Private efforts in these nations are incomplete and uneven. While there are agencies for some stigmatized groups, for others there are none, and even the private agencies that do exist often cater to only selected types of stigmatized people such as children and adults who can work.[28] In preindustrial and developing nations, then, expert meanings probably have little impact on the traditional conceptions of stigma that prevail.

In highly industrialized societies, however, organized intervention programs are legion; viewed in their entirety, they make up intricate and complex systems of services for the stigmatized of each nation. The scope of this bureaucratization and professionalization of such services can be illustrated with some data from our own country. In [... the United States] England, Sweden, Norway, Denmark, Holland, Canada, and Russia and to a lesser extent in France, Italy, and Spain. In these societies, especially the ones in which this movement toward bureaucratization and professionalization of responsibility for the stigmatized has been most rigid, expert meanings are beginning to pose a genuine challenge to the older, more traditional folk conceptions and stereotypes of stigma. At the same time, it is important to recognize the limits of this challenge. There is no existing delivery system of services anywhere that has succeeded in reaching the entire population of stigmatized people in a society, and there is some evidence that even the most elaborate of these systems probably reaches only a minority of all those who qualify or need services.[29] Moreover, the public education function, which is aimed at changing traditional attitudes of laymen toward stigma, is one of the least developed of all activities that helping organizations sponsor. By and large, public education campaigns involve little more than occasional advertising of the organization and its programs; very few of these campaigns make genuine efforts either to disabuse the layman of traditional conceptions about stigma or to clarify the nature of his complicity in contributing to the problems of stigmatized people.

The data suggest, then, that expert meanings have little significance in preindustrial and developing nations, that in most highly industrialized nations they are posing a genuine challenge to traditional ideas about stigma, and that in a few

countries they are actually emerging as dominant conceptions among laymen and experts alike.

A second gauge of the significance of professional ideologies about stigma is their impact on self-attitudes and behavior of stigmatized people on whom they are practiced. Although there is some dispute about the exact nature of the effects practice theories have on an organization's clientele, the data of three different studies all agree that these effects are profound. From their research on mental hospitals, Strauss *et al.* conclude that 'ideology makes a difference in the organization of treatment, in what is done to and for patients and in the accompanying division of labor.'[30] They find that professional ideologies affect such aspects of a patient's 'life chances' as the kind of treatments he gets, the frequency and direction of institutional transfers, and the times of discharge. Moreover, they note that 'if they [the patients] stay long enough they may enter into the ideological discourse of the professional staff, using psychiatric language to evaluate themselves and others.' (ibid. p. 373). I have come to a similar conclusion about the impact that agencies and organizations for the blind have on their clients. I found that

when those who have been screened into blindness agencies enter them, they may not be able to see at all or they may have serious difficulties with their vision. When they have been rehabilitated, they are all blind men. They have learned the attitudes and behavior patterns that professional blindness workers believe blind people should have. In the intensive face-to-face relationships between blindness workers and clients that make up the rehabilitation process, the blind person is rewarded for adopting a view of himself that is consistent with his rehabilitators' view of him and punished for clinging to other self-conceptions. He is told that he is 'insightful' when he comes to describe his problems as his rehabilitators view them, and he is said to be 'blocking' or 'resistant' when he does not. Indeed, passage through the blindness system is determined in part by his willingness to adopt the experts' view about self.[31]

I have concluded that 'gradually, over time, the behavior of blind men comes to correspond with the assumptions and beliefs that blindness workers hold about blindness.' (ibid.).

Goffman has also stressed the impact that professional ideologies have on patients in mental hospitals, although the nature of that impact which he describes is somewhat different than the ones found in other studies. He states:

> Mental patients can find themselves in a special bind. To get out of the hospital, or to ease their life within it, they must show acceptance of the place accorded them, and the place accorded them is to support the occupational role of those who appear to force this bargain. This self-alienating moral servitude, which perhaps helps to account for some inmates becoming mentally confused, is achieved by involving the great tradition of the expert servicing relation, especially its medical variety. Mental patients can find themselves crushed by the weight of a service ideal that eases life for the rest of us.[32]

These studies indicate that experts' practice theories have profound effects on the self-attitudes and behaviors of clients and inmates of institutions. Unfortunately, we do not know how enduring these effects are. There is presumptive evidence that they may be short-lived. This evidence lies in the findings of all three of the studies I have cited which show that patients and clients are strongly inclined toward 'making out' in the system by going along with their counselors. The implication is that when they are released, these patterns of behavior that they have deliberately or subconsciously feigned may disappear.

The process of constructing expert meanings

[. . .] From available materials and cases, it appears that few existing expert meanings of stigma were explicitly and consciously formulated. Experts may have tried to lay out these meanings in advance of beginning to work, but few such preconceived meanings have survived. They are modified, distorted, and stretched as efforts are made to mobilize financial and man-power resources and to deal with the daily problems of running a welfare agency. Only periodically do experts stand back to take a hard look at such things as the consequences of their actions or to attempt to codify the rationale for their activities and to construct explanations for them. It is important to see that when these meanings are codified, the process of doing so is one in retrospect. Meanings evolve which describe, explain, and justify what exists; but what exists has often come into being for reasons that are not entirely related to the problems of stigma. Norton Long has described this process at the community level. He writes, 'Much of what occurs seems to just happen with accidental trends becoming cumulative over time and producing results intended by nobody. A great deal of the communities' activities consist of undirected cooperation of particular social structures, each seeking particular goals and in doing so, meshing with others.'[33] This statement applies as aptly to the internal dynamics of the social welfare agency as it does to the dynamics of the local community. It is probably impossible for the expert to map out in advance all the implications of a proposed policy, of even to understand how such things as client problems, needs, and interests are modified, stretched, or changed by each successive decision. It suggests that expert meanings are not constructed in advance and by the ordinary rules of logic and scientific reasoning; rather, they evolve, often unconsciously as the expert 'muddles through' the day-to-day problems of running a welfare organization.[34] This in turn implies that one can only speak of 'constructed' meanings of stigma in the sense that they are genuinely man-made and do not inhere in nature or in the stigmatizing conditions to which they are applied

NOTES AND REFERENCES

1. [. . .] *Rehabilitation of the Disabled in Fifty-one Countries*, Washington, U.S. Department of Health, Education and Welfare, Vocational Rehabilitation Administration, 1964.
2. Wilensky, Harold L., and Lebeaux, Charles N., *Industrial Society and Social Welfare*, New York, Russell Sage Foundation, 1958, Part I.

3. Goffman, Erving, *Stigma: Notes on the Management of Spoiled Identity*, Englewood Cliffs, N.J., Prentice-Hall 1963, p. 3.
4. Haffter, Carl, 'The Changeling: History and Psychodynamics of Attitudes to Handicapped Children in European Folklore', *Journal of the History of the Behavioral Sciences*, 1968, pp. 55—61.
5. Hes, Josef P., and Wollstein, Shlomoh, 'The Attitude of the Ancient Jewish Sources to Mental Patients', *Israel Annals of Psychiatry and Related Disciplines*, 1964, pp. 103—16.
6. Davis, Kingsley, 'Sexual Behavior', in Merton, Robert K., and Nisbet, Robert A., (eds.), *Contemporary Social Problems*, New York, Harcourt, Brace and World, 1966, pp. 322—72.
7. From a conversation with Professor Roelf G. Boiten, Laboratorium Voor Werkuigkundige Meet-en, Regeltechniek, Technische Hogeschool, Delft, The Netherlands.
8. See Blank, H. Robert, 'Psychoanalysis and Blindness', *Psychoanalytic Quarterly* XXVI, No. 1, 1957 pp. 1—24; Carroll, Thomas J., *Blindness: What It Is, What It Does, and How to Live with It*, Boston, Little Brown. 1961; Cholden. Louis A., *A Psychiatrist Works with Blindness*, New York, American Foundation for the Blind, 1958; Cholden, Louis A., 'Some Psychiatric Problems in the Rehabilitation of the Blind', *Bulletin of the Menninger Clinic*, XVIII, No. 3, 1954, pp. 107—12.
9. Erikson, Seved, 'We Are Sure to Manage', mimeographed, p. 1.
10. *Ibid.*
11. *Op. cit.*, p. 2.
12. From an interview with Mr. Charles Hedkvist, Director, De Blindas Forening, Stockholm, Sweden. [. . .]
13. Scott, Robert A., *The Making of Blind Men*, New York, Russell Sage Foundation, 1969, pp. 80—9.
14. Anselm L. Strauss *et al.*, *Psychiatric Ideologies and Institutions*, New York, the Free Press, 1964, pp. 54—6.
15. Zald, Mayer N., *Social Welfare Institutions: A Sociological Reader*, New York, Wiley 1965, p. 141.
16. Marcus, Steven, 'Hunger and Ideology', *Commentary*, November 1963, pp. 389—93.
17. Goffman, *Stigma*, p. 7.
18. Goffman, *Asylums*, Garden City, Doubleday, p. 352.
19. Orlans, Harold, 'An American Death Camp', *Politics*, Summer 1948 pp. 162—7, 205.
20. Strauss *et al.*, *op. cit.*, p. 368.
21 *Op. cit.*, pp. 45—50.
22. Edgerton, Robert B., *The Cloak of Competence*, Berkeley, University of California Press, 1967. p. 3.
23. *Facts and Figures about Blindness*, New York, American Foundation for the Blind 1967.
24. Edgerton, *Cloak of Competence*, p. 5.
25. Zald, *op. cit.*, p. 555.
26 In this sense social welfare organizations have a much greater degree of flexibility than organizations that manufacture material goods. Material goods in a manufacturing firm are the most critical 'constituent' by virtue of the fact that they either sell and make money or do not. This condition cannot be changed, not can it ever be ignored. Companies are forced to be more responsive to profit and loss than to any other consideration. The 'material goods' in a social welfare organization are its clients. However, 'profits' and 'losses' or the definitions and the relativization of basic goals for the client are matters that are determined by social consensus; and one can alter this consensus by persuasion alone.
27. *Rehabilitation of the Disabled in Fifty-one Countries, op. cit.*
28. *Op. cit.*, pp. 9, 20, 22, 39, 53, for example.
29. Scott, *op. cit.*, pp. 69—70; Miller, Samuel M., Roby, Pamela, and de Vos van Steenwijk, Alwine A., 'Social Policy and the Excluded Man: The Prevalence of Creaming', mimeographed, June 1968.
30. Strauss *et al.*, *op cit.*, p. 361.
31. Scott, *op. cit.*, p. 119.
32. Goffman, *Asylums*, p. 386.
33. Long, Norton E., 'The Local Community as an Ecology of Games', *American Journal of Sociology*, LXIV, No. 3, November 1958, p. 252.
34. Lindbloom, Charles E., 'The Science of "Muddling Through",' *Public Administration Review*, Spring, 1959.

PART FOUR

Families with handicapped members

Introduction

For Part Four we have selected material expressing many of the different viewpoints of those involved with the families of handicapped people. To a great extent the situations, attitudes and problems under discussion are the same but often seem transformed or given added significance by the superimposition of another view of them. The first four items represent the view and advice of a paediatrician, a child psychiatrist, a consultant in mental subnormality and a multidisciplinary team working on behalf of the National Society for Mentally Handicappped Children. The remaining four items reflect on the experiences of the parents of an autistic boy, the mothers of handicapped children, the wife of a man who contracted multiple sclerosis in middle age and finally died ten years later, and a mother who was cut down by poliomylitis after the birth of her second child but survived to feel her family and her role within the home collapse around her.

The most telling commentary on the predicament of these families is probably that expressed in the feelings of one of the mothers, in Sheila Hewett's survey, about her child, 'You naturally wish they were normal' (p. 207). But in certain crucial respects they are not. This part is therefore in many ways an extension of the analysis of the stigmatized to those whom Goffman terms 'the wise'. But we have also included a chapter from Hewett's book on the type of services with which families were in contact and mothers' assessments of them. This data may be augmented by reference to Tizard and Grad's study of mentally handicapped children and their families, which is more comprehensive and considerably less encouraging.

MacKeith itemizes the likely feelings of parents and their professional advisers when confronted by a handicapped child, the reasons why such a child may be placed away from home, and the four main points of crisis in the life-cycle of a handicapped person in a domestic group. Bentovim adopts a very different prescriptive tone, which at times approximates to a professionally constructed form of double-bind trap for parents (see Bateson *et al.* 1956). In much of the diagnosis of domestic trauma there seems no escape from the Scylla of rejection and the Charibdis of overprotection, both stemming from a deep sense of parental guilt. Roith could be said to imply that this is one of the ways in which professionals construct their interpretation of reality in his exposure of the ways in which any action may be interpreted in this way. But he discusses it rather flippantly. In her book Hewett (1970 chapter 9) seems closer to the mark in her discussion of the adjustments required if a handicapped child is to be accepted satisfactorily into the family; firstly, adjustment to the fact of their child being handicapped, and, secondly, the establishment of a viable path between expecting nothing from the child and striving for the unattainable – what in residential care regimes Miller and Gwynne have typified as firstly 'warehousing' and secondly 'horticultural' models of care. Mrs Chalmers seems to exemplify a similar dilemma in postulating the unacceptable polarities of giving up or being permanently dissatisfied with one's performance and predicament. In fact, the lives of handicapped people and their families seem booby-trapped by these proverbial Janus-like judgements from which no escape is possible, and which have a relentless, self-sustaining truth to experience.

Several of the points made by MacKeith and Bentovim are also made in the advice to parents of mentally handicapped children, and stress is laid on the sorts of service required to alleviate the situation. The lack of a counselling service is acutely felt because what counts is how, not when, parents are told of their child's disability. General practitioners need more guidance if they are to provide the help expected of them. Parents also need to play a positive and practical role in the process of their child's care. A good example of the sort of parental counselling and children's playgroup that Bentovim recommends is the group for spina-bifida families that Hodges describes in Part 9. The lack of counselling is one of the chief features of Robert's parents' experiences. But they need more than this if the physical and economic burdens placed on parents, and on mothers in particular, and the restriction of their social activities and friendship networks are to be eased. Although, as Bayley (1973) indicates, close kinship ties are often strengthened by the presence of handicapped members in those families that can care for them in the community, other wider contacts are severely restricted and often curtailed. In fact, many handicapped children grow up in a social world restricted to their nuclear families and those encountered in the services with which they are in contact. The contraction of social networks which is a general experience in old age is the much earlier experience of their parents, with the result that the children never develop a wide extended network of human social resources upon which they may draw in later life. This is also the experience of those who become disabled as both Mrs King and Mrs Chalmers record. They knew nothing about available gadgets and only managed to achieve minor home modifications. It took all their time to keep their home and themselves going. Mr King's friends dropped away and Mrs Chalmers, by contrast, surrendered her role of wife and mother to her husband's parents and the staff that they were in the unusual position of being able to afford. Their own activities effectively ceased when one became the provider and the other almost totally dependent on others. The relevance of readings in Part Two is again apparent and the sort of good neighbour scheme discussed in Part 9 seems relevant to this situation. A set of case-studies of disabled housewives has recently been carried out on Merseyside by Earnshaw (1973) which includes a useful explanation of some common disabilities and their effects. Divergent views of the situation and role of families in modern urban industrial families when faced with domestic crises such as sickness, are provided by Parsons and Fox (1952) and Bott (1971), who may usefully be referred to by those interested in a more general sociological analysis.

REFERENCES

BATESON, G., JACKSON, D. D., HALEY, J. and WEAKLAND, J. H. (1956) 'Towards a theory of schizophrenia' reprinted in BATESON, G. (1973) *Steps to an Ecology of Mind, Collected essays in Anthropology, Psychiatry, Evolution and Epistemology*, London, Paladin pp. 173—98.

BAYLEY, M. J. (1973) *Mental Handicap and Community Care: A study of mentally handicapped people in Sheffield*, London, Routledge and Kegan Paul.

BOTT, E. (1971) 'Family and Crisis' in Sutherland, J. D. (ed) *Towards Community Mental Health*, London, Tavistock Publications, Chapter 2, pp. 17—30.

EARNSHAW, I. (1973) *Disabled Housewives on Merseyside: fourteen case studies*, London, Disablement Income Group Charitable Trust.

HEWETT, S. (1970) *The Family and the Handicapped Child*, London, George Allen and Unwin.

PARSONS, T. and FOX, R. (1952) 'Illness, therapy and the modern urban American family' *Journal of Social Issues* 8, 4, pp. 31—44.

TIZARD, J. and GRAD, J. (1961) *The Mentally Handicapped and their Families*, London, Oxford University Press.

13. The feelings and behaviour of parents of handicapped children *

RONALD MACKEITH
Paediatrician, Guy's Hospital, London and
Editor of *Developmental Medicine and Child Neurology.*

The behaviour of parents of handicapped children derives from many factors. These include cultural and social-class attitudes to children in general, to handicapped people and to teachers, social workers and to doctors and medical care in general. But to a major degree, their behaviour derives from their feelings about having a handicapped child.

Whatever the handicap, the reactions of parents to all the varieties of handicapped children have much that is similar.

The reactions will be influenced by whether the handicap is evident at birth or becomes evident later, after the parents have 'fallen in love' with the child. They will be influenced by whether there is a prospect of severe mental handicap or not. They will be influenced by whether the handicap is obvious to other people, and by the attitudes of other people — including lay people, teachers, social workers and doctors — to handicap and to handicapped people.

Parents' feelings
What may be the reaction of parents who find their child is handicapped? What will the feelings (and hence the behaviour) of a couple who find themselves in what may be called a 'classical' or typical situation? Consider the reactions of a young couple who have as their first child one

*From *Developmental Medicine and Child Neurology* (1973) *15*, pp. 524—7

with Down's syndrome or spina bifida — handicaps which are evident at birth. They have not yet 'fallen in love' in a way that means the child is part of them whatever happens to him. Their feelings will be mixed ones.

1. Two biological reactions: protection of the helpless; revulsion at the abnormal.

2. Two feelings of inadequacy: inadequacy at reproduction; inadequacy at rearing.

3. Three feelings of bereavement: at the loss of the normal child they expected, with almost infinite potentialities: (a) anger; (b) grief; and (c) adjustment, which takes time.

4. Feeling of shock.

5. Feeling of guilt, which is probably less common than many writers state.

6. Feeling of embarrassment, which is a social reaction to what the parents think other people are feeling.

Parents' behaviour
1(a) The biological reaction of protectiveness towards the helpless infant will tend to produce 'maternal' behaviour in both the mother and the father: (i) frequently there is warm normal care: or (ii) there may be highly protective care. Labelling highly protective care as over-protection is not an observation but a judgement and should involve the mother's need to behave in this way and the child's need to be highly protected.

(b) The biological reaction of revulsion at the abnormal is a normal reaction, even if in our

127

culture it is frowned upon. It will produce rejection of the child. Rejection may show itself as: (i) cold rejection; (ii) rationalised rejection, the parents suggesting that the child should be 'in a home with specially trained people to care for him'; (iii) dutiful caring without warmth; or (iv) lavish care from over-compensation of the feeling of rejection.

2(a) Feelings of inadequacy at reproduction can strike deep at a person's self-respect and may produce depression.

(b) Feelings of inadequacy at rearing can produce lack of confidence and hence inconsistency of rearing.

3(a) The anger of bereavement may cause aggressive behaviour towards those who are trying to help the parents.

(b) The grief may cause depression.

(c) The adjustment may come fairly quickly and though often stable is not always so in face of problems that arise later.

4. The sense of shock may cause disbelief and a succession of consultations at other clinics in the search for better news.

5. Guilt is frequently written about but it is not felt by all parents. It is a complex feeling with undertones, for example of punishment. It can produce depression.

6. Embarrassment can lead to withdrawal from social contacts and consequent social isolation.

The feelings and behaviour of professional advisers
Nurses, social workers, teachers, therapists and doctors faced with a handicapped person are often disturbed, as are most adults. As with parents, their behaviour will be influenced by their feelings. Social workers and doctors can feel revulsion at the abnormal and, having these feelings, show them in recommending the parents to put the child away into a home when this is not what the parents would choose. The family's advisers may be over-solicitous about the child and forget the needs of the rest of the family.

Doctors may reveal their own feelings of inadequacy at caring for the child by brusque dismissal of the child and parents. Doctors may also reveal their sense of inadequacy by objecting to the parents 'shopping around' for a further opinion. A doctor who feels he is reasonably competent and who has given adequate attention and time to the parents may regret that he has

failed to meet their needs, but he will understand why they feel they must ask for a further opinion. He may wonder where he failed them, but he will convey his understanding of their desire and will help them to see another physician. He will also convey very clearly that he is willing to accept them back again at any time.

Should the child go away from home?
Sometimes parents ask for this when they first know — at the birth of the child — that he is lastingly handicapped. It seems best to convey that there is no urgency to make a permanent decision. They may leave the child in hospital and later take him home, or they may take him home earlier with the knowledge that the physician will re-admit the child to hospital at any time.

Later on, the decision will depend on three principles which are presented to the parents.

(a) In our culture, most people live with their families and do better if they do so.

(b) People go away from home if thereby they are able to get treatment and education which are better — and sufficiently better to outweigh the disadvantages of being away from home.

(c) People go away from home if other people in the family are suffering from their continued presence.

These general principles can be conveyed over the years, long before any decision is urgently needed.

Crisis periods during the growth of the handicapped child
Crisis periods are important to know about, for the professional adviser can himself be prepared to act to diminish the difficulties of parents at these times. Furthermore, at the times of crisis, parents are often more open to receiving helpful guidance.

1. When parents first learn about or suspect handicap in their child. Until their anxieties are (to some extent) dealt with by full assessment and explanation, their child is 'not a person but a question mark'. This is a doctor's job.

2. When, at about age five, a decision has to be reached as to whether the child will be able to go to ordinary school, which would be a 'certificate' that he is more or less normal. This decision is reached by psychologists, educationalists and doctors in collaboration.

3. When the handicapped person comes to the

time of leaving school: both the parents and the handicapped person realise that cure is never going to happen and they wonder whether he or she will be independent and able to work, while the handicapped person wonders whether he or she will be able to meet girls or boys, make love and marry. Some of the explanation will fall on the employment services, some on social workers and some on doctors.

4. When the parents become older and are unable to care for their handicapped child. Parents will look ahead anxiously and they deserve to be reminded that there are statutory services which will give help.

Support for the parents

Support for the parents is one of the major needs that therapists, teachers, social workers and doctors have to provide. Perhaps the support given in the earliest days and months is of crucial importance for long-term acceptance by the parents. Their questions must be answered but they will also be greatly helped if they are shown how they themselves can be helping their child every day to move towards achieving his full potential.

For the community, there are economic benefits to be gained from giving full support and help to the parents but, more important, this is a compassionate and necessary part of the care of the handicapped person and his family.

14. Handicapped pre-school children and their families: effects on child's early emotional development [*]

ARNON BENTOVIM
Physician, Department of Psychological Medicine,
Hospital for Sick Children, Great Ormond Street, London.

As well as the known responses of the infant to the amount of warmth, empathy, efficiency, and control shown by the mother,[1] attention must be given to the quality of response from the child. The degree of activity, passivity, positive versus negative mood, ease of stimulation against difficulty of arousal, regularity versus irregularity, considerably affects the mother's response.[2] Problems which children have with particular handicaps may well in their turn specifically affect aspects of their development and their parent's attitude towards them.

Handicap and response

Though the blind child smiles at six weeks he does so less frequently and in response to touch rather than sight.[3] He cannot reach out and use his hand to locate objects, but has to wait to be touched by them. So that understanding of the world and particularly the definition of the self from the other cannot be reached through normal integration of sensations coming from hand, eye, and mouth.[4] Such difficulties mean that the blind child may prefer to rely on body stimulation and movement for pleasure — rocking, twisting, thumb sucking — rather than through the manipulation of objects, essential to the sort of play which leads to adaptation, control, symbolization, and learning about the world. The unknown is dangerous. The familiar provides reassurance for any child deprived of information about his environment — whether he is blind, deaf, autistic, or has cerebral palsy, spina bifida with difficulties in manipulating, moving and exploring, or is retarded with little interest or drive to explore.

For all these children a predictable routine of feeding and pleasure in body stimulation and body care by the mother may be more comforting and rewarding than the precariously controllable challenge of new situations. Such a routine may well be clung to in an obsessionally rigid manner and is found to be an important aspect of the emotional development of blind and sensorily deprived children. As a result there may be strong resistance to the move from being fed to self feeding, use of the pot instead of napkins. Being left in a play group may result in clinging, and overdependence with restricted social contact with other adults and children. Instead of meeting the mother's failures of adaptation with powerful forward moves the drive may be directed towards a struggle for control, sameness, and fixation to immature patterns of functioning.

Such rigid patterns can be altered by the appropriate intervention and stimulation (Wills 1970), but the parent who expects cues from the child about his readiness for the next step may become confused, discouraged, and anxious and may give up trying.

A similar situation may arise if unresolved parental feelings of hostility or fears of having caused the damage lead to overprotective attitudes, and attempts to prevent further harm. Too much care or 'too-perfect' adaptation to the child's needs mean that failure is not provided and the child is over-controlled, becomes over-dependent

[*]From *British Medical Journal* (1972) *3*, pp. 634–7

and infantile, and unable to respond to the stress inherent in development.

Effects on formation of early relationships

Paradoxically the achievement of a satisfactory degree of independence depends on the quality of the primary attachment between mother and child, and out of this comes a secure sense of identity and confidence in the world outside. During primary attachment a complete picture is built up of the mother in the infant's mind and he has to become aware of her many different aspects. She is experienced as a combination of the sight, sound, voice, warmth, smell, the feel of her skin, hair, mouth, lips. As a source of comfort at one time and of frustration at another, she is seen as two people at first, but later, through the growth of transitional phenomena and memory, as a whole person. Mothers can normally help their children through the anxiety and panic of this process. Nevertheless, if she is preoccupied, depressed, and grieving she may be experienced as a predominantly frustrating, uncomforting figure and the child may turn away from her — not feeding, failing to thrive, crying, not sleeping, or may turn to himself, with rocking and self stimulation.

For the child with some sensory component missing — for example, sight — there may be no relief from mother's angry word by the sight of her smile afterwards. Thus blind children do not maintain the idea of their parents as a constant object in their minds until a later period than normal (Wills 1970). This means that with their need for sameness and security the blind child may inhibit the normal show of assertiveness or aggressiveness for fear of provoking a frightening, punitive idea of his mother or father. The result may be a conforming, over-good child who is passive and lacking in maturity with negative feelings underground.

Although the deaf child[5] has vision intact, he may fail to develop the ability to communicate verbally. Ample reasons can arise for parents to feel frustrated and discouraged and for the child deprived of the transitional phenomena of sound, names, tunes, and stories to feel insecure. Children with similar language problems — whether from deafness, developmental language problems, autism, or severe deprivation — are handicapped in these respects, and in their later educational potential which is tied to verbal skills.

RESULTS OF FAILURE

The failure to integrate and comprehend verbally means that frustration may be poorly tolerated. Instead of the 'conforming' response of the blind child, there may be an explosive reaction. With the restriction of comforting communication, fantasy, and memory, an attempt is made to get rid of the source of frustration. Normal failures of adaptation are greeted with rage and tantrums; the birth of a sibling, changes of routine, admission to hospital, or separation (with the absence of mother) may be overwhelming and incomprehensible and lead to violent outbursts. In his egocentric view of himself there may be long-standing resentment at the relationship the parents have together or with a sibling. He may find sharing difficult and try to control the family. Socialization, toilet training may become a battleground. Attacks may be directed against the self, biting and scratching.

Similar problems may be seen in the brain-damaged or epileptic child, who has poor impulse control in response to frustration. If such difficulties are combined with overactivity and short attention span parents may find their child particularly hard to cope with, and may provoke considerable strain and hostility. A vicious circle can result with problems spiralling. There is a danger of such hostility and negativeness becoming the main language for communication. The rejected child who fails to get his needs met normally, may use similar mechanisms — a smack being as good as a hug in meeting his needs for recognition. The pre-school handicapped child in hospital without his mother has similar feelings. Stay in hospital and post-hospitalization responses of protest, despair, withdrawal, and apathy (with regression in socialization, clinging, fears, and distress) should be well enough known to be prevented by adequate visiting, rooms for mothers and child-centred nursing.

The severely handicapped child

The multiple handicapped child may have a combination of such problems. The child with rubella who is both deaf and blind may have such problems in synthesis and comprehension of the world that he fails to make a primary attachment to one person. A state resembling autism may develop with self-isolation, bizarre stereotyped behaviour, and self-stimulation and aloofness. Any severe impairment in communication together with severe enviromental deprivation — material or emotional — may result in a similar 'autistic' state.

The moderately or severely retarded child may present with several problems. These children and their parents appear to evoke a much less sympathetic response from the community than the physically handicapped. There may be greater tendencies to become frustrated and rejecting at the slow pace of development, with patterns emerging as described above. What may start as a difficulty — for example, gaining bowel and bladder control — can become a battleground. Alternatively, there may be a tendency to deny the slowness of development, as it may unfold relatively normally in sequence, problems then arising of acceptance of differences as school age approaches. Severely handicapped children are far more likely to be found among those placed in long-term residential institutions.

Emotional problems of the older pre-school child

The tasks to be accomplished by the older child are in the areas of sex definition and role in the community at large. There is the problem of finding an appropriate sexual identity. Long-standing contact with mother involving close body-care over a prolonged period may mean that the boy may tend to adopt a feminine role rather than an assertive masculine one. The rigid, passive attitude also favours a feminine identification. Frequent surgical or medical procedures — or the use of appliances, calipers, urinary bags — may also provoke feelings of being damaged or multilated and this too may emphasize feelings of being different. The girl may feel she will never be a mother and the boy never a father.

Attitudes to hospital may play an important part in general adjustment. On the one hand, there may be excess attachment to a nursing sister seen as the real mother, while the true one is rejected. On the other, there may be excess phobic anxiety when any hospital contact is necessary — with night-mares, clinging, and misery following each visit.

In making contact with other children the handicapped child may use his appliance or special diet to gain prestige, but he may meet rejection, fear, and disgust, and not find acceptance. Where physical excellence and skills are a sign of status the handicapped child feels a failure. He may talk a great deal about aggression, without entering the rough and tumble. He may instead focus on his body and its short-comings, and feel ugly, useless, and in need of care from his mother instead of facing competition from his father and the other children.

HANDICAPPED CHILD AND FAMILY FUNCTIONING

With increasing emphasis on the 'therapeutic' skills of the parent in helping their handicapped child, it may well be asked whether there is a risk from such intense involvement, from the prolonged period of primary maternal preoccupation. The rewards can be considerable for the mother who helps her partially hearing or deaf child to speak, her visually handicapped child to gain confidence in his world, the child with cerebral palsy to move sufficiently to gain concepts of space and size, or the mentally handicapped child to reach simple skills and self-help. With the aid of voluntary societies parents often become expert concerning their child and his special problems, and may even rival his medical advisers in the community. There may be an unwitting response and a danger of breakdown of communications.

Some parents have such an intimate knowledge of their child that they develop a special mutual non-verbal communication. Strangers are not felt to possess this ability and the parent may not wish to entrust his child to them. In this 'too perfect' adaptation or 'too-good mothering' there is a failure to appreciate that some degree of frustration is essential for a child to feel it necessary to communicate through speech, and to extend his social contact. Overprotection, overinvolvement, and overdependency may all occur. In some families the mother may well be aware of such a danger, but then finds her attempts to encourage independence undermined, and labelled cruel by her own mother who cannot allow herself to be as demanding. Instead of support and help in being firm, they condone making up for the child's impairment by spoiling.

FAMILY STRESS

Preoccupation with a handicapped child may well come to exclude, or be felt as excluding, the other parent or sibling, and stress in a marriage or a family may be very greatly increased. Professional help should be aimed at helping the child gain sufficient independence to relieve the family's strain. Special baby-sitting arrangements, nurseries, or day-care relieve the pressure. Periods away from the family may appear an attractive solution. But the families' guilt felt at the fulfilment of hidden rejecting wishes may result in unpredictable somatic and psychiatric symptoms — particularly depression — and there can be permanent rejection. Coping with separation for an immature child may result in severe problems when reunited with the family; increasing clinging, tantrums and regression in social skills.

Schaffer[6] has described the 'too cohesive family,' where not only the mother's life but also the father's and siblings becomes excessively centred on the handicapped child, to the detriment of the emotional growth and functioning of the family unit. This appears to be a way of avoiding damaging conflict and tension. It is possible for the normal sibling to become deprived as so much attention is given to the handicapped child. The normal child may respond with aggressive, attention-seeking behaviour. The birth of a handicapped child can become a factor in the distortion of the general family relationships. There may be a diversion of feelings and scapegoating of the normal sibling, who can be rejected where the handicapped child cannot. Consequently he may feel it was his fault, expect punishment, provoke it, or become anxious or depressed.

GENETIC COUNSELLING

Frequently parents limit the size of their family after the birth of a handicapped child, not always on realistic grounds. The importance of genetic counselling to clarify such problems may require several consultations and 'working through' particularly if there is a high genetic loading — for example, phenylketonuria or haemophilia. Marital and family tensions can develop in looking for the blame. Where the family 'mourning' is resolved by defining the handicapped child as needing indulgence, a sibling may be encouraged not to hit back, if attacked inappropriately.

All this may convince the handicapped child that he is always right, maintain his ideas of omnipotence and egocentricity and prevent the development of an empathic appreciation for the feelings and needs of others. Frustration is reacted to with justified aggressive outburst. Alternately with the urge to make sense of his own state of existence, his pain, discomfort, clumsiness, stiffness, or failure to comprehend or to be understood, he may attribute his difficulties to actions of parents and other children in the family or to his own 'badness.' This may lead to a variety of symptoms — aggressiveness, fears, and obsessionality.

Intervention in emotional problems

With the vulnerability of the pre-school handicapped child, above all, prevention is more important than cure. He should remain with his parents rather than be separated for specific educational help at 2 years. For a child without parents the substitution of a foster home or family group home is preferable to an institutional placement. Separation for medical intervention should be reduced to the minimum and parents should accompany their children whenever possible. Facilities have to be made available not only for the child with a specific handicap but also to help the family to participate in the process of treatment and to prevent the emotional problems which can arise with greater frequency among these children.[7] To achieve this a professional team is necessary and in the first place the paediatric clinic and the district assessment centre should fulfil the task. At a later date the community of general practitioner, welfare clinic, social services, and voluntary society has to provide the containing functions.

PRESENTATIONS

Emotional problems may present in several different ways. They may be noted by the teacher of the deaf, or the blind, the speech therapist, or physiotherapist — who comes across unexpected delays in learning or may be aware of mother's inability to co-operate in the therapeutic work with the child, or of tension between them. The family doctor, paediatrician or infant welfare clinic, or medical social worker may be presented with a child's management problem or come across the problem secondarily for psychiatric symptoms in the parent or another child, or in evaluating marital discord.

The health visitor or local authority social worker concerned with families at risk may note the quality of the relationship as it develops between child and mother and also be faced with problems within them or in the family. They may also be faced by requests to find a residential placement for a child who is rejected.

Each of these groups need to be aware of the nature of the child's and family's potential range of response so that appropriate treatment can be carried out. The 'crisis intervention' model of help[8] seems of particular value here, as complaint frequently arises when coping methods previously devised by the parent, child, and family to deal with the problems are breaking down. An opportunity then arises to ventilate feelings which have been unresolved over a long time and have them understood in an empathic, non-critical accepting way. More healthy coping methods may then become possible. In some families rejecting, hostile feelings towards the child are often most feared and difficult to admit to, but if faced and coped with can produce most relief. In contrast for the rejecting parent the loving affectionate feelings are often the hardest to find, as they confuse the initial request of wanting a child out of the family.

The value of seeing *both* parents when a crisis arises is often not recognized, and in some families seeing the unaffected siblings or grandparents may reveal unexpected sources of problems or of strength. In this way it is possible to clarify confusion and distortions which can affect the whole family functioning and well-being. One member — a mother, the child, or sibling — may be found to be carrying the grief and distress for the whole family, which if shared can be less of a burden.

INTERPROFESSIONAL CO-OPERATION

The group of professional workers involved with the family may also find additional strength in meeting to consider the family's needs and by co-operating rather than allowing themselves to be split and divided by the family or their professional roles. The regular clinic with a number of mothers attending can provide an informal 'extended' family for certain mothers and children. This mutual support has extended to the growth of voluntary societies — whether for autism, cystic fibrosis, mentally handicapped, spastics, spina bifida, rubella, blindness, deafness. Such organizations can help channel the powerful feelings aroused in the families to constructive reparative ends, whether through facilities provided or re-

search supported, meeting the needs to do something. There is a risk that in finding such an expression for grief and mourning, certain less obvious personal aspects of reactions may be avoided.

PRE-SCHOOL FACILITIES

So far as the children are concerned the provision of adaquate pre-school facilities is vital in prevention and dealing with difficulties as they arise. The pre-school play group principle, with the mother participating *alongside* staff, is a useful concept, and there may be a case for the mixing of normal and handicapped children at this young age. In the day centre for pre-school children attached to the Department of Psychological Medicine at the Hospital for Sick Children it has been found preferable to mix intellectually handicapped together with non-handicapped children with severe emotional problems. As well as the informal support gained from the communal staff-parent-child play-activity groups, individual or group casework or therapy with particular mothers and children is possible. Behaviour modification techniques can be used to control unwanted behaviour and encourage specific skills. Group work with the parents can be conducted — parents confronting and being confronted with both the impact of the child on themselves, and the effect of their attitudes on their children's behaviour — while individual therapy can help children or parents to understand their feelings or reactions.

Parents' groups[9] are being conducted in several centres with a variety of problems, and this may be a method of giving support and understanding when current and future crises occur before they become intense.

Finally, drugs may be needed for the brain-damaged over-active impulsive child. As the child approaches school age the parent may have to face the necessity for special education. They once more become aware of the discrepancy between their expectations and reality. With adequate pre-school educational provisions, and satisfactory solutions of earlier crises it should be possible for the transition to be less painful. Physical or mental impairment should not handicap the future emotional adjustment and development of the child.

REFERENCES

1. Brody, S., 1965. *Patterns of Mothering*. London, Bailey and Swinfen.
2. Thomas, A., Chess, S., Birch, H. G., 1968. *Temperament and Behaviour Disorders in Children*, New York, University Press.
3. Freedman, D. G., 1964. *Journal of Child Psychology and Psychiatry*, **5** p. 171.
4. Wills, D. M., 1970. in *Psychoanalytic Study of the Child*, Vol. XXV, London, Hogarth Press.
5. Dinnage, R., 1970 and 1972. *The Handicapped Child — Research Review*, Vol. I & II, London, Longman and the National Bureau of Co-operation in Child Care.
6. Schaffer, H. R., 1964. *International Journal of Social Psychiatry*, **10** p. 266.
7. Rutter, M., Tizard, J., Whitmore, K., 1970. *Education, Health and Behaviour*, London, Longman.
8. Parad, H. J., 1965. *Christ Intervention: Selected Readings*, New York, Family Service Association of America.
9. Parfit, J., 1971. *Spotlight on Group Work with Parents in Special Circumstances*, London, National Children's Bureau.
10. Caplan, G., 1963. *Prevention of Mental Disorders in Children*, London, Tavistock Publications.

15. The myth of parental attitudes *

A. I. ROITH
Consultant Psychiatrist,
Monyhull Hospital, Birmingham

It is a truism that the tragedy of a mentally subnormal child is always greater for the parents than for the child. In view of this it is rather surprising that, although there has been an abundance of material reported in the literature discussing the mentally subnormal child as an individual, comparatively little has been written concerning the parental attitude towards such a child. This applies particularly so to this country. Furthermore, much of what has been published is purely anecdotal in character or else based on mere impressions. And when one reads articles which purport to describe the feelings and reactions which parents of subnormal children have towards their offspring, one is immediately struck by the frequent occurrence of such emotionally charged words as guilt, shame, hostility, and remorse. So that it is hardly surprising that right at the outset one gets a completely biased and prejudiced impression of these parents and can hardly help being put on the defensive with regard to them.

And I must confess that this was the idea which I had when I first began working in the field of Subnormality and commenced interviewing relatives. I sat back and waited for the horde of guilty and aggressive parents to descend upon me. But now, after eight long years, I am still waiting for them . . .

Actually I have found the vast majority of the parents to be as normal as the parents of ordinary children. Although, as you know, there are some most peculiar parents of ordinary children going

around! However, granted a few of the parents were abnormal in one way or another, but most of them were able to discuss their children in a sane and sensible fashion.

What I think must have happened for this false idea to get abroad is that the authors of these articles have allowed these few parents to give them a misleading view of parents of subnormal children in general. They appear to have forgotten that you have to be very sure of your facts before making any sort of generalisation. Also it is generally accepted that traditional statements tend to get copied and repeated from one article and textbook to another, so that in this way false ideas are perpetuated and it is very difficult to stop this, once the ball starts rolling. Indeed it is the old story of giving a dog a bad name, except unfortunately the 'dog' in this case happens to be the poor parents.

The best way to bring out the woolly thinking and false reasoning in this matter is to go into the question of guilt. Why should the parents feel guilty? Some authorities allege that this sense of guilt is chiefly based on lack of knowledge of the possible causes of subnormality. It is maintained that the parents believe that subnormality is entirely caused by heredity and so the child must have inherited the condition from them and so they think they are to blame.

On the other hand other authorities claim that if the parents knew the condition was caused by heredity they would not feel guilty because, of course, there was absolutely nothing they could have done about it. But they state that these guilt feelings develop because the parents believe that some *external* factor, such as their drinking or

*Extract from *Journal of Mental Subnormality* (1963) 9, pp. 51–4.

write to the doctor asking for reports on their

Yet again there are writers who assert that the parents feel guilty due to their *love* for the child. But this is a guilty love because they feel, deep down, that is not they, but an evil spirit that has been working on them.

However, the exact opposite happens according to other writers. For these claim that the parents feel intense guilt not because they love their child, but because they have an impulse to *reject* it. In view of all this one could hardly be blamed for thinking that the cause of the guilt depends on which author you are reading!

At this point I thought it would be worthwhile to discover what the current thinking was with regard to this particular problem. So I attended as many meetings as possible at which Subnormality was discussed and whenever the speaker mentioned that the parents of subnormal children felt guilty, I noted down his reason for saying this. I was amazed to find that no matter what the parents did, it was construed to indicate that they had guilt feelings. For example the speaker at one meeting discussed the case of parents who write letters of complaint to their child's hospital or gambling habits, is responsible for the condition. child's condition. Here he said that they were doing this because they felt guilty and were attempting to project their guilt on to the doctor or hospital authorities. But at another meeting it was stated that those parents who never or hardly ever write to the hospital were also feeling guilty and were trying to repress these feelings by 'forgetting' about their child. Similarly if parents frequently visit their child in hospital it has been alleged that this was because they had a sense of guilt and that they were trying to overcompensate of make up for this. Whereas if parents only rarely visited their child why, once again I have heard it affirmed that this shows that the parents are guilty and are trying to hide their guilt by neglecting to see it and so they hope, put it out of their mind.

Finally, I have heard one psychiatrist state that if parents place their child in a hospital they will feel guilty because unconsciously this means that they are trying to get rid of him. Whereas another psychiatrist has maintained that if parents keep their child at home they will have guilt feelings because they are depriving it of the best medical and nursing care! [. . .]

16. The stress of having a subnormal child *

NATIONAL SOCIETY FOR MENTALLY HANDICAPPED CHILDREN

I Introduction

In post-war Britain it comes as a shock to parents to find themselves in a situation that is not fully covered by the welfare state. As long as the society in which we live accepts the [subnormal] child in principle but not sufficiently in fact, the problems of acceptance are made harder than they need be for the parents and for the child. It is not easy to accept a situation unless society itself also accepts it. Many public bodies appear to show antipathy rather than acceptance of subnormality. Rate-payers' associations protest against hostels for the subnormal in their district; adoption societies usually refuse a child to a family where there is already a subnormal child, even though it may be an adopted child; immigration officials reject a family with a subnormal child. The large isolated institution some distance from the parents' home is still the common pattern of residential care. It perpetuates conditions designed for custodial provision and to protect a society from a problem it was not yet particularly willing or interested to learn much about. There is still insufficient provision for the further training or employment of the subnormal adult; for hostel accommodation for subnormal adults unable to live with their own families, and for special care for those too grossly handicapped to benefit from the Junior Training Centre.

Much has been and is being done to improve and extend facilities for the severely subnormal, but society does not yet provide all necessary services for the SSN child and his parents as it does for the normal child and for the physically ill. Parents often complain that the degree of attention and quality of service given to their mentally handicapped child for other ailments or handicaps is markedly inferior to that given their normal children. It is against this background that the process of acceptance by the family must take place.

SOCIAL AND EMOTIONAL STRESS

There are certain types of social pressure which may seriously affect the psychological and emotional wellbeing of the family. They enter into the situation immediately subnormality is recognised.

Parents may learn of their child's handicap within a few days of his birth, at some time during the first year or in some cases not until the child reaches school age. It is not always possible for a precise diagnosis and prognosis to be given at this time. Indeed it is rare for this to be done when the parents are first informed.

A mongol baby can be recognised at birth and a diagnosis may be given before the parents have yet established their own personal relationship with the child. Many other cases do not receive specialist attention until the mother complains that her child is not making adequate developmental progress. Yet others are not diagnosed until school age when a teacher notices that the child seems unable to benefit in the normal school environment.

Knowledge of their child's disability may come as a bewildering surprise to the parents, or it may come after many frustrating attempts to interest their doctor in their suspicion that the child's

*From National Society for Mentally Handicapped Children (1967) *Stress*, London, part 2, pp. 5—18.

slowness grossly exceeds the margin of normal variations. It may come as forbidding information about a new baby whose 'normality' they have not yet had time to experience or belatedly as unbelievable information about an older child whose intelligence they have accustomed themselves to regard as normal, in spite of significant failure in the development of language and other skills.

From the very first moment that subnormality is recognised the parents are exposed to other people's attitudes to it, not only their friends' and relatives' attitudes, but also the doctors' and nurses'. At a time when they are extremely vulnerable to suggestion they are surrounded by a great deal of ill-informed and conflicting advice. In addition they may well themselves previously have shared the general association of subnormality with stigma.

Although much has been said and written about the harm that can be done if the parents' feelings are not sympathetically understood – it is still not unusual for parents to be told of their child's handicap in a manner which intensifies their natural distress and leaves them shocked, alienated and misinformed. [. . .]

> One doctor told a mother 'mongols make nice pets about the house', another told a mother to 'put her away and forget you ever had her'. Yet another told the father of a two month old mongol boy that 'his mind will not develop beyond that of an 18 month old baby' and the father killed the child.

STRESS IN PARENTAL REACTIONS

In order to protect themselves parents frequently withdraw from social life – from the comments, gratuitous advice, criticisms and the reactions of others, that intensify their feelings of isolation and shock and disappointment. Consequently they may also withdraw from those social services which are specially provided for children and are a constant reminder of their child's difference from others. Though the baby has not changed, his mother may no longer want to meet the other mothers at the ordinary Welfare Clinic and hear them talking of their normal children's progress.

Finding it difficult to share their experiences as parents with other people and deprived of normal social contacts, father and mother may find that the problem of subnormality dominates their emotional lives, unless they are helped at this time. It is more frequently a situation in which their own attitudes are likely to become entrenched than one which time heals. The first shock may after much time recede, but the attitudes formed then, may persist indefinitely.

One result of the way in which parents were informed is instantaneous rejection of the child. Another common attitude is rejection of the doctor who gives them the bad news.

> One mother of a mongol girl who had been advised by eight doctors she consulted to 'put the child away' persisted until she found a doctor who encouraged her to care for her normally. In her experience the eight doctors themselves rejected the child and that the ninth accepted her, gave the mother the support she needed.

Shattered hopes and feelings of humiliation make the parents extremely vulnerable to the doctor's manner. He lacks understanding of their feelings if he gives his diagnosis and tells them to get on with their job as parents and they feel without support.

A third attitude is a feeling of guilt – which may be projected as blame on to one or other of the marriage partners, or take the form of self-accusation.

Another attitude, which is quite common, is a pathological over-attachment to the child which Ounsted described as 'hyperpaedophilia'. Normal affection develops into a pathologically and grossly exaggerated devotion and over-protectiveness which subjugates the life and needs of other members of the family to the needs of the handicapped child. Holt (1975) describes two mothers having their normal children adopted in order to give their whole time to the defective child.

> In one family where the parents refused the offer of residential care for the severely handicapped child and were thus unable to care for their normal child properly, the mother worked a night shift while her husband minded the SSN child in order to pay for residential care for their normal child.

When subnormality is diagnosed only when the child is older, parents may refuse to accept that the child is handicapped.

One mother of a 17 year old SSN girl enquired about nursing training for her daughter. She described the girl's interest in nursing and talked about how well she was doing at 'school'. Not until it was discovered that 'school' was a training centre did she admit that her daughter could neither read nor write.

Parents frequently begin by saying 'my child is not mentally handicapped but . . .' as a preliminary to discussing the placement in education or in employment of a severely subnormal son or daughter.

In considering the essential experience of parents with mentally handicapped children we discussed whether there were any emotional reactions which were characteristic of this situation, unconditioned by social attitudes and expectations. It is possible that ethological studies might throw some light on a mother's instinctual reaction to her defective child.

It is notoriously unwise to generalise naïvely from the behaviour of lower animals to that of humans, since the higher the phylogenetic development of a species, the more complex and plastic are all aspects of its behaviour. However, some aspects of human activity can usefully be viewed from the ethological standpoint. We were particularly interested in work such as that of Prechtl (1958) and Lorenz (1940) suggesting that certain behavioural patterns in the infant are pre-requisites to a mothering response in human mothers. Bowlby (1958) suggests that human maternal behaviour is elicited by five instinctive responses on the part of the baby — crying, smiling, following, clinging and sucking. Other workers maintain that these responses must occur within certain critical periods for the mother's instinctual reactions to be aroused.

Since mentally defective babies are usually late in manifesting the essential responses it may be suggested that their mothers miss developing the instinctual reaction during the 'critical period'. These mechanisms have been shown to apply to animals. If they are involved in the establishment of 'appropriate' responses by mothers towards infants, incorrect nursing stimuli or disturbances in sequence may result in the mother failing to respond or doing so abnormally.

It may be therefore that the human mother whose baby does not present her with appropriate stimuli will fail to experience a normal development of maternal reactions at the instinctual level. She may express these reactions as a result of previous learning and cultural expectations, but in doing so may be dissociating between learned intellectualisation and full emotional involvement. In such a case tensions would be predicted and her subsequent behaviour may be interpreted in terms of 'defence mechanisms' aimed at reducing tension. She may, in fact, reject the child; she may, on the other hand, become over-solicitous.

These considerations are, of course, highly speculative. We include them because we think that it is necessary to study the emotional problems of parents at the instinctual as well as the socio-cultural level. Other severe handicaps may cause the parents similar social problems yet it is often felt by parents that there is a type of emotional stress peculiar to the presence of mental deficiency different from that associated with the other physical handicaps.

LACK OF ADVICE

While they may be given help and guidance when they are told of their child's handicap it is by no means uncommon for parents to be informed of his defect and then left to care for the child at home with no specialised help or advice during the pre-school years.

However much time and thought the specialist gives to the parents when he informs them of the diagnosis it will fall short of the time required for them to assimilate the diagnosis, ventilate their own conflicting feelings and anxieties and ask the things they want to know about what the diagnosis of subnormality is going to mean.

Although any one of the agencies with whom parents are in contact — the general practitioner, the local welfare clinic and health visitor — may give general advice about baby care, and, recognising subnormality, can refer the parents to a specialist, usually for a diagnostic examination, it is naturally extremely rare for any of these people to have practical knowledge of the management of the severely subnormal child in the home, or any specific experience of caring for these children.

While some local authorities are exceptional, it may be said that there is generally a paucity of services in the community for pre-school children. Except for consultation with the specialist who has informed them of the diagnosis, parents whose child's handicap is revealed before school age have no guidance and no means of sharing a problem about which they have no experience. They may be told that nursery training should begin as early as possible for the subnormal child, but day nurseries or play groups are rarely available to him. This dearth of services during the first five years increases stress and isolation at a time when the parents themselves are first going through the process of trying to accept their child's handicap. There is so little external evidence that the community has any interest in the pre-school needs of the handicapped child, that parents who might, with help, have cared for him successfully at home, ask at this early stage for him to be admitted to hospital. At present the parents feel very ill supplied with informed guidance about their management of the child and of their own feelings in relation to him. Apart from one or two notable exceptions where counselling clinics have been set up, nothing comparable to the child guidance service is available to these families.

In the first year or so of life, the mentally handicapped child is more vulnerable to illness than other children. The parents may have to make more demands on their doctor's services than they would with a normal child and they may need him to visit if it is difficult for them to take the child to his surgery. In these first years the parents are acutely sensitive to other people's attitudes. They are withdrawn socially, and their doctor's relationship with them may mitigate or confirm the anxiety and sensitivity they feel about the attitude of society as a whole. The general practitioner is, therefore, in an excellent position to help these parents. Unfortunately few GPs have had the training or experience or, indeed, the time to provide the understanding of their emotional problems and the counselling that is needed. Many consider that mental subnormality is the province of the specialist, and others that it is an irreversible condition and their time and skill could be directed more usefully to other patients.

The committee observed that the effect of this inability to get useful information from the authorities concerned was to increase emotional stress. The availability of information is not only essential for its practical usefulness, it is also an expression of the interest of the authorities in the problem.

II Recommendations
TELLING THE PARENTS
When a child is first found to be handicapped the parents' feelings as parents, the responsibility and love they feel, as well as the disappointment and distress must all be understood. The disaster is a part of their own experience with which they have to live and the physical removal of the child cannot alter this fact. They need to be told in a way which helps them accept the problem sufficiently to provide a basis for taking the child home and giving themselves time to establish a relationship with him and to discover as they go along how he develops. Decisions to be made in the future will be made with more conviction if they are based on considered judgment of the child's needs which can be formed only as his development proceeds.

In a situation so fraught with stress every effort must be made to reduce the strain on the parents, by listening to and answering their questions and giving them all the information they want about the existing services. The specialist concerned should arrange to see both parents and must be prepared to answer their questions and anxieties and arrange that counselling is available to them immediately afterwards. They need the most authoritative opinion available and the pediatrician or the psychiatrist will have the responsibility of telling them the diagnosis and of informing the family doctor and giving him guidance about what he may do to help the parents and about the counselling that has been given or arranged.

Once it is certain that a child is subnormal the following questions (and any others the parents raise) should be discussed. What does 'subnormality' mean and what effect is it likely to have on the child's development? What form of school or training is he likely to need and who provides it? They will want practical advice about how to help him now, in the immediate present, and they will want genetic information. They will need to be told that it is no-one's fault and they will need to discuss any anxieties they may have about future pregnancies and about the effects on siblings.

It is important that time is given to helping the parents understand the child's disability and accept it — otherwise the child himself will not be in a situation that allows for it and will suffer a great deal of confusion at the expense of his own developmental needs.

In practice the diagnosis may not make any difference at all to the immediate treatment of the child, but the doctor who makes it must be able to understand the needs of the parents for whom the diagnosis is always profoundly difficult to assimilate. Unless their questions are answered they cannot be expected to accept a situation in which, in all probability, no special treatment is likely to be advised until the child is of school age. Until that time his development will depend largely on what the parents can contribute to it.

Decisions about the child's future will normally have to wait until his development proceeds sufficiently for judgments to be made about the kind of care and educational help most likely to benefit him. This must be fully explained if the parents are to adjust themselves and their expectations to a reality which was not only completely unforeseen, but which may remain unforeseeable for some time. The specialist who tells the parents, must be able to help them towards a perspective in which they can postpone decisions that may have to be made about the child's care, until the appropriate stage of development is reached. [. . .]

ADVICE ABOUT PROGNOSIS
Parents are frequently misinformed, not only by friends and relatives, but also by doctors. They want to know whether their newborn mongol will ever learn to eat, walk, talk and acquire toilet habits; whether he will ever be able to go to school and what kinds of school or centre are available for him. They want to know what kind of skills he can be expected to have later on and what sort of life he will be able to lead as an adult.

If the doctor who informs the parents of their child's condition has not the experience and knowledge to answer these questions, it is essential that he refer them to someone who has. In many cases of subnormality prognosis may depend on developmental assessment which necessarily is spread over a period of time. During this period the parents may feel completely in the dark. The principle of assessment must be fully explained to them if they are to endure a prolonged period of uncertainty without frustration and anxiety. Not only the child's limitations, but also his assets, must be discussed. It is often not possible to give a

confident prognosis without continuing observation. Illingworth (1962) found that mothers respected sincerity, and were never critical when he made it clear that only further observation could determine the outlook for the child.

GENETIC ADVICE
Parents often need advice about the desirability of having another child and want to know whether the condition is hereditary or is likely to be inherited. They may need information about adoption and about birth control. Adoption cannot be offered as a simple solution in those cases where further pregnancies would be undesirable. At present adoption is not always permitted if a mentally defective child is in the house and he would have to be placed in an institution. This ruling, in our opinion, causes unnecessary hardship to families in a position to offer both the defective child and normal children a satisfactory home.

ADVICE ABOUT THE MANAGEMENT OF THE CHILD
The knowledge that a child is handicapped frequently makes parents over-protective. They may do for him things it is important that he is taught to do for himself. Their natural sense of the discipline a child needs to experience in the home may be inhibited in relation to him and behaviour difficulties due to spoiling can arise. Parents have to be shown how to relate both their training and their understanding of the child to his mental age not to his actual age and encouraged to stimulate his independence and the development of acceptable behaviour in the same way they would naturally use with a normal child of the same *mental* age. They need advice about play activities, and they usually need advice about speech development and about social behaviour. They may also need advice about the adjustment of their other children.

ADVICE ABOUT INSTITUTIONAL CARE
Parents may need to be informed about this, as about all the other services, should it seem probable that a particular child will eventually need residential care. It is important to sense the right time to discuss this possibility and the right time to say nothing about it. It may be necessary

to point out that a baby with no greater disability than mongolism will not have priority of admission to hospital and only time can show whether or not residential care really is what he needs and what his parents want for him.[. . .]

The question of when a child should be placed in an institution is a vital one. It must always be remembered that the affected child often does not benefit from institutional care, though his family may. Placing a defective child into hospital at birth may intensify feelings of guilt and leave the parents uncertain about the correctness of the diagnosis. It is usually better for the parents to try the effect of caring for him at home and make decisions about residential care only if home care fails, or if they find they cannot manage any longer. If the decision does have to be made, everything possible should be done to develop a good relationship between the hospital staff and the parents so that they do not feel their own relationship with him is altered by this decision.

It is helpful for the parents to know that residential care can be provided for short periods, if the mother needs a break or a holiday. She may not require any more relief from the SSN baby than from any other baby, but to know that the burden can be shared should it prove to be necessary, is reassuring to parents confronted with the as yet entirely unfamiliar and frightening responsibility of caring for a subnormal child at home.

ADVICE ABOUT EMOTIONAL REACTIONS TO THE HANDICAPPED CHILD

We do not consider that any of the parental reactions we have described are inevitable consequences of learning that a child is mentally subnormal and we think that most of these adverse reactions — rejection, over-compensation, guilt — can be avoided by helpful counselling at the time that the diagnosis is disclosed and for as long as necessary afterwards.

There may often be very little medical advice to give once a diagnosis has been made and the care of the child will usually proceed unchanged. Sources of advice about baby care already exist in the community services, but the special need of parents when they are first informed of the child's handicap is not met by 'child welfare' in the usual sense. They need help with their own adjustment; they need general information about a hitherto unfamiliar condition; they need an opportunity to discuss the reactions of those around them, and at a later stage they will need sufficient knowledge of child development to relate their understanding and management of the SSN child to his developmental age. There should be a continuing service, to which parents can refer at any time when developments in the family situations make new adjustments necessary.

In this situation, to reassure the parents and tell them 'not to worry' is far less helpful than telling them 'if you are worried don't hesitate to come and talk about it', or referring them immediately where they can get advice. The specialist who makes the diagnosis may not have the time counselling requires, and indeed may not be good at handling the anxieties parents do not always openly express. It is not necessarily his responsibility to counsel, but he should see that counselling is available and that the parents are referred to it.[. . .]

We have not considered it within our brief to describe in any detail the form that the counselling we recommend should take, but we suggest one or two aspects which we think are relevant to most families with mentally handicapped children.

First, we think that parents need help to regard and treat the subnormal child as they would another child. They may easily become over-protective, thereby retarding his development and allowing their subnormal child to dominate family life. They need to steer the same course between encouraging independence and helping that they steer with other children. Like all children, the handicapped child must be acclimatised to a family situation in which he will share attention and love with others. In most families the SSN child is greatly loved and in some he is favoured at the expense of the other children. It is always helpful to the mother to have some person who can discuss the needs of both objectively in order to balance them reasonably in the management of the family as a whole.

Second, the counsellor should always be aware that parents may be blaming themselves or each other for their child's condition. While all aspects of counselling do not require medically qualified people, we think that any discussion of the causes of the condition does so. The doctor should reassure the parents that neither of them is to blame, without waiting for them to express their feelings of guilt. It is important that both parents accept and understand the child's handicap — that they share the problem and give each other support; severe tension can arise if one parent blames the other's mismanagement .for backwardness which arises from the child's disability.

Stress always tends to expose and exaggerate existing conflicts within the individual, between the parents or within the family. This varies in character with the personalities concerned; with the age of the mother; the quality of support husband and wife give each other in the marriage; the social and financial situation in the home and the number of children. Sufficient help must be given at the beginning to lay the foundations for a satisfactory and progressive adaptation to the new problems as they present themselves at different stages of development, because at each stage adaptation in the present will depend upon the adaptations made in the past.

PHYSICAL STRESS
Emphasis on the social and emotional problems of the families of mentally handicapped children should not obscure that they, particularly the mothers, suffer actual physical stress because of the high morbidity of the handicapped child. Obesity and respiratory infections are commoner in handicapped children and dental problems are less easily overcome, though preventative treatment is particularly important. Often the mother is older than average and the physical effort of controlling a difficult, strong child, or of entertaining a bored child may tax her vitality. Physical stress increases for the ageing mother with a totally dependent adult.

Shopping and journeys to and from the clinic with a large but still infantile child can impose a forbidding strain that prevents her using fully specialist services she wants to use. Waiting for attention, which makes a normal child restless, can be an unmanageable ordeal for the mother when the child is handicapped.

All the normal work of housekeeping, washing, cooking, shopping and looking after other children becomes increasingly difficult when the mentally handicapped one needs constant attention. Housing conditions which are normally acceptable can become appallingly difficult if other children have to live in one room with the handicapped child, or if a very disabled child has to be carried up and down many flights of stairs, and the normal problems imposed by poor housing are often vastly increased for these families. In our experience, local housing authorities do not appear to place such problems high on the list of priorities for rehousing. Families often appeal in vain for better housing with ground floor accommodation and where a separate bedroom can be arranged for the handicapped child.

One of the greatest difficulties for parents with severely subnormal children is that they cannot look forward to any relief from the strain apart from placing their child in an institution. Those whose children are most difficult to manage are least likely to be able to have an occasional holiday to renew their strength. In an emergency, the child may have to be taken into an institution for a few weeks. However the effect of this on the delicate child must be considered. Lind and Kirman (1958) have described the high death rate of defective children in the immediate post-admission period and Illingworth (1962) describes being impressed repeatedly by the rapid and severe deterioration undergone by a defective child when placed in an institution for a short time, such as a month, when the parents are away or have some domestic crisis.

FINANCIAL STRESS
While one useful study of the special financial needs and difficulties of families with mentally handicapped children has been made (Tizard and Grad 1961), not nearly enough is known yet about this subject.

A careful comparison between families with handicapped children and those without is needed. Many homes depend on the mother's earnings for amenities over and above the necessities provided by the father's earnings and certainly depend on her vitality, ingenuity and management for the standard of living achieved at any income level. The social life of a family is to a great extent conditioned by its ability to conform or approximate to the social and economic pattern of other families in the same community.

There is no doubt that the family of a handicapped child suffers a serious disadvantage in our competitive community conditioned by rising cost and standards of living. The mother is both more tied and more burdened. Although she has nore need of relaxation and amenities, she is less able to contribute the means by which they can be obtained. She has problems of continual care, of transport and domestic difficulties, that the mother of a normal child does not have.

There is no financial help given to parents to enable them to meet the cost of making the special arrangements that have to be made for the mentally handicapped child if they are to have some freedom of movement themselves. The mother is rarely able to place her mentally handicapped child in a nursery while she gets on with the housework and shopping or if need be does part-time work. Child-minders and baby-sitters are very much harder to find for the mentally handicapped child and it may be much less easy to take him with her when she goes out than it is to take a normal child. Short stay care in emergencies or when a holiday is desirable is available at present only if a mental deficiency hospital bed can be found. The disturbance caused to the child by a short period of hospitalisation makes parents reluctant to take a holiday unless they are in a position to make better arrangements for their child in their absence.[. . .]

We do not assume that it necessarily costs more to keep a mentally handicapped child. The actual maintenance may indeed sometimes cost less than the maintenance of a normal child. However, financial problems may arise either in the home if the mother is burdened with the constant care of an SSN child or from the expenses involved in visiting regularly a child some distance away in hospital, laundry bills will be heavier and there is often destruction of clothing and equipment which must be replaced.

It is known that people looking after SSN children at home could rise from subsistence to average incomes if the child was in an institution. In a survey of these families in London almost twice as many families with the child in an institution had 'good' income ratings as those with a defective at home, while only half as many had 'poor' income ratings. 38 per cent of the families with a mentally handicapped child at home and only 13 per cent of those with the child in an institution were classified as 'poor' since the money available for housekeeping was little more than the amount which would have entitled them to receive National Assistance. This difference between these two groups could be accounted for

by the presence of the mentally handicapped child in the home in the lower income group (Tizard and Grad, 1961).

These figures give us information that merits further study, if we are to learn as much as possible about stress in the family. Some of the families, such as those described by Tizard and Grad living at a subsistence level, may be so conditioned to hardship that they may accept the great difficulties caused by caring for a very severely handicapped child without asking for help or hospital admission. People who are depressed by unrelieved strain and who are unsophisticated in dealing with official authorities are often those who need help most and are least able to obtain it.

III Recommendations

Parents of mentally handicapped children need the specialised counselling described earlier. They also need whatever welfare and practical help is available to any family whose practical problems and circumstances require help from the social services. In some circumstances they will require help sooner than other families would. Thus, as we have seen, housing difficulties and low incomes may be less readily supportable when there is a defective child in the home.

We think that local authorities should consult with the voluntary societies in the area in order to identify and co-ordinate the various types of help and services these may be able to provide and in order to give these voluntary agencies information about the special needs in the area that the local authority itself cannot meet. Unless there is mutual confidence and co-operation between local authority and voluntary societies, needs can remain outstanding which might have been relieved through the resources already active in the area. A great deal of voluntary energy and willingness could be evoked and canalised if the local authority discussed with the voluntary societies what help was needed, and what services they could contribute.

Resources vary from district to district, as do outstanding needs and the potentialities of such co-operation are considerable. They range from local authority grants to enable the local voluntary society to set up and maintain a day nursery for pre-school severely handicapped children, to youth clubs and special residential units for the handicapped. Even a simple measure such as regular 'baby-sitting' can make a very great practical difference to a mother otherwise tied to a child whose handicap prolongs the stage at which he needs constant supervision. It would also convey to the family the sense that other people do care about their problems. Voluntary services cannot be a substitute for planned services and the organised provision of nursery care for pre-school children. But they could relieve a situation in which the mother of an SSN child may be unable to have even the limited freedom of movement enjoyed by the mother of a normal pre-school child in similar circumstances. [. . .]

However, there are some services which are beyond the scope of the voluntary societies and which are urgently needed. [. . .] We wish to mention here *some practical measures which would help to meet the physical and financial stresses referred to in this chapter.*

1. Home Helps. The local authorities, Home Help service is provided to families when the housewife is unable to cope because of sickness. We suggest that this service should make special efforts to help housewives who are excessively burdened by a severely mentally handicapped child.

2. We recommend that the problems of these families should receive special attention by local housing authorities.

3. We emphasise the importance of widespread crèche or day nursery provision.

4. We recommend financial assistance in the following forms:

(*a*) Increased grants under SBC for the mentally handicapped (*cf* Blind and TB).

(*b*) Income Tax Reliefs for SSN handicapped persons in continuing training.

(*c*) Special grants for severely handicapped who require exceptional laundry or home nursing

(*d*) Subsidised holiday care.

5. *Lastly, we consider that either the local authorities or the hospital boards have the responsibility to provide satisfactory short stay residential units to assist families who look after severely subnormal children at home.*

REFERENCES

BOWLBY, J., 1958, 'The nature of the child's tie to his mother', *International Journal of Psycho-analysis*, 39, 350–373.

HOLT, K. S., 1957, 'The impact of mentally retarded children upon their families', M.D. Thesis, The University of Manchester.

ILLINGWORTH, R. S., 1962, 'Some points about the guidance of parents of mentally subnormal children', *Journal of Mental Subnormality*, 8, 2.

LIND, E. B., and KIRMAN, B. H., 1958, 'Imbecile children', *British Medical Journal*, 2, 1103.

LORENZ, K., 1940, 'Die angeborenen Formen moglicker Erfahrung', *Z. Tierpschologie*, 5, 235–409.

PRECHTL, H. F. R., 1958, 'The directed head turning response and allied movements of the human baby', *Behaviour*, 13, 212–242.

TIZARD, J., and GRAD, J. C., 1961, 'The mentally handicapped and their families', A Social Survey (Maudsley Monograph No. 7): Oxford University Press.

17. Who will help? The family and the social services, statutory and voluntary *

SHEILA HEWETT
Child Development Research Unit,
University of Nottingham

It is important that the parents are given continuing casework support by experienced doctors and social workers throughout, but especially in the first few months and years.

Mary Sheridan[1]

Families with handicapped children lead lives which in many respects are very like those of families with only normal children. However, there is one way in which their lives are almost inevitably different — that is, in their need to have much more contact with the various social services than most families. We found, for example, that the majority of the East Midlands children (74 per cent) had regular contact with consultants (mainly paediatricians), attending hospital outpatient departments at intervals ranging from one month to one year for this purpose. These routine visits often affect other members of the family and always present the mothers with something extra to be fitted into busy lives — father's role in this respect is usually negligible because he is at work, except when he takes time off to transport his wife, or when his shift coincides with a hospital appointment.

The existence of handicap also makes it likely that the family will become the concern of certain social work agencies, both voluntary and statutory, although this does not follow as inevitably as does contact with doctors. Spastic children who are also mentally handicapped become the responsibility of the mental welfare

officer, who is employed by the local authority to help and advise both the mentally ill and the mentally subnormal who are living at home. School medical officers and school welfare officers may visit the homes of children who are attending ordinary or special schools, to advise on questions relating to education. Again, school medical officers or psychologists may call to make assessments of the child's educability and special educational needs. Someone from the local authority's Welfare Department may visit to offer help with the problem of adapting ordinary homes to accommodate children who cannot manage steps, or, who can only be mobile in bulky wheelchairs — local authorities are empowered to make alterations to homes or to offer grants towards the cost of such alterations. Health visitor services are for the handicapped as much as for the normal. If the family has a child who is blind or deaf as well as physically handicapped, someone with a special responsibility for such children may visit as well. Voluntary bodies of all kinds offer services for people with specific handicaps, sometimes in cooperation with local authorities, sometimes independently. Thus, the fact of having a handicapped child means that one *can* become the focus of attention from all kinds of people who, but for that chance event, might never have been aware of one's existence.

The need for advice and counselling of parents who have a handicapped child is emphasized in all the literature on handicapped children, and we wanted to find out how much help of this kind had been made available to the East Midlands mothers and what they thought about it — in essence, a kind of consumer research. [. . .] At the

*From Sheila Hewett (1970) *The Family and the Handicapped Child*, London, George Allen and Unwin, chapter 7, pp. 155—72.

147

present time, people can be uncertain of the identity of the person who visits them. They are not always sure which local authority department the visitor represents or what kind of help they are entitled to expect from such a visitor.[2]

The exception is the health visitor. She is clearly recognizable in her uniform[3] and is expected to be able to give practical advice on the 'right' way to tackle problems such as difficulties with feeding babies or getting them to sleep. Mothers also expect that she will approve of some of the things they do with their children and disapprove of others[4] and that her concern is mainly with the physical well-being of the child. This may not be the image that the modern health visitor would wish to project, but it is one which seems to persist in the minds of many mothers. From the mother's point of view, the function and role of, for example, the mental welfare officer is not nearly so well defined, nor is that of the visitor from the Spastics Society or some other voluntary body.

All such visitors are referred to in the East Midlands survey as social workers. This will not satisfy those who would prefer to confine this designation solely to those who have had a casework training intended to enable them to exercise special skills in the detection and resolution of personal as opposed to practical problems. From the point of view of the clients, however, the difference is not one which is readily discernible, in respect of personnel or problems. Very few of the East Midlands mothers indicated that they appreciated the difference between the 'home visitors' from the Spastics Society Family Help Unit in Nottingham, who were not trained in casework techniques, and the Society's Regional Social Worker, who was. Both were simply from the Spastics Society. However, although the term 'social worker' is used in the text, it was not used at all in the questions put to the mothers.

In the quotation at the beginning of this chapter, the medical profession, too, is seen by one of its most distinguished and experienced members as having an important social work role. The way in which they approach their difficult 'social work' tasks of breaking the news of handicap to the parents, and of initiating and maintaining a relationship with them that will facilitate further discussion on a helpful level, is not always successful from the mother's point of

view. However, the views expressed there concerned the hospital consultants with whom the mothers had been in contact. The situation could be different in respect of general practitioners. We asked mothers how helpful they thought their family doctors had been with the handicapped child.

Twenty-five mothers (14 per cent of the whole sample) said that they had found their family doctors helpful in specific ways. Specific help included regular monthly visits by the doctor to see the handicapped child at home although he had not been asked to call (in seven instances). Some doctors had contacted various local authority departments on behalf of the parents and had concerned themselves with attempts to obtain temporary or permanent care. Active interest of this kind is very much appreciated by parents, particularly as most of them think of general practitioners as being over-burdened with work; the doctor's special concern for the problems of the handicapped is thought of as being extra to the service that can normally be expected of him.

Seventy-five mothers (42 per cent) said that they had found the family doctor helpful in a general sort of way although they could not think of any specific action he had taken. Far more often it was an attitude of understanding and helpfulness that had been conveyed to the mother, and a frequent comment in this context was that the doctor would always come when called to the handicapped child — as though some mothers half expected that he would not necessarily do so. Similarly, a doctor who will listen to mothers is valued very highly, even if he cannot actually do anything else. As with mothers' feelings about the helpfulness of consultants, their comments on helpful and unhelpful general practitioners seem to indicate that their perception of their relationship with their medical advisers is influenced very much by the doctor's ability to convey the idea that he is an ally, working *with* the parents, not against them. The sample was almost equally divided in its views on this matter, 56 per cent finding their family doctors helpful and 44 per cent not doing so. The comments that illustrate mothers' attitudes have been chosen so that this balance of views is retained.

Boy: 3 yrs. yes. I don't think I should ever have

got through without him. Well, everything I wanted to know, you know, he's tried to do his best for me. And he told me if I didn't let up at one time, where I would land up! I was getting a really — nervous wreck.

Boy: 2 yrs.
No, no help whatsoever. I went to him a few months back — I felt at screaming point with me own nerves and he said 'You'll find as he gets better, you'll unwind yourself and won't feel so tense.' He gave me nothing, no advice. I said, 'Is there anybody I can get in touch with about him?' I said, 'I've got to talk to somebody.' He said, 'I don't know anybody'. Didn't advise me or nothing. I mean, he *must* have known somebody I could have got in touch with.
(This mother later got in touch with the Spastics Society herself.)
[. . .]

Girl: 2 yrs.
No — but I think probably it's our own fault that he hasn't because we've never been to him, you see. I think with attending the hospital and having our drugs and everything from there, fortunately I haven't had to go to him at all and so therefore we haven't chatted — we did go once after we'd started going to the hospital and I must admit he did spend about half an hour talking to us about children like her — explaining to us about the attacks she had.

Boy: 4 yrs.
He simply is a doctor that . . . everyone seems to have the same opinion — you see, he seems to be writing out a prescription when you're walking in the surgery and he doesn't give you time to explain what's the matter and I feel a bit embarrassed going round — 'cause I don't know how to approach him, you know. I'm not one for going to doctors.
[. . .]

Girl: 7 yrs.
I always ask doctor if I want to know anything. (Interviewer: Your own doctor?) Yes — I talk to him like talking to my Dad.

The medical profession itself is well aware that there are problems to be solved and that the acknowledged difficulty of communicating technical facts to lay people (and worried lay

people at that) is a crucial one when it comes to establishing and maintaining a workable relationship with them. In an interesting discussion of the problem,[5] Dr T. A. Quilliam stresses the importance of the supportive role to be played by the general practitioner and points to two difficulties — first, that they may not 'possess the knowledge and experience to perform this task adequately' and second, that 'medical students are not instructed in the technique of communication with patients and those practitioners who have learned to do so with truth, tact and sincerity have only done so by trial and error after much conscientious effort and soul-searching'. These comments were made with particular reference to congenital heart conditions and heart surgery for children, but they apply equally to other situations.

Communication is never a one-sided affair, of course. Dr Errington Ellis, discussing 'What the Doctor has to offer'[6], points out that 'Some parents are relaxed and friendly, skilled communicators and good witnesses. Others are not but it is important to meet them all and to listen to them, because they are an important part of the child's environment and their attitude to their child's disability is probably the most important factor in his life.'

Turning now to other social workers and their significance in the lives of the East Midlands families, we found that only 10 mothers said that they were not visited by anyone at all. One hundred and ten of the rest were visited by more than one agency, 75 by two, 33 by three and 2 by four. To take the health visitor first, with her nursing training followed by specialist training for her work with families, she seems on the face of it to be the ideal bridge between the medical world and parents bringing up handicapped children in their own homes. As a member of a local authority department and a key worker in the fields of preventive medicine and public health, which are the local authorities' main contributions to the National Health Service, she has a unique opportunity to act as a co-ordinating agency between the three branches[7] of the health service and other local authority services. She knows how the departments work, what services they offer and how to go about obtaining these services. She also has a better chance of knowing which families have a handicapped child because she knows of all the babies born in her area and has a duty to contact all new mothers. Some local authorities give individual health visitors special responsibility for particular groups – the handicapped, the elderly or the mentally ill, for example – but their main concern in most areas is with normal babies and young children and their mothers. The number of handicapped children in the area looked after by any one health visitor will not be large, so that (like the general practitioner) she will not necessarily have the opportunity to become really familiar with the problems of managing such children at home. On the other hand, the fact that these children are few in number means that it should be possible for her to concentrate more of her time on them than on some of the well babies of experienced mothers who need her least.

We found that, according to mothers' reports, 75 per cent of the 55 children who were under 5 years old were being visited by health visitors at the time of interview – 40 per cent of them 'regularly, i.e. 3 or more times a year and 35 per cent 'occasionally', i.e. less than 3 times a year. Twelve of the 18 children who were 2 years old or less were being visited, 7 of them regularly. Most of these mothers had welcomed the health visitors and found them kind and helpful, in spite of the fact that they had been unable to solve particular difficulties: the mothers of children who were difficult to feed, for example, did not say that the health visitor had been able to offer any advice about this. A mother who wanted more advice about equipment for her child did not get it from the health visitor (or from anyone else). Some of the comments made by the mothers show that they do not really expect health visitors to be able to help them but that they appreciate the *intention* to help. Other comments show that some of them feel that the health visitors are avoiding them because they know that they will not be able to offer help and feel at a loss in the face of handicap.

Girl: 2 yrs.: first and only baby, very difficult to feed.
Oh, yes, yes, the health visitor; she's very nice, she is – it's the one I should see if I went to the clinic, you know. She comes to see why I haven't been – perhaps once in every 3 months. I think she comes to encourage me to go to the clinic, really, but she's very, very nice – you know – if

she could help in any way I'm sure she would, and she's asked if I wanted anything.
[. . .]

Boy: 2 yrs.
I don't know that health visitors are awfully well trained for this . . . I wouldn't dream of asking the health visitor because they've got too wide a field.

Girl: 2 yrs.
During the first 10 months of her life I expected her to come and I was longing to talk to somebody – or perhaps it was the first 6 months – I was absolutely longing to talk to somebody and every time she came up the road I thought 'Surely she's coming to see me this time.' Because I didn't know she was a spastic. She did all this screaming and nobody came anywhere near and . . . this probably put me against her (the health visitor) a little bit. I think she would be helpful if she could be helpful but – there's nothing much they can say. They don't seem to have a lot of experience in it and they just sympathize and say 'Yes, dear' and so on and I don't know that you feel a lot better for that . . . I don't suppose *she* would say that she knew a lot about it, if you asked her and therefore I don't have a lot of confidence in her . . . But I always welcome her – I welcome anybody – just breaks the monotony.

Boy: 6 yrs.
I couldn't tell you the last time she came. That does really – I *do* feel a bit upset about that. She did used to come odd occasions, but only very rare, never made a regular visit. It's 12 months since her – I've had plenty of help – I'm not grumbling – from other sources, but I do think that it wouldn't have hurt her to have called and seen how I was occasionally. I mean, if they can visit normal healthy children, I'm sure they can come and just have a look at these, that's how I feel about it.

The health visitor's duty to the normal child ends when he starts school and becomes the responsibility of the school medical services. This usually happens at 5 years of age – not many children attend state schools before that age. However, as we have seen, handicapped children are not always provided with appropriate education or day-care at the age of 5. More than a third of the East Midlands children who were 5 or older were not provided for in this way by local authorities and so were not benefiting from school health services, 46 children in all. Of these, 37 were known to have some degree of intellectual impairment. As we said at the beginning of this chapter, the responsibility for the welfare of mentally handicapped children lies with the local authority Health Departments[8] who employ mental welfare officers to visit the children and their families at home. Where the children are attending local authority day-centres or special care units, they are constantly under the supervision of the local authority or the hospital service and it might be argued that in these circumstances there is less need for the family to be visited by the mental welfare officer. Where the children are not being provided with day-care, both for the child and the family, the need for the advice and support of the mental welfare officer seems *prima facie* to be greater. In the East Midlands sample, the priorities appeared to have been reversed. Of the 18 mentally handicapped children who were aged 5 or over and who were attending day-centres, 16 were also being visited by the mental welfare officer. Of the 37 who were not attending day-centres, again 16 were being visited by mental welfare officers, 11 of the remainder were sometimes seen by the health visitor (often because there were younger children in the family) and 10 were visited by neither the mental welfare officer not the health visitor.

This might be an area where health visitors could be of great service, continuing to keep in touch with the children who are not in schools or day-centres after the age of 5, particularly in those instances where no other local authority social worker is in regular contact with the family. The concept of community care for the handicapped must seem to be no more than a bad joke to families such as these unless somebody translates the idea into practical action. Life is particularly hard for mothers caring for physically and mentally handicapped children if no day-care is provided for them, and it would appear to make sense to divert scarce social worker services from the families who already benefit from this day-time relief to those who do not.

As we have seen, mothers realize that the health visitor does not normally have special knowledge of handicap and are consequently not surprised

when she is unable to offer specific advice or help. The mental welfare officers, on the other hand, do have a special field and could, perhaps, more confidently be expected to have some expertise to offer to mentally handicapped children and their families. In practice, this did not seem to be so for the East Midlands children. Unless the mental welfare officer had been instrumental in helping parents to get either day-care or residential care for the children, the opinion of the mothers in many cases seemed to be that he was as little able as the health visitor to help in managing the child at home. This is not really surprising. There is a chronic shortage of workers in the field of mental health, relatively few of such workers as there are have professional social work qualifications and the distribution of trained workers is uneven throughout local authority areas.[9] In these circumstances, home visits must be less frequent than is desirable (15 families were visited by mental welfare officers three or more times per year, 26 twice per year or less) and continuing casework support cannot be possible. It is arguable whether all, or even most, families are in need of such support, particularly if adequate day-care is provided The comments that follow all refer to mental welfare officers.

[. . .]

Boy: 6 yrs. 11 mths. No local authority day-care.
Well, he doesn't have much to say. He just wants to know if there's anything he can do in any way to help, which he can't and that's about all that goes on.

Boy: 6 yrs. No local authority day-care
They would help, but I honestly can't see what they can do for him, you know. But it is through the help of the health officer that we hope we've got him in this training centre.

Boy: 6 yrs. Special care unit for 6 days per week
The mental health officer – he came and it was him that got him into this day-care, you see. But, I mean, apart from that I've not really got any problems with him at home. He's not really a big problem . . . I don't *count* him as a problem.

Girl: 7 yrs. No local authority day-care
Oh, he's only a very young man. He's very helpful – anything you ask. But of course, they're

not doctors. He's very good but it's not like dealing with anyone that's medically — that knows about these things.

The health visitors and the mental welfare officers are the local authority workers most likely to be in relatively frequent contact with families where there is a handicapped child. School medical officers or medical officers of health may make isolated visits for specific purposes — to make assessments of need for special education, for example, or for routine medical examination of children returning to special schools after the holidays — but these are not social work visits. The most highly specialized of the visitors to the families of cerebral palsied children are those employed by the Spastics Society itself. At the time the East Midlands survey was carried out, a 'home-visiting' service was in operation, using the Family Help Unit in Nottingham as its base. A more 'casework'-oriented service was then in the process of being set up and some mothers had been visited both by home visitors and by a social worker with a specific social work training. As we have already pointed out, the distinction between the two kinds of workers and the help they could offer did not seem to be apparent to the mothers concerned. When they were able to remember the names of the workers who had been to see them, it was possible to be sure that casework support had been offered to them, but not otherwise. All such visits have therefore been counted together. Twenty-six families had been visited 3 or more times in one year, and 126 once or twice in a year (83 per cent of the sample altogether). Thus, more mothers had seen someone from the Society than from any other single agency. The part played by other voluntary bodies of all kinds was a very minor one. Only 18 mothers (10 per cent of the sample) had visitors from these, mostly infrequent. The voluntary bodies concerned included the churches (11 mothers), mainly represented by vicars and priests, the National Society for Mentally Handicapped Children (2), Dr. Barnado's Homes (1), voluntary worker for a local group of the Spastics Society (1), voluntary worker for the deaf (1) and for the blind (1) (identity of organizations uncertain). One mother had been visited by someone concerned with running a weekly play-group for handicapped children.

The sample was almost equally divided into those who thought they were members, or were sure they were members, of local groups of the Spastics Society (91) and those who were not (89). There was doubt in the minds of some of the mothers about what it meant to be a member. When mothers said they were not sure, they were asked whether they paid a subscription to the local group or not. If they replied that they did, they were counted as belonging to the group, even if they took no part in its activities. The Spastics Society and its visitors make no distinction between members and non-members. The same help is available for all. Mothers had heard about the Society from a variety of sources. These are listed in Table 17.I.

Table 17.1

Mother's sources of information about the Spastics Society	No. of mothers
Consultant	29
General Practitioner	2
Physiotherapist	30
Almoner	1
Other parents or friends	18
Parents made contact on their own initiative	8
Spastics Society made first contact with parents	55
No contact	6
Other sources	31
Total	180

Comments on the helpfulness of visits by the Society's workers varied as did those on other kinds of visitors. Mothers hope that visitors will be able to give them advice about practical problems of management, about equipment and gadgets as these become available, about other sorts of help, such as short-term care. In some cases, they simply like someone to talk to who understands their problems, particularly in the earliest months of realizing that they have a handicapped child. A very basic need exists for more information of all kinds, both about the condition itself and about ways to meet the difficulties that arise from it. Until the recent publication of the book by Nancie Finnie,[10] there were few sources of specific advice which would be of real use to a mother with a child who was difficult to bath, change, feed and dress or could not be persuaded to sleep. The Spastics Society has published a small number of helpful pamphlets but these had found their way to only a few of the East Midlands mothers. Spastics News did not always reach even those who belonged to local groups. Table 17.2 lists the various channels through which mothers had obtained information about cerebral palsy.

Table 17.2

Sources of information about cerebral palsy	No. of mothers
Pamphlets or leaflets seen at hospitals	9
Spastics Society publications sent for by mothers	21
Spastics Society publications obtained via local groups	28
Books obtained from libraries	30
Books bought	17
Articles in the press, in magazines	69
Programmes on television and radio (particularly Women's Hour)	127
Other	25
None	11

Note: These figures do not add up to 180 because sometimes individual mothers had several sources of information.

It seems that relatively few mothers will turn to the printed word for information unless this becomes more readily available. One way to make certain that useful books and pamphlets actually reach the mothers would be for health visitors and social work visitors of all kinds to have these always available. They could then look *with* the mothers for solutions to particular problems and actually participate in applying suggested remedies or techniques to the difficulties of specific children. This would also help to meet the criticism made by some mothers, that social workers cannot help them because they lack practical everyday experience of handicapped children.

A difficulty arises if the kind of help which the family needs cannot be supplied by the worker, however resourceful he or she may be. This is inevitably the case when mothers would like good day-care for their children but there is no suitable provision available for them. The same is true when the temporary care that is available is of a kind that causes mothers to be wary of accepting it for their children, however much they may need the relief it affords. In this situation of scarce and inadequate provision, which applies particularly to

the mentally handicapped who also have physical handicaps, the case worker is in a very difficult position. Faced with a family who are suffering strain because the community services are inadequate to meet their practical needs, how can he or she approach them? The concept of supportive casework relationships, which has its origins in psychiatry, is surely inappropriate when the family is in distress, not through any inherent weakness in its relationships, but rather because it is being forced to function in circumstances which would test any family. How many of the 'anxious', 'aggressive' and 'possessive' parents, described by psychologists and doctors as 'rationalizing' their need to 'get rid of' their children when they attempt to obtain residential education or care, would simply 'disappear' if both day and residential care were equally good and freely available? If choice of provision were a reality, as it is for those parents of normal children who can afford to educate their children privately, would such adverse value judgments of parental motives be made? It seems unlikely — parents who send their children to public schools are seldom categorized in these ways.

There are some parents, however, who very much appreciate the fact that someone is interested enough in their children to call and see them. They find this expression of society's awareness of their problem sufficient justification for such visits, even if no practical help can result. No mothers said that they had asked any worker not to call again, however disparaging they had been of the usefullness of visiting. [. . .]

There were 32 mothers (18 per cent of the sample) who had no strong feelings about social work visits. They were not hostile to them, but it seemed to make no difference whether any one visited them or not. [. . .]

The rest of the mothers were either welcoming to social workers without reservation (52 per cent) or gave them a qualified welcome (23 per cent) — this last meaning that they made comments on the failure of the visits to have any useful outcome but that they welcomed the visitors just the same.

When we asked mothers whether they would like to be visited more often, almost 70 per cent of them replied that they would not (123 mothers). Fifty-seven mothers felt that they would like to be visited more often. Of this group, proportionally twice as many had children whose mental status had been classified (by us) as uncertain (36 per cent — 21/58) or who were known to be mentally handicapped to some degree (36 per cent — 28/77), as had children who were known to be of normal intelligence (18 per cent — 8/45). Forty-eight of the mentally handicapped and unclassified children had no day-care or had only voluntary day-care provision for one or two days per week. It is therefore not surprising that their mothers should feel that they need more contact with possible sources of help. We have already seen that those having no day-care were less likely to be visited by mental welfare officers than those who were at a junior training centre (p. 151 of this chapter). The mothers who would like more social work support thus include some of those who pose the problem for caseworkers that we have discussed above. Is this, perhaps, the reason why they are visited less frequently than they would like?

We asked mothers the question, 'If you needed help or advice, who would you turn to first?' thinking that their replies would reflect to some extent the importance to them of the various social service and social work agencies. The distribution of their replies is given in Table 17.3.

More mothers thought that they would turn to the Spastics Society than any other agency (32 per cent). Often this meant that they would contact the Family Help Unit in Nottingham to ask for emergency care, but sometimes secretaries of local groups of the Society were mentioned, too.

Second in popularity were the general practitioners (16 per cent). Local authority agencies, which included health visitors, mental welfare officers and the children's department (once) came third (12 per cent). Consultants and physiotherapists accounted for 18 per cent of choices between them and when it is remembered that almost 80 per cent of all the children in the sample were attending hospital out-patient departments it is remarkable that no one considered the hospital almoner or medical social worker to be the source of help that would spring to mind first.

The information supplied by the East Midland mothers appears to lend some support to the case for a single social service department to whom all handicapped children and adults would be entitled to turn. However, unless such a department were able to tap greater resources than are at present available, the end result from the point of view of the public whom it would serve would not be any different. If provision of services is basically inadequate, rationalizing the channels through which such services can be obtained will not affect the outcome. On the other hand, if the social workers who are detecting need are also part of the department which will supply those needs, it is possible that a greater sense of urgency will be generated, and it will not be possible to lay responsibility for failure and delay at other departments' doors. The exception here will be the provision of education and training which would lie outside the province of such a department.

Table 17.3 To whom mothers of spastic children would turn first for help

Spastics Society	Spastics Society	Other vol.body	Own G.P.	Consultant	School	Physio-therapist	Hosp. almoner	L.A. agency	D/K	Other	Total
Members	37	—	13	7	1	8	—	11	12	2	91
Non-members	21	1	15	11	2	6	—	11	10	12	89
Total	58	1	28	18	3	14	—	22*	22	14†	180

* In 9 instances, this means the mental welfare officer.
† 'Other' includes family and friends, a school headmaster, a teacher of the deaf, a maternal and child welfare clinic and a school medical officer.

NOTES AND REFERENCES

1. Sheridan, M., *The handicapped child and his home*, National Children's Home, London, 1965.
2. One of the best guides through this labyrinth is *The Consumers' Guide to the British Social Services* by Phyliss Willmott — a Pelican Original, Harmondsworth, 1967.
3. In some local authority areas uniform is no longer worn. In others, only the colour to be worn is specified, often the traditional navy-blue.
4. See Newson, J. & E., *Infant care in an urban community*, Allen and Unwin, London, 1963, for evidence of mothers' attitudes to health visitors.
5. Quilliam, T. A. 'Clinical Communication — a Contemporary Problem.' *Medical Biol. Illust.*, 15, 66—8, 1965.
6. Ellis, E. in *Teaching the Cerebral Palsied Child*. Ed. James Loring. Spastics Society, William Heinemann, 1965.
7. The hospital service, the family doctor service and local authority health service. These three are administered separately from one another, although unification of health service administration is under discussion.
8. Since 1970—71 this responsibility lies with the Local Authority Social Service and Education Departments.
9. Seebohm Report, Report of the Committee on Local Authority and Allied Personal Social Services. Cmmd. 3703, H.M.S.O., London, 1968.
10. Finnie, Nancie R., Handling the Young Cerebral Palsied Child at Home, Heinemann Medical Books, London, 1968.

18. Robert *

 recorded by his parents and edited by
Liz Cooper and Roberta Henderson
M.R.C. Unit for Non-Communicating Children

The family
[Robert is nine and has one sister two years older than he is. His father is a self-employed building contractor. His mother does not work outside the home. The family live in a terraced house with a garden surrounded by a six foot fence to keep Robert in. The house itself is arranged to give Robert as much space as possible to run around in.]

Mother
The changes Robert has made to our lives is incredible, for example the strain of seeing a very young child destroy our home, totally ignore us, in fact literally walk on us, was soul destroying, but as we wanted him our love overcame what could have been hatred. It has paid dividends — Robert is now very lovable, but we could so easily have made the mistake in those early years and disciplined him in a physical manner for the destruction and total rejection towards us, it was like having a demanding little monster ruling us.

It is difficult to realise those years existed, and I don't know whether it was our strength or weakness that got us through. It's hard for a mother to be one step ahead all the time but that is what it means, for safety reasons, in fairness to our daughter so the chip didn't rub off on her and distort our love as a family.

I personally found the screams (without tears) the most heartbreaking of all, no one could tell us the reason and he wouldn't let me comfort him, I couldn't touch, just watch.

It's even harder in some ways for a man, to come home to chaos and live with it evenings and weekends. I learned to switch off so as to keep my sanity because the feeling of being ignored, shut out and definitely not wanted I found unbearable. I would sit and sob for hours and nights — it doesn't do any good so I just existed through those years.

The rewarding part comes after years of torment when Robert first looked into our eyes — it was a breakthrough and he didn't look the same child, how wonderful it is to be allowed to cuddle him and feel he enjoys us, people!

Something wrong
When I had Robert they said 'You've got a lovely boy', it was a long time before he gave that first cry, and then I thought perhaps there was something wrong — I didn't know anything then obviously — they showed him to me, they said 'You've got a lovely baby boy'. Well, I've never seen a baby before that hadn't been washed and my first child was all washed and clean and lovely when I saw her and I thought she was marvellous. Well, whether it's because they showed him to me and he was like that, I didn't get a thrill, although the fact that I wanted a boy so much I felt I should have. [. . .]

When I had him back in the ward with me, I never for once watched him with the adoration like I did my first child; I was conscious of this. He didn't want me to feed him and I used to look at him and I used to think he looked like a little prize fighter. [. . .]

It was noticeable, if I called his name he never turned and his eyes never looked at me, not at any

*From Liz Cooper and Roberta Henderson (eds.) (1973) *Something Wrong*, London, Arrow Books, pp. 75—95.

time; I could hold his face, right up close to mine, nose to nose, looking into his eyes and whichever way I moved not even for a second could I get his eyes to focus on mine.

I think he walked at a year, in fact he ran at a year, he never ever crawled – he just got up and ran away from me, never towards me, always away from me. I think at 18 months I was pretty certain then, because there was no gurgling, no attempt to make speech or even contact; he hated to be cuddled – as long as he was left alone he was marvellous.

The doctors

I took him for all the usual check ups and injections and everything. When he was about 18 months, I couldn't understand why he would eat only when I could distract him; he had to be so distracted. I told the doctor 'He just will not touch food at all at any other time'. They said it was probably just a fad and that he looked a bonny child and not to worry, and because my daughter had been so very normal in all her timing of walking, speaking and everything, not to compare, so I tried to accept and comfort myself in this manner.

I went to my doctor's so many times and in fact when I look back on it I had it in a nutshell for them but they're obviously not to blame, there was so little known about autism nine years ago, and it is a specialist thing. I used to say to my doctors, I said Robert is a very contented child, he'll play as good as gold all on his own, I could leave him all day long like that. I told him I couldn't understand why he wouldn't turn to his name, and [the doctor] looked down his ears. I knew Robert wasn't deaf as he would turn to the sound of sweet papers or a ticking clock.

When I first asked him for a letter to go to a children's hospital he said 'Well, all right, I'll give you a letter to go to the ears, eyes and throat specialist', which indicated even more that he had no idea it was anything other than that.

I wanted to go partly because Robert had these terrible screams and I wasn't absolutely sure then it was claustrophobia, I was only guessing. It would have been feasible that it would have been a clot passing the brain, because he used to go like a stone; he was absolutely rigid, and a very high tense scream, no tears, and I would put my arms round him and the only way I can describe the

feeling and it's absolutely true, it felt as though I was getting an electric shock coming through him into me.[. . .]

For years he wouldn't cry, he didn't cry. He does now, it's lovely because he really does cry normally, and he'll come up to me and show me his knee to be comforted but he wouldn't ever, it was as though he was rejecting pain even. I told my doctors all this.

The hospital never really told me anything very much, they just said that the brain wasn't developing evenly. I asked them to do X-rays on the skull for tumours; anything like that [but they said] there was nothing whatsoever, there was no brain damage, which confused me at the time.

The word 'autism' came up when I first saw the psychiatrist. I'd never heard of it. I didn't really know anything about psychological things. I don't think I was very shocked then. The first visit I had I went up there on my own and when I came home and I told my husband that Robert had to see a psychiatrist he was terribly shocked; it hadn't shocked me. I don't know why, I don't really know why it hadn't. In fact, it was almost a relief because I had visions of some sot of blockage in the brain affecting the hearing and the speech and him having to have a major operation, you know, and whether the fear of that was a relief when they said he had to see a psychiatrist, I thought 'Oh, smashing, they'll talk him out of this sort of thing.' Oh dear! All the doctor could tell us without, obviously, he can't put himself on the spot, it's understandable because with autistic children you don't know how much they can develop or when, or when they're going to stop. [. . .] He said Robert may gradually grow, he didn't say grow out of it, no, he said that with help, there are special schools to train autistic children but they must have help because it's not something you can ignore, and he said the last thing you must do is leave Robert alone.

People can't say to you 'Oh, in so many years he's suddenly going to get better' or suddenly going to talk or something like that. Dr. —— is very very good and I appreciate the fact. He did say that Robert may never speak and I was able to accept it from that to fight it. I think if he'd told me 'Oh well, he will speak' over these years I would have lost so much hope that I would have been worse now.

I'm not altogether convinced now that my G.P.

didn't know there was something wrong. He may have been using some discretion whereas he thought it was better that I wasn't told then, I don't know. He may have thought that the longer it's left then perhaps the more Robert may develop and make it that much easier, but quite honestly in my opinion I think the younger you have some idea what you're up against the easier it is to try and help the child.

If it hadn't heen for my husband's rudeness and bluntness at the children's hospital we're convinced it would have been many wasted years instead of six months before we knew what autism meant. It seems such a terrific pity one has to be like this to get through to specialised people who are supposed to know what they are talking about — makes me wonder how many autistic children have been written off right at the start.

Father

I didn't take Robert to the doctor, my wife did, but she tells me afterwards very little as it happens, but from the information that I gleaned he had rather a lethargic attitude towards the whole situation. In other words well, give him another six months and we'll see how he goes, and when he's 45 perhaps we'll find out what's wrong, but nevertheless, I'll say this, that to the G.P., providing the child is sound in wind and limb and it's not immediately dying, he's not really interested.[. . .]

Now, we went for the EEG (electro-encephalogram) test with Robert and again there was a tremendous amount of ignorance and stupidity on the part of the medical profession, not so much the doctors, more the nurses. Now, they have a pair of pliers that puts a metal strip mechanically round the child's wrist. This thing is not only dangerous but is criminally stupid because a child who cannot be spoken to won't be restricted like that and will tend to rip it off and cut their wrists. I said to the nurse 'Please', in the kindest way I could, 'don't put that on his wrist, he'll cut himself'. 'Oh no he won't', she said. Now I knew he would cut himself, she was saying he wouldn't not knowing the child, never seen him before in her life. I tried to explain to her that he was mentally handicapped; it was like talking to concrete. So I said 'Miss, there's only one thing I can do, that is sit here and wait, and I'll tell you this, young girl: I'm his father, I love him, if that

child cuts himself I'll punch you right on the nose' and it frightened the girl. Now I'm a reasonably big man, why should I have to frighten a young girl? Eventually, she was certainly astounded and somewhat afraid, she cut the thing off his wrist and that was the only way, to threaten the girl to take it off his wrist.

We went into a room on the ground floor, there was a Dr. —— there and we were already somewhat sceptical about the attitude of the medical profession. Well, this particular ward was on the ground floor with louvred windows some 12′ by 12′, big enough for a man to get through let alone a child, and the windows were fixed in such a fashion they were like a ladder. Now, had a child climbed these louvred windows that are formed like a ladder and slipped he would have fallen in excess of twenty feet into a concrete area.[. . .] When I pointed this out to the doctor, 'No-one's fallen through it up till now', he said, but he'd never had a child like Robert before, in my opinion. We were still, my wife and I, trying to convince him how bad Robert was and he was still ignoring us and writing and he said 'You let him go, he'll be all right', he said, 'those doors are very very heavy, designed like it to stop children running away'. Well I agree these doors were 7′ 6″ in height, two doors 4′ wide each made of 2″ solid oak; they must have been very heavy. Robert rushed at them, he was about three years of age and he went through them like they were paper.[. . .] Again the same performance. We fetched him back and I said to my wife there's only one way to convince this man. I said to the doctor 'You're not big enough to move me so we'll shut Robert in there and give him two minutes'. 'Good God, no', he says, 'there's thousands of pounds of equipment'. I said 'We'll ignore you and your instruments, he's definitely going in there', and the man pleaded with me not to put him in there. Then I knew I'd got through to him. The EEG was finished at three o'clock. Ridiculous! To have to go to the trouble of threatening people.[. . .]

The teachers

[Attended clinic playgroup for six months, two mornings a week. Entered the Unit: 1967, aged 4½. Referred to Unit by clinic psychiatrist.]

It's difficult to tell at this stage what effect the new school is having on Robert because having the lapse, the six week break, this makes a lot of difference to all the children. They either send you insane over the six weeks' holiday or they're sent insane, the rest of us survive.[. . .]

If the new teacher can demand respect from the children from go he may be able to get through more at this state. No-one could have got through to Robert more than his first teacher did, he went there at 4½ with such withdrawment, he appeared deaf and dumb, there was no contact, nothing, you just couldn't get near him, but all the love and firmness that she gave Robert got through a terrible barrier.[. . .]

Special education is different. I think this master is a perfect example because he's come from a normal school teaching 11- to 13-year-old children. He's had to change his attitude and methods. I mean he couldn't possibly have gone to our school with the ideas that he's going to say to the children 'Right, sit down and do this', 'Do that'. It's absolutely out of the question. This is where someone skilled – they have to be adaptable, with any handicapped child a good teacher definitely has to change to get through to the child in the best way they know how.

I think they must first of all try to make the children have respect for them, and this is very difficult, I know. It sounds pretty absurd with our kids but they do have respect and they can be taught it because Robert from being a vegetable now knows that when I say 'No!' in a firm voice he stops dead and he will not do what I've said 'no' to. So I think mainly the teacher must, right from the start, aim for respect from the child, and also give it. They've got to treat the children as though there is something in their minds to be reached, there has to be a goal which for the teacher is to make the child as acceptable in society as much as possible or to make the child as normal, whatever that is.

I can't discipline Robert in the same manner he can be disciplined at school, mainly because I think I've given in to him for too many years, so I would have to change. Perhaps people could if they have a different personality but I can't be unkind to Robert. He does get smacks but there's no viciousness in it, not that I think that would do any good, but I think people at school could get through to Robert more than I can purely because Robert now can take me for granted, like a normal child.

I think it should also be given the option for the teachers, if willing, to come to the home and observe because I've had it said to me 'I've never seen Robert do that' when a teacher's visited here and they've been quite astonished. Even the social worker, I mean I've seen her for a couple of years now, and she said about how much a loner Robert is at school and that he doesn't seem to have any contact, and I've explained that I think this is because he is afraid of the other children. She visited here in the summer holidays and she was absolutely astonished at his happiness.

The community
I think you obviously get hurt along the line over silly little things. I don't even blame people for not understanding because I don't expect them to understand. You know, you can be in shops or in the Post Office and Robert, he'll give out sudden squeals which I know are startling, and you get people turn round and glare and he might struggle if we're in a queue because he hates the restriction again, you see; and you know, you hear people saying 'Oh, you're a naughty little boy' and things like this choke me because I think to myself straight away 'How can they possibly understand?' and I can't go into the details.

Everyone down this road's absolutely marvellous because they've known Robert from the beginning and, you know, they're very very kind to him. I've got new neighbours here and I was a bit worried because I've always said that if they've known the child right from the beginning, that's all right, and you can accept it as you go along, but if it's something that is suddenly plonked on you it is a bit startling. I was so concerned we finished up building a six foot fence all the way round.[. . .]

Our social worker is very good. I say to her that hearing all the different problems and people that she has to cope with; she's so involved with individuals, it's fantastic, but she is genuinely interested.[. . .]

Conspicuous? I think it's getting more apparent, I think probably now as Robert gets bigger. You know, on the bus he loves travelling and I'll take him on the bus to my mother's and he gets a bit cross at bus stops, you see, because if he goes out in the van with us we don't stop at bus stops and I go like that, if I touch his mouth and try to stop him he'll sometimes stop or I shove a sweet in his mouth. I don't think it really embarrasses me because I feel he is more important to me than other people are, but on the other hand I'm very conscious of, I'd never put anybody out or, you know, deliberately embarrass anybody which I feel that Robert probably does at times.[. . .]

The future

Nobody could love anyone more than I love Robert, but we have to be totally unselfish and unbiased for the child's sake so that you've got to look way ahead because he can't do it for himself, and to keep the child means that if you are ill or anything or when you die the child's going to be passed down through the family; this to me is utterly wrong, I maintain. I've got Janette and she's 11 now, she's been an absolute angel with Robert, she's helped a hell of a lot, but I would no more dream of letting Janette have this responsibility of Robert; I wouldn't, I just wouldn't have it. You know she says 'Oh, I'll look after Robert and I'll marry somebody rich and we'll take care of him', but the whole point is that if you've got a sick person in the house, it's a sick house, I don't care what anybody says, and it would give her no chance whatsoever of having a normal life.

I think if I could get satisfaction now, if I was told or mainly if I had in black and white from a Rudolph Steiner Home that they would take Robert, even at the age of 13, I could live with an easier mind now, knowing that there is somewhere for him to go rather than, he is able to stay at that school as long as they can handle him and then at the end of that there is absolutely nothing. So it's the uncertainty. It seems to me even if the best child there, if they could keep them until they're 16, that's the end of the road 'cos we're not offered anything else.

If he went to a Rudolph Steiner Home, we would be able to have him home for holidays for as long as we're here and he would be with his own kind because obviously all autistic children vary. Robert I don't think is ever going to speak which

is the main drawback. With some of the children obviously their parents would look at it in a different light because they might be able to get them to training centre and things like that, but something like this wouldn't be sufficient to my mind.[. . .]

The social worker is helping me and has written to numerous boarding schools, mainly Rudolph Steiner but also some that are run on similar methods. We've had replies that they have a two year waiting list and it's not practical to have it any longer because these children have a healthy, long life. The authorities have agreed to pay the money for Robert to go to boarding school which was a big barrier I thought. There just don't seem the facilities. To my mind, each child, although they have similarities, would be better off in a different place rather than all in one type of place, because of their different degrees and abilities, or lack of.[. . .]

I think there's still at least 30 per cent recoverable of Robert; I'm certain there's more there, you can see it in his eyes. I don't think we can reach it because we love him too much and we're too kind to him. Sometimes, I mean, Jan makes him obey much more firmly than I do and he responds to it, and he respects her for it, whereas I don't want him ever to be treated badly but I'm convinced that had he gone to this boarding school, for their sake and his, he would have had to have been disciplined firmly. I mean even that is just a step forward but that was why I wanted it to happen now, and I think the longer it goes the harder and the less likely they are to reach him. [. . .]

I mean you bring them into the world, you've got to do your best for them, and if he's not capable of doing it for himself, I mean for eight years at least I've had to think for him and be one step ahead. I feel that society owes you something when you try blooming hard as many years as you can. I'll hang on for as many years as possible, but I've got to see some future which I don't feel I can now; it's existing because I can't see any future.[. . .]

19. In memoriam *

SYLVIA KING
Housewife

'We are going to call it MS.' my husband was told at a London Teaching Hospital, after a second stay of a month in 1967. 'You can go home straight away.'

'Whatever is MS?' he asked me on the 'phone a few minutes later as he prepared to come home. Obviously this was only something trivial or something would have been done about it. It was not really a shock to me but I had dreaded this diagnosis more than anything. I knew all about Multiple Sclerosis, having been secretary to a neurologist some years earlier, but how could I explain? He died last month.

Everything dated back to 1961. He had been in Greece on his firm's behalf, when he panicked because he thought himself unable to write easily. The few letters that I received were anxious in tone, but I persuaded myself that the writing was more care-free than usual. Certainly it was not so precise — I had often teased him that he hesitated before putting pen to paper and was too meticulous for his own good.

More recently, I have pondered the question, 'Did he succumb to this illness because of his very character?'

When a mind is so methodical, is it not possible that small disturbances such as hot climates, unexpected air journies, anxiety about foreign food, responsibilities undertaken on behalf of the firm when abroad, family affairs generally, the novelty of having small children around the house, etc. all build up and start a chain reaction somewhere? No wonder that for several years after 1961 he was considered to be a neurotic by specialists and it was hinted to me that this was the verge of a nervous breakdown.

Several years passed, with visits to Physicians, Neurologists and Eye Specialists — and there was no diagnosis! Meantime the months passed with more and more frequent attacks of influenza and migraine, so called. As a family, we suffered severely. No plans could be made that included Daddy unless they were provisional. Trips abroad on firm's business continued until 1964, but each one became more distressing and I can understand that the effort needed to take responsibilites involved was excessive. There was always at least one episode of lethargy or sickness while he was away.

What a vicious circle! When the firm realised that the burden was too great, and left him at his desk, the frustration was enormous and depression overshadowed everything else. Around this time, the methodical mind began to lose control. How can a perfectionist be satisfied with second rate work? Rather than do something imperfectly, things were left undone, always to be done tomorrow. (Looking through personal papers and files now, I can trace this exactly). Depression increased.

We produced another child in 1966 to my delight, but that child knew from the moment he was born that there was trouble around him. He has always been the most demanding, yet most affectionate of the three children. He instinctively seemed to know that unless he insisted on my attention, he would not get a fair share of it. He

*From the first Megan du Boisson Memorial Prize Award (1971) DIG Occasional Paper No. 11, Godalming, Disablement Income Group.

161

has barely known his father, who died the week before he started school. For two and a half years, after my husband's premature retirement, the two of them battled for my constant attention. I am sure that my little son saved my sanity, as I had to be normal around the house and not get depressed myself. Now they are both gone within a week.

The diagnosis established in 1967, we set about facing the future, I hinted that this illness must be fought, not accepted passively but although he half understood this, it always seemed that he was waiting for the next day to arrive, when he would be feeling fitter. It was not until about 12 months later, when he had lost ground, especially as regards speech and balance, that the same London Teaching Hospital seemed to attempt to get a message across. And then it was getting late to face facts; all effort was needed to get up in the morning, face a day in the office and literally exist in an armchair all evening.

Perhaps the most difficult time for us all was in 1969, when the Personel Manager from my husband's firm brought him home after a bad fall and announced that the firm could no longer cope, or words to that effect. How long he had been a 'passenger' at the firm I never enquired. I had most carefully avoided such a topic of conversation with colleagues since I could guess that things must be as bad there as at home. For some months prior to this, there had been ever-increasing episodes of loss of balance and all the distress associated with this.

It had never occured to me before that shopping crowds on Christmas Eve would take it for granted that a man staggering and finally falling at the roadside, was drunk. But they did and who could blame them; I realised this after it happened. For months, I knew what to expect when he arrived home. It was a case of anxiously looking through the window to see if he had a cut head or face, was covered with mud, or if he needed an escort home. That final day at the firm, he had been missing for hours before anyone noticed the fact, and then was found half-conscious in a cloakroom, having fallen hours before and been unable to call out or get up unaided. Until this, he was driving the car each day and convincing everyone that he was safer in the car than on his feet (and I am sure he was right).

With the final withdrawal from working life, a rapid deterioration took place. I had feared this

would happen. No longer was it necessary to make an effort to get up each morning and soon it was midday before he roused. The incidence of falls increased and we never knew where we would find him, but always it was the same picture — when he fell, he lay completely still with eyes shut as if to pretend it had not happened. Great were my difficulties in getting him up unaided and the harm this period did to the two elder children cannot be judged.

Having realised that the downhill slide was not to be reversed, it occurred to me that a wheelchair was a necessity. Now began a new phase of difficulties as we were in touch with no-one connected with equipment. Our doctor arranged for an ambulance car to take us to the same hospital as previously in order that a chair could be ordered, but by the time the appointment came, it was impossible to get out of the car on two feet. This seemed an insurmountable problem at the time.

We then heard of the local Multiple Sclerosis Society and it was a great relief to me to have two members pay us a visit and to realise that there were other **victims** of MS in our district. An obvious solution to our chair problem was suggested — ask to borrow one from the local hospital pro tem. This arranged, we soon possessed a chair ourselves. As months passed, more and more items of equipment were needed for trials. We discovered gradually that there were Health Visitors, Social Workers, Welfare Workers, Occupational Therapists, District Nurses, etc. who could all make suggestions on and procure equipment from the County Council. So often it was a case of trial and error and we often called on father-in-law to make adaptations for us or to manufacture things which my husband, as an engineer, designed or latterly, described. We eventually collected together a comprehensive selection of aids to suit our particular needs and I give details of some.

Rails around the toilet became a necessity, but several types that arrived at the house were unsatisfactory, usually because there was no support for the head or because there was no foot room for me when lifting. A sani-chair became the solution as this gave support for back, head and arms and could also be transferred elsewhere in the house.

The greatest comfort was obtained from a

ripple mattress and ripple chair pad. Although my husband was helpless for many many months, we had no pressure sore problems. We bought a pillow roughly L-shaped and this proved of enormous value as it stayed where placed without slipping as two separate pillows must do. Likewise a neck pillow did double duty as neck support or eased discomfort in the legs when placed under the knees.

The manufacturers of melamine plastic tableware produced a range of 'crockery' for the disabled last year and we at once bought the special cup and dishes, which made eating and drinking easier while my husband could still manage his own meals. We discovered some Wangee cane which can be made into new large handles for cutlery.

A hoist provided by the local authority proved useless, as I was unable to fix such a helpless patient in the slings, pump the handle and support his head at the same time. Physical lifting was less distressing and quicker — it really was lucky that I proved strong enough to do this unaided, often over 20 times a day.

A clever invention of my husband was a secondary wheelchair for use upstairs, in the days before he had to use the dining-room as a bedroom. This consisted of a flat board with castors underneath, onto which was strapped a small armchair. For many months, I dragged him upstairs and as it was impossible to fold up a wheelchair and get it upstairs at the same time as my husband, this improvised wheelchair filled a great need — let me forget the awful struggle needed to lift a helpless person from the top stair onto a chair balanced precariously nearby.

There were some problems that we never did solve, but as the illness progressed, each was superseded by another more or less great.

An inter-com lent by a relative was of the greatest value to me as, except on particularly bad nights, it dispensed with the need for me to sleep downstairs. A bell is of no use if a patient can neither reach it nor handle it.

As time went on, many of our friends, though most sympathetic, gradually lost touch. Wives could chat to me when the occasion arose, but the husbands found it so difficult to converse with someone who could barely make himself understood. It seldom occurred to former colleagues to come in small groups and just chat generally. One newly-found local friend came regularly for the last 12 months and so kept up a continuity of small talk. How grateful I shall always feel for that.

How did the children cope with their father's disability? Our elder son obviously fared worst because he had known his father when he was active. He is now 13 and looking back, I realise that difficulties in the father/son relationship began to develop when he was about six years of age. A father, who had been a keen sportsman, refused to play ball games. To a child, this was almost a rejection and I admit that even to me it seemed a case of 'would not' rather than 'could not'. Gradually, in the next five years, contact was lost between father and son. There were two answers only to almost any question, 'I will think about it' and 'Not at the moment'. All concentration was being used up at the office desk. I was helpless to close the gap and my husband was very quick to notice if I appeared to take action against him. The situation was tragic and I think I nearly lost contact with our son too, when he felt I was being unsympathetic to him by seeming to side with his father. We were fortunate that in changing schools two years ago, my son came in contact with a most sympathetic house master.

Our daughter, now aged 10, wanted so much in the past few years to get to know her father properly. Until she was around the age of seven, she did not realise that all was not well, then the realisation came that we were not like other families with whom she came in contact. Our youngest child has been least touched by the long illness perhaps, although activities have always had to be restricted for him and he had to accept that I myself was never sure that I could be available to do things promised. He is obviously a bright child who can never be pushed into the background — it has been very hard work for the last two and a half years since my husband was at home permanently, but I cannot but be glad that I had a lively child round me to banish my moments of despair.

Despair I have felt so very often. Nobody can ever understand unless they have nursed a slowly declining husband, as I have done. Slowly the body systems ceased to function properly, but through it all the mathematical brain worked spasmodically on financial problems and gadgetry. How tragic it was when the voice was almost completely lost; I had to summon all my patience to get instructions into my unmathematical brain. Most of the time in the past 12 months, it would seem that there was no thought process, as there was little or no interest shown in things going on or in the children's progress, but obviously the brainpower was only dulled, not diminished. We never discovered whether the depression that had been talked of so many years before was still a factor in the case.

Yes, we had insurance to cover death, but not disablement. How many friends have taken note of our case and insured against disablement after seeing my husband's plight, I do not know, but I do know it made many people stop and think on these lines. We were to consider ourselves lucky that he had been with one firm for 20 years. This firm was very fair to us and a pension of half-pay was something to be grateful for, as I was completely unable to earn anything myself, never having left the house for more than two hours for two years. I lost count of the number of forms I filled in over the years of disablement. I was to be glad I had had secretarial training. I compiled long lists of in-coming and out-goings by week, month and year, in £.s.d. and £.p. Does no-one realise that every official form asks for the same information in different ways? Surely it would not

be impossible to give disabled persons a code number? I completed the same form three times for different departments of the County Council within two weeks at one stage. We watched the progress of the various government proposals to aid the chronic sick and disabled. Ironically, news came that we were to receive the invalidity allowance and the attendance allowance the week my husband died.

We joined DIG last year and through its literature alone was I able to get a clear picture of government proposals for people with problems such as ours. How little such matters concern journalists reporting in the national press is all too obvious. No doubt the general public will read an article through casually and not realise the confusion bad reporting can cause to others looking for help. On several occasions, I was handed articles from different newspapers by helpful relatives and discovered that the information given hardly tallied!

Now I am alone with our three children, gradually putting the house back to its former state, before the dining-room had to become a bedroom and wanting to think back to the years when we were a happy united family, though never forgetting the mental distress my husband suffered as a Disabled Person.

20. Victim invicta *

ROSALIND CHALMERS
Exhousewife

Polio caught me in 1950, an epidemic year in Birmingham, so I have been a 'Victim' for fourteen years now and really ought to have evolved an adequate working philosophy. It's odd, how the epithet 'Victim' is so often attached to people with polio: other diseases have sufferers, accidents have casualties, but we are Victims, and somehow the word has undertones other than physical: 'Victims of rape', 'Victimization at the factory', 'Victims of persecution'; these seem to contain moral implications hardly applicable to polio. But polio is recognized as a disease of civilized countries, which have improved their hygienic conditions to the point where many germs have been eradicated, and among them the odd weak polio germ which might have immunized against more severe attack. Perhaps there is a moral application there.

It is possible to write about physical handicap without being autobiographical, but not without being personal. The case of a man without the use of his arms is different from that of a man without the use of his legs, and the situation of the latter is preferable, unless of course he happens to be a ballet dancer or steeple-jack. However, paralysis is seldom as tidily disposed as that, and there are other factors which are almost as important.

In many ways I was a lucky Victim. I had several advantages, the most important being a good husband, an inquisitive or enquiring mind, some education and some money. My interests lay in reading and writing, not in dancing, tennis or

*From Paul Hunt (ed.), (1966) *Stigma: the experience of disability*, London, Geoffrey Chapman, Chapter 2, pp. 18–28.

climbing. But in other ways I was unlucky. I was a solitary, and enjoyed spending a lot of time alone. I was lazy and perhaps too fatalistic; at the same time I liked doing things for myself and hated asking for help. I disliked crowds, and anything more gregarious than the ward of an orthopaedic hospital it would be impossible to imagine. It was rather like living out an extended version of 'Have a Go', complete with 'characters', sing-songs, and earthy if not homely fun.

The problem is one of balance. It is disastrous to be too accepting (you give up trying), equally disastrous to be too dissatisfied (you don't make the best use of what you have). It is bad to be too dependent — obviously — but as bad to be too contemptuous of help, for a little at the right time is invaluable. But this correct balance is most difficult to achieve even when you are aware of the necessity, because the mind takes longer than the body to recover, not indeed can it ever be said to be 'normal' again. For there has been nothing less than a second birth, another expulsion from the womb.

It was easy to die that first time. I was a happy person, with a little girl of two and a baby of five weeks, a bit tired perhaps after his birth, but with a great deal of tether to run before the end of it was reached. Most people can stand a lot more than they believe possible, especially when their reserves of endurance are untapped. It wasn't difficult for me, with a loving family and an interest in experience (for I still hoped to be a writer) to face calamity. I expected to overcome it and continue as before. This polio, which we had feared for our children, was certainly unpleasant but only temporary. Then when I lay gasping in hospital I suddenly realized I was dying, and was at first very angry indeed. It seemed, when there was so much to see and do, to be entirely the wrong moment to die. Now, of course, I'm not sure; undoubtedly it would have been neater and swifter for us all. But the moment passed, and my anger changed into a determination to survive — at any cost. And God knows the cost has been high.

The iron lung contained its foetus. Unconcerned, I lay reciting poetry, of which fortunately I knew a large amount by heart, invariably becoming confused in the order of the verses in 'Ode to a Nightingale'. Why did Keats seem so appropriate? My husband made me a reading machine with a roll of Penguin books, for not being able to read was a bad deprivation. The moments of terror came only when the respirator was opened and I found the air cold and without breath. My world inside was circumscribed; I grew accustomed to it, and outside demands were few. Those began when I was expelled for the last time and, protesting and terrified, had to accept the bigger world again.

We had a splendid ward sister. Brisk, confident and scathing she fought like a tigress for us and with us. I had the impression that any back-sliding towards death would not be tolerated. Obediently I improved a little. It was obvious to others but not yet to me that I was not going to make a complete recovery. I was too busy being a patient.

After a year in that general hospital, and a year in an orthopaedic hospital, I went home. Things had not been static there either, of course. Both my daughter and the baby had forgotten me. My husband had been a constant tower of strength from the beginning at a cost to himself I couldn't yet appreciate. And the hardest part of the battle was in front of us.

We moved to a larger house which we could divide into two and share with my husband's parents, thus being separate but adjacent. We engaged a housekeeper who would also look after me, and a nursemaid for the children. And we had someone coming in daily to help in the house. If we hadn't been able to afford this the whole system would have broken down, or could not even have been initiated. This happened to a friend of mine at the orthopaedic hospital: her four small boys were put into (different) Homes and her husband left. She could have managed a bungalow with some help from her husband: although in a

wheelchair, she had very strong back and arms and could have looked after herself and the children. Her husband did not even try: but some did try and the strain and expense defeated them.

Our main purpose was to keep a home together for the children and somehow we managed it for the next twelve years; until, in fact, the day before yesterday, when with both children at boarding-schools, me in a nursing-home, and my husband eating with his parents, we have come to a full stop. Or it could be a semi-colon; we don't know yet. And we don't know either whether it was worth it, although I must think that it was. The comparison, after all, should not be with the norm, the happy Weetabix family on television (is anyone as happy as that?), but with my friend at the orthopaedic hospital, and others who lost everything they had, not just some things.

This article is supposed to deal with the problems of the Victim, so perhaps those of husband and children are not strictly relevant. But it is impossible to study one person in isolation; no man was ever less an island than a polio or other severely handicapped person. Or is it only that his dependence is made visible and beyond argument, obvious to the casual glance? Basically his needs are the same as anyone else's; the difficulty is, how far is he justified in pursuing them at other people's expense? It is the question of balance again.

In my husband's case he had lost his wife, but she was not conveniently dead and buried. ('Daddy has three children,' said our daughter pertinently, 'Me, Peter and Mummy.') He had an exhausting job but could not rely on peace and comfort in the evenings; on the contrary, there was generally another crisis to be resolved. He had to appear bright and confident with me, the children and the succession of housekeepers and helps. Life had become merely a matter of making-do.

As for the children, they had lost their mother. Instead of being desired for themselves they were someone's job of work which had to be attended to. Oddly enough it is the small things I remember most clearly and painfully. The children having to stop watching 'Toad of Toad Hall' in the middle because the nanny was going off duty; my daughter crying at the door and not being allowed in until the housekeeper was ready. When I heard one or other of them cry in the night I would try to judge the urgency of the cry to decide whether I should wake the housekeeper, who would not be pleased, and thus not likely to be very patient with them. But they didn't cry much; perhaps not as much as they ought to have done. I had very definite ideas about how they should be brought up, but most of those had to go by the board; plain survival took all our and everybody else's time. It afforded me a certain bleak amusement when I heard of other people's children refusing school dinners and insisting on coming home instead. That could not happen to us!

Yet no one was to blame for the situation. Housekeepers and nurses needed their time off, for they had their own lives to lead. No one was actively cruel to the children; some people were very kind. But one continuing, reassuring presence was lacking, and when they were hurt I couldn't put my arms round them.

It is a mistake to imagine that in such circumstances, and having to do so many things for themselves, children will grow up more independent than others. On the contrary, they will grow up less so. Having no basic security they lack confidence and grow timid and withdrawn, clinging to what little there is to cling to. It is the secure child who leaves his home and possessions confidently, knowing that they will be there when he returns. One tends, too, to load the child with material things, out of pity for him and a sense of guilt.

In theory I was in charge of the house. I didn't need much actual nursing and was in a wheelchair all day, but I needed someone to get me up, put me to bed and take me to the lavatory. I was occasionally ill (colds are a hazard for most polios) and then had to be in bed all the time. It is extraordinarily difficult to reprimand anyone when they also lift you on and off the lavatory like a baby several times a day! In addition I had to think of the repercussions on the children. It was hard to get housekeepers in the country, and a very little might cause them to give notice, which would mean more changes for the children. So I interfered as seldom as possible in the running of the house, and if that too was humiliating for me I considered my humiliation to be the lesser evil.

Now that I am alone it is easy to look back and see what was happening then and how certain things could have been done differently. But at the beginning I was capable only of thinking of myself, and afterwards it was a question of struggling on without thinking much at all. At least the family remained a unit, albeit a shaky one. My own feeling of guilt springs from the knowledge of having ruined three lives, whether wittingly or not, and being at last fully conscious of it. However, guilt without action is sterile, and will only cast general gloom if indulged in for too long. It won't help anyone, least of all yourself. But what will?

There are several practical steps which should be taken to help disabled people and their families. The wife should be entitled to a pension, for her incapacity is as great a catastrophe as would be that of the breadwinner, and if paralysed in an accident she could receive vast damages, as indeed could a single girl. The cause of the disability is of no relevance to the family's needs, which have to be catered for individually by the State at far greater expense if the family disintegrates.

There should be someone with up-to-date information about gadgets and equipment who would see each disabled person before he leaves hospital. This adviser should know about bungalows and how they could be acquired, about grants, and about holiday reliefs; he should also be able to give general advice about problems, with reference to how people similarly disabled have coped with theirs. This service could be provided by the almoner, but we never found hospital almoners to be the slightest use. They knew nothing and could do nothing. Snippets of information were picked up here and there, from the staff and other patients, from friends and from articles in the press. An enormous amount of worry and despair could be prevented if all this information was pooled, together with the conventional medical advice, and made available before the return home from hospital. It is only common sense to give all the practical help possible at the very start, in case some families find the whole thing too much for them before they have even begun. Going home is an even greater emotional strain than the initial adjustment to disability.

This advisory service should be continued when the patient leaves hospital. Physiotherapy or hydrotherapy, if needed, should be arranged, and contact should be maintained either by the adviser coming to the house or the patient going to the hospital or office. Thus he could be kept in touch with new gadgets and ideas, or could just talk things over. Such a service might avert a few crises before they developed, and for some people it might be enough to know it was there in reserve.

I know it is no use advocating a register of domestic helpers as there just are not enough to go round; but it might be possible to compile a list of people prepared to help for short periods, over holidays, or to give the disabled person and their full-time helpers a rest from each other. My dream holiday would be somewhere on the Mediterranean in a room with a balcony where (almost) unseen hands attend to my intermittent needs. The delight would lie in not having to be grateful to the 'hands' — the person would receive an exorbitant fee — in not having to feel guilty because something else was waiting to be done, in not being emotionally involved at all.

I think the various organizations for the disabled could do more in trying to supply temporary helpers and gadgets instead of concentrating so much on parties and pantomime trips. Of course in this matter I am prejudiced, being temperamentally ungregarious, but it seems odd that people are expected to enjoy being together merely because they are all incapacitated. They are probably as different from each other as people picked out at random from a crowd. Clinical details of my 'case' are the last thing I want to discuss with anyone, but the temptation to do this is surely stronger when surrounded by others similarly afflicted. I am convinced that such dwelling on one's disease is wrong, and that the whole endeavour of the Victim should be directed towards getting back, if not into step, at least into the company again at his own calculated pace. This means taking advantage of every practical aid available, and of as much human help as is fair to the givers, in order to get on with the business of living.

It seems essential to a man's self-respect that he should find himself of use, and it is no less necessary for a woman. On becoming disabled the man or single woman has probably lost the power to continue his previous job, and a wife the power to look after her family herself. Both are traumatic experiences, and something else to do must be found as soon as possible. Anything will do at first. Obviously the degree of paralysis affects the ease with which suitable tasks can be found, but there is always *something*. I used to encourage people to discuss their plans for the future with

me, and it seemed to help them to sort out their ideas. Later, when the Victim improves or his condition stabilizes it is time to look round for more things to do, and to try a few until it becomes clear which is the right one for him. (I doubt if basket-making would ever be the grand solution, but for some reason occupational therapists are mad about it!)

Even bedridden people should not allow their lives to dwindle to mere television watching — unless they intend to criticize it for the local paper. One possibility for them is to learn a language from the radio or long-playing records, and it might be feasible then to do translating work, perhaps using a dictaphone.

Of course if the Victim improves enough to go back to his own job, this is fine. He will feel an increased satisfaction in it, probably in ratio to the extra effort needed. But if it has to be a new venture it is important that this should be something which he can do by himself, or nearly so. I thought once I might do some cooking, but as that would have entailed so much collecting of tools by others and putting away again afterwards it wasn't worth it; not to me, for I wasn't that keen on cooking, and not to the household. In a specially constructed kitchen it might have been possible, or in a bungalow I might have managed some other chores, but we wished to go on sharing a house with my husband's parents, and we had to have a housekeeper anyway.

I know really that the one talent I ought to exploit is that for writing, and I try to, in the time not spent worrying about the family, knitting and mending.

Occasionally I imagine that the whole thing is some macabre joke, as in 'The Monkey's Paw', when the woman had two wishes granted, and then retracted them with the third. I can remember wishing, when the children were babies and I was so tired, that I would like to go to bed for a year. I did. And I also wished, though even less seriously, that I could be shut up somewhere — a hermit's or prisoner's cell perhaps — so that I could get some writing done. And I have been. I haven't had a third wish, and if I had I would be chary of using it. Didn't someone say that the worst thing that could happen to a man was to have his wishes come true?

I have said that no one, after emerging from a serious and cataclysmic illness, is the same person again. He might think he was or would be, but for good or evil he would be different. The components are still there, naturally, but reassembled, some diminished and some enlarged, until the result is a variation on the theme of his old self, which until he is familiar with the score he has to play by ear. At the same time he has the same family and commitments as before. They do not change.

The Victim's most important task is to put himself into perspective and, eschewing the king-like role of the patient, become merely a person again. His world-shattering experience has in fact shattered only his and his family's little world, and there are millions of people and millions of worlds. However, his attitude and behaviour afterwards can spread circles of influence far beyond his immediate situation, whether that is contained by four walls or not.

From the months in the general hospital my most vivid recollection is of the first time I was taken out of the ward and downstairs to the nurses' hostel to have a cup of coffee. On the way a door was open to the garden and I saw the grass. We stopped, and I stared at it in astonishment and exaltation. Its greenness was of a quality beyond memory and beyond imagination. I drank it in, and it was as though my body had lacked some mysterious chlorophyll of its own which it now recognized and absorbed. That moment should be put on the scales against all the previous pain and frustration and humiliation; and I think the scales would balance.

Of course the moment passed, like the bad ones. Not many Victims are destined for the life of a mystic or philosopher-saint, which is just as well, as it would be very hard on their relations. Nevertheless, such an opportunity to see everything freshly again is not easily forgotten. It is something to carry forward into the mundane struggle and days of inching progress, when, like Alice, it seems to take all the running you can do to stay in the same place. You have felt yourself, however briefly, to be linked to the universe, which would be the weaker if that link were broken. And you want to exclaim, with the woman to Thomas Carlyle: 'I accept the universe!'

Only, I hope, to receive the same reply: 'My God, she'd better!'

PART FIVE
The development and education
of handicapped children

Introduction

Probably the most critical event in the life of a handicapped person is the point at which the handicap is diagnosed, with the consequent implications for parents and relatives. The first item in Part Five by Illingworth, deals with the paediatric examination of infants, when handicap may be first diagnosed. An understanding of the medical terminology is not essential to the main point, which is that physical development and the development of motor skills are not as important in indicating intellectual handicap as qualities such as language development or powers of concentration. These latter qualities are primarily psychological ones, and the next item, a chapter by Mittler, discusses some of the issues relating to psychological assessment.

Like Illingworth, Mittler stresses the use of 'profile assessment', rather than a single quotient such as the intelligence quotient or social quotient But from his position that the main purpose of assessment is to serve treatment, Mittler points out that profile assessments which are also appreciably less reliable than quotients, still offer problems. He argues for the use of the experimental assessment of learning skills as the most helpful development in psychological work with handicapped children. Other items in this book exemplifying clinical and other forms of assessment for various purposes include Townsend, in Part Two, and the discussion of rehabilitation included in Part Eight. Psychological assessment will be required in the situations where a child or adult is handicapped in multiple ways. A wide range of relevant work in this field is reviewed in a symposium edited by Peter Mittler (1969).

How does a handicapped child think of himself? Richardson, Hastorf and Dornbush follow an interesting and imaginative approach to examine this question. Their findings suggest that handicapped children are realistic in their perception of their own situation, but that their appreciation of the nuances of interpersonal relationships is limited — perhaps through a lack of social involvement and experiences. It is important to remember that the findings of this investigation relate to American children aged ten to eleven years, in the context of a summer camp situation. But the enquiry was carefully conducted and the findings are provocative.

If a lack of social involvement and experience results in limiting the conceptual framework that handicapped children use, how can this lack be best remedied? It can be argued that bringing the handicapped person into the community as far as possible is a fundamental principle — and in childhood the community is the ordinary school. We do not know whether the children of the Richardson enquiry attended ordinary schools or not. But just as it is too easy to assume that all handicapped children need special schooling, so it is too easy to argue that all handicapped children should be educated in ordinary schools. Kershaw's article discusses the practical issues involved in this latter situation with care. He discusses the points of stress which will occur and he particularly emphasizes the importance of the perceptiveness and understanding of the teacher if a placement in an ordinary school is to be successful. Finally, he argues for the need of a team approach in which 'members of several disciplines forget demarcation lines and professional possessiveness'.

This last point is very much the theme of

Cotton's article. This outlines very briefly a Hungarian approach to the education of cerebral palsied children in which the barriers between the experiences of education, speech therapy, physiotherapy, are broken down and the child learns all these skills with the help of one person or 'conductor'. This is described in relation to a special school, but the principles advocated could be of much more general application. Considerable attention is paid to both the methods and the ways of organizing teaching for deaf and blind children in Part Six, and to the mode of formulating individual behaviour modification programmes in Part Eight.

The extract from Morgan's paper focuses particularly on the handicapped adolescent. It stresses that physically handicapped adolescents have the same needs and drives as non-handicapped adolescents. Leaving school is just as much of a critical point for them as it is for others and they need just as careful guidance and counselling in which their developmental needs are recognized and understood. One of these needs, and one which has been glossed over in the past, is for satisfactory relationships with the opposite sex. The last article in this part, by Shearer, opens up this question by discussing some of the issues relating to sex and marriage among handicapped persons.

A recent careers book for young people with handicaps, which has been written by a team of disabled men and women, to which reference may be made, is *Despite Disability: career achievement,* published in 1974 as one of the 'My Life and My Work' series by Educational Explorers, Reading.

REFERENCES

MITTLER, P., 1969, *The Psychological Assessment of Mental and Physical Handicaps,* London, Tavistock Publications.
Despite Disability: Career achievement, 1974, Reading, Education Explorers, 'My Life and Work' series.

21. The development of the infant and young child, normal and abnormal: interpretation*

R. S. ILLINGWORTH
Professor of Child Health,
University of Sheffield and
Paediatrician, The Children's
Hospital and Jessop Hospital
for Women, Sheffield.

Allowance for prematurity

In developmental assessment, it is essential that allowance must be made for premature delivery [...]. Development is continuing from conception to maturity, and birth is just an event in that development. If a baby is born prematurely, he misses development *in utero*, and proper allowance must be made. For instance, if a baby is seen for assessment at 4 months of age, and it is found that he was born two months prematurely, he must be compared not with an average 4 month old baby, but with a two month baby.

In theory allowance should be made for postmaturity, but this is not now likely to be of significant degree, because its dangers are well recognised.

Relative importance of different fields of development

Some fields of development are more important for assessment purposes than other fields. Below is a summary of my opinions on this.

Gross motor development

It is unfortunate that the aspect of development which is the most easily assessed and scored is the least valuable for the overall assessment of a child's development and capability. It would be quite wrong to suggest that gross motor development is useless as part of the developmental examination. It is of great value, but its limitations have to be recognised. It is true that defective motor development, as determined by head control in ventral suspension and the prone position, is commonly the first sign of abnormality in a child who is mentally retarded from birth or before birth. It is true that the majority of mentally retarded chiidren are late in learning to sit and to walk, but the exceptions are so frequent that one can hardly deny that the age of sitting and walking is only of limited value in assessing intelligence.

In Table 21.1 I have analysed the age at which mentally retarded children, seen by me at the Children's Hospital, Sheffield, learnt to sit for a few seconds without support, and to walk a few steps without support. None had cerebral palsy or other mechanical disability. None had any degenerative disease, so that there was no deterioration in these children. Mongols are kept separate from the others. The gradings 'seriously subnormal' and 'educationally subnormal' were based on IQ tests at school age.

It will be seen that the age at which unsupported sitting began was average (6 to 7 months) in 8.3 per cent of the ineducable children, in 6.7 per cent of the mongols, and in 10.7 per cent of those who were educationally subnormal.

*From R. S. Illingworth, (1972) *The Development of the Infant and Young Child, Normal and Abnormal*, fifth edition, London, Churchill Livingstone, Chapter 14, pp. 270–85.

175

Table 21.1

| Age in months | Age of sitting unsupported | | |
	Seriously subnormal Total 48 Percentage	Educationally subnormal Total 28 Percentage	Mongols Total 45 Percentage
6 to 7	8.3	10.7	6.7
8 to 9	14.5	39.3	31.1
10 to 11	2.1	7.2	26.6
12 to 17	35.4	39.3	22.0
18 to 23	15.0	3.6	} 13.4
24+	22.9	0	

| Age in months | Age of walking unsupported | | |
	Seriously subnormal Total 59 Percentage	Educationally subnormal Total 42 Percentage	Mongols Total 37 Percentage
Under 12 months	0	4.7	0
12 to 14	5.1	9.5	0
15 to 17	10.1	14.3	0
18 to 23	18.6	19.0	24.3
24 to 35	37.2	40.5	51.4
36 to 47	13.5	4.7	10.7
48 to 59	10.1	2.4	} 13.5
60+	5.1	4.7	

On the other hand the skill was not acquired until after the first birthday in 73.3 per cent of the ineducable children other than mongols, 35.4 per cent of the mongols, and 42.9 per cent of the educationally subnormal children.

The age of walking without support was average (12 to 17 months) in 15.2 per cent of the ineducable children other than mongols, and in 29.5 per cent of the educationally subnormal ones. No mongols walked as soon as this. On the other hand the skill was not acquired until the second birthday or after in 65.9 per cent of the ineducable children, 75.6 per cent of the mongols and 52.3 per cent of the educationally subnormal ones.

It has already been mentioned that there are great variations in the age of sitting and walking in normal children, some learning to walk without support by the age of 8 months, and some not until the age of 3 or 4 years. Early locomotion does not in any way indicate a high level of intelligence. Elsewhere I described a boy who

had uniformly advanced gross motor development, but his IQ score subsequently was only 88. All that one can say about unusually early motor development is that it probably excludes mental deficiency.

There is only a measure of truth in the view expressed by Abt *et al.* (1929) that there is a positive relationship between the age of walking and intelligence. Their figures indicate that the reason for the correlation is the fact that most retarded children are late in learning to walk. Hurlock (1956) wrote that, 'Babies who are slow in sitting up, standing up or walking generally prove, as time goes on, to be backward in intellectual development. On the other hand, those who are precocious in motor development prove to be, for the most part, intellectually precocious'. I think that the latter part of the statement is doubtful. One agrees with Shirley (1931) who wrote that 'Locomotor precocity, such as walking at an early age, certainly should not be used as a single criterion for predicting superior intelligence'. Terman, (1926) however, wrote that the average age of walking was 1 month earlier in gifted children than average children; yet an occasional child in his gifted group did not walk before the age of 2 years.

I would feel that the main clinical importance of delayed locomotion lies in the fact that it should make one extremely careful to look for signs of cerebral palsy or hypotonia though delayed locomotion may occur without discoverable cause. The main importance of unusually early locomotion is that it almost excludes mental deficiency and certainly excludes cerebral palsy.

Fine motor development (manipulation)

Though I have no figures with which to prove it, I feel that the development of manipulation is a better guide to the level of intelligence than is gross motor development. I have not seen notable delay in manipulative development in normal children. The only children in whom I have seen unusually early development of manipulation have proved to have a high IQ later. It is obvious that some children have certain aptitudes, irrespective of intelligence, and that some children are better than others in the use of their hands. I believe that this may be detected in the latter part of the first year in some children.

I have already said that if one sees good finger-thumb apposition and a definite index finger approach at 10 months, one is fairly safe in saying that the child is not mentally defective. I have not seen a mentally defective child with average manipulative ability, provided that he was defective from birth or before, and has therefore not acquired normal manipulation before the development of mental deficiency. I believe that the relationship of fine motor development to subsequent intelligence would repay further study.

Speech

The words speech and language are often used as synonyms, whereas they should really be distinguished from each other. By speech one denotes the use of words, but by language one means the expression of thought in words. The assessment of language from the developmental point of view is difficult, but the use of 'speech' as an indication of developmental level is relatively easy, the two chief milestones, as already stated, being the age at which words are first used with meaning, and the age at which words are first joined together spontaneously.

It is the experience of many workers that the early development of speech is a most important sign of a good level of intelligence. Terman (1926) wrote that 'Earliness of onset of speech is one of the most striking developmental characteristics of intellectually gifted children'. Abt *et al.* (1929) wrote that 'The development of speech and intelligence go hand in hand'. Anderson (1939) wrote that 'Early language development appears to be more closely related to later intelligence test scores than any other grouping of tests. A tentative conclusion may be drawn, namely, that the best indication of intelligence at 18 and 24 months of age is development in the use and understanding of language'. Spiker and Irwin (1949), found a good correlation between speech sounds and the level of intelligence, and between subsequent speech and the IQ. Catalano and McCarthy (1954) described work by Fisichelli, who made a phonemic analysis of tape recordings of the vocalisations of 23 infants in an institution, at the mean age of 13.3 months. They followed these children up and conducted Stanford-Binet tests on them at the mean age of 44.8 months. There was a strongly positive correlation between the infant sounds and the subsequent

Stanford-Binet tests, especially with regard to consonant types, the frequency of consonant sounds, the number of different kinds of consonant sounds, and the consonant-vowel frequency and type ratio. The correlation between the IQ and the number of different kinds of consonants gave a coefficient of .45 with the Stanford-Binet tests.

Ausubel (1958) wrote that 'intelligence is perhaps the most important determinant of precocity in speech, since it affects both the ability to mimic and to understand the meaning of verbal symbols'.

In my opinion the greatest importance should be attached to speech development as an index of intelligence. It has already been stated that the development of speech may be delayed in children of average or superior intelligence, so that it follows that delayed speech in itself can never be used as an indication of mental retardation. Advanced speech, however, is in my experience always an indication of superior intelligence. I should be most surprised, for instance, if I heard a child speaking well in sentences at 15 months, and subsequently found that his IQ was 100 (unless there was subsequent emotional deprivation, or other retarding factor).

It must be mentioned again that the understanding of words far outstrips the ability to articulate them. I should be just as impressed with a child who was able to point to a large number of objects in a picture book as an indication that he understood the meaning of words. I believe that there is a need for a new development test for children aged 12 to 18 months, based entirely on their understanding of the meaning of words.

Just as advanced speech can be regarded as a sign of superior intelligence, average speech can be regarded as a sign of at least average intelligence, though a child of 12 to 24 months with average speech may also prove to be of superior intelligence. The above opinion is important, because one sees children with delayed motor development, with or without some mechanical disability, in whom an assessment of intelligence is required. The presence of average speech immediately tells one that his intelligence is normal, even though he is also retarded in another field, such as sphincter control.

In the same way speech is important in the assessment of retarded children, and especially those with a physical handicap such as cerebral palsy. If, for instance, a child were severely retarded in all fields but speech, in which retardation was only slight, I should give a good prognosis with regard to his intelligence, because I would think that his IQ would be only slightly below the average. I have only once seen a possible exception to this.

Smiling and social behaviour

The age at which a baby begins to smile is of considerable importance in the assessment of a child. The mentally retarded child almost invariably begins to smile long after the age of 4 to 6 weeks, the average age. The mean age of smiling in a consecutive series of 62 mongols seen by me was 4.1 months. It is vital, of course, to make due allowance for prematurity in these early milestones.

I do not know whether unusually early smiling presages superior intelligence, or whether it is affected by the child's personality. I suspect that it usually presages superior intelligence.

There is some disagreement as to what the baby's early smiles signify. Bowlby (1957) regarded the smile as a 'built-in species specific pattern' — a view with which I agree. Bowlby implies that the smile is not merely a learned conditioned response, as has been suggested by some. It has been shown that the essential stimulus for the early smile is the face.

Whatever the psychological explanation of the smile, the age at which the baby begins to smile at his mother in response to her overtures is an important and valuable milestone of development, in that this is bound up with the child's maturity and therefore with his mental development. I agree with Soderling (1959) that smiling is in some way dependent on maturation, though environment must play a part.

It is important to note the age at which babies begin to laugh, to play games, to imitate, to draw the attention of their parents (*e.g.* by a cough), and their general social responsiveness. More important still are those features like the alertness, the power of concentration, the degree of determination of a baby (*e.g.* to obtain a toy out of reach, or to grasp a pellet when he is not quite mature enough). 'The child speaks with his eyes'. It is very difficult to convert many of these into scores: but they can be observed, and used in a

child's assessment. They are far more important than the readily scored sensorimotor items, which have been the basis of most of the tests used by those psychologists who found that developmental tests have no predictive value.

Sphincter control

This is of relatively little value for the assessment of a child. Mentally retarded children are usually late in acquiring control of the bladder, but not always, while many children of superior intelligence are late in acquiring control. Apart from constitutional and anatomical factors, the parental management has considerable bearing on the age at which control is learnt, and this is irrelevant in the assessment of a child's intelligence.

Chewing

I find that the age at which a child begins to chew is of considerable value in assessing a child. Mentally retarded children are always late in learning to chew. It is my impression that babies who begin to chew unusually early (the earliest being about 4½ months), are bright children, but I have no figures to support this.

It has already been said that an extraneous factor has to be considered (and eliminated by the history) and that is failure of the parents to give the child solid foods to chew. This would delay the development of chewing — or at least the age at which it is observed.

The relationship of one field of development to another: dissociation

In the assessment of the value of the history for diagnosis and prediction, it is important to balance one field of development against another. In the great majority of children the development in one field approximates fairly closely to the development in another. For instance, most children at the age of 6 to 7 months are nearly able to sit on the floor without support: they are able to grasp objects easily and they have recently learnt to transfer them from hand to hand: they have recently learnt to chew: they have just begun to imitate: they are making certain characteristic sounds when vocalising. In assessing any child, one automatically assesses his development in each field. Gesell remarked that the developmental quotient can be specifically ascertained for each separate field of behaviour and for individual behaviour traits.

In some children, however, the development in one field is out of step with that in other fields. It has already been explained that there are great individual variations in various fields of development, children learning some skills much sooner or later than others, though they are just average in other fields. For instance, some children are late in single fields, such as speech or walking, and yet are average in other aspects of development. I have termed this 'Dissociation' (Illingworth 1958). It is important for enabling one to determine the likelihood that the mother's story is correct, and it draws one's attention to variations in development, such as lateness in one field, which require investigation. The following case history may be cited as an example:

Case report. This girl, born at term, reached important stages of development at the times below:

6 weeks	Smile
5 months	Grasp objects voluntarily.
6 months	Chew.
1 year	Casting. Saying 3 words. Good concentration and interest. Very defective weight bearing; equivalent to that of average 3 months' old baby. Knee jerks normal. Marked general hypotonia.
Diagnosis.	Benign congenital hypotonia.

She walked without help at 5 years. Her IQ was 100.

Whenever one finds that a child is notably retarded in one field as compared with his development in others, a search should be made for the cause. In many, as has already been said, no cause will be found, but the cause will be found in others. Below is an example of dissociation.

Case record. Diplegia in an infant with minimal neurological signs.

This boy was referred to me at the age of 5½ months for assessment of suitability for adoption. He had been a full term baby. He began to smile at 7 weeks and to vocalise 2 weeks later. It was uncertain when he had

begun to grasp objects. He had not begun to chew. It was said that he was very interested when his feed was being prepared.

On examination he did not grasp an object. The head control was not full, being that of a 4 months old baby. He bore very little weight on his legs — being no better in weight bearing than an average 2 months old baby, though it was said that he had been given a chance to do so. I thought that the knee jerks were normal. The baby seemed alert. I advised the foster parents to let me see the boy in three months, and not to clinch the adoption until I had done so.

I saw him at 9½ months. He began to chew and to sit without support at 6 months. At that age he had begun to cough to attract attention, and to shake his head when his mother said 'No'. He could not nearly grasp the pellet between finger and thumb, but his grasp of a cube (with each hand) was average for the age. He was alert, vocalising well and sitting securely. He had begun to play patacake. Yet his weight bearing was seriously defective. I now realised that both knee jerks were definitely exaggerated and there was bilateral ankle clonus. The knee jerk was more brisk on the left than on the right. When I discussed this with the foster parents they remarked that he had always kicked more with the right leg than the left. The diagnosis was spastic diplegia, with a normal level of intelligence. The full implications were explained to the parents, who unhesitatingly decided to adopt him in spite of his physical handicap.

This case was interesting because of the minimal signs of spastic diplegia, discovered on routine developmental examination. There were no suggestive symptoms, and the only developmental sign pointing to the diagnosis was defective weight bearing. It may be that the inability to grasp the pellet was the only sign of truly minimal involvement of the upper limbs, for judging from his developmental level in other fields, he should have acquired finger-thumb apposition.

Below is another case report which illustrates the importance of balancing one field of development against another.

Case report. Mental retardation with anomalous features.

This girl was referred to me at the age of 14 months because the parents were unable to accept the gloomy prognosis given to them by a paediatrician in another city.

She was born a month after term by Caesarian section as a result of signs of foetal distress. The birth weight was 9 pounds 9 ounces. Pregnancy had been normal throughout. There were no other children. She was asphyxiated at birth and had 'several' convulsions in the first 3 weeks. She was kept in an oxygen tent for 5 days. The condition in the newborn period was such that the parents were given a bad prognosis with regard to her future development.

The subsequent history was somewhat confusing. She had never picked any object up. Both parents were uncertain whether she could see. She had been examined on that account by an ophthalmologist when she was under an anaesthetic, and no abnormality was found in the eyes. She was said to turn her head to sound at 3 months. She had begun to smile at 4 or 5 months, and to vocalise at 6 or 7 months. She was said to laugh heartily now. At 6 months she had begun to hold a rattle placed in her hand. She had begun to imitate sounds (a laugh, a song) at 8 months and to imitate the rhythm of songs. She said 'dadada' from 8 months. She had just begun to play with her hands, watching them in front of her face (hand regard). She had begun to chew at 11 to 12 months, and at that age would eat a biscuit.

On examination she was a microcephalic girl with a head circumference of $16\frac{7}{8}$ inches, which was very small when her weight at birth was considered. The fontanelle was closed. She was very obese, weighing 32 pounds and tall for her age. She showed no interest whatsoever in test toys, but was seen to smile at her mother when she talked to her. She was heard to make vocalisations (complex sounds with 'ch' and 'dada') such as one would expect to hear at 10 months. The grasp of a cube placed in the hands was immature. Her head control was that of a 3 months old baby. In the prone position her face was held at an angle of 45 degrees to the couch. There was head lag when she was pulled to the sitting position, with considerable head wobble when she was swayed from side to side. There were asymmetrical creases in the thighs. She played for a prolonged period with a rattle placed in the hand, but would not go for any object. She bore virtually no weight on her legs. It was difficult to assess muscle tone owing to the obesity, but the impression was one of hypotonia rather than hypertonia; and abduction of the hips was greater than usual. The knee jerks were normal, but there was bilateral unsustained ankle clonus. The optic fundi were normal. The X-ray of the hips was normal, and the X-ray of the skull showed normal sutures. The urine did not contain phenylpyruvic acid.

There were difficulties about giving a confident prognosis here, and these difficulties were explained to the parents, who were intelligent. The development history and examination indicated dissociation. She was severely retarded in manipulation and motor development, and there was no evidence that she could see — though it is difficult to be sure whether a severely retarded baby can see or not until he is old enough. On the other hand, in chewing, imitation, and vocalisation she was only moderately retarded and her IQ in these respects would indicate that she should fall into the educable range later. This strongly suggested a mechanical disability, and the unsustained ankle clonus suggested that she might prove to have the spastic form of cerebral palsy. Subsequent athetosis, however, could not be excluded. The relatively good development in speech and imitation suggested that the IQ would not be as bad as it appeared on the surface.

The second difficulty was the question of blindness. I was unable to say whether the child could see or not. Blindness would explain some of the features of the history and examination, and in particular the complete lack of interest in surroundings was out of keeping with the fact that the girl turned her head to sound from about 3 months.

The third difficulty was the history of convulsions. There was a considerable possibility that convulsions would occur later, possibly with mental deterioration.

I gave my opinion that the prognosis was bad, and that she would probably prove ineducable, but said that in view of the difficulties mentioned above she might prove better than expected — though possibly with the complication of cerebral palsy and perhaps with blindness. I arranged to see her in a year.

The significance of the development of speech in relation to other fields has been mentioned. In general the finding that speech development is relatively more advanced than motor development would make one look particularly carefully for a mechanical disability, such as hypertonia or hypotonia, though the occasional late walker has also been discussed.

The calculation of a score

Though it is very much a matter of opinion, I think that it is usually unwise to calculate a single figure for the DQ or IQ in the preschool child. The reason is that some fields of development are so much more important than others, that a single figure is apt to be fallacious. Ruth Griffiths used an interesting method. She used the term GQ, meaning the general intelligence Quotient, and to obtain this she worked out the quotient for each of 5 fields of development (the QA, locomotor quotient; QB, personal social; QC, speech; QD, hand and eye quotient; QE, performance quotient — which includes the ability to reason, or to manipulate material intelligently). She then added up all five quotients, divided by 5, and termed this the GQ. I consider that the method of working out the quotient in each field separately and showing a 'profile' (Figure 21.1) is excellent; but I disagree entirely with the idea of obtaining a GQ from the product of these 5 quotients, because that would imply that all fields of development are of equal importance. They are not.

Such a scoring method fails to take into account physical, mechanical or even environmental causes for retardation in individual fields — factors which have no bearing on the child's intelligence. If one were to calculate one overall score for a child with paralysed legs due to meningomyelocele, his score would be lowered by the fact that he could not walk.

Below is an example of the difficulty of assessing a child on the basis of one overall score.

I saw the girl for the first time at the age of three years five months. The following are extracts from the letter which I wrote to the family doctor:

There are several difficulties about giving a confident prognosis here. One is that there is a family history of late walking in both mother

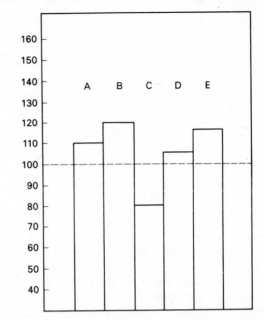

Figure 21.1 A developmental profile (*After Ruth Griffiths*). A to E represent five different fields of development.

and father, and it would not be surprising if the children were to take after them.

There was delayed motor development. She began to sit without help at 14 months and walk without help at 22 months. I have seen quite a few normal children who were unable to walk until after the second birthday. On the other hand her speech was good. She was saying single words under a year, and sentences at 18 months. I have never met a mentally subnormal child who could do that. Furthermore sphincter control began at 12 months. She has, however, been late in learning to manage a cup, and she has only just begun to do so, and she is not very good at dressing herself, but I am not sure whether the parents have given her a chance to learn these things. This is a difficult age at which to carry out developmental testing, but I have come to the conclusion that in one or two tests she was average, but in others she was retarded. There is, therefore, considerable scatter in her performance which makes a confident opinion about the future impossible. She looks normal. She concentrated well on a doll's house when I was talking to the mother.

Her head is of normal size. Her gait is normal. I explained that when a child has learned to walk as late as this, you must expect her to be unsteady in walking for quite a long time afterwards.

On the whole I think that Mary will prove to be normal, and not below the average, but one cannot be sure at this stage. I shall be seeing her again in about a year in order to re-assess progress.

I followed her progress with interest. By the age of four years she was reading well, and at five years she was assessed as having a reading age of 9½ years. Her manipulative, creative and physical ability were described by her teacher as excellent.

I would certainly decry the conversion of any scores into one figure to denote the IQ, because that would imply that the IQ is a static figure, which the child will always have. It has been amply shown that it is far from static, and that it may be profoundly affected by a wide variety of factors.

Gesell's term 'the developmental quotient' seems to be as good as any: it indicates how far the child has developed in relation to the average level of development at that age: and no implication is made that it will not alter as future years go by. By observing the rate of development and changes in the DQ, one can form a good conclusion as to how far the child is likely to develop, given good environmental circumstances. One assesses, in other words, his developmental potential.

I personally prefer to say in my letters to family doctors that a child has developed as far as an average child of x months: but I always qualify that by commenting on the individual fields of development, emphasising where relevant, that one is particularly concerned with his interest, powers of concentration, alertness, and speech, and much less concerned with his gross motor development. I might say, for instance, that a 36 months old boy has in general only developed as far as an average 24 months old boy but the fact that his speech is very much better than the 24 months old level, even though he appears to be below the 24 months old level in other fields, indicates that there is real hope that he is well above the 24 months level in potential growth, and that he may well do much better than superficially appears likely at present.

In some cases the difficulties of assessment are such that it is quite impossible to forecast the child's future without further observation. It is impossible, for instance, to predict the child's future development if there had been adverse environmental factors, such as prolonged institutional care or some serious debilitating disease, when an infant who is found to be uniformly retarded. A period of observation after the correction of these adverse factors is essential before any opinion is expressed about his developmental potential.

I was asked to assess the mental development of a 21 months old child with nephrogenic diabetes insipidus. He had not thrived, weighing only 15 pounds at the time. He had had repeated admissions to hospital. His general level of development was that of a 12 months old baby with little scatter in different fields, though he showed good interest in his surroundings and in toys — an important observation suggesting that he might well prove to have a normal level of intelligence. It was impossible to assess this child's developmental potential without serial observations of his rate of development.

He has been followed up since then. At the age of 6 years 4 months he is progressing normally in an ordinary school. Physically he is small, weighing 27 pounds 6 ounces (12.4 kilograms) and measuring 39⅜ inches (100 centimetres).

The experienced paediatrician will resist the temptation to attempt to give an accurate figure for the child's developmental quotient. He is merely deceiving himself if he thinks that he can distinguish a developmental quotient of 70 from one of 71. He can and should be able to place the child into an approximate position in the developmental range. Any attempt to be more accurate will only lead to inaccuracy.

Summary

Some fields of development are much more important than others for the purposes of developmental assessment.

Gross motor development, which is the easiest field of development to assess, and which was the field used more than any other in many studies, is the least useful for the purposes of prediction. Quite severely retarded children may learn to walk at the average age. Advanced motor development in no way presages a high IQ.

Manipulative development and the age of chewing are useful for predictive purposes.

The most valuable of all fields for prediction is speech (and pre-speech vocalisation), provided that it is recognised that retardation in speech development does not in itself portend a low IQ.

The age of beginning to smile, and social behaviour, are valuable fields for study. The age of acquiring clean toilet habits is of only slight value for prediction.

More important than any of the above are the baby's alertness, interest in surroundings, powers of concentration, and determination — all items which are difficult to translate into scores.

In all cases the development in one field should be compared and contrasted with that in another. If a child is notably out of step in one field of development ('dissociation') the cause should be looked for.

Because of the relatively greater importance of some fields of development than of others, it is usually unwise to express the whole of a baby's development in one score.

REFERENCES

ABT, I. A., ADLER, H. M., BARTELME, P., 1929, 'The Relationship between the Onset of Speech and Intelligence', *Journal of the American Medical Association*, 93, p. 1351.

ANDERSON, L. D., 1939, 'The Predictive Efficiency of Infancy Tests in Relation to Intelligence at 5 years', *Child Development*, 10, p. 203.

AUSUBEL, D. P., 1958, *Theory and Problems of Child Development*, New York, Grune and Stratton.

BOWLBY, J., 1957, 'Symposium on the Contribution of Current Theories to an Understanding of Child Development', *British Journal of Medical Psychology*, 30, p. 230.

CATALANO, F. L., McCARTHY, D., 1954, 'Infant Speech as a Possible Predictor of Later Intelligence', *Journal of Psychology*, 38, p. 203

GRIFFITHS, R, 1954, *The Abilities of Babies*, London, University of London Press.

HURLOCK, E. B., 1956, *Child Development*, London, McGraw-Hill.

ILLINGWORTH, R. S., 1958, 'Dissociation as a Guide Developmental Assessment', *Archives of Disease in Childhood*, 33, 118.

SHIRLEY, H. F., 1931, *The First Two Years*, Minneapolis, University of Minnesota Press.

SÖDERLING, B., 1959, 'The First Smile', *Acta Paediatrica (Uppsala)*, 48, Suppl. 117. 78.

SPIKER, C. C., IRWIN, O. C., 1949, 'The Relationship between IQ and Indices of Infant Speech Sound Development', *Journal of Speech Disorders*, 14, 335.

TERMAN, L. M., 1926, *Genetic Studies of Genius*, London, Harrap.

22. Purposes and principles of assessment *

PETER MITTLER
Director of the Hester Adrian Research Centre for the study of
Learning Processes in the Mentally Handicapped, University of Manchester.

This chapter has three aims:

1. To place psychological problems of assessment into the social and political context of a rapidly expanding demand for adequate assessment of handicapped individuals.

2. To discuss some of the assets and deficits of traditional assessment procedures, particularly those arising from the use of intelligence testing.

3. To present a brief account of a number of experimental developments which seem likely to provide alternative or supplementary assessment techniques.

1. The demand for assessment

The importance of adequate assessment procedures is widely accepted, but there is much confusion and uncertainty on the subject. Doubts are being expressed about the relevance and effectiveness of many of the well-established techniques, but attempts to develop better and more sensitive methods have not yet made sufficient impact to provide viable alternatives to traditional practice. As a result many psychologists who are strongly critical of established procedures cannot confidently recommend or adopt new approaches. This represents what is sometimes euphemistically described as a 'delicate transitional phase'. Unfortunately, this period of uncertainty happens to coincide with a revival of official

interest in assessment facilities for handicapped populations. Government encouragement is being given to the setting up of large numbers of assessment and diagnostic units in hospitals, clinics and schools. There is some evidence that psychologists are not being involved either in the establishment or in the day to day running of many of these units (British Psychological Society 1972). One of a number of possible explanations for this neglect of their skills is that the psychologist's contribution is either not understood or not actively sought.

Common to much of the current dissatisfaction is a concern for the separation that has arisen between assessment and treatment. Doctors are taught during the course of their training that treatment must be linked to diagnosis, but this rule applies more obviously in general medicine than in the field of the developmental disorders. It is easier to diagnose mental retardation, or even a common syndrome such as mongolism than to suggest what treatment should be provided either by the doctor, the teacher or the parent.

Psychologists on the other hand have over the years become associated with assessment, allocation and classification, but rarely with the design or application of specific programmes of treatment. Complex historical factors are responsible for this preoccupation with testing. In the early years of this century, intelligence tests were welcomed as positive instruments of social change, enabling 'pools of ability' to be discovered in working class communities, so that secondary and higher education could be made available on a

*From P. Mittler (ed.) (1973) *Assessment for learning in the mentally handicapped*, London, Churchill Livingstone, Chapter 1, pp. 1—21

broader basis. The most obvious example here is the use of intelligence tests in selecting children for different types of secondary education. Although these procedures have now fallen into disrepute, the tests themselves proved reasonably efficient selection instruments, given the educational system of the day (Vernon 1957). Nevertheless, much of the opposition to the whole machinery of selection was focused on intelligence tests which tended as a result to become discredited by association. Furthermore, much of the original optimism about the possibilities of achieving social change through the use of scientific selection procedures had to be modified when it became clear that social class differentials remained a powerful factor, not only in relation to selection at 11+, but throughout the whole educational spectrum.

The place of intelligence tests in the selection of children for special educational treatment is not easy to establish. The former category of educational subnormality (ESN) was not in fact strictly defined by IQ at all, but by educational attainment and need. It was therefore theoretically possible to classify a child as ESN even though his IQ might be as high as 100. Surveys have indicated that the average IQ of ESN pupils is in the 70s, and that many of them have IQs well above this point (Williams 1965).

For children being considered for the former Junior Training Centres now renamed 'Special Schools', the intelligence test tended to be the principle criterion determining exclusion from the educational system, the cut off being found around an IQ of 50 to 55. Ironically enough, psychologists were by no means routinely involved in decision-making; the tests were administered by school medical officers, who accepted the main responsibility for decisions on 'educability' (British Psychological Society 1966). School medical officers also played the principal assessment role in the selection of children for ESN schools. A recent government report estimated that it would be quite impossible even for a greatly expanded profession of educational psychologists to provide adequate assessment for children being considered for special schools (Department of Education and Science 1968).

This state of affairs forces the profession to reconsider its traditional monopoly of psychological testing. Special courses of training might be made available in universities or by the British Psychological Society, which would allow non-psychologists, particularly teachers and doctors, to become competent in administering and interpreting certain tests, including the principal standardised tests such as the Terman-Merrill and Wechsler scales. Psychologists would then be able to devote themselves to more specialised work, to the most difficult problems requiring experimental methods of assessment, and above all to attempts to design programmes of treatment or remediation based on the kind of detailed study of the individual for which they now have too little time (see Mittler 1970 for a fuller discussion).

It is apparent that a study group concerned with assessment of the mentally handicapped must take cognisance of the difficult transitional situation currently confronting professional psychologists. Educational psychologists now find themselves responsible for some 35,000 children in the new special schools and hospital schools. This number has to be added to the existing total of nearly 100,000 children already receiving or awaiting special educational treatment, of whom about half are already classified as ESN. Is it realistic to ask them to exercise 'positive discrimination' on the grounds that SSN children have previously been excluded from the educational service?

Without in any way underestimating the seriousness of the manpower problem, a case for the involvment of the educational psychologist can be made by stressing the opportunity provided by his new responsibilities to exercise new skills and to play a new role in the school system. It would be unfortunate if his first contacts with the new ESN population were to take the form of giving them all an appropriate intelligence test: in other words, if he played the part expected of him in the existing system. Even the briefest period of exposure to SSN children and to the schools in which they are educated should be enough to cause him to doubt the automatic relevance of a traditional intelligence test to the entire population. There may be a case for such tests in specific instances, particularly in the case of 'borderline' children about whose placement there is room for doubt. But most children placed in JTCs are undoubtedly severely subnormal, have IQs below 50, and must be regarded as biologically damaged individuals, usually by reason of structural or functional disorders of the central nervous system. All of them, by definition, have severe problems of learning and development, but the nature and type of the learning difficulty will vary greatly from child to child. Only a small proportion of the variance of such learning difficulties is attributable to measured intelligence. Many of them have particularly severe deficits in basic information processing, in attending to the relevant aspects of a stimulus display, and in making an appropriate response. Specific difficulties both in understanding and using language are commonly found, as are severe difficulties in the use of language in problem solving. Sometimes these deficits are more apparent in one sensory modality or channel than another. In some cases, it is difficult to assess the effects of a particular stimulus configuration or specific learning situation because the child has too limited a response repertoire to enable him to provide any behavioural evidence at all. Not only are many children unable to speak, but others either cannot or will not use non-verbal signals, such as pointing or eye-pointing (Mittler 1972a).

The severity of the handicaps encountered and the initial lack of response to testing may prove unduly discouraging to the psychologist, who may abandon assessment and fall back on the use of developmental charts or scales. The term 'untestable' may even be used, though this tells us more about the psychologist than about the child. The more handicapped the child, the greater the challenge to the psychologist to use and adapt his knowledge of psychological processes, and to display an experimental approach to the problems which are presented by severely handicapped children. This challenge could not come at a more opportune moment, since psychologists are becoming increasingly critical of the relevance and validity of the tests and procedures on which they were trained. Nowhere are these procedures less relevant than in the new ESN schools. The psychologist can therefore try out new methods and techniques, in a school environment with which he is unfamiliar, but which does at least have the merit of not expecting him to play a traditional role. The fact that the new special schools have little or no experience of psychologists is in some respects a happy coincidence, for it gives him the opportunity to establish a new role in relation to teachers. At least half of these

teachers have no appropriate training, and appear to welcome any help that the psychologist can offer, provided they appreciate its relevance to their own professional role and to the learning problems of individual children.

2. Assets and deficits of intelligence testing

It will be noticed that no formal presentation in this symposium has been exclusively devoted to the assessment of general intelligence. This seems a serious omission, if only because most of the energies of psychologists are devoted to attempts to obtain a reliable intelligence test result. The omission is deliberately designed to focus discussion on the assessment of specific cognitive and other skills, on the development of new techniques of assessment, and on attempts to link assessment with treatment. Nevertheless, it is important to consider the place of intelligence testing in assessment, because this is likely to remain the procedure of choice for many psychologists, whatever new methods and developments are eventually introduced.

A further reason for omitting the subject from a formal presentation is that a good deal of information is already available on this subject, and nothing short of a book could hope to do justice to a review of the achievements of intelligence testing, as well as a critical evaluation of specific techniques. Useful reviews of test procedures have recently been compiled by Brison (1968), Allen and Jones (1968), Shakespeare (1970), Gunzburg (1970) and D. Clark (1973), all written from a subnormality point of view.

CLASSIFICATION OF 'HIGH-GRADE' SUBJECTS

The main justification of an intelligence test lies in its value as an instrument of classification. It is well known that the American behavioural classification relates degrees of retardation to standard deviation units, unlike the British system, which distinguishes only between subnormality and severe subnormality.

In a broad sense classification by IQ has much to recommend it. Despite individual exceptions, it provides a reasonably accurate reflection of current levels of functioning, though its value as a predictive or prognostic instrument is more open to doubt (Windle 1962). There is also the danger of the self-fulfilling prophecy in which, for example, an individual with a low IQ is deprived of treatment or education on the grounds that he is unable to derive benefit from it. His subsequent failure to make progress is then held to justify the original decision to withhold treatment. Although many individual case histories of mistaken diagnosis and 'recovery' of hitherto unsuspected intellectual functions have been reported, there is little justification for abandoning intelligence tests and classification procedures for that reason alone. Even in normal children, the misclassification rate in selection for secondary schools is as high as 10 per cent (Vernon 1957); the probability of error in handicapped and difficult to test populations is considerably higher. The clinician must remain aware of the variables which are likely to lead to under-estimates (or over-estimates, for that matter), and to check his results by using other tests and scales, and above all by relating the results to the individual's skills in real life. Regular reassessment is also necessary, though shortage of psychologists frequently rules this out. Most hospitals or schools barely keep pace with the assessment of new admissions; here again, there may be a case for delegating routine retesting on simpler scales to suitably trained non-psychologists, such as nurses, teachers or psychological technicians. Marked changes in intellectual functioning in either direction can then be more carefully investigated.

The situation in Britain is complicated, in so far as the 1959 Mental Health Act, while stipulating that mental subnormality must include subnormality of intelligence, is disregarded in practice; many patients in subnormality hospitals are still being designated as subnormal even though their tested intelligence is well beyond the limits agreed by psychologists to constitute subnormality of intelligence (Castell and Mittler 1965). The upper limit of subnormality of intelligence is placed by psychologists at an IQ of 70, though allowance has to be made for a borderline group with IQs up to 80 (British Psychological Society 1963). Nevertheless, the average IQ of adult admissions to hospital appears to be around 72 on the Wechsler scales. Many of these patients have several social or behavioural handicaps; they need social education and rehabilitation and are in hospital mainly because of inadequate local authority provision. Official figures indicate that 60 per cent of adult patients are still graded as subnormal rather than

severely subnormal by the hospital staff. It is clear from surveys that the great majority of children in ESN schools with IQs above 55 are suffering from a wide range of social pathologies and difficulties over and above low intelligence or learning difficulties (Kushlick 1966, Tizard, 1970). They come predominantly from social class V, and tend to live in the central areas of towns and cities, frequently in poor housing conditions, with considerable overcrowding. Parental ill health, both physical and mental, is not uncommon, and other siblings, or even one or both parents, are also likely to have had educational difficulties. Nevertheless, about 70 per cent of ESN leavers succeed in adapting to the demands of society, and need little or no further help (Stein and Susser 1963). A minority find their way into subnormality hospitals, particularly between the ages of 16 and 20.

Reliable intellectual assessment is essential for this group, who not only still constitute a large proportion of patients in subnormality hospitals, but who will equally require skilled assessment in the context of community care, now the responsibilty of the new social services departments. It is important to establish the degree of subnormality and to assess educational and social skills, since the potential abilities of some high grade subnormals are easily under-estimated, especially if they are illiterate or socially immature. This applies most strongly to adolescents and young adults whose early upbringing took place in conditions of severe deprivation or poverty. The Clarkes reported substantial IQ increments in a population of this nature, apparently as a consequence of removal to hospital from grossly unstimulating home environments (Clarke and Clarke 1954, Clarke *et al.* 1958). Similarly, Kirk (1958) showed that working class retarded children gained relatively more from pre-school programmes than their middle class counterparts. Both these studies were more concerned with 'high grade' than with more severely handicapped subjects. There is as yet no convincing evidence that socio-economic variables (e.g. social class) exert the same kind of powerful effect on the cognitive development of more severely handicapped individuals (e.g. Carr 1970; Singer and Osborn, 1970).

CLASSIFICATION OF SSN SUBJECTS

Although accurate and thorough assessment of intellectual level is of prime importance for higher grade individuals, doubts can legitimately be expressed about the use of IQ assessments in more severely handicapped populations. Buddenhagen (1967) goes so far as to state that the IQ is probably one of the most trivial items of information to be ascertained about a severely retarded individual. This seems an extreme view, but it is probably fair to say that even within the narrow framework of classification, other approaches to assessment may yield as much information as IQ. Amongst these may be included behaviour ratings and measures of social competence, such as the recent *Adaptive Behaviour Check Lists* (Nihira *et al.* 1969) as well as established scales such as the *Vineland* or the *Caine-Levine Social Competence Scale*. Evidence for this point of view is to be found in census returns based on over 23,000 patients from 19 institutions conducted by the Western Interstate Commission for Higher Education (WICHE). In a preliminary analysis of a large amount of data, Johnson (1970) reported that SQ and IQ were equally effective in predicting the ability of patients to develop social and personal skills relevant to independence, including self help, helping others and also being considered suitable for specific training programmes by the staff. Neither IQ nor SQ were related to behaviour disturbances.

If measures of social competence are as effective as IQ tests in providing information about hospital patients, psychologists might consider training nurses and other staff in the use of scales which provide relevant information about behaviour and social development. The more detailed scales not only help to sharpen observational skills, but also provide a blueprint for a training programme. Gunzburg's (1966) *Progress Assessment Charts* are designed for this purpose, and are widely used in schools for the SSN. Parents can also be taught to make systematic observations of their own handicapped children by teaching them how to use detailed developmental charts, based on items derived from standardised tests of infant development (Cunningham and Jeffree 1971).

One reason why SQ and IQ are equally effective as predictors derives from the similarity of items constant at low levels of development. Factorial studies have identified a factor of 'sensori-motor alertness' which is particularly powerful in infant scales up to about 20 months, followed by a 'persistence' factor which lasts until 40 months (Hofstaetter 1954, Smart 1965). Although there is still uncertainty about factorial structure of infant scales (Cronbach 1967), there is in practice considerable communality of item content between the two types of scale, though differences become more apparent at levels corresponding to an MA of about four.

A further reason for doubting the value of IQ tests in more severely handicapped populations arises from the loss of discriminatory power the further away one moves from the mean — in either direction. It is apparent from work with the gifted that an individual with an IQ of 160 is not necessarily more fortunate than someone with an IQ of 140, though both do better than a third person with an IQ of 120. Other factors may be more important than genuine IQ differences, including personality, motivation and opportunity. Similarly, IQ is only one of several relevant variables in the mentally handicapped. Within the previous category of 'imbecile' (corresponding roughly to the IQ range 25 − 50), IQ has been shown to be a poor predictor of learning especially in the sphere of motor skills (Clarke and Clarke 1965). Much depends on the nature of the training methods used, and also on personality factors such as response to incentives.

Individual differences have also been insufficiently studied by psychologists. A group of SSN children will show considerable clinical and behavioural heterogeneity; consequently both within and between group comparisons are fraught with difficulty. Although IQ and MA matching are frequently employed to 'control' for this factor, intelligence only accounts for a small part of the variance ascribable to individual differences. Two groups or even two individuals may be well matched for IQ, MA, social class and other 'relevant variables' but may still respond very differently to the same training programme, for reasons that are either unknown or outside the experimenter's control. The ready availability of IQ measures has sometimes led to the assumption that groups have been equated or matched, although other critical factors have been neglected (Baumeister 1967, Clarke and Clarke 1972). Unfortunately, it is clear from a symposium devoted to this subject (Gagné 1967) that research workers have only recently begun a serious and systematic study of individual differences in learning, or questioned the assumption that such sources of variance could be dealt with by examining standard deviations. The recent emphasis on the role of experiential factors in cognitive development both of normal and handicapped children has highlighted the difficulties of isolating and identifying the complex variables which affect the development of intelligence, and led to caution in the interpretation of intelligence test data derived from individuals with histories of severe deprivation of experience, whether due to sensory and motor defects, institutionalisation or neglect. A particularly valuable attempt to specify the relationship between experience and development of SSN children was made by Stephen and Robertson (1965), who also discuss ways in which deprivation of experience might be compensated.

PROFILE ANALYSIS

An increasing awareness of the limitations of intelligence testing has led in recent years to a number of attempts to develop alternative approaches to assessment. One example is provided by tests such as the Illinois Test of Psycholinguistic Abilities (Kirk *et al.* 1968) and the Frostig Developmental Test of Visual Perception (Frostig *et al.* 1964). These tests reflect an attempt to isolate different aspects of cognitive performance in 'language' and 'perception', and to provide a breakdown of these global constructs into a series of specific skills and abilities. To a lesser extent, the new British Intelligence Scale also aims to develop a multi-factorial approach to the assessment of intellectual skills (Warburton *et al.* 1970), though this test is still at an early stage of development. Tests such as ITPA and Frostig are designed to provide an organic link between assessment and treatment. By providing a profile of a child's relative assets and deficits in respect of different language skills, a remedial programme can be designed, in collaboration with teachers, which is fitted to the needs of the individual child. The test has therefore been used prescriptively rather than merely for purposes of classification.

Although these tests represent a useful and challenging model of the assessment process, many problems remain to be solved, both of a technical but also of a more fundamental nature. In the first

place, there is reason to question whether, in the case of ITPA, Osgood's (1957) model can still be considered as a satisfactory basis of a test of language abilities. It is unfortunate that the revision of the test which was published in 1968 has taken no account of developments in the field of psycholinguistics, in particular the contribution of the transformational generative linguists and their psychological followers. Even if we agree to accept the ten subtests as a preliminary basis for a description of specific language abilities, factorial studies still suggest that between 45 and 65 per cent of the test is accounted by a general language factor, and that the claim of the test constructors to have provided undimensional subtests is not fully supported (Silverstein, 1967; Mittler and Ward 1970). Profile analysis is further complicated by the problem of the reliability of differences between subtests.

Perhaps the most serious problem is represented by the difficulty of designing a detailed remedial programme which is closely linked with the diagnostic profile provided by the test. The results of such programmes have been encouraging, though some of the earlier studies merely trained children to become more skilled at passing the post-test. A number of Frostig studies, for example, have demonstrated improvements on the test following the specially devised training programme, but without showing any appreciable effects on reading ability or other evidence of generalisation or transfer (Rosen, 1966; Clark 1972).

3. The use of experimental methods

Although assessment techniques have usually consisted of standardised and normative instruments, it is likely that more emphasis will in future be laid on the development of experimental techniques. Some of these will be more fully discussed by other contributors, but the rationale of this approach can be briefly considered, together with a number of relevant examples.

The need for an experimental approach derives in part from the inability of most standardised tests to provide information on the *processes* and *strategies* of problem-solving. Tests are usually scored in terms of a right/wrong dichotomy or, more rarely, by a graded points system. Although such methods are inevitable in the context of standardised test procedures, they could usefully be supplemented by a more detailed approach, characterised by the psychologist using his knowledge of developmental and experimental psychology to devise assessment procedures for a particular purpose or for an individual child in order to learn more about the nature of the underlying cognitive processes which appear to be involved in problem-solving. Such an idiographic approach has been advocated for many years by Shapiro (e.g. 1970) but has commanded disappointingly little support from educational or clinical psychologists (see also Gwynne Jones, 1970, 1971 for illuminating discussions of this point).

It can be argued that the rapid expansion of research in experimental child psychology during the past 10 years has provided a wealth of potential assessment techniques which have so far remained largely unexploited by applied psychologists. One obvious example can be taken from the work of O'Connor and Hermelin and their associates. These and other workers (see, for example, Reese and Lipsitt 1970) have in the course of what were never intended to be anything but research studies developed methods of assessing cognitive processes which could with only a little ingenuity be modified by the educational or clinical psychologist interested in learning more about an individual child's functioning than is provided by the usual intelligence test. A close study of their two major books (O'Connor and Hermelin, 1963; Hermelin and O'Connor 1970) should suggest ideas for a variety of assessment techniques which require little or no apparatus, and which have been shown to be within the competence of severely handicapped and far from co-operative individuals. Obvious examples can be found in their experiments on 'clustering' both visual and verbal material, in which the objective was to throw light on the extent to which subnormal and autistic children were able to impose order and structure on incoming material. Such techniques can be adapted to the individual case in order to study information processing systems and organisation strategies.

Another example of an experimental approach to assessment consists essentially of a small-scale but systematic attempt to teach the individual to carry out a skill or to learn a task which is unfamiliar to him. An early example of this approach can be seen in the Modified Word Learning Test (Walton and Black 1959) in which the subject is taught the meaning of 10 words immediately above the ceiling of his vocabulary knowledge. A further example of the use of a standardised test as the basis for a learning situation can be found in Schubert's (1967) design of a teaching programme based on the WISC Block Design Test.

Response to a 'mini-teaching' (learning) situation should be instructive, even though it is not easy to quantify. Some nonverbal tests lend themselves to this procedure — e.g. the Seguin Form Board is normally scored by reference to the fastest of three trials, but no account is taken of improvements from the first to the third trial, or — as an extension from a test to a teaching situation — from the fourth to the nth trial. Limited experiments can also be undertaken to assess transfer and generalisation.

The changing emphasis from testing to teaching as part of the assessment process is most clearly reflected in the behaviouristic approach. Although the strength of operant techniques derives from their interventionist strategy, and from the creation of a direct link between assessment and training by means of a systematic study of 'baseline' behaviours, their value as assessment techniques *per se* should not be neglected. In particular, the behavioural analysis approach has developed basically simple and straightforward observational techniques which can be used not only by psychologists but also by nurses, teachers or parents after appropriate training. The main aim of such observations is to observe the frequency of a given piece of behaviour. The use of film or videotape as a teaching aid is particularly valuable for this purpose; it allows observers to ignore irrelevant material and to learn to concentrate exclusively on the behaviour in question (Gardner 1971).

Conclusions

The revival of public, political and professional concern with the care and treatment of the mentally handicapped has led to a renewed insistence on adequate assessment, not only for its own sake, but as the basis of a programme of treatment in the broadest sense. Psychologists are not well prepared to meet this demand, partly because the mentally handicapped confront them with problems for which traditional assessment techniques seem inadequate if not actually irrelevant. Thus, the incorporation into the educational system of some 35,000 severely handicapped children should act as a catalyst to a reconsideration of the psychologist's role, to a crystallisation of an already existing awareness of the limitations of traditional procedures, and to an increasing readiness to experiment with new methods.

The need for alternative approaches to assessment springs on the one hand from failure of the intelligence test to provide information which can be positively harnessed to the design of a programme of education or habilitation but also arises from the need for assessment techniques which allow for an idiographic approach to the wide individual differences found within mentally handicapped populations.

What is needed at this stage is a combination between the normative tradition and newer methods that tell us more about the individual person. The intelligence test reliably and validly classifies and categorises the individual, and is reasonably successful — within fairly generous limits of error — in predicting future educational or occupational achievement. But it tells us very little about the person as an individual. Indeed, it seems curiously paradoxical that the educational and clinical psychologist whose prime concern is with the individual should have come to place such heavy reliance on a group of tests and techniques which do little more than compare that individual with the rest of the population.

One example of such an attempt to find a balance between the normative and the individual approach can be seen in the development of 'profile assessment' as found in ITPA, in which an attempt is made to describe an individual's assets and deficits in respect of different aspects of language skills and abilities, and to plan a programme of treatment accordingly. Detailed study of a very young or immature child can also be carried out with the aid of developmental charts concerned with different aspects of development; these too can be used as the basis of observation by non-psychologists, and a programme of planned experiences and activities can be devised with teachers, nurses or parents which is designed to help the child to reach the next stage of his development. These techniques reflect a shift from

formal testing to observation, either on the basis of developmental charts (incorporating norms) or towards a criterion-referenced type of observation of the kind recently advocated by Ward (1970), designed to answer questions on the child's ability in real life situations to carry out specific tasks (e.g. retrieve a hidden object, use a screwdriver etc.). Systematic observation of the frequency of specific behavioural events also characterises the operant approach to assessment. It will be apparent that the psychologist merely initiates such assessments, but that the actual observations can be carried out by others. This point is perhaps over-emphasised in this presentation, because it seems unlikely that trained psychologists can play more than an initiatory or advisory role, considering the nature of the problem and the size of the demand for assessment of handicapped populations.

If psychologists could be relieved of a substantial part of what has now become 'routine assessment', partly by delegating such procedures to others, the time thus saved could be devoted to more specialised psychological work. Although this would need to include psychometric examinations of the most difficult cases, and advice on the interpretation of tests by others, the psychologist could then devote more time to the experimental assessment of the individual case; he might modify and adapt techniques which, although developed by research workers, appear to offer promising methods of studying ways in which individuals attend to, organise, classify, store and transform incoming information. Such a process of translation has hardly begun, though some guidelines have been tentatively described (Clarke and Clarke 1972, Serpell 1972). Such procedures are designed to provide information on the processes and strategies which an individual uses to solve problems and to deal with specific situations. These processes may be no different in kind from those used by other people, whether normal or handicapped, but may nevertheless call for rather specific methods of remediation if the individual is to be helped in the direction of normality or at least towards the next stage of his own development.

It is worth emphasising in conclusion that the experimental study of the individual is not a development that is being advocated for the benefit of handicapped populations alone. It is just as relevant for the understanding of cognitive processes in normal children; indeed, this is one way in which the study of handicap might contribute to our understanding of normal development.

REFERENCES

ALLEN, R. M. and JONES, R. W., 1968, 'Perceptual, Conceptual and Psycholinguistic Evaluation of the Mentally Retarded Child', in Baumeister, 1968.

BAUMEISTER, A. 1967, 'Problems in comparative studies of mental retardates and normals, *American Journal of Mental Deficiency*, 71, pp. 869.

BAUMEISTER, A.(ed.), 1968, *Mental Retardation: Appraisal Education and Rehabilitation*, London, University of London Press.

BRISON, D. W., 1968, 'Definition, Diagnosis and Classification, in Baumeister 1968.

British Psychological Society, 1963, Report of Working Party on Subnormality, *Bulletin of the British Psychological Society* 16, p. 53.

British Psychological Society, 1966, 'Children in Hospitals for the Subnormal', London, British Psychological Society.

British Psychological Society, 1972, The contribution of psychologists to children's assessment units. Report of BPS Working Party. *Bulletin of the British Psychological Society*, (in press).

BUDDENHAGEN, R.G. 1967, 'Towards a better understanding', *Journal of Mental Retardation*, 5, pp. 40.

CARR, J. 'Mental and motor development in young mongol children' *Journal of Mental Deficiency Research*, 14, p. 205.

CASTELL, J. H. F., and MITTLER, P., 1965, 'Intelligence of patients in subnormality hospitals: a survey of admissions in 1961', *British Journal of Psychiatry* 111, p. 219.

CLARK, D., 1973, 'Psychological Assessment in Mental Deficiency,' in Ann Clarke and A. D. B. Clarke, eds *Mental Deficiency: the Changing Outlook*, (3rd ed). Methuen.

CLARKE, A. D. B., and CLARKE, A. M., 1954, 'Cognitive changes in the feeble-minded', *British Journal of Psychology*, 45, p. 173.

CLARKE, A. D. B., CLARKE, A. M. and REIMAN, 1958, 'Cognitive and social changes in the feeble-minded — three further studies', *British Journal of Psychology*, 49, p. 144.

CLARKE, A. D. B. and CLARKE, A. M. 1965, 'The Abilities and Trainability of Adult Imbeciles', in (Ann M. Clarke and A. D. B. Clarke eds) *Mental Deficiency: the Changing Outlook*, (2nd ed): London, Methuen.

CLARKE, Ann and CLARKE, A. D. B.1972, 'What are the Problems?' in A. M. Clarke and A. D. B. Clarke, (eds.) *Mental Retardation and Behavioural Research* London, Churchill Livingstone; Baltimore, Williams and Wilkins (in press).

CRONBACH, L. J., 1967, 'Year to year correlations of mental tests: a review of the Hofstaetter analysis', *Child Development* 38, p. 283.

CUNNINGHAM, C. C. and JEFFREE, D. M., 1971, *Working With Parents: Developing a workshop course for parents of young mentally handicapped children*, Manchester, National Society for Mentally Handicapped Children.

Department of Education and Science, 1968, 'Psychologists in Education Services' (The Summerfield Report), London, HMSO.

FROSTIG, M., LEFEVER, D. W. and WHITTLESEY, J. R. B., 1964, *Marianne Frostig Developmental Test of Visual Perception*, Palo Alto Consulting Psychologists Press.

GAGNE, R. M. (ed.), 1967, *Learning and Individual Differences*, Columbus, Ohio, Merrill.

GARDNER, W. I., 1971, *Behavior Modification in Mental Retardation*, New York, Aldine.

GUNZBURG, H. C., 1966, *Progress Assessment Charts*, London, National Association for Mental Health.

GUNZBURG, H. C., 1970, 'Severely Subnormal Adults' in Mittler 1970.

GWYNNE JONES, H., 1970, 'Principles of Psychological Assessment' in Mittler 1970.

HERMELIN, B. and O'CONNOR, N., 1970, *Psychological Experiments with Autistic Children*, London, Pergamon Press.

HOFSTAETTER, P. R., 1954, 'The changing composition of 'intelligence': a study in T technique', *Journal of Genetics and Psychology*, 85, p. 159.

JOHNSON, R. C., 1970, 'Prediction of independent functioning and of problem behavior from measures of IQ and SQ', *American Journal of Mental Deficiency*. 74, p. 591.

KIRK, S. A., 1958, *Early Education of the Mentally Retarded*, Urbana, Ill., University Illinois Press.

KIRK, S. A., McCARTHY, J. J. and KIRK, W., 1968, *The Illinois Test of Psycholinguistic Abilities*, (revised edition), Urbana, Ill.: Institute for Research in Exceptional Children.

KUSHLICK, A., 1966, 'Assessing the Size of the Problem of Subnormality', in J. E. Meade and A. S. Parkes (eds), *Genetic and Environmental Factors in Human Ability*, Edinburgh and London, Oliver and Boyd.

MITTLER, P. (ed.), 1970, *The Psychological Assessment of Mental and Physical Handicaps*, London, Methuen.

MITTLER, P., 1970a, in 'Assessment of Handicapped Children: Some Common Factors' in Mittler 1970.

MITTLER, P., 1972a 'New Directions in the Study of Learning Deficits', in A. D. B. Clarke and M. M. Lewis (eds), *Learning, Speech and Thought in the Mentally Retarded*. (IRMR Symposia series nos. 4 and 5), London, Butterworth.

MITTLER, P. 1972b, 'The Teaching of Language,' in A. D. B. Clarke and A. M. Clarke (eds), *Mental Retardation and Behavioural Research* Proceedings IRMR Study Group no. 4, London, Churchill Livingstone; Baltimore, Williams and Wilkins (in press).

MITTLER, P. and WARD, J., 1970, 'The use of the Illinois Test of Psycholinguistic Abilities with English four year old children: a normative and factorial study,' *British Journal of Educational Psychology*, 40, p. 43.

NIHIRA, K., FOSTER, R., SHELLHAUS, M. and LELAND, H., 1969, *Adaptive Behavior Scales*, Washington, American Association for Mental Deficiency

O'CONNOR, N. and HERMELIN, B., 1963, *Speech and Thought in Severe Subnormality*, London, Pergamon Press.

OSGOOD, C. E., 1957, 'A Behaviouristic Analysis', in C. E. Osgood (ed.) *Contemporary Approaches to Cognition*, Cambridge, Mass., Harvard University Press.

REESE, H. W. and LIPSITT, L., 1970, *Experimental Child Psychology*, New York, Academic Press.

ROSEN, C, 1966, 'An experimental study of visual perceptual training in the first grade', *Perception and Motor Skills*, 22, p. 979.

SCHUBERT, J., 1967, 'Effect of training on the performance of the WISC Block Design Test', *British Journal of Social and Clinical Psychology*, 6, p. 144.

SERPELL, R., 1972, 'Applications of Attention Theory to Teaching in Schools for the Severely Subnormal', in A. D. B. Clarke and A. M. Clarke (eds.), *Mental Retardation and Behavioural Research* (Proceedings IRMR study Group no. 4), London, Churchill Livingstone; Baltimore, Williams and Wilkins.

SHAKESPEARE, R., 1970, in 'Severely Subnormal Children', Mittler, 1970.

SHAPIRO, M. E., 1970, in 'Intensive Assessment of the Single Case: an Inductive-Deductive Approach', Mittler, 1970.

SILVERSTEIN, A. B., 1967, 'Variance components on the Illinois Test of Psycholinguistic Abilities', *Perception and Motor Skills*, 24, p. 1315.

SINGER, B. D. and OSBORN, R. W., 1970, 'Social class and sex differences in admission patterns of the mentally retarded', *American Journal of Mental Deficiency*, 75, p. 160.

SMART, R. C, 1965, 'The changing composition of intelligence: a replication of a factor analysis', *Journal of Genetics and Psychology*, 107, p. 111.

STEIN, Z. and SUSSER, M., 1963, 'The social distribution of mental retardation', *American Journal of Mental Deficiency*, 67, p. 811.

STEPHEN, E. and ROBERTSON, J., 1965, 'Normal Child Development and Handicapped Children', in J. G. Howells (ed.), *Modern Perspectives in Child Psychiatry*, Edinburgh and London, Oliver and Boyd.

TIZARD, J., 1970, 'The Role of Social Institutions in the Causation, Prevention and Alleviation of Retarded Performance', in H. C. Haywood (ed.) *Social-Cultural Aspects of Mental Retardation*, New York, Appleton Century Crofts.

WALTON, D. and BLACK, D. A., 1959, 'The predictive validity of a psychological test of brain damage', *Journal of Mental Science*, 105, p. 440.

WARBURTON, F. W., FITZPATRICK, T., WARD, J. and RITCHIE, M., 1970, in *Some Problems in the Construction of Intelligence Tests*, Mittler, 1970.

WARD, J., 1970. 'On the concept of criterion-referenced measurement'. *British Journal of Educational Psychology*, 40 p. 314.

WILLIAMS, P., 1965, 'The ascertainment of educationally subnormal children', *Educational Research*, 7, p. 135.

WINDLE, C., 1962, 'Prognosis in mental subnormals', *American Journal of Mental Deficiency*, 66, monograph supplement 5.

VERNON, P. E. (ed.), 1957, *Secondary School Selection: a British Psychological Society Inquiry*, London, British Psychological Society.

23. Effects of physical disability on a child's description of himself *

STEPHEN A. RICHARDSON

Research Director, Association for the Aid of Crippled Children, U.S.A.

ALBERT H. HASTORF and SANFORD M. DORNBUSCH

Stanford University, U.S.A.

The purpose of this study[1] was to examine empirically the effects of physical disability on a disabled child's conception of himself. The study stemmed from the following beliefs: (a) There is need for clearer understanding of the interpersonal world of the child — how he sees other children and himself — particularly in view of the common tendency of adults to impute their perceptual world to children. (b) This kind of study is needed to supplement the predominantly biological study of disability. (c) The effects of a physical disability are not confined to functional limitations but include social and psychological consequences that stem from the reaction of others to the disabled child.

Observational studies of children with and without disabilities and interviews with their parents have indicated that the disabled child receives less social and interpersonal experience, less responsibility, more maternal nurturance and protection, and that he has lower self-esteem than the non-disabled child (Barker and Wright 1955, Bell 1956, Goodman *et al.* 1963, Richardson 1963, Richardson *et al.* 1961, Shere 1957). How and to what extent are these reported differences reflected in children's free descriptions of themselves when they are asked, 'Tell me about yourself'?

Method

SUBJECTS
The children whose self-descriptions are reported here were white, Negro, and Puerto Rican boys (63 handicapped and 63 nonhandicapped) and girls

*From *Child Development*, (1964) 35, pp. 893–907.

(44 handicapped and 65 nonhandicapped), aged 9 to 11, who lived in low-income areas of New York City. They were studied at a summer camp that provided two- or three-week vacations for underprivileged city children. The camp population was divided almost evenly between children with and without handicaps. Each tent was similarly divided and children mixed in a decentralized program of activities determined largely by each tent of children with their counselor.

The handicaps of the children ranged from slight to moderate and included cerebral palsy, post-polio impairments, cardiac disorders, diabetes, and various orthopedic disabilities. The absence of both severe impairment and a single diagnostic category of disability reduced the likelihood of finding clear differences between children with and without disabilities. What differences were found must be attributable to the more general consequences of general physical disability on a child's growth and upbringing.

PROCEDURE
To obtain the children's descriptions of themselves, a nondirective type of interview was used. Prior to the interview the interviewer spent time gaining the confidence of the child by sharing in some of his activities. The interviews were conducted in a quiet room, and the child was told that the interviewer was interested in learning about children in the camp. The child was shown how the tape recorder worked and was encouraged to play with the machine and listen to his voice. He was assured that other children and counselors would not be told what he said. The child was then asked to describe two other children and

himself. For each description the question asked was' 'Tell me about Johnny,' or, in the case of the self-description: 'Tell me about yourself.' When the child finished talking, the interviewer, after a short silence, used follow-up questions such as: 'Tell me more,' or 'That's very interesting,' but no questions were asked which suggested a perceptual category to the child; that is, the interviewer could not ask: 'Are you happy?' or 'Do you like swimming?' because 'happiness' and 'swimming' suggest things the child could say about himself. The interviews were tape-recorded, and typed transcripts of the interviews provided the basic data for the analysis.

Our goal in content analysis was to stay as close as possible to the child's verbal report. It would have been impossible to analyze the verbatim record of the children's responses without a method for categorizing the words they used. To minimize the possible distortion that may have occurred through deductively imposing predetermined categories, we derived an empirically based set of categories from children's descriptions obtained in an exploratory study. Sixty-nine content categories were developed.[. . .]

The reliability of coding was high. For reliability analysis, specific interviews were selected at random and studies of reliability by the two coders were performed throughout the coding process. Reliability by the strictest criterion was 86.4 per cent (Beech and Wertheimer 1961). This means that any idea which one interviewer coded in a specific category was coded in the identical category by the other interviewer more than seventeen out of twenty times. If idea units for which both coders agreed on residual classification were to be included in the reliability analysis, the coding reliability would be over 90 per cent.

We employed two measures of category usage. The first was a binary concept: present or absent — that is, the category was used or not used by any child; E represents the percentage of the group who employed the category. The second measure was the proportion of a child's over-all description that fell into any one category, or

$$p = \frac{\text{Number of units in any one category}}{\text{Total number of units in entire description}}.$$

The measure p indicates the emphasis a child gave to any one category in his description. For example, if a child used 10 units and two of these

were 'physical agression' (No. 12), then p = .20. An average p, or P, can be obtained for any group of children by adding the individual ps and dividing by the number in the group.[. . .]

In addition to determining differences in category usage between children with and without handicaps, a second analysis was conducted. We have already pointed out that many of the perceptual categories are really continua in which the child can make *positive* or *negative* statements and that the direction of the statement was ignored in the coding. For example, 'I run very fast' and 'I run very slow' were both coded 'physical ability' (No. 53). On a random sample of children we coded all categories in which directional differences were possible. To provide some indication of awareness of others and egocentricity, still another analysis was undertaken on the same random sample of children to determine whether each statement in fact described the *child himself* or made reference to *other people* even though our question was, 'Tell me about yourself.' The findings of these analyses have been included in the results.

Results

Three concepts about the consequences of physical disability have been used to organize the differences found in category usage between children with and without physical disabilities in their self-descriptions. Each concept is stated below. The relevant categories are examined by comparing the handicapped group (H) with the nonhandicapped group (A) in terms of P and E measures, for males and females separately, to determine the extent to which the general concept is supported by the data. As mentioned earlier, to prevent the possibility of selecting only findings which support the concepts, we have included in the tables of results every comparison meeting the criteria of meaningful differences described above.

REFLECTION OF FUNCTIONAL RESTRICTION — PHYSICAL ACTIVITY

The most direct consequence of physical disability for a child is that he will be restricted in, or prevented from engaging in, certain activities. The restrictions may stem from the disability or may be imposed, rationally or irrationally, by adults or other children. Table 23.1 shows the category comparisons which are pertinent to physical

Table 23.1 Self-description: reflection of functional restriction — physical activity

Category	Male				Female			
	PH	*PA*	*EH*	*EA*	*PH*	*PA*	*EH*	*EA*
Handicapped greater								
6. Handicap	015	004	180	070	015	000	190	040
7. Health	015	009	220	170	026	022	370	370
11. Nonphysical recreation	035	032	470	410	045	028	410	390
10. Physical recreation	170	159	270	270	095	090	200	150
40. Competition	011	013	120	220	009	000	170	030
Nonhandicapped greater								
1. Spatial location	011	017	170	230	013	019	210	310
53. Physical ability	024	056	320	410	041	043	320	390
65. Occupation of the child	002	011	010	110	000	000	000	000

Note: H = handicapped, A = nonhandicapped (absence of handicap). Total number of cases in each group: Male: H = 63, A = 63; Female: H = 44, A = 65. E = proportion of group employing given category; P = proportion of each child's response units found in the given category, averaged for the group (see p. 196). Decimal points are omitted.

activity. Two categories, 'physical recreation' (No. 10) and 'competition' (No. 40), show the absence of differences in the direction that might have been expected. The other comparisons in Table 23.1 all support the general concept and are not very surprising. They strengthen our confidence that our research approach provides results that agree with what might be expected with minimal use of inference. This gives us some measure of assurance that differences in more subtle forms of category usage presented later are worth interpreting.

Handicapped boys and girls talk *more* about 'handicap' (No. 6).[2] This result was by no means predictable, since one could reason that a child with a handicap might try to develop a self-conception which shuts out the handicap. In interviews with one of the authors, a number of adults reported that they do not generally think of themselves as handicapped and that having this forced on their awareness is painful.

Handicapped boys refer to 'health' (No. 7) *more* often. The child with a disability is likely to have experienced more ill health and have his attention more focused on problems of health because of his disability. The evidence is clear only for boys, perhaps because handicapped boys have more health problems than girls or because of the greater emphasis that our culture places on physical activity for boys.

Handicapped girls speak *more* of 'nonphysical recreation' (No. 11). This activity, in which the disabled child is not at a disadvantage, is spoken about more only by disabled girls, probably because nonphysical recreation is more acceptable and encouraged by girls in the peer culture than by boys.

The categories reported thus far have all been used more by the handicapped than by the nonhandicapped. The following categories are used less by the handicapped.

Handicapped boys and girls speak *less* about 'spatial location' (No. 1). This suggests that restrictions imposed either directly by the handicap or indirectly by adults or peers limit their spatial awareness. This finding coincides with Barker and Wright's (1955) and Bell's (1956) observations that the handicapped child is not taken about or given as wide a variety of experiences as the nonhandicapped child.

Handicapped boys make less use of 'occupation of the child' (No. 65), probably because their disability prevents them from taking the type of job that 10- and 11-year-olds are able to obtain.

Handicapped boys talk *less* about 'physical ability' (No. 53). That the difference does not show up for girls may again be attributable to the greater emphasis placed on physical ability both for and by boys than girls.

For selected categories, we also coded the number of statements that were references to self or others and whether each of these was positive or negative. Two of these categories, 'giving aid' (No. 37) and 'physical ability' (No. 53), although they did not show over-all differences between children with and without disabilities, did provide evidence supporting the 'reflection of functional impairment — physical activity' and no category treated in this way provided negative evidence.

Boys, whether handicapped or not, talk more about their own 'giving aid' (No. 37) than about others' 'giving aid' (No. 37). Girls emphasize others 'giving aid' (No. 37) more than boys do, and handicapped girls emphasize others much more than themselves in comparison to girls who are not handicapped. This suggests that the way in which others give aid is more important for handicapped than nonhandicapped girls and that handicapped girls are attentive to others 'giving aid' (No. 37), possibly because it is easier for girls to receive help in our culture than it is for boys.

In the category 'physical ability' (No. 53), for which we have reported differences in over-all use, an analysis of self vs. other statements shows that with one exception all statements refer to self. In these 'self' references 40 per cent of the handicapped boy's statements are negative as compared to only 15 per cent for nonhandicapped boys. This suggests that the handicapped boy is showing realism in discussing 'physical ability' (No. 53) by not indulging in positive fantasies about his ability, and that he is not diverting attention from what may be a painful subject by speaking about others rather than about himself. That 32 per cent of handicapped boys use the category (even though less than the nonhandicapped) shows its power in the value system of the children. Even more

striking is the absence of difference in the use of 'physical recreation' (No. 10), when it would be rational to expect the category to be used less by the handicapped. From the same viewpoint the absence of difference for 'competition' (No. 40) is surprising. (Indeed, handicapped girls tend toward greater usage than nonhandicapped girls.) Taken together, the findings on categories dealing with physical activities suggest the acceptance and sharing by handicapped children of the majority peer value which so strongly emphasizes physical activities.

SOCIAL IMPOVERISHMENT

A number of studies have indicated that, compared to children without handicaps, handicapped children are impoverished in social experience and in interpersonal relations. We were interested in determining whether the children's self-descriptions would support this concept of social impoverishment. The differences found are shown in Table 23.2.

At first sight the finding that handicapped boys talk more about their 'relations with mother' (No. 27) does not support the concept of social impoverishment. For the handicapped, however, the greater use of this category may well reflect the greater need he has for care, which for 10- and 11-year-old children falls largely to the lot of the mother. It is also probable that if there is more

Table 23.2   Self-description: social impoverishment

Category		Male				Female			
	PH	PA	EH	EA		PH	PA	EH	EA
Handicapped greater									
27. Relations with mother	022	011	220	210		019	017	320	430
Nonhandicapped greater									
28. Relations with siblings	013	021	150	240		026	034	270	410
32. Membership in a specific collective	011	032	220	410		013	024	220	320
44. Interpersonal skill	006	011	120	150		011	011	160	200
23. Freq. of interaction: others and described	000	007	030	120		002	004	070	090
29. Relations with family members other than parents or siblings	002	006	060	130		002	006	110	200
31. Relations with non-family children	123	118	750	600		084	121	650	800

Note: H = handicapped, A = nonhandicapped (Absence of handicap). Total number of cases in each group: Male: H = 63, A = 63; Female: H = 44, A = 65. E = proportion of group employing given category; P = proportion of each child's response units found in the given category, averaged for the group (see p. 196). Decimal points are omitted.

than one child in the family the greater needs of the handicapped child and his physical limitations may lead to a splitting of the family on many occasions, with the father looking after the children who are not handicapped. That it is only handicapped boys who talk more about their 'relations with mother' (No. 27) may be because by 10 to 12 years of age the mother's relation with her nonhandicapped sons is usually less close than with her daughters, so her closer relation with the handicapped boy is more likely to be reflected in category usage.

Support for the idea that the handicap splits the family into two groups — mother and handicapped son, father and other children — is provided by the finding that handicapped boys and girls talk *less* often about 'relations with siblings' (No. 28). Boys and girls who are handicapped speak *less* about 'relations with family members other than parents or siblings' (No. 29). Although other categories dealing with the family did not show differences large enough to meet out formal criteria, none showed differences that suggest negative evidence for the explanation.

Outside of the family the handicapped child's social impoverishment is indicated by less frequent use of 'membership in a specific collective' (No. 32) for both boys and girls and of 'interpersonal skill' (No. 44) for boys. Again a review of all findings which just missed meeting the formal requirements for difference in category usage

revealed more evidence for the concept of social impoverishment. Handicapped boys use 'frequency of interaction: others and described' (No. 23) *less* and handicapped girls use 'relations with non-family children' (No. 31) *less*. No negative evidence for the concept could be found.

Upon classifying statements within categories on the basis of their reference to self or to others, if all self and other references are added up for all categories thus analyzed (Nos. 27, 29, 32, 44, and 31) both handicapped boys and girls use a lower percentage of references to others than do non-handicapped children (MH 7, MA 14, FH 11, and FA 27 per cent). This higher degree of egocentricity for handicapped children may well be related to their social impoverishment.

REFLECTION OF FUNCTIONAL
RESTRICTION – PSYCHOLOGICAL IMPACT
One would anticipate that the physical restrictions and social impoverishment which the handicapped children have reflected would have an important psychological impact on a child and would be reflected in expressions of personal inadequacy and uncertainty. Table 23.3. shows the differences obtained.

Boys who are handicapped speak *more* of 'humor' (No. 42). One of the traditional ways by which the handicapped person has gained some acceptance has been by becoming the jester and the buffoon. Hathaway (1943) has described with

Table 23.3 Self-description: reflection of functional restriction — psychological impact

	Male				Female			
Category	PH	PA	EH	EA	PH	PA	EH	EA
Handicapped greater								
42. Humor	013	006	170	150	011	011	210	240
46. Excitability	006	006	170	170	011	004	160	090
47. Confidence	013	004	220	160	006	004	130	180
51. Undifferentiated negative statements	004	000	090	060	011	002	100	100
116. Concern with past	022	011	390	150	015	009	250	240
Nonhandicapped greater								
2. Age	006	006	060	100	011	019	170	280
36. Generosity	007	004	090	040	006	011	140	230
108. Social comparison: self with others	000	017	000	260	002	006	090	160

Note: H = handicapped, A = nonhandicapped (Absence of handicap). Total number of cases in each group: Male: H = 63, A = 63; Female: H = 44, A =,65. E = proportion of group employing given category; P = proportion of each child's response units found in the given category, averaged for the group (see p. 196). Decimal points are omitted.

great sensitivity the use of humor in obtaining access to peer groups. All the handicapped boys' statements about 'humor' (No. 42) are about 'self' and are positive. This adds some support to this interpretation of the use of humor.

Handicapped boys speak more of 'confidence' (No. 47). At first sight this appears negative evidence, as the opposite finding would follow logically from the general conceptual view proposed. It must be remembered, however, that the statements were initially coded without reference to their direction, and statements about both confidence and lack of confidence are included. The separate analysis of category direction shows that for 'confidence' (No. 47) there are more negative than positive statements concerning self for both handicapped boys and handicapped girls. Thus handicapped boys talk of *lack* of confidence more than nonhandicapped, which means that this finding contributes positive evidence for the general conceptual viewpoint.

The greater use of 'undifferentiated negative comments' (No. 51) by handicapped girls in self-descriptions suggests greater self-depreciation, which the handicapped children also evidenced on another test (Richardson *et al.* 1961). The handicapped boys' difference on the same category is in the same direction, although it does not meet the formal requirements. We do not understand why the handicapped boys are not higher. Why handicapped girls use 'excitability' (No. 46) more is also not clear.

Handicapped boys and girls talk *more* about 'concern with the past' (No. 116). Sociometric data on the children in the study indicate that the handicapped children have lower status. This, combined with the peer-group emphasis on physical activities, provides the handicapped children with an environment that is probably more threatening and less rewarding than it is for the child without a handicap. Given this set of conditions, it seems natural that the handicapped child should turn in his descriptions to the more familiar and less threatening environment of his home and neighborhood.

Handicapped girls talk *less* about 'age' (No. 2). For a child the mention of his age implies a wide variety of expectations dealing with appearance (height and weight) and accomplishments (behavioral and intellectual). The handicapped child who has difficulty in living up to these normative expectations is likely to avoid use of the category. Three times as many girls as boys use 'age' (No. 2). This suggests that the result is obtained for girls and not for boys because at ages 10 and 11 girls are more advanced physically and socially and thus more aware of their immaturity.

Girls with handicaps make *less* use of 'generosity' (No. 36). This finding supports the earlier suggestion that the handicapped are more egocentric. In terms of 'self' and 'other,' only nonhandicapped girls emphasize the 'generosity' (No. 36) of others.

Handicapped girls make *less* use of 'social comparison: self with others' (No. 108). For boys the difference is in the same direction but not large enough to meet our criteria. There may be two reasons for this. One is that the handicapped child knows fewer children; the other is that in such comparisons he is likely to feel he will come off second best, reflecting indirectly a form of self-depreciation.

An over-all analysis to determine whether statements in all the selected categories are positive or negative suggests another psychological impact. Handicapped boys and girls have a higher proportion of negative statements about themselves (MH 13, MA 8, FH 17, and FA 11 per cent). Although the differences are not large, they are suggestive of self-depreciation.

DIFFERENCES NOT RELATED TO THE THREE MAJOR CONCEPTS

Differences not readily fitting the three main concepts are shown in Table 23.4. A striking difference occurs in the use of aggression. In general, handicapped boys use aggression more, whereas handicapped girls use it less. From other research done with the same children, there is some evidence that the boys who talk most about aggression are those who tend to be targets of physical aggression from the other boys. This suggests that the handicapped boys speak of aggression more than the nonhandicapped because they tend to get picked on by others. It is known also that girls make more use of verbal aggression than boys, and in verbal aggression the handicapped girls are not disadvantaged. They may, however, feel less secure in the camp situation through their more marginal position (as determined independently by sociometry) and therefore be more restrained in their use of aggression.

Table 23.4 Differences not related to three major concepts

		Male				*Female*			
Category	PH	PA	EH	EA		PH	PA	EH	EA
Handicapped greater									
12. Physical aggression	035	024	320	320					
13. Verbal aggression	007	007	160	120					
14. General aggression	013	006	120	150					
69. Residual						194	177	940	840
Nonhandicapped greater									
12. Physical aggression						013	015	220	270
13. Verbal aggression						006	013	110	210
14. General aggression						006	011	090	220
69. Residual	166	250	420	920					

Note: H = handicapped, A - nonhandicapped (Absence of handicap). Total number of cases in each group: Male: H = 63, A = 63; Female: H = 44, A = 65. E = proportion of group employing given category; P = proportion of each child's response units found in the given category, averaged for the group (see p. 196). Decimal points are omitted.

It is possible that the results reported may to some extent be due to the handicapped children's being less talkative and using fewer categories than the nonhandicapped. The handicapped child made higher use of 44 per cent of the categories, whereas the nonhandicapped child made higher use of 56 per cent. This difference does not appear to be of any special significance.

Discussion

The picture that emerges from the self-descriptions of handicapped children as compared with those of nonhandicapped children is consistent with evidence from observational and interview studies. Both emphasize the physical functional restrictions imposed by the handicap, its psychological impact, the deprivation of social experience, and the limitations on involvement in the social world.

In this study we were interested in discovering the effect of the restrictions imposed by the handicap on the handicapped child's description of himself. It might be argued that the child who is forced to stand aside from social activities will attempt to gain his social satisfactions in part vicariously and hence will develop a high sensitivity in observing human behavior. If this were so, we would expect a rich and diverse set of perceptual categories dealing with interpersonal behavior. This richness might also be further extended by the development of a rich fantasy life to compensate for his lack of social involvement. The alternate possibility is that lack of social involvement and experience would lead to an impoverishment of the child's category usages pertaining to interpersonal relations. This second conceptualization seems to be borne out by the results. It appears that for these children, aged 10 and 11, direct experience in social interaction is a prerequisite for the full development of perceptual categories dealing with human relationships.

The handicapped children are very realistic in their self-descriptions. Although they share in the peer values, they are aware that they cannot live up to the expectations that stem from the high value placed on physical activities. Handicapping does not have the same consequences for boys and for girls. For example, the handicapped girls may turn to nonphysical recreation, where they are not disadvantaged, but this alternative is perhaps less acceptable to the boys because among them physical activity is more highly valued. Possibly because of this, they express more difficulties in interpersonal relations and make more use of humor to gain some measure of acceptance. Handicapped boys also express more concern about aggression than do handicapped girls, possibly as a consequence of being more often targets of physical aggression, which is used less by the girls.

Both handicapped boys and girls show greater concern with the past than do nonhandicapped boys and girls, possibly because of the greater uncertainty and threat in the present. They both reflect more physical restriction and less social experience within and without the family.

NOTES

1. This paper was presented in shorter form at the biennial meeting of the Society for Research in Child Development at Berkeley, California, April 1963. We gratefully acknowledge the assistance of James Block, Caroline Conklin, Anne L. Constant, Matthew Friedman, Norman Goodman, Abraham Ross and Rebecca Vreeland in the collection and analysis of a portion of the data. In addition we wish to express our gratitude to the agencies and institutions which made this work possible. This research was supported by the National Institute of Mental Health (Grant No. M-2480) and the Association for the Aid of Crippled Children.
2. Comparisons of this sort always refer to handicapped vs. nonhandicapped. Where cross-sex comparisons are made they are so specified.

REFERENCES

BARKER, R. G., and WRIGHT, H. F., 1955, *Midwest and its children: the psychological ecology of an American town*, New York, Row, Peterson.

BEACH, L., and WERTHEIMER, M., 1961, A free response approach to the study of person cognition, *Journal of Abnormal and Social Psychology*, 62, pp. 367—74.

BELL, J. E., 1956, The nature of social depreciation and of defenses against being adjudged: a study of the cerebral palsied child in his family. Unpublished report submitted to the Association for the Aid of Crippled Children.

GOODMAN, N., RICHARDSON, S. A. DORNBUSCH, S. M., and HASTORF, A. H., 1963, Variant reactions to physical disabilities, *American Sociological Review*, 28 (June).

HASTORF, A. H., RICHARDSON, S. A., and DORNBUSCH, S. M., 1958, The problem of relevance in the study of person perception, in Tagiuri, R., and Petrullo, L. (eds.), *Person perception and interpersonal behavior*, Stanford University Press, pp. 54—62.

HATHAWAY, K. B., 1943, *The little locksmith*, Coward-McCann.

RICHARDSON, S. A., 1963, Some social psychological consequences of handicapping, *Pediatrics*, 52, pp. 291—7.

RICHARDSON, S. A., GOODMAN, N., HASTORF, A. H., and DORNBUSCH, S. M., 1961, Cultural uniformity in reaction to physical disabilities, *American Sociological Review*, 26, pp. 241—7.

SHERE, M. O., 1957, The socio-emotional development of the twin who has cerebral palsy, *Cerebral Palsy Review*, 17, pp. 16—18.

WRIGHT, B. A., 1960, *Physical disability — a psychological approach*, London, Harper.

24. Handicapped children in the ordinary school *

JOHN D. KERSHAW

Consultant W.H.O., formerly Medical Officer of Health,
Colchester; Divisional School M.O., North-East Essex;
Consultant Physician, Myland Hospital;
Chief, Rehabilitation Unit, United Nations Secretariat.

Stress is a part of life; the art of living consists in the achieving of equilibrium within a balance of stresses. And because the nature and intensity of stresses are constantly changing, an important requirement is the ability to foresee those changes and adjust and adapt to meet them. It follows that learning to live must include experience of stress, experience which must be controlled so that in any situation the stress is enough to challenge but not so great as to overwhelm. Precise graduation is usually impossible and one must assume that the child will have sufficient resilience and tolerance to recover without harm if he should happen to be temporarily overstressed.

This process postulates the existence of an informed group of educators — prominent among whom are parents and teachers — who will strike a balance between too much protection and too much exposure and will guide and advise the child in dealing with stresses. The home and the school are ideally partners in providing a structured environment which progressively introduces the child to challenging stresses and leads him on to the point at which he can stand on his own.

When a handicapped child enters an ordinary school, a special situation arises. A large school cannot be infinitely flexible in organisation. Its buildings, its staffing and its administration are provided on the assumption that the pupils' requirements as individuals will vary within only a comparatively narrow range and that by a compromise between the adaptability of the pupils and the adaptability of the school system the needs of most will be met without either children or school suffering unacceptable strain.

By definition, a handicapped child is one who suffers from a disability which, because of its nature or degree, places him at a disadvantage as compared with normal children in the same circumstances. His disability must be accepted as a fact and therefore, initially at least, an ordinary school will have to accept the strain of having to adjust somewhat beyond its normal range to give him what he needs. The aim of the school, in the long run, must be not only to educate him in the ordinary sense of the term but to teach him to accept and adapt to the total circumstances of living.

He has several special points of vulnerability. His total powers of adaptation are restricted. His special disability may be a point of weakness in that too much stress may actually increase the disability. One of the important elements in the normal child's learning to bear stress is that in school most of his stresses are shared by others and a stress which is common is more easily tolerated. A stress which is special to oneself carries an element of 'unfairness' which makes it harder to bear and it is just this kind of stress which the handicapped child must face.

To understand this vulnerability it is useful to

*From *New Society*, 11th May (1972) *20*, No. 505, pp. 295—6

*From V. Varma (ed.) (1973) *Stresses in Children*, London, University of London Press, Chapter 1, pp. 1—20 consider what it means to be handicapped. First and foremost there is a limitation of performance. There are some things which a handicapped child cannot do at all. There are others which he can do just as effectively as a normal child. In between there are many things which, though he can do them, he will do less well or more slowly than a normal child, or at the cost of pain or greater effort. Some activities are essential; others are not. Some, while not essential, are pleasant or socially desirable; others are less so.

Essential activities must have first priority. If the child cannot perform them himself then someone else must do them for him. If he performs them only imperfectly or with difficulty it becomes necessary to decide whether others must do them or whether he should deal with them himself and pay the price in time, fatigue or pain. Among the non-essentials it is necessary to help the child to a choice based upon priorities and upon his desires and his capacity to bear fatigue or pain, remembering always the possibility that the putting of too much of himself and his time into a non-essential, however pleasant, may reduce his ability to deal with essentials.

Many workers in this field, myself included, have urged in the past that we should concentrate on the achieving of maximum independence and that we should teach the child to see himself though 'different' as not necessarily 'inferior'. In view of the changing patterns of disabilities and the increased prevalence of multiple handicaps this approach can no longer be defended as realistic. In the sense that a handicapped child must have some essential things done for him by others – or be helped by others in the doing of them – he is dependent and must accept some measure of planned dependence. In the sense that he is unable to engage in some activities which normal children enjoy or are part of the accepted pattern of social life he is inferior to the normal child.

The necessity to accept dependence and inferiority is a producer of emotional stress in itself. To come to terms with a disability involves the acquiring of a special personal set of values which will differ from those of the group. To forego some highly regarded activities is to become isolated from the group in those parts of its life. But the development of satisfactory personal relationships is usually achieved through partici-

pation in group activities; it follows that the handicapped child is likely to be disadvantaged in this essential part of growing up.

Because his activities must be restricted and because the things which must be done must not involve excessive strain it is important that the handicapped child must so order his life, or have it so ordered for him, that as far as possible it shall be regular. It must be realised that any substantial unusual activity, when it has to be undertaken, should be foreseen and planned for and even some occasional special activities which the normal child can take in his stride may, for the handicapped, involve a good deal of quite detailed preliminary work. This considerably reduces the handicapped child's adaptability and his power to tolerate change; it is unfortunate for the individual and helps still further to limit his chances of fitting in with the normal majority.

Choice of school

The medical officer who is charged with advising the local education authority on the education of a handicapped child will approach his task with the feeling that it is desirable that every child should live in his own home and attend an ordinary school. Whether in fact he recommends special educational treatment will depend upon whether the child has some essential need which cannot be met while he lives at home and attends an ordinary school. The essential need or needs which are considered may be educational, social, emotional or therapeutic.

In making a choice it must be remembered that the ordinary school may carry certain important advantages, as compared with the special school. Its curriculum is probably wider and its ultimate standard of attainment is in some respects substantially higher. Socially it offers the child better prospects of learning how to adjust to life in a community of non-handicapped people, closer contacts with the community in which he will later have to live and probably more practice in activities of daily living. These certainly justify some degree of bias in favour of the ordinary school.

It follows, therefore, that handicapped children admitted to ordinary school will fall into two main groups. The first, and larger, is that of children whose disability is comparatively minor in character and degree and who can be confidently expected to benefit by normal education if they are understandingly managed and if a few small adjustments can be made to the curriculum and the general daily round. The second group consists of children regarding whom there is some element of doubt; it is considered that they will probably be able to succeed in an ordinary school but their initial placement is a quite deliberate trial procedure.

In addition, there are two smaller groups which must be borne in mind. The first consists of children whose disability is such that they will probably be able to profit by ordinary education in the easier atmosphere and at the moderate pace of an ordinary infant or even junior school but who are likely to need transfer to a special school when they reach the age at which stricter routine and educational pressures impose unacceptable stresses. For these the ordinary school offers opportunities for maturing, educationally and socially, without the disadvantages attendant upon early separation from their home and their normal peer group.

The second of these groups, fortunately very small, consists of children who unquestionably need special education from an early age but whose parents refuse to allow them to go to a special school. Compulsory powers exist to require their attendance at a special school but it is often a lesser evil to permit them to go to an ordinary school than to enforce special school attendance with inevitable conflict between home and school. Often, though not always, the time may come when the parents accept that the child cannot benefit by ordinary school attendance and acquiesce in special education. Until that time arrives these children, with comparatively severe disability, may present serious problems.

In the first three groups — those must likely to be met with in ordinary schools, the following will be the commonest disabilities:

moderate motor defect;
partial sight;
partial hearing (with or without hearing aids);
minimal cerebral dysfunction;
moderate intellectual disability;
minor or well-controlled epilepsy;
slight or moderate chronic illness (e.g: asthma and diabetes).

It is worth mentioning that there is a growing tendency to transfer some quite severely handicapped children from special schools to ordinary schools for the final years of their education. In some cases the principal reason for this is to enable the child to make the transition from a specialised environment to ordinary community life in two stages rather than to discharge him direct from the protection of a special school to the rough-and-tumble of working life. In other cases the intention is rather to give the child the opportunity to have fuller secondary education in special subjects which are not taught to an advanced level in the special school.

The stress periods

Some disabilities generate quite specific patterns of stress for the children affected and where this is so it is possible to predict the child's response and take anticipatory action. Indeed, this is part of the *raison d'être* of the special school. This is most likely to be the case where the child has a severe major disability but no other significant defect.

Handicapped children who are placed in an ordinary school are not likely to show this specificity. The picture is most often of a child whose disabilities make him generally vulnerable to stress and whose immediate trouble is that he has difficulty in coping with the stresses which are normal to school life. The importance of the nature of his disability lies mainly in the way in which it may affect the pattern of his stress symptoms and, also, in determining the lines on which care and therapy may be most profitably carried out.

All school life — one might indeed say all life — contains elements of stress, but the impact of the normal school stresses tends to be specially marked at particular periods; predictably periods when change is impending or taking place.

SCHOOL ENTRY

The effect on the child of his first entry to school has not received the detailed study it deserves. It is only within the past decade that workers in the school health field have realised that many perfectly normal children go through phases of what is coming to be described as 'school shock' and 'first-year failure'. The former is a period of behaviour disorder or emotional disturbance occurring in a child who has hitherto appeared quite well adjusted. There is no standard pattern. The disturbance may show itself both at home and at school, but it is by no means uncommon for the child to be perfectly behaved in school and grossly disturbed at home, or *vice versa*. If this happens, it can set parent and teacher at odds, with the one imputing all the blame to the other, and the consequent antagonism between home and school adds to the child's problems.

It is probable that the main causes of school shock are to be found in the sudden change from family life to a group situation or from a home where the child's every wish has been met to a place where at any rate some rules have to be imposed impersonally by a stranger. The trouble does not usually last long and may well be over by the end of the first term or early in the second.

'First year failure' is probably to some extent a special form of school shock. A child who is, with reason, considered to be of average or high intelligence simply fails to manifest that intelligence in his school activities. He may have a spell of overt behaviour disorder, but the failure to progress may be the only outward sign. The trouble may persist throughout the first year but this is hardly surprising since in the permissive atmosphere of the reception class in a British school the challenge to the intellect builds up somewhat slowly. It has been suggested that one element in the picture is an inadequate relationship between child and teacher and that there is a more or less deliberate refusal to learn as a manifestation of hostility to the teacher. Needless to say, a refusal to learn hardly endears the child to the teacher and the relationship does not improve. It is perhaps significant that these children often suddenly leap ahead in the second year when promotion to a new class brings about a change of teacher.

Obviously, a child with a handicap is likely to start school at a disadvantage. In the first place it is probable that his disability will have restricted his social experience. He may have been impeded in joining with his peers in play, his parents may have taken him about in their normal activities less than they would have done if he had had no disability, he may have been helped in normal activities of daily living or he may have been overindulged at home. Any or all of these may have left him socially immature for his years and thus unready to fit into the group environment.

Social immaturity in itself is a substantial disability, but his handicap imposes other difficulties. School activities, inevitably in a systematised education, are based on the assumption that every school entrant will be capable of an average range of performance. The handicapped child is disadvantaged in some of the general activities in which he is expected to take part and probably for the first time in his life he has to face the fact that in some things he is inferior in performance. This is not a matter of failure in competition; the competitive element in education does not arise until appreciably later. Slowness in feeding, difficulty in coping with dressing and undressing, stumbling when one runs, clumsiness in handling simple classroom apparatus, all these may mark one as inferior. They certainly make a child feel 'different' from the others and if, in addition, his disability impedes him in communication or in joining in games or if it necessitates his receiving special attention from the teacher, the other children in the class will tend to see him as different from them and group integration will be retarded.

He may have a disability which specifically impedes his learning; if so the teachers will make appropriate allowances. What is not yet fully realised, however, is that *any* disability may make a child a slow learner. Education has moved out of the era in which children were bombarded ceaselessly with repetitive instruction in the hope that some of this would eventually adhere to them, and the keynote now is participation and activity, even to the point at which activity is recognised as a help to the acquisition of language. Any substantial disability impedes participation or activity with the inevitable consequences.

CHANGE OF SCHOOL

In the British system the ordinary child will expect two changes of school — from infant to junior at 7+ and from junior to secondary at 11+. The first of these gives little cause for concern; in the larger schools in urban areas it usually involves no more than a transfer of a group of contemporaries from one department to another within the same school. In rural areas it may require that the child moves from a small village school to a somewhat larger centralised junior school, but he is still moving with his established peer group to a school which is not too large and in most cases the only extra stress is that of daily travel to and fro. It is consequently easy to underrate the stress this transfer may present to a handicapped child.

Since an important concomitant of disability is diffidence and difficulty in making personal relationships a handicapped child will become more dependent upon those relationships which he does form. Even in the infants department he will have to receive some special attention and consideration from his teacher, with the result that he tends to have a much more close — and even dependent — relationship with his teacher than do normal children. This relationship may often extend to other members of the school staff who have had to give him particular attention — the auxiliary who has helped him in the lavatory, the canteen assistant who has ensured that he is not crowded or impeded at mealtimes, the playground assistant who has kept a helpful eye on him.

For such a child, mere promotion to a higher class may have been a little traumatic because of the change of teacher; it is quite common for a handicapped child to retain a relationship with his former teacher until he gets used to the new one and so long as he is in the same department or school this is practicable. Transfer to a different school at the age of seven or so requires that he must learn to live with a whole new set of adults, and however helpful and sympathetic they may be, they are still strangers for the first weeks and they have to learn his peculiarities just as he has to learn theirs.

Again, he may be vulnerable to the atmosphere of the junior school. It expects pupils to be more self-reliant and somewhat more responsible than they have been in the infant department. It also takes education more seriously; specific subjects begin to emerge, new skills have to be developed and inevitably there come the beginnings of educational competition as learning becomes less play and more work. During an acclimatisation period of one or two terms he may be reminded rather forcibly of difference and inferiority.

However, the most potentially traumatic change period is that from junior to secondary school. The comprehensive school system has much to commend it, but inevitably the comprehensive school must be large and draw its pupils from several primary schools. The pupil moves to it with his peer-group of classmates but this group may be only a small part of the new entry and the child has to learn to get on with a large number of contemporaries who are strangers to him. The age-gap between newcomers and seniors is greater than in his previous schools; he may well feel that he is under the shadow of young men and young women. Certainly even a normal child may be daunted by the change from being a big fish in a small pond to being a small fish in a big pond.

The handicapped child has new cause for feeling inferior. However much individual attention the teachers may give him, they do not yet know how to manage him, nor does he know anything of them. In any event, though he may have found an individual identity for himself in a community of perhaps two or three hundred he will have to start searching anew when he finds himself only one in a community of perhaps a thousand or more.

He has, one hopes, learned how to get around in his previous small school building with a minimum of physical difficulty. Now he must learn his way about something much larger and more complex which presents new practical problems. And, because he is among strangers, with a substantial age-gap between him and the majority of others, he cannot expect the little, understanding concessions and acts of consideration which have made it possible to adjust to day-to-day school life. All in all, there is good reason to expect a period of emotional and social regression, quite probably associated with a spell of general or specific learning difficulty.

THE LAST YEARS AT SCHOOL

It is probably just as well that the first years of adolescence coincide with the last years at school; the child has at least the probability that he will be facing adolescent turmoil, physical, emotional and social, in an environment which offers him protection from the consequences of his most serious errors, some degree of understanding surveillance and even some perceptive guidance. On the other hand, it is unfortunate that he should be compelled to leave school in the middle of what is probably the most difficult stage of adolescence.

The normal child manages to survive this period of schooling successfully and, in the long run, makes the transition to adult life in the community without suffering too greatly. It cannot, however, be assumed that because the educational system does well by the normal pupils one can be complacent about the handicapped ones.

It must be remembered that the handicapped child who has reached stability is still only conditionally stable. He has learned how to live with his disability within his environment at the moment. To do this he has almost certainly had to restrict his environment, in the sense of limiting his activities to those within his range and, also, limiting both the extent and the nature of his social contacts with his peers. Essentially, his capacity for adjustment to deal with sudden changes and emergencies is below average and his physical and mental powers may be fully taxed in maintaining his equilibrium.

Physical and emotional instability are essential elements in the picture of adolescence. The handicapped child, on his tired or moody days, has no reserves left to meet the extra strain which comes from the sudden impact of the unexpected. To make matters worse, it is not uncommon for the changes of adolescence to exacerbate his actual disability — diabetes or epilepsy may temporarily slip out of control, asthmatic attacks become more frequent, irregular physical growth impose extra strain on a weak limb and so on. All in all, therefore, it is to be expected that an adolescent with a disability will be under multiple stress during these years and that, to make matters more difficult, the stresses will be variable rather than constant. Emotional and social problems, and also school performance, are almost certain to suffer.

Competition takes on a new form and a new significance. The adolescent naturally begins to experiment with his growing powers and matching himself against his peers is now to him a serious business. Group aggregation is also becoming a serious part of life.

This, in the early stages, probably bears more hardly on the handicapped boy than on the girl. The standards of the male adolescent herd at this point tend to be oriented towards physical sports. If a boy is to be highly esteemed among his peers it is necessary for him to be more competent than average at one of a small number of such sports. Conversely, if he is unable to join in any one of them at a level of moderate competence he has no social standing in the major groups. The criteria of the majority are in fact such that a lad who shows interest and ability in his school work or in the less physical and more intellectual pursuits may be in some degree ridiculed and looked down upon; more urgently than ever before he finds that a physical disability, whether in vision, coordination or motor power, sets him among the inferior minority.

The girl is less likely to suffer in this way, because among girls physical sports are taken less seriously. Her problems come later but are no less painful. Competition enters the sexual field as the 'teens' come on. To achieve the highest esteem in his social group a boy must be good in sport *and* find himself a girl, but he will not suffer much if he concentrates on sport and makes girls his secondary hobby. A girl, however, has no such choice; she must find her boy or be branded as unsuccessful. To make matters worse, while the handicapped boy can often find a girl to take an interest in him — even though that interest be based on an element of sympathy or pity rather than on sexual attraction — the majority of boys at this age judge girls by superficial standards and the girl who is ungainly or unbeautiful, even if the thing which mars her appearance is nothing more serious than the wearing of a hearing aid or strong spectacles, is at a great disadvantage in the competition for personable boy friends. The results of this can be quite disastrous and may lead to long-lasting deformation of her ability to enter into normal relationships with the other sex.

Further disadvantages beset the handicapped in the final year at school. This is when the 'moment of truth' is approaching. It is normal and proper for the young to have optimistic daydreams about the future, with quite unrealistic ambitions for a career. The great majority settle quite comfortably for something short of these ambitions. The non-handicapped youngster has the assurance that he will find a job without great difficulty and that he can afford a period of trial and error when he goes into employment. The handicapped one begins to realise that the actual employments which some of his peers will find will be outside his powers, and even that finding work at all may be difficult for him. What he may not realise — but those in charge of him must be constantly aware of this — is that he cannot risk a period of trial and error. If he goes into a job and fails, not only is this a severe blow to his self-esteem and confidence, but the fact of his failure can too easily suggest to other prospective employers that he is a poor prospect because of his disability.

School has offered the handicapped child some measure of shelter and security within an ordered programme of living. If he is at all capable of forethought, he will realise that when he leaves school he will find life in general more difficult. The normal young person looks forward to leaving school with a considerable degree of eagerness. The day of leaving will bring 'grown-up' status, freedom from being treated as a child in that everything is arranged for him, and the prospect of having money of his own to spend. The handicapped youngster by contrast, knows that he will have new and undefined problems, that he will be going out into a community which will have comparatively little sympathy for his disabilities and shortcomings and that his earning power is somewhat dubious. It is hardly surprising if his fears take charge and he shows signs of social regression or attempts to compensate by becoming rebellious.

Care and management

Generalisations are dangerous in this even more than in other fields of child care, child health and education. However, it is reasonable to indicate a few general principles which can serve as a useful guide, provided that in applying them one does not lose sight of the uniqueness of the individual.

Because of his disability a handicapped child tends to be below the average in resilience. After any experience of stress he is likely to take longer to recover his confidence and his equilibrium than would most normal children. If a new stress strikes him before he has recovered from the previous one, his recovery will again be delayed and the cumulative effect of successive stresses may effect lasting damage. The aim should be to see that as far as possible he is not asked to face stresses beyond his capacity and that he should not be faced with more than one source of stress at any one time.

The time of school entry is outstandingly the one at which a child has to meet simultaneously a number of different stresses and the key to success lies in prevention and anticipation. It is particularly important that he should not be exposed at the same time to the sudden impact of group life, a formalised environment and the need to start learning school subjects, even though the teaching of these may be simple and not intensive. If he can be introduced by degrees first to group life, second to formality and then to being taught, his liability to school shock is greatly reduced.

Well before school age, therefore, he should begin this introductory process. Probably the best sequence would be part-time attendance at a play group, progressing to a nursery school and then entering an ordinary school. The paucity of nursery schools makes this sequence impossible in many places; an alternative is for him to go from nursery or play group to a nursery class. In some cases the latter may be preferable; if the nursery class is associated with the school to which he will go later he may become accustomed to the idea of school before he has to face schooling as such.

This process is more than acclimatisation. It offers a chance of assessing him and discovering his strengths and his weaknesses and observing his progress toward maturity. His future teacher should be given full information about him by those who have had charge of him and desirably she should, before he enters school, meet them and him and get to know him personally.

It should go without saying that he ought not to enter school as such until he is socially and emotionally mature enough to do so. Provided that he is having adequate group life and social experience he will lose nothing by starting school six months or a year after the standard age. If, however, there are no facilities for group experience other than in school it may be better for him to start part-time school attendance at the age of five.

Experience suggests that it is better for him not to enter school at the beginning of term. For the first weeks of term the reception class is going through a settling down process and to introduce a vulnerable child to a group which has not yet reached some sort of stability is bad for the group as well as for the child himself; not only will the staff be unable to give him much individual attention but the normal children, not yet having learned to accept each other, will be far from ready to accept him.

It not infrequently happens that a handicapped child, over quite a substantial period, is unable to tolerate school life for the whole day. If half-day attendance is permitted for too long there is the risk that he may begin to fall behind the other children educationally, and thus there exists the danger that he may have to face the extra stress of catching up with them or knowing that he is falling behind them. In these circumstances, an expedient worth trying is to combine half-day school attendance with part-time home teaching until the child is ready for whole-time schooling.

In the early days of schooling it is common for a handicapped child's disability to seem more handicapping than the history would suggest. This is partly because he is attempting some unfamiliar tasks and having to perform even the familiar ones in new surroundings. It may also be that part of the 'shock effect' of school entry is causing him to regress somewhat and to shelter behind his disability.

Whether this occurs or not, it is usually undesirable that he should be completely excused from any school activity which he is capable of attempting, even if it is obvious that he is not going to be able to do it as well as, or as fast as, the other children. He should be encouraged to try it and should be helped with it and his imperfections accepted. The reasons for this are fairly obvious – the longer he waits before trying, the more likely he is to assume that it is beyond him and observation of his attempts will help in the assessment of both child and disability.

However, he needs the confidence that only achievement can bring and it is most important that the school should discover as early as possible something which is part of the general pattern of class activities and which he can do competently, and let him have as much opportunity as possible to engage in it.

So far as giving him help is concerned, whether in classroom work or in daily living activities, full use should be made of any aids which will make tasks easier for him. Even so, he will probably need some assistance from one of the staff and initially it is desirable that all such help should come from one person. Not only is it going to be easier for him to learn to relate to one individual; it is important that the helper should be familiar with his powers and disabilities – and his idiosyncrasies – and know both how to help and when to help. Later, when he is beginning to settle down,

the other members of staff may undertake the helping role.

At this age, normal children accept the presence of a handicapped child quite well, so long as he does not actively interfere with or impede their own activities, but the acceptance is passive rather than active. It is reasonable that they should be taught to show him some consideration, but the further, and important, stage of acceptance, the giving of positive help, must not be expected to arrive until the second or third school year.

Transfer from infant to junior department must be considered well in advance. It is desirable, from the point of view of his self-esteem, that he should not feel that he is being held back but it is equally desirable that he should not suddenly be faced with challenges which are likely to be too much for him. Where the two departments are in the same school, gradual transfer may be possible; he may, for a while, spend part of his time in the infant department and part in the junior. If, however, transfer is going to involve a move to a different school, with the need to find his way around a new building and to get used to different staff, there may be a good case for retaining him in the infants department as an 'over-age' child for one or more terms. In general, one year should be the maximum retention period; if he is not mature enough to move at the end of a year it is probable that placement in an ordinary school was not, after all, suitable and transfer to a special school should be considered.

By this time his assets and liabilities should be fairly well known to the staff and full information about these and any special needs should be passed to the junior school well in advance, so that appropriate provision may be ready from the day he starts life as a 'junior'. If this is done, it is probable that no substantial new problems will arise during the first three junior years. However, this is the period during which school work is becoming a more serious matter and a careful watch should be kept for the appearance of any specific learning difficulties so that these may be investigated and remedial teaching introduced if necessary. On this point it is worth mentioning that if there is any doubt the help should be given sooner rather than later; if one waits till failure is obvious the child will already have felt the stress of that failure.

The last year in junior school should be a time

of special assessment and preparation, especially for the handicapped child. He is likely already to be somewhat apprehensive about his impending move to the secondary school and the staff should be looking ahead to the possible special difficulties he may meet there and considering how these may be minimised or circumvented. Consultation with the secondary school staff is highly desirable. Among the questions which need to be asked one must include whether the building will present any problems of getting about from classroom to classroom or from classroom to toilet block, whether the teachers whom he will first encounter have the right attitude and approach, whether the classes are unduly large and whether the pupils as a community are 'tough' or tolerant. It may be desirable for him to transfer to a secondary school other than the usual one which covers the catchment area in which he lives; if so, possible travel stress and the emotional difficulties which might arise from his being thrown into a community composed entirely of strangers must be balanced against the possible advantages.

A special point worth watching arises in the case of a handicapped girl. Not only does a girls-only school tend to have less of a 'rough and tumble' atmosphere than a mixed secondary school, but the social and emotional problems already referred to, which arise out of competition over 'dating', may be less important. Even so, before specially assigning a handicapped girl to a school for girls only it is worthwhile remembering that girls have to learn to mix with boys at some time and that perhaps introduction to the opposite sex may be best effected in the controlled environment of a school.

Since any secondary school will contain a large proportion of children from junior schools other than the one the child has attended, the importance of a child's being transferred at the same time as the rest of his class is less than at the time of infant—junior transfer and it is consequently much easier to hold the immature junior back for a year, or even longer, to let him ripen for secondary education. This is specially useful if the secondary school to which he is to transfer is a large comprehensive school, as the flexibility of the good comprehensive school makes it fairly easy for it to accept a child whose attainment level is one or even two years behind the average for his age.

The good secondary school offers a fair range of choice in its curriculum and there should be little difficulty in finding for the handicapped child a choice of subjects which will fit the pattern of his abilities. The choice, however, must be forward-looking. It is well worth while, if his disability is substantial, to enlist the aid of the Youth Employment Service quite early — at the age of thirteen or possibly even twelve — for preliminary advice. It is not to be expected that any precise vocational assessment can be made at this age, but it is often possible to define certain broad areas of employment which would be either quite unsuitable or dangerously stressful for the child and others which might offer good prospects. If this can be done, then it is possible to orient the child's educational programme appropriately and achieve two useful ends — first to channel his interests and ambitions into the realm of the realistically possible, and second, to prepare him for that particular field of occupation and thus give him some advantage over the children who have had no purposeful preparation.

Given understanding care, guidance and management during the pre-teen years the moderately handicapped child will have learned his powers and limitations and will know how to live within the latter. The natural competitive instinct will tempt him now and again to venture beyond his powers and fail, but this need not be grossly traumatic. It is, in fact, part of the normal process of learning by experience and one can only discover one's limitations by a process of trial and error. The most difficult part of learning to live with a handicap is learning to accept it and, as already indicated, the worst dangers that face the handicapped teenager are those arising out of frustration and isolation.

To overcome or avert these it is essential that he should, by some means or other, attain an average or above average level of competence and achievement in some activity which has significance for him and is valued by at least some of his peers. There are very good reasons why this should be sought in the field of recreation. This field is a wide one and within it there is something which would be appropriate for virtually everyone. In every type of recreation there are group linkages which are particularly important socially and emotionally because they are based on common interests entered into of one's own free will and desire. They are among the very few parts of human activity where competition and cooperation go hand in hand, so that the expert is eager to welcome, help, encourage and train the beginner. They usually cut completely across most of the common social barriers. And, not least important from the point of view of the handicapped youngster, they have continuity. One of the most dangerous stress factors in adolescence is the complete and sudden break which comes on leaving school and leaves the handicapped young person groping for new contacts in a strange setting. If, before he leaves school, he has been initiated into the brotherhood of the swimmers, the model engineers, the stamp collectors, the bird watchers or any of a hundred others, he will have friends ready-made when the interruption of other relationships is imposed by leaving school.

The target of those who are working with and for him in the later school years should be to find some recreation which is congenial and for which he has the basic ability and aptitude. If it is possible to find more than one, so much the better. In the case of a boy it is desirable that one of his recreations should be in the physical field, because of the special value which young males attach to physical sports.

In the large, progressive comprehensive school there may well be a wide range of facilities provided, with staff available to give help, training and guidance. In the smaller secondary school, whether facilities are available for anything outside the few 'standard' competitive sports depends too often on whether the school is lucky enough to have individual staff members who are interested in some of the less orthodox and traditional school recreations. In the latter event — and even in the former — the school may have to enlist the help of local clubs outside the school. This, however, is good rather than bad because it gives the youngster a footing in the outside world before he reaches leaving age.

Special disabilities

The foregoing general discussion has covered most of the problems of stress which will have to be faced by any handicapped child in an ordinary school; it is worth reiterating that since his disability is minor or moderate his essential difficulties will arise from the fact that normal stresses have a greater than normal impact upon him.

However, some kinds of disability may specially affect either his problems of adjustment or the task of the school in meeting his needs and these may be briefly indicated.

PARTIAL SIGHT

In the infant department the pace is comparatively slow, much work is oral or practical and the books in general use have large print. The majority of partially sighted children have little difficulty in coping with its activities whether in work or play, so that it is usual for these children to start their career in an ordinary school. At junior level, however, not only does the intensity of work increase but the actual techniques make greater demands on visual acuity. Not only does stress increase quite suddenly at this stage, but the work of the school includes basic processes which are fundamental to all the child's future education. That such a child has kept up with his peers in the infant department does not imply that he will be able to continue to keep up and transfer to a special junior school must be seriously considered. Many such children, given special school help during these critical years, may return to the normal school without undue stress in the secondary years.

PARTIAL HEARING

A partially hearing child, with an appropriate hearing aid if necessary, may have little trouble in keeping up with school work without stress. Much of it is visual and oral teaching, is usually given clearly and may be supplemented with visual demonstrations. However a level of hearing which is adequate for comparatively static class work may not be adequate for the general conversation of child with child outside the classroom. This means that the child may have difficulty in intercourse with his peers and may tend to become isolated from the group. This can lead to isolation and retarded social development. Moreover, ordinary conversation is one of the main agents in fostering language development and retardation in this can have repercussions on school work. There is no easy way of overcoming this difficulty. One solution which has been tried with varying degrees of success is the setting up of integrated partially hearing units within ordinary schools. Apart from the educational value of these, they offer the child the company of a special peer group — that of the other partially deaf children — where he will not be socially isolated to anything like the same extent.

Some children, especially those who have been fitted with a hearing aid rather late, are over-conscious of the aid as an outward sign of 'difference' and tend not to use it. In such cases the extra cost of providing an inconspicuous ear-level aid may be completely justified by the way in which it enables the child to mix successfully with the normal children in play as well as in work.

If, however, it becomes evident that a partially hearing child, though keeping up with the class in work, is substantially impeded in social contacts and integration one must accept the possibility that the experiment in placing him in an ordinary school has failed and transfer to a special unit or school must be considered. It is not desirable to retain him in the ordinary school in the hope that he will overcome his difficulties spontaneously. If, after such transfer, he improves rapidly and becomes socially mature in the special environment, re-admission to an ordinary school may later be considered.

PHYSICAL HANDICAP

An intelligent child with average vision and hearing, and with one normally functioning hand and another hand which can be used for steadying his work material, can be expected to cope with the general classroom activities of a normal school. There has been a general — and praiseworthy — tendency in recent years to place many such children in ordinary schools and this is, in fact, the only group of handicapped children of which a substantial number with really severe disabilities are likely to enter such schools. Given transport to and from the school and within the school they will have little trouble with their work. They will, however, be disadvantaged in extra-curricular activities.

Crippling disabilities are a matter of physically obvious fact. They are 'socially acceptable' by normal people, whether children or adults, and the handicapped child himself will perforce have become to some degree reconciled to them before he enters school. There are certain social-emotional risks which arise directly from these facts. The child himself may have become reconciled to inferior status before school age, and may already be convinced that competition is not for him. The

kinds of help he needs are plain to see and not difficult to provide; too often the school as an entity and the other children, collectively and individually, rush to offer too much help too quickly.

If such a child is not to be emotionally and socially ruined for life the school must, from the start, face him with direct challenge. Initially, while he is facing the sudden impact of school, it is reasonable to indulge him somewhat and give him a little more help than is strictly necessary. Nevertheless, even at this stage the school must be assessing his abilities — of course in close collaboration with those who are providing medical or surgical treatment — and trying to determine what is the absolute minimum help or protection that he needs. As soon as he begins to settle down in school the help and protection must be gradually reduced toward that minimum.

The crippled boy will be likely to feel his position acutely as he comes to the age when physical sport is of special importance to boys in general. In the case of most severely crippling conditions it is probably best to have started the process of diverting the boy's interests toward non-physical recreations before he reaches the age of eleven or twelve. If, however, there is *any* physical sport at which he can hope to become competent, he should be helped to do so. The leg-cripple in particular may have potential for swimming. Many boys who are competent in other sports may make little progress in swimming and the crippled boy who is coached into competence in this sport can derive much moral support from the fact that he is succeeding where many normal youngsters fail.

RESPIRATORY DISABILITIES

'Chestiness' in children has many causes. Cystic fibrosis is a severe, mainly physical, disability which demands that the child shall have some special care and protection. Asthma has components in both the physical (infective and allergic) and emotional fields. Much respiratory illness diagnosed as 'chronic bronchitis' probably also has some emotional component.

Parents of children with respiratory disabilities lean toward overprotection and are often likely to keep a child away from school if he has only a slight cough or cold or if the weather is a little chilly or damp. This overprotection in itself may intensify any emotional instability in the child, while its repeated interruptions of education may delay his school progress and place him under strain in keeping up with his class. The only practical action which can be taken is to have the child's condition carefully assessed through the medical services — including, if necessary, the child guidance service — to determine whether and to what extent pressure should be brought to bear on the parents to ensure more regular school attendance. The earlier in school life that this can be done, the better for all parties; the child is initially likely to prefer coming to school to staying at home, but if the parents' over-protection continues too long he can easily become something of a hypochondriac.

DIABETES
Many diabetic children have their condition stabilised on a combination of insulin and special diet and attend a normal school quite successfully. If the diabetes is at all severe, however, the child may require a regular routine which can be somewhat irksome to him and restrict his participation in some activities. He may well try to depart from the routine in order to be 'normal'; the consequence is commonly excessive fatiguability, with the risk of physical stress leading to emotional stress. The only safeguard against this is to gain his understanding cooperation in the early years.

The physical changes of puberty may cause temporary instability in a diabetic who has been previously well stabilised. This may first show itself as an inability to keep up the pace, in work and play, with the children with whom he has previously mixed as an equal. The possibility of this should be borne in mind and his physical condition investigated before competition stress has become significant.

EPILEPSY
Something like two-thirds of all epileptic children can now have their fits adequately controlled by drugs to the point at which they are able to attend ordinary schools. Occasional fits remain a possibility and the fear of them, together with the shock of their actual occurrence, often makes the child emotionally uncertain. One of the basic essentials is that such children must learn to live with their disability and the best and most important action to this end is that the manifesta-

tions of the disease should be accepted in school in the most matter-of-fact way. The other children quickly learn to do this; the difficulty may well lie in apprehensiveness in the teachers. Such apprehensiveness is understandable, for a child who may have fits imposes considerable responsibility on those in charge of him. When a child with epilepsy, however well controlled, enters an ordinary school, the staff should be fully advised and warned. To press for the admission of such a child to a school where the staff feel themselves already under such strain that they cannot accept the responsibility is unfair to both staff and child. If this is the case in the school which normally serves the neighbourhood in which he lives, admission should be sought in a school which is able to be more tolerant.

Puberty may bring a diminution of the epilepsy or may make a previously stabilised child unstable. In the latter event it is often better for the child to be temporarily transferred to a special school for a period of investigation and re-stabilisation than to try to re-stabilise him while he is attending an ordinary school. Not only are the special facilities more comprehensive but in a special school he is facing his crisis in the company of children who have the same kind of problem.

MINIMAL CEREBRAL DYSFUNCTION
This not uncommon condition is still too little understood. Present opinion inclines to the view that it is in many cases due to a minor degree of brain damage, though sometimes it may be accounted for by a combination of minor intellectual defect with emotional disturbance.

Typically, the child with minimal cerebral dysfunction presents a combination of intellectual 'slowness', physical clumsiness, physical hyperactivity and emotional instability. In some cases it appears that the intellectual disability is irregular, in that the child may be at or above normal level in certain aptitudes but substantially below in others.

The most difficult aspect of the child's situation is that no single aspect of his disability may be severe enough to attract special attention in the early years of life. Any one of them — and often all of them, considered separately — may be within normal limits, or at least no more marked than might be expected in a child who had been somewhat deprived of social contacts and normal play activities or over-indulged by his parents. The consequence is that in many of these children no disability has been suspected before the age of school entry, so that they tend to be presented automatically to ordinary schools without any suggestion that there is anything special about them. The many-sided challenge of school life suddenly finds out all their weak spots simultaneously and they may consequently suffer from 'school shock' in a quite severe form. The school tends to hope and expect that they will settle down and they may not be brought forward for special investigation until late in the first year, when general retardation is becoming well established.

By this time the child is facing the situation of slight but definite all-round inferiority to his peers. Since all the disparities are slight he will be confused and even bewildered by the inferiority and may already have begun to 'contract out' of school life. The risks of incompatibility between child and school is specially marked when the intellectual deficit is patchy. It is both easy and natural for a teacher to assume that if a child has taken easily to reading, for example, but is failing with numbers he is an intelligent child with selective laziness who needs to be pressed in his weak subject or subjects.

Some of these children will inevitably need special education. Others, given special attention, appropriate remedial teaching and, possibly, drug therapy, can expect to succeed in an ordinary school. It is of paramount importance that schools should be aware of the existence of this bizarre disability, not only because those of its possessors who need special education should be identified early, before they disrupt the life of the class, but because those who are potentially educable in an ordinary school should not be allowed to add maladjustment to their problems by having suffered a year or more of frustration and misunderstanding.

There are no sovereign or universal techniques for helping children with minimal cerebral dysfunction through ordinary schools. Those who are in fact of normal school potential will, in general, be children who make slow all-round progress. Though somewhat below average in intelligence they can learn. Their clumsiness will grow less as they gain practice in motor activity and their emotional instability will be reduced as they settle into a stable social environment. Their predicament is perhaps best seen as one of slow maturing. If the disability is detected early after first entry it may be wise to transfer them to a nursery school or class for a year and, after they become established in the ordinary school setting, to re-assess their maturity every time promotion is due — even from class to class — and retain them for a year or so if necessary until they are considered really mature enough to move up.

There is always the possibility that they may have periodical episodes of regression, especially in behaviour, after any traumatic experience — a crisis in the home, an interruption of schooling by illness, a misunderstanding with a teacher. Again, no universal rule for dealing with this possibility can be suggested. The need for emotional experience for these children is certainly at least as important as that of any other children and excessive shielding is just as damaging. Certainly, if experience suggests that a given child is specially vulnerable to a particular type of experience it is worthwhile trying to anticipate the occurrence of such a situation and to minimise its impact. Often these critical situations have several elements and it may well be possible, as the situation builds up, to reduce at any rate some of the elements.

Perhaps more than in any other group of handicapped children the closest of understanding and collaboration between home and school is to be sought. A word of warning from parent to teacher or from teacher to parent that the child has had some disturbing experience which has put him on edge on one particular day, either in the home or at school, may make it possible to avoid adding any other stress which, though mild in itself, may light the fuse and precipitate the explosion.

In conclusion it is worthwhile to return to and emphasise something which has been implicit throughout this chapter; namely that the most important element for success in coping with any handicapped child in an ordinary school is the perceptiveness and understanding of the teacher. Too little is still being done to stimulate and develop those qualities. The training of teachers still assumes too easily that handicapped children go to special schools and many training colleges give little more than passing mention of the problems of handicapped children in their syllabus of general teacher training. This deficit needs to be remedied.

Even with such training, two dangers persist. One is that not every teacher has the special qualities of personality needed in the management of a child with a disability. The other is that even if she has that personality and training a teacher may be working under such general pressure or in such unpropitious circumstances that she cannot make use of her assets as she should. The placing of a handicapped child in an ordinary school should therefore be preceded by as thorough an assessment of the child and discussion with the school staff as one would enter into before special school placement.

The School Health Service is not merely a clinical assessment agency, though that is still one of its important functions. In partnership with the pre-school health services and in collaboration with the school and other agencies it will prepare the child for schooling, discuss the selection of the school, prepare the school for the child's admission and serve as the continuing provider of surveillance, advice and guidance. The care of any handicapped child, however minor his disability, is a task for a team working in the harmonious relationship which subsists when members of several disciplines forget 'demarcation lines' and professional possessiveness and join in the common pursuit of the total aim — ensuring that the child shall have the best possible chance of realising all his potentialities.

25. Integration of treatment and education in cerebral palsy*

ESTER COTTON
Consultant Physiotherapist to the
Spastics Society, London

Cerebral palsy is normally treated by specialists who, in turn, deal with the specific symptoms of the condition. Each will pursue his own special interest, but they come together as a team to discuss the child; his symptoms, progress, and prognosis. This structure of treatment was changed by Professor Andras Petö, founder of The Institute for Conductive Education of the Motor Disabled,[1] by creating a new profession: the teacher/therapist (the conductor); and by developing a new learning method: 'rhythmical intention'.

Existing structure of treatment and education

It will help the understanding of Professor Petö's contribution, conductive education, if we examine the structure of treatment and education in our centres and schools. This is as follows.

1. Education and treatment are the responsibility of different departments.

2. Treatment is divided into:

    physiotherapy;

    occupational therapy;

    speech therapy;

    recreational activities.

3. Treatment and tuition are given individually.

4. Therapists and teachers may or may not have specialised training in cerebral palsy.

5. In some schools and centres teachers and therapists will meet as a team to discuss the children's progress and prognosis.

Advantages of this structure are that each child may be treated by highly skilled personnel and

*From *Physiotherapy*, April (1970), pp. 1–5

that his progress may be carefully discussed by a team.

Disadvantages are as follows.

1. An insecure child must adapt himself to a large number of adults.

2. The therapist must struggle for the attention of the child in order 'to get the best out of him' in the limited time at her disposal. Stimulated by toys and other incentives, the child is the centre of attraction. He will be spoiled – not motivated.

3. The teachers and therapists may have received different types of training and may, therefore, disagree about the best method of treatment.

4. Symptoms are treated in isolation. This is not only confusing for the child but also physiologically wrong. For example, the vexing problem of a tongue thrust is not an isolated symptom but part of a whole syndrome and will only improve if treated as such. Selective movements of lip and tongue must be made to fit into the entire feeding programme consisting of sitting balance, grasp and release, the movement of hand to mouth, and head control with head in midline.

Conductive education

Unity of disciplines is the key to conductive education and is the foundation of Professor Petö's theoretical concept of cerebral palsy. He suggested that the child with cerebral palsy is a child with learning difficulties, a child who has to learn actively and consciously all skills, including those which come naturally to the normal child by maturation and stimulation. Conductive education is, therefore, a learning method and is founded on the findings of Pavlov, who explained how learning processes take place by the forming of conditional reflexes. We know ourselves from experience how any higher skill is learnt by continual practice of the whole skill and parts of the skill, e.g. finger exercises for piano playing, clutch control for driving. Continual daily practice is also needed to maintain proficiency in higher skills as in ballet dancing or football. Similarly, within conductive education the child with cerebral palsy will learn to sit, stand, walk, feed, dress, and speak by practising these skills in 'task series' for many hours a day.

Pavlov has stated that we need quiet, concentration and repetition to form conditioned reflexes (Frolov 1937). Petö so organised conductive education that the children work in groups, guided by one teacher/therapist (the 'conductor') in a quiet room with sufficient time for practice and repetition, so fulfilling Pavlov's requirements for learning.

This milieu arranged for learning is an important part of conductive education. This does not resemble our normal classroom or nursery where the children, surrounded by toys and materials, learn by exploration and stimulation. As one English school-teacher said, 'We bring the world to the children.' Professor Petö might have answered, 'I normalise the children so I can take them out into the world.'

The conductor works with a group of children of similar handicap and age. She teaches the children all tasks of daily living as well as speech, language, and academic subjects. She understands all the mental and physical problems of the children in her group so that she is able to guide the work of each child according to his capacity. (As the Institute is residential, the conductors function on a shift system.)

It is within this structure of one conductor, one group, and a planned programme that the children overcome their greatest handicap, lack of *motivation*. Visitors to Budapest often comment on the motivation of the children. This is how a visitor described her first impression of the Institute: 'I was met by the astonishing sight of a line of small athetoid children walking with great difficulty up the corridor counting one-two, one-two, as they wobbled along. They were utterly concentrated, smiled cheerfully at us as we passed, and continued on their way. There was nobody supervising them.' A remarkable thing is the apparent lack of

supervision; a group of children walking and practising without interference of passing adults. It is taken for granted that if a child has to learn to walk well he must practise walking for many hours a day.

The motivation arises from a number of different factors within the sytem.

1. Working in a *group* is important as it is stimulating and makes the children ambitious. A group, however, is not the same as a class of children who all work at different tasks at different levels. In the group the children are all learning in the same way to overcome the same difficulties in order to arrive at a solution of the same task. When, therefore, one child manages to take her first step or learns to feed herself, the other children will understand how she learnt and this will motivate them to work harder to achieve the task themselves. Although taught in this uniform way, the children are shown many different solutions to a problem, e.g. five or six different ways of sitting up from supine; in the end each child will choose the way that suits him best in daily life.

2. The correct task series will also act as a motivator, or rather *success* achieved by the accomplishment of a task will motivate the children to further efforts. The 'task series' must, therefore, be constructed so that the children can manage to fulfil the task or part of the task.

The task series must be worked out so that they stretch the ability of the children in the group, but must not be too difficult so that the children get bored. It is of no use copying 'exercises' seen in Budapest or elsewhere, as these may be quite unsuitable for the specific children at hand. The task series must be built on an understanding of the children's disabilities, a knowledge of their stage of development, an understanding of Professor Petö's principles, and an analysis of the movements involved in the functions being taught in the programme.

It may take some time before a child will participate well enough to achieve a success. This may be the fault of the conductor, because the programme is unsuitable, or because the child has previously had too much attention and supervision from adults and has lost all initiative. The working ability of the child does not depend on his intelligence but on his inner drive and desire for work. Professor Petö did not select the children according to intelligence but according to their ability to participate in the work of the group.

3. The conductor and her personality is a motivator. She must show respect for the children's work, and as, Petö said, 'be kind but detached'. Being with the children all day and every day, she will know all their accomplishments and will be able to reinforce their learning in all situations. She will not destroy a child's initiative and motivation by carrying him if he can walk, or disrespectfully pulling off his coat when he is manfully struggling to take it off himself.

4. *Rhythmical intention* also acts as a motivator. This learning method involves the child's motor, linguistic, and intellectual abilities. Petö learnt from Luria (1961, Luria and Yudovich 1959) how small children use the second signalling system to help them solve a difficult problem. When forming conditioned reflexes, the second signalling system (speech) acts as the conditioned stimulus. The child will learn to use speech, or effort of speech (the intention), to guide his movements towards new motor sequences while counting to five (the rhythm). First the conductor says the command, 'I stretch my elbows' then the children repeat the command slowly with her, and at last they perform the movement while counting to five or while using the operative dynamic word 'Stretch, stretch, stretch'. The *intention* puts the children in a state of preparation for the coming task and acts as an important motivator.

As the command often includes references to the children's bodies, the method (rhythmical intention) leads to an accurate idea of body image and position in space: 'I hold my ears', 'I turn on my left side'. Rhythmical intention also helps the children to concentrate and to think; above all it makes them vocalise, and the continuous sound heard in the Institute is a welcome contrast to the quiet of many spastic centres.

Physiotherapy

The motor disfunction of the child with cerebral palsy is normally treated by a physiotherapist in the physiotherapy department. Within conductive education the motor disfunction is treated in conjunction with the functional, linguistic, and academic problems as part of the child's education. Physiotherapy, as such, has therefore no place in conductive education. When discussing

with Professor Petö which of our many professionals might be best suited to act as conductors, he preferred the occupational therapist, 'who thinks of function, not muscles', or the teacher 'who knows how to break up a task so that the child can learn'.

The children never do exercises, but each function and physical task is accomplished by working through many 'task series' while actively using rhythmical intention. A programme and time-table is worked out for each group of children, athetoids, double hemiplegias, hemiplegias, etc. All tasks — physical, functional, linguistic, and academic — are included in this programme and the task series are planned to lead to these accomplishments. Many tasks will be interrelated and the learning of one will help or reinforce the learning of another, e.g. a task series leading to the learning of grasp and release will include grasping with both hands which will further symmetry and bring the head into midline while inhibiting the extensor pattern.

The task series always contain movements and positions directly related to the children's main problems. The spastics will learn to part their legs and to keep their legs apart while moving to the side to prone, to sitting or standing, or while working with their hands. The athetoids will learn to grasp and to maintain the grasp for fixation so that they can perform selective movements and learn to hold on themselves instead of being held by others, an important step towards independence. When the child cannot fix himself the conductor may fix a limb to facilitate movement, but very little manual help is given as the child must learn to work actively himself. Similarly, only very little mechanical help is given. A limited amount of simple splinting is used, and the furniture consists of chairs with ladder-backs used for sitting, standing and holding, walking and pushing. Also slatted plinths are used as tables and beds and for task series in lying and sitting.

Margaret Parnwell describes in detail (1967) task series leading to writing: how writing starts with the learning of grasp and release, symmetry and normal asymmetry, head control with head in midline, and good sitting balance.

Two different aspects of sitting may be considered here to demonstrate as an example why conductive education succeeds where conventional methods fail.

The actual task of sitting is often practised successfully in the physiotherapy department. It involves learning to sit on the floor, chair, or box, to sit up from supine and prone, and to stand up from a chair and sit down again. The child must learn to flex and extend his hips, to dorsiflex his feet and put them flat on the ground, and to put his hands at his sides or on the table while stretching his elbows and leaning forward.

The difficulty arises when the child returns to the classroom or the dining hall. As soon as he speaks, uses his hands, or even thinks, his feet come off the ground, his hands go up in the air, he leans backward and the sitting balance is lost.

Sitting must, therefore, be taught in the room in which the child works. The task series leading to sitting should be intimately connected with the work the child is performing in sitting, as well as with speaking and singing. It must be part of the education of the whole child. I once said to a group of children, 'You have done your hand exercises very well and above all your feet are flat on the floor. Try and remember to keep them like that when you are working in the classroom,' and a little boy said, 'It doesn't matter in there,' by which he meant that in the classroom keeping the feet on the floor was not part of the day's work.

One child came to The Lady Zia Wernher Centre, Luton,[2] at the age of eight; a severe quadruplegia with athetodis, tonic spasms, and fluctuating muscle tone. He had received physiotherapy since he was 10 months old and had attended school since he was five. When he arrived he could not sit unstrapped on a chair or pot, nor use his hands for any function. In six months he learned to sit alone on the pot, to stand grasping a chair in front of him, to sit freely at a table using his hands to push objects around.

Later on he learned simultaneously to sit, to grasp and to speak. This is how the whole child is educated. This is the essence of conductive education.

NOTES

1 The Institute for Conductive Education of the Motor Disabled and Conductor's College was founded in Budapest by Professor Petö in 1945. Since his death in 1967, it has been under the leadership of his pupil and co-operator, Dr. Maria Hari. The Institute is a Rehabilitation Centre for many hundreds of patients, the majority of whom are residential; 200 children with cerebral palsy, several groups of spinal bifidae and muscular dystrophies. It also houses adult paraplegias and hemiplegias, and has a large out-patient department for babies and adult neurological cases.
   As far as the children are concerned, the Institute is neither a hospital nor a school but is regarded as a pre-school training centre from where they move into suitable schools as soon as possible. The Institute is also a 'Conductor's College'. The training of conductors takes four years and is divided between the Institute and the University of Budapest. The girls are accepted on selection; 'A' level qualifications are needed as well as aptitude for the work.

2. Conductive education as practised in Budapest has not yet been tried in England as we have no trained conductors. Integration of disciplines using the principles of Professor Petö was practised in The Lady Zia Wernher Centre, Luton, from 1966—68 with a group of athetoids. Similarly Claremont School for Spastics, Bristol, is using Professor Petö's principles in a day school. The first residential group is working at Craig-Y-Parc, a Spastics Society boarding school, and a day group is being tried at the Centre for Spastic Children, Cheyne Walk.

REFERENCES

LURIA, A. R., AND YUDOVICH, F. I., 1959, 'Speech and Development of Mental Processes in the Child',
London, Staples Press.
LURIA, A. R., 1961, *The Role of Speech in the Regulation of Normal and Abnormal Behaviour* in J.
Tizard (ed.), London, Pergamon Press.
FROLOV, Y. P., 1937, *Pavlov and his School: The Theory of Conditioned Reflexes*, London, Kegan Paul,
Trench, Trubner.
PARNWELL, M., 1967, 'From Hungary: the Petö Method', *Special Education*, 56 p. 4.

26. Like other school-leavers?*

MARGARET R. MORGAN
Head of Social Work and Employment,
Spastics Society, London

[. . .] I would like to look briefly at some of the *developmental needs* and *social problems* facing handicapped young people. These are, indeed, common to all adolescents but they are not always recognised as being important or relevant as far as handicapped boys and girls are concerned.

1. *Identity and self-determination.* Here I would like to remind you again of what I said earlier about stereotypes and to emphasise the complications involved in trying to establish one's own identity when there is an accepted stereotype about the sort of person that the general public expects you to be. It is particularly difficult for handicapped adolescents to discover exactly who they are and, perhaps more importantly, to discover what sort of men and women they are going to be in adult life. And do not those of us who are directly involved, perhaps with the best intentions, tend to protect young people from the reality of the situation and, in doing so, confuse the issue still further? Is it not sometimes easier to pretend that the handicapped boy or girl is going to be a perpetual Peter Pan who never grows up and so avoid some of the thorny problems that will arise in adult life?

2. Another major need of all adolescents is that of *independence*, of becoming a separate individual apart from parents and other people. We know from the experience of normal teenagers how strong this drive is and how intense the battles to win through to some form of real separation and liberation from parents. Yet, as I have pointed out earlier this need is particularly difficult to meet when handicapped young people have to be dependent on others in many different and subtle ways. It seems essential, therefore, that parents and all types of staff dealing with handicapped young people should be guided and helped to see how important this is in the maturation process and advice should be given on how to encourage independence of spirit, even if physical dependence is inevitable, by enabling and encouraging the young people to make choices and decisions for themselves and by trying to identify and limit the areas in which dependence is necessary.

3. A further need of adolescents is for *respect*, both from their own peer group and from other people. And by respect I mean genuine understanding and empathy, not patronage or sentimental sympathy. Young people need to feel that they are valued for themselves and that their views hold some weight, both with young people of their own age group and with older people as well. At this stage of development, young handicapped people who have attended normal secondary schools may need an opportunity to be with other young handicapped people for a short period, in order to regain lost confidence and to see themselves as one of the more lightly handicapped members of a larger group.

4. *Work and appropriate outlets for self-expression are needed by all young people.* Here I would like to put in a plea for more adequate provision of work centres for those who are more

*Concluding section of paper read at the thirty-first National Biennial Conference/Course of the Association for Special Education (now the National Council for Special Education) held at Cardiff on 24–27th July, 1972, pp. 7–10.

heavily handicapped and are not likely to be able to compete in normal employment, but where they can do useful, productive work to the best of their ability and enjoy the company and stimulation of being with a working group. In addition to providing work outlets, it is extremely important to extend the provisions for further general education and for study courses covering a wide variety of subjects, in order to enable those young people who wish to continue their education or to spend their time in cultural and intellectual pursuits to see their futures positively and not to be left feeling that all that can be provided for them is a life of continued enforced leisure.

5. The final basic need of all adolescents is for *satisfactory relationships with the opposite sex*. Fortunately, nowadays, nearly all schools are co-educational and very many of the further education, training and residential centres also cater for both sexes. Where mobility and personal independence are limited, however, it is especially difficult to make adequate friendships with other people of either sex and many handicapped teenagers are therefore deprived of the normal opportunities for experimentation and testing out their relationships. Sex education in this specialised field is very neglected and there is a great deal of work to do in helping parents and school staff to understand and cope more adequately with this very important aspect of the boys' and girls' development. There seems to be a real need for more discussion at all levels about the problems of personal relationships for handicapped young people and more opportunities for group and individual counselling with parents, other involved adults and the young people themselves.

Finally, I would like to summarise my suggestions for future discussion and development:

A. *Preparation for adolescents and for school-leaving*. Do we start this early enough and who should be involved? So often, discussions about post-school plans are left until the last year, or even the last term at school. The young people and their parents will, however, often have been speculating and worrying about the future for some years, though they may have been apprehensive about raising the topic themselves, for fear of disappointment and disillusionment. There is a good argument for starting general counselling in the pre-adolescent phase at a time when boys and girls are likely to be less emotionally involved and more ready and able to accept the reality of the situation.

B. *The need for a careful, frank and realistic appraisal* of the boy's or girl's assets and disabilities is extremely important. Although, clearly, the reports and views of those most closely connected with the young people are very valuable in building up the whole picture, the fresh appraisal at adolescence may be best undertaken by people who have not been closely involved with the child during the growing-up process.

C. *Consistent counselling* during adolescence and immediately after school is also very important if we are to help both parents and the young people towards a good adjustment in early adult years. So often, unfortunately, in spite of an apparently united team approach, different members of staff give different advice. Young people and their parents are obviously going to turn to those who offer the most optimistic future and it is human nature to shop around until they find someone who is prepared to suggest that 'a little job must be available somewhere'.

D. As our previous speaker has pointed out there is a *great need for more further education and vocational training facilities* for physically handicapped young people. Time is an extremely important factor and most handicapped young people are not ready to complete their education by the age of 16. Remaining at the same school that they have attended for many years, however, does not seem to be the best solution, and the development of a much greater variety and number of further education schemes and centres seems long overdue.

E. *Consistent support and help with placement* after leaving school are also very necessary. There has been some discussion about who are the most appropriate professional people to provide this guidance and help. The Local Authority Careers Officers are responsible for this area of work, but they usually have large case loads and, although some authorities have appointed specialist officers to work with handicapped young people, many Careers Officers have no specialised knowledge of disabling conditions and their effects on the boys and girls concerned. In the case of heavily handicapped boys and girls it may be more appropriate for a Social Worker from the Local Authority Social Services Department to provide the link between school and the community, but more co-operation is needed all round, as there are at present both gaps and overlapping in the services.

F. *Research is urgently needed* in order to discover new outlets for the working capacities of severely physically handicapped people. With the developments in aids and gadgets of all types and more adequate practical help and support, many more young people can make a useful economic contribution in the world of work even if this is in special centres or at home. There are, however, a number of heavily handicapped people who find any form of productive work in competitive conditions a very great strain, and here I think we have a responsibility to try and find suitable alternatives to work that are respectable and acceptable and not merely filling in time.

G. We need to extend the *social contacts* of these young people and to enable them to mix and make friends with a real peer group. Social Clubs, holidays both at home and abroad, group projects and many other activities enable handicapped young people to mix together and also to meet on equal terms with un-handicapped teenagers. There is a good deal of discussion these days about the value of integration, but I think we sometimes stress the need for social integration to the disadvantage of the handicapped young people themselves. We have found from experience that many young people prefer, at certain stages of their development, to be with other handicapped young people, where they can be more at ease and self-assured and where they may have a real contribution to make in helping and advising each other. The opportunities are not often available to

them in settings which are dominated by un-handicapped young people, who are probably there in helping roles and not as true equals.

H. Most young people *leave home* eventually, either for further education, training, work or when they get married. Handicapped young people may also reach the stage when they, too, want to move from the parental home and lead a rather more independent life. If you are heavily handicapped this is extremely difficult and opportunities are very limited. There is a need for a much greater variety of residential provisions: hostels, flatlets, and residential centres of all types, with more flexibility and more opportunities for spending short periods in communal living and then returning to one's family home again. Up to now, a major decision has usually had to be made about 'going into care' and once young handicapped people are accepted into residential centres, it is assumed that they will stay either in that centre or in other centres until the end of their days. It seems to me that there are times in the evolution of a family when it may be particularly difficult to contain a handicapped member, but as the family composition changes and ideas develop, what might have appeared impossible at one stage may become a practicable proposition at another. It is also essential that handicapped people themselves should have more choices, to decide not only whether they want to leave home or remain with their family, but about the centre and area in which they would like to live, and what type of facilities they would best enjoy.

27. Sex and handicap *

ANN SHEARER
Social Services journalist and founding member of the
Campaign for the Mentally Handicapped.

A most severely disabled young man, who is bound to a wheelchair, recently married a 'normal' girl. An elderly couple in their block of flats speak of him as 'that gentleman we've seen you with' when they meet his wife: the exact nature of the relationship is too embarrassing to contemplate. His wife, when she asked their GP for a pill prescription, met horrified incredulity at the thought of this pair having sexual relationship. She is now getting used to people trying to put a martyr's crown on her for marrying a disabled man. He is getting used to resentment from able-bodied men at his landing a normal wife.

Of all the problems that disabled people come up against in their dealings with society, our attitudes to their emotional and sexual needs are probably least discussed of all. We talk increasingly of offering mentally as well as physically handicapped people as 'normal' a life as possible, and as long as we stick to exhortations about community care or job opportunities, it's a good enough yardstick. But when it comes to offering opportunities for emotional and sexual expression, we prefer to duck.

Physically handicapped people have exactly the same range of feelings as the rest of us. The only difference may have to be in expression. Even the most severely mentally handicapped people, we're now finding out, need heterosexual emotional relationships.

Yet even workers with the handicapped people will bluntly deny that these normal needs exist —

*This article is based on the author's *A Right to Love?*, published by the Spastics Society and the National Association for Mental Health (1972). From *New Society*, 11th May (1972) *20*, No. 505, pp. 295–6

or, alternatively, claim that appetites are so exaggerated that society, as well as the handicapped individual, needs protection. Both views are myth, and by perpetuating them we are making life harder for handicapped people trying to meet an intolerant society, as well as offering an emotionally barren life to those who live in our institutions. We are adding emotional handicaps to those that already exist. More than that, we are also forcing handicapped people into the double-bind of having to live up to the stereotypes we have of them.

Why do we do it? The GP who was horrified at the thought of sex and disability can't be unique. Probably the link is disgusting to most of us. Classic psychoanalytical theory explains this by reckoning that the sight of physical disability stirs up old castration fears from childhood. A social worker with spastics suggests that as we strive more and more towards an ideal of sexual performance — egged on by explicit handbooks, films, and so on — we become increasingly worried by the thought of 'damaged' people in a sexual situation, perhaps reaching greater fulfilment than we can.

There are social fears as well — which are sometimes personal fears distanced into social acceptability. One of the main incentives for our building both large and isolated institutions, after all, was the imaginary danger of 'national degeneracy' if mentally handicapped people were not prevented from breeding. It was only just over a decade ago that the Mental Health Act, 1959, abolished the parole system for the certified subnormal — and with it, the condition that licence was to be revoked immediately if the parolee formed any relationship with the opposite sex.

We now know that very few of the defined forms of severe mental handicap are inherited, and we are wary enough of our social classifications of mild mental handicap to look carefully at the families so defined. We know that mentally handicapped people are not promiscuous. In fact their sexual activity seems to be less, the greater the degree of handicap. Nor do they breed faster than the rest of us. Indeed, one recent study of mentally handicapped couples showed they had only roughly half the birth rate of a comparable 'normal' population.

Yet little of this knowledge seems to have made much impact on popular mythology. Mentally handicapped people are still widely believed to have abnormal and dangerous sexual appetites. The risk to neighbouring children is still a standard objection to having a home for mentally handicapped people in the neighbourhood.

So it's not surprising — given the reluctance to tackle the subject found even among professionals — that our institutions for the mentally handicapped still reflect the old misconceptions. Mixing of the sexes is allowed only under the most rigidly controlled circumstances in most of them. At the last count, less than a quarter of even occupational departments in subnormality hospitals were for both sexes. While psychiatric hospitals are introducing mixed-sex admission wards, a couple of 'experimental family units' in subnormality hospitals allow mixing only by day and one rejected a man as he showed too much interest in the women.

Some of this has spilled over into attitudes to, and provision for, the physically handicapped. It wasn't very long ago, for instance, that Sweden forbade marriage between epileptics who hadn't first been sterilised, though the risk of epilepsy for first degree relatives was only 4 per cent compared with 1 or 2 per cent among the normal population. It wasn't long ago, either, that one group of homes for the physically disabled forbade residents to be alone together. The penalty for disobedience was sending one of the couple to another link in the caring chain. Segregation of the sexes has, after all, a long and dishonourable history in our caring institutions, from the Poor Law onwards.

Staff in old institutions commonly claim that mixing the sexes is impossible for purely physical reasons. The lavatories and washing facilities, they say, cannot be adapted. But the unwillingness of women staff to work on male wards and men on female is probably a better clue to what staff really feel about allowing their residents greater freedom. This staff mixing is only beginning now in most institutions for the mentally handicapped. Even in modern homes for physically handicapped people, where their right to privacy and freedom is theoretically accepted, staff attitudes are no less ambivalent than those of society outside. In one home, the wardens said firmly that their residents were far too immature to form relationships with each other, and that, in any case, this was something that never came up. Yet in the same home, six young couples were at that very time going through the agonies of adolescent engagements that seemed doomed for want of a sympathetic hearing. In another home, according to one of the wardens, 'there's far too much snogging.' This man will frisk the belongings of his residents for contraceptives if he 'suspects anything.' The gulf in attitudes between his predominantly middle aged staff and the young people in his charge is striking. Staff elsewhere will say unhesitatingly that their residents have a right to emotional relationships — but it's impossible not to hear the unspoken rider 'as long as they just hold hands.'

Not surprisingly, residents don't feel free to lead their own emotional lives. Time and again they speak of staff who come into their rooms without knocking, who always seem to know exactly who is where at any one time, who interrupt meetings in the sitting rooms. They feel that they are treated as children, that their emotional lives are not respected, that their attachments to each other are held up to ridicule by staff. Some say — particularly those in homes which depend on charitable funds — that they feel forced to repress normal desires because of accepted standards of 'respectability.'

This sort of atmosphere must inevitably have its effect. James Loring, director of the Spastics Society, has noted that where emotional attachments are formed in homes for the disabled, they often have a 'coarse and comic' quality about them. Staff talk of epidemics of engagements, of public snogging sessions. It doesn't seem to occur to them that they may be provoking such behaviour by their own lack of respect for privacy and expectations of residents' behaviour. At an even more basic level, it is surely unrealistic to expect 'mature' emotional and sexual behaviour without the knowledge on which to base it. Normal adults may complain about the lack of sex education that they received in adolescence. Physically handicapped adults have even more cause to complain, and their need for realistic discussion of their own sexuality may be even greater.

If physically handicapped people are forced into fulfilling our stereotypes of them, this is even more true of the mentally handicapped. Sweden, in its pursuit of 'normalisation' in the lives of mentally handicapped people, has a quarter of its daily living groups for mixed sexes. Experience here shows that where men and women live together, aggression becomes less, consideration towards each other increases, and unacceptable behaviour like open masturbation stops. Sexual and emotional expression is allowed. Couples, both heterosexual and homosexual, can share bedrooms.

The result is not — though it may be hard to convince British workers of this,— a sexual orgy. On the contrary, sexual activity is less than was expected, while affection and warmth have increased.

From this evidence, it seems that our own policies of segregation are actually creating the behaviour which justifies keeping them. Our reluctance to think in terms of active sexual and emotional guidance for mentally handicapped people can have other effects too. Swedish experts now reckon that much of the disturbed behaviour of mentally handicapped adolescents results from fear at the changes in their own bodies. They lay great stress on sex education.

If, then, we really mean what we say when we talk of offering handicapped people as normal a life as possible, we are not going to be able to duck a recognition of their normal emotional needs for much longer. This will mean more than providing the flatlets for married couples, that some voluntary societies are now very slowly beginning to build beside their homes for the physically handicapped. More, too, than local authorities investing in sheltered housing and social support. It will mean more, even, than admitting that the old institutions for mentally handicapped people can never be adapted to provide the privacy that is a first essential and replacing these altogether. It will mean a far more honest appraisal of our own motives and preconceptions about handicapped people.

For it would, of course, be hard to stop there. Physically handicapped people are increasingly beginning to demand not only emotional fulfilment and marriage, but children — if the nature of their disability allows this and makes caring for the child a possibility. The same is going to be true of many mentally handicapped people as we recognise their rights to a 'normal' life.

Perhaps it is this prospect that holds us back from more modest acceptance of emotional rights. Yet the few studies that have been made of the families of physically and mentally handicapped parents show that it is very hard to justify our demand that this small section of the community should discipline itself against reproduction. A small study of the children of blind parents in Australia shows that their problems — and 15 out of 18 families were reckoned to have them — could not be linked to the parents' disability alone. An American study of mentally handicapped parents (given the changing definitions of what constitutes mental handicap) shows that ability to cope with a family is not related to the handicap so much as to family poverty.

There's no denying that handicap brings its problems. One physically disabled father found that both his children were very disturbed by his handicap and suffered until their late adolescence from, in the boy's case, shame — and, in the girl's, excessive protection — in their attitudes towards him. A recent study of mentally handicapped couples illustrates that these families need a good deal of social support. But 'non-handicapped' families also have their inter-personal problems, and they also need a good deal of social support.[1] We don't discourage the children of broken homes from marriage and children, or those on low incomes.

How much longer will we be able to justify discouraging those people whose likely problems in coping are so much less well documented?

NOTE
1. Mattinson.

REFERENCE
MATTINSON, J., 1970, *Marriage and Mental Handicap*, London, Duckworth.

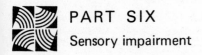

PART SIX
Sensory impairment

Introduction

Whilst it is possible for a person with unimpaired sight or hearing to simulate the immediate experience of sensory deprivation by closing his eyes or by using a pair of ear plugs — and few people have not tried one or other experiment at some time — the very simplicity of the operation may mislead them into an entirely false appreciation of the real implications of lifelong blindness or deafness. To be born without one of the two primary senses through which a person mediates between inner needs and the external environment affects and restricts his whole development as a person and necessitates the acquisition of quite different modes of adjustment from those of a normal person.

Vision and hearing are the most important of man's senses. They are the only senses that can give him information of objects and events at any distance away from him. Their primary functions in normally equipped people are different and they interact closely and to a limited extent are interchangeable. Man is unique in having two such highly efficient distance senses. Vision is directional. We must focus to see and we are continually re-focusing, gaining information about a small section of the world immediately in front of us and then moving on.

Hearing is multidirectional, continuously scanning the environment for new signals and, unlike vision, it cannot be 'switched off' at will. Indeed, it is still on the alert even when we are asleep. When awake even a faint unexpected sound will draw the head round to refocus as sharply as though twitched by a string attached to the end of the nose.

Vision is a 'snapshot' sense although we think of it as being concerned with space, and the impression that we normally have of being at the centre of a stable, continuous, surrounding environment depends in large measure upon the complementary interaction of the two distance senses, even although stimulation comes to the ears in temporal sequences, here now, then gone for ever.

When one of these senses is lacking, the complex and subtle system on which we depend for the satisfaction of nearly all needs, cannot function. Impairment of one of these primary senses may even have a damaging effect upon the remaining one (although popular mythology holds the reverse to be true). Myklebust and Brutten (1953) found that when hearing is deprived in early life, visual perception is disturbed. Yet it becomes necessary for the remaining distance sense to take over, with some support from the tactual, olfactory and gustatory senses, all the main functions of the missing one *as well as* continuing to perform its own. This leads to conflicting claims upon the attention. A deaf student cannot use his eyes to 'hear' a lecture and *at the same time* take notes, and he certainly cannot monitor the environment for alarm or interest signals as well. A one-channel input must always carry only half the information supplied by two, and for the sensorily impaired person everything takes at best rather longer. This may be one factor influencing the generally lower educational achievement of sensorily impaired children by the time they leave school. Also both handicaps can have serious implications for the child's present and future personal development and social opportunities.

231

Five of the papers in this part are concerned with education. Denmark provides a carefully reasoned argument in favour of supplementing the oral education of deaf children by manual means. It includes a highly condensed history of deaf education and a review of some of the literature relevant to his main theme. For a fuller treatment of the history and a classic exposition of the principles and methods of oralism by two of its chief pioneers in this country, readers are referred to Irene and A. W. Ewing (1956) *Speech and the Deaf Child*, Manchester University Press.

Then the two papers that follow, by the experimental psychologist Conrad, throw light upon the approach and methods of experimental research and upon the value of the contribution that is beginning to emerge from this source. These papers report and discuss the findings of two from a series of elegant experiments conducted by Dr Conrad on the memory processes of deaf children (references to earlier papers will be found at the end of each article). Starting with a question posed by Furth[1] (1964) 'What do the deaf think in?', Conrad sought a scientifically meaningful way of answering it. Drawing upon his own earlier work on memory processes in normally hearing people, he began by presenting deaf children with tests of short-term memory using sets of letter sequences which might be confused with each other if the child encoded the memory in some kind of visual image or code (KXYZ). He compared the number and kinds of errors they made with the results from tests which used letters (BCT and XH) which might be confused if the children encoded in some internal representation of their own efforts to articulate. The kind of 'inner voice' coding that his hearing subjects appeared to use was of course ruled out by their deafness. He also compared the results when children were required to read the test material silently or aloud. He found that some children (and these were in the main children whose teachers rated them as 'above average' in speech quality) performed equally well under both conditions, while others, of whom the majority were rated below average for speech, memorized less successfully when they had to read the stimulus letters aloud. Two conclusions are indicated: (1) deaf children do not all memorize in the same code, and for some it may be quite different from that used by their teachers, and (2) if memorizing in some children is impaired by

reading aloud, each individual child's educational needs require assessment and new teaching methods should be explored.

This very condensed and oversimplified summary does little justice to Conrad's work, but may help to set the scene for the items included in this section, which report further studies in the same field and discuss their possible educational implications. Gill Rimmer's paper is entirely different and reviews the problems of the hard-of-hearing in Britain from the standpoint of a practising social worker. It is fresh, forthright and very challenging.

Of the three items on visual impairment, two are concerned with the structure of the educational services. The first is an extract from the DHSS publication: *The Education of the Visually Handicapped* (The Vernon Report) published in 1972, the second a critique of the report produced jointly by the National Federation of the Blind of the United Kingdom and the Association of Blind and Partially Sighted Teachers and Students. It is always a valuable exercise to compare the views of those advising the providers with the views of the consumers. Although the Vernon Report moved further from the idea of segregation in education than any previous officially inspired publication in this country, it was still a long way from meeting the aspirations of visually impaired people, who felt that it bent over backwards to maintain existing forms of educational provision. Further discussion of the general aims and means of achieving the integration of handicapped children in ordinary schools may be found in Part 5.

Roy Fitzgerald's paper is a study of the immediate reactions of 66 newly blinded adults, and demonstrates the need for very prompt support in the face of what for many people is a profoundly traumatic experience. Some blinded people would argue that the need is wider. Blindness, like deafness, is something which may attack anyone, but the traumatic response is at least in part a product of the blinded person's expectations of what his blindness may mean for his whole future pattern of life. This in turn is a product of our society's attitudes to the handicapped person and his status and value to the community, and may usefully be considered in relation to Part 3 of this book. A recent book, to which reference has already been made (in the introduction to Part 3) is Minton's account and criticism of the official blind welfare and rehabilitation services in Britain. The United States aspects of these are discussed by Chevigny (1946), a journalist who, like Minton, suddenly lost his sight after the detachment of his retina. Scott's article in Part 3 is also relevant to Part 6.

NOTE

1. H. G. Furth has himself made a major contribution to the experimental psychology of deafness. e.g. (1973) *Deafness and Learning: A Psychological Approach*, Belmont California, Wadsworth Publishing Co.

REFERENCES

CHEVIGNY, H. (1946, reprinted 1972) *My Eyes have a cold nose*, London, Yale University Press.
CONRAD, R. (1970) 'Short-term memory processes in the deaf', *British Journal of Psychology*, 61, pp. 179—95.
FURTH, H. G. (1964) 'Research with the deaf: implications for language and cognition', *Psychological Bulletin*, 62, pp. 145—64.
MINTON, H. G. 1974, *Blind Man's Buff*, London, Elek.
MYKELBUST, H. R. and BRUTTEN, M., 1953, 'A study of the visual perception of deaf children', *Acta Oto-laryngolagica*, supplement 105.

28. The education of deaf children*

JOHN DENMARK
Consultant Psychiatrist, Department of Psychiatry
for the Deaf, Whittingham Hospital, Lancashire

'Nor is there any easy method of teaching or persuading the profoundly deaf.'

Lucretius, *De Rerum Natura*

Deafness is a blanket term covering many different clinical pictures, depending upon such variables as degree of deafness, age of onset, rate of onset, and the presence of other handicaps. For example, the sudden onset of profound bilateral deafness is an extremely traumatic experience usually producing severe depression, whereas the basic problem of the child who is born profoundly deaf is that he cannot acquire language normally. This paper is concerned largely with profoundly deaf children whose handicap dates from birth or early age, before the development of laguage.

The normally hearing child first develops auditory language. The deaf child, on the other hand, will not develop language unless given special education and even then it is a most difficult and slow process. If a child does not hear, then language must be developed through the sense of vision — through lip-reading or through the written word.

But lipreading is extremely difficult. It presupposes a knowledge of the language and, moreover, many of the sounds produced are not seen, while the position of the lips for other sounds is ambiguous. Ability to understand the written word requires maturation of the nervous system such as is not usually attained before the school years. In consequence the prelingually profoundly deaf child with no useful residual hearing begins to acquire language very much later than his hearing peers and then only very slowly.

If we compare a young deaf child with his hearing peers we find a markedly different situation. The average hearing child at five years has a vocabulary of some 2,000 words and uses these in a grammatically and syntactically correct manner. He is able to communicate easily simply because he can hear. He has a body of general knowledge and has developed a code of social behaviour. The deaf child, on the other hand, cannot hear. He has little language and so is unable to express himself; his general knowledge is limited and he is socially immature. In consequence the teacher of the deaf has a far more difficult task than the teacher of normally hearing children. He has not only to teach the usual academic subjects but has to teach language and communication skills. More than that he has to teach social skills and a great deal of general knowledge, all of which the hearing child acquires so easily.

F. L. Denmark wrote, 'When one considers the handicap under which the born-deaf child lives, the marvel is not that he has such a poor command of language but that he is able to accomplish as much as he does under such adverse conditions' (Denmark, 1929).

It is not surprising that the majority of prelingually profoundly deaf school leavers are educationally retarded, have poor language and because of their difficulties with speech and lipreading have

*From *Hearing*, September (1973), *28*, pp. 3–12.

to rely upon manual methods of communication — upon finger-spelling and signing.

At the time of the Caesars deaf children were thrown into the Tiber to drown and for centuries they were thought to be ineducable. In mediaeval Britain deaf mutes were classed with idiots, forbidden to manage their own affairs or to bequeath their own property.

The earliest attempts we really know of to teach deaf children date back only to the sixteenth century when in Spain a Benedictine monk, Pedro Ponce de León (1520–1584) taught a few carefully selected pupils. He did it for money and would only work for the rich. There are references to sporadic attempts to educate the deaf in various countries from that time onwards, but it was not until two centuries later that their education started to be systematised.

About 1760 a French abbé named de l'Epée began to teach deaf children employing a sign language — each sign representing a word or a phrase. He argued, and the same argument is relevant today, that language is necessary for speech and the understanding of speech, and that the priority in deaf education is the teaching of language.

At about the same time as de l'Epée was teaching deaf children by signing, Samuel Heinicke (1729–1790) was teaching in Germany by a purely oral system, arguing that if the deaf were to take their place in society they had to speak and to lipread. Thus began the controversy between the 'manualists' on the one side and the 'oralists' on the other, which continues to this day and which culminated in this country, in the setting up of a committee under the chairmanship of the late Professor M. M. Lewis by the Secretary of State for Education and Science to investigate the 'Possible Place of Finger Spelling and Signing in the Education of Deaf Children' (1964–1968). In the United States of America, about the same time the Secretary of Health, Education and Welfare set up an Advisory Committee under the chairmanship of Homer D. Babbidge (1965) to make a similar investigation.

The nineteenth century saw the development of schools for the deaf throughout Britain and America and the communication methods used have varied in these schools and in those of other countries also. In Germany, the pure oral method has been used since the time of Heinicke; in America some schools are rigidly oral while others use combined oral and manual methods. In this country some schools used oral methods and others manual methods until, towards the end of the nineteenth century, most schools were at least paying lip-service to the employment of purely oral methods.

Great impetus to the use of purely oral methods was imparted by the International Conference of Teachers of the Deaf which convened at Milan in 1880 (Report of the Proceedings of the International Conference on the Education of the Deaf 1880). One resolution which was passed and through which the congress became a landmark was the following: 'The congress, considering the incontestable superiority of speech over signing in restoring the deaf mute to society, and in giving him a more perfect knowledge of language, declares that the oral method ought to be preferred to that of signs for the education and instruction of the deaf and dumb.' The French, for example, were totally converted to the oral system and it became, by decree, the standard method of teaching in deaf schools in France after 1886.

Delegates from Great Britain returned equally full of enthusiasm and a new Society came into being in 1886, the Ealing Society, where deaf children were taught by 'The German Method' (as oralism was first described) and teachers trained alongside them. Another Society, the 'Association for the Oral Instruction of the Deaf and Dumb and Training College of Teachers of the Deaf', had pre-dated the Milan Conference by ten years and in 1915 these two Societies amalgamated. Later this body became known as the Oral Foundation but this too was absorbed following the establishment of the National College of Teachers of the Deaf. The NCTD is still extremely influential in deaf education policy matters and its official attitude remains rigidly oral.

Unfortunately this narrow oral approach to the education of deaf children has led in this country and in others also to a great division between the teachers who advocate purely oral methods and psychiatrists, psychologists and social workers who find that in their dealings with deaf people they are forced to use manual methods in order to establish communication with them. The former it seems identify with the understandable but sometimes unrealistic wishes of parents that their deaf children will learn to speak and lipread and therefore integrate fully into society. The latter are brought face to face with the reality of the situation when they meet many deaf youngsters and adults with poor linguistic attainment (and therefore difficulty in lipreading) and unintelligible speech unable to integrate into a hearing society which does not understand their problems and with which they are unable to communicate.

The principal argument of those who advocate a purely oral approach to the education of deaf children is that if children are allowed to use manual communication methods they will do so in preference to speech and lipreading. They agree that facility in manual communication is easier for deaf children to acquire than are oral skills but do not pause to consider the psychological significance of this. They argue that deaf children will employ the easier method, will not make efforts to speak or to lipread and will be unable to integrate into hearing society.

There is, however, no evidence to support the contention that exposure to manual communication methods will have an adverse effect upon speech and lipreading skills. Montgomery (1966), Research Psychologist to Donaldson's School, Edinburgh, gave three standardised tests of speech, lipreading and intelligence, to 55 deaf school leavers who were independently rated for speech, lipreading and manual communication by their teachers. The distribution of ratings showed an overwhelming preference for, and fluency in, manual rather than oral methods of communication. The results showed statistically that manual methods had no adverse effects upon the development of oral skills.

Stuckless and Birch (1966) conducted an enquiry into the relationship between early manual communication and the later achievements of deaf children. Although this work has been the subject of some criticism we cannot ignore their conclusion that early manual communication – 1. appears to have no influence on the intelligibility of deaf students' speech, 2. facilitates the acquisition of language as manifest through comprehension and in reading, 3. facilitates the acquisition of speech-reading skills, 4. facilitates the acquisition of language as manifest through written expression, and 5. has no negative influence on the psycho-social development of deaf children and possibly has the effect of producing a psycho-

social adjustment superior to that of a deaf child without such a communication system.

Meadow (1966) studied two groups of deaf children from different (American) family backgrounds in an effort to determine the effect of early manual communication on the social and intellectual development of deaf people. She found that deaf children of deaf parents scored significantly higher on the self-image test than did the deaf children of hearing parents. The children of deaf parents also showed an average superiority to those with hearing parents of 1.25 years in arithmetic, 2.11 years in reading and 1.28 years in overall academic achievement. Ratings by teachers and counsellors at the school favoured children with deaf parents on items related to maturity, responsibility and independence, sociability and popularity, appropriate sex-role behaviour, and written language. No significant differences were found on lipreading test scores, nor on ratings for lipreading and speech proficiency.

Quigley (1969) compared two groups of deaf children, one of which had been taught by oral methods, the other by combined oral and manual methods. He found at the end of four years that there were differences in favour of the group using combined oral and manual methods in respect of language development, speech reading and general academic achievement, and that the admission of manual communication methods had no adverse effect upon speech.

More recently an interim report of a research project undertaken by the Research Development and Demonstration Centre in the Education of Handicapped Children at the University of Minnesota by Moores *et al.* (1972) to evaluate programmes for hearing impaired children is interesting. The study, begun in 1969, intends to compare the results of seven schools for the deaf each considered to represent different educational philosophies and methodologies. It is scheduled to continue until 1974 when four years of longitudinal data will have been gathered.

Results to date show that children received information most efficiently when it was presented simultaneously through speech and signs (72 per cent), followed by simultaneous speech and fingerspelling (61 per cent). The most inefficient means were covered speech (34 per cent) i.e. when the child was not allowed to observe the face but had to rely on hearing alone. The addition of speech reading improved findings to 56 per cent. It appears that the addition of each dimension, sound plus speech-reading plus finger-spelling plus signs, adds an increment to intelligibility.

It was also apparent that the use of manual communication does not detract from oral skills. Children who scored well in receiving oral/manual messages also scored well in receiving oral messages and there was no evidence that the use of manual communication causes the child not to develop speech reading skills. When children who have been exposed to manual communication are faced with a situation in which manual communication is not used, they still tend to be at an advantage. Moreover the evidence suggests that manual communication employed from an early age does not detract from the child's ability to utilise residual hearing.

Perhaps the most important finding in this piece of research is that children exposed to the spoken word signs and finger spelling tended to score higher than children exposed to the spoken word and finger spelling alone when tested in reception of the spoken word and finger spelling. The use of signs therefore does not detract from a child's ability to receive information through speech and finger spelling. In fact the evidence does not support any decision to withold manual communication at a very early age, nor is manual communication inappropriate for, or harmful to, children with substantial residual hearing. This important piece of research, the final results of which are awaited with interest, gives the lie to the old argument that the poor language of deaf persons is the result of signing. It confirms the opinion of those who advocate combined oral and manual methods that it is the handicap itself which leads to poor language development. This is evident also from the fact that deaf people who have not been exposed to sign language are invariably linguistically retarded.

All workers would agree that the aims of education of deaf children should be to help them to achieve their full potential and to integrate as far as possible into hearing society. The important words here are 'as far as possible' for unfortunately most prelingually profoundly deaf persons are unable to integrate fully into hearing society. The communication difficulties in a hearing community can be so frustrating and stressful that many are fully at ease only in the company of other deaf people.

Speech attainments were studied in a survey of 359 children born in 1947 who were in schools for the deaf in 1962 and 1963. The survey included 276 children with hearing loss of more than 70 decibels over the speech frequencies. Of these children, excluding six who became deaf after the age of five, only 11.6 per cent had clear intelligible speech and good lipreading ability. (*The Health of the School Child* 1962 and 1963).

The majority of profoundly deaf children make an adjustment and become stable and productive members of society; some marry and successfully raise families. However, their communication difficulties prevent their full integration into hearing society and they form a subculture usually based upon the local Institute for the Deaf. Witness to this is the continuing success of the many local, regional, national and international societies for the deaf which cater in the main for the deaf without speech. Some deaf individuals have severe communication difficulties e.g. those with additional handicaps, and often live only a peripheral existence.

Many 'deaf' children do acquire oral skills but a high proportion of these are partially hearing and some are children severely deafened after the normal development of language and speech. A very few are profoundly prelingually deaf children of good intelligence with stable home backgrounds who, given intensive auditory training in their early years, do manage to make optimal use of their residual hearing and this, combined with their mental alertness which enables them to master lipreading, lays the foundation for their oral success. The majority of profoundly deaf children however appear not to be able to make use of their residual hearing to this degree. There are a variety of reasons for this including the presence of other subtle handicapping conditions.

Moreover, even some of those deaf children who are regarded as oral successes, i.e. with fair speech and lipreading ability, find difficulty in integrating into hearing society. Communication may present no real difficulties at school or in the home where special efforts are made to communicate with them. Strangers, however, are embarrassed by the communication difficulties and tend to avoid them. Such deaf individuals find great difficulty in making and keeping friends and so they fall between the world of the hearing on the one hand and the world of the deaf and dumb on the other. It must be remembered also that the speech of many of the post lingually deaf often deteriorates in spite of speech therapy. Not surprisingly many partially hearing and post lingually deaf people overcome their isolation by acquiring manual communication skills and some of them have contributed greatly to the quality of life of the prelingually deaf community.

The fundamental questions are how best to overcome the barriers that face each individual child, and how best to enable him to reach his full potential. Unfortunately the tendency to regard the problems of all hearing impaired children as similar qualitatively and differing only in degree has led to a narrow approach to educational methodology.

Schools for the deaf in the United Kingdom during this century have, as already described, largely employed purely oral methods. Some are rigidly oral, not allowing children to use manual methods even in out-of-school activities while others, though paying lip service to oralism, have allowed individual teachers some latitude in finger spelling and signing. The Lewis Report (1968) indicated that a 'substantial proportion (of schools) made some use of manual media', and in an enquiry into the use of manual communication methods in schools for the deaf in England and Wales in 1970, 34 of 46 schools admitted some use of manual methods (Dept of Education & Science 1970). Significantly only six of these schools employed teachers who were said to have received 'some training' in these methods. Although a high proportion of all teachers will agree in private conversation that there is a place for manual communication methods with some deaf children very few will acknowledge this in public or in writing.

In practice many teachers of deaf children are not able to communicate effectively with their pupils. Many have to rely upon non-oral methods, but because of lack of training in manual communication methods they use them in a slipshod fashion. Most deaf children develop manual communication skills acquiring them surreptitiously from each other, but sadly most teachers are unable to understand what their children are saying in this medium.

There is, it seems a danger of expecting too much of some deaf children, of setting for them goals that are beyond their reach. Obviously a child who is deafened at the age of, say, six years who has already acquired language and speech, presents an entirely different educational problem to the born deaf child who does not know what sound is and whose main problem is the development of language.

It is the contention of many (including the author) that for many deaf children integration into hearing society through lipreading and speech is an impossible goal, and that combined oral, aural and manual methods of education from an early age would better enable them to achieve their full potential — in language development, in emotional maturity and in social skills. When the most important channel of communication (hearing) is partly or wholly blocked, all other channels should be used simultaneously i.e. lipreading, finger spelling and/or signing, gesture and the exploitation of useful residual hearing, if any, through hearing aids. Gesell (1956) wrote: 'It is not normal to be deaf, but the deaf can be remarkably normal as individual personalities if we guide them into the right methods of managing their handicap. Our aim should not be to convert the deaf child into a somewhat fictitious version of a normal hearing child, but into a well-adjusted non-hearing child who is completely managing the limitations of his sensory defect. If we lose sight of this principle are we not sometimes in danger of teaching speech with too much intensity?'

It is important to remember the necessity for a medium of communication in the early formative years. Every child has a need to be understood and to understand. But it is well recognised that profoundly deaf children do not develop verbal language until the formative years are passed. Their lack of verbal language precludes communication through speech and lipreading so that some other medium of communication has to be used.

It would appear, unfortunately, that many parents and even teachers do not appreciate the difficulties of lipreading for the prelingually profoundly deaf child. Deaf children and adults frequently do not understand when spoken to, but do not say so. Some children cannot explain that they do not understand, but often the situation appears to be that they realise the difficulties of communication, take the easy way out, and *pretend to understand*. The author would strongly recommend that parents and teachers should confirm that their children have understood what has been said to them. Such an exercise can be most enlightening.

Another point of controversy which exists in the management of deaf children is the question of residual hearing. The benefits that have accrued from advances in otology and audiology and the use of hearing aids are immeasurable. However, many authorities e.g. Whetnall and Fry (1970), mistakenly believe that *all* deaf children have useful residual hearing and this is just not true. Earlier Whetnall herself had found that five out of a sample of 491 children had 'total' deafness [quoted in] Robin (1964).

It can be stated categorically that some children are indeed totally deaf due to such causes as congenital absence of the labyrinth. Others have residual hearing which even when amplified is of no help for speech discrimination. F. G. W. Denmark (1972) stated that residual hearing lying below the 90-95 decibel level is 'of very doubtful value, if any at all'. He points out that 'in practically all cases of congenital deafness any residual hearing lies at the low-frequency end of the hearing spectrum and as speech intelligibility depends largely on consonant sounds, all of which have important high-frequency components, it means that in such cases any residual hearing which may become viable by the use of a powerful hearing aid is, in effect, 'vowel' hearing. Even so the vowel sounds will be heard imperfectly — for analysis of the pure tone components of vowel sounds shows that they also have some high frequency components. It has been claimed that, as vowel sounds are modified by preceding and following consonant sounds, (speech being a continuous flow of sound rather than a series of separate sounds), 'clues' to unheard consonants can be obtained by the severely deaf from the corresponding modification of the vowel sounds. It would appear to me that this, if it applies at all, would only be to a very limited extent.'

It seems that technological advances have unfortunately led to the neglect of those deaf children who cannot derive any benefit from hearing aids. Such children are very unlikely to achieve oral competence. In the past many schools for the deaf used to prepare these children for life after school by providing trade training such as tailoring, carpentry and boot repairing for the boys and sewing, tailoring and laundry work for the girls. Very few schools now provide vocational training and children in consequence have great difficulty in finding suitable employment when they leave.

If we confine our attention to those children who suffer from early profound deafness, who have no useful residual hearing and who have no additional handicap there is a strong case both for employing combined oral and manual communication methods at an early age and for a re-appraisal of the curriculum of many schools. It seems that in some cases valuable time is spent in futile attempts to give some children speech and lipreading skills which could be better used in imparting basic knowledge and social skills.

The barrier of deafness makes the teaching of deaf children a difficult task and it would seem that every channel of communication should be utilised to the full. Moreover such are the difficulties of the prelingually profoundly deaf child in acquiring general knowledge that the curriculum must also be geared to the individual child's needs. It is unrealistic for example to attempt to teach a child even simple geographical or historical facts if he is unable to manipulate money when he leaves school. For far too long in many schools has the child been required to fit the standard pattern instead of the pattern being chosen to fit the individual child.

The difficulties of educating deaf children are such that teachers must be, and are, very dedicated. Their total involvement and identification with their pupils, however, frequently appears to colour their appreciation of the real situation. The achievements of deaf children are often enormously magnified and there is a danger that this may lead to complacency. Only continual comparison of the achievements of deaf and hearing children will highlight the different levels of attainment and stimulate teachers to explore new and better methods for teaching deaf children. There is indeed a strong case for teachers of the deaf to undertake periods of teaching in normal schools, especially since so many enter immediately into the narrow field of deaf teaching as soon as their training is completed. It would also be helpful if teachers made more efforts to keep in touch with their pupils after they leave school and even into adult life. It is a sad reflection that the majority of teachers of the deaf have never visited a club for the deaf.

Deaf children have for too long been regarded as a homogenous group. Because some deaf children, i.e. many of the post lingually deaf, the partially hearing and the few severely deaf children who can obtain a little benefit from hearing aids may be capable of differing degrees of speech and lipreading, so it is reasoned that *all* deaf children are similarly capable. That this is not so is abundantly evident. Deaf children differ according to many variables and many have additional handicaps.

In the enquiry into the Use of Signing and Finger Spelling in schools for the Deaf in England and Wales undertaken by the Department of Education and Science in 1970, 398 of 938, i.e. 40 per cent of deaf children, had additional handicaps and of these more than half were regarded as of low intelligence, while Myklebust (1964) concluded that at least 10 per cent of all children in schools for the deaf required special programmes designed for those who have an intellectual handicap in addition to their deafness. The assessment and management of deaf children therefore requires a multidisciplinary approach. Unfortunately comprehensive assessment rarely takes place and the management of deaf children is usually left entirely in the hands of teachers.

Deaf children vary greatly as regards their potential and their needs must necessarily differ. An intelligent partially hearing child who can benefit from an aid to hearing may manage perfectly well with a purely oral approach and may achieve high academic standards. On the other hand a prelingually profoundly deaf child with no useful residual hearing aid and with an intellectual handicap is bound to suffer severe linguistic retardation. This type of child must not be denied manual communication and must be given a curriculum geared to his particular needs. Gunzberg (1968) stresses the need for the mentally handicapped to receive social education and these tenets hold also in many cases of deaf children.

The presence of an additional handicap is often not appreciated when the deaf child first enters school so that many such children are to be found in schools for the deaf.

A few schools have special classes for the more obviously additionally handicapped children and there are some schools which cater especially for such children. Examples are the Pathways Unit at Condover Hall School in Shropshire which caters for deaf children with visual handicaps: Bridge House, Harewood, Yorkshire which accepts deaf boys over the age of eight years with intellectual handicaps; Larchmoor School, Stoke Poges, which accepts maladjusted deaf children.

In spite of these provisions some deaf children are not accepted for schooling while others are rejected after a brief trial. As a result many do not receive education geared to their particular needs while others receive no education whatsoever. There is clearly a need for better facilities for deaf children with additional handicaps.

The approach to the problem of deaf children in often unscientific. It is, for example, not uncommon practice to describe some children as profoundly deaf who can hear very well with hearing aids. Investigators not uncommonly, and quite incorrectly, use the results of audiometric testing as their criteria rather than functional hearing ability.

The position of some authorities in relation to manual communication methods is ambiguous. Ewing, an international authority on the education of deaf children, acknowledged in his evidence to the Lewis Committee (Ewing, 1968) that some children require manual communication methods yet in all his writing he makes no mention of this. Indeed it is surprising that most of the textbooks on the education of deaf children since the last war make no mention whatever of manual communication methods, and when Mrs Thatcher the Minister for Education and Science was asked in the House of Commons in August 1972 whether any provision was available for trainee teachers of the deaf to study manual methods her reply was an almost tart 'No'.

Finally there is the important question of counselling and guidance for parents of deaf children. Counselling may be regarded as a process whereby the parent is gradually helped to come to an understanding of the implications of the child's handicap in terms of the effect of that handicap for the child, his parents, his siblings and others.

Guidance, on the other hand, is the giving of practical advice. In practice, counselling and guidance go hand in hand. Parents require this help from the time the diagnosis of deafness is made, throughout school life and even after the child has left school.

Counselling should be undertaken by social workers who have had training in case work techniques and specialised training in the problems of deafness. They should be members of the multidisciplinary team responsible for the management of the deaf child.

In the author's experience few parents of deaf children have the benefit of such counselling. Many receive no guidance at all. However, this may be better than the unrealistic and over-optimistic guidance which is so often given. Ewing and Ewing (1967) in a chapter entitled 'Parent Guidance Principles and Methods' in their book *Teaching Deaf Children to Talk* advocate that the question 'You do want your baby to talk, don't you?' is put to all parents. Similarly, Williams (1970) in a booklet entitled *You Can Help Your Deaf Baby* published by the National College for Teachers of the Deaf for parents of deaf children also asks the identical question and Moseley (1964) in a paper given at a Conference convened by the National Deaf Children's Society on the subject of Guidance to Parents of Deaf Children stated 'It is important to realise that, even though the child is handicapped, it is possible for him to learn to understand, to talk and to develop mentally'.

It is, of course, natural for the parents of any deaf child to hope that he will reach a good standard of education and be able to speak coherently and lipread satisfactorily. Unfortunately, the majority of children who suffer from prelingual profound deafness fall far short of this ideal and guidance which leads parents to believe that their child will so overcome his handicap, may be harmful. One does not need to be blessed with too much imagination to understand the irremediable damage this may do to the parents of those deaf children who never do acquire intelligible speech. Failure to attain the goals set for the child often produces in the parents feelings of guilt, with subsequent over-protection or it generates a belief that the child has failed and this may result in overt rejection. The very fact that parents have to learn to communicate manually with their

children after they leave school is surely an indictment of a system which provides exclusively for one method of education for all deaf children.

During the past decade there has been a great deal of publicity given to the question of methodology in the education of deaf children. It is most significant that 'there were no witnesses (to the Lewis Committee) who wished to claim that exclusively oral methods were appropriate for all deaf children at all stages of education.' In other words, everybody agreed that there were some deaf children who required to use manual communication methods. However, in spite of these findings, most of the authorities in this country remain rigidly oral and there is little evidence of any appropriate action being taken by the training colleges for teachers of the deaf. An illustration of this persistent attitude and the lack of appreciation of the basic problems of deaf children can be seen in the current issue of *Talk*, the journal of the National Deaf Children's Society, by Ivimey (1973), a lecturer in the education of deaf and partially hearing children. He minimises their difficulties: for example, he writes 'The fact that many deaf children do acquire normal language shows that it can be done. Deafness is not a total barrier — it just makes the path of learning a bit rougher'. He apparently believes that all deaf children can acquire language through hearing and can 'talk fluently if given the opportunity'. The attitudes of Ivimey, the Minister of State for Education and Science, and such bodies as The National College of Teachers of the Deaf, at the present day, five years after the publication of the Lewis Report and after some one hundred years of enforced oral education of deaf children in this country, is very hard to understand.

The development of language for many deaf children is so immensely difficult that merely to increase the number of teachers of the deaf with the same outlook as has been constantly suggested is not enough. Fortunately it seems that more liberal attitudes towards the use of manual communication methods are slowly developing. Many more authorities now accept that there is a place for such methods.

Most of these still hold however that purely oral methods must first be tried. Ewing for example in oral evidence to the Lewis Committee stated that he believed that only in exceptional cases would it be appropriate to consider introducing non-oral methods. He said that he would regard combined methods as 'a last resort for children failing to achieve any score in language after all that was possible had been done for them' and Fisch (1972) writes 'children with additional learning difficulties, especially multiple handicapped children, find it extremely difficult to learn language orally and to speak. In such cases it is necessary to change over to a manual method. It is not easy to decide in the early stages which child will be successful with the oral method, but when it is clear that at the age of eight or nine years, little progress has been made with the oral method, one should consider seriously the need for a change to a manual method, i.e. by sign language, which is much easier to learn.'

It is easier to learn. Should we not ponder on this and wonder why we should want to teach a very young child by the most difficult method available? Moreover there is no objective evidence that manual communication inhibits the acquisi-

tion of speech and all the evidence suggests that combined oral and manual methods should be employed from the earliest years — years when a meaningful form of communication is so vitally important for future emotional and intellectual development. Many authors have stressed the important part that combined methods should play in the field of preventive mental health (Sharoff (1959), McClure (1968), Mindel and Vernon (1971), Denmark, J. C. (1972)).

The most profitable step that could be taken at the present time would be for those who advocate a purely oral approach and those who are convinced of the value of combined methods of communication to come together with an open mind in an attempt to arrive at a better understanding of this basic problem. The time is long overdue for the holding of such a conference and until this takes place we are far from doing our best for all deaf children.

REFERENCES

DENMARK, F. G. W., 1972, Personal Communication.

DENMARK, F. L., 1937. 'The Development of Language in the Born Deaf Child' in *All About The Deaf*, The National Institute for the Deaf.

DENMARK, J. C., 1972. 'Surdophrenia', *Sound*, 64, pp 97—8.

Advisory Committee on the Education of the Deaf. 1965. Report to the Secretary of Health, Education and Welfare. Washington, US Department of Health, Education and Welfare.

Department of Education and Science. 1968. *The Possible Place of Finger Spelling and Signing*. London, HMSO.

Department of Education and Science. *Enquiry into the Use of Manual Communication and Methods in Schools for the Deaf in England and Wales in 1970*. London, HMSO.

EWING, SIR A., 1968, *In the Education of Deaf Children. The Possible Place of Finger Spelling and Signing*. Department of Education and Science, London, HMSO.

EWING, SIR A. and LADY E. C., 1967, *Teaching Deaf Children to Talk*, Manchester, Manchester University Press.

FISCH, L. (1972). *The Deaf Child* in Maxwell Ellis (ed.) *Modern Trends in Diseases of the Ear, Nose and Throat*, 2, London, Butterworth.

GESELL, A., 1956, 'The Psychological Development of Normal and Deaf Children in their Pre-School Years', *The Volta Review*, 58, pp. 117—20.

GUNZBERG, H. C., 1968, *Social Competence and Mental Handicap*, London, Baliere, Tindall & Cassel.

HEALTH OF THE SCHOOL CHILD 1962 AND 1963. The Report of the Chief Medical Officer of the Department of Education and Science, Survey of Children born in 1947 who were in Schools for the Deaf in 1962—63. Pp. 60—71. London, HMSO.

IVIMEY, G. (1973). 'Teach Your Child to be Deaf and Dumb', *Talk* 68, pp. 22—23.

McCLURE, W. S., 1968, 'Mental Health for the Deaf in a School Setting', in *Mental Health and the Deaf: Approaches and Prospects*, Altschuler, K. Z. and Rayner, John D. (eds.) Washington, US Department of Health, Education and Welfare.

MEADOW, K. P., 1966, 'Early Manual Communication in Relation to the Child's Intellectual, Social and Communicative Functioning', *American Annals of the Deaf*, 113, pp. 29–41.

MINDEL, E. D. and VERNON, McC. C., 1971, *They Grow in Silence. The Deaf Child and his Family*, National Association for the Deaf, Maryland.

MONTGOMERY, G. W. G. 1966. 'The Relationship of Oral Skills to Manual Communication in Profoundly Deaf Adolescents', *American Annals of the Deaf*, 111, pp. 557–66.

MOORES, D. F., MCINTYRE, C. K. and WEISS, K. L., 1972, *Evaluation of Programs for Hearing Impaired Children*. Research, Development and Demonstration Centre in Education of Handicapped Children, Minneapolis, Minnesota. US Department of Health, Education and Welfare.

MOSELEY, N. H., 1964, 'Experience in Parent Guidance in Proceedings', Proceedings of a Conference on Guidance to Parents of Deaf Children.

MYKLEBUST, H. R., 1964, *The Psychology of Deafness* (2nd ed.), New York, Grune and Stratton.

QUIGLEY, S. P., 1969, *The Influence of Finger Spelling on the Development of Language, Communication and Educational Achievements of Deaf Children*. Institute for Research into Exceptional Children. University of Illinois.

Report of the Proceedings of the International Conference of Teachers of the Deaf held in Milan, 1880. London, Allen.

ROBIN, I. G., 1964, 'The Medical Causes of Deafness' in *Proceedings of a Conference on Guidance to Parents of Deaf Children* convened by the National Deaf Children's Society, London, Pitman.

SHAROFF, R. L., 1959, 'Enforced Restriction of Communication. Its implications for the emotional and intellectual Development of the Deaf Child', *American Journal of Psychiatry*, 116, p. 443.

STUCKLESS, E. R. and BIRCH, J. W., 1966, 'The Influence of early Manual Communication on the Linguistic Development of Deaf Children', *American Annals of the Deaf*, 111, pp. 452–63.

THATCHER, THE RT. HON. MRS M. (1972). *Hansard*. Written answers, 9 August, p. 450.

WHETNALL, E. and FRY, D. B., 1970, *Learning to Hear*, p. 35, London, Heinemann.

WILLIAMS, K. M., 1972, *You CAN Help Your Deaf Baby*. London, National College of Teachers of the Deaf Publications.

29. The effect of vocalising on comprehension in the profoundly deaf *

R. CONRAD
M.R.C. Applied Psychology Unit,
University of Cambridge

A group of hearing and a group of profoundly deaf school children were tested for comprehension after reading prose passages either silently or aloud. The deaf subjects were known, from previously published studies, to comprise a subgroup who primarily relied on articulatory coding to memorize verbal material, and another subgroup who seemed more to rely on a visual code. Neither the hearing controls nor the deaf articulators showed a significant effect of reading mode. The 'visualizers' comprehended significantly less when they read aloud than when they read silently. Though the two deaf groups performed equally well after silent reading, after reading aloud the comprehension difference was significant at better than the 0.001 level.

It is now well established that certain kinds of learning are facilitated when the material to be learned is heard or read aloud by the subject rather than read silently (Murray 1965, Conrad & Hull 1968, Murdock & Walker 1969). However, in the reported cases it is recognized that the effect is limited to the most recently perceived material. [. . .] For the period of time when the acoustic information is still available, this provides an advantage over material which is only read silently.

Strong supporting evidence for this type of model was provided by Conrad (1970), who gave visually immediate serial recall tests of consonant sequences to profoundly deaf subjects. Conrad reported that analysis of errors indicated two clearly identifiable groups of subjects. One group

*From *British Journal of Psychology*, (1971) *62*, 2, pp. 147–50.

evidently used an articulatory code in memory — confusing BCT and HX — but, unlike hearing subjects, showed no recall differences between reading the test sequences silently or aloud. [. . .] A second group of deaf subjects did not confuse BCT or HX, but confused KXYZ. Conrad (1970) suggests that these subjects did not use articulatory coding but probably held the material in a visual code. This latter group recalled significantly worse when reading aloud than when reading silently.[. . .]

The fact that approximately half the subjects tested were hindered in recall performance when obliged to read the test material aloud is relevant to widely used procedures in the education of deaf children. Where (as is common) there is strong emphasis on speech training, a great deal of ordinary school learning is accompanied by overt vocalization. It seems possible therefore that many children, who may or may not improve their speech thereby, might very well be handicapped in their learning. This was clearly so for immediate recall. The present study considers the case where more complex material is involved, namely prose passages read for comprehension.

Method

Subjects Twenty-three profoundly deaf schoolboys who had been used in the study reported by Conrad (1970) were again used. On the basis of their memory errors each subject had previously been classed as either primarily using articulatory coding in short-term memory (A group) or primarily using visual coding (non-A group). There were 12 subjects in the A group (mean age: 13½ years), but only 11 were available to form the non-A group (mean age: 14½ years); this exhausted the school's population for which classificatory coding data had been obtained. The hearing loss of all subjects was such that it is safe to assume no auditory feedback when vocalizing at ordinary reading amplitude levels.

Twelve hearing children (mean age: 9½ years) were taken at random from an ordinary state school.

Materials Six prose passages, each of about 300 words, were selected from a standard school collection of intermediate comprehension passages. Whilst a rough attempt was made to equate for difficulty, the experimental design was such that this was not a requirement. The passages were partly narrative and partly dialogue. For each passage, eight questions were prepared concerned with matter in the appropriate passage. Each question was in the form of four-item multiple-choice, with only one choice correct in every case. There was a separate question sheet for each passage. The form of the questions was such that the correct answer was not explicitly given (e.g. proper names). Above chance correct response could only be achieved through original comprehension of the meaning of the prose. The passages themselves were typed in double-spacing and pasted on to a card so that the final line was on the reverse side. This was an attempt to minimize rereading, but in fact the results indicate that this was not a relevant factor.

Procedure The deaf subjects were tested either individually or in pairs. Even when reading aloud this was quite acceptable because of their absence of hearing. The general procedure was that the subject was given a passage, told to read it either silently or aloud, and as soon as he had finished was given the question sheet to complete. Exactly the same procedure was followed for the hearing subjects, with the proviso that subjects were individually tested.

The complete experimental design was such that 'silent' and 'loud' passages were alternated for

each subject. Each of the six passages was read both silently and aloud equally often in the overall design as well as being completely counterbalanced for order of presentation. This design called for 12 subjects for completion. This was possible for the hearing subjects and the A group deaf subjects. As has been mentioned, only 11 non-A group deaf subjects were available, and the final row of the design was omitted. Though of course statistical purity was thereby lost, it seems unlikely that one more subject could have affected the empirical outcome to any serious extent. Since each subject was tested on every passage, he was tested on only half the passages reading silently, and half reading aloud. A complete test session took about 30 min. per subject, including a short preliminary separate practice passage which ensured that the instructions were fully understood.

The instructions were given in writing to the deaf subjects and verbally to the hearing subjects.

Results

The measure used to compare reading silently with reading aloud was the percentage of wrong answers. Table 1 shows this for the hearing subjects, the deaf A group and the deaf non-A group. Although the hearing subjects were 4–5 years younger than the deaf, they showed much better comprehension overall. This particular comparison is irrelevant to the inquiry and the effect is in line with many published data (Furth 1966). The main inquiry concerns the effect of reading mode.

When the distributions of errors as between the two modes are compared for the three subject groups, there is no difference between those for the hearing subjects and A group deaf, but the non-A deaf group is significantly different ($P < 0.05$) from either. Where the former groups show improved comprehension when reading aloud, the non-A group deaf perform better when reading silently. In fact, the silent-loud difference does not reach the 0.05 level for the hearing and A

Table 29.1

Percentage wrong answers

Reading silently			Reading aloud		
Hearing subjects	A group deaf	Non-A group deaf	Hearing subjects	A group deaf	Non-A group deaf
41.6	58.0	61.0	37.2	51.4	69.7

group deaf, but it is significant in the opposite direction for the non-A group deaf ($P < 0.05$).

The most striking comparison perhaps derives from the quite fortuitous fact that when reading passages silently, the difference in comprehension performance between the A group and the non-A group deaf subjects is not significant ($\chi^2 < 1$), i.e. the two groups are effectively matched. But when the reading mode is aloud, the difference, to the disadvantage of the non-A group, is significant at the 0.001 level ($\chi^2 = 19.26$).

Discussion

Unlike data from short-term memory studies, when prose is read for comprehension — and very much more material presented — there seems little advantage in overt vocalization for hearing subjects with this type of material.[. . .] For those deaf subjects who appear to use articulatory coding when committing verbal material to memory (A group), again overt vocalizing makes little difference to comprehension. This entirely agrees with Conrad's (1970) data, which showed the same effect for immediate recall. One can use the word 'agrees' here because the absence of effect in the short-term memory task was attributed to absence of auditory feedback. It would simply have been puzzling had the A group deaf comprehended

more through reading aloud. The crucial result is the non-A group's performance. For these subjects reading aloud is clearly detrimental to comprehension of what they are reading. The reason for this might well be that suggested by Conrad for the detrimental effects of vocalizing in short-term memory; namely the distracting nature of vocalizing when the input processes for the material being learned are visual or analogues of visual. The fact that in silent reading there is no difference between the A group and non-A group is proof enough that the material can be learned. Vocalizing damages something somewhere along the learning line.

Impaired performance in some profoundly deaf subjects has now been shown on two widely different verbal learning tasks when these subjects are obliged to vocalize. Since at present we do not understand what it is that determines whether a particular deaf subject predominantly uses articulatory coding or 'visual' coding in these tasks, we have no *a priori* estimate of the relative proportions of these populations amongst the deaf. Were there evidence, either inferential or empirical, that the so-called non-A population were large, the results of these studies would cautiously contribute a qualification to universal oral instruction of the deaf that would be hard to ignore.

REFERENCES

CONRAD, R., 1970, 'Short-term memory processes in the deaf', *British Journal of Psychology*, 61, pp. 179–95.
CONRAD, R. & HULL, A. J., 1968, 'Input modality and the serial position curve in short-term memory', *Psychonomic Science*, 10, pp. 135–6.
FURTH, H. G., 1966, *Thinking Without Language*, London, Collier-Macmillan.
MURDOCK, B. B. & WALKER, K. D., 1969, 'Modality effects in free recall', *Journal of Verbal Learning and Verbal Behaviour*, 8, pp 665–76.
MURRAY, D. J., 1965, 'Vocalization-at-presentation and immediate recall, with varying presentation-rates', *Quarterly Journal of Experimental Psychology*, 17, pp 47–56.

30. Short-term memory in the deaf: a test for speech coding*

R. CONRAD
M.R.C. Applied Psychology Unit,
University of Cambridge

A study was carried out to examine the feasibility of identifying by a short test whether or not any particular profoundly deaf school child uses a speech code in short-term memory for verbal material. Consonant sequences were visually presented, drawn alternately from a set of letters which had high acoustic/articulatory similarity (AS), and from another of low similarity on this dimension, but with high shape similarity (VS). Relative recall performance from the two vocabularies is taken to represent the extent to which speech coding is used.

Almost all control hearing subjects recalled more from the VS set; almost all deaf subjects recalled more from the AS set. The test thus provides a quick method of assessing the level of oral memorizing in one situation which has pedagogic relevance. Some validity is provided by the further fact that deaf subjects selected for oral facility yielded scores which were significantly different from those of deaf subjects not so selected — and different in the direction of hearing subjects. Just the same, the most oral deaf, as a group, approached nowhere near the level of speech coding used by the hearing subjects.

Caution is suggested when comparing memory span of deaf and hearing subjects using verbal material, since it can be shown that with some consonant vocabularies, the deaf may show larger spans than the hearing.

Evidence is now accumulating that profoundly deaf school children use quite different coding

*From *British Journal of Psychology*, (1972) 63, 2, pp. 173–80.

strategies from hearing subjects for immediate recall of consonants or words. Whilst hearing subjects seem largely to use a speech code — reported by Conrad (1971) to begin to emerge about the age of 5 years — strong evidence has been found in the deaf both for dactylic and visual (shape), as well as for speech coding. Conrad (1970) discussed some of the educational implications when teachers and pupils remember — and probably think — in different codes.

Conrad & Rush (1965) compared error matrices for large groups of hearing and deaf subjects, showing overall differences. Conrad (1970), examining error matrices of individual deaf subjects in one school, showed that this method could be used to determine the predominant code used by individuals. This procedure, though, is tedious and interpretation somewhat arbitrary, since generally relatively few errors per single subject may be distributed amongst many cells of an error matrix. Locke (1970) set up letter-pairs in a delayed recall paradigm using pairs which were similar either phonetically or visually or dactylically. In this case, coding strategy is determined simply by comparing the number of errors observed with different types of letter-pair. Grouping all subjects, Locke reported consistent effects which though statistically significant were quantitatively quite small.

Two practical developments from these studies now seem desirable. First, a simple more sensitive test which would permit a reasonable assessment of the code used by individual subjects, and from this, some large-scale screening of deaf populations. The latter, as well as providing pedagogic data, would be a necessary step in the search for

247

correlates of coding strategy, such as degree of hearing loss, age, etc.

Method[1]

Studies by Conrad (1965) confirmed a hypothesis that hearing subjects use a speech code in short-term memory for visually presented verbal material, by comparing recall performance of test material with varying degrees of acoustic similarity. Effectively a similar rationale provided the basis for the present procedure.

Two consonant vocabularies were selected, each of six letters. One (B C D P T V) was designated AS, referring to assumed high inter-letter similarity on an acoustic/articulatory dimension. The second (K N V X Y Z) was designated VS, referring to visual similarity. The basis for the AS vocabulary was data for listening errors (Conrad 1964). The VS vocabulary was essentially intuitive depending on the presence of the diagnosis, but supported by data from Fisher *et al.* (1969). Though not ideal, it would nevertheless be useful merely to classify subjects into those using a speech code and those who clearly did not. The former would show more errors with the AS vocabulary. The validity of the VS designation is then not crucial. But if it is acceptable, then a subject giving more errors with the VS vocabulary would be assumed specifically to be using shape of letters as a principal memory code. The use of acoustic coding would effectively be ruled out with profoundly deaf subjects.

Using each vocabulary, letter sequences were constructed of length four to six letters. No letter was repeated in a sequence and each letter occurred equally often in each serial position. For each sequence length a test comprised 18 AS sequences and 18 VS sequences alternately presented. The letters themselves were 1.6 in. high, printed in black on white card. A sequence was presented by slotting the required cards into a concealed frame, which was then displayed to subjects. In this way all letters were simultaneously available for a duration equivalent to 1 sec. per card. At the end of this period the sequence was again concealed, and subjects reported in writing on prepared answer sheets, under a forced guessing instruction.

Hearing subjects ($n = 32$) were drawn from a state primary school and were aged 10–11. Hearing was assumed to be within normal limits. Deaf subjects were drawn from two schools. School 1 is a small private school to which entry at 11 years is governed by educational attainment, profound hearing loss and assessed ability to benefit from oral teaching. The entire school population ($n = 40$) aged 11–16 was tested. School 2 is a state school with pupils aged from 5 to 16 with no entry conditions except profound deafness, absence of mental subnormality or other known handicap. Fifty-six subjects aged 9–16 were tested. All subjects knew the names of the letters used in the test.

Subjects were tested in groups of up to eight with the deaf, and of 16 with hearing controls. Instructions were given by whatever means seemed appropriate and adequate, and enough practice trials were made to ensure that all subjects had fully comprehended, and that the experimenter knew which sequence length was most suitable for the particular group. Since the groups were approximately homogeneous for educational attainment, this presented no serious problem. Sequence length was arbitrarily assessed on the basis that there would probably be enough errors from each subject to make feasible comparison between the two vocabularies, but not so many that the task was clearly impossibly difficult. For each group, this length was of course the same for both vocabularies.

Results

Although for each subject the numbers of letters per sequence was constant throughout the test, some subjects had four- and some six-letter sequences, reflecting age and ability. Since span itself was not an issue, sequence length is irrelevant; the crucial measure is relative recall performance. This is shown in Table 30.1.

Table 30.1 shows the mean percentage of wrong letters for the three schools according to vocabulary and sequence length. Wilcoxon matched-pairs signed-ranks tests were made to assess the difference between AS and VS sequences for all schools and all lengths (except for the subgroup where $n = 5$). For the Deaf six-letter case, $P < 0.05$; for all others $P \leq 0.01$ (two-tailed). But the difference for the hearing subjects is in the opposite direction from that for the deaf. On average the hearing subjects had much more difficulty in recalling AS letters; the deaf subjects much more difficulty in recalling VS letters.

Table 30.1 Percentage wrong letters for various sequence lengths

	Four letters			Five letters			Six letters		
	n	AS	VS	*n*	AS	VS	*n*	AS	VS
Hearing	—	—	—	32	20.3	8.8	—	—	—
Deaf 1	—	—	—	25	9.8	20.0	15	13.3	17.9
Deaf 2	24	16.4	34.4	27	17.2	38.7	5	22.6	40.0

Table 30.2 Number of subjects in each bracket of the Articulatory Index (AI)

	n	0—0.20	0.21—0.40	0.41—0.60	0.61—0.80	0.81—1	Mean AI
Hearing	32	0	1	9	9	13	0.70
Deaf 1	40	9	12	14	4	1	0.37
Deaf 2	56	13	35	7	1	0	0.32

In order, to some extent, to examine individual differences concealed in these mean scores, a simple Articulatory Index (AI) was used to permit comparison of subjects tested with different lengths of sequence. Computed for each subject, the AI was the proportion of all errors which were AS errors. Thus a high AI score would indicate a subject who found the AS vocabulary difficult to recall — a subject whom we infer to be using principally a speech (acoustic and/or articulatory) short-term memory code. A low AI value indicates a subject who, relatively, is not disturbed by acoustically dissimilar items and indeed recalls them better than letters which may be accoustically dissimilar. The kinds of memory codes that might be used in this case will be discussed later.

What the AI gains in simplicity it does of course lose in accuracy, being particularly misleading when there are very few or very many errors with both vocabularies. For the middling range of scores, though, it reasonably reflects what it is meant to. For the purposes outlined in the introduction this is quite adequate. If the AI is to be used clinically with individual subjects, suitable error levels can be obtained by adjusting sequence length. For large screening exercises, some ambiguity can be tolerated; and where it cannot be, retesting of individuals can be resorted to.

Table 30.2 shows for each school the number of subjects whose AIs fall within different levels between 0 and 1. It may be noted that a Mann—Whitney *U* test shows the AIs for the two deaf populations to be significantly different

($z = 6.04$; $P < 0.001$). Nevertheless the most 'verbal' deaf group has a mean AI far below that of the hearing group. The distributions in Table 30.2 show clearly that the vast majority of hearing children were using a speech short-term memory code, and the vast majority of deaf children, regardless of school, were not. Only four hearing subjects had an AI below 0.50 (two of these were marginal). In the Deaf 1 school where all teaching was oral, 32 out of the 40 subjects had an AI below 0.50, and in the Deaf 2 school only a single child was not in this category.

In line with a previous indication (Conrad 1970), there was no evidence that the degree to which profoundly deaf children use articulation in memorizing this kind of material was related to either age or intelligence. For example, at the Deaf 2 school, the 28 oldest children had a hearing loss in the better ear (averaged over the frequencies 250, 500, 1000, 2000, 4000 Hz) of 94.9 db (and a mean AI of 0.32). The 28 youngest children had a mean hearing loss of 94.5 db and exactly the same mean AI. At the same school, subjects were classified into two IQ groups: 'high' and 'low'. The difference between the AIs of the groups was not significant. There are two obvious points to note here. The IQ scores were taken from school records; they represent several different texts and many different testers. A more refined classification than twofold would have been inappropriate. Secondly, few children with IQ above 115 would be likely to be found at this school since selection at age 11 years would have placed most of such deaf children in one of the grammar-type schools for the deaf — such as Deaf 1.

The higher AI of the Deaf 1 school could easily be reflecting an intelligence difference; reliable assessment was not available. But oral ability was also a criterion for entry, and they are probably correlated. Degree of hearing loss was similar to that of the Deaf 2 school. Again, AI was not significantly related, at the 0.05 level, to a twofold age split, though at the 0.1 level it was; the older subjects having higher AI (0.34 *v*. 0.39). Although for the older subjects mean AI was still far below that of hearing children, the small age effect need not be surprising in an 'oral' school. But before accepting that this effect is due to emphasis on oral instruction, one would need at least to be sure that entry criteria had stayed constant over several years.

Few deaf subjects in either school had a mean hearing loss in the frequencies referred to above of less than 80 db. At these profound levels from a preverbal age deafness did not seem to be related to AI. A more detailed study of AI and deafness was made using the classification procedure proposed by Risberg & Mártony (1970) which takes into account hearing loss at each frequency tested. Again AI appears not to be related to hearing at any particular frequency.

Discussion

In so far as this relatively simple short-term memory test can be accepted as indicative of types of code used in memorizing — at least at the level of whether or not it is acoustic/articulatory — the main purpose of the study has been achieved. That this is the crucial distinction has been discussed elsewhere (Conrad 1970). The case is based principally on the fact that regardless of quantitative levels of recall performance the speech code is the one overwhelmingly used in this situation by hearing people. It was used by the hearing controls of this experiment, and it has been shown to have a developmental history starting at about 5 years of age (Flavell 1970, Conrad 1971). In this simple 'thinking' task, the deaf do not 'think' like the hearing.

Nevertheless, the use of speech coding is not all-or-none. It is inconceivable that it should be; inconceivable that subjects totally ignore all the other identification cues present in verbal material visually presented or not (Conrad *et al.* 1965,

Baddeley & Dale 1966, Dale & Gregory 1966). A few hearing subjects and a few deaf subjects have an AI close to 0.50, which — unless this merely reflects performance sampling error — suggests either an ill-defined code preference or some quite idiosyncratic code. In view of the simplicity of the test material, we prefer the former alternative. Then, of course, the test is one of memory, not perception. Regardless of code used, some items will be forgotten; speech coding will not preclude forgetting of items which are phonologically dissimilar. The rationale requires no more than that in this case they would be more resistant to forgetting.

It would be surprising were there not AI differences within each of the three subject groups. That the AIs of the two deaf populations differ significantly is of greater interest. We have effectively ruled out effects of age (within the present limits). Degree of deafness, beyond the dichotomy, profoundly deaf/ normally hearing, is not a variable here; there are practically no partially hearing subjects in the samples. But it is virtually certain that the two deaf populations are significantly different in intelligence because of the explicit selection criteria for entry into the schools. Learning the articulations of speech sounds is a skill which must present formidable problems to those lacking useful auditory feedback. Few hearing subjects are ever required to learn any analogous skill. So it is hard to believe that intelligence is not one critical factor in this. Again this does not necessarily mean that at the level of skill attained, articulation would provide these subjects with the most useful memory code. The results themselves are against this. Just the same we shall point out later that there are independent reasons pointing to an advantage for the use of speech coding when memorizing words, letters or digits. The two deaf populations are also known to differ in 'oral ability'; another selection criterion. We have no real idea whether this ability is independent of intelligence. With the deaf it seems unlikely to be. In any case these population differences, with age and hearing loss equated, would probably be enough to account for the AI difference. What needs to be emphasized is the very large difference in the short-term memory codes used by the 'best' deaf subjects and the hearing subjects.

It may be necessary to point out that the

arbitrary device of the AI is quite irrelevant to the conclusions to be drawn from the results. Table 30.2 could just as well have been expressed in terms of the number of subjects who recalled more AS items and the number who recalled more VS items. The AI used here merely permits a finer classification and highlights the extent of the deaf—hearing difference without the need to present all of the individual subjects' data.

A previous study carried out in an 'oral' school for the deaf (Conrad 1970) suggested that about half of the pupils were using speech coding. The arbitrariness of the classification procedure then used was mentioned earlier. It now appears that this value may be an overestimate. Table 30.2 does show that about half of the Deaf 1 subjects overlap with the hearing controls. But most of this is in the 0.40—0.60 band of the AI which is the most equivocal region. What needs to be stressed is that the pupils at the Deaf 1 school are drawn from that section of the national deaf population most likely to be 'articulate', and that this section is the minority section of the national deaf population, those judged to be likely to profit from grammar-school type of education. The evidence of this study then is that it is probably that the vast majority of deaf children who have mean hearing losses above about 80 db use quite different memory codes from those of the hearing world.

By describing the two vocabularies used in the experiment as AS and VS the clear assumption has been made that in this test deaf subjects who do not use articulatory coding do use a visual code. This is a distinction with some *a priori* validity but which needs special qualification. At the Deaf 2 school finger-spelling and signing, as well as speech, were commonly used during teaching. Manual means of communication were commonly used between pupils. During test administration many children were observed to finger-spell letters both during the presentation of sequences and during report of them. The extent of the use of a finger-spelling code in memory needs serious consideration.

Very little study has been made of the perceptual confusability of finger-spelled letters of the alphabet or of manually signed words. The symbols used in Britain are to a large extent different from those used in the USA. No such study at all has been reported for Britain. Locke

(1970) has reported a restricted study of finger-spelling confusions for the one-handed American alphabet, but for a British school population we do not know which letters seem 'like' other letters. Europe and the USA use the same printed alphabet and there are many studies of shape similarity (Cornog & Rose 1967, Fisher *et al.* 1969, Thomasson 1970). It is relatively easy then to specify a group of letters which have marked shape similarity. But because to some extent the configurations of a number of letters in the British finger-spelling alphabet resemble their printed appearance, interpretation of the memory code is equivocal with the vocabularies used in this study. One obvious example is the letter X, which in finger-spelling crosses the two forefingers. The VS categorization, whilst reasonably correct, quite definitely does not exclude similarities other than visual. Indeed no set of alphabetic characters can be entirely free of ambiguities of this kind. This weakness, though, does not bear on the limited objectives of this study. We have unambiguously shown that deaf and hearing children use different memory codes. Just what those used by the deaf are, is a separate issue. Elsewhere we have argued that it is likely that the profoundly deaf with poor oral facility do not have available for memorizing a single code as highly developed and adapted for the purpose as speech coding is for the hearing (Conrad 1972). If this is so, we must expect more volatile coding systems in the deaf than in the hearing; more varied coding both between and also within subjects.

These results, together with many others, imply that for the hearing, speech coding is well adapted for short-term memorizing of verbal material. There has also been in the past a considerable research effort concerned with relative memory spans of deaf and hearing subjects (Furth 1964). It is perhaps worth elaborating on these two observations. Typically, the deaf have a smaller digit-span than the hearing. Digit names are auditorally more discriminable than are those of the 10 most discriminable consonants (Conrad 1972). But the curvilinearity of many of the digit shapes presents considerable difficulty in visual discrimination (Cornog & Rose 1967). On a digit-span test with visual presentation, a subject naming the digits to himself would be using a more durable code than would a subject forced to rely on the appearance of the digits; and this would be true regardless of any intrinsic biological advantage for speech coding over visual. The conventional digit-span test, then, penalizes the deaf subject, and for the same reason this may also be true when letters are used. Similarly, whilst no spoken language could tolerate much homophony amongst its words, in English there is very considerable shape-similarity amongst common words: few different lengths, and few different letters occupying the crucial first two and last positions (Baddeley *et al.* 1960). There are of course other language-based reasons why the deaf would have poor memory spans for verbal material, but these are largely independent of the coding question.

The hazards of using specialized vocabularies to make practical assessments of memory span can be perfectly exemplified by drawing from our own data. Using the scores from the VS vocabulary, we can match two groups, each of 18 subjects, one drawn from the Deaf 1 school, the other from the hearing subjects, and all tested on five-letter sequences. Both groups have a mean error score of 6.3 per cent. The hearing subgroup, as it happens, are a little better than the whole hearing group, whilst the deaf subgroup are the best of their population. But this is beside the point. On the AS vocabulary, the deaf subjects have an error score of 3.8 per cent; the hearing subjects, 13.7 per cent. The difference is highly significant. Now if for some reason the two groups had been tested only using the AS vocabulary we should have been able to report the unique, and bizarre, 'fact' that the profoundly deaf had a better memory span for letters than the hearing. It is simply that our AS vocabulary is well adapted for non-speech coding.

That some subjects, profoundly deaf from an age before they could have had useful spoken language experience, do learn to use articulation in their mental verbal behaviour must be indisputable. But even when we have included a selected 'oral' group we have comfortable evidence of not many more than 6 per cent. True, the total sample is small (96); true, the behaviour sample (short-term memory for letters) is narrow. But this restricted evidence could be pointing to a massive problem of 'oral' deficiency. We are neither assessing nor discussing speech quality nor verbal comprehension here. In some ways it may be thought that the pedagogic problem is more serious, since it is possible that the vast majority of these deaf children have no capability for thinking verbally. True, as Furth (1966) has shown, thinking does not require words. Furthermore, in effect, it is only the speech representations of words that the deaf may lack. But the nature of the educational procedures most likely to succeed with children who do not use speech forms in thinking — and are unable to — merits consideration. At a more tractable level, one might merely wonder what determines whether a profoundly deaf infant does come to learn to use articulatory correlates of words in thinking, and what are the consequences for, for example, reading in their absence?

NOTE

1. Because of the remote possibility of ill-informed comparisons being made, which are not implied in the results, the author prefers not to name the schools where this study was made. But he is most grateful for the generous collaboration offered by the staffs and pupils of all of them. Mrs. J. I. Phillips and Mrs. B. C. Weiskrantz assisted at all stages.

REFERENCES

BADDELEY, A. D. & DALE, H. C. A., 1966, 'The effect of semantic similarity on retroactive interference in long- and short-term memory', *Journal of Verbal Behaviour and Verbal Learning*, 5, pp. 417—20.
BADDELEY, A. D., CONRAD, R. & THOMSON, W. E., 1960, 'Letter structure of the English language', *Nature*, 186, pp. 414—16.

CONRAD, R., 1964, 'Acoustic confusions in immediate memory', *British Journal of Psychology*, 55, pp. 75—84.

CONRAD, R., 1965, 'The role of the nature of the material in verbal learning', *Acta psychologica*, 24, pp. 244—52.

CONRAD, R., 1970, 'Short-term memory processes in the deaf', *British Journal of Psychology*, 61, pp. 179—95.

CONRAD, R., 1971, 'The chronology of the development of covert speech in children', *Developmental Psychology*, 5, pp. 398—405.

CONRAD, R., 1972, 'Speech and reading', in Kavanagh, J. F., & Mattingley, I. G., (eds.), *Language by Ear and by Eye: the Relationships between Speech and Reading*, MIT Press.

CONRAD, R., FREEMAN, P. R. & HULL, A. J., 1965, 'Acoustic factors versus language factors in short-term memory', *Psychonomic Science* 3, pp. 57—58.

CONRAD, R. & RUSH, M. L., 1965, 'On the nature of short-term memory encoding by the deaf', *Journal of Speech and Hearing Disorders*, 30, pp. 336—43.

CORNOG, D. Y. & ROSE, F. C., 1967, *Legibility of Alphanumeric Characters and Other Symbols*. II. *A Reference Handbook*, Washington, National Bureau of Standards.

DALE, H. C. A. & GREGORY, M., 1966, 'Evidence of semantic coding in short-term memory', *Psychonomic Science*, 5, pp. 75—6.

FISHER, D. F., MONTY, R. A. & GLUCKSBERG, S., 1969, 'Visual confusion matrices: fact or artifact?' *Journal of Psychology*, 71, pp. 111—25.

FLAVELL, J. H., 1970, 'Developmental studies of mediated memory', in Reese, H. W., & Lipsitt, L. P. (eds.), *Advances in Child Development and Behavior*, Vol. 5, New York, Academic Press.

FURTH, H. G., 1964, 'Research with the deaf: implications for language and cognition', *Psychological Bulletin*, 62, pp. 145—64.

FURTH, H. G., 1966, *Thinking Without Language*, New York, Free Press.

LOCKE, J. L., 1970, 'Short-term memory encoding strategies of the deaf', *Psychonomic Science*, 18, pp. 233—34.

RISBERG, A. & MÁRTONY, J., 1970, 'A method for the classification of audiograms'. Paper read at Symposium on Speech Communication Ability and Profound Deafness, Stockholm.

THOMASSON, A. J. W. M., 1970, *On the Representation of Verbal Items in Short-Term Memory*, Nijmegen, Drukkerij Schippers.

31. The hard of hearing in Britain: are their needs being met?*

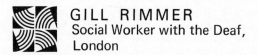

GILL RIMMER
Social Worker with the Deaf,
London

If a person is described as a cripple, certain expectations are aroused and behavioural responses are determined by the degree of handicap encountered. The generic term 'deafness' does not give the same preparation. Even if the presence of deafness is indicated by a hearing aid, the extent of disability is not evident so reaction to it is not obvious, defined or understood. Misunderstandings are very often gross. When answering questions about my work several people have asked me if I travel about teaching deaf people Braille. Some typify another common reaction, humour, and when I say I am a social worker for the deaf, they reply 'Pardon?'. The strange thing is that they all think they are being terribly original.

The misunderstanding is not confined to the general community. It permeates the social work field too. The full spectrum which the term 'deafness' embraces is not appreciated, and there is a tendency to consider the services a 'fait accompli' if the extremes, the hearing and the prelingually profoundly deaf, are catered for. Those in the middle are the ones that suffer and the ones who attract the least attention. It is at this group that I would now like to take a look.

As yet there is no clearly defined, accepted system of classification of deafness as the systems vary according to the purpose of the definition and may be based on type, cause, age of onset or degree of impairment. For the purpose of this paper I have accepted the classification of the Medical Research Council (1947) which divided hearing loss into seven categories based on the

social criteria of method of communication. Categories 3–6 were considered to be included in the blanket term 'Hard of Hearing'. All in this group used speech but the hearing loss ranged from totally deaf, able to hear amplified speech, able to hear loud speech, to difficulty hearing in the group situation.

Within this group are further sub-divisions identified by the combination of age of onset of deafness and its nature of 'impact'. The partially hearing person is one whose loss has been present since childhood although the cause may make the degree progressively severe. Another group is those whose deafness occurs after normal speech and language have developed, the onset being slow and insidious, but causing increasing loss with time. The third group is those 'deafened' persons whose hearing is affected severely and with traumatic suddenness.

To evaluate differences of need, the overall functioning of the person concerned has to be considered, communication, self-image, interpersonal relationships flexibility and adaptability. This may be best achieved by looking at the essential problem of each group and the ways it affects the individual in the four situational areas of education, family, employment and leisure.

By considering the prelingually profoundly deaf person briefly first, it is hoped to show that their needs differ from those of the hard of hearing and while similarities and overlapping exist between the partially deaf, progressively deaf and deafened persons, the problems hold differing degrees and types of significance.

Levine (1960) defines the essential problem of the prelingually profoundly deaf person: 'The

*From a paper held by the Polytechnic of North London, pp. 1–15.

254

great handicap lies in the fact that permanently impaired hearing occurs during the most vulnerable time of life — from birth through early childhood — and is so severe that it deadens the most powerful stimulus of all, the sound of the human voice'.

Upon this voice usually depends the development of language which is an important factor in inter-personal relationships and the socialization process. Thus the need is for the adoption of communication methods suited to the individual child to overcome the induced deprivation.

The educational system is not that flexible. It tends to be oral, segregated from the normal community, often residential with day pupils ferried by special transport, all of which restrict opportunity for experience. Further education, technical and professional training are extremely limited, and impoverished language and communication inhibit effective participation in courses for the hearing.

The crisis of the deaf child occurs within the family rather than within the child itself. The amount of constructive support available to the child depends on the adjustment capacities of the parents, their acceptance and understanding of the handicap, subsequent relationship and communication with the child and the ability to reconcile his needs with those of siblings and other family members. Guidance, although a generally recognized need, is subject to uneven quality and quantity of distribution and the apparently conflicting views and emphasis of the professionals involved.

A close correlation has been found between family environment and the adjustment of the deaf person to the work situation (Friend and Haggard 1948). His employment opportunities are also limited by the poor academic competition the deaf person makes with the hearing, misguided community attitudes with negative stereotyping and unsuitable in-service training schemes. He is often restricted to traditional trades, shows low occupational mobility and has limited opportunities for promotion. He depends on social workers rather than employment exchanges because of the lack of understanding and communication which extends to rehabilitation and assessment units as well as Government training schemes. (Lunde and Bigman 1959, Rodda 1966, M. Vernon, 1970).

The profoundly deaf person is, however, likely to have the company of a deaf spouse and rely heavily on clubs for the deaf for leisure activities. There he has ease of communication with friends, his handicap is neutralized, he can participate fully and he has access to the social worker for the deaf, an accepted source of help should he need it.

Overall, then, these people tend to communicate manually, accept their deafness having known no alternative and identify with other deaf people. Communication, restricted experience and environmental influences tend to retard them educationally and emotionally, creating a leaning towards introverted, egocentric inflexible behaviour, lacking sensitivity to role demands and expectations, characteristics often associated with institutionalization. Although this impairs relationships with the hearing, they are able to gain security from the stable interaction with other deaf people.

Denmark (1966) clarifies the differences between the profoundly deaf and hard of hearing groups: 'Those suffering from a prelingual profound deafness suffer a sensory deficit, those deafened in adult life suffer a sensory deprivation. The problems of the one are developmental, of the other traumatic. They cannot be equated'.

The early development of the progressively deaf person is entirely normal. Education and childhood relationships have followed the normal progression. It is likely that he has achieved a recognized status in employment, marriage and family life, has established both financial and psychological security and lived up to a particular personal and social identity.

Hunt (1944) maintains that when a diagnosis of progressive deafness is made in such circumstances, this can only be superficial. The true diagnosis should read 'fear.' He elaborates 'fear of ridicule, fear of people, fear of new situations, chance encounters, sudden noises, imagines sounds, fear of being slighted, avoided, made conspicuous.' This person has been a fully fledged member of the community. He understands the stigma attached to deafness which threatens the established personality, dignity, security and normality.

His reaction to the threat can be illustrated by Meyerson's experiments (1948) with experimentally deafened people who exhibited the classic symptoms associated with a progressive loss, withdrawal, aggression, suspiciousness, bluffing, inappropriate reactions, misunderstandings, restlessness and uncertainty.

Welles' experiments (1932) showed a synthesis of these reactions with the original personality into three chracterstic groups within the hard of hearing namely, the social inadequates, the depressives and those with paranoid tendencies.

The essential need of these people is, therefore, rehabilitation which Hunt (1944) defines in this context as: 'the process of restoring the individual to himself.'

In 1948 Wilkins (Social Survey, 1948) concluded that the 'provision of hearing aids without a supportive scheme of training in their case would result in a waste of public money.' Denmark trains Hearing Therapists to provide this service. As well as giving information, explanation, preparation, they are equipped to teach speech reading, speech therapy and to understand the emotional components. As soon as the crisis is reached, when the patient realizes his loss is both permanent and progressive, this avenue is open and available. Britain provides no such equivalent.

The technician at the hospital is trained to issue hearing aids and maintenance advice. He often has no time or experience in the other areas nor knows where they may be obtainable. The social worker for the deaf is likely to be shunned by the patient as representing the deaf world he is fighting against, and the patient not accepted by the social worker who denies responsibility for the non-manual client. The generic social worker is neutral in the eyes of the client but probably lacks insight and knowledge of the problem, while speech therapy is seen as a priority for children and lipreading classes subject to the term system of night school provision.

Although a few areas such as Stoke-on-Trent have established a social worker for the hard of hearing, such provision is rare and rapid increase, although necessary, is unlikely. A compromise could be reached with the co-operation of the professionals involved and an increase in the use of group work methods.

The group could provide first a natural channel to help. Further explanation of the particular loss could be given, for example, that the conductive loss, perhaps the loss of otitis media or otosclerosis, tends to respond better to treatment and amplification than a perceptive loss, maybe caused by presbycusis virus drugs, which affect the nerve cells that cannot regenerate. The maintenance of the aid could be elaborated, with time for practice

changing cords and batteries — very important for old people who may be afraid of mechanical things. The fact that different receivers can alter the power of the aid is often not appreciated, nor failure of aids to discriminate sounds, the distortion of which is common, the avoidable interference such as clothes rub. Other devices which contribute to independence such as flashing door bells, baby alarms, vibrating pillows, television and radio attachments, and the loop system could be available for trial. Expression of feeling and problems may be encouraged by the support of and identification with a small number of people in similar circumstances, promoting stimulation for constructive striving rather than self pity, and more incentive to adjust to aids, many of which at present find their way into the nearest drawer.

The group could also prove useful to the family where a block to communication brings severe unrest. A member could be invited to attend meetings with the deaf person and could also benefit from the educative function, encouraging understanding both of the problem and their own feelings. They need to know about the use of lighting, reduction of room reverberation, the greater reliance on expression to compensate for loss of tone, the need to attract the attention before speaking and then to talk clearly without shouting, the advisability of giving the individual a 'lead-in' to the conversation and the importance of keeping him informed of the small talk as well as the headline news within the circle. Acceptance of the problem is vital for the stability of both individual members and the family unit.

Misunderstandings lead to friction, anxiety and tension. One lady I met was infuriated by the fact that her husband, after a half-hour telephone conversation with their married daughter some distance away, would merely inform her that 'all is well'. Another husband lost his temper when his hard of hearing wife 'refused to open the door' when he forgot his key. The onus lies with the deaf person too. It was not surprising that the hearing partner in one family hit his wife during a row after she closed her eyes and thus effectively denied his presence as well as his argument. A physical approach was the only contact he could make, he explained afterwards.

There may be need for role changes and

without awareness, conflict may be the result. If a wife is suddenly expected to negotiate with insurance agents, discuss financial arrangements with building societies, etc., and take a more dominant role than previously, both may resent the new status and responsibilities unless they can discuss it in a rational fashion and accept each other's limitations. It is a family adjustment, including children, which is required for they too have to accept a parent who is not as easy to communicate with as before, and as such differs from friends' parents. This indicates the need for family casework where more intensive help is required.

Employment may be an obstacle in itself if hearing is an essential function of the type of work, especially if this is something which the person has been trained for, is good at and from which he derives psychological and financial satisfaction. The social worker has a role in three areas in this setting, the individual, the family and community. Financial doubts and fears will naturally have repercussions in the family sphere at a time when the deaf person most needs encouragement and support. Both family and individual need acceptance of the situation, information, clarification and motivation to make appropriate responses. Help may mean joint discussion with present employers to see if obstacles may be overcome. The Disablement Resettlement Officer and units for assessment such as Industrial Rehabilitation Unit and Government Training Centres may need more information about the handicap and its implications to achieve relevant advice, training and suitable placement. For example, the confused audio-visual balance may make the client seem slow and uncertain at times. Tinnitis and vertigo may give a negative picture of affect unless appreciated. Both are subject to misinterpretation. In interviews for new employment a social worker may be able to reduce anxieties of fearing to misunderstand and be misunderstood, discuss limitations and encourage the person to assert his abilities more confidently. Talks to groups such as Rotarians or Masons encourage insight with possible future employers, and there is a need for the education of the Department of Employment and Productivity to provide specialist workers to analyse possible openings in industry for the hearing impaired and encourage training facilities. Most important for

the client and his family is hope, knowledge of sources of help and reassurance that he is not a relic for the scrap heap.

Leisure is a particularly difficult area. While a profoundly deaf person and his wife are well established socially, the progressively deaf person may experience the need to be continually adapting or even to completely change his leisure habits. Adjustment may mean a change of interests to the more creative and less dependent on hearing. Some get-togethers with friends may need to be more focussed, perhaps on cards for example, to enable the deaf person to participate more fully. The clubs for the Hard of Hearing may attract some who gain support from others similarly handicapped. A problem could arise whereby the hearing partner clings to established friends while the deaf one seeks the self-help group, neither feeling very at ease in the other instance. Marginality is a very real problem to this group. Sussman (1965) explains 'the hard of hearing can never be sure in advance if they can perform in a particular social situation because the limitations they must accept are relatively undefined and depend on such vagaries as the amount of light in the room or the level of street noise'. He claims the profoundly deaf do not suffer the same ambiguity, uncertainty, confusion and eventual withdrawal which is the pattern of the hard of hearing. He quotes research which indicates that the condition itself is not as upsetting as the marginality of the individual. The relationship between the individual, family, extended family depends on the acceptance, understanding, joint exploration and participation to find ways round the difficulties, and the support and facilities available to help them prepare.

To summarise, the self image is that of a normal person with undermined prestige, status and confidence. Welles found them 'significantly more emotional, more introverted, less dominant than the average of their hearing friends'. Relationships must suffer. As Levine (1960) says 'from the tensions imposed a rift is apt to develop between the hearing impaired individual and his hearing environment. Isolation is not a psychic defence to escape anxiety but rather the environment which is escaping the perceptive grasp of the individual'. Communication is obviously impaired receptively but the inability to monitor speech and maintain speech quality is both traumatic and demoralizing.

Hence the need for therapy and increase in supply of teachers of lip-reading.

Looking at the circumstances of these people, who can deny first that there is a need and second that it is specialized? Perhaps another role for the social worker whom Goffman (1968) would describe as 'wise' is to so convince the hierarchy, the planners of the services.

The need is as obvious for the deafened person. He too shares the normal background of those with a progressive loss. Bergman (1951/2) defines the difference: 'the abruptly deafened adult experiences in one highly concentrated measure all the pangs and agonies of years of progressive deafness. Again, it is a moot question which is the more taxing human experience'.

Cornell (1950) describes the sudden jump into a world of silence mixed with distorted and unfamiliar sounds as 'one of life's most terrifying experiences'. It involves the sudden loss, or gross impairment of all sound psychologically important to the individual on Ramsdell's levels of primitive, warning and symbolic. We are unconsciously appreciative of the primitive level of background noise. We rely on conscious signs and signals for behaviour as a warning to maintain security, and the symbolic level represents the systematized combination of sounds for communication, the level vital for relationships.

Rehabilitation closely correlating that suggested for the progressively deaf person seems to be indicated but with greater emphasis on some factors. The first of these lies within the educational area and involves the acquisition of more knowledge by the professions concerned of the nature and implications of the particular handicap.

Research on the causes and effects of such a swift blow to functioning seems to suffer from the diversity of views and areas of interest of the researchers. Knapp (1948) feels 'medicine has maintained its basically dualistic contrast between "organic" and "functional" and has paid little attention to possible interaction of psychic with somatic factors in the realm of hearing'. Levine disagrees and feels that, as a result of the high incidence of psychogenic auditory disorder amongst the war-deafened — the subjects of Knapps' research — 'relegated to more or less secondary position were investigations of the inter-relationships between personality and straight organic hearing loss'.

It would seem to me that the important fact which is revealed from these two opposing views is that deafness is always relative to the individual and cannot be considered on the grounds of a below average audiogram. Levine (1960) seems to suggest that Knapp's results are less valid because 'quite likely the full impact of sudden hearing loss was somewhat watered-down as a result of the rehabilitation services at their command'. Surely this supports the need for rehabilitation but for appropriate help at the optimum time. To treat a patient with a psychogenic loss by assuming the loss to be perceptive and helping him to accept it, is a denial of his problem and the professionals need to be educated to be aware of this.

Knapp identified four groups within the deafened people he worked with. Unrelated cases referred to those with a straight organic loss with no psychiatric overtones. Depressive reactions dominated in the group which exhibited neurotic reaction to physiological loss. The third group was mixed cases with characteristics of neurosis exacerbated by a psychogenic increase of hearing deficit and the fourth was the purely psychogenic loss. Knapp developed tests to identify the differing roots of the problems but this involves a multidisciplinary approach or, at least, a swift referral system and ease of inter-disciplinary communications so that the crisis at onset can be acted upon while motivation and learning drive are high. If not readily available the personality adopts a pattern of defences which may unhealthily display withdrawal, apathy or disturbance which once established does not readily respond to influence. T, aged twenty-three, illustrates the point, Deafened by meningitis at sixteen, rejected by the family, hospitalized for several years, it is now virtually impossible to ascertain the relationship between his hearing loss and his present psychotic behaviour.

The shock of traumatic deafness is perhaps most sorely felt within the family. Knapp showed that the most affected areas lay in relationships, the most significant feeling tone being loneliness, the most singular fear to be thought stupid, and the height of anxiety, the insecurity of social situations. Crisis intervention with family casework could channel high motivation 'to compensate perceptually and use latent sensory facilities, intellectually to broaden creative interests, emotionally to sublimate anxiety into healthy psychic devices and volitionally to succeed because of the handicap, not in spite of it' to quote Menninger (1924). Most important too is to listen. One boy, deafened due to an accident, said he was sick of being told and just wanted to tell. Most important to him was the fact that he could no longer talk to his girlfriend in the dark. Objectively this would seem relatively a minor problem so it must be stressed that the loss is not objectively viewed by the sufferer.

The dramatic change which such a hearing loss produces extends to the employment situation. The insidious handicap of the progressive deaf person may slowly bring changes in performance which are misinterpreted as incompetence or lack of concentration which produce reactions of irritability, loss of patience and frustration amongst colleagues. The deafened person's problem is more defined and may produce more sympathy, a greater willingness to help. This must be utilized. The same approaches may be necessary as with the progressively deafened but the emphasis here is much more heavily laid on speech.

The abrupt transition from hearing to 'deaf' may exacerbate the ambiguity of marginality which, as shown, greatly affects social relationships and leisure pursuits. Upon communication hinges the greatest question. While manual communication for receptive purposes may seem easier to the outsider, the identification that this brings with the 'deaf' may prove too much of a psychological burden. The change of sensory focus from ears to eyes may prove difficult especially for older people with resulting difficulty learning manualism even if accepted in principle. The answer therefore does not lie in bracketing the severely deafened person automatically with the manually communicating but by working with the family and the individual to help them define problems and acceptable solutions.

While personality and self image are savagely attacked by the sudden onset of deafness, researchers such as Knapp have concluded that the acute nature of onset may in fact improve prognosis. 'My impression was that chronicity causes a less dramatic sense of loss but a more warping one'. Like the former group, relationships, flexibility and adaptability will depend on personality, acceptance, adjustment and the services available.

While the problem of the prelingually pro-foundly deaf person is developmental and of the other groups adjustment and learning to live with a handicap, the partially hearing child's problem lies somewhere between the two. Levine believes that he 'fares worse than any other age, level, or category of auditory disability, worse even than his far more seriously handicapped deaf peer.'

On the surface he appears normal as he may have sufficient hearing to get by. He is probably unaware of any deficiency himself and therefore in no position to understand the reactions to his behaviour which have been described in my experience as lack of concentration or co-operation, stubbornness, defiance, day dreaming, inattentiveness, shyness or sullen nature. The stratagems which are employed to correct the 'character traits' provide an adverse educational and social climate for his emotional, psychological and intellectual development.

Detection of the root of the problem is likely to be easier if external symptoms present like a speech 'impediment' or disturbed behaviour that prompts the search for medical help as in the case of one five year old I met described by his mother as a 'monster'. The extension of audiometric screening by peripatetic teachers or local health authorities is also helping, and improvements can be witnessed in children with a slight loss who sit at the front of the classroom and whose parents and teachers are aware of the problem.

Often early detection is avoided to the disguise of what Levine calls the 'camouflage defence' whereby the child restricts his life experience to situations with which he can cope and to areas within which he appears superficially to function. By adolescence the pattern of personality under-development is set and attempts to rehabilitate by issue of hearing aid or change of school may cause severe psychological upheaval. The essential need is therefore for early detection and compensation for the combination of sensory deficit and deprivation.

The marginality with which he is faced is reflected in the educational provision. Groups of hearing impaired children who are, according to Lewis (1968) educationally rather than medically homogeneous, may be attached by units to either hearing schools or schools for the deaf. The relative association must influence identification and hence self image.

The way in which units function internally and

in relation to the main school also vary as illustrated by the Department of Education and Science Education (1967) Survey on Unit Provision. Seven variations were noted with considerable differences in educational principle exemplified by the extremes of total integration with main school with only tutorial support from the unit, to separate unit function with integration only for practical subjects. Difficulties such as large age, ability and disability ranges in classes, misunderstanding of function of main school, lack of awareness of unit staff of the curriculum and standard of the main school contribute to inadequate progression. Twenty junior units were found to lead to no secondary provision at all. Mary Hare Grammar School may be able to offer places to a limited few and some, if they have the psychological stamina to bear being 'different', may be able to join normal further education provision with the help of technical aids, e.g. radio microphone link such as a Russaid, and co-operative staff. But the result of haphazard provision was seen in 'retardation of all but the most able pupils.' A College-based meeting with some of the 'more able pupils' showed their satisfactory progress was realized by mammoth perserverance and application educationally to the detriment of other areas of functioning. The partially hearing are a betwixt and between group subjected to stress and strain to a greater degree much earlier than the other groups of hard of hearing people.

A lesser degree of loss does not demand the same urgency for parent guidance although relationships can be affected just as radically by a child who 'hears when he wants to'. Peripatetic teachers are likely to be more involved with the child in school. Social workers are seldom associated with the group as, firstly, referrals are few, and, secondly, it is often considered outside their area of operation. The need is shown by Department of Education and Science who found parents who 'in spite of being aware of the severity of the impairment, did not realize the degree of retardation which was impeding progress'.

Another component worth considering is stressed by Lysons (1965). He believes in the need for research into the psychosomatic and somato-psychic reactions to deafness. The former influences the extent to which other physical disabilities eg, ulcers, headaches, are brought on by strain through deafness, and the latter the effect that fatigue, tinnitus, distortion and deprivation of sound have on the mind.

Much could be done through group meetings of parents of children in a particular class or on a wider basis at Parent Teacher Association meetings. These could offer education to parents of hearing children which may then percolate through to the poor group. The factors which need to be stressed are often simple, to talk to the child, show interest in his work and activities, be sensitive to what appears to worry him, encourage him to talk and join in conversations, take him to meet new experiences and encourage confidence, give him a secure, stable base from which to venture out, fill in gaps in knowledge which could otherwise accumulate, and prepare him for life by nurturing his independence.

The first step into 'life' occurs when he leaves school. Without preparation from home and school this can present a vast unknown threat. Preparation in the form of occupational knowledge and experience, vocational guidance and training are part of some schools' curriculum, engendered by the staff, youth employment service and careers guidance. This could be extended to individual and group work using situational role play, psychodrama supported by trips to places of employment, even holiday placements. I found employers helpful in this respect once aware of the need. If the youngster's and the community's fears and fantasies can be alleviated by preparation, there is more hope for placement, a constructive work relationship and satisfactory vocational adjustment.

I found contacts with Youth Clubs with co-operative leaders one means of encouraging integration. More creative, action based activities reduce the strain of uncertainty and communication and present equal opportunity for achievement and success, the confidence builders. With support from home and school a more mature personality may be able to cope better with mimicry, teasing and scape-goating.

The self-image of the partially hearing child is undermined by the disparity between his apparent normality and the effort required to maintain this image. Communication could often be eased if the child had the confidence to subject himself to contact, accept his hearing loss, admit it and tell others how to reduce its problem potential. This confidence must not be shattered especially from avoidable sources such as the reclamation of post-aural aids should repairs be needed when he has left school.

Relationships will be affected by his attitude which in turn depends on his experiences. Like the profoundly deaf child, a certain rigidity and lack of adaptability will be reflected if the climate in which he has grown up has offered no alternative.

Again, need is glaringly apparent if thought about. Much controversy occurs in such circumstances over 'who does, could, should and shouldn't do what' to provide for the need. The first priority would seem to be a get-together of professionals including teachers, social workers, parents and planners to decide roles so that gaps can be filled and an adjustment programme from child dependence to adequately functioning adult is smoother and more natural.

Withrow's (1965) studies show how the partially deaf tend to make a poorer adjustment than both hearing and deaf peers, but as yet very little is being done to help them.

My aim has been to show that hard of hearing people cannot be classed with the born deaf as their needs are completely different. Neither can they be regarded as hearing, without a denial of their problems. Their difficulties are those of the hard of hearing person and as such they are misunderstood, ignored or unrecognised, subject to continual non-acceptance of responsibility by the social services.

A definition of need, roles and responsibility is called for which involves co-ordination and co-operation of medical, technical, psychiatric, psychological educational and social work fields to develop a comprehensive service with channels of appropriate help not only available but invitingly obvious.

Greater use of levels on intervention is required to influence not only the individual but the family, community planners and residential fields too, to make life a more viable and enjoyable prospect for the hard of hearing.

The extent of the problem is great. There are two totally deafened people to every one born deaf without taking into account those with lesser degrees of loss whose need may be equivalent. The Royal National Institute for the Deaf estimate that one in six people will suffer some sort of hearing problem. If we cannot accept responsibility on moral grounds, perhaps we should consider our own future needs.

REFERENCES

BERGMAN, M., 1951/2, 'Special Methods of audiological training for adults'. *Acta Otolaryngologica*, 40, Facs. V/VI

BRUNSCHWIG, L., 1936, *The Study of Some Personality Aspects of Deaf Children*. New York, Columbia University.

CORNELL, C. B., 1950, 'Hard of hearing for seven days', *Hearing News*, 18, p. 14.

DENMARK, J. C., 1966, 'Mental Illness and Early Profound Deafness', *British Journal of Medical Psychology*, 39, p. 117.

DEPARTMENT OF EDUCATION AND SCIENCE, 1967, *Education Survey 1: Units for Partially-Hearing Children*. London, HMSO.

DEPARTMENT OF EDUCATION AND SCIENCE, 1968, *The education of deaf children: the possible place of finger spelling and signing* (The Lewis Report) London, HMSO.

DEPARTMENT OF EDUCATION AND SCIENCE, 1969, *Education Survey 6: Peripatetic Teachers of the Deaf*. London, HMSO

EWING, A. W. G. and EWING, I. R., 1958, *New Opportunities for Deaf Children*. London, University of London Press.

FRIEND, J. and HAGGARD, E., 1948, *Work Adjustment and Family Background*. Applied Psychology Monograph. Washington DC, American Psychological Association.

GELLMAN, W., 1965, Vocational Adjustment and guidance of Deaf People. In *Research on Behavioural Aspects of Deafness*. Washington DC, U.S. Dept. of Health Education & Welfare.

GOFFMAN, E., 1968, *Stigma: notes on the management of a spoiled identity.* London, Penguin.

HUNT, W. M., 1944, 'Progressive deafness and rehabilitation'. *The Laryngoscope, May.*

KNAPP, P. H., 1948, 'Emotional aspects of hearing loss'. *Psychosomatic Medicine*, 10, p. 203.

LEHMANN, R. R., 1954, 'Bilateral sudden deafness', *NY State Journal of Medicine*, 15 May, p. 1481.

LEVINE, E. S., 1960, *The Psychology of Deafness: techniques of appraisal for rehabilitation.* New York, Columbia University Press.

LUNDE, A. S. and BIGMAN, S. K., 1959, *Occupational Conditions among the Deaf.* Washington, Gallandet College.

LYSONS, K., 1965, *Some aspects of the historical development and present organisation of voluntary welfare societies for adult deaf persons in England, 1840—1963.* Unpublished M.A. thesis, University of Liverpool.

McCALL, R., 1967, 'The Deafened', *Hearing*, 22, p. 324.

MENNINGER, K. A., 1924, 'The Mental Effects of Deafness'. *Psychoanalytical Review*, 11, p. 144.

MEYERSON, L., 1948, 'Experimental injury: an approach to the dynamics of physical disability'. *Journal of Social Issues*, 4, p. 68.

RAMSDELL, D. A., 1956, in H. DAVIS (ed), *The Psychology of the Hard of Hearing and Deafened Adult*, London: Staples Press.

RODDA, M., 1966, 'Social adjustment of hearing — impaired adolescents'. *Volta Review*, 68, p. 279.

WILKINS, L. T., 1948, *Survey of the prevalence of deafness in the population of England, Scotland and Wales*, by Social Survey, London, CO1.

SUSSMAN, M. B., 1965, 'Sociological Theory and Deafness: Problems — Prospects' in *Research on Behavioral Aspects of Deafness.* Washington DC, US Dept. of Health Education and Welfare.

VERNON, M., 1970, 'Potential, Achievement and Rehabilitation in the Deaf Population'. *Rehabilitation Literature.* 31, 258.

WELLES, H. H., 1932, *The measurement of certain aspects of personality among hard-of-hearing adults.* New York, Columbia University.

WITHROW, F., 1965, 'Current Studies of Personality Adjustment of Deaf People'. In *Research on Behavioral Aspects of Deafness.* Washington DC, US Dept. of Health Education and Welfare.

32. Organisation of schools for the visually handicapped[*]

 (THE VERNON REPORT)

Introduction

In considering the organisation of schools a number of questions arise. Should visually handicapped children live at home and attend school daily or should they go to boarding schools? Should they be educated with full sighted children, with or without other handicaps? Should blind and partially sighted children be in the same school? Should boys and girls be educated together? Should there be variations of educational provision according to age, ability and additional handicaps?

We realised at the start that our conclusions on certain aspects might have implications for other aspects, for example in relation to the size of schools. We have taken into account throughout our basic premise that children should live at home if possible, or failing that should board as near home as practicable (see pages 263—4), but otherwise we decided to consider each aspect on its merits in isolation and then at the end to look at the cumulative effect of the conclusions reached.

Day attendance or boarding
THE PRESENT POSITION

In addition to the Sunshine Home schools for young blind children, which were considered in the previous chapter, there are 12 boarding special schools for blind children. There are no day special schools but in January 1971, 35 day pupils

*From Department of Education and Science (1972) *The Education of the Visually Handicapped*, report of the Committee of Enquiry appointed by the Secretary of State for Education and Science in October 1968, (Chairman: Professor M. D. Vernon) London, HMSO, chapter 5, pp. 34—57.

attended the boarding schools. For the partially sighted there are 5 boarding and 14 day special schools. There are also 2 boarding schools which cater for both blind and partially sighted children.

In many boarding schools, children are not merely allowed to go home at some week-ends but are encouraged to do so every week-end. This system is generally known as weekly boarding.[. . .]

CONSIDERATION OF THE ISSUES

We believe that all blind and partially sighted children, except some of those with multiple handicaps or poor home conditions, could and should live at home if their home is within an hour's journey of a suitable school and provided their parents can be given guidance on child management. The exceptions cannot be stated more categorically because so much depends on the attitude of individual parents to their handicapped child and to boarding education for him, and on their ability to cope with him at home. Competent professional advice should be available to help parents to see what is in the best long-term interests of their child and, if boarding is indicated, to accept this without feeling it casts a slur either on their competence as parents or on their child's ability. This advice could appropriately be given by the peripatetic teacher for the area, working in association with the regional assessment team[. . .][1] Where boarding education is decided on, it is most desirable that the parents and the child should visit the school well in advance of the time when he is due to go there.

Where day attendance is impracticable, weekly

boarding seems to us the best way to maintain the links between children and their homes. It also makes it easier to recruit staff.[. . .] It is important that schools should provide adequately for the occupation and recreation of children who stay at boarding schools at week-ends.

The type of boarding accommodation required will vary according to children's age. Older boys and girls need to be prepared for leaving the protective atmosphere of a school and going out to a more independent life in the world. The separate sixth form block at Chorleywood provides one method of inculcating independence.

We also consider that all boarding schools should be prepared to accept children for boarding for short periods, where there is a domestic crisis or parents need a respite for other reasons.

Education in ordinary schools

The inclusion of some handicapped children in the ordinary classes of ordinary schools is often described as 'integrated education' (sometimes as 'open education'). This description is usually applied to children living at home, but some children boarding away from home also obtain their education in ordinary classes of ordinary schools. Another possibility, which we consider as well, is to organise special classes of visually handicapped children as part of ordinary schools.

THE PRESENT POSITION

Only a very few blind children are known to have been placed in ordinary classes of ordinary schools while living at home. The number of partially sighted children so placed, who would generally be considered to require to attend a special school, is larger.[. . .]

At St. Vincent's School for the Blind and Partially Sighted, selected blind children have since 1961 been going daily to local grammar schools to take academic courses; they are assisted by an education counsellor and there are satisfactory arrangements for transcription of books into braille. Partially sighted children at St. Vincent's, however, who require academic courses are transferred to Exhall Grange. Since 1969 six selected pupils from Tapton Mount School, Sheffield, which takes blind children aged 5–12, have proceeded for secondary education to a nearby comprehensive school, while living in a hostel on the campus of Tapton Mount. Apart from the

full-time schemes based on these two schools, in a few special schools for the blind and the partially sighted some of the older children are sent part-time to ordinary secondary schools or colleges of further education, e.g. for 'O' and 'A' level courses in certain subjects.

Special classes No special classes for blind children exist, so far as is known. One reason presumably is that, when age-range is taken into account, there are not sufficient blind children in the area of any ordinary school to make up a satisfactory special class. In January, 1971, there were 9 special classes for partially sighted children attached to 8 ordinary schools, containing 86 children in all; 7 of the 9 classes catered for children of primary age.

EVIDENCE RECEIVED

[. . .] In most European countries blind children are segregated for their education from sighted children. But in the USA a survey by Nolan and Ashcroft (1969) indicated that 59 per cent of over 20,000 children registered as blind were in sighted schools. (The different criteria for registration used in the United States result in a greater proportion of children than in this country being registered as blind.) In general, special provision was made for them by means of 'resource rooms' and/or itinerant teachers for teaching braille, etc., though the bulk of the teaching was undertaken by non-specialist teachers in ordinary classes. But the visual acuity of these children was in general greater than that of children in special schools for the blind (Jones 1961). Even totally blind children in sighted schools were found by McGuinness (1970) not to be inferior to those in special schools when their braille reading was tested; and the former were superior to the latter, in social maturity and social integration. However, another study by Havill (1970) showed that the estimated sociometric status of blind children was inferior to that of their sighted classmates, and they were less well accepted; above average achievement improved the status of blind children. Lukoff and Whiteman (1970) found that blind children in special schools showed a lower degree of independence than those in sighted schools. But those for whom family influences were unfavourable to the development of independence benefited most from special education.

Avery (1968) has described the deficiencies in integrated education for the visually handicapped in the USA. He said that the needs of the sighted were considered first in sighted schools. The visually handicapped child might remain in the same grade year after year because he did not progress at the same rate as the sighted. Some teachers were too sympathetic to the visually handicapped, and had too low an expectation of his progress; thus they were satisfied with minimal performance. Other teachers had too high an expectation and were too critical of slowness in the visually handicapped. Library and musical facilities and physical activities for the visually handicapped were inadequate. Courses in mobility were seldom available and there was no specific training in acquiring daily living skills. The sighted and the visually handicapped did not mix easily, and the former did not like helping the latter. However, the older visually handicapped children profited more from integrated education than did the younger, because there was more social accept-ance. A child and his parents might feel a loss of face if he did not do well in a sighted school and it was recommended that he should attend a special school. On the other hand, residential schools tended to be slow to relinquish to integrated education their more intelligent and socially acceptable children. Magleby and Farley (1968) compared 59 visually handicapped adults educated in residential schools for the blind with 39 educated in sighted schools (all were handicapped before 3 years). Almost twice as many of the former were blind as of the latter; but the former had had a more prolonged period of education than the latter. More of the former could read braille and had received vocational training. Their social contacts were wider and their attitudes to life more positive.

Special Classes [. . .] Tobin (1972) found that teachers of sighted children often knew little about the problems involved in teaching the visually handicapped and had no desire to teach them. The account also indicated that the special facilities needed by the partially sighted, including lighting, low visual aids and medical supervision, may not be provided; and staffing may be a problem. [. . .]

Overseas, the most common practice is for partially sighted children to be educated in special classes in ordinary schools. In Holland there are special schools for the partially sighted, both day and boarding.

In 1971 a report by Elizabeth M. Anderson was published under the title 'Making ordinary schools special' on the integration of handicapped children in Scandinavian Schools, based on a visit in September, 1970 to Sweden, Norway and Den-mark. All three countries are committed to a policy of integrated education, and special classes within ordinary schools are one of the forms of provision that are being extensively developed. Although the report concentrates on provision for the physically handicapped, mention was made of special classes for children suffering from other disabilities including those whose sight was im-paired; and what was said about factors making for the success of special classes appeared to be of general application. The following were listed as pre-requisites for good staff relationships.

(i) a head who was interested but not necessarily experienced in the education of the physically handicapped pupils;

(ii) a common staff room;

(iii) a willingness on the part of the special staff to keep the ordinary teachers well in-formed about what they were doing;

(iv) a time-table and staffing ratio which allowed the special teachers to do some teach-ing in the ordinary classes and those of the ordinary staff, who were interested, some spe-cial class work.'

The report continued: 'It was suggested that when the ordinary children know the special teachers, and are also aware that their own teachers work in the special classes, they are more willing to accept the handicapped children on an equal basis. Both the amount of time which physically handicapped children spend with ordinary pupils and the quality of the interaction between them are important . . . one of the most useful pointers as to whether the child would fit in socially in the ordinary school appeared to be the extent to which he joined or was joined by children from the ordinary classes in the dining-room and play-ground.'

CONSIDERATION OF THE ISSUES
The current trend is to emphasise that handi-capped children are, above all, children, with many needs that children without handicaps have too. This approach however has its dangers as well as its merits, since it can lead to a demand that

handicapped children should be given exactly the same educational treatment as other children; and we realise that it is impossible for visually handicapped children to progress satisfactorily in a sighted school unless they are given special facilities. We recall however the importance which the Royal Commission of 1885 attached to blind children having 'free intercourse with the seeing'[. . .] and we are deeply impressed by the argument that, if visually handicapped children are to be fitted through their education to live in the world with sighted people, the best way for them to acquire the necessary ability and confidence is to mix as freely as possible with sighted children during their schooldays. Social events arranged with neighbouring sighted schools may help a little, but contacts tend to be artificial or at least superficial; in order to get to know sighted children and to feel at home with them, a visually handicapped child needs to be in the same school as they are.

Comparatively little experience has been gained in this country of educating visually handicapped children in ordinary schools. Before any firm judgments can be made about the extent to which integrated education is possible for these children, we believe that further systematic experimentation, with education both in ordinary and in special classes, is desirable within the context of the national plan which we recommend[. . .] should be drawn up. Some doubts have been cast on the whole concept of a special class by the failure of some of the existing ones for partially sighted children to achieve full integration with their parent school, but we are ready to believe that it is not the concept which is to blame but rather the human and material factors operating in individual cases. We hope that the Scandinavian experience with special classes will be found relevant to classes in this country. Moreover, it is difficult to see what other form of day provision would constitute a realistic alternative to special classes in an area where there are 20–30 partially sighted children of all ages and no special schools for other handicaps which might be suitable for them.

Further experiments with integrated education should test the validity of fears expressed on various counts, for example about the services likely to be available for technical and medical support. The Tapton Mount scheme demonstrates that, even for 6 children, technical supporting services are at present required which are far in excess of those normally available or necessary in schools for the blind. If a prohibitive amount of voluntary help is not to be called for, the amount of brailling required will have to be reduced[. . .] and arrangements will have to be made for a single set of support services to serve a large number of children. For the partially sighted too, facilities are needed for producing typed lesson notes and clear maps and diagrams and for recording books and materials on tapes. On the medical side, there are serious risks that the specialised care of visually handicapped children may fall short of the high standards desirable. The distance separating the ordinary school from the special regional assessment centre may be considerable. As a result there may be little expert supervision of spectacles or low visual aids; and, with probably only one resource teacher and little medical assistance, continued visual assessment may be poor. Another fear, where blind children live during the week in a school for the blind (or a hostel attached), is that some of them may be unsettled by dividing their time between three environments – an ordinary school, a school for the blind and their home at week-ends.

Particular care should be taken to ensure that the specialised medical and ophthalmological supervision reaches the same standard as that found in special schools for the visually handicapped. Besides adequate support services, vital factors in the success of a scheme of integration appear to be that:

(a) the children should be of stable personality and of at least average intelligence;

(b) regular reviews should be undertaken at each stage of their education to ensure that adequate progress is being made;

(c) their parents should support the scheme;

(d) the ordinary school should not merely welcome the children but the staff should be ready to take time and trouble to integrate them – and specialists in the education of the visually handicapped should be responsible for giving advice and support;

(e) special equipment should be provided on a generous scale, including for the partially sighted suitable lighting and low visual aids; and

(f) special arrangements should be made for mobility training and physical education.

In addition, for special classes three further points need to be emphasised:

(g) there should preferably not be more than two age-groups in a class, though family grouping can work well where the required teaching skills are available;

(h) the staff of the school must be prepared for visually handicapped children to work alongside sighted children for certain subjects and activities; and

(i) the staffing of the school must be sufficiently generous to enable the classes in which visually handicapped children are working to be smaller than their counterparts.

Education with children suffering from different handicaps
THE PRESENT POSITION

Nine special schools primarily for the delicate or physically handicapped take some partially sighted children. The East Anglian School, Gorleston-on-Sea, caters for partially sighted and deaf children in separate departments. Exhall Grange School contains a number of physically handicapped children, of whom 90 per cent are also partially sighted. There are 3 special school campuses which include a special school for partially sighted children — two in Birmingham and one in London.[. . .]

CONSIDERATION OF THE ISSUES

We have discussed at some length a broader scheme of school organisation into which schools for the visually handicapped might fit. Experience at Exhall Grange and some of the special schools primarily for delicate or physically handicapped children has shown the advantages which some of us think lie in mixing groups of children suffering from different handicaps, provided the staff take the trouble to become knowledgeable about these. An alternative way of mixing children, which is more suited to a regional pattern of special school provision, would be to have several schools and units for different handicaps and combinations of handicaps on one or two campus sites near centres of population with good communications, sharing medical services and certain educational facilities and ancillary services. One or two ordinary primary and secondary schools should be near at hand. Others of us have considerable misgivings about assembling large crowds of handicapped children and about putting children suffering from certain handicaps in close proximity, even if they are not in the same school, for example, the blind, the severely physically handicapped and the maladjusted. It would, of course, mean that in most areas the schools would have to be residential, but taking day pupils. So far too, the sharing of facilities on the existing campuses is said to have fallen short of expectations.

It would be a pity if the whole idea of a variety of schools on a campus site was rejected because of the inability or unwillingness of some special schools on existing campuses to work closely together. It may be that schools have not realised the benefits of co-operation in terms of enjoying teaching, medical and physical resources that would be beyond the reach of one school on its own; or the possibility of combining co-operation with a high degree of autonomy. We commend the idea that a committee of teachers should be set up representing all the schools involved, which would have responsibility for the use of the resources of the campus and would help to create a greater understanding of the needs of children with different handicaps. We all agree that one or two experiments on campus lines would be of great interest as and when it becomes possible to concentrate on one site some of the special schools to serve a region.

Education of the blind and partially sighted in the same or separate schools
THE PRESENT POSITION

The 1934 Report of the Committee of Enquiry into problems relating to partially sighted children[. . .] recommended that the partially sighted should not, as a general rule, be sent to schools for the blind. There are now only 2 special schools, both all-age, where blind and partially sighted are educated in the same school — the School for Visually Handicapped Children, Bridgend, Glamorgan and St. Vincent's School for Blind and Partially Sighted, Liverpool. In both cases there were special reasons for retaining provision for both groups, the school at Bridgend being the only provision for visually handicapped children in Wales and the school at Liverpool the only school for Roman Catholic children. Viable schools would have been impossible if an attempt had been made to cater for Welsh and RC blind and partially sighted children separately. [. . .]

CONSIDERATION OF THE ISSUES

We all agree that the blind and the partially sighted each have some special needs. In acquiring their skills of reading and writing, and in compensating for the different degrees of visual handicap, the approach to learning is different for the two groups. The learning of mobility for blind and for partially sighted children is based on a different variety of experiences: for the blind, early training in tactile exploration is essential; for the partially sighted, insistence on the maximum use of vision at the earliest moment is equally vital. At this learning stage, direct association in the same classes may restrict the independence of each group.

If the special needs of the blind and the partially sighted, at the time when they are acquiring different skills for reading, writing and mobility, could be met in a combined school with two departments, we all agree that there would be substantial advantages in educating the two groups together. We are particularly impressed by the scope that would be created for keeping blind children nearer home (with some of them able to attend schools as day pupils) and for dealing flexibly with children who are on the borderline between educational blindness and partial sight or who need to employ visual and tactile methods for different kinds of work. Further, the larger numbers resulting should make it possible to provide better facilities, e.g. specialist teaching and class-rooms, swimming pools, medical rooms and administrative and technical resources. Teachers trained through Birmingham University course to teach both blind and partially sighted children will be particularly valuable in combined schools. [. . .] combined schools. [. . .]

[. . .] Since, however, they consider the handi-caps of blindness and partial sight to be different and distinct as outlined in paragraph 5.43, they [two of our members] would view the reorgani-sation into combined schools as a retrograde step which would militate against the interests of each category in the fields of research, mobility, involvement in the community and above all learning experience. They are convinced that the number of children in the borderline category is small; and they consider that the needs of the blind with good

residual vision and the severely partially sighted can be met by imaginative treatment within each category and closer co-operation between schools within the same region or on the same campus site. They, therefore, have been unable to subscribe fully to the conclusions reached in paragraph 5.45.

Co-education
THE PRESENT POSITION

All schools except the two selective schools for the blind provide for both boys and girls. [. . .]

CONSIDERATION OF THE ISSUES

We are in no doubt that co-education is desirable for all visually handicapped children throughout, including blind boys and girls pursuing academic courses up to the age of 18 or 19. Since they have been in a mixed primary school, certain — though not all — of the special dangers feared by Chorley-wood [the grammar school for girls] should be minimised. Some dangers are inevitable; adole-scence is a turbulent time even for sighted boys and girls.

All-age or separate primary and secondary schools
THE PRESENT POSITION

Twenty-three out of 39 schools for the visually handicapped are all-age. The proportion for schools for the blind is 3 out of 18, for the partially sighted 18 out of 19, with 2 all-age schools providing for both the blind and the partially sighted. Schools for the blind in the North of England were reorganised in the late 1940s in order to separate provision for primary and for secondary education. [. . .]

CONSIDERATION OF THE ISSUES

We believe that visually handicapped children, particularly the blind, will benefit from a change of environment to widen their experience before going out into the world. In some cases it may be sufficient to secure this at the stage when boys and girls leave school and go on to further education and vocational training. Children who need select-ive secondary education will necessarily have to move to another school. For many children besides these some of us think that a change of school at 11 or 12 is desirable. Others of us consider that visually handicapped children benefit from the stability of life and the social continuity of an all-age school.

Since there is some doubt whether all-age schools or separate primary and secondary schools are generally desirable, we suggest that there should be a mixed pattern varying according to local circumstances. All-age schools, however, are in our view certainly preferable where they would enable a substantial proportion of children to attend as day pupils instead of boarding away from home, or as weekly boarders instead of going to a boarding school further away where week-end visits home would be impracticable.

In what circumstances will the existence of an all-age school make it practicable for children to live at home or, if boarding is inevitable, to be weekly boarders, whereas otherwise they could not? The claim that in most areas there are sufficient visually handicapped children to form viable all-age schools, but not primary and secondary schools, needs to be treated with some caution. Taking partially sighted children in day schools first, if there are fewer than about 80 children of all ages in an area, even an all-age school will not be viable (except where, e.g. on a campus site, teachers for certain subjects can be brought in from other schools); and if there are more than about 100 children, separate primary and secondary schools will be possible. Where however there are about 80—100 partially sighted children in an area, numbers will support an all-age school and only such a school. Schools for the blind are boarding schools and most of them serve a whole region. Where there are about 80—100 blind children in a region, an all-age school might be the only alternative to children going to schools outside the region and thus not being able to go home at week-ends. Moreover, even where numbers would be just enough for separate primary and secondary schools, an all-age school of that number would have a significant advantage in the greater teaching resources that it could call on for the benefit of particular groups of children.

Where all-age schools are established, there should be flexibility in the age of transfer from the primary department; some children of 11 or 12 have had such a chequered medical history that they are not ready for secondary education. Two points need to be carefully watched — the quality of the secondary education provided and the opportunites for widening children's experience, since it is easy for the atmosphere of a secondary department of an all-age school to become cosy and undemanding. The secondary department needs to be 2-stream if there is to be satisfactory classification of pupils and an adequate range of specialist teaching. The stimulation which can come from a change of school must be secured in other ways. The secondary department of an all-age school should be carefully planned to provide a different environment as well as continuity of care. To enrich the children's experience, teachers should be brought in from other schools on a part-time basis and arrangements should be made for children to participate in lessons and activities of other educational establishments.

Selective or comprehensive secondary education
THE PRESENT POSITION
Two single-sex schools for the blind are selective and recruit on a national basis. The Royal Normal College has had a mixed school department taking children of 'average to good intelligence,' but the school is going to close at the end of the summer term, 1972. Exhall Grange serves both as a national grammar school for the partially sighted and as a regional school for partially sighted children who need other types of secondary course.
[. . .]

CONSIDERATION OF THE ISSUES
[. . .] We regard it as inevitable that advanced academic courses should be restricted to a very few schools. There is only a small number of children requiring such courses and there is a shortage of specialist staff. It is important that there should be suitable accommodation for all children likely to profit from GCE 'O' and 'A' level work. There has been some difficulty with regard to these courses for partially sighted children considered to be suited to them: some have not been presented for admission to Exhall Grange and others have failed to secure places there. Other schools should be prepared to cater for children who want to take CSE courses.[. . .]

We consider that the 2 single-sex selective schools for the blind are too small (both have about 70—75 children). There are several ways of meeting this criticism on a co-educational basis. One would be to combine the schools into a single-selective school. Another way would be for both to accept a somewhat wider range of ability and vision so as to offer courses for children who develop late and whose interest might be kindled by the presence of brighter children and specialist staff. It would also be possible to turn them into comprehensive schools without interfering with their national intake for academic courses. Just as Exhall Grange serves, for the partially sighted, both as a national grammar school and as a regional school for children requiring other courses, so there could be two other schools with a regional intake for blind children suited to non-academic courses as well as with a national intake for those needing an academic course.

Visually handicapped children with additional handicaps

THE PRESENT POSITION

All special schools for the visually handicapped contain some children with additional handicaps.[...] The new special schools, which were formed in 1971 out of former training centres and schools for the mentally handicapped, contain a number of visually handicapped children. Some indication of the proportion is provided by a survey carried out in the North Midlands in 1970–71 which showed that, out of 2,300 children in the new day special schools (excluding hospital schools), about 80 had a visual handicap. Since 1971 a considerable number of children in other institutions who suffer from both mental and visual handicaps – and possibly others – have been coming to light. In addition, there are units for children with defects of both sight and hearing attached to special or ordinary schools in the London area and Newcastle; and there are 3 special units in hospitals – one admitting 40 mentally handicapped blind children at Reigate in Surrey, one with 30 mentally handicapped blind children, 15 of whom are also deaf (Dr Simon's unit at Lea Hospital, Bromsgrove) and the third with 24 places for maladjusted-blind children of primary age (Dr. Williams' unit at Borocourt Hospital, near Reading). Dr Simon's and Dr Williams' units primarily provide assessment and short-term education.

EVIDENCE RECEIVED

The prevalence of additional handicaps is shown in Dr Fine's survey which covered children born in or after 1951 attending special schools for the blind or special schools or classes for the partially sighted. Additional handicaps were found in over 50 per cent of the blind children and in over 40 per cent of the partially sighted. Physical handicap was the commonest additional handicap, followed by low intelligence. Although the percentage deemed to be maladjusted was 9 per cent of the blind and 7 per cent of the partially sighted, the teachers interviewed considered 36 per cent of the blind and 32 per cent of the partially sighted to be emotionally disturbed, indicating a need for psychological and psychiatric investigation.

It was commonly accepted that, where the additional handicaps were mild and the children concerned would fit in with the regime of the general schools for the visually handicapped, these schools could and should accommodate such children. Equally, however, there were some children to whom this did not apply, because their physical or mental handicaps, deafness or maladjustment were so severe.[...]

CONSIDERATION OF THE ISSUES

In view of the many different combinations of handicaps possible, with different degrees of severity, we believe that a variety of provision is essential for visually handicapped children with additional handicaps. Where the additional handicaps are predominant and prevent a child from fitting into the normal pattern of a school for visually handicapped children, day special schools for the multiply handicapped should be prepared to admit some of these children provided that their visual handicap is recognised and specialised care is maintained. We recognise however that there will be some children whose combination of handicaps would not enable them to fit into either a general school for visually handicapped children or a special school for the multiply handicapped. There will consequently be a continuing need for a few schools specifically for visually handicapped children with additional handicaps. For particular combinations of handicaps, either a single unit like Pathways serving the whole country or a number of strategically situated ones is required. We believe that some of the mentally handicapped blind children need to be accommodated in special local units; and that several more units are required outside the Midlands to accommodate children suffering from mental handicap, deafness and blindness, on the lines of Dr Simon's unit. Since Dr Williams' unit for the maladjusted-blind is usually not full, the only further provision needed for these children is somewhere where they can receive education and treatment for as long as they require it.

[. . .]

Recommendations

We recommend that:

(1) all blind and partially sighted children, except some of those with multiple handicaps or poor home conditions, should live at home if their home is within one hour's journey of a suitable school and provided their parents can be given guidance on child management (paragraph 5.09);

(2) where day attendance is impracticable, weekly boarding should be adopted and local education authorities should help with travel home (paragraph 5.10);

(3) all boarding schools should be prepared to accept children, who normally attend school by day, for boarding for short periods to meet domestic emergencies (paragraph 5.12);

(4) further systematic experiments should be carried out, within the context of the national plan, with the education of visually handicapped children in ordinary schools, either in ordinary or in special classes (paragraph 5.31);

(5) experiments are desirable, in order to meet regional needs, in the grouping of several schools for children with different handicaps on campus sites, sharing a full range of educational and medical resources, with ordinary schools adjoining (paragraphs 5.36–5.37);

(6) [1] blind and partially sighted children would benefit from being educated in the same schools, though they need to be in separate classes at the junior stage (paragraph 5.45);

(7) co-education should be adopted for all visually handicapped children throughout their school careers (paragraph 5.50);

(8) all-age schools are to be preferred where their existence would enable a substantial proportion of children to attend as day pupils instead of boarding away from home, or as weekly boarders instead of going to a boarding school further away where week-end visits home would be impracticable. Otherwise, there should be a mixed pattern of all-age schools and separate primary and secondary schools, varying according to local circumstances (paragraph 5.57);

(9) places should be provided for all visually handicapped children likely to profit from GCE 'O' and 'A' level work; courses would be required in only a very few schools, none of which should be as small as the 2 single-sex selective schools for the blind. Other schools should be prepared to cater for children who want to take CSE courses etc. (paragraphs 5.64–5.65); and

(10) a variety of special schools and units should be available for visually handicapped children with additional handicaps. Where such children are accommodated in special schools for the multiply handicapped, due attention and care must be given to their visual handicap (paragraph 5.71).

NOTE

1 Two members dissent from this recommendation.

REFERENCES

AVERY, C. D., 1968, 'A psychologist looks at the issue of public vs residential school placement for the blind', *New Outlook*

HAVILL, S. J., 1970, 'The sociometric status of visually handicapped students in public school classes.', *A.F.B. Research Bulletin* No. 20, pp. 57–90.

JONES, J. W., 1961, 'Blind children: degree of vision, mode of reading', *Bulletin* No. 26, United States Office of Education

LUKOFF, I. F., and WHITEMAN, M., 1970, 'Socialisation and segregated education'. A.F.B. Research *Bulletin* No. 20, pp. 57—90.

MAGLE, F. LE G. and FARLEY, O. W., 1968, 'Education for blind children', *Research Bulletin* No. 16.

MCGUINNESS, R. M., 1970, 'A descriptive study of blind children educated in the itinerant teacher, resource room and special school settings', *A.F.B. Research Bulletin* No. 20, pp. 1—56.

NOLAN, C. V. and ASHCROFT, S. C., 1969, 'The visually handicapped.' *Review of Educational Research*, 39, (1), pp. 52—70.

TOBIN, M. J., 1970, 1972, 'The attitudes of non-specialist teachers towards visually handicapped pupils', *Teacher of the Blind*, 60 (2).

Committee of Enquiry into Problems relating to Partially Sighted Children, 1934, *Report*.

33. Education provision for the visually handicapped: comments on the Vernon report*

 National Federation of the Blind of the
United Kingdom and the Association
of Blind and Partially Sighted Teachers and Students

A: The need for an education boost

[. . .] The first of our more concrete proposals in this connection is that all visually handicapped pupils should continue in full-time education up to the age of 18. We do not mean that they should all necessarily remain in *school* up to that age, and indeed it would almost certainly be better in many cases that they should complete their full-time education in further education, technical or commercial colleges, and that for some, the education should include an element of vocational or pre-vocational training in the later years; but we believe that right up to 18 the stress should be on 'education' rather than on 'training'. We know that some support will be forthcoming for our proposal on the alleged ground that at present visually handicapped children in this country are on average some two to three years behind unhandicapped sighted children in educational attainments at the age of sixteen.[. . .]

Our second concrete proposal in this connection is that the state shall assume financial responsibility for ensuring that any person suffering from serious visual handicap, or indeed serious handicap of any kind, shall be enabled at any time of life to pursue without financial difficulty for himself or his family any desired course of study at or under the auspices of a recognised institution of further or higher or adult education, provided only that in the opinion of the institution in question that person is suitably qualified to pursue that course of study.

B: The educational deprivation of visually handicapped children

Large numbers of visually handicapped children grow up to become mature, deeply engaged and competent persons, but too often the process of doing so is accompanied by unnecessary strains and difficulties, goes less far than it otherwise would, and leaves the visually handicapped person in a job (if he is lucky enough to have one at all) which is far below the average in pay and status and far below his potential — partly at least because of the extent of educational deprivation amongst the visually handicapped. We believe that the great majority of visually handicapped children today suffer educational deprivation in some or all of the following forms.

(1) Due to lack of parent counselling and educational facilities, many visually handicapped children of pre-school age suffer from lack of stimulation and lack of encouragement to explore their environment and to develop adequately varied and full social relationships. The Vernon Report recognises this form of deprivation and in our view makes constructive proposals to deal with it[. . .]

(2) Virtually every blind child in this country at the present time, if he is to have schooling, has to spend the whole of his childhood and adolescence, from the age of five if he is then blind to the age of 16 at least and often to the age of 18 or 21, away from home during term-time, in special residential schools or training centres. Many

*Jointly submitted to the Secretary of State for Education and Science by the National Federation of the Blind of the United Kingdom and the Association of Blind and Partially Sighted Teachers and Students, October (1973), Part 1, Chapter 2 'The report's deficiencies', pp. 3—13.

partially-sighted children, too, have to live away from home for the greater part of their childhood to attend school. This means that visually handicapped children are deprived to a very substantial extent of the possibility of growing up in their own families and in their own local communities, and of the very important educative effects of doing so.[. . .] The Vernon Report clearly recognises that this *is* an important form of deprivation.[. . .] The Report, however, fails to make the one recommendation whose implementation could result in creating schools suitable for the visually handicapped within an hour's journey of the homes of the great majority of visually handicapped children – namely, the recommendation that selected local schools be made suitable by being developed as 'integrated' schools with the establishment within them of units for the visually handicapped.

(3) Furthermore, because the schools attended by the overwhelming majority of visually handicapped children are not 'integrated' but 'segregating' schools – i.e. schools catering *only* for blind or partially-sighted children – these children are also deprived *within* their schools of a very fundamental element in the education of the handicapped, namely, the opportunity to come to know and understand, and to learn to live and work with, a wide range of their unhandicapped peers. Most handicapped adults in this country today want to live and work 'in the world', and in any case have to do so. To do so successfully they have to have help of various kinds, but they do *not* need or want to be shut off from the world at large in a highly sheltering 'special' environment of their own. But to live as a seriously handicapped person in a world predominantly composed of unhandicapped people is something which has to be learnt. Far from promoting this important kind of learning, the prolonged segregation of visually handicapped children stands in its way, and in fact artificially intensifies the problem. Time and again our members have testified to the enormous difficulty they have found on leaving their special schools in trying to bridge the gulf between themselves and fully-sighted people which they felt their long immersion in these schools .had opened up. Again, as will be seen under 'D' below [. . .], the Vernon Report makes some acknowledgment of this major defect of the present system, yet fails firmly to propose the

remedy which it itself clearly indicates, or indeed any remedy at all.

(4) Finally, there is reason to believe that even on the narrowest interpretation of the term 'education' the majority of visually handicapped children are to a significant extent unnecessarily under-developed educationally. In an appendix (Appendix F) the Report itself provides some evidence of this with regard to the reading skills of blind pupils of secondary school age. This summary of the results of a survey carried out in 1969–70 shows (i) that whereas all 11-year-olds in the sighted control group were able to begin the reading test administered, approximately 36 per cent of the visually handicapped 11-year-olds were unable to do so; (ii) that 40 per cent of all the pupils between the ages of 10 and 16 in all the schools and colleges in England and Wales for the visually handicapped where braille is used as a medium of education were 'unable to cope with the test'; and (iii) that in 'comparative age-groups of sighted and visually handicapped children', 'while differences in mean comprehension scores were slight and not statistically significant, mean reading rates differed very significantly, those of the sighted being slightly more than twice those of the visually handicapped' – i.e. of the visually handicapped who could read at all. The report of the survey itself indicates that whilst the presence of mental handicap in a 'substantial number' of the visually handicapped pupils, and also late entry to, and frequent absences from, school were obviously contributing factors to findings (i) and (ii) above, also contributory were educational factors amongst which we would call attention particularly to 'lack of conviction of the suitability of braille for individual children' and 'lack of policy with regard to braille reading, particularly apparent in the break between primary and secondary school' (Appendix F, para. 3). The seriousness of these findings does not seem to us, however, to be adequately reflected in the body of the Vernon Report, which also expresses no concern at all at the fact that the majority of schools for the blind in this country are no longer even *trying* to teach blind pupils to write braille efficiently by hand, and which more generally simply fails to raise the question of the quality of the 'academic' education and training being provided for visually handicapped pupils at the present time. This is the more surprising since

members of the Vernon Committee must have been aware of the allegation which is sometimes made — and for which, *we* have been told, there is some concrete though unpublished evidence — that generally speaking, visually handicapped school-leavers are at least two years retarded, compared with sighted school-leavers, in terms of measurable educational attainments — i.e. that even on the narrowest interpretation of 'education', the educational equipment of visually handicapped school-leavers, far from being *above* the average as seems desirable, is actually on average well *below* the average. The impression formed in our organisations from the experience of our members is that whilst the allegation of two years' retardedness may be an exaggeration or at least to some extent misleading with regard to the visually handicapped who suffer from no serious additional handicap, the fact is that, excepting the grammar schools which do, however, suffer academically as well as in other ways from their grossly excessive smallness and their vulnerability to staff resignations, the majority of schools for both the blind and partially sighted, judged as institutions of formal education, are poor — unambitious and unstimulating.

[. . .] The lack of realism of which we have accused the Report consists largely in that it does not adequately reflect this fact. Too often its view of its subject-matter seems to be a view at an obscuring, administrative distance. It conveys no impression, for instance, of the extent to which many schools for the blind and for the partially-sighted, though no longer the harsh prisons they once were, not so long ago, are now pervaded by a debilitatingly undemanding and unstimulating atmosphere where the relentlessly easygoing pace, apparently so genial and humane, is (to the children themselves) all too clearly expressive of the devastating judgment — 'Nothing much can be expected from these children'. It may be said that the Vernon Committee was not complacent about the present situation. In 5.73 of the Report they say: 'The existing pattern of schools for the visually handicapped will require to be altered in many respects if our recommendations on school organisation are to be put into practice'; and their recommendation of a national plan does indeed imply the need for major changes. Yet — and this is part of what we have in mind when we speak of its indecisiveness and inconsistency — the language

and substance of much of the Report also suggests that throughout a considerable part of its deliberations the Committee was content to assume that things will and should remain very much as they are.

C: The right to non-selective schooling

An important and particularly surprising illustration of the Vernon Committee's readiness to assume that things should continue much as they are is its failure properly to discuss the question of whether the present highly selective system of secondary education for the visually handicapped should continue unchanged, with its channelling by 11-plus selection procedures of a small percentage of visually handicapped pupils into special grammar schools for the visually handicapped and the rest (for the most part) into special 'secondary-modern' type schools for the visually handicapped which can only be described as 'educational dead ends'. We call these latter schools 'dead end' schools, first because there is no direct access from them to higher education, and secondly because what they do lead straight to, especially in the case of the blind, is confinement within a tiny group of low-paid, low-status, insecure, and above all 'blind alley' jobs, and for just these reasons it seems to us imperative that these schools should be abolished. It has long been recognised that whilst visually handicapped people with higher educational qualifications have a reasonably good chance of entering the employment pyramid at a relatively high level and of finding there relatively satisfying and secure work, those without such qualifications are on average much likelier than the unhandicapped to remain stuck for life at the bottom of the pyramid. If, therefore, it is intolerable that unhandicapped children should be consigned at 11-plus or any other age to secondary or upper schools which do not prepare pupils for entry into higher education — and that it is so seems to be the judgment of virtually the whole nation today — then such streaming is all the more intolerable in the case of the visually handicapped; and if the alternative is the making available of comprehensive secondary education to all, then room must be found for the visually handicapped in that 'all'. This entails not only the abolition of the 'dead end' schools for the visually handicapped, but also the closure or transformation of the existing, highly selective, segregating grammar schools for the visually handicapped; for if segregated education continues to be the normal form of education for the visually handicapped, then comprehensive secondary schools for the visually handicapped could not be made viable if a large fraction of abler visually handicapped pupils were still to be 'creamed off' into special, non-comprehensive grammar schools; and if, as we would wish, segregated education were to come to an end, then these grammar schools, as segregative, would have to be closed or transformed. Nor is this a case of sacrificing the few for the many. We believe the visually handicapped pupils of the selective, segregative grammar schools would not only benefit from de-segregation, but also from the greater variety, in terms both of population and of courses offered, of good comprehensive schools as against the present very constricted special grammar schools.

D: The need for integration

The view of the overwhelming majority of the members of both our organisations is that the key necessity with regard to the education of the visually handicapped at the present time is that steps should forthwith be taken to do away with separate schools for visually handicapped children and to establish in their place, in a number of primary and secondary schools predominantly for unhandicapped children well distributed throughout England and Wales, a network of units for visually handicapped children, blind and partially-sighted, which, properly staffed and equipped, will be able to provide special teaching for the visually handicapped as required, but which will be oriented to encouraging and supporting the fullest possible participation by the visually handicapped pupils in the work of the ordinary classes of unhandicapped pupils. In short, the pre-eminent need just now is for 'integration' instead of 'segregation'.[. . .]

The Vernon Committee [p. 266] states what must count as a decisive consideration in favour of integrated schooling unless, as we have said, exceptionally weighty counter-considerations can be adduced. The Committee deploys no such counter-considerations. On the contrary, whilst stressing that there are a number of steps which should be taken to ensure the general success of integrated education (see particularly [pp. 266−7]), the Committee eschews any suggestion that such schooling must be impracticable or harmful, and cites some if by no means all of the evidence which shows that in a number of varied countries, in some cases over long periods of time, supported integration of unselected populations of blind and of partially-sighted children within schools predominantly for unhandicapped children has worked well.

All this being so, it comes as a deeply disappointing shock that the Committee should conclude anti-climactically that 'Before any firm judgments can be made about the extent to which integrated education is possible for these (i.e. visually handicapped) children, we believe that further systematic experimentation. . . is desirable within the context of the national plan' [p. 266]. The sole reason offered for this conclusion is that 'comparatively little experience has been gained in this country of educating visually handicapped children in ordinary schools' [p. 266]. But in the first place the Committee has not adequately reported or collected all the experience that *has* been gained of integrated education in this country − in particular, the 'Glasgow experiment' and its successes in the 1930's is barely mentioned, and the more recent experience with St. Vincent's pupils in Liverpool is quite inadequately considered. Secondly, the Committee gives no reason at all for treating as largely irrelevant to this country the considerable experience of integrated education gained in the U.S.A., in Scandinavian countries and in a number of 'developing' African and Asian countries. Such experience really puts beyond all serious question the issue of the 'possibility' of integrated education for blind and partially sighted children other than those suffering also from serious additional handicaps.[. . .] Thirdly, the Report does not even *raise* essential questions about these experiments[. . .]. The fact that such questions are not even touched upon in the Report inevitably suggests that at this crucial point in their deliberations the Committee suffered a loss of nerve, and that the recommendation of 'further systematic experimentation' really represents a half-hearted compromise between the desire firmly to recommend a full-scale transition in this country to integrated education of the visually handicapped and the desire not to hurt or antagonise those institutions and individuals closely bound up with the operation of the prevailing system of segregated education.

On the Report's own showing, however, there should be no such compromise, for this compromise can only be at the expense of visually handicapped children who, as the Report itself shows in the passage [printed on p. 266] above, will be deprived by segregation of 'the best way' of acquiring the 'ability and confidence' necessary to their learning to 'live in the world with sighted people', and who will also have forced on them by continued segregation the unnecessary suffering and loss involved in having to leave home for school for long periods from a very early age. For, as we have already pointed out [p. 276], the Committee's timidity about integration has prevented it from proceeding consistently as it claims to have done – i.e. from the 'basic premise' that 'children should live at home, or failing that should board as near home as practicable' [p. 263]. For the establishment of the system of integrated education which we are urging would undeniably permit far more visually handicapped children to live at home throughout their schooling than any system of segregated education, and would permit the remaining minority whose homes were not within practicable travelling distance of an integrated school to live much nearer home, on average, than would be possible if they were attending special schools. The reason for this is of course that units for visually handicapped children in ordinary schools are viable with much smaller numbers of visually handicapped pupils than are needed to make special *schools* viable, and therefore do not have to be so widely scattered and few in number. It is therefore nothing short of astonishing that throughout the chapter on organisation of schools (Chapter 5), the Vernon Report makes virtually no mention of this marked and major advantage of integrated over segregated education, despite the Committee's claim to have 'taken into account throughout' the 'basic premise that children should live at home if possible' etc. Had this really been treated as a 'basic premise', this by itself again would have been sufficient to determine the issue between integration and segregation in favour of integration.

There are other ways, too, in which lack of incisiveness on this central issue has reduced the coherence and effectiveness of the Report as a whole. For instance, the Committee was clearly and rightly worried about schools for the visually handicapped being too small, but its nervousness about integration has driven it to propose remedies – segregated *combined* schools for the blind and partially sighted, and also all-age schools – which are patently unsatisfactory, both because there are grave objections to these kinds of schools to which the Committee has been able to make no effective reply, and also because such schools can only escape being too small by being too far from the homes of many of their pupils. Yet again, the Committee has rightly advocated co-education of the sexes, but by assuming the continuance of segregation of the visually handicapped has been unable to answer objections which do point to difficulties which are always likely to be acute where there is co-education in special schools, particularly where they are residential, but which loom much less large in the context of a school integrating handicapped with unhandicapped pupils.

Let us make our own position quite clear. We do not deny the usefulness of 'systematic experimentation' in connection with integrated education. Indeed, we believe that there is need for such experimentation to determine the extent to which, and the ways in which, the visually handicapped with serious additional handicaps can be involved in integrated education. We also believe that it would be useful to investigate experimentally questions such as the best training and best modes of functioning for the special teachers in the visually handicapped units in (a) the primary schools, and (b) the secondary schools; the best ways of preparing the rest of the staff and the unhandicapped pupils in an integrated school for working with visually handicapped pupils in integrated schools, the provision of necessary resources, etc. etc. But investigations of this kind – or more generally the investigation of how to make a system of integrated education work at its best – presuppose and cannot precede the establishment of such a system. But enough is already known now, we claim, to make it clear that such a system should be established here without further delay.[. . .]

E: The proper valuation of the visually handicapped

Mention must be made of what seems to us to be

one other major weakness of the Vernon Report, namely this: that, as it seems to us, it is pervaded by under-valuation of the assets, achievements and potentialities of visually handicapped, and in particular blind, people. Such an under-valuation, we believe, underlies the undue equanimity of the Committee in the fact of the educational deprivation of the visually handicapped discussed in B above (see esp. [pp. 274–5]), and also, we believe, the Committee's excessive caution about integration, and its unquestioning acceptance of 'selectivity' as right for the visually handicapped at a time when it has very widely come to be thought unacceptable for others.[. . .]

Our view is that certain assets are characteristically (though not of course universally) associated with pronounced lack of sight at least amongst children, young adults and the middle-aged — this being a handicap serious enough to stimulate to special effort and not so overwhelming as to kill all hope. These assets are a special eagerness to learn, and a special eagerness to be active and contributing, rather than passive and receiving. These seem to us valuable assets in pupils, on which educators can build much if they do not first destroy them.

In addition, visually handicapped people who have lived with their handicap for some time with some success are likely to know a lot more than others about how to cope with this handicap, and this must be a major asset in all matters connected with the education of the visually handicapped. *Our* view therefore is that visually handicapped children who are not deadened by discouragement and over-insulation and who, on the other hand, have ready access to necessary resources and special help when required, are likely to display especially *good* educational potential, so that educational retardedness of a marked sort should not be regarded as inevitable or acceptable in the visually handicapped who are unhandicapped mentally, and educators of such pupils — and not just of the exceptionally bright amongst them — should be ambitious for them and seek to stimulate educational ambition in them. Again, it is our view that for the reasons indicated, visually handicapped adults *do* have a distinctive and indispensable contribution to make to the education of the visually handicapped as teachers, as counsellors and as members of boards and committees.

34. Reactions to blindness: an exploratory study of adults with recent loss of sight *

ROY G. FITZGERALD
Research Fellow,
National Institute for Mental Health, U.S.A.

Blindness is a disability that irrevocably changes the course of a formerly sighted person's life. There have however, been few systematic studies of the psychological effects of loss of sight, and none have considered in a comprehensive manner parameters such as the early psychological reaction, changes in socioeconomic status, persisting visual and other intrapsychic phenomenology, and adjustment and rehabilitation factors.

The present investigation was designed to study reactions to loss of sight in a group of newly-blinded adults of working age. For a representative sample, everyone living in a large and contiguous region of metropolitan London meeting the below criteria was selected. On the basis of a survey of the literature on reactions to blindness (see comments), discussions with interested caregivers in the blind welfare field in England, and a pilot study of verbally fluent and intelligent newly-blind persons, an interview was designed to explore the condition of the newly blind.[...]

Subjects and methods

The subjects were drawn from a region of metropolitan London subsuming a total population of 1.98 million people, or about one fifth of the city's population (Census 1964). The region included inner urban, outer, and more suburban residential areas, and all socioeconomic groups. The subjects all had been certified as blind by a consultant ophthalmologist and registered with a central agency. An individual was regarded as blind

if he was 'so blind as to be unable to perform any work for which sight is essential' (Register of blind persons or partially sighted persons 1962). The register was thought to be greater than 90 per cent complete for the working group.

The study included all persons who had been registered as blind within the preceding year, who were 21 through 65 years of age, and who were able to communicate in spoken English. From these the following persons were excluded: two who were congenitally blind, four who had been blind more than five years (10 to 30 years), two who were deaf, two who were mentally retarded, four with severe organic brain damage from various causes who suffered from confusion, disorientation, and probable anosognosia, or aphasia, and two who had died. The median duration of blindness for those eligible was 1.2 years (Table 34.1).

All eligible persons were visited by a member of their local authority welfare department and asked to participate. Four persons refused to be interviewed. They were similar demographically to the rest of the sample, but were felt by their welfare workers to be among the most upset. The data from the blindness registration form (1962) were recorded for those agreeing to be interviewed. I interviewed the subjects in their residences.

The interviews were informal and semi-structured. Demographic data and personal and family histories before the onset of blindness were obtained. The subjects were encouraged by open-ended statements and questions to describe the details of loss of sight. Subsequent experiences, attitudes, feelings, and relationships were probed in detail and clarified with family members when necessary.

*From *Archives of General Psychiatry*, April (1970) 22, Chicago, American Medical Association, reprinted in *New Beacon* (1971) 55, pp. 31–7.

Table 34.1   Range and median duration of visual problems and of blindness*

Duration of:	Range	Median
Visual problems before blindness	3 months-64 years	7.6 years
Blindness when registered	1 month-4.3 years	9.7 months
Blindness at interview	3 months-5 years	1.2 years
Registration as blind	1 month-17 months	4.0 months

*In relation to date of registration as blind and to the present interview for 66 London adults.
†This time interval was longer than the 12-month maximum initially selected because of delays in arranging some interviews.

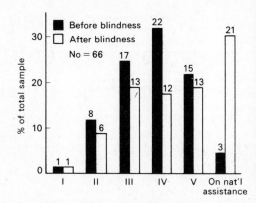

Figure 34.1   Change in socioeconomic status of 66 London adults with blindness.

Results

CHARACTERISTICS OF THE FINAL SAMPLE

Sixty-six subjects (35 men and 31 women) were interviewed. The median age of the subjects was 55 and two-thirds were over 45. The age-sex distribution closely follows that for the total blind population of southern England (*Annual Report 1966–67*), with a preponderance of men over 50 and women under 50. There 9 widows, 4 men who were separated or divorced, 31 married, and 22 single persons. Seventeen (26 per cent) were foreign-born — the largest groups being from Ireland and Jamaica (four each). There were five negroes.

Socioeconomic status based on occupation and standard of living before loss of sight was determined (Census 1964, Classification of occupations 1961, Miller 1962) and compared to status at interview. This group of blind persons were generally of lower socioeconomic status before blindness than the general population from the same area and age group. Figure 34.1 compares the socioeconomic status before onset of blindness with that at the time of interview. There was no rise in socioeconomic status, and the percentages experiencing a fall were from highest to lowest: class I, 0 per cent; II, 25 per cent; III, 35 per cent; IV, 55 per cent; and V, 40 per cent. The great increase among those on National Assistance after blindness were three, nine, and six subjects from classes III, IV, and V respectively.

PRIOR VISION AND TIME COURSE OF LOSS OF SIGHT

In any unselected group of blind persons there is great variation in previous amount of sight as well as in the course of onset of blindness itself. This group was no exception. Prior to onset of blindness, one-half the group had normal vision while 30 per cent wore correcting glasses. The remaining one-fifth had greater visual difficulty uncorrected by aids. A few subjects had had poor eyesight since birth or early childhood in one or both eyes. Furthermore, 11 (17 per cent) had been registered as partially sighted *prior* to onset of blindness.

The course of visual loss varied from very gradual to sudden. There was a gradual loss of sight over one year or more in two-fifths of the subjects. One-quarter lost their sight over a course of two weeks to 12 months. One-fifth rapidly became blind in one to 14 days. The remaining 15 per cent had a sudden loss of vision over 24 hours or less. Interestingly, the intensity of the initial reactions to the loss seemed unaffected by either the rapidity of the loss or the amount of previous sight in all but a few individuals. There was variation in duration of blindness as well (Table 34.1). The mean duration of blindness for subjects when interviewed was 1.5 years and seven (11 per cent) had been blind six months or less. Since nearly one-third of the subjects (no. = 20) gave the onset of their blindness as the same time as the certification-examination-registration procedure, and since one-half of these 20 had a slow loss of sight, this is an important time on which to focus. These events, with their implications of irrevocability of the loss, together with the ritual of recognition of a new identity as 'blind' (registration) were more important in defining onset of blindness than the loss of sight itself for some.

ETIOLOGY OF BLINDNESS AND REMAINING VISION

There was the usual variety of illnesses causing loss of sight for this age group (Sorsby 1966). For example, the most frequent was diabetes (12 subjects). There were no cases of blindness due directly to injury. Sorsby (1966) notes that injury accounts for less than 1 per cent of blindness.

It is a common misconception that those registered as blind have no remaining sight. Although this is largely true for the war-blind (Wittkower and Davenport 1946, Diamond and Ross 1945), it has not been the situation in surveys of civilian populations (Sorsby 1966, Bauman 1964, *Estimated Statistics on blindness* 1966). In the present study, visual acuity as found at interview was compared to that on the ophthalmologist's report and was the same or somewhat deteriorated; it never had improved. Table 34.2 gives an approximate and generous estimate of remaining sight in the subjects. Many of the subjects had severe visual field defects as well. In short, this was a severely visually-handicapped group without exception, all functionally blind.

INITIAL REACTIONS TO LOSS OF SIGHT

A major dysphoric reaction to loss of sight occurred in 61 out of 66 (92 per cent) recently blind adults. The interviews with these subjects illustrated dramatically that loss of sight results in a dynamically unfolding process, not just a fixed state of depression. Many subjects reported aspects of initial absolute disbelief that they were losing their sight, or had, in fact, become blind. While some asserted they had acknowledged the onset of

their blindness, various behaviours demonstrated that a partial denial or protest of their condition was present initially or persisted with pining for the sighted state. They sought second ophthalmologic opinions, resisted using a white cane, attempted to continue work for which sight was essential, etc. As disbelief and protest gave way, these seemed to be replaced gradually, suddenly, intermittently, or concomitantly, with depression and other intrapsychic distresses. This varied in intensity from moderate upset to the frequent and severe incapacitating states in which depression with suicidal ideation, anxiety, weight loss, sleep disturbance, and even paranoid thinking occurred. Recovery from depression or other distress began at various times after onset. A few subjects began coping with their loss, at least partially, within days or weeks, while most took many months to begin to recover.

These four distinct phases of the reaction — disbelief, protest, depression, and recovery — seemed to occur in the order mentioned, but without clear dividing lines between them. In fact, there was usually overlapping of phases.

Time of onset

The time of onset of distress varied. One fifth of the subjects became upset as their sight began to deteriorate while one subject was distressed when registered as partially sighted prior to blindness. Others experienced their loss reaction with onset of blindness (33 per cent) or following ophthalmologic consultations (15 per cent) or following registration as blind (12 per cent). Some did not react until sometime after these events: four were distressed by their loss of sight only after they had lost their jobs and physical health, while three could not identify the stimulus beyond saying such things as 'I finally realised I was really blind' and 'I couldn't keep from facing the facts any longer'. So, with regard to onset of the loss reaction, there were those who anticipated and those who denied the inevitability of blindness.

The percentage of subjects having each of the principal features of the reactions is listed in Figure 34.2. Not all subjects had the same symptoms. For instance, only 56 out of 66 reported feeling depressed following loss of sight. But five of those ten who did not report depression did report increased anxiety, paranoid ideas, suicidal ideation, etc.

Table 34.2 Amount of blindness at interview in 66 London adults, optimal available lighting conditions and glasses permitted*

Acuity scale	Definition	% of subjects
0	Absolute blindness	1.5
1	Light perception or projection	6.1
2	Motion perception up to 5/200; count fingers at 3 feet	54.5
3	5–10/200; count fingers at 3–10 feet	30.3
4	20/200	7.6
Total		100.0

*Acuity scale after Baumann (1964).

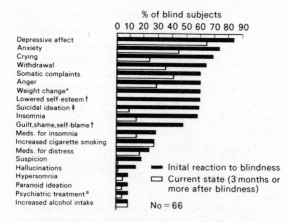

% of blind subjects
0 10 20 30 40 50 60 70 80 90

Depressive affect
Anxiety
Crying
Withdrawal
Somatic complaints
Anger
Weight change*
Lowered self-esteem†
Suicidal ideation‡
Insomnia
Guilt,shame,self-blame†
Meds. for insomnia
Increased cigarette smoking
Meds. for distress
Suspicion
Hallucinations
Hypersomnia
Paranoid ideation
Psychiatric treatment[a]
Increased alcohol intake

■ Inital reaction to blindness
□ Current state (3 months or
more after blindness)

No = 66

*Weight loss was reported by 31 subjects. The median loss by their estimates was 28 pounds (12.7 kilogrammes). Nine subjects gained an estimated median of 17 pounds (7.7 kilogrammes). The subjects' quantitative estimates must be regarded as tentative and unreliable and the duration could not be determined.
†There was recovery of self-esteem and lessening of guilt, shame, and self-blame with remission in other indicators; endpoints, however, could not be identified.
‡This group included two persons who made three serious, life-threatening suicide attempts for which they were hospitalised, one in a psychiatric hospital and the other twice in a general medical hospital.
[a]Three persons underwent psychiatric hospitalisation following loss of sight – this includes the subject mentioned above. They spent 5, 6 and 19 months each continuously in the hospital. Three persons had psychiatric treatment on an outpatient basis for 1, 6 and 60 month intermittently during the time of visual difficulties through loss of sight.

Figure 34.2 Percentage of 66 blind subjects with each of the principal features of the reaction to blindness present in the initial reaction compared with presence at interview.

No reaction
Five subjects had no significant reaction to blindness. These five had 0 to 2 distress indicators present (Figure 34.2). Of these, one, a 59-year-old widow, was still in the hospital four months after sudden loss of sight secondary to an intracranial haemorrhage. She had somatic complaints and marked weight change, two positive items from the list in Figure 34.2. These items, however, were due to secondary diabetes insipidus. It is not entirely clear why this subject had no reaction to

loss of sight. The fact that she had worked in this same hospital for 20 years, had been a patient here before, and was finding this a totally familiar and non-threatening environment may have been crucial. The other four subjects seemed to anticipate blindness while losing their sight slowly over many years, but without the affect-laden 'anticipatory mourning' as described in parents of leukaemic children. (Chodoff, Friedman, Hamburg 1964). These four had all acknowledged early their ultimate blindness, and had arranged their occupations and domestic lives so as to be only minimally affected by this sensory loss. One was a 23-year-old woman blind from a macular degeneration. She had trained as a physiotherapist (a profession traditionally available for the blind in England) while still partially sighted and had made mostly blind friends. Another was a 49-year-old single immigrant slowly blinded from a familial chorioretinal degeneration associated with myopia. He was tolerantly accepted as a tool carrier by his foreman, and had lived with his partially-sighted brother for years.

It is important to note, however, that there were 21 others with slow loss of sight who could have similarly anticipated their blindness, but instead became upset, depressed, and anxious, as did the rest of the subjects in the sample.

Turning point
There was a noticeable improvement in the initial distress reaction of 62 per cent of those reacting to loss of sight (38 subjects). The reaction was akin to mourning in that it seemed to end with healthy resolution of the crisis. Seven of the 38 healthy subjects seemed to be in a transition phase with diminution of the intensity of their distress, but without replacement by positive feelings about themselves. A typical remark was, 'Yes, I still feel sad, and sometimes cry when I'm by myself, but I don't feel so bad as I did the first several months [after blindness].'

The turning point was associated with increased self-esteem from attempting and mastering self-sufficient acts, and with the establishment of important interpersonal relationships with care-givers and other blind persons. In the 31 subjects with a marked change, the depression had largely lifted, and other painful feelings and behaviour such as angry outbursts, crying, and social withdrawal had disappeared. A typical remark about he turning point, from a recently retired 62-year-old man, was, 'No, I just don't feel depressed or wish I were dead any more. In fact, since I've been going to the social club [a local welfare service for the blind], I've felt much better. I even forget that I've lost my sight at times!' Other persons attributed the positive change in their feelings to leaving home to spend several months in a residential rehabilitation centre for the newly blind, or to relationships with social workers who got them involved in handicrafts, or to their spouses insisting that they do things for themselves as making tea, washing dishes, etc. This group was by then experiencing positive feelings about themselves, and, in varying degrees, making future plans, coping, and working as discussed below. The subjects who had experienced relief of their distress seemed to be moving toward a healthy resolution of the crisis in their lives caused by blindness.

Of those distressed, 38 per cent had experienced no significant decrease in their psychic upset (23 subjects). Some of these had developed clearly pathologic syndromes as described below. And, of course, the duration of the distress was longer in these subjects. The most prolonged unrelieved reaction was 96 months in a negro immigrant carpenter.

PRESENT STATE
There was much disability at the time of interview, even in those who declared their distress to be passed. This was the case of course for those most recently blind; it was also so for many who had been losing their sight for many years, and for many of those blind over one year, as illustrated in Figure 34.2. The following were among the rateable items often present, although of generally lessened intensity: feelings of depression, increased anger and irritability, insomnia, and need for medications for sleep and for nervousness. For most of the items for which it was determined, the median duration was around nine months except for three items whose median durations were around one year — anxiety, suspiciousness, and insomnia. Most of those who had increased their consumption of tobacco and alcohol following loss of sight persisted in doing so.

A direct comparison can be made of the number of distress items present at onset of reaction and at the time of interview in Figure 34.3.

At the time of interview, seven persons were largely without distress (only one item present). At the high frequency end, 30 persons had ten or more items positive initially while only four did at interview. No subject reported an increase in the total number of items of distress, although two who disclaimed depressive affect initial reaction felt depressed at interview. There were two subjects with no change in their responses. They both had been moderately depressed, and still felt that way, though less so; they both had some sleep disturbance, anxiety, and hyperirritability.

The blind subjects related the onset and persistance of a number of symptoms to their disability as shown in Table 34.3. All of these symptoms — eye discomfort, eye pain, and headaches — were usually related to attempting to see, to trying to read a newspaper or watch television, or especially to see with the eye with least remaining sight.

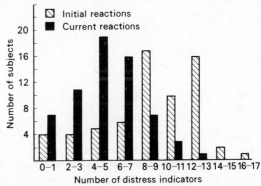

Figure 34.3 Frequency distribution of number of psychic distress indicators of 66 recently-blind adults.

Table 34.3 Distribution of eye symptoms among 66 newly blind adults

Item	% of subjects
Somatic symptoms:	
itching lids, soreness of eyes, eyestrain, tears from eyestrain, feelings of eye irritation	23
Pain in one or both eyes	21
Headaches:	
more often than every two months and newly arisen since blindness	48

Acquisition of new skills and occupational status
Use of the freely provided white cane (Table 34.4) is regarded as a good indicator of adjustment

Table 34.4 Occupied status and acquisition of new skills and aids by 66 recently-blind adults

Occupational status	% prior to blindness	% at interview
Full-time gainful employment	62	14
Part-time gainful employment	17	6
Housewife	18	
Full duties		9
Partial duties		9
Formally retired		17
Unemployed, plus non-functioning housewives	3	45

Skill	%*
Use of white cane	53
All other skills and aids	35
Talking Book	14
Blind crafts: basket-making, pottery, etc	9
Touch typing	
Learning	5
Proficient	14
Braille	
Learning	17
Proficient	5

*Multiple use frequent

(Thume and Murphree 1961). Only one-half the subjects, however, were willing to use it for travel and identification. Nor were many of them skilled in the techique of its use. Those with greater visual acuity (Table 34.2) did *not* have increased range of mobility. A *t*-test was run and there was no significant difference in restrictions on travel between those groups with virtually no remaining sight (acuity ratings 10, 11, 12), and those with acuity ratings of 13 and 14. Many of the latter had an unexpectedly limited range of mobility, and it appeared that the determining factor was the non-acceptance of the finality of the loss. Acknowledgement of the realities of blindness, however, was associated with willingness to acquire other skills and aids for blindness and to be employed. Table 34.4 shows the relatively small percentages who were employed and who had acquired such skills and gadgets; there was multiple use in this group. It was often the same person who was both learning braille and to type, or who had a Talking Book and was engaged in braiding and cane-work. None had or were planning for guide dogs.

Faith healing

Most unexpected was the finding that 23 persons (35 per cent) had been to faith healers (no. = 18) or religious shrines (no. = 5) for the express purpose of regaining their sight. Fifteen of these 23 subjects had been to a series of different faith or spirit healers as successive ones had failed or had been exposed publicly as frauds. These persons generally felt it had been a 'waste of time' or 'delayed my making a good adjustment to my blindness' and delayed pursuing other ways of coping. Eight others were still attending faith healers or had stopped after feeling they had been helped. This group of eight felt it had given them peace of mind, and several even thought their progressive loss of vision had been arrested or slowed down, although this could not be verified.

Psychiatric disability

Blindness was associated with severe psychopathology and social maladaptation in a number of persons in this sample. A four-point scale of distress and disability based on current mental status, subjective reports of recent distress, and history of psychiatric treatment since blindness was devised. The distributions on the scale are given in Figure 34.4. No identifiable recent distress or disability is indicated by 0. Those subjects with awareness of intermittent distress when reminded of loss of sight and the attendant disablement but without major psychiatric symptoms or additional secondary disablement by this distress are indicated by 1. Subjects were given a score of 2 if their subjective and conscious distress was constant, and there were psychiatric symptoms as depression or insomnia, hypersuspiciousness, and intermittent or partial disablement by this distress. A score of 3

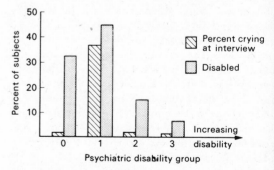

Figure 34.4 Percentage of 66 blind London adults who cried at interview in each psychiatric disability category, as explained in the text.

indicated considerable distress and total psychiatric disability.

Figure 34.4 also shows that the percentage of subjects crying at interview varied among the above groups. It was most frequent among the mildly distressed (scored as 1) and uncommon in the more distressed groups. This is perhaps because the midly distressed were mourning their loss most effectively while groups scored as 2 and 3 were, as yet, unable to acknowledge their handicap and its consequences. The one person who cried with a score of 0 did so on being reminded of her dead father for whom she was still mourning.

The following case illustrates the onset of an acute paranoid psychosis following sudden onset of blindness. This and the next case are scored as 3.

Case 1. This patient was a 47-year-old separated negro man who had immigrated to England some 13 years before. He had been working as an office clerk, (socioeconomic group IV) and, though socially isolated, had been a regular participant in church activities. With minimal warning he became suddenly and totally blind with bilateral retinal artery occlusions associated with hypertensive disease. Three months later he underwent psychiatric hospitalisation for an acute paranoid psychosis. At interview, several weeks after discharge, he was still hypersuspicious, deluded, grandiose, feeling he had been deserted by all female friends, withdrawn and depressed, and confining himself to his bed in a rented room where the welfare workers brought him meals. He was readmitted to the mental hospital for an extended period shortly after interview with the same symptoms.

This next case, also of an immigrant, shows severe disability with psychic and psychosomatic symptoms and multiple ophthalmic consultations as a form of denial of blindness.

Case 2. This patient was a 58-year-old woman who had been a widow for 14 years and who had immigrated to England from the Near East ten years before. She was in the second highest socioeconomic class and lived with her nephew. Always hypochondriacal and myopic, she began to lose her sight three years earlier from senile cataracts. She became blind following retinal detachment post-cataract extraction, and was registered as blind two months later. She refused to accept the poor prognosis for restoration of sight given by four ophthalmic surgeons in three different countries. She was planning a trip to the United States for another consultation. She denied she had been registered as blind. Following the most recent consultation, as with each of the ophthalmic consultations, she had severe peptic ulcer symptoms and a hysterical conversion syndrome. These were treated by general practitioners on an emergency basis. She remained depressed, tearful, anxious, socially isolated, with frequent nightmares about becoming physically crippled. She said, 'If I have to be blind, it's not worth living'.

Comment
VALIDITY OF SAMPLE

The sample interviewed was comparable to the total population of the registered blind in southern England (*Annual Report, 1966–67*) in age, sex, and incidence of blindness per London borough. If the area studied is typical of urban areas, and there is no reason to doubt this, then it seems reasonable to regard this sample as representative of the urban newly blind for the purposes of this study. One might then expect similar groups of newly-blind persons to have reactions comparable to those in this report.

Individuals in this sample of newly-blind were, however, older, had a higher proportion of unmarried to married, (Census 1964) and were over-represented in the lower socioeconomic groups (Partial census 1966), than the general population from which they came. There was also a slightly higher proportion of immigrants (Census 1965). A lengthy examination of factors affecting the demographic and socioeconomic groups is not pertinent to this study. It is probable, however, that the uppermost socioeconomic groups as well as housewives are under-represented among the registered blind. It is possible, too, that the upper classes have a lower incidence of blindness due to more prophylactic medical care and the ability to pay for whatever might be necessary. Similarly, for housewives there is not the pressing economic need for the welfare and rehabilitation services available through registration.

One also must ask whether blindness or the illnesses that cause blindness are more common in the poor. Except for a group of four juvenile-onset diabetics, the lower socioeconomic status before blindness in a larger proportion of the subjects was not due to downward movement in occupation before onset of blindness as determined by work history.

The fall in socioeconomic status with blindness (Figure 34.1) did not occur so frequently in the two uppermost groups as in the lower ones. The upper groups' advantages and material resources protect them against the misfortune of blindness while those in the lower groups have few such cushions and can fall to the levels of subsistence and total dependence on welfare.

With regard to marital status, it is well known that the single have higher mortality rates from most causes of death than the married. Reasons have been advanced elsewhere for this (Shurtleff 1956, Kraus and Lilienfeld 1959). It may also be that, for the same reasons, the single, widowed, and divorced or separated have a higher incidence of the disease leading to blindness, and they may become blind more often as a complication of these same diseases. Two cases suggestive of this were men who had retinal detachments within weeks of their wives' deaths. [. . .]

DENIAL PHENOMENA

Examples of apparent partial denial of blindness and prolonged false hopes for recovery were numerous: subjects who did not accept the consultant's prognosis and sought multiple opinions; those who persisted in attempting to read, to watch television, or to work at jobs requiring sight. These denial phenomena persisted indefinitely; some said they did not realise that they had been registered as blind in spite of much evidence to the contrary. Many asked how the interviewer thought they could go about regaining their sight at the end of a discussion of permanent loss! As many authors have written (Blank 1957, Carroll, 1961) such continued denial seems to be maladaptive.

Turning to faith healers seemed an obvious illustration of how false hopes for sight and continued denial of blindness were prolonged in the 23 subjects who sought miraculous restoration of sight. It is salutary that eight out of these 23 attributed the resolution of their distress to the faith healers. The most obvious explanation seems to be in the nature of the relationship effected with those newly blind by the faith healers. They were sensitive and skilled students of human misery and magical thinking, and trained to provide and foster dependency relationships, giving much advice of a practical nature during the crises.

While the results of this study and the discussion of the findings have emphasised the maladaptive aspects of behaviour that deny the finality of blindness, another aspect must be kept in mind. Denial or partial denial of a loss can be adaptive during the initial periods of crisis with increased stress; this allows the subject gradually to come to terms with major changes, and to learn new ways of coping without being overwhelmed.

The loss model for the reaction to blindness seems to find support both in the present study and in the literature on reactions to blindness. There is support as well in studies of bereavement, maternal deprivation, deafness, and amputation cited above. The worth of any such psychosocial model is its usefulness in further research and in helping the subjects themselves, their families, and other involved caregivers to cope with loss. One would hope that by pointing out the character and possible extent of the reaction to loss of sight, the professional caregivers could better educate the subject, family, and friends. The goal is to recognise what is normal and what is pathological, what needs only the balm of time, and what requires crisis intervention, as well as who are the most in need of help by professionals. [. . .]

REFERENCES

Age, marital conditions and general tables, Census 1961, London, HMSO 1964.

BAUMAN, M. K., 1964, *Adjustment to blindness*, State Council for the Blind, Department of Welfare, Commonwealth of Pennsylvania, September.

BLANK, H. R., 1957, 'Psychoanalysis and blindness', *Psychoanalytic Quarterly* 26, pp. 1–24.

CARROLL, T. J., 1961, *Blindness — what it is, what it does, and how to live with it*, Little, Brown & Co., Boston.

CHODOFF, P., FRIEDMAN, S. B. & NAMBURG, D. A., 1964, 'Stress, defenses and coping behavior — observations in parents of children with malignant disease', *American Journal*, 120, pp. 743—9.

Classification of occupation 1960, HMSO, 1961.

Commonwealth immigrants in the conurbations, Census, 1961, England and Wales, HMSO, London, 1965.

DIAMOND, B. L. & ROSS, A., 1945, Emotional adjustment of newly blinded soldiers, *American Journal of Psychiatry*, 102, pp. 367—71.

Estimated statistics on blindness and vision problems. The National Society for the Prevention of Blindness Inc., New York, 1966, p. 10.

Examination for admission to the register of blind persons or to the register of partially sighted persons, Form BD8 1962, G.R.G. Limited, 769/5, London.

KRAUS, A. S. & LILIENFELD, A. M., 1959, 'Some epidemiologic aspects of the high mortality rate in the young widowed group', *Journal of Chronic Diseases*, 10, pp. 207—17.

MILLER, E., 1962, *Social class and related concepts — a preliminary review*, Document no. 594(a), Tavistock Institute of Human Relations, London.

SHURTLEFF, D., 1956, 'Mortality among the married'. *American Geriatrics Society Journal*, 4 pp. 654—66.

Socioeconomic status, Partial Census, 1966, HMSO, London.

SORSBY, A., 1966, *The incidence and causes of blindness in England and Wales, 1948—1962*, Ministry of Health Reports on Public Health and Medical Subjects, no. 114, HMSO, London.

THUMP, L. & MURPHREE, O. D., 1961, 'Acceptance of the white cane and hope for the restoration of sight in blind persons as an indicator of adjustment', *Journal of Clinical Psychology*, 17, pp. 208—9.

Twenty-ninth annual report, 1966—67, Southern Regional Association for the Blind, 1968.

WITTKOWER, E. & DAVENPORT, R. C., 1946, 'War blinded — their emotional, social, and occupational situation', *Psychosomatic medicine*, 8, pp. 121—37.

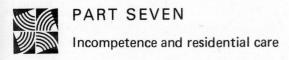

PART SEVEN

Incompetence and residential care

Introduction

Mental handicap, alias retardation, defect or sub-normality, is one of the labels most clearly associated with social *mores* and expectations because, in a great number of cases, it has no particular causes or prognosis. Whereas severely handicapped children and adults are relatively evenly distributed across the population and have generally come to the notice of public services before adulthood, the opposite pattern is shown for the more mildly handicapped. The latter, as Susser (1968) has indicated, tend to have come from the poorest and most deprived families rather than from all social classes, and their numbers fluctuate in a way that requires one to refer to their administrative rather than true prevalence. They emerge as a rate explosion at the critical point in their lives when they proceed through adolescence, leave school and fail to find work. Their numbers then decline with their absorption into jobs and marriage in the community, so that a smaller proportion actually continue in contact with official services and are placed, with those more severely handicapped, in various types of residential care when their parents grow old, infirm and die.

In Part 7 we have devoted attention to the social problems of being seen as mentally handicapped in the community and to recent developments in forms of residential care and their evaluation. Small-scale residential establishments in the community are only a part of the spectrum of care some mentally handicapped people need, but until recently they have remained a pipe-dream compared to expansion of training and occupational units and the lowering bulk of the nineteenth-century certified institutions. Other parts of this book refer to different aspects of mental handicap and forms of residential provision and training for people handicapped in other ways, e.g. Grunewald and Shearer in Parts 1 and 2, several items in Parts 4 and 5, and Townsend in Part 9.

Dexter proposes why mild mental handicap should be seen as a social problem in a society which places great store in the use of many technical devices and in social status achieved by means of education. When the technique of learning has become an end in itself, those who are incompetent at it have their difficulties and misbehaviour attributed to this, and a negative self-image is developed to the point where it becomes self-generating. He suggests a need for finding different ways in which they may accommodate to their society because if they follow the normal channels they cannot but be losers. Edgerton describes just how ex-hospital patients did in fact try to pass as normal and deny their past in seeking to weave a cloak of competence in the community to cover their stigma and lowered self-esteem. Such status as they had was based on being a hospital 'high grade' yet they eschewed hospital contacts if possible for fear of social contamination. They had difficulty in finding a job, and a spouse and in affording the possessions they desired to accumulate as a sign of normal success such as furniture, books and a car, and their everyday life involved constant negotiation to avoid being shown up in telling the time, using money and filling in forms. In fact they were in important respects dependent on normal people – their spouses, kinsmen, landladies, employers and, in a few cases, professional social workers.

Edgerton's sample was of course a residual one. In the first place it naturally excluded those who had never been put away in hospital and also those who could not be traced, both categories most likely to include the most competent social performers who had joined the ranks of the normal population. Mattinson's follow-up of English ex-hospital patients who got married when they were discharged into the community is less discouraging, but this category of patients is, as Edgerton indicates, a small proportion of the mentally handicapped adults in the community.

In planning the provision of services it should be considered essential to establish the likely scale and type of need to be met. This has been Kushlick's responsibility in the Wessex Hospital Region. Having estimated, and subsequently established the accuracy of, prevalence rates, his research team proposed an experimental feasibility scheme which has been implemented. All mentally handicapped children in need of care in certain areas have been admitted to a residential hostel near their home regardless of the severity of their condition, whilst other areas have continued to use the hospitals as before. The success of these mixed-disability hostels has itself had an impact on the internal policies of the hospitals but they are short of staff and remote from community services, extramural activities and patients' families. Like Anne Shearer (see Part 2), Kushlick sees no future in crash programmes to erect wards of the wrong sort in the wrong places and yet, as Townsend describes in Part 9, because of its central government funding, this is the only part of the 1971 White Paper that is being generally implemented! The rest is left to local authorities.

Raynes and King carry this comparison of hospitals and hostels much further by investigating the ways in which residential care regimes differ, why this should be so and, by implication, what effect they must have on the children in them. Using a scale of institutionalization derived from Goffman's analysis of total institutions, they were not only able to differentiate clear, if overlapping, patterns of hospital and hostel care but also able to account for some of these differences. In particular they found a correlation between senior staff roles and types of child management associated with the nursing sister or matron's involvement in activities with the children, her mode of

interaction and her training and past experience of child care, chronic or acute sickness.

The significance of different models of care is borne out in Miller and Gwynne's book, and by Grunewald in Part 1, and in the article by Scott in Part 3. The system of residential care in Lancashire's hostels for mentally disordered adults was characterised by no conscious or coherent model other than the potentially conflicting aims of providing a happy home for all the residents and a temporary hostel for developing the potentialities of those who could progress to work and lodgings outside the local authority's care. Alison Rosen summarizes the findings of her research. After initially receiving ex-hospital patients the local health divisions soon switched to local admissions from the community as crises occurred due to the loss of key caring persons. Those who had relatives and friends interested in them when they left hospital came to live closer to and had more contact with them, but those with no one remained without just as they did in hospital, although they got out into public places and activities in the community much more often. Hostel residents had a pronounced preferential gradient for their own homes, hostels and, at worst, the hospital, and set their sights on work and lodgings that remained unfound in most cases.

It also emerged that, although hostel residents did many more things for themselves than was permitted in the hospital wards to patients of a similar capacity, in most cases they did not progress after their first few weeks or months adjusting to the expectations of their new environment. With a static view of their role few hostel wardens, or for that matter training-centre staff, had developed social or other forms of training programme for individual residents, or trainees.

Kushlick stresses the need for such programmes, which are indicated by forms of behaviour modification (see Part 8), but they are equally necessary within all services for the maintenance of purpose essential to resident and staff morale. It must also, however, be understood that patients' moral and social careers tend to be written in terms of the services available and the staff they happen to encounter (Boswell 1973). Although the Lancashire hostels discharged some residents into the community, they sent as many back to hospital, including both mildly and severely handicapped residents. The situation in Salford was exactly the opposite, however. Selection techniques were different and the responsibilities assumed by the two local authorities were apparently very different. There is little sign that long-stay hospitals are ceasing to be dumping grounds for social misfits and nuisances who deserve and have rights equal to those who fit more amenably into the existing expectations of a stratified system of care.

REFERENCES

BOSWELL, D. M. (1973) 'Residential care and opportunities for adults', in Campaign for the Mentally Handicapped (eds.), *Effective Services for the Mentally Handicapped,* London, Dr Barnardo's, pp. 26–53.
DEPARTMENT OF HEALTH AND SOCIAL SECURITY (1971) *Better Services for the Mentally Handicapped,* Cmnd. 4683, London, HMSO.
MATTINSON, J. (1970) *Marriage and Mental Handicap*, London, Duckworth.
SUSSER, M. (1968) *Community Psychiatry: Epidemiologic and Social Themes*, New York, Random House.

35. A social theory of mental deficiency[*]

LEWIS ANTONY DEXTER
Kate Jackson Anthony Trust,
Miami, U.S.A.

Mental deficiency may usefully be regarded as a 'social problem' in the technical sense in which sociologists use the conception 'social problem' (Rose 1957). In most, if not all, societies, mental defect tends to constitute a social problem because mental defectives fail to learn (or are supposed to be incapable of learning) the 'right meaning' of events, symbols, or things; in all societies, certain 'meanings' attached to events, things, or symbols, are regarded as highly significant or sacred, and those who fail to learn them therefore naturally create uneasiness or shock. In our society, mental defect is even more likely to create a serious problem than it is in most societies because we make demonstration of formal skill at coordinating meanings (reading, writing and arithmetic) a requirement for initiation into adult social status, although such formal skills are not necessarily related to the capacity for effective survival or economic contribution.

There is a distinct possibility that many mental defectives become concrete social, legal, or economic problems simply because of the direct or indirect consequences of *this* requirement for initiation into social status and for no other reason. The indirect consequences of the high valuation placed upon such skill manifest themselves in discrimination and prejudices against the 'stupid' which leads them to acquire a negative or hostile self-image of themselves and therefore to live according to a self-definition of themselves as worthless or contemptible. If this hypothesis is in fact valid, a substantial proportion of the cost and

trouble resulting from the presence of mental defect in our society is a consequence, not of the biological or psychological characteristics of mental defectives, but of their socially prescribed or acquired roles and statuses. For clinical and diagnostic purposes, it might then become vital to differentiate those aspects of the behavior of individual mental defectives arising out of social factors from those traceable to biological and psychological bases; in concrete cases, operationally, the effects of the social factor are just as real of course.[1] But the therapy and control might well be different.

The propositions here put forward are designed to aid in the development of a social theory of mental defect; but like any other 'armchair' formulation need to be refined and tested by actual field work, using systematic methods of observation and recording.

1. *Mental deficiency may usefully be regarded as a social problem in the technical sense in which sociologists use the notion* (Rose 1957). As contemporary sociology uses the term, a social problem exists where a significant[2] proportion of the people in a society or sub-society act (a significant proportion of the time) *as though* they regard some existent behavior[3] of others as dangerously or undesirably 'abnormal'; such disapproval may be expressed in any way from frequent frowning to capital punishment.[4] The words 'act as though' in the foregoing sentence are deliberately stressed; the segregation of dull children in special classes or the institutionalization of the 'feeble-minded'[5] means, whatever the motivation, rationalization, or reasoning of

[*]From *American Journal of Mental Deficiency*, (1958) 63, pp. 920–8.

those who make the decisions, that the dull and feeble-minded are likely to feel that they have been treated as 'abnormal' or 'bad.'

2. *The mental defective tends to constitute a social problem in society because he has failed (or is supposed to be incapable of learning) the 'right meanings' attached to events, symbols, or things in that society.* All societies regard it as right and proper that the young should learn the right ways to react towards symbols, things, and events — including the events of desiring food, sexual experience, attention, elimination and 'power.' In a given society, the properly educated person responds to perceptions not only in terms of physical reality but in terms of social expectations and propriety (Sherif 1936). Shame and modesty for most persons in our society illustrate the point (Piers and Singer 1953).[. . .]

Complex societies usually develop procedures for 'handling' careless, unlucky, unorthodox, criminal, and alien persons who do not automatically give the 'right responses'. H. G. Wells in *The Country of the Blind* (1947) switched the notion 'in the country of the blind, the one-eyed man is King' to 'in the country of the blind the one-eyed man has to put his eye out or he will be treated as dangerously mad' to show one method of dealing with the unorthodox.

Our society has, however, found it quite difficult to handle and classify 'psychotics' and 'mental defectives'; we punish or stigmatize those who won't learn the right meanings in terms of a conception of responsibility; and we regard these two groups as lacking in responsibility, so we don't quite know what to do about them.

Forty years ago, however, the mentally defectives were regarded in the United States — in what is now universally considered an exaggerated form — as constituting a tremendous social menace (National Conference of Charities and Corrections, 1916, Dexter 1927, Shaw *et al.* 1938[6]). Indeed, some of the literature of that period about mental defectives sounds like fulminations against the politically unorthodox or Jews in more recent periods. It has been suggested that the most violent and unreasonable-sounding attacks on those who violate accepted social patterns or rôles may be made by those who themselves fear that they do not really belong (Shils 1956, Allport 1954). If this general hypothesis be correct, it may well be that the most extreme fear of the 'menace'

of mental defectives was expressed by those themselves uncertain or insecure of their acceptance as 'intelligent'.

The media of public communication have altered their emphasis on mental defect as a menace since; but the underlying attitude of uneasiness, hostility, and contempt for mental defectives appears to be still fairly widely prevalent.

3. *In a society like ours which emphasizes as an end in itself formal demonstration of skill in the technique of symbolization and coordinating meanings a far higher proportion of mental defectives are likely to be treated as cases of a social problem than would be so treated in a society emphasizing some other set of values, for instance the capacity for survival or effective economic contribution.* To some extent, inability to learn 'the right meanings' and to act according to them would in any society make some mental defectives 'social problem cases'. But in our society learning the right meaning is of value, not only because of its consequences, but because *the technique of learning has become a value in and of itself*[7] [. . .]

We find, that is, that many mental defectives become social problem cases, even though they do in fact learn enough of the right meanings to 'get by', because they do not demonstrate formal command of the technique of learning.

Of course, many mental defectives have such a low degree of skill at symbolization and communication that they would not learn the right meanings anyhow. But the maladjustment of high grade mental defectives in our society is probably not due as much to this fact as to the following circumstances:

(1) In fact, modern technology and the interdependence of the modern world makes skill at coordinating symbols far more vital than it once was; the modern soldier or automobile driver ought to be able to read maps or signs exactly; whereas their 14th century counterparts had no such needs.

(2) We require that young people learn complex symbols in order presumably to make themselves good citizens and in order certainly to establish their claim to social status. We live in a society which allocates social status according to achievement[8] based upon educational skill. Those who do not even make the first rung of this ladder or

do so with great difficulty create a serious problem, for this reason alone.

Nevertheless, several studies show that a fair proportion of special class students or those released from institutions (Charles 1953, Kennedy 1948, Matthews 1922), once they have passed school-leaving age and the onerous requirements of formal education, get along well enough. A subject of one of these studies (Charles 1953) is quoted as saying: 'I can't do much with words but give me a pile of flour and cinnamon and makings and I can turn out good bread'.

Such development in adult life of those regarded as more or less mentally defective in adolescence may be explained in several different ways. First, some type of 'delayed maturation' may occur; that is they may grow intellectually more slowly but nevertheless grow.[9] Second, the intelligence tests are obviously subject to error for various reasons; and in addition may be administered in a careless or error-producing fashion. A third hypothesis – and one more relevant to our effort to develop a social theory of mental defect – is that the intelligence which the intelligence tests test is not in fact a measure of ability to make an economic contribution or to survive, but merely of the type of intelligence and clerical aptitude which enables people to do well at school.

(3) It also happens that if a person of low intellectual ability gets into some sort of trouble the difficulty is more or less automatically attributed to 'mental defect' whereas if a person of 'normal intelligence' gets into a similar difficulty, it is not regarded as symptomatic of anything in particular. Consequently, attention becomes focused upon the mental defectives as people who get into trouble; we have no real evidence as to whether they do (or for what reasons) in any greater proportion than do normal individuals of similar socio-economic statuses. It may be that mental defect is significant as a trouble-creating factor only because of the social attitude towards it, not because of the defect itself – *in the case especially of high-grade mental defectives.* This statement is probably exaggerated; but not necessarily more exaggerated than the customary attitude towards mental defectives the other way about.

4. *The self-image of the mentally defective in a society which stresses aptitude at intellectual*

achievement is likely to be negative because the 'looking-glass self' principle operates and they learn from their social contacts and experiences to look down upon and distrust themselves; in consequence difficulties are created, derived from the social role of the defectives rather than from anything inherent in the bio-psychological nature of defectives. [. . .]

In a society where people in a given category are restricted in role, made fun of, looked down upon, and subjected to great obstacles, the people in that category are likely to learn to feel considerable self-doubt; this self-doubt may express itself in helplessness, lack of ambition, or erratic, impulsive, and highly negative behavior – 'kicking out' at a world in which 'the generalized other' – the typical or modal other person as they have experienced him – has frustrated, bewildered, or oppressed him. These undesirable or anti-social types of conduct are not *per se* the result of any particular abnormality, low status position, or deviation from conventional conduct; they are rather responses to the way people are treated who are regarded as abnormal, of low status, or undesirably unconventional. [. . .]

There is however a particular class of persons who are not completely members of any group, either because their ancestry is so physically mixed that in a society where 'race' is important they are regarded by almost everybody as outsiders, or because their life history has been such as to make them outsiders everywhere, neither fish nor fowl. Sociologists and novelists have devoted a good deal of attention to these persons, called 'marginal men' (Stonequist 1937, Forster 1924) and it may well be that the problems of the marginal many are the problems of the high grade mentally retarded. If this hypothesis is correct, it may turn out that *the* significant therapy for the high-grade retarded is to find some place where they can be accepted completely and that the explanation of the success of those graduates of institutions and special classes who have succeeded in adult life will be discovered to be that by good fortune they found a place where they could be accepted without any sense of being left out.

But those who differ in such a way as to be regarded negatively by the people with whom they spend the greater part of their lives, their kin groups, work groups, or age mates, do not have such 'moral support'; so they are likely to develop an image of themselves as incapable or of other people as being hostile, an image which extends beyond the specific areas of incompetence or hostility which actually exist and suffuses most of their behavior.

Mental defectives are probably more likely than any other group in our society to develop such negative self-images; the nearest analogue which comes to mind is perhaps the person afflicted by compulsive homosexual drives. In other societies, persons with certain diseases – e.g. leprosy (Mercier 1915, Ackernecht 1947[10]) – may have been likely to develop similar images of the self and of others.[. . .]

It is probable that a considerable proportion of the social burden and economic cost of mental defect arises, not out of lack of intellectual ability as such but out of the accommodation (Park and Burgess 1941) that mental defectives learn to make to the consequences of such lack. The problem of mental defect, so envisaged, would then become *in part*, and in different amounts, a problem of learning different methods of accommodation. On such a hypothesis, one would expect to find that the less the mental defective is exposed to conventional pressure for scholastic or equivalent success, and the less he is exposed to ridicule, the greater, on the average, the adult social and economic success experienced.[. . .]

5. *The foregoing propositions remain to be tested after further clarification and comparison with alternative sociologically based propositions about mental defect.* (It should again be stressed that the present effort has been confined to a *social* theory of mental deficiency, and therefore probably has more pertinence to high grade mental defectives than to others.) The propositions here put forward assume that there is a bio-psychological condition which can properly be identified as 'mental defect', just as there 'is' a biological condition of having scarlet fever (Crookshank and Richards 1938[11]). This may not in fact be the case; it may well be that we have, for sociological reasons, fallen into the error of treating members of a null class, people who lack or appear to lack some particular characteristic, as though they have positive characteristics in common. We know that there is no scientific sense in talking of 'foreigners' or 'anti-Communists' or 'criminals' as though all the persons in any one of these groups have anything much positive in common. Similarly, it may be that all that mental defectives (or even high-grade mental defectives) have in common is that they have gone through the experience of being treated as mental defectives and are undergoing deviant role-status experiences because of the existence of mental defect.[. . .]

NOTES

1. Of course, empirically, social and biological factors will be inextricably intermixed. Our purpose here is to try to devise a set of analytic explanations which may help in making etiological differentiations where it may be therapeutically desirable to do so.
2. 'Significant' should be here defined in terms of 'significant *influence*' as well as significant numbers.
3. 'Behavior' must be here defined very widely – 'existence' is a form of behavior, and extreme 'racists' may regard the mere existence of another race as *per se* creating a social problem.
4. In essence a social problem may be said to exist when a considerable number of members of society say in effect through their actions 'What you do (or are) is so bad that something ought to be done about it', in such a way that the implicit threat is regarded seriously by a good many of those engaged in the disapproved behavior and/or by a good many of those doing the disapproving.
5. Strickland (1948–9, p. 510) says: 'In practically all cases it can be assumed that before admission (to an institution for mental defectives) the patient has been through experiences highly charged with emotion – enforced separation from parents, appearances in court, etc., and is finally taken to an institution where people are vaguely said to be mental, there to stay for an undefined period. . . .' If this is not punishment, what is? The vagueness will persist and the difficulty, particularly for defectives, in knowing what they have to do to get out presumably adds to the unpleasant nature of the experience and the feeling that one must have done something wrong.

6. See the reference to 'moron' as an epithet similar to 'brute' or 'beast' in journalistic usage, (Shaw *et al.* 1938, p. ix).
7. Rose (1957) is very illuminating on this point.
8. 'Open society' here used as referring to a society in which there is considerable competition for achieved statuses ('a career open to the talents'). (See Linton 1936.)
9. I am indebted for awareness of this idea to personal conversations with Dr E. Doll 1949, 1951. He puts the notion within a general framework of mental deficiency in his valuable review (Doll 1940, see pp. 408—10).
10. Especially pp. 142—3: 'Even the notion of disease itself depends on the decisions of the society (rather) than on the objective facts', followed by a discussion of pinto and ague (Ackernecht 1947).
11. Pp. 337—55 analyzes critically the notion that a pathological condition 'has' 'innate' 'biological properties'.

REFERENCES

ACKERNECHT, E., 1947, 'The Role of the Medical Historican in Medical Education', *Bulletin History of Medicine*, 21.
ALLPORT, G., 1954, *Prejudice*, Boston: Beacon, pp. 382—408.
CHARLES, C., 1953, 'Ability and Accomplishment of Persons Earlier Judged Mentally Deficient', *Genetic Psychology Monograph*, 47: 9—19, review of literature; citation, p. 55 and p. 58.
CROOKSHANK, F., 1938, Supp. II., to Ogden, C., and Richards, I. *Meaning of Meaning*, New York: Harcourt.
DEXTER, L., 1947, 'Examinations as Instruments of, and Obstacles to, General Education', *School Review*, 55: 534—41.
DEXTER, R., 1927, *Social Adjustments*, New York: Knopf, pp. 151—2.
DOLL, E., 1950, 'The Nature of Mental Deficiency', *Psychological Review*, 47: 395—415, reprinted in *Training School Bulletin*.
FORSTER, E., 1924, *Passage to India*, New York: Harcourt.
KENNEDY, R. J. R., 1948, *Social Adjustment to Morons in a Connecticut City*, Harford, Conn: Mansfield-Southbury Training Schools.
LINTON, R., 1936, *The Study of Man*, New York: Appleton, Century, pp. 115—131.
MATTHEWS, M., 1922, 'One Hundred Institutionally Trained Male Defectives in the Community Under Supervision', *Mental Hygiene*, 6: 332—42.
MERCIER, C., 1915, *Leper Houses and Medieval Hospitals*, London: H. Lewis.
MILLER, N., 1932, 'Initiation', *Encyclopaedia Social Science*, 8: 49—50.
National Conference of Charities and Corrections, 1916, *Feeble-Mindedness and Insanity*, 205—300.
PARK, R. & BURGESS, E., 1921, *Introduction to the Science of Sociology*, Chicago: University of Chicago Press, Ch. X, Accommodation, pp. 663—733.
PIERS, G. and SINGER, M., 1953, *Shame and Guilt*, Springfield, Illinois, Chas. C. Thomas.
ROSE, A., 1957, 'Theory for Social Problems', *Social Problems*, 4: 189—99, — bibliographical notes list several leading references.
SHAW, C. et al., 1938, *Brothers in Crime*, Chicago: University of Chicago.
SHERIF, M., 1936, *Psychology of Social Norms*, New York: Harper's.
SHILS, E., 1956, *The Torment of Secrecy*, Glencoe, Illinois Free Press, pp. 77—89, (section on xenophobia).
STONEQUIST, E., 1937, *Marginal Man*.
STRICKLAND, C., 1948—9, 'The Social Competence of the Feeble-Minded', *Am. J. Mental Deficiency*, 53: 504—515, p. 510.
WELLS, H. G., 1947, *Country of the Blind*, London, Longman's.

36. Residential care for the mentally retarded *

NORMA V. RAYNES
Formerly Research Sociologist, Child Welfare Project,
Institute of Education, University of London

ROY D. KING
Lecturer in the Department of Sociology and Social Administration,
University of Southampton

A. The measurement of child management in residential institutions for the retarded

A substantial number of retardates require residential care. In England and Wales, this is currently provided for them under the National Health Service, either in Hospitals, which are the responsibility of Regional Hospital Boards, or in Hostels, which are the responsibility of our Local Health Authorities.[1] Residential care is also provided for retardates, outside the National Health Service, by a number of voluntary and independent organizations.

We set out to study existing residential institutions, in terms of a number of dimensions, such as their child management practices, their size and their organizational structure. In this paper, I am going to discuss the development and application of a scale, for the measurement of one of these dimensions, namely the way in which inmates in residential institutions are cared for.

I shall discuss firstly the theoretical background to this scale, secondly, the methods used in its construction, thirdly, its expansion and finally, the results of its application to a range of institutions for severely retarded children.

THE THEORETICAL BACKGROUND

The conceptual framework behind the development of this scale, is contained in an essay by

*From First International Congress for the Scientific Study of Mental Deficiency (1967) Montpellier, Surrey, Michael Jackson, pp. 637—49.

Erving Goffman, entitled 'On the Characteristics of Total Institutions', (Goffman 1961). In this essay, Goffman pointed to the similarities between seemingly disparate institutions, which he labelled 'total institutions'. The institutional model he developed, resembles what has come to be regarded as the typical, bleak institution associated with the last century. We have argued that the management practices included in his description of this institutional type, represent but one end of a possible continuum of management practice, along which institutions may vary. We have termed the practices he described, *institutionally oriented*. We have argued further, that at the opposite end of this continuum are practices, which are *inmate oriented*.

Our scale attempts to measure the degree of inmate or institution orientation in management practice in four areas of the regime, experienced by children in institutions. These are:

1. Rigidity of routine
2. Block treatment
3. Depersonalization
4. Social distance

Management practice, in each of these areas, has been defined operationally, in terms of both inmate and institution orientation. Here, for the sake of simplicity, I shall present the definitions, only in terms of institution orientation.

Rigidity of Routine

We mean the inflexibility of management practices, so that neither 'individual' differences among inmates, nor unique circumstances, are taken into account by the staff, in their interaction with the children. We asked for example, if the children's getting up and going to bed times were unchanged throughout the week. We asked also, if there were set times at which they could use their bedrooms and the garden and at which their parents could visit them.

Block treatment

We mean the regimentation of inmates together, as a group, before, during or after, any specific activity. We asked here, if the children were regimented on getting up, before or after bathing and toileting, and before or after meals.

Depersonalization

We mean, the absence of opportunities for inmates to have personal possessions, or privacy, or of situations, in which there is opportunity for self-expression and initiative, on the part of the inmate. We asked, for example, what was done with the personal possessions the children brought with them to the institutions. We asked too, if after admission, the children had personalized clothing and toys of their own and places in which to keep these. (Strict ownership was not required. The definition used is contained in a paper by Brown and Wing 1962). We also asked, if the children had pictures of their own in their rooms, and whether the children were taken on outings.

Social distance

We mean the limitation of interaction between staff and children to formal and specific activities and the use of physically separate areas of accommodation by the children, and those who care for them. We asked here if the staff ate with the children, and watched television with them, and whether the children had access to all the rooms in the cottage or ward in which they lived. We also asked how the children were bathed and toileted. That is, whether they were supervised by one member of staff, or alternatively by several, one person undressing the child, another bathing it and so on. [. . .]

THE APPLICATION OF THE SCALE TO SIXTEEN INSTITUTIONS

[We studied] sixteen institutions comprising eight Local Authority Hostels, five Hospitals and three Voluntary Homes, [which] accommodated children between the ages of 5 and 16 who were severely retarded, that is, had Intelligence Quotients of less than 50 points. The majority of the children, 92 per cent of the sample population, were fully ambulant and over half of them had been resident in the institutions for between 1 and 5 years.

The techniques used in the collection of data, the scoring of items for the child management scale, were repeated in the study of the sixteen institutions. Reliability studies were carried out on both the interviews and observations. The level of agreement between interviewers was 94.2 per cent and between observers was 92.0 per cent.

Fifteen items, in addition to those already in the scale, met Maxwell's criteria and were thus added to the existing scale. A coefficient of correlation of 0.92 was found to obtain between the fifteen original and fifteen additional items. The new thirty item child management scale gave us a possible range of scores from 0 to 60.

RESULTS

The sixteen institutions scored within a range of 3 to 47 points on the scale. An analysis of variance on these scales scores produced a value of H., significant at the 0.01 level (H = 10.80, p = $<$0.01, df = 2).

The establishments were then grouped by institutional type, i.e. Local Authority Hostels, Voluntary Homes and Hospitals. The mean scale score and standard deviation for the Hostels as a group was $\bar{x}$ = 11 points S.D. = 6.7 points, for the Voluntary Homes $\bar{x}$ = 27.7 points S.D. = 13.5 points and for the Hospitals $\bar{x}$ = 43 points S.D. = 4 points. The difference between the mean scale score of the Hostels, as a group, and the Hospitals, as a group, was significant at the 0.001 level. (t = 8.90, p = $<$ 0.001, df = 12). The lowest scoring Voluntary Home, with 14 points, came well within the range of Hostel scores. The highest scoring of the Voluntary Homes with 41 points, came within the range of the Hospitals' scores. One Voluntary Home, scoring 28 points on the scale, was outside both the range of scores obtained by the Hostels and Hospitals.

CONCLUSION

To conclude, in this paper I have described the development of a scale to measure child management practices in residential institutions. The use of this scale in a number of such institutions, indicated that there exist at least two clearly differentiated patterns of care, one of which we have called inmate oriented and the other, institution oriented. When we used this scale in a study of sixteen residential institutions for retardates, the Hostels in the study appeared to provide a regime for their children which represents the pattern of inmate orientation. The Hospitals, on the other hand, appeared to provide a regime which represents the pattern of institution-orientation. One of the Voluntary Homes in this study was characterized by the pattern of management found in the Hostels; a second by that in the Hospitals; a third Voluntary Home appeared to provide a pattern of care which was unlike that found in either the Hostels or the Hospitals. [. . .]

B. Some determinants of patterns of residential care

In this paper I am going to present some material, collected in our survey of sixteen institutions, in an attempt to account for the observed differences in patterns of care. At least two main types of factors may be invoked by way of explanation: (a) selective factors and (b) social structural factors including the numbers of available staff.

SELECTIVE FACTORS

It might be argued that differences in management practices result from the differences in age and mental or physical handicaps of the populations which have been selected as suitable for each type of institutional care. Such an argument presupposes that severely handicapped patients require different management practices from those required by less handicapped patients. In extreme cases there is probably some truth in this. However, elsewhere we have shown that children with different handicaps were cared for in the same way in the wards of a large hospital (Tizard *et al.* 1966; King and Raynes 1967a), and that groups of children with comparable handicaps were cared for differently in different types of establishments (King and Raynes 1967b).

SOCIAL STRUCTURAL FACTORS

I shall discuss some social structural features of the institutions studied in two sections. Firstly, characteristics such as the size of the institution, the size of the child care units, and the staff-child ratios; secondly, some aspects of the internal social organization in different types of establishment.

Institutional size

At first sight it is apparent that the child management scale scores are related to the overall size of the institutions, as measured by numbers of patients (Figure 36.1). The rank order correlation between size of institution and child management scores is .76 which is significant at the one per cent level, and it might be argued that size of institution in some way affects the patterns of care found. However, if we examine size and scale scores within types of institution, this relationship no longer holds.

The Hostels, on the left of Figure 36.1, vary in size from 12—41 patients and have a range of scores from 3—22 (r = —.05, p = N.S.). The Hospitals, on the right range from 121 to 1,650 patients yet vary in scores only between 37—47 (r = —.375, p = N.S.). Within the range of 12—41 patients, and 121—1,650 patients, size has no systematic effect on scale scores. There is, of course, no overlap between institutions either in scores or overall size, and it may be that below 41 patients and above 121 patients are critical points for determining management practices. But again we have shown elsewhere that institutions with over 300 inmates can have inmate oriented patterns of care (Tizard *et al.* 1967; King and Raynes 1967a).

Size of child care units

More plausible as an explanation of differences in patterns of care is the possibility that they result from the size of the actual units, wards or cottages, in which the children live. Here there is a rank order correlation between child management scale scores and size of units: this time of .45 which is significant at the five per cent level (Figure 36.2). But if, once more, we look within types of institutions the relationship between scale scores and unit size disappears. The Hostels, in the lower diagonal, vary in unit size from 8—41 patients, but none scores higher on the scale than 22 points (r = .04, p = N.S.).

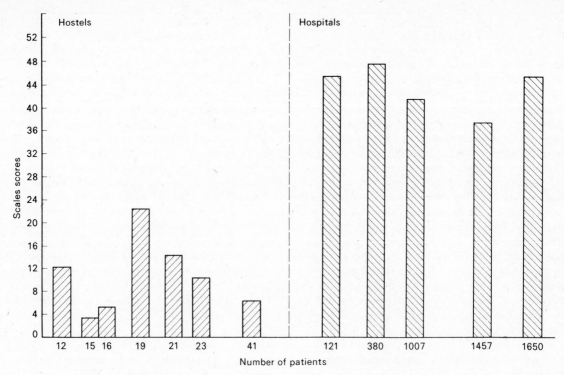

Figure 36.1   Scale scores by size of institution

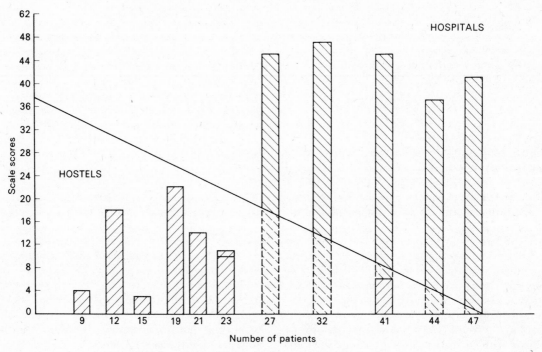

Figure 36.2   Scale scores by size of child care unit

The Hospitals in the upper diagonal range in size of wards from 27—47 patients, but none scores less than 37 points on the scale (r = −.68, p = N.S.). There is a clear overlap in unit size between the two types of institution but the patterns of scale scores are markedly different.

We would argue that the apparent associations between scale scores and both overall and unit size, are by-products of the association between scale scores and institutional type.

Staff-child ratios

A third possible explanation for management patterns could be differences in staff-child ratios. We have calculated crude staff-child ratios, excluding domestic helpers and night staff, for the week in each institution when the field work took place. (Each person who worked 40 or more hours per week was counted as 1 full-time staff. Those working between 30—39 hours counted as .8; 20—29 hours as .6; 10—19 hours as .4; and less than 10 hours as .2 staff.) There is no correlation between child management scale scores and crude staff-child ratios (r = .03, p = N.S.) and there is no significant difference in staff-child ratios between Hostels on the one hand and Hospitals on the other (t = .06, p = N.S.). Indeed one Hostel with a ratio of 1 staff to 8.9 children scored 6 on the scale whilst one Hospital with a ratio of 1:34 scored 45.

The differences in scale scores cannot therefore be satisfactorily explained by overall size, the size of the child care groups, nor the staff-child ratios. I turn now to a discussion of some aspects of the internal social organization of the institutions which may help to explain the differences in the patterns of care between the Hostels and the Hospitals, and the idiosyncratic patterns in the Voluntary Homes. I shall examine first the role activities of the person in charge of each unit, secondly the way they perform those activities and finally their training.

Staff roles

From our earlier investigations we developed the hypothesis that in inmate oriented establishments the person in charge of the child care unit would be highly involved with the actual care and supervision of the patients. In institutionally oriented establishments we predicted that the head of the unit would be more concerned with adminis-trative and domestic activities, while the actual care of children would be delegated to her subordinates.

To test this hypothesis we observed the activities of the heads of units for regular intervals, while the children were in the unit, over a period of four days. Her activities were classified into five categories: Administration, Domestic Work, Supervision of the children, Physical Child Care (by which we meant bathing, dressing, undressing children and so on) and Social Child Care (which included educational and recreational activities with children). Each category was denotatively defined by a check-list of activities. Inter-observer reliability was 95.95 per cent. Here I can give only a few summary results. The higher proportion of total activities which the head of the unit spent in Social Child Care and Supervision of the children the lower were the scores of those units on the child management scale. For both of these the correlation was −.55, which was significant at the five per cent level. On the other hand the higher the proportion of activities spent in Administration the higher were the scores on the scale (r = .63, p < .01).

When we combined activities which involved the heads of the units with the children and compared them with those that did not, a similar result was obtained. The greater the proportion of the role formed by Social and Physical Child Care and Supervision the lower were scale scores (r = .64, p < .01), while the greater the proportion formed by Administrative and Domestic activities the higher were scale scores (r = .54, p < .05).

The differences in the proportion of total activities spent in each of these categories by the heads of units in Hostels as compared with Hospitals were very significant. The role activities of heads of units in Hostels involved a much higher proportion of Social and Physical Child Care and Supervision of the children than did the role activities of their counterparts in Hospitals (t = 3.61, p = <.01). Conversely heads of units in Hospitals did proportionately more activities of an Administrative or Domestic kind than was the case in Hostels (t = 3.18, p = <.01). The heads of units in the Voluntary Homes tended to follow the patterns of activity for the Hostels, or else to have a unique pattern of their own.

Staff role performance

A second hypothesis was that regardless of the actual activities carried out by the heads of units, *the way in which they were performed* would be different in inmate oriented and institutionally oriented establishments. In particular we predicted that heads of units in inmate oriented places would interact with the children, both physically and verbally, more frequently than heads of units in institutionally oriented places. Using the same observation technique, we recorded as one measure of role performance whether in each ½ minute time interval the head of the unit spoke to any child. Inter-observer reliability for the coding of verbal contact was 96.62%. This measure of role performance was significantly related to scores on the child management scale, high rates of verbal contact being associated with inmate oriented patterns of care ($r = -.83$, $p < .001$).

Once again striking differences obtained between the Hostels and the Hospitals with much more verbal contact in the former ($t = 5.29$, $p = <.001$). On this measure, however, one Voluntary Home conformed to the Hostel Pattern, one to the Hospital Pattern, while one was quite idiosyncratic. Very similar results were obtained with a second measure of role performance, namely the total amount of interaction with the children.

Our data suggest that the Hostels have a related pattern of staff roles, role performance, and management practices which is quite distinct from the pattern of these variables in the Hospitals. The Voluntary Homes tend either to follow the pattern of the Hospitals or the Hostels or else have a distinctive pattern of their own.

We are at present examining various features of the formal organization of the institutions which in turn may be related to staff activities. We expect to find that the actual activities carried out by heads of units are a function of the demands placed upon them by the wider institution in which they work. With regard to role performance, we expected that the way in which activities were carried out, would be strongly affected by the emphasis given to interaction with the children in the training which heads of units received. We have accordingly examined our data in terms of the training received by heads of units. We have classified our staff in charge of units as follows: those who have had nursing training and no other

(5 Hospitals and 3 Hostels and 1 Voluntary Home) and those who have had training in child care regardless of whether they have been also trained as nurses (5 Hostels and 1 Voluntary Home). One Voluntary Home had a head of unit who was untrained. There were significant differences between units having Nursing trained heads, and those with Child Care trained heads, both for rates of verbal contact ($t = 2.78$, $p = <.02$) and for scores on the inmate management scale ($t = 3.97$, $p = <.01$).

There was a striking similarity between the role performance, as measured by verbal contact, of heads of units and the patterns of management in their units, when looked at from the point of view of training of staff. In Figure 36.3 the inter-relationship of training heads of units, type of establishment in which they worked and scale scores is shown. A similar inter-relationship was found for degrees of verbal contact.

What is particularly interesting in Figure 36.3 is that Hostel Units with Nursing trained staff, score much lower than Hospitals, but not quite so low as Hostels with Child Care trained staff. In the Voluntary Homes, one with a Child Care trained unit head follows the pattern of Hostels with a similar training, while one with a Nursing trained head tends to fall between the two extremes on all measures. The Voluntary Homes in which the unit head was untrained scored within the range of the Hospitals.

I would like to conclude with the statement of an hypothesis which links these findings together. That is, that among Local Authority Homes a model of care for retarded patients has been taken over from traditional care of deprived children. Each Hostel converges upon that model because of the socialization undergone by unit heads in the form of training, and because of the system of inspection and other constraints imposed by the Local Authority Organization. Hospitals for subnormals, on the other hand, have taken over a model of care based partly on that for acute cases and partly on the tradition of care of the chronic sick. Each ward converges upon that model because of the training undergone by staff, and because of inspection by superiors and other constraining demands of the Hospital. In the Voluntary Homes studied none was part of a wider organization. They had a choice of models of care, but no regular system of training or inspection

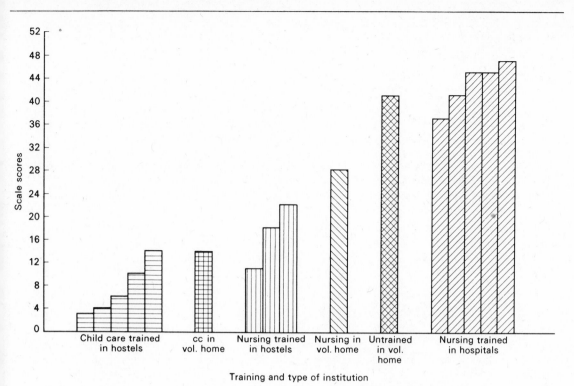

Figure 36.3   Scale scores by training of head of unit and type of institution

designed to produce conformity to the chosen model. This lack of systematic constraint from a wider social organization may help to explain the greater variation, and in some cases idiosyncratic patterns, found in the Voluntary Homes.

SUMMARY

In this paper I have discussed a number of structural characteristics of sixteen residential institutions for retarded children in an attempt to account for observed differences in their management patterns as measured by the child management scale.

I began by showing that the differences could not be explained by (1) the overall size of establishments nor (2) the size of the child care units, when the factor of institutional type was taken into account. Nor could they be explained by any differences in staff-child ratios.

I went on to show that patterns of care were closely related to the role activities of the person in charge of each unit, and their role performance as measured by rates of verbal contact with the children.

Finally I pointed out that there is an inter-relationship between training of staff, type of institution, role performance and patterns of child care. Nursing trained staff in Hospitals had low rates of verbal contact with the children and their units were characterized by institutional patterns of care. Child Care trained staff in Hostels, had high rates of verbal contact and inmate oriented patterns of care. Nursing trained staff in Hostels held an intermediate position on both these variables.

NOTE

1. Since the reorganization of the NHS and local government in 1970—74 the hospitals have become the responsibility of the new Area Health Boards within the Regions, and the hostels have become the responsibility of the new Social Service Departments or, in cases where they share premises with a school, of the Local Education Authorities.

REFERENCES

BROWN, G., and WING, J., 1962, 'A comparative clinical and social survey of three mental hospitals', *Sociological Review Monographs*, No. 5, July.

GOFFMAN, E., 1961, On the characteristics of total institutions, in *Asylums*, New York, Anchor Books.

KING, R. D. and RAYNES, N. V., 1968a, 'An operational measure of inmate management in residential institutions', *Social Science and Medicine*, 2, 1, 41–53.

KING, R. D. and RAYNES, N. V., 1968b, 'Patterns of institutional care for the severely subnormal', *American Journal of Mental Deficiency*, 72, 5, 700–9.

MAXWELL, A. E., 1961, *Analysing qualitative data*, London, Methuen.

TIZARD, J., KING, R. D., RAYNES, N. V. and YULE, W., 1967, 'The care and treatment of subnormal children in residential institutions', *Proceedings of the First International Congress of Special Education, London, July, 1966*.

37. The need for residential care*

ALBERT KUSHLICK
Director of Health Care Evaluation Research Team,
Wessex Regional Health Authority

This paper aims to illustrate:

that we already know much about the size and nature of the problem of severe subnormality (IQ under 50), and about the need for residential care;

that the available statistics, although crude, enable us to make useful and valid predictions of the real problems of providing care;

that the problem of residential care must be considered in relation to that of caring for the mentally handicapped in their own homes; and

that this applies whether they are in hospital wards or hostels. For this reason hospital wards and hostels will be referred to by the general term 'living-unit'.

The case will be made that while any new residential facilities should be provided in the geographical areas where the families live, conditions in existing hospitals could be vastly improved if, in addition to increasing staffing levels on living-units, residents were to be relocated in living-units on a geographical basis, in place of the existing practice of grouping by functional incapacities.

The importance of geographical relocation of residents in existing hospitals will be illustrated.

It will be argued that personnel are the most important component of any facilities, and that they must be enabled to collaborate effectively wherever there are handicapped people, regardless of the administrative structure of the service or where the facilities are located.

*From Victoria Shennan, (ed.) (1972) *Subnormality in the 70's: action for the retarded*, London, National Society for Mentally Handicapped Children and World Federation of Mental Health, pp. 13–26.

This paper will only touch upon some of the problems associated with the residential care of the mildly subnormal person, IQ score 50 and over. It concentrates on the severely subnormal (IQ less than 50), and particularly on the profoundly retarded, IQ under 20.

The numbers and the proportion of these people in residential facilities for the retarded are increasing, and they form the great majority of people on waiting lists for admission to residential care.

The need for residential care of the SSN person arises when their families for any of a number of reasons are no longer able to cope with the problems of caring for the handicapped person in the family home.

Although the expression 'family rejection' still occurs in much of the literature and psychological reasons are advanced for this behaviour, there is now considerable, well-documented evidence of the very serious problems presented to the family by a retarded person, and of the relative failure of the social, welfare, medical and educational services to deal with these problems (Tizard and Grad 1961, Moncrief 1966).

Very briefly, the family's problems arise from the discovery that a child for whom there have been hopes and expectations for the future will not be able to meet them, from the increasingly difficult logistics of caring in a busy household for a child whose social development is much slower than that of the other children, from a lack of easily available norms for dealing with the child's behaviour, from conflicting advice from relatives, friends, social workers and doctors on how to deal with the problems which arise, and from a lack of resources, financial, personnel or outside facilities, which might enable the families to solve some of these problems.

Substitute homes

Despite these problems, all surveys show that, far from 'rejecting' these children, most families wish to keep them at home (Tizard and Grad 1961). In addition, those families who have placed their children in residential care continue, in spite of the grave difficulties involved, to maintain an interest in them. Thus, in England and Wales, 80 per cent of SSN children and just under a half of the SSN adults are at present being cared for at home (Kushlick 1966). This proportion appears, contrary to general belief, to have increased since 1927 when Lewis undertook his classical survey of mental handicap in England and Wales (Kushlick, in press, Lewis 1929).

In England and Wales the function of a substitute home for those people whose families cannot maintain them at home, is undertaken largely by the psychiatric hospitals for the subnormal. At present only a very small proportion of their care is provided by Local Authority hostels or 'private homes'. Some of these people are also cared for in district general hospitals or psychiatric hospitals for the mentally ill.

The profound difficulties faced by the staff and residents of these hospitals have been documented recently in an official inquiry into one such hospital, (Cmnd. 2975, 1969) and a NSMHC sponsored study of these facilities on a national basis by Dr. Pauline Morris (1969). A policy statement on the future of the service in England and Wales is now awaited in the form of a Government White Paper (Cmnd. 4683, 1971).

Much is known about the size and nature of the problem of mental handicap from studies conducted in England and Wales.

Table 37.1 summarises some of this information. The data are taken from a survey conducted on behalf of the Wessex Regional Board in 1963 by myself and Miss Gillian Cox (Kushlick and Cox 1969). The survey was financed by the Department of Health and the Nuffield Hospital Trust Fund.

The figures show the size of the administrative problem for a total population of 200,000. They are presented, for the purposes of this paper, in the form of an existing hospital for the retarded serving this population.

The hospital has about 300 places. It has been divided into seven wards or living-units — one of

Table 37.1

Structure of a comprehensive hospital for 300 residents serving a total population of 200,000			*Comparison figures of mentally handicapped known to be living at home in a total population of 200,000*	
1 Children's living unit			**Children**	
40 places serving	12 NA		10 NA	
	10 ALL SB		10 ALL SB	
	6 SI		4 SI	
	12 CAN	40	52 CAN	76*
4 SSN Adult living units			**SSN adults**	
Each 40 places serving	3 NA		1 NA	
	7 ALL SB		1 ALL SB	
	3 SI		— SI	
	27 CAN	160	23 CAN	25
2 MSN Adult living units			**MSN**	
Each 50 places serving	2 NA		1 NA	
	4 ALL SB		— ALL SB	
	1 SI		— SI	
	43 CAN	100	76+ CAN	76+

*A further 84 mentally handicapped children would be at home but unknown to the special agencies.

Key:
NA	Non-ambulant	CAN	Continent, ambulant, no severe behaviour disorders
ALL SB	Ambulant but with severe behaviour disorders (may also be severely incontinent)	SSN	Severely subnormal IQ under 50
SI	Ambulant, no severe behaviour disorders, but severely incontinent	MSN	Mildly subnormal, IQ 50+

40 places for children, four of 40 places for SSN adults, and two of 50 places for MSN adults.

Most existing hospitals are bigger than this. Thus, a complex of 600 beds serving 400,000 total population would be twice this size, and a complex of 1,500 beds serving a total population of one million would be five times this size.

The national picture for England and Wales can be derived by multiplying the numbers in Table 37.1 by 250.

The picture for 200,000 total population has been used because it presents a 'human' scale from which it is a little easier to comprehend some of the complexities involved in developing and in running a comprehensive service.

Table 37.1 also shows the social and physical incapacities of the people concerned. A substantial minority of the 40 children in residential care are CAN, that is continent, ambulant and without severe behaviour disorders. The majority are, however, in our classification called CAN'T, that is, non-ambulant – NA; ambulant but severely behaviour disordered, often also severely incontinent – ALLSB; or ambulant, without severe behaviour disorders, but severely incontinent – SI.

However, the vast majority of the adults, even those who are severely subnormal, are CAN. Indeed, half of these adults, in addition to being CAN, are also able to feed, wash and dress themselves without help.

Residential care can only be usefully considered in relation to the handicapped who are living at home. The right-hand column of Table 37.1 shows the numbers living at home, per living unit in the hospital. Thus the children's unit of 40 places serves a total population of 200,000 where there are 76 such children known to be living at home; a unit of 40 places for severely subnormal adults serves a total population of 50,000 (one quarter of 200,000), where there are 25 such adults known to be living at home.

To summarise:

the numbers needing care at any time are finite and comprehensible in relation to a population of 200,000;

it appears feasible, if it were considered desirable, to provide a comprehensive service covering both those in residential care and those living at home from the same population area;

the majority of children, particularly the CAN,

and a substantial minority of CAN'T children, live at home;

a slight majority of SSN adults are in residential care, and there are many more CAN people in hospital than there are CAN'T people at home;

waiting lists for residential care for a population of 200,000 are about 12 – six children and six adults;

in addition, these data enable possible predictions to be made of the problem of providing residential care.

The Wessex experiment

However, hospitals are not organised as in this table. There is evidence that it would be feasible to do so.

It is not often that the epidemiologist has the opportunity to be heard, to have his advice acted on or, and more alarming, to have the advice and predictions tested. The Wessex RHB and the Department of Health and Social Security agreed to test the feasibility of the recommendations for children arising from these data.

Two living-units of 20–25 places, designed to provide for *all* residential care needs for *all* of the mentally handicapped children from a total population of 100,000 (one half of 200,000) have now been set up – one in Southampton and one in Portsmouth. These units, like all other wards of existing subnormality hospitals in Wessex, are administered by the Coldeast and Tatchbury Mount HMC. However, they are situated in the centre of the areas served, and therefore near to the children's families. The children are cared for by staff whose main skills are in child care.[1] The front line medical care is provided by a local general practitioner, at two sessions per week. Additional help is provided by a local authority medical officer, social workers, educational psychologist as well as by the parents and local volunteers. A physiotherapist does two sessions per week. The consultant in mental handicap is responsible for the overall care of the children. Other specialist medical care is sought when necessary by the GP as it would be for children living at home. Half of the children, those acceptable to the local training schools for the mentally handicapped, attend in the same way as children living in their own homes.

This is an experimental evaluation of this form of care. After initial assessments of *all* of the SSN children in these towns and their families, children living on the experimental side of the towns were transferred to the new units either from existing hospitals or from their own homes. The children living on the other side of the town are the 'control' children, as are matched children living at home. We have not yet assessed the progress made by all of the children or by their families. However, some early findings have some illustrative value.

This is a trial of feasibility. It had been predicted by some that units of this sort could not work because:

it would be impossible to find suitable sites, because of local neighbourhood opposition;

it would be impossible to find and retain staff;

the admission of children would have to be selective, i.e. only CAN children or those not needing 'skilled medical and nursing care', as in the Brooklands experiment conducted by Professor Tizard, would be admitted. The severely physically handicapped, 'non-responsive' children and those presenting severe behaviour disorders would not be containable in the new units, and would have to be excluded and returned to the existing hospitals. If not excluded, the severely behaviour disordered children would harm the frail children and upset the entire programme;

the majority of children in hospital are helpless, non-responsive idiots who would be incapable of appreciating their environment or inherently destructive of the fabric of the building;

if the admissions were non-selective, it would become impossible to avoid in the new units anti-therapeutic qualities of care found by Raynes and King (1968) in existing hospitals for the mentally handicapped, such as block treatment, where residents do everything simultaneously and in large groups, getting up, dressing, toileting, eating, recreating and so on. Rigidity of routine would mean that exactly the same activities would go on irrespective of the day of the week or the month or season of the year. Depersonalisation would result from the residents not having personal clothing, toys or effects, and social distance would continue if staff wear uniforms, eat and live away from the residents and seldom communicate with the residents other than to give orders or to intervene in crises. Staff move from one unit to another at frequent intervals;

the running costs would be prohibitive;

the administrative problems would be considerable;

the original statistics would not be valid in practice, i.e. the characteristics of the real children would be very different from those suggested by the statistics.

Experience in the Wessex experiment

It has been possible, as a result of collaboration between officers of the Regional Hospital Board, Hospital Management Committee and Local Authority Planning and Health Officials to find sites for children's and adult hostels. One is in a residential area, one on the site of a centrally situated psychiatric hospital for the mentally ill, two on district general hospital sites and one on a local authority site. No opposition and some support was encountered in one area where a public meeting was called. Minor opposition, over-ruled by the council, was encountered after a public day of enquiries to the planning department in one area.

Minor opposition, overcome after explanations, was encountered from within the medical profession itself in relation to one hospital site. In one area, planning committee permission to build on the site of an existing hospital was reversed by the council after a deputation led by that hospital's chaplain was heard by the council. It is significant that in this town, local neighbourhood soundings by the planning officers had shown that the neighbours were in favour of the unit being built by 84 to two against.

No major difficulty has so far been found in recruiting staff.

No child has so far been excluded from either of the two units after admission. One child from the eastern half of Southampton, however, could not be transferred to the unit from an existing hospital. She has fairly frequent attacks of status epilepticus during which she requires an injection of an anti-convulsant. The Southampton unit has no staff member who is legally qualified to give such an injection. This child is much more able than most of the children in the unit and has no severe behaviour disorders.

Thus, the absence of nursing staff qualified to give injections from these units, effectively prevents the admission of one out of 40 children at present receiving hospital care.

There have been no major problems arising

from children with severe behaviour disorders, children with multiple physical handicaps or from caring in the same unit for children with a wide range of handicaps. Very little damage has occurred to the domestic furnishing and equipment. Carpets remain undamaged and in good condition in spite of the presence of incontinent children. In addition, children who required feeding or had, in the existing hospitals, to be tied to their chairs at meal times because of their tendency to wander or steal food from others, were found on arrival at the new units to be able to feed themselves and to be left untied to chairs because there were hostel staff sitting at the table eating with them who could quickly intervene and correct inappropriate behaviours.

Children becoming seriously acutely ill have been quickly and easily admitted by the GP for short periods to the local paediatric hospital. In addition, children referred by the GP for orthopaedic advice have had tenotomies performed and have been fitted with appropriate appliances.

No child has been found to fit the descriptions of 'helpless idiot', 'vegetable' or 'non-responsive' in spite of the fact that only a minority have speech or can even score on an IQ test. All are in need of and are capable of responding to individual training programmes on operant conditioning lines but lack of expertise and insufficient staff (in spite of the unusually generous staff ratios) prevent these from being fully implemented.

The staff ratio allows the avoidance of 'block-treatment'; 'rigidity of routine'; as well as of 'social distance' — in addition to the absence of uniforms, staff on duty eat together with the children and once recruited with the collaboration of the head of the unit remain attached only to that unit.

'Depersonalisation' is also being avoided because the staff ratio ensures that adequate care can be taken of the individual clothes worn every day by the children. Staff have limited authority to purchase clothes from certain wholesalers with exchequer monies, and from retail firms with children's pocket money where the doctor prescribes sufficient to allow this. In addition, parents are giving and are encouraged by staff to give much of the personal clothing which can be adequately stored in individual cupboards (not lockers), carefully laundered in washing machines provided on the living units. The work of storing,

maintaining and laundering clothes is done jointly by child-care and domestic staff.

The running costs of the new units have still to be carefully analysed. Preliminary results in Southampton suggest that they are about £29/week/child. For children attending local authority training centres there is an additional cost of £6 to £7 per week. This compares with costs of about £28/child/week in a children's annexe of an existing hospital.

Survey estimates

The administrative problems are also being examined. No major difficulties have arisen so far, and the HMC's and RHB's administrators do not appear to be daunted by the prospect of having more such units.

The original survey estimates of the characteristics of the hospitalised children from a total population of 100,000 agree remarkably well with the actual characteristics of the hostel children found in existing hospitals and whose families live in the areas served by the hostels.

Where the children are slightly younger than expected, the proportion of non-ambulant children is higher and the proportion of CAN children slightly lower than expected. The number of severely incontinent children and those with severe behaviour disorders is as expected.

It is worth remembering that these children represent a cross-section of *all* children at present in hospitals for the retarded. They therefore include the most difficult and profoundly retarded of *all* the children from the area.

In addition, these are the most difficult and retarded adults of the future. The prevalence of SSN adults is increasing. However, the increase is largest among the CANS while among the N-A it is virtually stationary (Kushlick and Cox 1969).

It is not here suggested that this is the only or the ideal method of providing such care.

It is used only to provide some pointers as to why important components of what is agreed to constitute high quality care are attainable in these new units, but so difficult to implement in existing hospitals.

The Wessex Regional Hospital Board has now accepted for *all* hospitals for the retarded the policies originally worked out for the new units. We have been observing the difficulties of trying to implement them in existing hospitals.

Staffing difficulties

These findings may be helpful. The evidence suggests that all new residential facilities would be most usefully developed in the areas where the families live, and where the complementary services exist. However, it will take some time before such alternatives are provided, and in the meantime existing hospitals will continue to provide the bulk of care. Steps are needed urgently to make it possible for them to do so.

Moreover, there are signs that efforts to get rid quickly of the 'scapegoat' problems of 'overcrowding' by building what is euphemistically referred to as 'temporary' accommodation on existing hospital sites could well exacerbate the real problems and further delay alternative action.

The evidence suggests that the key problems in existing hospitals arise from two interrelated difficulties. The first is staff shortage on the living units. (The Wessex Regional Hospital Board's recommended staffing levels needed to achieve reasonable care are shown in Table 37.2.) They have not yet been achieved in the hostels but are lower in the hospitals. This shortage of personnel is aggravated by their dislocation from the areas where the families live and from which other important services are organised.

Table 37.1 shows an existing hospital with living-units serving geographical areas within the hospital's catchment area. Hospitals, however, are never organised in this way.

First, catchment areas of existing hospitals have often changed during the long lifetime of the hospitals. Thus hospitalised people from any geographical area are likely to be found, not in one, but in a number of hospitals, often scattered over many miles outside the area from which the residents come. This is particularly the case where hospitals select by sex, men only or women and children only, or by incapacity, only high grades or low grades. Over 500 of the 3,000 hospitalised retarded from the Wessex Region were in hospitals 60 to 100 miles outside the region of two million people.

Table 37.2. Recommended staff levels in each type of living unit

Children's living unit

Residents		Care staff* Day	Night	Domestic staff
NA	12	2.4		= 40 × 6.1 hrs/wk
ALL SB	10	5.0		= 244 hrs/wk
SI	6	1.2		ie 7 establishment
CAN	12	2.4		
	40	11.0	2 at any time	

Establishment = (11 × 2.6) + (2 × 2.4)
= 28.6 + 4.8
= 33.4
= 1:1.2

SSN adult living unit

Residents		Care staff Day	Night	Domestic staff
NA	3	0.6		
ALL SB	7			= (13 × 6.1) = 79 hrs/wk
SI	3	5		(27 × 3.5) = 95 hrs/wk
CAN	27	1.4		= 174 hrs/wk
	40	7	2 at any time	

Establishment = (7 × 2.6) + (2 × 2.4)
= 18.2 + 4.8
= 23
= 1:1.7

MSN adult living unit

Residents		Care staff Day	Night	Domestic staff
NA	2	0.4		
ALL SB	4	2.0		= 7 × 6.1 = 42.7 hrs/wk
SI	1	0.2		45 × 3.5 = 158 hrs/wk
CAN	45	2.2		= 200 hrs/wk
	52	4.8	1 at any time	ie 5.6 establishment

Establishment = (4.8 × 2.6) + 2.4
= 12.5 + 2.4
= 14.9
= 1:3.4

*Care staff = nurses, child care staff, assistants etc.

Second, within the hospital itself living-units take people, not on a geographical basis, but on functional criteria, i.e. wards for so-called 'low grades', the physically handicapped, the psychotic or 'disturbed' and so on.

Not only does this policy create collections of the most difficult people with the most bizarre and disagreeable behaviour, it also dislocates caring staff, the nurses, from continuing relations with the key people outside the hospital, whether these are professionals or parents. Because the nursing staff are cut off from the key personnel outside, decisions appropriately made by nursing staff at living-unit level must be referred centrally to people off the living-unit. The nurses cannot possibly, because of the area involved, make contact with the families of handicapped people still living at home. Moreover, Local Authority personnel, bewildered by the geographical spread of their clients over many living-units and hospitals, are unable to plan and develop their services on a rational basis.

The absence of overall information leads to conflicts on which agency, hospital or Local Authority, is responsible for providing services, on who needs 'specialist medical and nursing care', and contradictory assertions as to who needs what service continue untested.

Professional staff availability

The present crisis in residential care for the retarded is now very serious. We cannot afford any longer to view residential care separately from the care of the handicapped at home. Nor can we afford to waste effort by allowing the staff concerned inside and outside these facilities to go about their work in separate, water-tight compartments.

Table 37.3 shows the total professional hospital staff available per living-unit of a 'low' hospital for the mentally handicapped in England and Wales on a week-day (Kushlick 1970). 'Low' means the 14 hospitals in England and Wales with the lowest nurse-resident ratio — these 14 hospitals include the largest and most prestigious hospitals for the mentally handicapped in England and Wales. An average living-unit will have, as we have seen, between 40 and 50 residents.

These people are, on average, being looked after at any time by 2 3/7ths nurses. The staff-resident ratios on adult living-units will be lower than this,

while those on children's units will be slightly higher. Pauline Morris (1969) found no children's units where there were at any time of the day more than one staff to five children.

In addition, virtually all decisions concerned with admissions, discharge training, therapy, pocket money etc. of residents, needs or contacts with the social services outside the hospital are made through or by the 1/14 consultant in charge of all of the residents in the hospital.

The first column of Table 37.3 shows the key professional staff available in a total population of 400,000 outside the hospitals for the mentally handicapped. In column 2 these have been divided by 14 as if they had been shared out equally among the 14 living-units in a manner that assumes that they have collectively the responsibility among their other commitments, for looking after the residents only on a single living-unit.

Thus the total number of handicapped people cared for by the personnel in the first two columns of Table 37.3 can be seen from Table 37.1. These would include the people on a single living-unit, plus those from the same area who are at home (Table 37.1). Even if the people in column 2 of Table 37.3 could only visit their living-unit once a week, or even once a month, they could increase many times the overall existing provision of professional skills to that living-unit. This is particularly the case in relation to medical and social work resources, but also in the others.

Moreover, a substantial improvement to existing conditions could be made if only one of the ten possible GP's, and only one of the three possible social workers were to collaborate with the hospital unit; each unit could then have its own GP and social workers. Since a unit for 40 children serves a total population of 200,000, the possible contribution to a single children's unit from 'outside' personnel can be seen in the first column of Table 37.3. This would include two consultant paediatricians or child psychiatrists and 13 child care officers, half the numbers in column 1.

Additional resources

For those who doubt the validity of these statistics, it may be of interest that the two children's experimental units which I mentioned earlier have their own GP and continuous working contacts not only with the consultant paediatricians from the local district general hospital but also with the senior mental health social worker, senior medical officer for mental health and the educational psychologist from the Local Authority. In addition, decisions concerning admissions, discharges, education, special investigation and treatment are taken regularly by case conferences operating at living-unit level. Among other personnel available are, of course, also the residents' families and local volunteers.

What prevents this type of concentrated collaboration between the staff inside existing hospitals and those outside? It is often said by each side that the other is not keen on, or actively obstructs, such collaboration. It is likely that this is partly the case. Thus, the Chairman of the Royal Medico-Psychological Association, MD Section, has warned of the dangers of 'interdisciplinary egalitarianism' (Shapiro 1970).

The evidence, however, suggests that even if all concerned were to favour this type of joint activity, it would at present be very difficult to implement. Residents from the same geographical area are now scattered far and wide in different hospitals many miles from one another, and from their local areas. Alternatively, they are on different wards or living-units of the same hospital. For example, a social worker from Southampton wishing to talk to the staff caring for *all* of the 19 institutionalised children from east Southampton can now do so by making only one visit to a unit one mile from his office, or by means of one telephone call to the unit. Before this unit was set up, the same social worker would have had to visit seven different living-units at five different hospitals or private homes over a distance of some 60 to 70 miles — the hospital living-units have not even got telephones with lines to outside

Table 37.3 A comparison of professional staff available outside NHS hospitals for the mentally subnormal and those within such hospitals

	Average staff available outside hospitals for the MH for a Total Population of 400,000	Average staff available per living unit on a weekday (number of residents = 40–50) In a total population of 400,000 there are 14 living units	
		Outside hospitals* for MS	Within 'low' hospitals for MS

Medical	160 GPs
	20 LHAMOs
	14 Phys. or Psych.
	4 Paed. or
	  Ch. Psych.
		10 GPs
		1½ LHAMOs
		1 Phys. or Psych.
		²⁄₇ths Paed. or
		  Ch. Psych.
		(2 per children's unit)
			$\frac{1}{14}$th consultant
			
			$\frac{1}{10}$th other

Psychologists	4	²⁄₇ths	$\frac{1}{28}$th
Social workers	12–20 MHSW 20–28 other 26 CCO	1–1¾ths MHSW 1¾ths–2 other 2 CCO (13 per children's unit)	$\frac{1}{42}$nd
Teachers and occupational therapists	36 (20/children's unit 16/adult unit) 16/adult unit)	2½ (1¾ths children's unit 1¹⁄₇th adult unit	¾ths (2/children's unit $\frac{1}{6}$th adult unit)
nurses	72–80 HN 48–64 HV	5¼th–5⁵⁄₇ths HN 3¾ths–4²⁄₇ths HV	2²⁄₇ths

*Calculated by dividing numbers in first column by 14.

Key:
GP	General practitioner
LHAMH	Local health authority medical officer
Phys.	General physician
Psych.	General psychiatrist
MHSW	Mental health social worker
CCO	Child care officer
HN	Home nurse
HV	Health visitor
'Low hospitals'	14 hospitals with the lowest nurse-patient ratio in England and Wales. Includes the most prestigious hospitals.

he hospital. It is not hard to see why his predecessors did not try to visit regularly.

The evidence suggests that relocation on a geographical basis of residents in existing hospitals, as shown in Table 37.2, would allow us to unlock a major potential of personnel resources. Without these additional resources existing hospitals may well continue to flounder because of the tremendous tasks facing such a small number of personnel if the job is to be done adequately.

Other advantages of geographical relocation of residents within existing hospitals might be:

the spreading out of the most dependent and difficult residents among those more able, who could also contribute to their care;

bridging the traditional gap at operational level between home and institutional care —

parents from any area would know which unit serves their particular area, and the living-unit staff might get to know the families with children still at home in that area;

bridging the gap between hospital and local authority and GP services — GP's, paediatricians, social workers, teachers, home nurses and health visitors from an area might know the unit and the staff serving their particular area;

local councillors and parents' societies might also be able to identify with one or two living-units or wards, and take a special interest in achieving, maintaining and improving standards on that unit.

We are coming to think that advantages originally ascribed to the size of the living-units, small better than large, are in fact much more related to the numbers of staff available to care for the residents on the living-unit, and the ability of the staff to take decisions on the many aspects of the day-to-day lives of the residents and their families.

Location of residents on living-units by geographical area appears an important ingredient to achieving both of these aims.

Overcrowding

There is, however, an opinion that existing hospitals would overcome all or many of their difficulties, if only the 'overcrowding' were reduced.

To this end, it is suggested that the immediate 'decanting' of residents of 'overcrowded' wards into 'temporary' buildings erected at the existing hospital is more important even than increasing staff-resident ratios on the living-units. On this scale of priorities, geographical relocation of residents, or establishing links with general hospital or local authority personnel outside the existing hospital feature very low, if indeed they feature at all.

If existing low staffing levels encourage rigid routines involving 'block treatment' because even existing rooms cannot be staffed simultaneously, and everybody has to be kept in only one of the available rooms, rapid provision of extra accommodation without increasing staff establishment, will merely spread available staff more thinly and aggravate the existing negative characteristics of ward routine.

By this measure, residents will be still further randomly dispersed, and the 'overcrowding', now the main stimulus to improvement and change in the facilities, will have been 'relieved'. Calls for further resources needed to follow up the 'temporary' moves may thus be more easily neglected.

Conclusion

The needs of the mentally handicapped at home and their families are intimately related with those of the people in residential care. Moreover, the complex of medical, educational, welfare, nursing or care skills required to implement policy are the same in both situations. It appears to be in the interests of the people providing the services to collaborate in their provision and use.

While the new accommodation needed urgently in the areas where the families live, will allow this form of collaboration to take place comparatively easily, there is every reason to believe that geographical relocation of residents in existing hospitals, together with staff increases at living-unit level, will permit dramatic improvements in the quality of care in existing hospitals, and the setting up of a truly comprehensive and dynamic service. The need is no less for the profoundly retarded than for anyone else.

Finally, the problem of mental handicap looks on close examination to have much more in common with the major problems facing mainstream medicine and social welfare than has been recognised before, namely the problems of helping the chronic handicapped person and his family.

Table 37.4 compares the size of the problem of mental handicap in a total population of 100,000 with those found among the elderly in the same

Table 37.4 Total population 100,000

Elderly (aged 65+)			Mentally subnormal (all ages)		
Bedfast	350	(220)	21	(8)	Non-ambulant
Confined to home	1,410	(1,300)	31	(7)	Severe behaviour problems
Mobile outside with difficulty	1,020	(910)	14	(4)	Severely incontinent
None of above	9,240	(9,100)	247	(142)	None of above

Brackets show those living at home

population. The figures on the elderly are taken from the national study undertaken by Townsend and Wedderburn (1965). The figures on the mentally handicapped are taken from the Wessex Survey (King and Raynes 1968).

Since more is known about the size and nature of the problems of mental handicap than about the other conditions, and since mental handicap is a comparatively small and discrete problem, the retarded present us with an opportunity for planning and developing solutions equally applic able to these other problems. The personne involved outside of the hospitals for the mentally handicapped are also intimately involved with these other problems, and valid solutions for the retarded could make important contributions in these other areas.

NOTE

1. The warden of the first unit is a nursery nurse and the deputy has had experience in Local Authority hostels by the mentally handicapped. In the second unit the warden is a paediatric trained nurse, and the deputy is a mentally nandicapped trained nurse.

REFERENCES

Department of Health and Social Security, 1969, *Report of the Committee of Inquiry into Allegations of Illtreatment of Patients and Other Irregularities at the Ely Hospital, Cardiff*. Command 2975, London, HMSO.

Department of Health and Social Security 1971, *Better Services for the Mentally Handicapped*, Command 4683, HMSO.

KING, R. D. and RAYNES, N. V., 1968, *Social Science and Medicine*, 2, p. 41.

KUSHLICK, A. 1966, *Social Psychiatry*, 1, p. 73.

KUSHLICK, A. 1970, *Journal of the Royal Society of Health*, 90, p. 225.

KUSHLICK, A. *The Care of the Profoundly Retarded Person*, In press. To be published by Nuffield Hospital Trust Fund.

KUSHLICK, A. and COX, G. R., 1969, in *Provision of Further Accommodation for the Mentally Subnormal*. Wessex Regional Hospital Board.

LEWIS, E. O., 1929, *The Report on the Mental Deficiency Committee being a Joint Committee of the Board of Control: Part IV, – Report on an Investigation into the Incidence of Mental Deficiency in six areas, 1925–27*, London, HMSO.

MONCRIEF, J., 1966, *Mental Subnormality in London, A survey of Community Care*. London, PEP.

MORRIS, P., 1969, *Put Away*, London, Routledge and Kegan Paul.

1970, *Report on Measures to Improve the Hospital Services for the Mentally Handicapped*. Wessex Regional Hospital Board.

SHAPIRO, A. 1970, *British Journal of Psychiatry*, 116, p. 353.

TIZARD, J. and GRAD, J. C., 1961, *The Mentally Handicapped and Their Families,* London, OUP.

TOWNSEND, P. and WEDDERBURN, D. 1965, *The Aged in the Welfare State.* London, Bell.

38. Residential provision for mentally handicapped adults *

ALISON C. ROSEN
Formerly Research Psychologist, Department of Social
and Preventive Medicine, University of Manchester.

1. Introduction

The Mental Health Act, 1959, placed a duty on local authorities to provide a comprehensive range of community services for the mentally handicapped. Most authorities have concentrated on providing training facilities as a first priority, and the demand for training centre places has to some extent been met. The need for residential accommodation is, however, still overwhelmingly great. At the end of 1969, according to the White Paper, *Better Services for the Mentally Handicapped* (Cmnd. 4683, 1971), only 43 of the 174 local authorities in England and Wales had residential accommodation of their own for both mentally handicapped adults and mentally handicapped children. Twenty-eight authorities still had no residential accommodation of their own for either age-group. Hence the renewed call in *Better Services for the Mentally Handicapped* for local authorities to provide such residential accommodation. One authority that responded in more than a cursory manner to the earlier call of the Mental Health Act, 1959, to provide a range of services for the mentally handicapped was Lancashire County Council. During the 1960s Lancashire County Council set up a variety of services for the mentally handicapped, including 16 mixed-sex hostels for mentally handicapped adults. A research project was begun in 1965 to evaluate the care provided by these hostels and the situation of their residents as compared to that of patients in

*From G. McLachlan (ed.) (1972) *Approaches to action: a symposium on services for the mentally ill and handicapped*, London, Oxford University Press for the Nuffield Provincial Hospitals Trust, chapter 7, pp. 71–80.

mental subnormality hospitals. The observations of the present paper are based in the main on the findings of this research project from 1965 to 1968. These findings will be related wherever possible to current thinking on services for the mentally handicapped as set out in the recent White Paper.

2. Intake of hostel residents according to their previous place of residence

At the inception of the Lancashire hostel-building programme it was thought that large numbers of residents would enter the hostels from mental subnormality hospitals. The number of patients eventually discharged to the hostels was, however, considerably less than originally anticipated. This was due in the first place to a lack of agreement and understanding between hospital and local authority personnel as to the nature and purpose of hostels and the sort of patient who might benefit from hostel residence. Hospitals tended to put forward patients in their 50s, 60s, or even 70s, often with a long history of institutionalization. For such patients transfer to a hostel might be seen as a reward for years of work on the wards. Most hostels, however, were hoping for younger patients with reasonable prospects of rehabilitation and employment in the community at large. Hospitals seemed disinclined to put forward younger patients due to fears of sexually promiscuous behaviour in establishments that were to be mixed-sex. Hospitals seemed disinclined also to put forward lower-grade (severely subnormal) patients on the assumption that such patients would not adapt to a hostel environment. This again excluded from consideration many patients whom the local authority might have been willing to accept. Had there been more precise specification of the aims of the hostel service and the sort of person being catered for, much of this confusion might have been avoided.

The number of hostel residents discharged from subnormality hospitals was further limited by hostels not always being willing to accept patients unless the hospital in question guaranteed to readmit them if they proved unsuitable as hostel residents. Hospitals were often not willing to give such a guarantee. Joint planning and co-operation between hospital and local authority personnel as advocated in *Better Services for the Mentally Handicapped* should do much to obviate this difficulty.

A third factor limiting the number of patients discharged to the Lancashire hostels from mental subnormality hospitals was the demand for hostel places from mentally handicapped people living at home (with one or both parents), with relatives or friends, or in other residential establishments in the community (children's hostels, voluntary homes, etc.). The proportion of residents admitted to the Lancashire hostels from the community at large increased from 31 per cent of all admissions in 1965 to 69 per cent of all admissions in 1967 (Campbell 1968c). The main reason for admissions to the hostels from the community at large was the loss through death or, less often, long-term hospitalization of the key person (usually the resident's mother) previously caring for the resident. Twenty-three per cent of the 186 admissions direct from the community to the 14 Lancashire County Council hostels operative at the beginning of 1968 fell into this category. Other major reasons for admissions to the hostels direct from the community at large were incapacity or illness of the key person previously caring for the resident (17 per cent of all admissions from the community at large up to the beginning of 1968), and behaviour problems such that the resident had become beyond this person's control (16 per cent of all admissions from the community at large up to the beginning of 1968). The 'behaviour problems' leading to hostel admission consisted mainly of aggressive outbursts and temper tantrums. Significantly more severely subnormal (as opposed to mildly subnormal) residents were admitted to the hostels from the community at large than from mental subnormality hospitals,

and residents admitted from the community at large were also significantly younger than those from mental subnormality hospitals ($p < 0.01$ in each case). There was also a tendency ($0.10 > p > 0.05$) for residents admitted from the community at large to come from a higher social class, as judged by father's occupation, than residents admitted from mental subnormality hospitals, which suggests that middle-class families are more willing to place a mentally handicapped relative in residential care when this takes the form of a community-based hostel rather than the traditional mental subnormality hospital.

Admitting residents to hostels directly from the community at large can be regarded as a 'preventive' use of hostels, ie it prevents mentally handicapped people in need of residential accommodation but not in need of hospital facilities or nursing care from being admitted to mental subnormality or other hospitals simply for want of anywhere else to go. Should the person's health or behaviour deteriorate then admission to a hostel may prevent admission to a hospital only temporarily, but for the majority of residents admitted to the Lancashire hostels direct from the community the hostels have become long-term homes. Admission of residents from the community at large rather than from mental subnormality hospitals has continued since 1967, for whenever a hostel vacancy arises there is invariably someone living at home or elsewhere for whom hostel care seems highly desirable. In view of this there is a risk that until more hostels are provided the claims of hospital patients potentially suitable for discharge to hostels will be disregarded. Such patients may well remain on waiting-lists for transfer to hostels indefinitely.

3. Criteria and procedure for selecting hostel residents

There is no general agreement from one local authority to the next as to criteria for selecting residents for mental health hostels. Those in charge of admissions to any particular hostel however tend to have very definite ideas as to the sort of person who will (or, more often, will not) fit amicably into the social organization of that hostel. Few hostels (the Lancashire hostels included) accept residents who are incontinent or who are not able to go out to work or to attend a training centre or other such establishment during the week. Some hostels set an upper age limit for admissions (for example 50 years of age), and some hostels will not accept residents with a history of epilepsy. Some hostels cater only for the mildly subnormal; others cater only for the severely subnormal; still others take in residents of all degrees of handicap. It would be foolish to try and lay down rigid or comprehensive criteria for the selection of hostel residents since different hostels will be catering for different needs. It would, however, be advantageous if people were less ready automatically to exclude certain categories of people from consideration as hostel residents. Thus Kushlick (1970) has challenged the widespread belief that hostels are not intended for or should not be expected to take in residents who are severely incontinent, or who have severe behaviour disorders, or who are unable to attend a training centre or to go out to work but simply 'stay at home' all day.

With regard to the procedure for the selection of hostel residents this is typically carried out by medical, administrative, or social work staff. Residential staff, the people most intimately involved with the residents, are typically not involved at all. Thus Apte (1966) in a study of 25 short-stay hostels for the mentally ill found that in only 6 of these 25 was the warden given any say in the selection of residents. Four of these 6 hostels were run by voluntary bodies, which characteristically give more responsibility to wardens than do local authorities. Many hostel wardens would like a say in resident selection but the objection to this is that wardens may have personal prejudices against candidates put forward as potential residents. While this may be true such prejudices are not going to disappear simply because someone else does the selecting, and staff and residents do have to live together. Hence it would seem desirable for wardens to play some part in the selection procedure.

4. Residential accommodation for the aged mentally handicapped

The majority of local authority hostels for mentally handicapped adults accept residents from the age of 16 upwards with no upper age limit, although there tends to be a bias against admitting people who are 'too old'. Residents have, however, been admitted who are in their 70s. Hostel staff often feel that whereas they can 'do something'

with younger residents in the way of social rehabilitation and the development of personal and social skills they 'can't do anything' with older residents other than provide them with a place in which to live. Older residents are thus often seen by staff as 'less rewarding'. To admit only younger residents, however, leads to problems of its own. If the hostel is newly established, and is to be a long-term home for most of the residents, then in time it will be a hostel of predominantly aged residents all of whom may be making considerable and perhaps excessive demands on staff time and patience. And if there is an upper age limit on admissions (typically 50 years of age) what is to happen to mentally handicapped people older than this who are in need of residential care? Are they to be hospitalized even although not in need of hospital facilities or nursing care? Or do we set up special hostels or residential homes for the aged mentally handicapped? Ordinary old people's homes do not seem a likely prospect for large numbers of the aged mentally handicapped due to the demand for places in such homes from non-mentally handicapped people, although some local authorities do set aside a proportion of places in their old people's homes for the mentally infirm. The Lancashire hostels manage to cope adequately with a resident population of widely varying ages and older residents are not required or expected to leave unless or until they are in need of nursing or other care that the hostel cannot provide. Problems can arise, however, when older residents become incapable of putting in a full day's work at the training centre, although they are otherwise still quite acceptable as hostel residents. Some rearrangement of staff hours and duties could enable such people to stay at home in the hostel all day, possibly helping with the housework if they are sufficiently capable and so inclined. It is surely anomalous that mentally handicapped people over retirement age are not able officially to 'retire' but must continue to attend a training centre five days a week in order to qualify for hostel residence.

5. Residents' contacts with family and friends

One argument in favour of community care for the mentally handicapped is that in the community a person can maintain contact with family and friends. Mental subnormality hospitals tend to be geographically remote, or set back from the road and away from the public gaze. In either case this fosters social isolation. It is possible, however, for residents in community-based hostels or residential homes to be just as socially isolated as patients in the most remote mental subnormality hospital if they neither receive nor pay any visits. A study was undertaken in Lancashire to determine whether mentally subnormal adults transferred from mental subnormality hospitals to the Lancashire hostels were less socially isolated from family, friends, and the local community than comparable mentally subnormal adults (matched for age, sex, grade of subnormality, and length of institutionalization) still in hospital (Campbell 1968b). The one variable on which the two groups differed significantly was the distance of their next-of-kin from their present place of residence. The hostel group lived significantly closer to their next-of-kin ($p < 0.001$), it being county policy to place residents in hostels as close to their own home areas as possible. The hostel group had significantly more contact with family, friends, and the local community than did the hospital group ($p < 0.001$, $p < 0.05$, and $p < 0.001$ respectively). Hence, on the argument that social isolation is in itself detrimental to mental health, these results can be taken as a vindication of the policy of community care for the mentally handicapped. The most striking thing, however, about the contacts of both hostel residents and hospital patients with outside friends was that 76 per cent of the former group and 92 per cent of the latter group had no outside friends at all.

With regard to contacts with family a later study (Campbell 1969) found that for residents with families definitely interested in their well-being (as rated by hostel and local authority personnel) family contacts were significantly more frequent for residents with next-of-kin less than 10 miles from the hostel than for residents with next-of-kin more than 10 miles from the hostel ($p < 0.001$). This amply vindicates the policy of having hostels as locally based as possible as far as residents with families definitely interested in their well-being are concerned. For residents with families not particularly interested or definitely not interested in their well-being, family contacts are infrequent in any case, and independent of the distance of the hostel from the resident's next-of-kin ($p > 0.20$). This is not to say, however, that one need not worry about placing these residents

in hostels near their own home areas. Although a resident's family may show little interest in him at one stage there is always the possibility that their interest may revive, and if this happens then geographical proximity would facilitate contact. And even if a hostel resident entirely lacks effective kin he will still have more meaningful contacts with his own home area than anywhere else.

6. Views of the mentally handicapped themselves

In the summer of 1966 there were 316 residents (252 mentally handicapped and 64 mentally ill) in the 13 Lancashire County Council hostels for mentally disordered adults then in operation. Of these residents 57 per cent had come to the hostels from hospitals, 25 per cent from their own homes, and the remaining 18 per cent from other residential accommodation in the community at large. Of these 316 residents, 304 were interviewed in an attempt to assess their attitudes and feelings with regard to their present and past situations, and with regard to the type of residential care they themselves might prefer (Campbell 1968a). Of former hospital patients, 88 per cent preferred hostels to hospital. Typical of the reasons given for such a preference were 'you are more free here'; 'you get better food here'; 'they lock you up in hospital'. Hostel accommodation was also preferred to other residential accommodation in the community. Hostel accommodation was not preferred to living at home ('home is of course best of all', as one resident put it). A longing to live at home was expressed to a like degree by all residents irrespective of their previous place of residence and irrespective of whether they had a home any more. Even residents who had been in hospital for more than thirty years and who had had no contact with their families for many years expressed a desire to go back home. Belief in home and family seemingly transcends all abandonment, rejection, and neglect.

Each of the hostels had an adult training centre alongside, which the majority of residents (90 per cent) attended. Of those attending training centres 55 per cent would have preferred to be in outside employment, mainly for such reasons as 'there is more money in a job'; 'you can meet new people out at work'; 'the things we do here in the training centre are dull and boring and not proper work'. Many of the residents expressing a desire for a job were certainly being unrealistic, but a considerable number did seem fit for outside employment (and were acknowledged as being thus fit by training centre staff) given a suitable job and a 'sympathetic employer'. More attention could be paid to the finding of jobs for the mentally handicapped, whether hostel residents or not, for having a job, no matter how menial, helps prevent the segregation of the handicapped and enables the handicapped to feel more normal members of society.

7. The ultimate purpose of services for the mentally handicapped

Official statements concerning services for the mentally handicapped (Ministry of Health 1959, 1963) lead one to the conclusion that the ultimate purpose of such services is to enable the mentally handicapped to lead as normal a life as possible and to develop their potential, however limited, to the utmost. The extent to which local authority and other services achieve either or both of these goals is a matter of some consequence: if they are not being achieved, or only partly achieved, then some reorganization of services may be desirable. In this connection it has been observed (Campbell 1971) that in many hostels staff tend to do things for the residents (washing their hair, lacing their shoes, etc.) that many residents could with training, or even without training, do for themselves. Staff tend also to supervise residents' activities (bathing, dressing, leisure-time pursuits) unnecessarily, in the sense that the residents are demonstrably capable of undertaking these activities satisfactorily without supervision. This tendency for staff to do things for residents that the residents might well do for themselves is acknowledged by some hostel wardens, but it is apparently a very difficult thing to eradicate. Most staff have no special training for the job, and junior staff in particular (who often have most to do with the residents) tend to have but a limited appreciation of the over-all aims of hostel care. The net result is that the residents' independence in many areas is quashed rather than nurtured and this effectively prevents them from developing their potential to the full.

With regard to leading as normal a life as possible, staff routines and administrative convenience can militate against hostel residents doing various household chores that people normally do

at home. People living at home can usually make a cup of tea if they feel like it, for example, which is not always possible in a hostel. A further point is that few people living at home have their place of work on their very doorstep, within their own grounds. It has always been official policy to have hostels and training centres on separate sites, but in many cases the difficulty or the expense of finding separate sites has led to the two establishments being built adjacent. This may be administratively convenient, but it is unfortunate from the point of view of providing hostel residents with as normal an environment as possible.

8. Misplacement of residents in mental health hostels

The White Paper, *Better Services for the Mentally Handicapped*, notes that lack of experience in the running of hostels may lead to hostel places being misused in the sense that people are in them who could manage with far less support. It can also happen that people who could manage with far less support are occupying hostel places simply because the hostel has been successful in achieving its aim of developing the independence of residents who were initially in need of a sheltered environment, and no real thought has been given to what happens to these residents now. It is ultimately against the residents' own best interests to stay in a hostel if he no longer needs the support that a hostel provides. Not only is such a person stunting his own potential development but he is also blocking a place that could usefully be taken up by someone else. One problem that arises here is that hostels are generally so comfortable in material terms that residents can understandably be reluctant to leave. It is also not unknown for staff to discourage residents who could lead a more independent life from leaving a hostel, due either to a misunderstanding on the part of staff as to the whole aim of hostel care or to a misguided belief that one ought not to 'break up the happy home'. What seems needed here is some sort of review mechanism whereby residents are periodically assessed and once deemed fit for a more independent way of life they would then *have* to move on to some less sheltered form of accommodation provided either by the local authority or privately. The need for a range of residential accommodation has long been recognized, and one form of alternative accommodation that might suit such people is a group home, ie a residential home for perhaps 6—10 people, without residential staff, but with some support and supervision from social work or other agencies. A number of such homes exist for the mentally ill but relatively few for the mentally handicapped. Mentally handicapped people who have moved on from hostels to a group home are generally reported as showing marked gains in personal independence, which after all is one of the things that community care for the mentally handicapped is all about.

REFERENCES

APTE, R.,Z., 1966, 'The transitional hostel in the rehabilitation of the mentally ill', in McLachlan, G. (ed.), *Problems and Progress in Medical Care*, Second Series, pp. 155—85, Oxford University Press for the Nuffield Provincial Hospitals Trust.

CAMPBELL, A. C.*, 1968a, 'Attitudes of mentally disordered adults to community care', *British Journal of Preventive and Social Medicine*, 22, no. 2, pp. 94—9.

CAMPBELL, A. C.*, 1968b, 'Comparison of family and community contacts of mentally subnormal adults in hospital and in local authority hostels', *British Journal of Preventive and Social Medicine*, 22, no. 3, pp. 165—9.

CAMPBELL, A. C.*,1968c, 'The "preventive" use of mental health hostels', *Medical Officer*, 120, no. 10, pp. 137—9.

CAMPBELL, A.,C.*, 1969, 'Family contacts of mentally subnormal and severely subnormal adults in local authority hostels', *Medical Officer*, 122, no. 14, pp. 183—4.

CAMPBELL, A C.*, 1971, 'Aspects of personal independence of mentally subnormal and severely subnormal adults in hospital and in local authority hostels', *International Journal of Social Psychiatry*, 17, no. 4.

Department of Health and Social Security, 1971, '*Better Services for the mentally handicapped*', Cmnd 4683, London, HMSO.

KUSHLICK, A., 1970, 'Residential care for the mentally subnormal', *Royal Society of Health Journal*, 90, no. 5, pp. 255—61.

Ministry of Health, 1959, '*Mental Health Service*', Circular 9/59.

Ministry of Health, 1963, '*Health and Welfare: the Development of Community Care*', Cmnd 1973, London, HMSO.

Present author's maiden name.

39. Passing and denial: the problem of seeming to be normal *

ROBERT B. EDGERTON
Assistant Professor of Anthropology, Department of Psychiatry,
University of California at Los Angeles, U.S.A.

We, in our everyday affairs, regularly and easily accuse others and ourselves of stupidity. We joke about real or fancied incompetence, we estimate the IQ's of our friends and foes, we make invidious comparisons of all kinds about the intelligence of many persons with whom we come into contact. Usually we mean little by these remarks and usually neither we nor the victims of our speculations or accusations suffer very much as a result.

For the ex-patient of an institution for the mentally retarded, however, matters are very different. The ex-patient *must* take his intelligence very seriously, for he has been accused and found guilty of being so stupid that he was considered incompetent to manage his own life. As a consequence, he has been confined in an institution for the mentally incompetent. This research has shown, and our common sense would agree, that such an accusation of stupidity has a shattering impact. The stigma of having been adjudged a mental retardate is one which the ex-patients in this study reject as totally unacceptable. Hence, their lives are directed toward the fundamental purpose of denying that they are in fact mentally incompetent. These former patients must at all times attend to the practical problems of seeming to others to be competent and of convincing themselves that this is so. The label of mental retardation not only serves as a humiliating, frustrating, and discrediting stigma in the conduct

*Extract from Robert B. Edgerton, (1967) *The Cloak of Competence: Stigma in the Lives of Mentally Retarded*, University of California Press; London, Cambridge University Press, Chapters 4 and 5, pp. 144–71, 193–204.

of one's life in the community, but it also serves to lower one's self-esteem to such a nadir of worthlessness that the life of a person so labeled is scarcely worth living. Thus the 'moron' who is released from Pacific State Hospital must 'deny,' must 'pass' with himself. He cannot, and he does not, accept the official 'fact' that he is, or ever was, mentally retarded.

To understand the processes of passing and denial in the period following the ex-patients' release from the institution, we must first review prior events in the life experiences of these persons. In an earlier study, the pre-hospital and hospital careers of the same patients who formed the cohort for this research were examined (Edgerton and Sabagh 1962). It was rarely possible to reconstruct the pre-hospital biographies of these patients in adequate detail, yet it was possible to determine that their pre-hospital experiences were typically highly mortifying. These experiences commonly involved both direct and indirect communication by normal persons to the retarded person to the effect that his or her intelligence was deficient. Parents, peers, teachers, neighbors, and even strangers presented a consistent refrain of rejection and humiliation. Notwithstanding this concerted onslaught, the retardate resisted the accusation that he was mentally retarded, and he usually found allies in the form of parents or peers who would aid him in denying that his intellect was subnormal.

However, entry into Pacific State Hospital presents the retarded person with a new dilemma. Although he is by now thoroughly familiar with mortification and has probably developed means of self-defense against suggestions of mental deficit, he is surely not prepared for the experiences that the hospital will inflict upon him. The cumulative impact of the initial period of hospitalization (at the time of the research) was greatly mortifying, leaving the patient without privacy, without clear identity, without autonomy of action, without relatives, friends, or family, in a regimented and impersonal institution where everything combines to inform him that he is, in fact, mentally inadequate. A typical patient reaction is seen in the following words of a teen-age boy who was newly admitted to the institution: 'Why do I got to be here with these people? I'd rather be dead than in here' (see Edgerton and Sabagh 1962 p. 267.).

At this point, when the hospital's impact has taken full effect, the patient's self-esteem has probably reached its low point. However, at this critical point, circumstances arise to provide the patient with an opportunity to aggrandize himself and reconstruct his damaged self-esteem. This opportunity results from (1) the presence in the hospital of large numbers of manifestly severely retarded persons with whom comparisons of intellectual ability may profitably be made — the newly admitted mildly retarded person is clearly superior to most of the more severely retarded patients in the hospital, thus it is not surprising that he concludes that he does not really belong in a hospital that contains such patients; (2) friendly, accepting peer-group relationships that, in comparison with pre-hospital relationships, sustain a positive conception of self — these relationships often provide the patient with the first instances of acceptance by peers that he has ever experienced; (3) contacts with well-meaning employees who encourage favorable self-esteem — many of these employees not only provide acceptance and affection but also do much to provide authoritative assurance that the patient truly is not retarded (Edgerton and Sabagh 1962).

The patients in the research cohort, then, had an opportunity to rebuild and even to aggrandize their self-esteem while in the hospital. Nonetheless, they felt acutely uncomfortable about being in the hospital and hoped for release. There is no necessary contradiction implied. The patients were able to aggrandize their self-esteem by being in the hospital, but a vital feature of their own aggrandizement was their contention that they did not belong there in the first place. In addition, the patients seldom appreciated either hospital confinement or its regulations. As a result, freedom from institutional confinement was a primary goal for every patient in the cohort.[1]

Release, when it came, was always received as an expression of justice, long overdue. Again and again, the words 'I never belonged there in the first place' were recorded. As one ex-patient put it: 'I was never mental like the others that couldn't remember nothing or do nothing.' Members of the cohort commonly saw their release as confirmation of the error of the original diagnosis of mental retardation that had sent them there, and as affirmation of their right as 'normal' persons to live their own lives, 'without anybody telling me what to do.' Release from the hospital was indeed the beginning of their right to live 'like anybody else,' but it was emphatically not the end of their problems, nor of their need for passing and denial. They now had to face the multiple challenges of living independently in the 'outside' world. Each former patient knew that failure to meet these challenges would not only be ruinous to self-esteem — it might also lead to a forcible return to the hospital. Consequently, the outside world was entered cautiously and fearfully.

One of the first needs of the ex-patients was concealment of their institutional history, a 'past' which, if revealed, could be gravely discrediting. This concealment was regularly attempted through a stereotyped 'tale' which explained and excused their confinement in the hospital by revealing the 'real' reason they were there.[2] Such excuses were collected from all of the forty-eight ex-patients. The excuses fell into nine categories. The excuses, with the number of persons who gave them, are as follows: 'nerves' (2), mental illness (2), alcoholism (3), epilepsy (4), sex delinquency (5), criminal offences (5), physical illness — usually a need for surgery — (7), need for education (8), and the enmity of, or abandonment by, parent or relative (12). The first four categories of excuses admit of some degree of mental or physical abnormality; the last five excuses admit nothing more than errors of conduct, and sometimes admit nothing at all. [. . .]

Entering the world outside the hospital, or as the ex-patients put it, 'life on the outs,' means facing an often bewildering array of demands for competence. The reaction to this initial contact with the outside world is typically a kind of 'release shock.' (see Goffman 1961).[. . .]

For some, the initial period of release shock was overcome in a few weeks; for others it lasted for many months. But despite the shock of finding oneself alone in the outside world, each ex-patient immediately had to come to grips with his or her need for passing and denial — for dealing with the practical problems of seeming-to-be-normal. As mentioned earlier, the ex-patient faces the two related problems of denying to oneself that one is mentally retarded, and of 'passing' with others, so that they neither suspect nor accuse one of exceptional stupidity.

Passing

The second of these problems — the 'passing' problem — will be dealt with first. The practical problems of everyday life have to be solved, not simply in order to get along, to live successfully, but also because, as every patient saw it, failure would lead to a forcible return to the hospital. But the demands of everyday life also had to be coped with in order to 'pass,' simply because no ex-patient was willing to seem to others to be mentally retarded. What follows is a discussion of the practical problems these retarded persons encountered in meeting the challenges of everyday life in the outside world. [. . .]

MAKING A LIVING

Finding a job when one has no demonstrable skills is difficult enough, but when the job-seeker also has a past that would tend to discredit him in the employer's eyes, the difficulties are increased many times over. Obviously, very few employers are looking for employees who, in addition to being unskilled, are also mentally retarded. The ex-patient approaches a job interview burdened with his discrediting past and with extreme anxiety. The following quotations are typical:

(A woman) 'When I try to get a job they always ask me where I'm from. I don't tell nobody I'm from there (Pacific State Hospital) — I say I'm just an 'outsider' like anybody, but I've been working in the East. They want to know how long I've been away and I say that it's been pretty long. I don't tell anybody where I'm from, or I'd never get a job.'

(A man) 'I get jobs by walking the streets and answering ads. I know I'm not qualified but I lie to

them. I figure that once I get the job I can learn it. Sometimes they find out about my past and fire me and sometimes they don't. A man's got to eat.'

(A woman) 'I've got to find a job but I just can't. I go down somewhere and fill out the application, but then when I have an interview I just tense all up because I know they'll find out that I've lied on the application about never being in the hospital. I just break down and cry. I can't ever hide it — they always find out about me. How can I get a job?' [. . .]

Finding a job means more than making a living to many patients. Those who continually fail to find employment suffer a serious loss of self-esteem. A man put it this way: 'When you been out of work so long and can't seem to get no job you really worry: Is there something wrong with me or something? A man's got a right to work. Besides, you're better off when you're doing something. It puts your mind at ease, makes you feel like you're as good as everybody else.' [. . .]

All but a very few of the patients complain about the job they currently have, arguing that it compromises their claim to normal mentality by suggesting somehow that they are less than normal. Some representative complaints follow: [. . .]

(A woman) 'On the last job I was supposed to be a stock clerk, you know, putting things on the shelf and all that, but my supervisor made me do the sweeping and clean the toilets all the time. She treated me like I was an idiot. I wasn't getting paid to clean toilets. I just quit that place.'

(A man) 'I do real good on a job as long has they leave me alone, but they always start telling me what to do just like I was a little child. That makes me so nervous I got to quit. I can't stand everybody treating me like a child — I got to be my own boss.'

Despite the acute difficulties of finding a job, and then in finding self-respect on the job, by far the most formidable problems relating to work lie elsewhere. They have to do with the proper attitudes for work: punctuality, regularity, zeal, industriousness, and sober responsibility. When asked to recall the worst problem faced in adjusting to the outside, all but two members of the cohort mentioned these attitudinal problems as being among the most difficult to deal with. [. . .]

A man summarizes the problem this way: 'I made good on the outside for just one reason. I learned to work hard, do what I'm told, get to work on time and go to work every day. Most of the people from the institution never had to work like that, so they have a real hard time getting adjusted. Lot of them never make it.' Unfortunately, this verdict is correct. Many of the ex-patients who have sufficient skills to hold a job have never developed the requisite work attitudes.

FINDING A MATE

For many reasons, it is imperative that the ex-patient find a mate – if possible, a marriage partner. Ideally this mate should be a normal person. A woman discussed the matter this way: 'Every girl wants to marry an outside guy. I know I did. I tried everything to find one. I bought nice clothes and tried to talk right, and I went to nice places. And I didn't go around with no hospital guys either. When I finally married an outside guy I knew my troubles were over.' A man sees it as follows: 'A guy usually wants to get married, but mostly he can't meet no outside girls. He can only get hospital girls or whores or something. I'm still single because I ain't found no outside girl yet.' Another woman states the matter as succinctly as is possible; when asked if she knew another ex-patient in the cohort she said: 'Oh yeah, she's doing real good. She's really made good. She married an outside guy.' [. . .]

Marriage for the ex-retardate is a highly meaningful status to achieve. Not only does it partake of most of the meanings it possesses for normal persons, it also serves dramatically to emphasize their newly won status as free and full members of the outside world. As patients in the hospital they had been denied the right to marry, or to bear children. By the time of the research, all but fourteen of the forty-eight cohort members had married. But bearing children continued to be a problem.

Forty-four of the forty-eight ex-patients had undergone 'eugenic' sterilization before their release from the hospital. Indeed, during the period of their institutionalization, sterilization was generally viewed by the administration as a prerequisite to release (Sabagh and Edgerton 1962).[3] [. . .]

A few ex-patients, almost without exception the single men, approved of sterilization on the grounds that it gave them greater freedom to enjoy sexual relations without fear of pregnancy. As one male put it, 'It ain't so bad. This way I can play around with the girls and I don't have to worry about getting into no trouble.' However, most of the ex-patients held strongly negative feelings about sterilization. They objected to it because it suggested to them their mortifying, degrading, and punishing past; sterilization for them had become an ineradicable mark of their institutional past. As such, it served as a permanent source of self-doubt about their mental status. One woman gave expression to this doubt in the following typical fashion: 'I still don't know why they did that surgery to me. The sterilization wasn't for punishment, was it? Was it because there was something wrong with my mind?' (Sabagh and Edgerton 1962 p. 220). Another woman gave these words to her torment: 'I love kids. Sometimes now when I baby-sit, I hold the baby up to myself and I cry and I think to myself, 'Why was I ever sterilized?'

But more important to the present discussion is the extent to which sterilization impedes the course of 'passing.' As the following characteristic remark should indicate, it sometimes does so to a marked degree:

(A woman) 'Naturally, when a girl comes out of the hospital and meets a guy and gets married – well, if she is sterilized, then the guy wonders why she can't have no children. She's either got to tell the guy the truth or lie to him and say, "Well, I had an accident," or something.' (ibid. p. 219).[. . .]

Men, too, can suffer this same dilemma. One man was inordinately proud that he had courted and married a normal girl. He had revealed nothing of his past to her, least of all his sterilization. But after several childless years of marriage, he was feeling immense guilt and anxiety about his infertility. 'It almost worried me to death. I was scared she would find out about me and divorce me.' Then, without his knowledge, his wife went to a doctor and discovered that *she* could not have children. He was tremendously relieved and has still not told his wife anything about his own sterility.

It is evident, then, that sterilization can complicate the problems of passing by standing as a permanent and visible mark of a secret and humiliating institutional past.

MANAGING MATERIAL POSSESSIONS

Whether married or single, ex-patients face some unusual difficulties in the management of material possessions. They enter the outside world without any of the large or small possessions which normal persons accumulate. Many normal folk may come to regard these possessions as impedimenta, but the released retardate sees them as the essential symbols of being normal in the outside world.

For one thing, the ex-patient lacks the ordinary souvenirs of a normal past. When he leaves the hospital he ordinarily has few, if any, souvenirs that could be displayed in the outside world. The ex-patients recognize this lack and make efforts to remedy it. It is quite common for souvenirs, photos, and oddments of all kinds to be picked up in junk shops or trash cans. Others are borrowed from friends. And more or less legitimate memorabilia of trips or experiences are collected with a passion, as though to make up for lost time. For example, one married woman had a photograph album filled with photos of assorted relatives, friends, and family — and not a single photograph in the album was legitimate. She had accumulated the photos from several old albums at a church rummage sale and was now happily representing the album to be a record of her allegedly normal, almost illustrious, past.[. . .] A man had over a dozen trophies of supposed skills in golf, bowling, tennis, and even archery, presumably dating back to a happy, athletic boyhood; these too were acquired in junk shops. [. . .]

The ex-patients also acquire actual souvenirs at a great rate. When they visit a fair, amusement park, or any tourist attraction, they buy inexpensive items, bring them home, and display them proudly. When they acquire a photograph of themselves or some relative or friend, they often have it framed and then display it in a conspicuous manner.

Still the search for memorabilia continues and most of the ex-patients feel the lack acutely. For example, one woman who is married to an ex-patient keeps the following lists in a small, grimy notebook. She keeps the lists up to date and proudly shows them to visitors. The lists are given opposite just as she wrote them.

Reading is something which few of the ex-patients do adequately and only one practices as a recreation. In general, beyond the occasional picture magazine or newspaper, reading is simply not done. However, many of the ex-patients recognize that books and magazines are read and displayed by some of the normal people they meet in the outside world. These ex-patients pick up

Things I have made	*Things I found*
12 dish towels	cloths pins
8 pillow cases	dish pans
6 scarbes	knife
3 bed spread	silver ware
2 pot holders	ash trays
1 clothes pin bag	pillows
1 rug bag	skirts
2 pillows	underware
1 quilt	
7 curtanes	

Things I bought for home	*Things we are interested in*
soap	sex
bleach	sports—baseball
starch	sewing
2 salt and pepper	gardening
shackers sets	music Western
silver ware set for six	match covers
"rolla way bed"	ash trays
egg beater	picture taking
table cloth	collecting odd ends
coffee pot	
2 potato pealers	*Things given to us*
dish drainer	lamp
ice cream scoop	dresser
silver serator	dish
blankets (sheet)	2 trays
books on sex	

used magazines here and there, look at the pictures, and then keep them around as display items. Others acquire and display books in the same way. Large, pretentious book displays were maintained by five of the married couples (ex-patients married to each other); these books were *never* read. [. . .]

The receipt and display of mail is something else which concerns these former patients. Very few send or receive mail, and when they do send it, they usually need help. All, however, love to receive mail, because receiving mail is 'what outside people do all the time.' The living quarters of the former patients often seem virtually littered with mail that was apparently addressed to the occupants. This curious fact does not accurately represent the volume of mail received; most of the ex-patients very seldom receive mail. It is this lack of mail that causes the ex-patient to surround himself with real or fraudulent letters: 'I like it to look like I get a lot of letters. You know, like people you see in the movies. So I keep lots of mail around – most of it ain't mine, but some of it is.' One woman regularly looks for discarded letters in the trash cans around the apartment where she lives. When she finds a letter or an envelope, she brings it in, folds it neatly, and adds it to a stack of letters she keeps on a small desk near the door. A man has but one letter – a legitimate one – and he keeps it prominently propped up against a lamp in his living room. He admits that he recently had to recopy and replace the original envelope because it was beginning to yellow and grow dirty. He says the newly addressed envelope 'looks a lot better.' Even bills from utility companies are often retained and displayed as though they represented the invoices of a busy commercial enterprise.

One final problem concerning material items must be mentioned – the problem of the automobile. The automobile represents perhaps the most enticing yet unattainable of commodities for the ex-patient. Nothing else so represents the cultural focus of the outside world, yet nothing else is so difficult to acquire, legally operate, or properly maintain. For the ex-patient the automobile is the ultimate symbol of success, but for all except a very few it is a symbol quite as elusive as the Holy Grail.

In the first place a serviceable car is expensive, and no member of the cohort was able to purchase a car that ran with any regularity. At the time of the research three ex-patients had cars, but all these vehicles must be described as wrecks that ran seldom, if at all.[. . .]

Even more forbidding than the expense of buying and maintaining an automobile are the requirements for a driving license. So formidable is the licensing process of written exams and driving tests that only one member of the cohort has ever obtained a license (and he has never owned a car). Only three others have ever attempted to pass the tests, and they have all refused to attempt the tests more than once. The lure of driving is sufficiently great, however, that five men and three women drive automobiles occasionally without benefit of an operator's license. [. . .]

And so the unattainable automobile is surrounded by excuses: 'I wouldn't have one of them cars – they cost too much.' 'It's much easier to get around on the bus – cars are too dangerous.' 'I'd

rather walk, you know – cars are too much trouble.' 'I'm not interested in cars; those things just cause you trouble.' Under more sensitive questioning, however, the lure of the automobile is readily admitted. It attracts *all* the ex-patients as surely as a lamp does moths. The following two statements are typical of their unguarded feelings about cars:

(A man) 'I'd give anything to have me a car of my own. I could ride around wherever I wanted and do anything and really feel great, if I could only get a car.'

(A woman) 'Me and my husband (cohort member) are shooting for the moon. We're saving our money so someday we can get a car. Then we can go places and be just like anybody else.'

INTERPERSONAL COMPETENCE

Of all the ways in which the ex-patient's competence is challenged, none is more serious than the multiple demands that are posed in interpersonal relations. Here the ex-patient must contend with demands for intellectual skills that he does not possess. In an effort to produce the competencies demanded, the retardate must often dissemble, lie, or fake in most ingenious fashion. Here, in its most classic form, we see 'passing.' And here also we see the constant danger of failure, disclosure, and shame.

One of the major concerns of the released retardate is the avoidance of any public association with other retardates. This kind of association could be highly discrediting, as the following typical remarks show:

(A woman) 'I guess once a girl's been out – the real bright ones that has a lot of sense – they don't like to talk to the girls or boys they knew at the colony. They just don't hardly want to be seen with them. I remember one time I was in San Diego. I guess I went to buy a pack of cigarettes or something. Well, I seen a girl in there I used to know at the colony. I turned around and walked out, then I snuck back in there to be sure she was the one I used to know. She was the one, all right, so I got out of there. I didn't want nobody to see me with her.' [. . .]

Association with 'outsiders' carries an obvious burden: demands for social competence and consequent danger of disclosure as an incompetent. One of the first demands is for appropriate speech. A male ex-patient states the problem: 'I just don't

associate with very few State hospital people —
maybe I want to get out and associate with more
of the outside people. Maybe you've noticed the
different change in me since I've associated with
outside people. I more or less speak a little
different than what the State hospital people does.
Maybe you've noticed that I've got class now.'

'Class' in speech requires that hospital jargon be
avoided. Lapses into this jargon can be dangerously discrediting: 'I always got to watch myself
that I don't slip and use some words which
somebody would know I'm from the hospital. One
day I called somebody a 'low-grade,' then I almost
bit my tongue off, because outsiders don't use that
word. I'm usually real careful about that.' 'Class'
also depends upon the use of 'all the big words'
and a liberal infusion of 'sayings' — in both instances, solecisms predominate. [. . .] But most of
the ex-patients manage their verbal deficit by
saying as little as possible when they are in public.
Naively paraphrasing the well-known saying, one
man put it this way: 'The best way to get by when
you're with outsiders is just to keep your mouth
shut. You know, if you just keep your mouth shut
you won't say nothing foolish — if you talk you're
just gonna say the wrong thing.'

Reading and writing also present enormous
problems for the 'passing' retardate. Everyone in
the cohort was able to read and write, at least in a
rudimentary way. But rudimentary skills are often
not enough, especially where reading is concerned.
Everyday life offers a variety of situations in which
the retardate's reading ability may prove insufficient, for example, reading bus destinations, using
telephones, shopping in markets, deciphering signs
or notices, or reacting to newspaper headlines. The
ways in which an ability to read may prove
necessary in a modern city are almost infinite. For
the ex-patient to fail such a challenge in the
company of normals with whom he is trying to
pass would be damaging indeed. Fortunately, the
ex-patients have developed serviceable excuses for
most contingencies. For example, one woman was
twice observed to excuse her inability to read
labels in a market by saying that she had been
drinking and couldn't focus her eyes very well. But
one excuse is almost universally valid, and the
ex-patients use it often. When the challenge to
read cannot be avoided, the retardate simply
fumbles about for an instant, then says that he's
forgotten his glasses and can't see the words in

question. The obliging normal usually can be
depended on both to accept the excuse and to
read aloud whatever is needed.

Writing can also be a problem but it arises as a
problem much less often than the need to read.
The ex-patients are seldom called upon to write in
public. They can all sign their names so that is no
problem. Some have developed a hasty and ille-
gible scrawl that they use if called upon suddenly
to write something that is beyond their ability.
Others rely upon retreat in the face of difficult
requests such as filling out forms or applications;
faced with such a request, one simply pleads
illness, forgotten glasses, or, occasionally, the need
to put pennies in a parking meter, and walks out.
If the need for writing is important but can be
delayed, the ex-patient can always wait for the
assistance of a benefactor. [. . .]

By far the most difficult challenge for the
ex-patient lies in the use of numbers. Without
exception, the members of the cohort had difficulties with numbers; some had more difficulties
than others, but all found that numbers — both in
the form of counting and in temporal relationships — were serious obstacles to passing.

Numbers obtrude into the ex-patients' lives at
frequent and regular intervals, and when they do
they are usually important. For example, most of
the ex-patients carry little bits of paper on which
they have written their address and phone
number — few trust their memories for such long
numbers. However, one man has responded to this
problem by memorizing all the significant dates in
his employment history and can easily provide the
beginning and ending dates of every job he has
ever had. He admits that he 'practices' the dates
almost every day. A more serious problem is
telling time. It has already been pointed out that
getting to work on time is a serious problem for
the ex-patient. This is in part an attitudinal
problem but it is also a problem in telling time. A
few ex-patients can tell time without difficulty,
but most — justifiably so — must take precautions
against getting to work late. The most common
precaution is having an alarm clock set by their
employer or friend: 'My boss sets this old clock
for when I should get up, then I just get up and go
on over to work.' Others have their clocks set by
friends. At one time or another, thirty-four of the
cohort members have relied upon alarm clocks set
by others to get to work on time.

In other circumstances, however, when the ex-patient is unsure of the time of day, he must ask. This raises problems because to ask simply, 'What time is it?' would be dangerous. Answers to this question can be exceedingly confusing. For example, 'It's twenty of nine,' or, 'It's eight forty,' may refer to the same time, but the effect of such intricate temporal distinctions upon the ex-patient is usually vast confusion. To avoid such potentially confusing answers, many of the cohort members employ a similar technique. The device probably derives from the hospital culture, where it also exists, but regardless of its provenience, it meets the need. Instead of asking 'What time is it?' the ex-patient asks, 'Is it nine o'clock yet?' The answers to this question — 'No, not for a few minutes,' 'It's way past nine,' or 'It's only eight' - — are much less likely to be confusing. Consequently, the retardate usually asks for the time in this latter form, often holding up his or her own watch, saying 'My watch stopped.' Most of the retardates, even those who can't tell time, wear watches. It helps greatly, in asking for the time, to be able to look at one's watch and ruefully remark that it has stopped running. As one man, who wears a long-inoperative watch, put it: 'I ask 'em, 'Is it nine yet?' and I say that my old watch stopped, and somebody always tells me how close it is to the time when I got to be someplace. If I don't have the old watch of mine on, people just act like I'm some kind of bum and walk away.'

But if telling time is a difficult problem, dealing with money is a greater one still. Again, the degree to which the ex-patients suffer from the problem varies, but all do suffer. It is not simply that, as the apothegm would have it, 'a fool and his money are soon parted,' but also that earning money, counting it, spending it, banking it, and owing it are all problems of the highest seriousness. For one thing, few of the cohort members are capable of counting money at all well. This makes for multiple problems, such as the case of one man who never knew how much he was earning: 'I make a dollar an hour — that's more than four hundred dollars a month,' (How many hours do you work?) 'Oh, about two or three a day, I guess.' (How can you make four hundred dollars then?) 'Oh, ain't that right? Maybe it's one hundred dollars. I don't keep such close track.' Such confusion is not uncommon.

Purchasing items, as in a market, can also be baffling. Only one of the female cohort members has any confidence in her ability to shop. And when this woman was accompanied on a shopping trip, her alleged competence vanished. She did not know prices, could not calculate change, and had to rely upon the honesty of the employees. She finally admitted: 'When I go shopping I just take what I want, then I go up to the check stand and give them the biggest bill I've got. If it's enough, they give me change; if it isn't, I give them another one.' Indeed, many of the cohort members spend money as some tourists do in a foreign country — by spreading it out on a counter and letting the shopkeeper take what is owed him. Unfortunately, not everyone is honest, as some of the ex-patients have been made to realize.

Of course, jobs requiring that money be handled are usually beyond their capacity, as witness the previously mentioned woman who served as cashier for a day until she rang up seventy-seven dollars instead of seventy-seven cents and gave twenty-three dollars change for a one-dollar bill to a customer who uncomplainingly accepted the windfall. Another man had similar problems as a gas station attendant; he lost that job when his inability to make change made itself apparent in the discrepancy between receipts and cash on hand.

Banking is not a problem in one sense because no member of the cohort had a checking account and those who had a savings account were always assisted in its use. The confusion of being paid by check is overcome easily enough by presenting the check to a nearby bank and having it cashed. But before some of the ex-patients discovered that banks would cash checks honestly, they lost a good deal of money cashing their checks at various markets and liquor stores. [...]

Denial

It should now be apparent that the ex-patients meet some challenges to self-esteem well and others not so well; they pass in some circumstances and not in others; they 'get by' in some instances but by no means in all. As a result they cannot fail to realize that their competence in many aspects of everyday life is clearly less than that of the normals with whom they must associate. Such a realization is potentially devastating to their self-esteem, and if the integrity of the self is to be maintained, imputations of stupidity must be denied. The process of denial is continuous.

For a few ex-patients, denial appears not to succeed. [. . .]

Overwhelmingly, however, they give the appearance of success in denying to themselves that they are retarded. They succeed by turning their institutional past to good use. They say, and they appear to believe, that they are relatively less competent than normal people because they have suffered the depriving experience of having been confined – wrongly of course – in Pacific State Hospital. This single excuse is sovereign. It serves in any need and it serves well. [. . .]

By attributing their relative incompetence to the depriving experience of institutionalization, and by insisting that the institutionalization itself was unjustified, the ex-patients have available an excuse that can and does sustain self-esteem in the face of constant challenge. To what extent they 'really,' in any psychodynamic sense, accept their own denial is exceedingly difficult to estimate. They usually give the appearance of being successful in their efforts to answer their own questions about themselves, but at the same time they give indication that, fundamentally, they either know or strongly suspect that they are mentally retarded. Probably the most accurate understanding of the ex-patients in their struggle for denial is to see them as participants in a self-instructive dialogue that is in a constantly changing balance between highly rationalized denial and gnawing self-doubt.

One point remains. One absolutely essential component of the ex-patients' armamentarium for passing and for coping with problems has been mentioned only now and then. This essential component is a 'benefactor,' the normal person or persons without whom the ex-patients could not maintain themselves in the community.

Aid with passing
Although the aid that benefactors provide is vitally important to the former patients' ability to cope with the practical demands of everyday life, the aid of benefactors is not limited to problems of coping. Benefactors regularly serve the ex-patient by assisting them with passing and denial. [. . .]

In order to assist with the task of passing, the benefactor sometimes becomes an 'insider,' someone privy to an ex-patient's secret institutional past. In such a situation, there is an active collaboration, usually involving a benefactor who is a spouse, a relative, a professional person, or an employer. Either these persons have prior knowledge of the ex-patient's diagnosis and hospitalization, or, as is the case with some spouses, the ex-patient has told them. [. . .]

The 'insider' benefactor is often concerned with problems of biography management, particularly with concealing the ex-patient's discrediting past. Aid with this problem can take the form of helping the former patient fill out an official form (for employment, welfare assistance, credit applications, etc) so as to conceal past hospitalization, or simply to intervene when a stranger comes to the door, not merely to help manage the situation but also to prevent disclosure of the ex-patient's past. For example, this statement from a landlady who is an 'insider':

'I keep a pretty close watch on their door, just in case some stranger comes along. You know, someone could really take them if they found out they used to be in a hospital for the retarded. Besides, I think that is their private secret and I don't think anyone should be asking questions that might make them admit something that would really shame them.'

Benefactors also contribute to the concealment of deficits in everyday competence such as appearance, dress, or speech. However, the benefactors' aid most often concerns the ex-patients' inability to read, write, or manipulate numbers. Again, the emphasis can be as much upon passing as upon coping. [. . .]

As an 'outsider' benefactor put it: 'She gets so embarrassed when she has to do things in public, so I go along and help her out. She always comes and asks me if I'm busy. So I go along, and that way she never feels ashamed because she doesn't know how to act in public or how to do things like read and write.'

Aid with denial
Still more important than aid in passing is the benefactors' role in aiding denial. The need to deny to oneself the humiliating admission that one is in fact mentally deficient is for these ex-patients constant and essential. [. . .] Denial is accomplished, and accomplished surprisingly well, by arguing to oneself that the very fact of hospitalization is the cause of whatever current incompe-

tence the ex-patient sees in himself. Nonetheless, the need for confirmation that one is not retarded repeatedly arises, and here the benefactor can be invaluable. A direct approach for reassurance is apparently rarely attempted, but indirection is often employed. The ex-patients' approach usually takes the form of a slip or hint – a self-deprecatory remark that is casually tossed off with the express hope that the benefactor will argue to the contrary. For example, the following exchanges between former patients and bene-factors were overheard: [. . .]

(Ex-patient, remonstrating with herself and bursting into tears about burning a shirt she was ironing) 'I'm just so stupid; I can't do anything right.' (Husband, a normal man) 'Cut that out. Anybody can burn a shirt. Don't talk that way, You're good enough to be my wife so don't talk that way.' [. . .]

(Benefactor, a roommate) 'Did you get the job?' (Ex-patient) 'No, well, they said they'd let me know. You know that means I don't get it. Hell, nobody's gonna hire an idiot like me that don't know nothing.' (Benefactor) 'What d'ya mean? The whole country's full of people with no jobs. You think they're all idiots? You're as good as anybody – it's just hard times,' (Ex-patient) 'Yeah, I suppose that's it. I was only kiddin' anyhow. You know that. It's just that I got no luck.'

[. . .] A related contribution of the benefactors must not be overlooked. In the ex-patients' efforts to establish their worth as normal human beings, they are greatly in need of the affection and respect of normal persons. Through these affec-tionate responses, the ex-patient is better able to regard himself as a worthwhile person. In order to convey affection without seeming to be patro-nizing, the normal benefactor must be highly sensitive to the ex-patients' need for self-respect. As the preceding material should have made clear, most of the benefactors are very successful in providing affection *with* respect. The following exchange is characteristic:

(Benefactor, an employer) 'Hi, Bertha, you're looking real pretty today.' (Bertha, blushing hap-pily) 'Oh, you're always talking that way to the girls, I betcha.' (Benefactor, smiling and walking away) 'You know that's not so, Bertha. You're my girl. You look very nice today, pretty as a picture, in fact.' (Bertha, to a researcher who had over-heard the conversation) 'He is so nice. He always makes me feel like I'm appreciated. He really is the nicest man. I'm always happy when I'm around him, because I know he likes me.' Later, the benefactor made this comment to the researcher:

Sometimes, it's pathetic the way these re-tarded people eat up anything nice you say about them. They're like puppy dogs. They'll lap up affection as long as you can give it out. I've had half a dozen of these Pacific people work for me over the years, and they've all had such a need to be loved – I guess you could say – that it's hard to deal with them. You've got to give them attention and affection every minute or you disappoint them terribly. It's the price you've got to pay if you're going to have them around. You've got to give them love every minute and you've got to mean it. I can do it because I do like them and they know it.

Who are the benefactors?

It is clear that benefactors aid the ex-patients in several ways and that their aid is important. But who are these persons and why do they give their aid? At the time of the study there were fifty persons who were regularly and frequently giving assistance to the ex-patients. These fifty, then, stand in an established benefactor relationship. Thirty of these benefactors are female, twenty are male. Of the female benefactors nine are employ-ers, five are landladies, four are social workers, three are neighbors, three are sisters, three are mothers, two are stepmothers, and one is a wife. Of the males, eleven are husbands, three are employers, two are roommates, three are step-fathers, one is a lover, and one is a doctor. The mean age of the women is forty-seven; of the men, it is thirty-eight. Sixteen of the women and four of the men were known to have had prior experience with persons who were mentally ill or mentally retarded.

The question of the motivation of these bene-factors is extremely difficult to answer. Between the extremes of crass exploitation and perfect altruism lie innumerable intermediate motivations, all of which are difficult to assess. The benefactors were asked about their reasons for befriending and aiding the ex-patients, but their answers were by no means either clearly or candidly phrased. When queried about their motivations for serving as benefactors, the benefactors regularly phrased their answers in terms of one or another altruistic purpose. Searching cross-examination was out of the question. However, some measure of the accuracy of their claimed motivation may be had by examining what is known of their actual conduct. Twelve of the benefactors are employers working in sanitariums or restaurants that regularly recruit employees from State hospital dischargees. Indeed, many of these places are licensed and supervised by the State. All of these employers have good practical reasons for attempting to stabilize their employees and maximize their work potential (e.g., they are very low cost workers); but in addition, all these employers went beyond such obvious practical needs by becoming truly concerned and sympathetic benefactors. Without exception these employers showed a high degree of altruistic concern for their retarded employees.

Thirteen of the benefactors are spouses or lovers. Here, too, the motivation and necessity for benefaction can be inferred from actual conduct. Several of the eleven husbands involved admitted directly or indirectly that they were isolating or secluding their wives not simply to protect these women from public obloquy or derision but also to protect themselves from public disclosure that their wives were mentally retarded. Furthermore, most of these husbands appeared to enjoy their extremely dominant relationship with their retarded wives. Hence, it seems fair to conclude that while the motivation of the spouse-benefactor is always mixed, it is not simply altuistic.

Ten benefactors are close relatives. Here the motivations vary still more widely – from strong affectionate concern on the part of some, to a transparent desire to degrade, control, and reject in at least one case. Such variability was noted that it is impossible to characterize either the ostensible or the 'real' reasons why those close relatives become benefactors.

Ten benefactors are neighbors or landladies. All the benefactors in this category are women. For the most part, these women appear to have a profound and selfless interest in the welfare of persons whom they perceive as being desperately in need of their help. In only two instances did it appear that a neighbor or landlady was exploiting an ex-patient. Five benefactors are professionals. Their 'reasons' for becoming benefactors, however, always transcended professional duty. None was even remotely required to act as he or she did; each one had a sincere personal interest in the well-being of the ex-patient that somehow made the sacrifice of time, effort, and money worthwhile.

In conclusion, while it is clear enough that a few of the benefactors maintained basically exploitative motives for their benefactions (e.g., the controlling parent, the *quid pro quo* landlady, the self-protective husband, the neighbor who enjoyed psychological dominance), and perhaps all incorporated a modicum of such feeling into their reasons for acting, nonetheless, most of these persons appear to have acted out of motives that were predominantly compassionate.

If it is not obvious why the benefactors acted as they did, it is certainly clear that their aid is important. They assist with the practical problems of coping as well as with the highly delicate matters of passing and denial. In all three areas they did yeoman service. Few of the ex-patients – perhaps three, and at the very most ten – could cope with everyday life adequately without the aid of a benefactor. It is impossible to measure the importance of the benefactors' contributions to passing and denial, but it is certain that these contributions – especially toward effective denial – are important. It would not be an exaggeration to conclude that, in general, the ex-patient succeeds in his efforts to sustain a life in the community only as well as he succeeds in locating and holding a benefactor.

Since much of the activity of the benefactors is secretive, the benefactors' role might even be thought of as a conspiracy. If so, it is indeed a benevolent conspiracy.

NOTES

1. A few patients were not eager to be discharged from hospital supervision after they were living in a community on 'work leave' status, but all patients in the cohort wanted to leave the confines of the hospital itself.
2. For an introduction to the concept of the 'sad tale' see Goffman 1961.
3. Not only is eugenic sterilization no longer performed at Pacific State Hospital as a routine prerequisite to release, but currently employed medical and psychological criteria for performing such surgery are so demanding that very few patients are now being sterilized.

REFERENCES

EDGERTON, R. B. and SABAGH, G., 1962, 'From mortification to aggrandizement: changing self-concepts in careers of the mentally retarded', *Psychiatry*, 25, 263–272.

GOFFMAN, E., 1961, *Asylums: essays on the social situation of mental patients and other inmates*, New York: Doubleday; London, Penguin edition, 1968.

SABAGH, G. and EDGERTON, R. B., 1962, 'Sterilized mental defectives: a look at eugenic sterilization', *Eugenics Quarterly*, 9, 213–22.

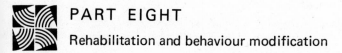

PART EIGHT
Rehabilitation and behaviour modification

Introduction

In one way or another every part of this book is relevant to rehabilitation, or in some cases initial habilitation, and there are specific items to which reference will be made here. We are concerned with the operation and efficiency of the formal rehabilitative services, and various means of achieving physical redevelopment as well as the adoption of physical and social skills by children and elderly people. In Part 1 we have indicated the aims of providing the opportunity for autonomy and normalized living, and in Part 2 reference is made to the ways in which handicapped people wish to achieve this situation through appropriate services directed to these ends. In Part 5 Illingworth and Mittler discuss various forms of assessment and their significance as interpretations of normal development and potentialities, and in Part 7 Kushlick and Rosen indicate the need for clear objectives even in complex situations such as the use of residential care. Only with such objectives can both staff and their clients work towards some achievement.

Nevertheless one is aware of the extent to which services fall short of this. In a recent paper, Blaxter considered that

> There is, in the British system, so complex a network of possible pathways through rehabilitation services that the process by which a client finds himself in one sub-system rather than another may appear to be wholly arbitrary. Obviously, the points of transfer represent crucial positions for the client. The way in which he was defined as he entered will be important in deciding what direction he is sent in. . . . Tossed as the client may be between one sort of agency and another, it must not be assumed that the processes of definition are wholly passive; the patient himself is also involved . . .

> The ideal client for all rehabilitation services is co-operative, motivated to using his residual capacities to the full, has acknowledged his disability and had it legitimated. This man is fighting for legitimation. (Blaxter 1970 pp. 19—20).

But, as the author indicates, those who don't fit the system and therefore get labelled as 'difficult' may be equally in need of it or something like it. It is a Procrustian bed.

The Tunbridge report on the existing services was highly critical of their lack of development since the previous Piercy recommendations. They are orientated, where they are developed, to occupational restoration although two-thirds of the demand comes from geriatric and psychiatric patients. They are also highly dependent on the enthusiasm of individual practitioners because of poor organization and the lack of effective follow-up even after intensive hospital rehabilitation programmes. The remedial professions are very dependent on medical practitioners who may be ignorant of their potential contribution. The small amount of data that is available is not encouraging. Sommerville indicates why intensive therapy is vital to the recovery of those facing life after a stroke, but also, by contrast, how much less is achieved without it. Forder, Reti and Silver (in Part 9) describe the bungling muddle and general ignorance of the various services supposedly responsible for the continuing care of paraplegic patients when discharged. The Johnsons' paper, which showed the extent to which the services were failing paraplegics discharged from hospital in Scotland, had an important influence leading to the full application of the 1970 Act to Scotland, i.e. the duty of local authorities to ascertain the numbers, and provide facilities in the homes of the disabled and chronic sick.

But because too little is attempted and achieved, it is necessary to consider what could be done. The Director of the Disabled Living Research Centre, Phillip Nichols, outlines the sort of functional assessment required by each patient prior to discharge and the range of daily living requirements they need to fulfil in their own home, and in their daily working routine and social activities. Although superficially similar to the much briefer mode of assessment used by Sainsbury, Jefferys and Harris, and referred to in the introduction to Part 2, it is important to distinguish this form of specific remedial assessment from basic prevalence studies required for general administrative purposes.

Nichols and others have stressed the importance of motivation and we have seen the extent to which existing services and procedures fail to deliver what is desired. But those such as Meyerson and Lindsley, who argue for behaviour modification programmes, have extended the scope of such services by considering ways of modifying the environment to induce motivation along a structured path. Through the use of case examples, Meyerson *et al.* indicate not only how autistic children may be helped, after others have failed to establish relationships and given up (see also Wolf *et al.* 1967), but also how children with other problems may be encouraged to overcome their disabilities. The essence of the method is assessment of the situation, the establishment of goals, careful monitoring and inducement of progress in the specified direction, and the establishment of a more regular and acceptable pattern of behaviour. What is unfortunately not discussed by either Meyerson or Lindsley is the way in which staff may also be motivated to have the appropriate goals. Because of the extent to which clients lose control of their environment in such programmes, it becomes of even greater importance to establish what appropriate goals may be and why staff wish to achieve them. One feels that the main reasons why old people, dumped in geriatric wards, have nothing decent to wear or eat, nothing to think about and nothing to do is because it suits too many people to have them put away cheaply. A lot of what Lindsley argues for as a form of prosthetic environment could be equally justified as a civil right that should be claimed in order to achieve an acceptable standard of living for elderly people. Some of these questions were raised in Part 2 and we return to them in Part 9.

REFERENCES

BLAXTER, M. (1970) 'Disability and Rehabilitation: some questions of definition' in Mead, A. and Cox, C. (eds) *The Sociology of Medical Practice*, London, Collier-Macmillan.

WOLF, M. M., RISLEY, T. R. and MEES, H. L. (1967) 'Application of operant conditioning procedures to the behaviour problems of an autistic child' in Bijou, S. W. and Baer, D. M. (eds) *Child Development: Reading in Experimental Analysis*, New York, Appleton-Century-Crofts, Chapter 16, pp. 173–83.

40. Concepts of rehabilitation and reasons for the failure of the present provision*

 (THE TUNBRIDGE REPORT)

[...] 86. We have deliberately avoided any attempt to re-define rehabilitation. In 1958 the World Health Organisation stated that 'Medical rehabilitation has the fundamental objective not only of restoring the disabled person to his previous condition, but also of developing to the maximum extent his physical and mental functions.' It aims not only at 'physical cure' but also at 'social cure' (Carstairs et al. 1956). While we approve of this as a comprehensive statement, we consider that it is important to avoid the risk of rigidity inherent in any definition, and for this reason we have confined ourselves to a statement of principles as we see them and not attempted to finalise the concept of rehabilitation by a new definition.

87. Although the principles of rehabilitation as propounded by Piercy and others have not changed, there has been a dramatic change in the problem to which they relate. The pattern of disease and disability has altered over the past thirty years, and the emphasis in rehabilitation has shifted from a primary concern with restoring physical fitness to members of the working population to a much wider concern with four main groups of disability: recurrent illness and progressive unstable disability; definitive disability; psychiatric conditions; and the multiple disabilities due to the degenerative changes associated with

*From the Department of Health and Social Security, Welsh Office, Central Health Services Council (1972), *Rehabilitation: Report of a Sub-Committee of the Standing Medical Advisory Committee*, (Chairman: Professor Sir Ronald Tunbridge) London, HMSO., Chapters 3 and 4, pp. 21—32.

advancing years. With the exception of the latter these disabilities are found in all age categories and rehabilitative measures are equally necessary for all to enable the individual to lead as full and independent a life as possible.

88. The essential features of any rehabilitation programme are that in addition to restoring the individual patient to the highest level of functional activity, both mental and physical, in the shortest possible time it is necessary to consider the programme in terms of the individual's morale, motivation, and relationship to the society in which he lives and to which he will return. Even for the individual with one of the more readily assessable disabilities, for example loss of a lower limb, the degree to which rehabilitation is possible and successful will depend not merely on the individual's age and general mental and physical health, but also the kind of work and mode of life he is expected to pursue, the social environment, the attitude of dependants and friends, his own latent abilities and interests and the extent to which he is motivated to achieve a purposeful and satisfying life.

89. It is often stated that doctors should take into account the problems of rehabilitation on first contact with the patient. This is clearly untenable for many patients either because of the severity of their condition and the urgent need for immediate treatment or because the existence of multiple pathologies, particularly in persons over the age of 60, often makes immediate assessment difficult. However, the need remains for the doctor responsible for care to keep in mind the concept of total patient care so that as soon as

practicable he initiates rehabilitation procedures and when necessary seeks the advice of those more experienced in the problems that may be encountered in the rehabilitation of his patient.

90. Rehabilitation implies more than therapeutic supervision including the application of physical methods; there is the need for dynamic leadership, clinical competence combined with a sensitivity to individual needs and awareness of the patient's socio-economic environment. Few doctors other than those specialising in rehabilitation can be expert in all the intricacies of a complete rehabilitation service but they should be made aware of the potentialities of such a service and be willing to seek and utilise the experience of those with specialised knowledge at the earliest opportunity.[. . .]

Reasons for the failure of the present provision
[. . .]
GENERAL LACK OF APPRECIATION OF THE IMPORTANCE OF REHABILITATION
47. During our deliberations we have been concerned by the failure on the part of administration, the medical and para-medical professions and the general public to appreciate the importance of effective rehabilitation. To some extent this failure has been concealed by circumstances. In the recent past full employment has masked the problem amongst males of working age; because it has been relatively easy to find work, there has been no pressing need to recognise the importance of good rehabilitation and little demand to provide it. Paradoxically the improved social security benefits which have done so much to alleviate financial anxiety during sickness sometimes militate against the incentive to return to work.

48. Many of the rehabilitation facilities that exist are based on the objective of a return to employment as soon as possible but a major change has taken place which makes this no longer the sole or even primary goal of rehabilitation. Two-thirds of the demand for the rehabilitation services comes from geriatric and psychiatric patients, for many of whom return to employment is not a relevant consideration. In these two specialties, the need for rehabilitation in the widest sense has been recognised and although the services are still inadequate, much pioneering work in the provision of rehabilitation services has been done in these fields. However other patients who

do not have return to employment as a target but nevertheless need rehabilitation, for example, housewives and adolescents, have not fared so well.

LACK OF INTEREST IN REHABILITATION
49. Within the context of lack of interest, the medical profession must take due share of the blame. While there are some first class facilities in this country, they tend to be isolated and largely dependent upon the drive and leadership of an individual doctor and sufficient interest has not been created elsewhere for others to follow. Although much advice has been issued by the health departments, this has not been implemented generally by health authorities. There has been a general failure to appreciate the changing nature of the problem or the growing need, and unless doctors are interested and prepared to press the interest, there is little or no effective pressure on hospital boards to provide the necessary rehabilitation facilities and to appoint a consultant to be in charge of them.

50. The British Association of Physical Medicine and Rheumatology comment on this aspect in their written evidence to the sub-committee:

> 'The main hindrance to the development of rehabilitation services at the present time is the low level of interest in the medical profession as a whole and divided views concerning the need for and roles of the medical, paramedical and other categories of skilled staff in the rehabilitation services. Consequently in medical advisory committees the ever pressing need for additional accommodation, equipment and staff for diagnosis and definitive treatment tends to be given priority and the provision of additional facilities for rehabilitation postponed more or less indefinitely.'

We consider this to be fair comment.

51. Many people fall into the trap of associating rehabilitation mainly with the management of permanent disability and the present services tend to be orientated towards provision for the rehabilitation of people with relatively severe but stable conditions such as loss of limbs, sight or hearing, and with crippling disorders. Less thought is given to patients with temporary incapacity due to illness or accident and to the prevention of further incapacity. This is well illustrated by a study which was done on absence from work after

fractures of the wrist and hand (Brown and Wing 1962). This showed that patients with temporary incapacity were taking far too long to return to work and that greater awareness of the disability in relation to the patient's work was necessary. In some conditions little or no rehabilitative treatment is required, but medical counselling is essential and in many cases instruction in simple rehabilitation exercises commenced in hospital and continued at home will speed recovery.

52. There is also much less professional and public awareness of what can be achieved in the rehabilitation of patients with chronic disorders which are liable to recrudescence or progressive deterioration with increasing disability, so that neither medical treatment nor social or industrial resettlement can be finalised. The medical profession and the public must appreciate how much can be done to ameliorate such conditions and ensure that the requisite facilities are available and used.

53. Curiously enough, no Executive Council circular was issued to general practitioners to bring the recommendations of the Piercy Report to their attention although a year later in July 1959 'Rehabilitation of the Sick and Injured' was issued. [. . .] Nevertheless, it seems to us that partly because of the heavy demands on the general practitioner's time and partly because of the poor communications between the branches of the health service, he is seldom referred to during the rehabilitation period of his patient's treatment at hospital. The general practitioner, in fact, receives little encouragement from his hospital colleagues to be involved in the rehabilitation process and, coupled with minimal teaching in the subject during medical training, perhaps it is not surprising that he may fail to make use of the facilities available.

MEDICAL EDUCATION

54. The Piercy Report recommended better medical education in rehabilitation and better organisation of the rehabilitation services, and we consider that these two requirements remain the essential basis for a good rehabilitation service. However, with few exceptions, medical schools have not followed the Piercy recommendations to include rehabilitation as an integral part of undergraduate training or of postgraduate study. Until they do, rehabilitation will never become part of the young doctor's thinking.

POOR ORGANISATION

55. During our discussions we became aware that the division of responsibility for rehabilitation between several government departments had a deleterious effect on the rehabilitation services as a whole and that this situation was aggravated both by the internal organisation of the Department of Health, which divides responsibility for the service both organisationally and by specialty, and by the fact that the role of this Department, unlike the Department of Employment, is to give advice rather than instructions. At the centre there is an absence of direction and this is reflected in the service provided in the hospital.

56. [. . .] The division of responsibilities between the Department of Employment and the Department of Health has created fairly clear demarcation lines which are not always in the best interest of patients during the interim period between illness and return to employment, and it appears that there is a gap in the provision of facilities for some patients in the interval between the termination of medical and the beginning of industrial rehabilitation. Both Departments are aware of this problem and the Department of Health is sponsoring some research designed to determine the nature and extent of the gaps in facilities. We note this development and consider such research to be important since any delay or break in continuity in the provision of rehabilitation services may cause the patient to regress, lower his morale and greatly increase the length of the rehabilitation period, making the transition back to work more difficult.

57. A major complaint in all the evidence was the general failure in coordination and communication between the hospital, the general practitioner, the community services and the services of the Department of Employment, and the unnecessary delays in starting rehabilitative treatment which result from this. We have referred to the results of the questionnaire to hospitals which indicated clearly that many hospitals do not have a nominated consultant in charge of rehabilitation in spite of the recommendations in the Piercy Report and the advice given by the health department. We can only assume that the medical profession generally and others concerned with the health services have not appreciated the importance of such an appointment and the organisation that springs from it. The need for better communica-

tion will be even greater now that one hospital may be dealing with several social service teams within an area authority.

[. . .] It is relevant when discussing reasons for certain failures in the present services to pinpoint deficiencies that arise from unsatisfactory organisation which are aggravated by the absence of a consultant in charge of rehabilitation:

(*a*) Physiotherapy and occupational therapy departments are often physically as well as organisationally separated and frequently operate as independent units. Time will eventually correct the division as new hospitals are built with fully integrated rehabilitation departments, but the existing badly co-ordinated remedial services could be greatly improved.

(*b*) The lack of clinics to assess a patient's progress also contributes to unsatisfactory rehabilitation, because these clinics are the main link between the various services, and they provide an opportunity for continuing review.

(*c*) Lack of co-ordination results in poor communication and unnecessary delays, not only within the hospital itself but between the hospital and the many other services involved in the total rehabilitation process, i.e. the artificial limb service, industrial rehabilitation and employment services, local health and social services, housing, education, and the voluntary services.

59. Further difficulties in organisation arise from the confusion over the correct distinction between the terms 'case conference,' 'resettlement clinics,' and 'medical interviewing committees.' We have been told that similar confusion is caused by ignorance about the role and function of the disablement resettlement officer. We have heard criticisms that these officers fail to provide the vital linking service between the hospital facilities and the facilities provided by the Department of Employment. For their part, the disablement resettlement officers say that they may discover patients who need medical advice but they do not know to whom they should be referred. The result of this confusion is that the services provided are not used to their full advantage. [. . .]

NATURE OF LEGISLATION AFFECTING
LOCAL AUTHORITY PROVISION
63. [. . .] Local authorities have a duty to provide

the necessary services for those patients who remain disabled, sometimes severely, after their intensive period of hospital rehabilitation, and need one or more of the many community services which can be supplied temporarily or permanently for both the physically and mentally sick and disabled. A large range of services are available, some of them continuing the rehabilitation process but mostly providing assistance in daily living, such as home adaptations and aids, special accommodation such as homes for the elderly, and hostels for the mentally handicapped, and occupation through sheltered workshops and day centres.

64. Without the community facilities much of the intensive rehabilitation of disabled people undertaken in hospital can be rendered all but useless. For example, unless those physically and mentally disabled persons who cannot be found a place in normal employment can be placed at sheltered workshops or at day centres on discharge from hospital, they are likely to deteriorate, and risk the loss of incentive to live as full a life as their disabilities will allow; if there is no suitable accommodation available in the community the patient may have to remain in hospital. The evidence we have received indicates that many local authorities are failing to meet the need.

65. Much of the dissatisfaction with local authority services turns on what is usually described as the 'permissive' nature of the legislation. The Royal College of Nursing blame the situation on the terms and wording of the National Health Service Act 1946, which they say, 'accounts for the fragmentation of the various aspects of the local authority services and for the tremendous differences in the policy of local authorities up and down the country'. The College go on to say that 'according to the Act each local authority is free to interpret its responsibility to provide services according to its philosophy, finance and ancillary services.'

66. We have been told by the health department that as local authorities were placed under a duty to exercise their powers under Section 29 of the National Assistance Act, these powers are therefore not permissive. It would, they suggest, be clearly impossible to legislate for the exact level of service needed by any individual in particular circumstances; the type and intensity of service to be given can only be determined in the light of a knowledge of local needs and resources, and must

therefore be matters of local administrative judgement. While we accept this as a statement of fact, we nevertheless consider that the result is the same.

THE SIZE OF THE PROBLEM

67. The absence of comprehensive figures is a serious impediment to demonstrating the inadequacies of the existing services. While we accept that there are difficulties in the collection of statistics relating to rehabilitation, in our view their absence gives rise to a major problem. It is hard to make a case without supporting evidence, and in a situation where facilities and services are in constant competition for limited resources, those facilities and services which cannot demonstrate first necessity, and second results, tend to remain forever at the bottom of the list of priorities.[. . .]

70. Statistics on duration of incapacity are collected by the Department of Health and Social Security, and we have been provided with information on the number of patients with certain selected conditions on sickness benefit for up to 3 months (Table 40.1). However, [. . .] these figures exclude men over 65 and women over 60 who are retirement pensioners, all men over 70 and women over 65, members of the armed forces, mariners while at sea, most non-industrial civil servants, married women and certain widows who have chosen not to be insured for sickness benefit, so their value for our purposes is severely restricted.

71. Not only are there virtually no figures, there is also a paucity of research on the requirements of rehabilitation and the evaluation of rehabilitative treatment and techniques. Evidence we have received suggests that where research is done, there is difficulty in obtaining acceptance for publication because the subject matter is not considered to be of sufficient interest compared with other research.

PSYCHIATRY AND GERIATRICS

72. So far we have not considered the particular problems of rehabilitation in the psychiatric and geriatric fields. Psychiatric and geriatric patients make the greatest demand on the rehabilitation services, and those responsible for the provision of facilities have been slow to realise this. The changed emphasis in the main role of the psychiatric hospital from the provision of custodial care

to the preparation of patients for return to life in the community has made it essential to carry out successful rehabilitation initially in the hospital environment. In the main, this rehabilitation has been directed to those patients whose primary psychiatric disabilities are aggravated by the secondary social disabilities of institutionalism but increasingly the problem is becoming one of rehabilitating those with unstable psychiatric disabilities who may have spent only a short time in a hospital environment, and of applying psychological principles to rehabilitation problems in general. [. . .]

75. The geriatric rehabilitation services are more bedevilled by chronic staff shortages in all professions, medical, remedial and nursing, than by lack of interest on the part of geriatricians in the problems of the rehabilitation of the elderly. The British Geriatric Society consider that 'where the consultant geriatrician organizes his own service there is usually no lack either of interest or organisation,' but they claim that 'where he depends on a service organised by a (non-geriatric) colleague there is sometimes lack of interest and in those cases the geriatric department is often the first to suffer in times of staff shortage.' The very nature of geriatrics, with the ever increasing number of elderly patients entering hospital, creates an awareness in this specialty of the need to get such patients back to the community and, in consequence, the value of progressive patient care, in which rehabilitation plays a vital part. However, too often patients arrive too late for effective rehabilitation to take place, and many of those who are rehabilitated cannot be discharged because there is nowhere for them to go.

THE REMEDIAL PROFESSIONS

76. The Committee on the Remedial Professions was set up in 1969 to consider the function and inter-relationship of occupational therapists, physiotherapists and remedial gymnasts in the National Health Service and their relationship to other personnel concerned with rehabilitation. [. . .] In their statement the Committee has identified four main problems that confront the professions.[1] These are:

(i) the low level of remuneration in comparison with other professions of equivalent responsibility;

Table 40.1. Sickness Benefit Statistics. (Great Britain) Duration of incapacity up to 3 months in the period 6th June 1966—3rd June 1967

	Units	Males								Females							
		All spells in the year	Less than 4 days	4 to 6 days	7 to 12 days	13 to 18 days	19 to 24 days	25 to 48 days	49 to 78 days	All spells in the year	Less than 4 days	4 to 6 days	7 to 12 days	13 to 18 days	19 to 24 days	25 to 48 days	49 to 78 days
Mental, Psychoneurotic, and personality disorders																	
Psychoneuroses and psychoses	Number	181260	4340	22960	38420	29640	17100	32680	14160	99520	1800	11140	22120	16980	9240	17800	7300
	Per cent	100	2	13	21	16	9	18	8	100	2	11	22	17	9	18	7
Psychoses	Number	14300	360	700	1500	1100	1180	2440	1900	5740	160	340	520	260	280	800	420
	Per cent	100	3	5	10	8	8	17	13	100	3	6	9	5	5	14	7
Anxiety reaction without mention of somatic symptoms	Number	48660	1180	6600	11400	8180	4880	9020	3760	25760	540	3280	6140	4620	2540	4420	1580
	Per cent	100	2	14	23	17	10	19	8	100	2	13	24	18	10	17	6
Other psychoneurotic disorders	Number	118300	2800	15660	25520	20360	11040	21220	8500	68020	1100	7520	15460	12100	6420	12580	5300
	Per cent	100	2	13	22	17	9	18	7	100	2	11	23	18	9	18	8
*Disorders of character, behaviour and intelligence	Number	2660	40	240	300	260	160	480	420	440	20	40	60	60	—	80	120
	Per cent	100	2	9	11	10	6	18	16	100	5	9	14	14	—	18	27
Diseases of the nervous system and sense organs:																	
Vascular lesions affecting central nervous system	Number	7180	40	280	520	360	140	880	760	560	—	20	100	20	20	100	60
	Per cent	100	1	4	7	5	2	12	11	100	—	4	18	4	4	18	12
*Multiple sclerosis	Number	1680	40	100	120	240	100	260	180	680	—	80	80	80	60	120	40
	Per cent	100	2	6	7	14	6	15	11	100	—	12	12	12	9	18	6
*Paralysis agitans	Number	1340	—	100	80	160	60	180	80	220	—	20	20	20	20	80	6
	Per cent	100	—	7	6	12	4	13	6	100	—	9	9	9	9	13	—
*Cerebral paralysis	Number	5500	20	220	480	260	160	540	700	840	20	60	60	40	20	60	60
	Per cent	100	—	4	9	5	3	10	13	100	2	7	5	2	2	7	7
*Epilepsy	Number	8040	440	1100	1520	980	520	1340	680	3140	100	240	600	340	260	440	300
	Per cent	100	5	14	19	12	6	17	8	100	3	8	19	11	8	14	7
*Migraine	Number	15780	2420	4280	4320	2260	1100	980	240	9840	740	3100	2960	1400	380	880	240
	Per cent	100	15	27	27	14	7	6	2	100	8	32	30	14	4	9	2
*Other diseases of central nervous system	Number	3820	—	140	320	420	280	680	600	940	100	80	80	120	120	120	120
	Per cent	100	—	4	8	11	7	18	16	100	4	9	9	13	13	13	13
*sciatica	Number	44760	820	4620	9720	8580	5160	9460	3540	6480	140	780	1400	1360	620	1260	380
	Per cent	100	2	10	22	19	12	21	8	100	2	12	22	21	10	19	6
*Other diseases of nerves and peripheral ganglia	Number	22740	1300	3600	5120	3680	2420	4020	1300	8100	380	1340	1700	1420	680	1580	400
	Per cent	100	6	16	23	16	11	18	6	100	5	17	21	18	8	20	5
Diseases of the respiratory system:																	
Bronchitis	Number	620700	16100	86800	168200	129680	65220	87760	27300	124640	2900	22260	38740	26520	11500	14180	368
	Per cent	100	3	14	27	21	11	14	4	100	2	18	31	21	9	11	30

Diseases of the digestive system:

Category																
Diseases of stomach and duodenum, except cancer	Number	459500	34560	98400	118900	35120	56020	21260	104800	6080	30720	31400	14400	65400	9780	3080
	Per cent	100	8	21	26	8	12	5	100	6	29	30	14	6	9	3
Ulcer of stomach	Number	58160	1320	6120	10580	6160	11720	700	3340	740	320	540	300	560	440	360
	Per cent	100	2	11	18	11	20		100	22	10	16	9	17	13	11
Ulcer of duodenum	Number	45900	1520	4800	8300	7680	9600	5160	3040	480	520	480	240	640	440	360
	Per cent	100	3	10	18	17	21	11	100	16	17	16	8	21	14	12
Gastritis and duodenitis	Number	239740	23780	63100	70180	38980	20510	4180	23700	4560	9100	3940	5180	1060
	Per cent	100	10	26	29	16	9	2	100	33	32	13	6	21	7	1
Other diseases of stomach and duodenum, except cancer	Number	115700	7940	24380	29840	18100	8600	6220	27480	1400	6360	7480	4240	2060	3400	1280
	Per cent	100	7	21	26	16	7	12	100	5	23	27	15	7	12	5

Accidents, poisonings and violence (nature of injury)

Category																
Accidents, poisonings, and violence (nature of injury)	Number	79860	362240	1472260	224940	1393320	71220	103180	35960	142140	5460	29200	40180	22580	12200	18420	7180
	Per cent	100	5	18	28	17	9	13	5	100	4	21	28	16	9	13	5
Fracture of skull, spine and trunk	Number	15320	920	1920	2320	1740	4240	1920	1880	240	120	240	200	220	440	360
	Per cent	100	6	13	15	11	28	13	100	20	13	6	13	11	23	19
Fracture of upper limb	Number	29240	860	2560	3140	42280	11120	4640	6120	260	560	800	520	2000	1220
	Per cent	100	3	9	11	15	38	16	100	9	8	13	8	33	20
Fracture of lower limb	Number	35320	940	2080	2520	2460	7380	6020	5620	180	440	1400	340	900
	Per cent	100	3	6	7	11	21	17	100	3	8	6	25	16
Dislocation without fracture	Number	5620	400	740	620	780	1640	700	820	40	120	100	100	220	160
	Per cent	100	7	13	11	14	29	12	100	8	6	27	20
Sprains and strains of joints and adjacent muscles	Number	265360	13740	58840	83480	51820	24780	6180	42080	1660	9920	12700	7520	3300	4660	1240
	Per cent	100	5	22	31	20	9	2	100	4	24	30	18	8	11	3
Head injury (excluding skull fracture)	Number	34440	1000	5680	10760	5760	4280	1580	7320	200	1360	2100	1200	740	1120	320
	Per cent	100	3	16	31	17	12	5	100	3	19	29	17	10	15	4
Laceration and open wound of face, neck and trunk	Number	4740	880	1780	700	420	440	100	740	20	180	320	100	60	40	20
	Per cent	100	18	38	15	9	9	2	100	3	24	43	14	8	5	3
Laceration and open wound of upper limb	Number	16920	2780	6380	3740	1400	1520	420	2600	100	600	1020	360	220	160	80
	Per cent	100	16	38	22	8	9	2	100	4	23	39	14	8	6	3
Laceration and open wound of lower limb	Number	9000	1840	3060	1600	760	960	360	2280	40	360	520	440	260	420	100
	Per cent	100	20	34	18	8	11	4	100	2	16	23	19	11	18	4
Laceration and open wounds of multiple location	Number	8280	700	1020	560	280	320	80	820		160	220	160	120	140	20
	Per cent	100	9	21	31	10	9	2	100	20	27	20	15	17	2
Contusion and crushing with intact skin surface	Number	42300	3360	11180	13200	6640	3580	560	8280	560	2560	2660	1100	620	520	200
	Per cent	100	9	26	31	16	8	1	100	7	31	32	13	7	6	2
Foreign body in eye and adnexa	Number	2360	740	740	660	200	160	60	20		20	20		
	Per cent	100	31	31	28	8	7	3	100	100	100	
Burns	Number	13020	2440	3680	2360	1380	1760	480	4940	200	1000	1780	900	340	440	120
	Per cent	100	20	28	18	11	14	4	100	4	20	36	18	7	9	2
Injury of other and unspecified nature	Number	321760	15240	59060	93620	57240	29270	12880	58620	2640	12460	17480	9620	5080	6860	2440
	Per cent	100	5	18	29	18	9	4	100	5	21	30	16	9	12	4
Contacts with infectious diseases(a)	Number	400	20	60	120	120	40	20	200		100	30	40		
	Per cent	100	5	15	30	30	10	5	100	50	10	20	20	

*Part of the residual Group C 49 (Other specified and ill-defined diseases).
(a) Persons who were not sick but who were excluded from work.

(ii) poor career prospects;
(iii) the lack of clarity over professional role;
(iv) the lack of critical assessment of treatment
      techniques and the serious lack of research.

77. We have been particularly concerned with the role of the remedial professions in rehabilitation. All three professions have been affected by the changes in patterns of disability and the consequential changes of emphasis in treatment, yet insufficient attention has been paid to these changes. In many centres there has been a persistence in the use of obsolete methods to the detriment of more modern techniques, and many of the treatments applied by the professions have an historical rather than a scientific basis. There is a considerable amount of overlap in the work undertaken by the three professions, and while this is inevitable to a certain extent, there are indications that the present level is hindering the development of the future role that the professions will be called upon to play.

78. Although the remedial professions have developed separately the problems they have encountered are strikingly similar. All three professions work to medical prescription and this may vary in precision from the highly specific to the merest indication of the treatment required. Surprisingly few doctors have sufficient experience of the range of modern occupational therapy, physiotherapy and remedial gymnastics to be able to prescribe in detail the most effective treatments and those who have the necessary experience rarely have time to see the patient sufficiently frequently to vary the treatment as soon as the need arises.

79. Many doctors are not prepared to delegate reasonable responsibility to the therapist to adjust treatment to the changing condition of the patient. The traditional relationship between the doctor and members of these professions is such that all too often it is difficult for them to challenge the medical direction as they feel they should, not only in the hospital but also in the training schools where teachers feel obliged to instruct students in the types of treatment they will be asked to give, even though some of these are of doubtful value. The absence of research into and evaluation of these treatments exacerbates the situation.

80. Despite an annual increase in the numbers in posts in each of the three professions, hospitals continue to complain of shortages of staff. The shortage is related to the fact that the remedial professions are predominantly female,[2] and this makes them extremely vulnerable to loss of skilled staff through marriage. While marriage in itself should not compel a woman to cease work, many newly qualified therapists find neither the career prospects nor the net level of remuneration sufficient to compensate for the inconveniences of combining domestic duties with a full-time or major part-time job. The low salary scale and poor career prospects also deter men from entering these professions.

81. The training schools also face problems. There is increasing competition for students with the educational attainments required for entry into the remedial professions, and it is no longer realistic to rely on a sense of vocation and personal service to provide sufficient numbers of suitable recruits for the professions. While a sense of vocation and a desire to help the disabled will always be factors in recruitment, they are no longer sufficient in themselves to withstand the pressure from the attractions of further education on the one hand and other careers with better prospects and higher salaries on the other. Consequently the standard of recruits to the remedial professions and their number is placed in jeopardy.

82. The pattern of training based on a number of relatively small schools has not changed significantly since 1948 and has been determined largely by clinical opportunism. The present pattern is useful for clinical work but teaching facilities are limited and the majority of existing schools are isolated from other educational establishments, as well as from each other. As a result, there is a tendency for schools to lag behind developments in teaching, and students in the remedial professions are deprived of the companionship of their fellow students in other disciplines. Many schools have difficulties in recruiting staff: the hours of work are long, the work load is heavy, and few teachers have the time for study, preparation and research which is necessary for the maintenance of high standards.

CONCLUSIONS

[. .] 84. The end result of the weaknesses and unevenness of the rehabilitation services is that both the patient and his family suffer. Further the temporarily ill patient or disabled person may take longer than necessary to return to work, those with permanent or unstable disabilities may suffer delays in being trained for alternative work, may not be rehabilitated to their maximum possible function and may be discharged from hospital with no proper provision made for their continuing care in the community. In total, this adds up to a complex social and economic problem, which is wasteful not simply of resources and facilities but more significantly, which is destructive of the quality of people's lives. [. . .]

NOTES

1. Statement by the Committee on the Remedial Professions, 1972, HMSO.
2. The ratio of women to men in the three professions in England, Scotland and Wales is as follows:

Profession	Number	Whole time equivalent
Occupational therapists	23.5:1	22.3:1
Physiotherapists	9 :1	7 :1
Remedial gymnasts*	1 :2	1 :2

*Remedial gymnasts are predominantly female in the younger age groups. The ratio for those under 40 years old is 3:1.
[Figures taken from an unpublished census conducted by the Department of Health and Social Security in 1969.]

REFERENCES

BROWN, G. W., and WING, J. K., 1962, 'A comparative clinical and social survey of three mental hospitals'. *Sociological Review Monograph*, 5, 145–171.
CARSTAIRS, G. M., O'CONNOR, N., and RAWNSLEY, K., 1956, 'Organisation of a hospital workshop for chronic psychotic patients', *British Journal of Preventive and Social Medicine*, 10, 3, pp. 136–40.
Department of Health and Social Security, 1973, *The Remedial Professions: A Report*, London, HMSO (The Macmillan Report).
Ministry of Health, 1959, *Rehabilitation of the Sick and Injured*, prepared by the Standing Medical Advisory Committee for the Central Health Services Council (July), London.
Ministry of Labour and National Service, 1956, *Report of the Committee of Enquiry on the Rehabilitation, Training and Resettlement of Disabled Persons*, Cmnd. 9883, London, HMSO. (The Piercy Report.)

41. The rehabilitation of the hemiplegic patient *

J. G. SOMERVILLE
Medical Director, Medical Rehabilitation Centre, Camden Road, London, and Farnham Park Rehabilitation Centre, Buckinghamshire.

The problem of living with a stroke is not a new one, but there has been a very significant change in emphasis in recent years in relation to the management of such patients. People with this condition should not be allowed to wait for recovery. They should be encouraged to live the fullest life possible, consistent with their disability.

It is difficult to obtain accurate statistics concerning the number of hemiplegics involved. However, it seems likely that there are at least 800,000 at any one time in the United Kingdom.

The prognosis in the individual case, must depend on the cause, the age, the site and size of the brain lesion, the general health of the patient and the family situation in which the patient is involved. The extent of functional recovery is also influenced by the presence or absence of a speech defect, the degree of sensory damage and the degree of intellectual impairment. To differentiate between cerebral thrombosis, cerebral embolism and the sequelae of the rupture of an aneurysm as the cause of a hemiplegia is extremely difficult. It can involve thy use of techniques which may, of themselves, cause complications which would be to the detriment of the patient. In view of this I have never insisted on such a differentiation when collecting statistics.

In an attempt to give you some factual information I have analysed the treatment of 444 hemiplegic patients treated at the Medical Rehabilitation Centre, Camden Road, London, between 1957 and 1965. This group represents about 1? per cent of the total number of patients treated during these nine years (Table 41.1).

Table 41.1

Total cases	444
Male	316
Female	128
Side – right	241
left	203
Aetiology:	
Medical	397
Surgical	23

It is interesting to note the analysis of these patients in relation to age (Table 41.2).

Table 41.2 Analysis of patients in relation to age

Under 25	28
26–35	23
36–45	62
46–55	155
56–65	143
66–70 plus	33

There is little doubt that at least 75 per cent of all patients who survive a cerebro-vascular catastrophe require intensive medical rehabilitation to achieve maximum functional recovery in the shortest possible time. It is also clear that the sooner such treatment is afforded to the patient the more likely it is that such treatment will succeed without undue delay.

In this series it is clear that the majority of the hemiplegic patients were referred very late rather than very early (Table 41.3).

*British Council for the Rehabilitation of the Disabled, London.

Table 41.3 Time under treatment before attending the Centre

Under 2 months	43
2–4 months	44
4–12 months	160
Over 12 months	197

Over 85 per cent of the patients were found, on commencing treatment, to have serious problems in relation to ambulation and independence. The time spent in hospital seems to have little influence in this respect (Table 41.4).

Table 41.4 Time as hospital in-patient

Under 2 months	156
2–4 months	120
Over 4 months	125

It is quite incredible how many patients are allowed to leave hospital completely dependent from an ADL point of view. For months a junior nurse has cut up their food and even fed them when co-operation between the nursing staff and the occupational therapists would have resolved this problem in a matter of weeks or even days.

To achieve independence requires the united efforts of the patient, the family and the treatment team. Experience has shown that at least 80 per cent of patients with a stroke can achieve independence within a few weeks if they co-operate fully and have the necessary guidance and sufficiently intensive treatment. A further 10 per cent will achieve this end, but take longer to do so. The remaining 10 per cent will be unlikely to achieve it however long one persists in treatment. It is equally important to define this group in order to save treatment time being spent on patients who cannot possibly benefit. In general this group have severe pre-frontal damage to the brain which prevents their assimilating or retaining instruction, and may also have sensory damage, especially in relation to spatial appreciation.

All the patients who attend either of my Medical Rehabilitation Centres do so on a whole-day basis, 9.15 am–4.30 pm five days per week. The patients at Camden Road attend on a day basis; 60 beds are available at Farnham Park for patients who cannot attend as day patients. Each patient is medically examined on admission, and then an individual programme is worked out which is designed to resolve the problems of that patient.

A joint functional assessment unit deals with the initial problems of mobility and ADL. In this room a physiotherapist and an occupational therapist work together to assess the problems and consider the solution. Patients are treated in the physiotherapy department, gymnasia or in the workshops, and speech therapy is provided if required. [. . .]

I have no doubt that it is only such intensive assessment and treatment which solve the problems involved satisfactorily. Intermittent out-patient treatment is rarely effective, and can and does prove wasteful, both in relation to the effective deployment of staff and also in relation to its efficiency in resolving the problems in a reasonable time, if at all (Table 41.5).

Table 41.5 Time at centre

Under 2 months	219
2–4 months	131
Over 4 months	94

The average duration of stay of 444 hemiplegic patients involved in this series was approximately 11 weeks. Some hemiplegics are able to achieve independence with the minimum of help and encouragement, but the vast majority need a great deal of stimulation and careful handling to obtain satisfactory results. It is most important to deal, not with the disability alone, but with the total situation. The co-operation of relatives and friends is as essential to success as the assessment of the home conditions of the patient, for example.

The first objective is to establish rapport — co-operation is essential to success. This can take several days or weeks. The whole treatment team must discuss the problems involved and then speak with one voice to the patient and the relatives. All should aim at handling the patient in a firm yet sympathetic manner. They must appreciate the mood-swings that such patients have, and make due allowance for them.

One of the major problems which you have to meet is the presence of a speech defect. The total number of hemiplegic patients who had a speech defect in this series was 201. This represents approximately 45 per cent of the series. Such a high proportion emphasises the magnitude of the problem which faced the staff. The areas most

Table 41.6 Speech therapy

	Male		Female		Total
	Dysphasia	Dysarthria	Dysphasia	Dysarthria	
Speech therapy cases of working age with hemiplegia admitted 1957–62 (non-intensive speech therapy)	98	26 (Total 124)	19	9 (Total 28)	152
Male patients of working age who returned to work 1957–62	21	6 (Total 27)			27
Percentage of male patients of working age who returned to work 1957–62	22%				
Speech therapy cases of working age with hemoplegia admitted 1963–65 (intensive speech therapy)	24	3 (Total 27)	8 (Total 8)		35
Male patients of working age who returned to work in 1963–65	14	1 (Total 15)			15
Percentage of male patients of working age who returned to work 1963–65	55%				

commonly involved, when a speech defect appears as one of the focal signs are:

1. Temporal lobe of dominant hemisphere — this produces aphasia, dysphasia or difficulty with language.

2. The brain system — this produces dysarthria or difficulty with articulation.

3. The larynx — this produces dysphonia or difficulty in voice production.

The loss of speech means the loss of a powerful means of communication between the patient and those around him. A speech difficulty can alter the patient's whole personality and his approach to recovery. The re-building of morale involves all who are concerned with his welfare — the rehabilitation team, the family, the friends and even the potential employer. Close co-operation is essential between the speech therapist and the occupational therapist. This results in each playing her full part in achieving progress as rapidly as possible. An occupational therapy department provides excellent opportunities for the patient to receive verbal stimulation from those working around him. Pattern drawing and writing practice can be carried out in the department. Paper stabilisers can be provided by the occupational therapist.

It is essential that speech therapy be provided at a realistic level. In this respect the implications of inadequate treatment are identical to those in physiotherapy and occupational therapy.

I have had the results of speech therapy analysed from this point of view; comparing non-intensive speech therapy — i.e. treatment lasting for about one hour three times per week with treatment which involves patients in speech therapy three times per day, five days a week. Although the latter group is still too small for fair comparison, the difference in the number of male patients of working age who resumed work in each group is striking (Table 41.6). [...]

Independence

Basic activities should be taught first and no attempt should be made to achieve too much at one time, otherwise the patient becomes overtired and discouraged. Almost all actions can be carried out with one hand, if adequate stabilisation takes the place of the paralysed hand. The patient must be persuaded that it is more appropriate to achieve independence using the unaffected hand than wait for the affected hand to recover. He or she must be told that there is no disadvantage in learning one-handed methods — if the affected hand recovers, nothing has been lost, but independence has been achieved in the meantime.

Mobility

Exercise tolerance must be built up gradually. If a stick is required, it is a help if a loop of elastic is attached to the handle. The hand is then left free to grasp a rail, insert a key, accept change or turn a door handle. Suitable handrails may have to be provided in the patient's home, possibly on stairs and in passage-ways, bathrooms and toilets. They should not be less than one inch in diameter and at least 1½ inches clear of the wall. The normal heights for such handrails is 2′ 9″, from the ground level. If a hemiplegic can walk to a bus stop, a bus trip is usually possible, once the fear of such an undertaking has been overcome by practice. Hemiplegic patients can drive cars if they are suitably adapted.

Personal hygiene, dressing and undressing, eating, cooking and housework all present problems to the hemiplegic patient. Such problems can be overcome in most cases[. . .]

The work involved in rehabilitating patients cannot be pursued in splendid isolation. The co-operation of many statutory and voluntary bodies is essential to success. The role of social rehabilitation centres or occupation centres and social clubs is now accepted, and they prove particularly valuable in maintaining patients in the older age groups.

What are the results achieved by a total approach to the problem? (Table 41.7).

It should be noted that housewives are not included under the heading of original work. Although it is believed that many of them were completely independent and remained so, it was

Table 41.7 Results of treatment

	Number	Percentage	
Original work	70	15.6	
Different work	61	13.8	
D.R.O.	38	8.4	78.0%
I.R.U./training	6	1.4	
Function improved	172	38.8	
Hospital/further treatments	56	12.7	
Home/further treatment	31	7.1	
Self-discharge	7	1.6	
No progress	3	0.6	
Total	444	100.0	

difficult to be certain that no assistance was afforded in the home. Although this lowers the percentage of patients in the first category, at least it errs on the side of caution.

It has been estimated that of every hundred patients who survive a stroke, ninety will be able to walk again. Only ten will recover useful function in the affected hand. The time taken to achieve useful hand function may vary from a few weeks to several years. Many patients never recover useful function in the hand.[. . .]

'There is no point in adding years to life unless you add life to those years.'

42. Paraplegics in Scotland: a survey of employment and facilities*

GILLIAN S. JOHNSON
Social Worker,
Renfrew County Social Work Department.

RALPH H. JOHNSON
Senior Lecturer in Clinical Neurology, University of Glasgow,
and Consultant Neurologist, Western Regional Hospital Board.

Summary

The results of a survey of employment facilities and social services available to 50 paraplegics living in Glasgow or the surrounding counties are reported.

The degree of unemployment in the group (74 per cent) was far greater than has been reported in other surveys and although the general unemployment level in the area is high, services to help the disabled gain employment were only partially utilized.

Liaison between social workers was not always successful. Some paraplegics were visited at home by both a medical social worker and a local authority social worker, while others were not supported by either. There was no apparent attempt by local authorities to identify the disabled as is required in England under Section 1 of the Chronically Sick and Disabled Persons Act (1970) and several paraplegics lacked facilities which are covered by Section 2 of the Act. It appeared that the exclusion of Scotland from Sections 1 and 2 of the Chronically Sick and Disabled Persons Act might widen the differences between the two countries as the Scottish legislation is less specific.

*From British Journal of Social Work, (1973) 3, 10,
pp. 19—38

(This work led to the Chronically Sick and Disabled Persons (Scotland) Act, 1972; see note, p. 364.)

Introduction

The British Government has been frequently pressed in the past few years to take more action to help the disabled, and the demands have been accompanied by damning evidence that the disabled form a seriously disadvantaged section of our society. (Leader, *Lancet*, 1971.)

The passage through Parliament, in 1970, of the Chronically Sick and Disabled Persons Act highlighted growing concern that the needs of the disabled have been neglected. We have carried out a survey, in the West of Scotland, of a homogeneous group of disabled people in order to examine the limitations which their disability has imposed upon them. The disability of paraplegia was chosen because individuals with this disorder have a relatively static medical condition and their mental processes are unaffected.

Paraplegia is paralysis of the limbs which results from injury or disease to the spinal cord. The level at which the nerves which pass up and down the cord are damaged or severed, together with the degree of completeness of the lesion, determines the extent of disablement. For example, those who have high lesions in the neck (cervical) region may lose the use of their arms and hands as well as their legs. In such cases the condition may be termed quadriplegia. Paraplegics with lower lesions retain the use of their arms. The trunk is also paralysed below the lesion and this often means that bowel and bladder control and sexual function are affected. In addition, the loss of feeling and restricted movement of the body makes the paraplegic susceptible to skin pressure sores and also to injuries such as burns. The medical management of paraplegics has greatly advanced because the large number of casualties resulting from the Second World War prompted research in this disorder. During the First World War only those cases survived in whom the spinal lesion was a partial one (Cushing 1927). Even in 1944 it was said in America that there had been no striking advance in the late care of spinal cord injuries (Everts and Woodhall 1944). The most important development took place in the U.K. and was the foundation, in 1944, of the National Centre for Spinal Injuries at Stoke Mandeville, near Aylesbury, Buckinghamshire, under the direction of Sir Ludwig Guttmann. Previously few paraplegics had survived more than a few weeks or months after their injury, but with this and similar developments the prognosis has become more favourable. The history of the Centre was reviewed by Guttmann in 1967 by which date out of 3,000 patients only 343 (11.4 per cent) had died as a direct result of their paraplegia and many of these died in the Centre's early years (Guttmann, 1967).

Since the War, hospitals elsewhere in the U.K. have established units which specialize in spinal injury. These include Edenhall Hospital, Edinburgh, and Philipshill Hospital, Glasgow.

We wished to determine the extent of facilities outside hospital available to this disabled group in Scotland. This could be of particular importance because not all of the sections of the Chronically Sick and Disabled Persons Act (1970) apply to Scotland. Part of the study therefore examined whether or not the difference in legislation between Scotland and the rest of England and Wales might give rise to less favourable provision of facilities in Scotland. The results have been briefly reported (Johnson and Johnson, 1972).

Survey procedure

Fifty paraplegics living in the West of Scotland were visited and personally interviewed. The paraplegics were living in the City of Glasgow (23) and the neighbouring counties of Lanarkshire (8), Dunbartonshire (4), Renfrewshire (11) and Ayrshire (4).

The sample included only those paraplegics who had left hospital after initial treatment and returned to their homes or to other accommodation in the community. It was drawn from several sources, mostly from names of patients discharged from Philipshill Hospital, Glasgow, and Edenhall Hospital, Edinburgh, but also from names supplied by other paraplegics. A sample technique could not be applied as there was no complete register of the disabled in the area. The Local Authority Social Work Departments were not approached for names as this would have produced a group who were known to have applied for or be using social services. A lower age limit of 15 years, the present school leaving age, was set as we wished to consider problems of employment, finance and social independence.

The paraplegics were contacted to explain the purpose of the survey and were asked if they would be prepared to be interviewed. 58 paraplegics were approached of whom 50 were included in the survey (86.2 per cent): the others failed to reply. A questionnaire, which was designed to allow information to be standardized, was completed at the time of interview, while at the same time freedom was given for individual comment. Interviewing took place between November 1970 and June 1971.

Details of subjects

There were 44 male and 6 female paraplegics aged 16—26 years (Figure 42.1). All had been paraplegic for at least a year and more than half the sample (28) had been disabled for up to 6 years. The

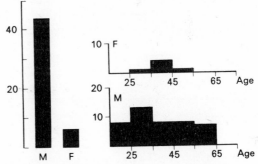

Figure 42.1 Age and sex distribution of paraplegics

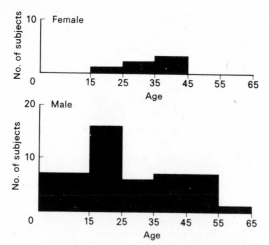

Figure 42.2   Age at onset of paraplegia

onset of disablement was most common in the 15—25 year age group (Figure 42.2) and industrial and road traffic accidents were the most frequent causes. All those involved in industrial accidents were employed in manual occupations and were usually undertaking construction work.

Thirty-three of the group had paralysis of the lower limbs; of these 28 had complete paralysis and 5 had some limited movement in the lower limbs, but only one was able to walk with calipers. Seventeen of the subjects had lesions of the cervical spinal cord but not all of these were quadriplegic with paralysis of arms as well as legs. Eight had incomplete lesions and 4 of these could use their arms and hands. 60 per cent had been re-admitted to hospital because of complications, urinary infection and pressure sores being the most common causes.

There were 27 married and 21 single paraplegics; one had been widowed before injury and one had become separated from his wife since his injury. Four of the men had married after injury and 3 more were engaged to be married. Twenty-three had children born before the patient became paraplegic, but only one child was born to a paraplegic. She had had three children before her injury and gave birth to another child five years later. Three couples, where the husband was the paraplegic, had adopted children, two through a local authority department and the third through an adoption society. One of them found difficulty in obtaining an adoption order because of dis-

ability and was refused by an adoption society, but later accepted by a local authority.

COMPARISON WITH OTHER REPORTED GROUPS

The group was similar to other reported groups of paraplegics. It is usual for the proportion of males to females to be about 5:1 (Thompson and Murray, 1967) and the majority are between the ages of 16 and 30 or 35 (Guttmann, 1965; 1967). Guttmann reported that in his series there were 23.6 per cent with lesions of the cervical spinal cord but he stated that their proportion was increasing. Injuries in other groups were also mainly incurred at work or on the road (Thompson and Murray, 1967). The situation in other countries is similar, e.g. in Switzerland (Gehrig and Michaelis, 1968).

We had a higher proportion of patients (60 per cent) re-admitted for management of complications, than has been reported elsewhere. Forder, Reti and Silver (1969) were prompted to study this problem as 3 out of every 8 patients discharged from the Liverpool Regional Paraplegic Centre, Southport, required re-admission. It is uncertain whether our group actually had more complications or were managed more cautiously.

The marital and reproductive lives of our paraplegics were also representative. Guttmann (1964), writing from his experience at Stoke Mandeville, considered that the pessimism existing about the possibility of motherhood in paraplegic women was unfounded. Nevertheless the occurrence of a successful pregnancy in a female quadriplegic is uncommon (Hardy and Warrell, 1965). The difference of attitude of agencies concerned with adoption has previously been recorded in Scotland by Thompson and Murray (1967) who pointed out that successes should be publicized in the hope that the 'climate of opinion of Adoption Societies and others responsible might thereby change'.

It has become apparent from statistics elsewhere that the proportion of disabled in the world population is rising. In Switzerland the increase in patients developing traumatic paraplegia appears to be between 2 per cent and 4 per annum (Gehrig and Michaelis, 1968). The figures are probably similar in the U.K. but the absence of a disabled persons' register prevents them from being available and makes forward planning almost impossible. Our figures indicate that the number of paraplegics increased in the last six years. This suggests that there is a need for frequent reassessment of the services available for this group.

Employment

Before disablement the majority of the 50 paraplegics were in paid employment (40) and only one man was unemployed. Most of the working group were manual workers. The effect of disablement on the pattern of employment has been considerable, leaving only 7 paraplegics working. Thirty-seven of the group were unemployed (Table 42.1). Those who were working after disablement were all in full-time remunerative employment. Four had the same type of occupation as before disablement, 1 having retained her job; they were all professional or skilled workers. Two of the other paraplegics who were working were in sheltered employment. Not all the paraplegics who were unemployed were seeking work. Several said that they did not wish to work and some (7) were physically unfit. There were, however, 13 paraplegics who had unsuccessfully tried to obtain employment. Six of these had cervical lesions and no individuals with such lesions were in employment.

Table 42.1 The effect of disability upon occupation

Employed	Before disability	After disability
Professional	5	2
Clerical	2	–
Manual – skilled	13	3
Manual – unskilled/ semi-skilled	15	–
Apprentices	2	–
Military service	3	Sheltered work 2
	– 40	– 7
Unemployed	1	37
Other		
Housewives	3	2
Education	5	4
Pre-school	1	–
	– 9	6
Total	50	50

USE OF DEPARTMENT OF EMPLOYMENT SERVICES FOR THE DISABLED

The paraplegic who is seeking work may be registered by the Disablement Resettlement Officer (D.R.O.) of the Department of Employment. There were 44 paraplegics who were potentially employable when discharged from hospital, but only 21 had been in contact with a D.R.O. and 4 others obtained work for themselves. However, 19 paraplegics for whom employment might have been possible, never saw a D.R.O. The cause for this is uncertain but it appears that many paraplegics were not referred to the D.R.O. by the hospital. In many cases contact with the D.R.O., even though made, was minimal, sometimes because the D.R.O. indicated that there was little hope of finding employment in the area. On the other hand, 5 paraplegics who were referred to the D.R.O. refused help and stated that they did not want employment.

Even those who managed to find work through the D.R.O. did not always retain their jobs. Four resigned at an early stage giving medical reasons or complaining that the work was unsatisfactory and badly paid. The remaining 3 were still working, but only 1 of them was in the job originally obtained in a Sheltered Workshop. Thus 6 of the 7 jobs held by paraplegics at the time of interview were obtained independently. Only 8 paraplegics were offered industrial rehabilitation and 2 of these refused the offer (Figure 42.3). Of the other 6 who went onto an Industrial Rehabilitation Unit 3 were then offered re-training facilities. Those who received industrial rehabilitation were males under

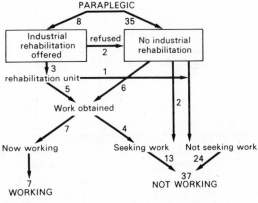

Figure 42.3 The use of rehabilitation services by paraplegics and its effect on their employment.

25 years of age at the time of injury; most had experienced some form of training and were skilled workers. In some cases retraining was possible for work similar to their pre-injury employment, although severe disability sometimes prevented this. One paraplegic failed to seek employment despite rehabilitation and another held his job for only 3 weeks; these men were offered jobs which bore no relationship to their chosen occupation prior to injury. Two others had to discontinue their work owing to long periods of hospital treatment. Two-thirds of the group not offered industrial rehabilitation (24) stated that they did not want to work. In the total group of potential workers there were, however, 13 who were trying to obtain work and 10 of these had neither had a chance of industrial rehabilitation nor vocational training.

OTHER REASONS FOR UNEMPLOYMENT

There were several factors which appeared to influence the paraplegics' approach towards employment.

Disability caused a burden due to its associated restriction on movement and extra requirements for careful body management. The availability of extra time and energy was critical for the completion of tasks. As many paraplegics commented, the process of getting up and dressing in the morning was so exacting that in order to arrive at work on time it was necessary to rise an hour or more before an able-bodied man. Travelling to work and manoeuvring a wheelchair into and out of a car added further physical strain even before the working day began. One paraplegic relinquished his job because he found a 20-mile journey to work exhausting. Another very fit and active paraplegic said that he did not feel able to meet the demands of an 8-hour working day.

Many paraplegics expressed anxiety about difficulties which might be encountered at work due to confinement to a wheelchair. They were particularly concerned with moving about their work place and coping with bowel and bladder function. The experience of those paraplegics who were working was that such anxieties were easily overcome. Minor alterations could be made with little effort; for example, the installation of ramps or the re-positioning of work benches. All commented on their good relationship with workmates, receiving help from them when needed and

saying that at all times they were treated as a 'normal' person.

The difficulties of coping with a full-time job, however, should not be underestimated. One paraplegic was interviewed just two weeks after he had acquired a new job. He was delighted with his work as a radio technician and had met no difficulties, but he was anxious that he might be spending too long sitting still in his wheelchair without relieving the pressure on his buttocks. Some weeks later this paraplegic was admitted to hospital for treatment for a pressure sore and he was unlikely to return to work for two months. It appeared that uncertainty of continuous availability, rather than doubt of ability to do the job, was more likely to dissuade employers from accepting a paraplegic as an employee.

The degree of motivation to seek employment appeared to be related to *age*. All but one of the 13 seeking work had been under 40 years of age at the time of injury and 10 had been under 30 years. At the time of interview 9 still looking for work were less than 40 years old. 18 of those who were not wanting work were over the age of 40 years.

The long period of initial hospital treatment may have made the paraplegic reluctant to revert to the discipline of regular employment or to participate in activities outside the home. 68 per cent of the group spent more than 6 months in hospital immediately following their injury and a few were in for over 18 months. Although the patients were usually offered occupational therapy in hospital they were rarely compelled to be very active and on return home could be looked upon as an invalid by others in the family, so lapsing further into inactivity. This often caused dissatisfaction in young paraplegics, but older ones were more contented and stated that they were not wanting employment. One married man, aged 39, commented.

> My first year home I spent in getting used to living with my family again, after that I had recurrent bladder trouble and I never looked for work.

Lack of transport was cited as a reason for not seeking employment, but the paraplegics who felt this were often severely disabled and had poor use of their hands. This would make a hand-controlled car difficult to drive. The Department of Health and Social Security will provide an invalid vehicle

Table 42.2 Main source of income of unemployed paraplegics

Income	Work sought	Not seeking work	
Industrial injury benefit	—	6	adequate income
Compensation	—	2	
Industrial injury + compensation	5	7	
War pension	—	2	
Sickness benefit	6	low income 6	
Supplementary benefit	1		
Private income	1	—	
None	—	1	(Husband earning)

or help with the conversion of a motor car for any disabled person who needs conveyance to their place of work. All the paraplegics who were in employment were travelling to work in their own car or invalid vehicle. There was, however, no evidence of other transport for disabled workers.

Financial incentive also influenced the paraplegic's decision to accept work offered. Those who did not want work were often receiving an adequate income from Industrial Injury Benefits, compensation, or War Pension (Table 42.2). A low income was a considerable incentive to 7 paraplegics seeking work. One paraplegic stated that he had refused a job offered to him because he was awaiting the result of a compensation claim. Three more paraplegics, who did not seek work, were still awaiting the result of their compensation claims, 2 years, 3 years and 5 years respectively, after injury. There was, however, no evidence that this was their main reason for not working. If a paraplegic was able to take up the same occupation as before injury he was more likely to work. Thus professional people and others who had been trained with further education were more likely to seek employment and to obtain it.

Well-paid jobs were hard to find for those who lacked full use of their hands and who were unable to use previously acquired skills. Unemployment might then be preferable to a badly paid, low-status job, as the sentiments expressed by a 23-year-old man suggest:

I spent 3 years learning a trade, being an apprentice and going to night school. Now they ask me to spend the day sticking labels on bottles.

When high job expectations were not fulfilled disappointment and disincentive to work appeared to result.

COMPARISON WITH OTHER REPORTED GROUPS

There is a marked difference between the employment statistics of our group and those reported from elsewhere. Guttmann (1962) reported that 66 per cent of all paraplegics discharged from Stoke Mandeville were employed; this included some in further education and in part-time occupations. In 1965 and 1967 he amplified these findings and reported that if he discounted patients who had retired and were over age, who were under treatment in hospital, physically unfit or had died, then only 14.6 per cent were not working at all. This compares with our figure of 60 per cent. Thompson and Murray (1967), who have carried out the only comparable survey in Scotland, did not examine this problem in detail.

Even greater differences are found on considering the problem of employment of quadriplegics. None in our group, which included 9 complete and 8 incomplete lesions, was working, although one was receiving further education. A study of 188 quadriplegics discharged up to 1968 from Stoke Mandeville found that 44 per cent were in remunerative employment and 7.4 per cent were students (Robinson, 1970). A survey carried out at the Institute of Rehabilitation Medicine, New York University Medical Center, on 131 quadriplegics aged 18–60 years, who had been patients between 1962 and 1967, found 34 per cent were employed and 47 per cent were receiving higher education (Siegel, 1969).

The poor employment situation that we have found in the West of Scotland is related to a local unemployment rate above the national average. Nevertheless it may also be related to poorer facilities compared with more prosperous areas. Alternative transport to work could have altered the position for the severely disabled. Other areas provide an ambulance or car service to transport such disabled people to and from work. This might not always be possible in outlying districts but in such situations help can be made available towards transport costs by the Department of Employment. In many instances, however, the paraplegics were unaware of the possibility of such aid.

Our results indicate that the Disabled Persons

(Employment) Acts (1944, 1958) which require employers of 20 or more workers to employ a quota of registered disabled are not providing an answer in the West of Scotland. Dunham (1964) has already suggested that what is done under the Acts is only dependent upon goodwill.

The figures also suggest that many paraplegics were not referred to a Disablement Resettlement Officer and few were offered industrial rehabilitation. Moreover, those who did use these services were generally dissatisfied with the type of work offered. Studies elsewhere have revealed similar situations. Robinson (1970) found that only 11 out of 84 employed quadriplegics had obtained work through the D.R.O. and only 2 had received industrial rehabilitation. A recent survey of work and housing for the disabled in Great Britain found that of 146 unemployed who sought help from the D.R.O. only 5 obtained work through this service (Buckle, 1971).

One of the main problems up to now has been that local Disablement Resettlement Officers are usually part-time workers. Fortunately, however, the National Advisory Council on the Employment of the Disabled has agreed to reorganize the service. Under the new proposals resettlement work is becoming a full-time duty and officers will be trained for this purpose. The difficulties that the paraplegics in our group have had over rehabilitation and resettlement indicate the necessity of this development.

Social work services
The duty of local authorities to care for the disabled has been made clear in the Chronically Sick and Disabled Persons Act (1970). We therefore examined:

1. The contact between social workers and paraplegics.

2. Services made available to the paraplegic and family at home.

3. Provision of housing and house adaptations.

CONTACT BETWEEN SOCIAL WORKERS
AND PARAPLEGICS
During their period of hospital treatment, 49 paraplegics were seen by a medical social worker (Figure 42.4). Only 1 paraplegic did not see a medical worker as he was nursed at home. Forty-one paraplegics were visited at home by a local

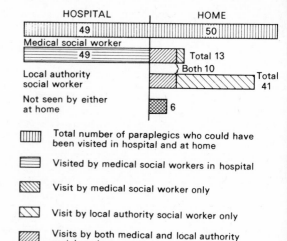

Figure 42.4   Contact between social workers and paraplegics in hospital and at home. The central vertical bar divides visits in hospital on the left from those at home, on the right.

(Reproduced from Johnson and Johnson (1972) by kind permission of the *British Medical Journal*.)

authority social worker. Thirteen paraplegics were visited by the medical social worker after they had been discharged from hospital and 10 of them were in contact at home with both social workers. Thus 3 paraplegics saw only the medical social workers at home. No paraplegic was visited in hospital by a local authority social worker although several families were contacted by their local authority before the patient's discharge, in connection with re-housing and home adaptations. Only 7 paraplegics received a routine introductory visit from a local authority social worker on arrival home from hospital. Others were visited at their own request to discuss house adaptations and aids. Often the paraplegics had regular contact with a local authority worker while arrangements were made for house alterations, but no further visits once the work was completed. On no occasion did a medical social worker and a local authority social worker visit a paraplegic's home together. Only 8 said that they were still contacted periodically. One young paraplegic, who had worked as a miner before his injury, had additional contact with the Coal Industry Social Welfare Organisation whose social worker visited regularly. Six had no contact with any social worker once they had left hospital.

The paraplegics who were at risk were those who lost contact with all social workers in the process of transferring from hospital to home. An example of this group is as follows:

A 52 year old married woman had been disabled for 8 years and was living in very poor social surroundings. As her husband was working she spent most of each day alone, relying on a married daughter to visit daily to help with housework and shopping. The front door and hall of the house were so constructed that she was unable to open the door to callers or to go out unaided. There was no telephone or other way to summon help. Throughout the interview this paraplegic sat on a bed-pan in her wheelchair as it was the only way she knew how to manage her incontinence. She seldom bathed as her husband could not lift her and she had to ask her daughter to bed-bath her. A local authority social worker had visited the house before the paraplegic was discharged, but never after her return home.

Communication between the hospital and the community services should be such that between them they provide a comprehensive service for the paraplegic and his family. There was often, however, a closer link maintained by the paraplegic with the hospital services than with the community services because doctors and social workers outside the spinal centres lacked detailed knowledge of paraplegia. Only 5 received regular visits from their doctor and it was therefore possible that general practitioners were not fully aware of their patients' problems. Similar difficulties were found in a study of the rehabilitation of 10 paraplegics discharged from the Liverpool Regional Paraplegic Centre at Southport, Lancashire (Reti, 1969; Forder, Reti and Silver, 1969). The study was mainly concerned with co-operation between medical personnel in the National Health Service and the authors concluded:

the study revealed many features in communication which resulted in frustration and hazards for the patients and their relatives.

In our group problems of communication were not purely medical. In hospital the medical social worker invariably saw the patients and their families. After discharge, however, we found evidence of inadequate liaison between social workers and the paraplegics and between social workers themselves. In particular some families underwent considerable anxiety when the patient was discharged, showing a greater need for emotional and practical support at this time.

Three wives reported their experience as follows:

When he came home the first time the ambulance man just dumped him and left. I didn't know how to look after him and he had to try to show me what he had learned from the nurses. It was a matter of trial and error.

We had been married three years and had a year-old baby. They brought him home from hospital and I didn't know how to cope. It was terrible.

It would have helped to have met other wives in the same position who could have given me advice.

A visit from the local authority social worker to the paraplegic in hospital and to the family shortly after his discharge would have allayed some of these anxieties. Teaching of simple nursing care, together with a booklet on the subject would have helped many (Forder, Reti and Silver, 1969). Further, to ensure continuous support of the paraplegic and his family, there is a need for information about the paraplegic to be given direct to the local authority Social Work Departments and for a member in each department to have special concern for the problems of the disabled and the services available for them.

Under Section 1 of the Chronically Sick and Disabled Persons Act (1970), which came into force on 1 October 1971, local authorities in England and Wales must assess the numbers and needs of chronically sick and disabled persons in their area and publicize the services which are available to them. This should provide the social services with a comprehensive register of disabled persons which was not previously achieved under the permissive powers of registration of Section 29 of the National Assistance Act, 1948. In conjunction with the Act a circular has been sent to local authorities requesting that they be imaginative and generous in the provision of services. They have also been recommended to undertake local sample surveys of the needs of disabled people, to launch publicity campaigns and to submit progress reports to the Secretary of State.

Unfortunately Section 1 of the Chronically Sick and Disabled Persons Act (1970) does not extend to Scotland. In Scotland the cover provided by this section is understood to be available as a result of Section 12 of the Social Work (Scotland) Act (1968), the terms of which are far more general:

> It shall be the duty of every local authority to promote social welfare by making available advice, guidance and assistance on such a scale as may be appropriate for their area. . . .

There is no specific reference made in the Scottish legislation to the registration and needs of the disabled. As a result we feel that this group may continue to have low priority in the apportionment of social services and that services available to the disabled will continue to vary from area to area.

We found paraplegics with whom the local authority social worker had not kept in touch and who were not informed of services available to them. The implementation of Section 1 of the Chronically Sick and Disabled Persons Act should help to overcome these problems in England and Wales, but there is no comparable legislation to provide a more efficient information and advisory service for the disabled living in Scotland.

SERVICES AVAILABLE TO THE PARAPLEGIC AT HOME

Section 2 of the Chronically Sick and Disabled Persons Act (1970) requires local authorities to consider the provision of facilities in the home. This is the first time that legislation has detailed services to be provided for disabled persons where there is need. Thus Section 2 provides for:

(a) Practical assistance in the home.

(b) Wireless, television, library or similar recreational facilities.

(c) Lectures, games, outings, recreational facilities outside the home and educational facilities.

(d) Assistance in travelling to use services outside the home.

(e) Assistance with home adaptation.

(f) Holiday facilities.

(g) Meals at home or elsewhere.

(h) Telephone or any special equipment necessary for its use.

Section 2, like Section 1, does not apply to Scotland. Because of this we wished to see to what extent these services were being provided in our area.

Many paraplegics already had one or more of the facilities specified (Figure 42.5), but there were some cases of need and there was little evidence that local authorities were going to assist with their provision. The most noticeable inadequacy was in the provision of telephones. Thirty-seven paraplegics had privately owned telephones. They provided an essential method of communication with medical and social services and also relieved the isolation of those who were partly housebound. Twenty-two paraplegics had obtained a telephone after disablement. On 4 occasions installation had been rapid (2—3 weeks after application) despite the Post Office's long waiting list. This was often due to intervention on behalf of the paraplegic by social workers and medical practitioners, but none had received financial help

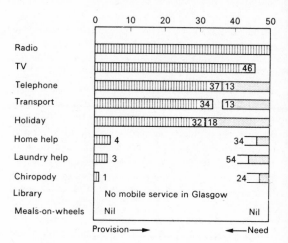

Figure 42.5 The provision of some of the facilities covered by the Chronically Sick and Disabled Persons Act (1970). The number of paraplegics is indicated on the horizontal scales.

(Reproduced from Johnson and Johnson (1972) by kind permission of the *British Medical Journal*.)

from the local authority. Thirteen had no telephone and the need for one was expressed by them all. Under normal circumstances, 74 per cent ownership for telephones would be considered high (*The Family Expenditure Survey for 1968* showed only 29 per cent of British households possessing this amenity (Source: Table 194, *British Labour Statistics*)), but Section 2 of the 1970 Act recognizes the telephone as an essential facility for the disabled. Only one local authority in the survey area plans to provide telephones for the chronically sick and disabled, setting aside £1,000 for this purpose (*Glasgow Herald*, 3 June 1971).

Thirty-four paraplegics possessed either an invalid vehicle or an adapted car. Three others lived with a car-owner, but 13 paraplegics had no form of transport readily available to them. We found no evidence of local authorities providing transport services on a comprehensive scale in accordance with Section 2(d) of the Chronically Sick and Disabled Persons Act. Some paraplegics (11) had been on holidays arranged by welfare or voluntary organizations, but 18 others had not been away, mainly because of cost. If more help had been made available to those who had not had holidays, several might have accepted it. The assessment of other needs which were not covered was more difficult (Figure 42.5). A number of paraplegics, besides those indicated in the figure, might have benefited from some services if these had been more widely available.

A survey of the handicapped in a quarter of a million households estimated that although 3 out of 4 were assisted by at least one service there remained 2,000 very severely handicapped and 90,000 others who were living alone and not receiving services (Buckle, 1971). A writer reviewing that survey found consolation in the Chronically Sick and Disabled Persons Act and commented:

> the situation revealed in the report may soon be improved.
>
> (Leader, *Lancet*, 1971.)

We are concerned that improvement is less assured in Scotland where the provision of these services is not guaranteed by legislation.

HOUSING AND HOUSE ADAPTATIONS

Section 3 of the Chronically Sick and Disabled Persons Act, 1970, lays a new duty on local authorities, including those in Scotland, to consider the particular needs of the chronically sick and disabled when planning the provision of housing. Special houses are to be distinguished in planning proposals.

In the group of paraplegics, 35 had moved house because of their disability (Table 42.3). This was usually arranged before discharge. Twenty-one obtained accommodation through their local authority and local authorities also assisted 33 paraplegics with aids and interior alterations. There were, however, still a number of paraplegics whose homes were inadequate. Seven had an upstairs bathroom and W.C. to which they had to be carried and one family had no bath. Two paraplegics had their beds in the living room as this was the only ground-floor room. They, and 2 others, could not leave their homes unaided because of front door steps too steep to be ramped. Six of these families had never been rehoused and 4 had been inappropriately rehoused by the local authority.

Section 3 of the Chronically Sick and Disabled Persons Act (1970) places a duty on local authorities when considering new housing to:

> have regard to the special needs of chronically sick or disabled persons . . . and distinguish any houses which the authority propose to provide which make special provision for the needs of such persons.

This section of the Act came into force on 29 August 1970, shortly before our survey commenced. Nevertheless, local authority provision of purpose-built housing in the area is still very limited and none of our paraplegics occupied such

Table 42.3 Housing of paraplegics after disability

No change		11
Local authority rehousing		
Before discharge — adequate	13	
After discharge — adequate	1	
Before discharge — inadequate	7	
Special housing	Nil	
	Total	21
Private housing		14
		46

Note: 4 paraplegics moved for reasons unrelated to their disability.

accommodation. One authority has integrated special bungalows into a new housing scheme and at least one other plans to provide such facilities. In Glasgow the City Factor holds information on houses that have been structurally altered for the handicapped so that these might be appropriately re-allocated, but no special houses have been included in new developments.

Conclusion

In examining the social consequences of disability in 50 paraplegics in Scotland we have had the advantage of studying a group with obvious handicap. We would suggest that the difficulties in obtaining employment and social services may be greater for subjects with less clearly defined disability. It would appear that the exclusion of Scotland from Sections 1 and 2 of the Chronically Sick and Disabled Persons Act (1970) may place disabled people in Scotland at a disadvantage compared with those in England and Wales.

Note. As a result of the summary article in the *British Medical Journal* on this work (25 March 1972), Dr. Dickson Mabon (M.P. for Greenock) introduced a Private Members Bill in the House of Commons on 30 March 1972, to extend Sections 1 and 2 of the Chronically Sick and Disabled Persons Act (1970) to Scotland. The Bill received a third reading on 16 June 1972, and Royal Assent on 27 July, 1972.

REFERENCES

BUCKLE, J. R. (1971) *Work and Housing of Impaired Persons in Great Britain* (part II of *Handicapped and Impaired in Great Britain*), H.M.S.O.

CUSHING, H. (1927) 'The Med. Dept. U.S. Army in World War I', *Surgery* 11, Part 1, 757 (quoted by Guttman, 1965.

Department of Employment and Productivity (1969) *Family Expenditure Survey. Report for 1968*, London: H.M.S.O.

Department of Employment and Productivity (1971) *British Labour Statistics: Historical Abstracts 1886–1968*, London: H.M.S.O.

Department of Employment and Productivity (annual from 1971), *British Labour Statistics Yearbook* (annual data from 1969), London: H.M.S.O.

DUNHAM, C. (1964) 'Employment from a Wheelchair', *Paraplegia* 2, 40–2.

EVERTS, W. H. and WOODHALL, P. (1944) 'The management of head and spinal cord injuries in the Army' *Journal of the American Medical Association,* 126, 145.

FORDER, A., RETI, T. and SILVER, J. R. (1969) 'Communication in the Health Service: A case study of the Rehabilitation of Paraplegic Patients', *Social and Economic Administration,* 3, 3–16.

GEHRIG, R. and MICHAELIS, L. S. (1968) 'Statistics of Acute Paraplegia and Tetraplegia on a National Scale', *Paraplegia* 6, 93–5.

GUTTMAN, L. (1962) 'Our Paralysed Fellowmen at Work', *Rehabilitation* 43, 9–17.

GUTTMAN, L. (1964) 'The Married Life of Paraplegics and Tetraplegics', *Paraplegia* 2, 182–8.

GUTTMAN, L. (1965) 'Services for the Treatment and Rehabilitation of Spinal Paraplegics and Tetraplegics in Great Britain', in *Trends in Social Welfare*, p. 319, Pergamon Press: Oxford.

GUTTMAN, L. (1967) 'History of the National Spinal Injuries Centre, Stoke Mandeville Hospital, Aylesbury', *Paraplegia* 5, 115–26.

HARDY, A. G. and WARRELL, D. W. (1965) 'Pregnancy and Labour in Complete Tetraplegia', *Paraplegia* 3, 182–8.

JOHNSON, R. H. and JOHNSON, G. S. (1972) 'Differences in opportunities for the disabled in England and Scotland: A survey of paraplegics in Scotland', *British Medical Journal*, 1, 779–82.

'LANCET' LEADER (1971) 'Help for the Handicapped', *Lancet* i, 1169.

RETI, T. K. (1969) 'Role and Communications in the Rehabilitation of Paraplegics'. Report for Liverpool Regional Hospital Board, 71 pp. (unpublished).

ROBINSON, R. S. (1970) *Survey of Employment for Quadruplegics (United Kingdom)* National Spinal Injuries Centre, Stoke Mandeville Hospital, Aylesbury, Buckinghamshire (privately circulated).

SIEGEL, M. S. (1969) 'Planning for Employment for the Quadruplegic', *Proceedings of the 17th Veterans Administration Spinal Cord Injury Conference, New York*, 230–3.

THOMPSON, M. A. and MURRAY, W. A. (1967) *Paraplegia at Home: A Pilot Survey*, E. & S. Livingstone: Edinburgh and London.

43. Assessment of the severely disabled*

P. J. R. NICHOLS

Director of the Disabled Living Research Unit at the
Nuffield Orthopaedic Centre and of the Oxford
Rehabilitation Unit, and Consultant in Rheumatology
and Rehabilitation

General assessment

One of the most difficult problems in the management of the severely disabled is to establish an assessment of the long-term prognosis. Many of the disorders leading to severe disability have their own unpredictable variations (for example, rheumatoid arthritis). Others, which are known to be progressive, such as muscular dystrophy and motor neurone disease, proceed at varying rates. So-called static disabilities (for example, traumatic paraplegia) are subject to intermittent intercurrent problems, particularly urinary infections, which have a dominant influence on the patient's capabilities, while others, such as multiple sclerosis, are associated with many other disabilities deriving from the same underlying pathology. Furthermore, there is increasing evidence that many disorders are polymorphic and the disability is an interaction of environmental and inherent factors which will interact differently, according to the circumstances. The complexity of these factors makes a comprehensive appraisal not only very important but also very difficult. With physical limitation of rehabilitation services and shortage of staff, it is necessary to indicate quantitatively which patients will benefit from rehabilitation and which patients are likely to remain uninfluenced.

Walking can be said to be dependent upon strength and endurance, rather than co-ordination,
whereas upper-limb function is more dependent on co-ordinated muscle activity. Difficulties in walking may arise from many possible causes; for example, hemiparetic patients may have interference with balance, or muscle weakness, or spasticity. Balance may be disturbed by lesions of the cerebellar systems or the visual system. Muscle weakness of trunk, abdomen, hip, knee or foot muscle groups may all seriously affect walking. Similarly, spasticity in lower-limb muscle groups, flexors or extensors, will seriously impair locomotor function. Walking ability is also related to mental alertness, but incontinence, cardiovascular disease, joint degeneration and sensory deficit may individually or collectively have a significant effect. Thus the assessment of a patient's mobility potential must include an appraisal of all these motor and sensory aspects of the patient's condition.

The functions assessed under the activities of daily living are relatively standardized; feeding, dressing, personal hygiene, writing, typing and simple manual tasks. Charts of activities can be graded to indicate levels of activity, and if correlated with the initial level of function, successive assessments will give a record of changes and indicate the degree of recovery or the effectiveness of rehabilitation measures.

Most occupational therapy departments have their own charts of activities of daily living and many departments have added to these records a system of scoring. Quantitative assessments expressed numerically offer the attraction of ready

*From P. J. R. Nichols, (1971) *Rehabilitation of the Severely Disabled, Part 2, 'Management'*, London, Butterworths, Chapter 2, pp. 19—37, 371—5

comparison; patient with patient, or capability with capability. But the assumption that the physical assessment of competence in activities of daily living provides a simultaneous assessment of a patient's functional capabilities is merely naïve. The practical domestic situation is much more complex.

As yet, there is no detailed analysis of the inter-relationship of clinical records, muscle charts, joint range and competence in activities of daily living. There is no analysis of the inter-relationship between competence in, say, putting on a vest, eating bread and butter, and controlling a wheelchair. Furthermore, competence in any particular activity achieves different levels of significance in different sets of circumstances. For example, the ability to walk from wheelchair to toilet may have more significance for domestic independence than the ability to walk from house to shops.

In order to obtain a comprehensive functional assessment, detailed records of function are necessary; but these can become so complex that processing the data presents almost insuperable problems, outweighing the value of the possible results. But functional assessment can provide a comprehensive index of a patient's capability, giving a realistic appraisal of the patient, more relevant than simple records of joint range and estimation of muscle power.

The primary object of assessment is not necessarily description or classification, but an exploration of the functional variables which may serve to help predict responses to treatment. By reviewing daily living activities in near real-life situations, it is possible to achieve a considerable exposure of the important but intangible and immeasurable variables which are often the most important; the patient's willingness to co-operate, his tolerance of failure, levels of aspiration, ability to understand new situations, awareness of limitations and capabilities, his level of intelligence and education, in short, his motivation.

Such practical tests as the occupational therapist can carry out in assessing activities of daily living can be developed into graded orders: ability to adapt to decisions made, accuracy and endurance. They can give a very clear understanding of the patient, although they do not provide an IQ or a 'mental status' quotient. In all functional assessments the patient's capabilities are more important than their disabilities and the changing patterns of competence present a pragmatic measure of recovery.

Successful response to treatment depends very largely on the patient's ability to understand, adjust and accept the treatment. For this reason emotional and intellectual status influence the final result. There are likely to be definite patterns in the pre-morbid state, and an understanding of the patient's normal mode of living and capabilities obtained by direct questioning of relatives and neighbours when compared with his current ability will lead an experienced therapist to a shrewd quantitative assessment of the standard of attainment which can be achieved.

Sometimes clues can be derived from social or welfare workers, sometimes from direct personal knowledge such as school reports, and all possible sources should be explored to enable a firm appraisal of the pre-morbid personality.

Patients' potentials for recovery and for rehabilitation are as diverse as the patients themselves and their disorders, ranging from the achievement of a single function, such as the ability to 'transfer', to the return to full-time employment. There are no objective criteria available by which the clinician is enabled to predict the potential of rehabilitation or to determine which patients will achieve much and which patients will achieve little. The most a detailed clinical reappraisal will yield is general guidance regarding the progress of the disability.

Physical assessment

After the general clinical assessment, attention can be directed towards the patient's independence and functional capability. The physical features of the patient's clinical condition determine the intensity of rehabilitation activities and delineate the aims of management. Because of the complexity of problems inherent in the management of the severely disabled, a full clinical examination and record is essential. For many patients, a muscle chart (usually graded 0–5 in accordance with the Medical Research Council scale) is a useful base line. But also it is important with many severely disabled patients to record muscle contractures as these may determine handicap and may be amenable to improvement by physiotherapy or surgical measures. [. . .]

Flexion deformity of the wrists, whether from changes consequent upon rheumatoid arthritis or a congenital deformity such as radial club hand, may put the hand in a functional position as regards feeding. Very careful assessment of function is necessary because correction of the deformity may render the patient unable to feed, although producing a meaningful improvement in power of grip. To compensate for the correction of wrist flexion, an increase in elbow or shoulder range may render the patient once again independent for feeding. The flexed wrist compensates for loss of elbow flexion and conversely in the presence of limited elbow movement, correction of the wrist deformity demands a functional improvement in elbow movement to retain function.

Furthermore, it is only by detailed clinical reappraisal that the effectiveness of various alternative methods of management can be compared. Much time can be spent in devising complex wheelchairs or gadgetry, or in altering the domestic situation, whereas it may be possible to achieve some significant improvement in function by a surgical procedure. Sometimes an appropriate splint can be devised to simulate the end-result which surgery hopes to achieve and a functional assessment of the efficacy of this splint indicates the improvement which surgery is likely to produce.[. . .]

Functional assessment

Clinical assessment is based on a stylized system of 'history taking', clinical examination, muscle-power charting and so on, without which significant details may be missed. Functional assessment can be systemized and formalized, based on Activities for Daily Living charts and graded activities. Although much information can be acquired by questioning, observation of activities is more helpful. A patient may state that he is completely independent for dressing and undressing and yet under direct observation, it may soon be clear that either he has taken a certain amount of help for granted, or he cheats by failing to complete some aspects of the task, or he is unrealistic (euphoric) and lacking in insight about his handicap. This distinction is only available after direct functional assessment and may give the clinician quite a different appraisal of the situation from that which he gained in the out-patient department or on examining the patient in a hospital ward. Sometimes it is sufficient to know that the patient is able to carry out a particular

activity, but on other occasions it is essential to record the details of how the task is performed as trick movements may be a risk if new techniques are introduced or the functional anatomy altered by surgical procedures. It is in this field that film records can be invaluable, allowing for careful study of movements without overtiring the patient, and allowing for repetitive analysis.

Preliminary functional assessment can be directed towards the main areas of activity as follows:

Personal care	Nursing Feeding Toilet Dressing
Mobility	Walking Wheelchairs Transfers
Household	Cooking Housework
Hobbies/recreation	
Outdoor activities	
Work	

Enquiry will enlarge upon some of these activities, particularly home conditions, general mobility and upper-limb function.

Home conditions

Type of house, flat, bungalow, Residential Home

Main problems, access-steps, stairs, bathroom upstairs and so on

Family living at home, relatives or friends near

Mobility

General pattern

Lie, sit, stand, walk

Walking unaided, aids, appliances

Implications at home, ramps, steps, kerbs, distances

Lie, sit, wheelchair, method of transfer, suitable chair

Method of propulsion

Outdoor transport, private, public

Upper-limb function

Reaching, lifting, carrying, handling

Having obtained an over-all impression of the patient's problems, direct detailed observation will enable the therapist to build up a picture of the patient's handicap under the following headings:

Personal care
>Washing, including hair, nails, shaving or
>>make-up
>Toilet
>Bath
>Dressing
>Eating and drinking

Communication
>Speech, telephoning, writing, typing
>Public transport, shopping, social functions

Domestic activities
>Basic meal preparation and housework where
>applicable for men and women.

Work/education/training
>Including job of running a home
>Problems related to patient's particular job and
>place of work or education.

Leisure activities
>Personality and mental attitude:
>Positive or negative attitude
>>Quick or slow reaction
>>Anxious or relaxed
>>Co-operative or resentful
>>Dependent or independent.

These headings form the basis for the therapist's preliminary assessment.

When the main problems lie in personal independence a more detailed analysis of activities of daily living is called for (*see* Appendix I).

As far as home conditions are concerned, it is always preferable for a therapist to carry out a domiciliary visit, but where this is not practical, it is probably simpler to ask the domiciliary occupational therapist employed by the local authority or the appropriate welfare officer, or social worker to complete a prepared questionnaire so that relevant details are not missed. Appendix 2 sets out a sample proforma for domiciliary assessment. [. . .]

For more detailed functional assessment, graded tests can be devised, but it is particularly important that these activities should be planned in the context of the patient's disability, home conditions, social background and likely resettlement. The process of getting up in the morning; sitting up in bed, getting out, going to the toilet, washing, dressing and grooming, may appear to repeat many of the functions observed in the preliminary assessment; but as a related sequence of events to be performed in reasonable time, this requires considerable perseverance and may un-

cover factors such as fatigue, pain or spasm not apparent when these activities are performed separately. As well as observing the physical function involved, step by step, points such as the following should be noted:

(1) How much of this sequence could the patient manage safely without help?

(2) Could any accident risk be reduced by the provision of aids such as grab rails?

(3) Would adjustment in heights of his bed, chair, or toilet help him?

(4) Would simple adaptations to his clothes help him?

(5) Was any pain, fatigue, or spasm noticeable and if so, was this due to any particular task in the sequence, or was it due to the sustained effort?

(6) Could the routine be simplified to make it less tiring or to reduce the time required?

(7) What was the patient's attitude, did he give up easily or did he persevere?

(8) Was he distressed by failure, was he angered by it or did he accept his limitations?

Household tasks such as planning and cooking a family meal, or washing, hanging out clothes and ironing can be used in a similar way.

Assessment for work

It is seldom possible to simulate the patient's job in an occupational therapy department, except perhaps for home-making, but it is possible to examine his work potential. Firstly, it is necessary to go carefully through the patient's daily routine by question and by definitive practical tests where necessary and when possible.

>Patient's occupation
>When last at work
>Getting up in the morning; can this be done in
>>reasonable time
>With or without help
>Main difficulties
>Mobility; walking, with or without aids
>Wheelchair; independent or needs help negotiating kerbs, crossing street
>Leaving the house; steps, slopes, rough grounds
>Public transport; distance to bus stop or train
>Mounting bus or train
>Any problem sitting in bus or train
>Distance from transport stop to place of work
>Private transport; car, invalid tricycle
>Getting in and out; with or without help
>Getting wheelchair into vehicle

Difficulties with driving

Adaptations needed

Parking; distance from parking place to work

Sufficient space to off-load and transfer into wheelchair

Access to place of work and circulation; steps, slopes

Heavy swing-doors, narrow doors

Narrow passages, awkward corners

Circulation within working area

Atmosphere; heat, cold, damp, exposure to weather, any problems

Toilet; distance to toilet

Access to toilet; walking/wheelchair

Independent or needing help for toilet

Clothing; any difficulty with protective or special clothing

Food; distance and access to canteen

Any difficulties in eating

Confidence to eat in public

Facilities for eating packed meal

The general patterns of work activity need to be considered both as related sequences and as a series of tasks in separate contexts.

Architectural hazards are numerous and situations similar to those at work can usually be found without much difficulty. Specific work situations, prolonged standing, carrying, lifting, manual dexterity and so on may be tested by mock-up in an experienced rehabilitation centre. A therapist who has assessed the patient and seen him at work in the physiotherapy department and occupational therapy department can often tell directly what are the likely problems. A visit to the place of work and discussion with the employer, or employees in similar work may be of considerable help. Although these situations are more relevant to the less severely disabled, the principles apply to all disabled patients, at the stage when resettlement in work is being planned.

To avoid mistakes, frustrating to patients, therapists and employers alike, detailed assessment and planning is essential. For example, office work does not only involve typing or writing; filing letters, handling small cards, telephoning and taking down messages while sitting at a desk, lifting down and handling books, interviewing other people are all involved. Most patients have never had to consider and analyse work in this detail and often may find it difficult to describe or demonstrate it without the help of systematic

enquiry. Successful resettlement can be a complex activity for patient, therapist and rehabilitation or resettlement officer.

Social assessment

Social and welfare problems often predominate among the problems of the severely disabled. Once adequate clinical care has been instituted, the social and welfare aspects become increasingly important, particularly in the home situation. The majority of the severely physically disabled are cared for at home, and the family bears the brunt of the load of nursing and general care. The amount of support which the family receives depends on the family, and on the local organization. This varies considerably from area to area.

The majority of the problems are either concerning the handling of the disabled patient, particularly during the day when the able members of the family have to be at work or at school, and the housing. Patient-handling can be eased by the provision of various aids and appliances, hoists, commodes, special beds and by assistance from district nurses, domiciliary therapists and services such as Meals on Wheels. Most of the housing problems derive from difficulties of access and lack of manoeuvring space. The patients are often amenable to alterations, either minor or major structural changes, or to rehousing.

Rehousing may often appear to be an attractive solution from the physical handicap aspect of the problem; but such recommendations should be made only after careful assessment of the family relationships, and the likely support for the patients from the family and neighbours. Conversely the lack of family and local support is equally of importance in the over-all appraisal, because rehousing may not be helpful if it means leaving the neighbourhood where the patient has friends, neighbours and family connections. For the physically handicapped, much can be done with grip rails, ramps, re-hanging doors and the installation of suitable washing, toilet and bathing aids. The majority of housing adaptations are carried out within a year of recommendation, but rehousing takes considerably longer in most instances. [. . .]

No matter how the social assessment is achieved, it is a *sine qua non* in the total assessment of a severely physically disabled patient.

Personality and intellect assessment

Some authorities consider that many of the patient's personal characteristics are the result of external factors and that if the social environment and family background are supportive, the outcome of rehabilitation is likely to be successful. But lack of achievement may be associated with a lack of personal drive and endeavour as well as lack of opportunities or support from family, friends or community. The patient's reaction to the combination of all the relevant factors is often referred to under the general term 'motivation'. There is no evidence that there are particular personalities associated with specific disabilities, but some physical conditions have a direct organic effect upon the brain and central nervous system and thus may be associated with changes in intellect and personality.

It becomes important to record these faculties, never an easy task but doubly difficult in the case of disabled patients for whom many of the available 'test-batteries' are unsuitable. It is inappropriate to ask a wheelchair-bound patient dependent upon others to move him from place to place, about his aspirations for action and community activities.

Patients with painful joint conditions such as rheumatoid arthritis, voluntarily restrict their activities to avoid pain, and thus enquiries related to achievement and activities may produce inapposite answers. Standard questions such as 'Would you be unhappy if you were prevented from making numerous social contacts?' are clearly inappropriate.

Physical disability, whether painful or not, will undoubtedly induce a reactive depression in many instances; furthermore, severe disability in childhood will interfere with education and thus influence the assessment.

There is evidence that some of the most severely physically disabled patients have stable personalities, because they no longer have to struggle, they are cared for. But progressive lack of social activities accompanying disability is often associated with an increasingly introverted personality.

The correlation between educational levels and achievement is definite. Patients who have had a higher education are predominant among those who achieve maximal activity in spite of severe disability. This feature is closely linked with the social status and the consequent opportunity or support for education. Certain disabilities, particularly strokes and multiple sclerosis, are associated with organic damage, intellectual deterioration and personality change, impairment of memory, lack of insight into the disability, and an inability to adapt or to accept training, all of which mitigate against rehabilitation techniques; and it is an essential part of the total assessment of the patient to delineate these features. A full psychological assessment can often give a clear indication regarding the possible outcome of rehabilitation or indicate the particular lines of management likely to give best results.

There is a need to establish standard personality, educational and intellectual status tests applicable to the physically disabled and there is a wide field of activity for collaboration with clinical psychologists in the field of physical rehabilitation.

Records, reports and communication

[. . .] A clearly set out assessment of functional activity and the other relevant factors can be a more useful record of handicap and achievement than lengthy muscle charts and clinical examinations. The example given here illustrates how such a report gives a complete picture of the patient against which all therapy and management can be appraised.

Occupational Therapist's Report

Preliminary Assessment: date

Name: Mr. B . . . . .   Age: 50   Ward G

Diagnosis: Rheumatoid arthritis

Home conditions

Lives in an old cottage with his wife, who works as a secretary, and son aged 16 years who is studying for 'O' levels. Three steps at front door; patient can no longer manage these. Outside toilet, approach slippery and uneven. Mr. B sleeps downstairs. Neighbours bring him his midday meal.

Mobility

Patient is virtually chairbound and only stands and shuffles three or four steps to transfer from bed to wheelchair to toilet. Has 8G wheelchair and Invacar.

Upper-limb function
Generalized loss of power and loss of precision function of both hands. Loss of joint range in shoulder and elbows limits his reach to mid-range.

Personal care
Can wash face and hands only, shaves himself, wife washes him. Bathroom upstairs. Cannot get off toilet. Has difficulty cleaning himself.

Dressing
Dependent on his wife, who dresses him before she goes to work every morning.

Communications
Has to be helped into Invacar, but does go out to friends. No other problems.

Work
Was an electrician, and was still working part-time until 15 months ago.

Mental attitude
Mr. B. resents being dependent on others, and is worried because his wife is the wage earner. He is friendly, easy in manner and appears eager to get some work.

Suggestions
Occupational therapist to meet domiciliary occupational therapist and welfare officer at cottage *re* roughened concrete path to toilet and (?) sloped concrete path from gate to back door. To try out toilet heights and grab-rails. To look into dressing and clothing problems. Possibility of some part-time work discussed with medical social worker. Occupational therapist to test his aptitude for figures (his writing is clear though slow) and (?) adding-machine and typing.

THE NEED FOR REPEATED ASSESSMENT
Assessment is not an isolated single episode, but a continuing sequence of examinations, studies, consultations, appraisals, and reviews of the patient's capabilities and handicaps, based upon complete evaluation of the physical, functional, educational, psychological and social attainments. The personnel involved in obtaining this comprehensive review is large, and only relatively few patients require the full range of studies. Therefore, it is probably appropriate that such assessments should be carried out in special centres which are closely associated with a regional clinical centre. Because of their special experience, such centres should also be able to provide postgraduate training for therapists and other ancillary staff. The first task lies in identifying the problems. The initial selection of the patients is important, referral being necessarily selective, and this is followed by the comprehensive assessment, then the planning of rehabilitation in all its aspects, therapy, appliances, training and resettlement. From the centres, there would emerge continuing studies of the disabilities, and a continuing programme of teaching and research. But for the work to remain clinically and practically orientated, the most important step is the follow-up. This only becomes realistic if it is taken right into the patient's home, or other place of domestic resettlement. For it is at home, about a year after the last admission, that the real test of success or failure lies.

The need for continued detailed reassessment is illustrated by the two case histories, No. 582 and No. 54.

M.M.L. No. 582   born 1946   male
Diagnosis: Osteogenesis imperfecta

This young man was a classical example of osteogenesis imperfecta. He was small, intelligent with a relatively large head and characteristically high-pitched 'metallic' voice.

His limbs were small and deformed from numerous fractures and his trunk foreshortened with a marked kyphoscoliosis and 'keeling' of the chest wall. He had a remarkably objective view of his disability and of life in general.

Throughout his life, he had been cared for by his mother, and had achieved an educational level suitable for university entrance. The problem now was whether he could achieve enough independence to take up his university place. Clearly, the two main problems were mobility and personal care.

After many discussions, a university was found which could both offer him a course suitable to his academic capabilities and interest, and also was prepared to collaborate in organizing suitable accommodation.

At this time, he was using a child-size front-wheel-drive self-propelling wheelchair and a Barret light-weight outdoor motorized tricycle. He was unable to get his wheelchair into the tricycle and his parents were lifting him for all transfers. He needed help with washing and toilet, and having led a very sheltered life, was somewhat unrealistic both about the problems he might face and possible solutions.

The first problem was that of the wheelchair and his transfer techniques. Eventually, after much practice, a special chair was ordered with the following specifications:

Wheels. 20 in (50 cm) diameter front propelling wheels with solid tyres; 8 in (20 cm) castor wheels at the rear

Seat. 13 in (32 cm) × 13 in (32 cm) and 18 in (46 cm) height from the ground

Cushion. 2 in (5 cm) hard based

Back. 'Zip' back with the zip set 4 in (10 cm) from the right-hand side of the back canvas. The zip to be operated from the front and to open from the top downwards, and to have 2 in (5 cm) overlength to ease replacement after opening.

He was able to lift objects of up to 3 lb (1.36 kg) in weight, so from a household point of view, he could manage to cook light meals. Long-handled pick-up appliances made him independent for many other activities. A pair of specially made portable ramps were also provided and enabled hime to achieve universal access to home and university. This chair was based on a lightweight folding frame and proved to be highly successful. With this chair he was able to transfer independently, using a sliding board, into bed and in and out of his outdoor tricycle.

The toilet was a problem, but he could transfer on and off through the back of the chair providing the seat was between 20 and 22 in high (50—57 cm). On the toilet he used a 'child's' seat. If the toilet was lower than 20 in (50 cm) he used a specially made 'overseat', which was 20 in (50 cm) high at the front and 22 in (57 cm) at the back (the University toilet seats were 17½ in (44 cm) high).

Washing was achieved with a long-handled sponge. He was independent using a wash-basin 26 in (66 cm) high with 21 in (52 cm) clearance underneath for the wheelchair. Bathing was accomplished by a double bath seat made to fit the bath available at home and at college. An occupational therapist from the Unit went with the patient and a local social worker to the University and discussed all the likely problems with the medical and welfare authorities.

The University was able to allocate special accommodation and make some minor structural alterations once they were convinced that the assessments made were realistic. For example, the wardrobe doors were altered so that he could reach the handle, the mirrors were lowered, and gantry tables were provided at the correct height. His special toilet seats were provided in two suitable toilets and in one the door was removed and a curtain provided.

COMMENT

A detailed assessment and comprehensive plans of function followed by willing collaboration from University authorities and local authority social and welfare authorities, enabled him to achieve university education.

At follow-up a year later, he had moved out of the special accommodation into some standard quarters which he found himself and could manage. This brought him into the general life of the University rather than segregating him in special accommodation and isolating him from University community life. This illustrates how the well-motivated patient will progress with his independence once given the facilities and help to take the first steps.

M.M.L. No. 54   born 1947   female
Diagnosis: Poliomyelitis; Keratoconus; Eczema; Ehlers-Danlos syndrome.

At 2 years of age, this girl had an attack of acute anterior poliomyelitis which left her with severe weakness of both legs. She eventually was able to walk with crutches and calipers, and various orthopaedic procedures were undertaken to maintain her mobility. At the age of 10 years she had rotation osteotomy of the right femur and at 15 years of age she had transplantation of tibialis anterior to the os calsis.

Her childhood was spent mostly at a school for physically handicapped children. She rarely went home as her mother had remarried, achieved a new family, and found it increasingly difficult to manage her. Her schooling had frequently been interrupted by treatment and she was pleasant but a rather frustrated, aggressive and difficult child.

While in hospital, she began to have recurrent dislocation of the right hip, and later the same year this was arthrodesed. She had great difficulty during her post-operative rehabilitation period. Her sight was deteriorating because of keratoconus, eventually requiring a corneal graft in 1965. She was by now having repeated dislocation of the left hip and a pseudarthrosis was performed.

From 1965 onwards, she was admitted to the Disabled Living Unit at intervals, usually during each school holiday. On the first admission, she was supplied with a semi-reclining self-propelled wheelchair with elevating footrests and 25 in (63 cm) diameter rear wheels. It had to be reclining with elevating legrests, because of the arthrodesis of the right hip and cushioning was complicated. At this time, she was able to transfer from bed to chair by means of a sliding board, and direct from chair to toilet if the seat was at 21 in (52 cm), and had an old-fashioned wooden surround.

She was accepted as a pupil at a special school for physically handicapped older girls; she settled in very well and achieved GCE 'O' levels in English language, English literature and history. However, her increased activity precipitated painful symptoms in her right shoulder. The apparent weakness was at first thought to be due to muscular dystrophy, but estimation of the serum creato-kinase and electromyography were normal, and clinically it was considered that she was a mild case of Ehlers-Danlos syndrome.

By December 1966, she was having so much trouble with her shoulder that self-propelling was an increasingly slow and painful procedure. It was therefore considered justifiable to issue her with an electrically-powered indoor chair, with a similar frame and cushioning to the self-propelled one.

She was now doing well at school, the electric chair gave her considerable independence and opened up many possibilities for her. On total review, it was decided that her future lay only in a wheelchair existence and thus it was reasonable to convert the previously arthrodesed right hip to a pseudarthrosis and to fix the painful snapping scapula, and these operations were carried out during the school holidays.

These two operations and the subsequent rehabilitation produced further over-all improvement. She returned to school and achieved a total of 6 GCE 'O' levels. After she left school in the summer of 1968, she was accepted for further education at a technical college to work for GCE 'A levels. Much of the education was planned to be done on a correspondence basis and with visiting tutors, and with transfers organized by hospital friends she attended the college weekly for practical sessions.

In January 1969, she entered a residential home to make a new life, continuing her further education, contributing to the life of the Home and ultimately making a career for herself.

Although severely physically disabled and with very poor sight (officially registered as a blind person), she is an excellent cook with active hobbies of reading, needlework, cookery, music (including playing the clarinet).

This outcome was the combination of repeated re-assessments, orthopaedic surgery and rehabilitation, adapting her appliances and independence techniques to her current capabilities and finally undertaking surgery to allow her to adapt to increasing disability.

APPENDIX 1

Checklist of activities of daily living

Bed activities
Ring bell
Roll on to right side
Roll on to left side
Roll from back to stomach
    and back
Sit up from lying
Sit erect in bed
Sit erect with feet over
    edge of bed
Use bedpan or get out of
    bed to commode

Wheelchair activities
Propel forward
Propel backward
Turn
Use brake
Propel chair on uneven
    ground
Mount kerb
Propel chair up slope
Propel chair down slope
Cross street at traffic lights
Wheelchair to bed
Bed to wheelchair
Wheelchair to toilet
Toilet to wheelchair
Wheelchair to bath or
    shower
Bath or shower to wheel-
    chair
Open and close door
Reach floor
Wheelchair to car
Car to wheelchair

Standing and walking
Bed to standing position
Standing position to bed
Wheelchair to standing
Standing to wheelchair
Chair to standing (state
    height of chair)
Standing to chair
Toilet to standing
Standing to toilet
Bath or shower to standing
In and out of car
Walk less than 5 yd on
    even ground
Walk 5—10 yd on even
    ground
Walk more than 10 yd
Walk independently
Walk with sticks; crutches;
    aids
Walk on uneven ground

Walk up slope
Walk down slope

Personal care
Blow nose
Wash face
Wash trunk and arms
Wash below the waist
Clean teeth
Brush or comb hair
Clean nails
Shave or make-up
Turn on taps
Manage bottle
Manage toilet
Use paper
Flush toilet
Get in and out of bath

Dressing
Fastening Velcro
Fastening zips
Fastening buttons
Fastening press-studs or
    hooks
Put on clothes over head
Put on trousers or slacks
Brassiere
Roll-on or corset
Stockings or socks
Shoes
Jacket or cardigan
Tie
Orthopaedic appliances

Eating
Use fork or spoon
Use both together
Cut own food
Drink with straw
Drink from cup
Reach and pick up plate

General activities
Turn pages of book
Write name and address
Fold letter and seal
    envelope
Open envelope and remove
    letter
Type
Strike match and light
    cigarette
Switch light on and off
Use telephone
Wind watch
Handle money

Laundry
Wash small clothes in sink
Rub clothes
Wring clothes
Use washing machine
Use spin dryer
Peg clothes on to line
Carry laundry basket
Ironing
    Erect ironing board or
        prepare table for
        ironing
    Switch on iron
    Iron handkerchief,
        pillow-slip
    Iron shirt
    Refold ironing board

Kitchen
Turn on gas/electric taps
Open oven door and move
    shelves
Lift cake trays in and out
    of oven
Lift kettle of water
Turn on tap
Fill saucepan/kettle at tap
Open tins
Cream fat and sugar
Rub in fat and flour
Roll out pastry
Cut loaf of bread
Carve meat
Spread butter
Peel vegetables
Wash up, wipe up
Open refrigerator door

Housecleaning
Sweep floors
Vacuum-clean
Mop
Polish
Dust surfaces, high, low
Clean sink, basin, bath,
    toilet
Make beds

APPENDIX 2

Therapist's report on home conditions

Name: Age: Address:

Diagnosis: Equipment:

Neighbourhood   *Housing*
Rural; suburban; urban   House; flat; bungalow
Distance from shops   Owned; rented; tied
Transport available   Council; private ownership
                                          Pre-war; post-war
                                          State of repair
                                          Occupiers
                                          Who gives care
Access
From street to house
To front door (if used)
To back door (if used)

Circulation in house
Adequate space
    narrow passage; easy turn into rooms; awkward corners

Flooring   *Doors*
Types — carpet; lino   Widths
    polished surface
Condition   Thresholds
Level

Stairs   *Rails*
Straight; turned   One side; both sides
State tread   Are they adequate?
Rise
                                          Alteration potential
Lighting   House structure
Dark corners; passages   Furniture — heavy;
                                              light, too much

Details of rooms   *Attitude of family*   *Garden*
Kitchen   Flexible; understanding;   Cultivated; otherwise
Surface heights — table   co-operative   used (*e.g.* children,
                cooker   Unco-operative; over-protective   washing)
                sink   Approximate size
Storage — larder; refrigerator; cupboards (doors, shelves)   *Patient's activities*   Paths — level; steep;
Are facilities adequate?   Additional requirements: Responsibilities   smooth; rough; firm;
                                        children   soft; wide; narrow
Bathroom   dependent relatives   Is there a garage; shed;
Up; down; none   Height of bath   business   fuel store?

Lavatory: *Main problems*   *Occupational needs*
Up; down; outside   Height of seat
                                                               Hobby needs
Patient's bedroom
Circulation space   Height of bed   *To be done*   Being dealt with by:
    adequate; insufficient

44. Behaviour modification in rehabilitation*

LEE MEYERSON, NANCY KERR
AND JACK L. MICHAEL
Arizona State University, U.S.A.

The treatment of handicapped persons in rehabilitation centers often requires them to engage in activities that are difficult, effortful, or unpleasant to perform. It is not surprising, in view of this factor alone and without consideration of other possible influential variables, that many rehabilitation clients resist rehabilitative efforts. Nor is it surprising that rehabilitation personnel complain frequently of 'lack of motivation' in their clients or that the proportion of cases discharged from rehabilitation centers for this reason is relatively high.

Characteristically, the patient whose behavior fails to conform to the expectations of the rehabilitation staff is referred to the psychologist for 'evaluation.' Much of the work of the psychologist in rehabilitation is at present devoted to the routine evaluation of client intelligence, personality, and achievement, in the belief that these data are 'good things' to know and that they may help the staff do better work. Most of the data obtained, however, seem strikingly unrelated to the behavior required in the rehabilitation center. They may lead the psychologist to believe that he 'understands' better why a client acts as he does, but the data lend little aid in changing unacceptable behavior to more acceptable behavior. Most often the psychologist confirms the observation of others that the client is unmotivated, and he assigns a reason for it. This reason is usually some inaccessible trait of the client: 'He hasn't accepted his disability.' 'He isn't bright enough or mature

enough to understand what is best for him.' 'He is overly dependent.' 'His super-ego is weak.'

Sometimes such evaluations are accompanied by vague directions to give the client 'psychological support,' to coax him more, or counsel him so that he will understand himself better. More often they seem to result in a decision to discharge the client as unmotivated or as having reached the maximum medical benefit that is possible without long-term psychotheraphy which may or may not change the underlying or 'real' personality problems.

This kind of approach to rehabilitation not only places an overwhelmingly, needless, and often unfulfillable responsibility on the client to be the architect of his own rehabilitation, but also neglects two other basic variables that can be manipulated for the client's benefit: his environment and, as a result of the manipulation of his environment, his behavior.

Most rehabilitation psychologists will accept formula B = f (P, E), or behavior is a function of a person's interaction with his environment. In concentrating on the P term in the formula, however, it is easy to neglect the fact that the formula has three terms and that B and E can be independent variables also. Among psychologists who strive to do more than measure and categorize the traits of disabled persons, present practice is to attempt to direct changes in the person by counseling and verbal psychotherapeutic procedures. It is not generally perceived that equally indirect changes of the psychological situation by manipulation of the environment may be equally valuable and far more feasible. It may be better, for example, to assist a physical therapist in achieving

*From S. W. Bijou, and D. M. Baer (eds.) (1967) *Child Development: Reading in Experimental Analysis*, New York, Appleton-Century-Crofts, Chapter 19, 240—59.

his goal of restoring functional use of an arm or leg than to attempt to deal with the inferiority feelings or dependency status that may be engendered in a person because he lacks such functional use. Counseling and psychotherapy were developed in an attempt to modify abnormal reactions to normal situations. It is by no means clear that they are the treatments of choice for normal reactions to abnormal situations.

Following the pattern of previous experimentation (Meyerson & Kerr, in press), in which operant conditioning techniques were used to obtain striking behavioral changes in rehabilitation clients, we accepted at face value the behavioral problems referred to us by other members of a rehabilitation-center team. We gave no tests; we made no evaluations; we held no interviews; we took no history. In fact, we generally knew nothing at all about the person referred to us except that he was not engaging in some behavior that was desirable for his rehabilitation. In addition, almost all of the experimental work was conducted by first year graduate students who had had no previous experience in clinical psychology or rehabilitation, but who did know learning theory.

We were guided in this work by the theoretical formulations of the Workgroup on Learning of the Miami Conference on Psychological Research and Rehabilitation (Meyerson, Michael, Mowrer, Osgood and Staats, 1963). In particular, we took seriously the following statements:

Motivation may be considered the task of specifying adequate reinforcers (p. 91).
If an individual 'should' do something . . . you must provide strong reinforcers contingent upon his behavior . . . (p. 92).
One of the most important things that we can offer . . . is a frame of reference which induces (psychologists in rehabilitation) to look for adequate reinforcers and to apply them correctly, skilfully and subtly . . . if this approach were followed, many presently difficult problems might become readily amenable to solution (p. 101).
Psychologists in rehabilitation (should) look for causal, manipulable variables in a situation which they would then use to facilitate the generally accepted goals of rehabilitation workers (p. 78).

Some of the problems referred to us were remarkably simple ones that could be solved immediately by the application of a single behavioral principle. Others were much more complex, and the results reported here can be considered only a beginning in the application of behavioral principles to some rehabilitation problems. As in other beginnings, our initial experiments have been crude, lacking in the precision and elegance of design, the data collecting and the reporting that are desirable, but a start has been made, and the fruitfulness of the approach may be apparent.

Case 1.
Lack of motivation in a traumatic quadruplegic adolescent

Background:
John K. was in an automobile accident when he was 16 years old. After he had spent four months in what was medically diagnosed as a decerebrate condition, recovery of function began to occur. At the time he was first seen by us, at the age of 18 he was unable to walk and tremors in the upper extremities were severe. Binocular vision, speech, memory, attention span, and muscular coordination were reported to be impaired.

Problem:
The occupational therapist had selected the task of learning to type, by hunt and peck, as an intrinsically interesting and useful one which would also improve the client's hand-eye coordination. Although the client verbally expressed interest in learning to type, in practice, he did not attend to the task. He would type a few letters, stop, and then call the therapist with a complaint or a question or simply wait for her to approach him and ask why he was not working. He did this with a frequency that allowed little time for actual typing behavior, and hand-eye coordination did not improve. In addition, his 'need' for attention made it difficult for the occupational therapist to function effectively with other patients. In view of the client's behavior and his failure to make progress, the therapist believed that maximum functional benefit had been reached and the client should be discharged.

Observation:
The client never worked for longer than 5 to 7 minutes at a time. He would then stop or call for

the therapist's attention. The therapist invariably responded by coming over to where he was working, answering his question or complaint, and talking with him for a few moments before coaxing him to return to work.

Behavioral analysis:

The occupational therapist was reinforcing the disrupting behavior. The client 'liked' to talk and recieve attention from the therapist more than he liked to engage in the difficult typing task, and he controlled the situation because the therapist invariably responded to his demands.

In this case, as in others, there were four basic questions to be answered:

1. What is the 'desirable' behavior? This question must be answered with precision in terms of objectively (observable) actions. An answer that the client should 'do more' or 'show more interest and spunk' is insufficient unless what he should do more of or what he should show more interest in is specified. In this case it was desired that the client engage in more typing behavior.

2. What is the criterion for success? This question must be answered in terms of frequency of specified actions, time spent at the task, speed or accuracy or adequacy of the performance, or some combination of these. Under automated conditions it would have been possible to use the increase in the number of letters typed as a criterion. Since automated equipment was not available, however, a more global set of criteria were specified as follows: (a) The client should attend to the typing task for at least 30 minutes. (b) During this period he should not demand the therapist's attention. (c) The work output in terms of lines typed should increase. (d) Accuracy of typing should improve. Of course, only the first two of these criteria were the focus of the experiment. The latter two criteria would be met, in some degree, if the first two were met; although great improvement in speed and accuracy undoubtedly would require a separate analysis and special attention.

3. What behavior must be generated, extinguished, or altered? If desirable and undesirable behavior are incompatabile, one might expect that reinforcing the desirable behavior would be sufficient to maintain it in strength. This question deserves attention, however, because the training of rehabilitation personnel to be responsive to

'human needs' may lead them to reinforce undesirable behaviors concurrently with their reinforcement of desirable behaviors without being aware of what they are doing. They may not perceive that the undesirable behaviors must never be reinforced. In the present instance, for example, the occupational therapist did give moderate attention to the client for typing while he was typing, but she was also responsive to his demands for attention and was rather incredulous that paying no attention to the latter might have positive effects on the former. Extinguishing incompatible behaviors is especially important in cases of relearning, where the desired behaviors are usually present in at least minimal strength. In cases of new learning where the desired behaviors are absent, altering behavior by means other than extinction is more important.

4. What will serve as a reinforcer? In the absence of knowledge of what has been reinforcing to the client in the past, the behavioral engineer may attempt to use an extrinsic reinforcer such as money, trading stamps, trinkets, food delicacies, or any activity of consumption that therapists may report the client engages in. Apparatus for programming and reinforcement delivery usually is required for effective extrinsic reinforcement. Social reinforcement is also possible. The latter is particularly effective with many rehabilitation clients since much of their behavior appears to be under aversive social control, and they have been deprived, sometimes for long periods of time, of the positive social reinforcement they experienced prior to disablement. It also has the advantage of not requiring programming status. In general, a good reinforcer often is that reinforcing stimulus that has been maintaining undesired behavior. In the present case, it was social reinforcement which was maintaining the client's disruptive behaviors and which could be used just as easily to reinforce behavior.

Behavioral treatment:

Treatment in this situation consisted of making two changes: (1) Moving the typewriter and the client from the large occupational-therapy room where non-typewriting behavior had been reinforced to a smaller, more-isolated room. This was done partly to help weaken the past behavior by introducing new discriminative stimuli and partly to decrease the response alternatives that were presented by the presence, activities, and conversation of other people. (2) Making social reinforcement contingent upon engaging in typing behavior. The client was given 5 minutes of social interaction, on a 'man to man' basis, at the end of each 30 minute therapy session in which the client typed more lines than in the previous session. (Sessions were held semi-weekly.) The talk during the break was of cars, sports, and other topics of masculine interest which were not otherwise available to the client within the institution. Although he was 18 years old, his slight physique and unsophisticated manner had led the staff to treat him as a child.

The task was sufficiently difficult for John so that if he stopped typing for several minutes during the session, he could not possibly exceed his previous output; in that event, of course, no social reinforcement was given. In addition, the experimenter attempted to avoid demands for attention by giving reinforcement for smaller units of work. He did this by walking into the room about every 5 minutes and, without interrupting the client, estimating the number of words typed. If output per minute of time appeared roughly to have increased over the previous period, he would make some positive remark such as 'You're doing very well' and then walk out.

Results:
After a single 30-minute session in which variable-interval reinforcement was given but demands for attention were ignored, the client no longer attempted to engage the experimenter in conversation during the working period. After the ninth session, the client asked the experimenter not to dispense the variable-interval reinforcements because they slowed down his output. Three additional 30-minute sessions were then held without the variable-interval reinforcement contingency.

During each session from the second to the twelfth, John attended to the typing task for the entire 30 minutes. He neither stopped work nor demanded the therapist's attention. In addition, his typing output increased from 5 lines in the first session to 12 lines in the twelfth session, and his error rate decreased from 3 errors per line to ½ per line.

From the thirteenth through the fifteenth experimental periods, the duration of typing activity was increased to one hour with only a 5-minute reinforcement break at the half-way point. The client's close attention to the typing task was maintained without decreasing the production rate or increasing the error rate. He now appeared to be 'well-motivated' and it was clear that further gains were possible if the regular therapist, to whose care he was now returned, gained skill in maintaining the reinforcement contingencies.

Case 2
Fear of falling in a cerebral-palsied child

Background:
Tom was born with multiple congenital anomalies. In addition to nystagmus, ptosis, scoliosis, and three-fingered hands without thumbs, he was diagnosed as a 'mild spastic with left hemiplegia.' He was one of several seven-year-old cerebral-palsied children participating in an experiment concerned with investigating the process by which tokens (poker chips) might be established as generalized conditioned reinforcers.

In rehabilitating handicapped children, it is often necessary to generate new behavior or to strengthen weak behavior. Since these children are not deprived of primary reinforcers, and since it is usually impossible, for social and administrative reasons, to place them under such deprivation, it is not easy to find conditioned reinforcers of powerful and continuing effectiveness. The ideal reinforcer should be of the kind which can be easily dispensed by the experimenter or therapist and delivered immediately contingent upon the appropriate behavior; it should be non-satiating or low in satiation so that many can be dispensed in a short period of time; it should be non-distracting or low in distraction by reason of its own intrinsic reinforcing properties; it should be appropriate for the many different deprivations which may exist in any subject and be capable of use in a variety of situations. Money has these characteristics for adults. Tokens exchangeable after the experimental or therapeutic sessions for a wide variety of social and material reinforcers may be equally effective for handicapped children who are given some experience in a 'token culture.'

The main experiment, in which Tom participated, showed that tokens which were exchangeable for toys were effective generalized conditioned reinforcers in shaping increased attention span, speed and accuracy in two behaviors:

(1) hand-eye coordination in coloring and (2) manipulation in a nut-bolt-washer assembly.

Problem:

Tom would not stand unless he had something to hold on to, and he would not walk unless he held someone's hand. It was believed by the child's physician and physical therapist that he could walk alone, and recurrent but unsuccessful efforts had been made in the past to induce him to do so. It was said that he had an extreme fear of falling, but the child refused to attempt the exercise that would teach him to fall without discomfort or injury.

Observation:

Observation confirmed the fact that Tom never stood or walked unassisted. Attempts were sometimes made to coax him or goad him into walking. He smiled shyly and was good humoured in these situations until ultimately someone took him by the hand and walked with him. Tom had 'insight' and 'acceptance' of his disability. He talked freely and at some length to many people about his inability to walk alone.

Behavioral analysis

The adults in the environment were reinforcing the non-walking behavior. The child was at the center of the stage and received a great deal of attention, which he seemed to enjoy, for not walking and for refusing to fall.

The terminal behaviors, their criteria, and the conditions for their occurrence were as follows: (1) Desired Behaviors: The child should stand and walk independently, and he should learn how to fall safely. (2) Criteria for Success: He should walk unassisted to and from the experimental room, and he should fall, in the approved way, on command. (3) Behavior to be generated, extinguished, or altered: The problem appeared to be one of overcoming the fear of falling and having the child experience the freedom of unassisted walking — to get them over the hump so that the naturally reinforcing contingencies in the environment that are available to one who walks alone could exert their effects. It was decided that these behaviors could be generated by reinforcement more powerful than the child was receiving for not walking. However, the social reinforcement given for not walking was so widened within the

rehabilitation center, and of such long standing, that it was not considered feasible to try to extinguish this behavior in the staff. (4) Reinforcer: Tom came strongly under the control of tokens in the main experiment mentioned earlier, and there was evidence that they would serve for him as generalized conditioned reinforcers.

Behavioral treatment

Treatment was begun by reinforcing with tokens successive approximations to independent walking. First, while engaged in a coloring task, Tom was given two extra tokens if he scooted in his chair from his work table to the experimenter's correction desk and pulled himself up to a standing position. If he chose not to come to the desk to have his paper corrected, the experimenter went to his table, but he received no extra tokens. After one reinforcement for coming to the desk, Tom refused to let the experimenter come to him. After a dozen reinforcements for this behavior, Tom was offered extra tokens for standing at the desk without holding on. He met this contingency in one 20-minute session and thereafter would stand unassisted. During the shaping process, the child's verbal behavior changed from comments about being unable to walk, to statements such as 'Look, I can stand by myself.'

The next step was to place two chairs back to back close enough so that Tom could hold onto one chair, turn, and grasp the other chair without letting go of the first chair. He was reinforced with tokens for this behavior. The chairs were then gradually moved apart until it was necessary to take one or more steps without support to get from one chair to the other. At the end of the first 20-minute session, Tom was walking three unsupported, unassisted, consecutive steps from one chair to the other.

At the next session five days later, Tom walked into the experimental room unassisted, and it was obvious from his verbal behavior that walking, in itself, was now reinforcing. It was not possible to trace what had occurred in the institution during those five days. It seems probable that some unassisted walking had occurred which provided the opportunity for the physical therapist, who was also working on this behavior, to give massive, positive, social reinforcement. Combined with the intrinsically reinforcing effects of walking itself, the consequences were sufficient to maintain the strength of the behavior. It was evident that the child was now walking freely all over the institution, and although it was believed that the experimental effort provided the catalyst, we could not be sure that it was the behavioral treatment and not some adventitious occurrence that was responsible for the result.

Accordingly, attention then turned to a behavior that was non-existent in the subject's repertory — falling on command, correctly and safely. The physical therapist had given up trying to teach this behaviour, and she agreed not to attempt to teach it again during the period of the experiment. The physical therapist stated that the ability to fall voluntarily was an important behavior to develop inasmuch as incoordination resulting from the spastic paralysis probably would result in the child's falling from time to time. It would be beneficial if he would learn to fall correctly and safely. However, she had been unable to induce Tom to engage in falling exercises under any circumstances.

In accord with the physical therapist's instructions to the experimenters, falling was broken down into three phases: (1) Placing the subject's hands and knees on the mat and having him roll his body to one side. (2) Placing the subject on his knees with his body in an erect position and having him fall forward on his hands and then roll to his side. (3) Standing the subject beside the mat and having him fall to his knees, then to his hands, and then having him roll his body to one side.

Tom was told and shown the successive approximations to falling behavior outlined above. Tokens were then dispensed contingent upon his performing the required behavior upon command.

Results

The results are shown in Table 44.1. It will be seen that after the rolling response was well established, it was possible to proceed quickly to the behaviors of falling from the kneeling position and falling from an upright position. More rapid acquisition of the desired response might have been possible. At the end of the first session, Tom was reluctant to stop and asked the experimenters if he might try, 'for tokens,' the falling from an upright position exercise. This was not permitted because of the complexity of the response and the inexperience of the investigators in physical-therapy activities. It is perhaps sufficiently noteworthy that

Table 44.1 Frequency of the component parts of the falling sequence during four sessions of training

Sessions (20 minutes)	Rolling to side	Responses Falling from knees to hands and rolling	Falling from upright to knees, hands and rolling
1	8	3	—
2	2	2	7
3	3	—	4
4	—	5	6

an important behavior that had been unobtainable previously by traditional physical-therapy methods was obtained in just four sessions of 20 minutes each by utilizing principles of behaviour theory. Moreover, the behavior was engaged in willingly, almost eagerly, and with little or none of the emotionalism that the subject was reported to have shown in previous attempts to teach him to fall.

The rapidity with which the falling behavior was obtained lends some support to the belief that the tokens functioned as strong, generalized conditioned reinforcers. As in the walking study, the desired behavior was manifested immediately after token reinforcement was put into effect.

Case 3
Inability to walk in a mentally retarded child

Background

Mary was a nine-year old girl who, in addition to having other behavioral deficits, didn't walk, didn't talk, and wasn't toilet trained. She was classified by the residential institution in which she lived as 'congenitally mentally retarded.' She was reported to have crawled when she was two years old, but she never walked. At the time of first observation, she would not stand on her feet unless someone lifted her by the hands or arms and supported most of her weight.

It wasn't clear why Mary didn't walk. She was somewhat bow-legged, as if she had had rickets at the age when most children begin to walk, but there were no other physical abnormalities now that would tend to interfere with walking or standing unsupported.

To the institution, however, it was an old and familiar story. Many mentally retarded children do not walk. It is believed to be one of the 'characteristics' of severely mentally retarded children that is related not to their muscular strength but to their not being smart enough or sufficiently coordinated to learn to walk. An inquiry sometimes follows this pattern:

'Why doesn't Mary walk?'

'Well, she's severely mentally retarded, and it is not uncommon among the severely mentally retarded that they don't walk.'

'I see, but what is the reason for it?'

'She's slow in development.'

'I see. And what is it that is responsible for her slow development?'

'It is the fact that she is mentally retarded.'

'I see. And how do you know that she is mentally retarded?'

'Why you can see for yourself. She doesn't walk, she doesn't talk, she isn't toilet trained and doesn't do many other things like a mentally normal child.'

There may be many reasons for the impoverished behavioral repertoire of long-institutionalized children. Not the least of these variables are the impoverished environmental contingencies to which the child must respond appropriately either to receive reinforcement or to avoid punishment. A diagnosis of mental retardation, however, which by definition is an 'incurable' disorder, tends to lead to the easy acceptance of the inevitability of behavioral deviance and behavioral deficits and to choke off some simple rearrangements of the environment which might lead to the generation of more adequate behavior.

Observation

Mary, except for her very thin, bowed legs and lack of muscular development in the calf, seemed physically capable of walking. Her primary mode of locomotion, however, was scooting across the floor on her buttocks by pushing with her feet and hands. She could be pulled to a standing position if the experimenter supported most of her weight, but she could not be induced to move her legs, and she would drop to the floor as soon as support was removed or relaxed.

Behavioral analysis

For physical reasons, Mary may not have had the capacity to walk when she was younger. The acceptance of her as 'a child who doesn't walk,' however, led to neglect in providing environmental contingencies which would shape up and maintain walking. At present there were no important positive consequences contingent upon walking, or aversive consequences contingent upon not walking. She was carried or wheeled in a chair wherever it was necessary for her to go.

The behavior desired from Mary was that she should stand unsupported and walk independently; first, upon request of the experimenter in the experimental room and, later, in response to the naturally reinforcing contingencies of the ward. The task here, as with Tom, was to get her over the hump of initiating the strange and strenuous effort of walking so that this ultimately less effortful mode of locomotion could be experienced and so that the naturally reinforcing contingencies in the environment that are available to one who walks could exert their effects. No attempt was to be made to induce the ward attendants not to carry Mary or not to push her in a wheelchair, since these efforts would introduce uncontrolled variables. Since Mary was highly reinforceable with edibles such as popcorn, raisins, crackers, nuts, and ice cream, it was believed that these reinforcers would be sufficient to generate walking behavior and that the reinforcing effects of walking itself would maintain the behavior on the ward.

Behavioral treatment

Mary was seen twice a week in experimental sessions usually lasting 20 to 45 minutes. In the initial sessions, resting periods of 5 to 15 minutes were as long as or longer than working periods; but later, as her muscles became stronger, the walking periods were about twice as long as the resting periods.

In Phase 1, lasting one session, Mary was lifted to her feet and given a reinforcer while she was standing. Gradually the experimenter released his support. In the beginning, when the child supported on her own legs even a small portion of her weight for a fraction of a second, she was reinforced with an edible. Later, the contingencies were modified to require higher degrees of weight-bearing over longer periods of time, until at the end of the first session she would stand unsupported for 5 to 15 seconds at a time. Detailed records were not kept of this session.

In Phase 2, two folding chairs were placed approximately 30 inches apart, back to back. Mary was placed on the floor between the chairs while an experimenter stood behind each chair. She was told and shown how to pull herself to her feet by grasping the back of one chair, then turn around and grasp the back of the other chair first with one hand and then with both hands. When Mary was standing, the experimenter behind her would say, 'Mary, come over here.' If the command was followed, she was reinforced with an edible. If it was not followed, or if she dropped to the floor and scooted on her buttocks to the other chair, a reinforcer was not dispensed.

When Mary was effectively making the transfer from chair to chair upon command, the distance between the chairs was very gradually increased until it was impossible for her to move from one chair to the other while holding on to either of them. Initially she was able to release one chair with one hand and, standing unsupported, lean over until she could grasp the second chair with the other hand. As the distance between the chairs increased, however, it was necessary for her at first to take one unsupported step and later several, before she was reinforced. In the seven sessions of Phase 2, the greatest distance between the chairs was 45 inches.

In Phase 3, the chairs were removed and the procedure was as follows: One experimenter would hold Mary's hand while the other experimenter, a few feet away, would hold out a reinforcer. When she had taken a few steps toward the reinforcer, the first experimenter would release her hand while the second experimenter walked backwards away from her. Initially, Mary was given a

reinforcer after taking three of four steps, but this requirement was gradually increased at each session. By Session 12, for example, reinforcement was contingent upon taking at least 25 steps. The number of steps taken was recorded as 'Steps from Supported Start.' In addition, an attempt was made to keep Mary walking for additional reinforcements as the experimenter moved away from her. The steps taken under this contingency were recorded as 'Steps from Unsupported Start.' These categories were not really meaningful after Session 11, as by that time it was Mary who released her hand from the experimenter's hand rather than vice versa.

Table 44.2 Progression in alternating between chairs during phase training

Session	Commands*	Reinforced transfers between chairs	Standing unsupported between chairs	No. of unsupported steps between chairs
1†				
2	66	34	6	
3	64	39	18	
4	23	18	1	
5	57	32	24	
6	68	32	25	17
7	20	7	3	3
8	39	9	0‡	28

*The number of commands given provides a rough index to the length of a working session. Sessions 4, 7 and 8 were shorter than others.
†Session 1 was part of Phase 1 and consisted only of reinforcement for standing unsupported for a short time. Records were not kept.
‡The chairs were separated by a distance that required one or more steps for completion of the task.

Table 44.3 Steps reinforced with supported and unsupported starts in phase 3 of training

Cumulative session*	Steps from supported start	Steps from unsupported start	Total steps	Reinforcements	Steps reinf.
9	190		190	31	6.1
10	560		560	36	15.5
11*	790	223	1013	61	16.6
12	414	249	663	20	33.1
13	422	391	813	29	28.0
14	806	111	917	22	41.7
15*	445	40	485	10	48.5

*Each session was 45 minutes long except Session 11, which ran for 70 minutes, and Session 15, which was interrupted after 30 minutes.

In Sessions 13, 14 and 15, the procedure was modified further by placing the second experimenter across the room rather than having him lead the child by a few steps. If, when she was called, Mary walked across the room without sinking to the floor, she received a reinforcer. If she sat down, no reinforcement was given, she was walked back to the starting point, and the command was given again. The same attempt was made as before to keep Mary walking for additional reinforcements as the experimenter moved across the room.

Results

The results are shown in Tables 44.2 and 44.3 and in Figures 44.1 and 44.2. It will be seen in Table 44.2 that there was a gradual but consistent shift from

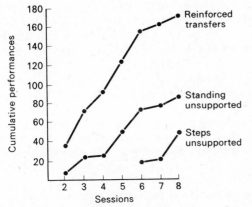

Figure 44.1 Alternations between chairs by Mary in Phase 2.

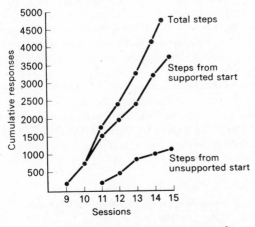

Figure 44.2 Walking by Mary in Phase 3.

transferring from one chair while holding on to the other, to standing unsupported between the chairs, to taking unsupported steps between the chairs. By the end of Session 8 of Phase 2, and after the expenditure of less than 200 minutes of experimental time, Mary had taken 28 unsupported steps in one session. The cumulative performances under the Phase 2 contingency are shown in Figure 44.1.

Table 44.3 shows that a gradually increasing total number of steps was obtained in each succeeding 45-minute session. Session 11 lasted for more than an hour and resulted in an unusually large number of steps, while Session 15 was terminated after 30 minutes. The table also shows the gradually increasing number of steps obtained per reinforcer as the reinforcement contingency was raised, from six steps in Session 9 to 40 consecutive steps in Session 15. Figure 44.2 presents the same data in cumulative record form.

By the end of the last session, the institutional attendants reported that Mary was taking unsupported steps in the ward. No attempt was made, as would ordinarily be desirable, to generalize the walking behavior to the ward or to fade out gradually the food reinforcers and replace them with other reinforcers. At the present writing, however, six months after the training sessions were completed, Mary is walking freely and frequently throughout the institution. Less than 9 hours of experimental effort had removed a behavioral deficit of 9 years' standing.

Case 4
Self-destructive behavior in an autistic child

Background

Phil was a 4-year-old child physically small for his age, who was confined to a crib in an institution for the mentally retarded. He attracted the attention of visitors, when he was not restrained, by the forcefulness with which he slapped and punched himself on his cheeks and mouth, banged his head, and scratched his body. These behaviors, which left visible injuries, were part of his almost ceaseless motor and tactual activity during most of his waking hours.

Problem

Physical assault on one's own body, sometimes to the point of injury, is not uncommon among autistic children. Such children are often confined in strait-jackets or restrained in other ways. It would be desirable to extinguish or alter such self-destructive behavior, but the variables that control it are not well understood.

Observation

Systematic observation of the unrestrained, unstimulated child for three 10-minute periods led to the identification of 20 different motor and tactual behaviors. These included hitting, slapping, kicking, scratching, biting, and rocking himself, sucking on thumb, finger, hand, arm; rubbing or flipping fingers against teeth and other parts of the body, chewing on bedsheet, banging head against the bars of the crib, and others. Several of these behaviors were sometimes manifested simultaneously, and once begun, a particular behavior such as finger-flipping or rocking might continue for several hours.

Simultaneous observation by four observers, each recording the frequency and duration in seconds of five different behaviors, revealed that during three 10-minute periods the child was stimulating himself in some way for an average of 44 seconds out of every minute.

Behavioral analysis

Phil's behavior did not appear to be a socially reinforced operant. His behavior was accepted by the institution's attendants as 'characteristic of that kind of child,' and little attention was paid to it except for periodic imposition of mechanical restraints. It was speculated that sensory deprivation in this child was of such a degree that tactual stimulation, even of a painful kind, was reinforcing in itself; and self-destructive behavior might be reduced if an external source of tactual stimulation were available.

It was desirable in this case to reduce the frequency of self-destructive behaviors and to determine the functional relationship between such a reduction, if it occurred, and two kinds of tactile stimulation which would be applied for brief periods. As in other behavioral alteration experiments in which the stimuli controlling the undesired behavior are not known and extinction procedures therefore not possible, the intent here was to generate a behavior that was incompatible with self-destruction — namely, lying quietly.

Experimentation, Phase 1

Four observers gathered around the child's crib.

Each observer was responsible for recording the frequency and duration of five of the 20 self-destructive behaviors that the child had exhibited in the past. A 50-minute experimental period consisting of alternating 10-minute periods of stimulation with 10-minute periods of non-stimulation had the following format: 1. No stimulation. 2. Vibrating pillow applied to child's back. 3. No stimulation. 4. The experimenter scratched the child's back gently. 5. No stimulation. There were two such 50-minute sessions spaced one week apart.

Results, Phase 1

The results of alternate periods of stimulation and no stimulation are shown in Figure 44.3. It is evident from inspection that applying stimulation from an external source was an effective means of reducing the behaviors that were classified as self-destructive in various degrees. The kind of stimulation appears to have been less important than its ordinal position within the series. Back-scratching was more effective than vibration in reducing self-destructive behaviors when vibration came second in the series and back-scratching came fourth, but vibration was more effective than back-scratching when the order of the stimuli was reversed. This phenomenon, when combined with the striking reductions in the duration of self-destructive behaviors during periods of stimulation in Session 2 as compared to Session 1 (which did not occur during periods of no stimulation) lent support to the sense that it reduced some and eliminated other self-stimulating activities. The distributions of the durations of the several behaviors during periods of no stimulation and stimulation show quite clearly the shift from more self-destructive classes of behavior to less self-destructive classes of behavior. The distributions for Sessions 1 and 2 are shown in Table 44.4. It will be seen that during periods of stimulation, almost the entire activity time was accounted for by the minimally self-destructive behavior of keeping fingers in mouth. This was a behavior that did not occur at all during the periods of no stimulation, although other, more self-destructive behaviors were manifested.

Experimentation, Phase 2

If a stimulus is reinforcing, it increases the frequency of the behavior that was emitted

Table 44.4 Distribution and duration in seconds of self-destrucive behaviors observed under two conditions in alternating ten minute trials

	Finger flipping	Ear pulling	Slapping hitting	Kicking	Scratching	Chewing on sheet	Rocking	Sucking	Tooth rubbing	Fingers in mouth	Total secs.	Average per min.
Condition												
Session 1												
No Stim.	7	0	0	12	90	0	392	45	5	0	551	55.1
Vibrator	0	0	0	0	0	0	0	0	0	385	385	38.5
No Stim.	9	0	40	96	19	0	82	120	22	0	388	38.8
Back Scratch	15	0	0	8	20	0	0	20	0	52	115	11.5
No Stim.	0	0	0	5	0	0	520	18	0	0	543	54.3
Condition												
Session 2												
No Stim.	41	0	76	37	34	32	97	215	9	0	541	54.1
Back Scratch	0	0	0	0	0	0	0	0	0	106	108	10.8
No Stim.	0	133	0	34	0	0	390	407	0	0	964	96.4
Vibrator	0	0	0	0	1	1	0	0	0	2	3	.3
No Stim.	0	0	0	0	20	20	511	5	0	0	536	53.6

immediately prior to its presentation. It seemed important, for two reasons, to know if external tactual stimulation was intrinsically reinforcing. First, tactual stimulation is not presently included in the list of known primary reinforcers, although some reports of sensory-deprivation phenomena indicates that it might well be one. Second, if

tactual stimulation is a primary reinforcer, it offers a powerful tool for altering the self-destructive behaviors of children like Phil, and it becomes potentially possible to modify and improve a tremendous range of behaviors in children for whom tactual deprivation may be a naturally occurring phenomenon.

Back-scratching does not lend itself very well to precise programming or automation, but a vibratory stimulus does. Inasmuch as the results in Phase 1 did not indicate compelling reasons for preferring one kind of tactual stimulation to the other, experimentation was continued with vibration.

To assess the reinforcing properties of vibratory stimuli, a vibrator embedded in a pillow was sewn immediately beneath the surface of the mattress in the child's crib. The vibrator was controlled by automated programming equipment which turned it on for 10 seconds of vibratory stimulation after each light pressing of a foam-rubber-padded, leather-covered, oblong lever, 8½ inches by 5½ inches in size, that was mounted on the side of the child's crib. The lever was mounted a few inches away from one of Phil's arms so that he would be likely to hit it by chance while engaging in the gross motor activity that he frequently exhibited, but his hand would have to turn at a sharp angle in order to strike the lever with his fingers or palm.

The vibration was contingent on pressing the lever, so if vibratory stimulation was reinforcing, after a few reinforcements resulting from adventitious lever pressing, Phil would be expected to strike the lever with increasing frequency. Two one-hour sessions, spaced one week apart, were run.

Results, Phase 2
The cumulative records are shown in Figure 44.4. It will be seen that the results of Session 1 were strikingly successful. It appeared evident that vibratory stimulation was reinforcing. Temporary satiation seemed to occur after 5 or 10 minutes of stimulation, but recovery was rapid. Records of the topography of the lever pressing response showed that all except the first few presses were made by hand and fingers and were clearly not accidental.

Figure 44.4 also shows the cumulative record of the first 20 minutes of Session 2. The lever-pressing behavior that was so evident in Session 1

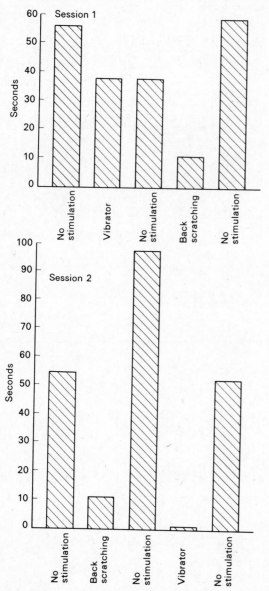

Figure 44.3   Average duration of self-destructive behaviors per minute under natural and tactually stimulating conditions.

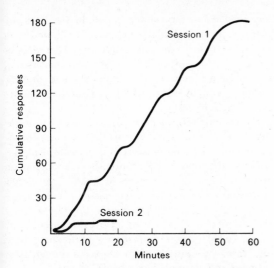

Figure 44.4 Cumulative record of lever-pressing for vibratory stimulation by an autistic child.

was no longer present. Moreover, attempts to hand-shape the response by delivering vibratory stimulation for successive approximations to lever pressing were unsuccessful. No progress toward reinstating the lever-pressing response was evident after 60 minutes of experimental effort.

Discussion

Case 4 was included in this paper to indicate that behavioral experimentation is not always, or even usually, a hop, skip and jump from isolating a problem, to devising a procedure, to successful outcome. In every case reported, there were some false starts and some difficulties of greater or lesser degree that had to be solved. In Case 4, we may or may not be on the track of important phenomena. It is clearly evident, however, that the problem has not been solved; nor is there a clear interpretation for the data obtained. Additional experimentation is necessary. It is now planned to place the lever and the automatically recording vibratory apparatus in Phil's crib on a 24-hour-per-day basis over a period of several weeks to determine if a longer period of experimentation will yield more interpretable data. The reader may conceive of other procedures that would be equally promising or better.

The responses of behavioral scientists, medical personnel, parents, and others to the kind of experimentation and applied psychology that is exemplified by the cases reported have been very encouraging. The psychologist in rehabilitation who tests, evaluates, classifies, and describes the strengths and weaknesses of candidates for rehabilitation services is not uniformly valued by his colleagues or those he serves. There appears to be an increasing demand for psychologists who have the knowledge and the ability to modify behavior – to generate desirable behavior when it is not present, to maintain good behavior in strength, and to extinguish or alter undesirable behavior. The role of the psychologist in rehabilitation of the future clearly requires a specialist in behavioral engineering who by open, clearly specifiable, non-esoteric, and non-subjective procedures can alter human behavior and thereby contribute more fully to the improved functioning of disabled persons.

Helping a child learn to work productively in activities that will improve his hand-eye co-ordination, to fall safely, and to walk, when these behaviors were not present previously, is surely beneficial. Some individuals, however, appear to have strong emotional reactions to the procedures that are used in the experimentation that was described and doubts about the value of what was done. It may be of value to discuss two spontaneous, but perhaps unthinking, objections that are most frequently made.

1. 'I don't believe in bribing children.' Critics who make this comment appear to be expressing the belief that children should 'voluntarily' engage in certain behaviors because 'it is for their own good,' or 'it is the right thing to do' and that it is somehow dishonest, evil, ineffective, or contrary to some immutable moral law to offer them extrinsic inducements to behave as they 'should' behave.

Such critics appear to forget that infants and children learn to behave in ways that the significant others in their lives consider right and good – they are not born with such behaviors. The learning is accomplished as a consequence of thousands and thousands of materially and socially reinforced responses and exposure to the naturally reinforcing or punishing contingencies of the environment.

For various reasons, some children do not receive the kind or frequency of reinforcement that shapes the behavior of most children to the ordinary demands of the social environment.

Other children, because of the physical or social effects of disabilities, or other fortuitous circumstances that are presently relatively unexplored, do not come under the control of the naturally occurring contingencies in the environment. The critical choice for those who work with children whose behavior is maladaptive is whether to view the problem as a scientific, valuatively neutral task of facilitating the learning of more adaptive behavior — even though the behavior 'should have' been learned earlier — or to view it as a moral problem of the childrens' own making which requires that they be consigned to limbo in preference to 'bribing' them to behave more adaptively. The scientifically oriented psychologist should experience no conflict in making this choice. [. . .]

One may attempt to distinguish the behavior required of rehabilitation clients from these examples on the grounds that rehabilitative therapy is for the client's own good and 'should be' engaged in without payment, but this is not tenable. It is for their own good that college students 'should' acquire as much knowledge as possible, and children 'should be' polite and unselfish without the aid of symbolic or social payment. But these behaviors must be learned, and it is necessary in the learning process to reinforce them.

[. . .] However, as Michael (1964) has remarked, 'If behavior which 'should' be engaged in without extrinsic reinforcement is not, in fact, occurring, a program of extrinsic reinforcement must be evaluated, not in an absolute sense, but in comparison with the common alternative approaches: increased aversive control, or simply accepting failure.'

On a similarly practical level, some professional persons are not so much concerned with the moral implications of dispensing extrinsic reinforcements as they are with the likelihood that the behavior obtained will be temporary or cease abruptly when the reinforcement is discontinued.

It is not possible here to describe the processes by which behavior comes under the control of secondary and so-called intrinsic reinforcement, but the transition to secondary reinforcement is often necessary for long-term persistence of behavior under natural conditions. If such additional learning does not occur, and the behavior does not come under the control of

naturally occurring reinforcement in the environment, it is true that the behavior developed and maintained by experimentally manipulated, extrinsic reinforcement will cease. We deceive ourselves if we believe that any behavior that is without consequences will be maintained indefinitely. [. . .]

When long-term persistence is desired for some behavior that does not receive primary reinforcement from the environment, it is necessary for the behavioral engineer to ensure that the behavior comes under the control of readily available secondary reinforcement. To ensure the maintenance of some behaviors in handicapped persons, it may be necessary to construct prosthetic environments. There are no approaches to learning that are free of these requirements, although the terminology employed may be different.

2. 'What is the value of changing one or two discrete bits of behavior? The children are still physically handicapped or mentally retarded, aren't they?' It would be delightful if varied, complex, and poorly understood disorders could be put completely right at one blow, but that process is called a miracle, and people who believe in it generally resort to prayer. The scientific process tends to proceed by slow accretion and the step-by-step solution of discrete problems.

From an immediate, practical standpoint, when one compares the time, effort, and resources that are necessary to care for ambulant and non-ambulant, toilet-trained and non-toilet-trained, self-destructive and non-self-destructive, or hyperactive and non-hyperactive children, it seems clear that changing one or two bits of discrete behavior should not be despised.

In addition, the objection quoted neglects the fact that no learned behavior appears in full bloom. It is learned bit by bit from the moment of birth, or earlier, and refined by thousands and thousands of repetitions. The learning of congenitally physically handicapped or retarded persons may be obstructed or impeded by insuperable physical barriers, chance exposure to conditions that are detrimental to learning, lack of knowledge of how to facilitate learning under unusual conditions, or perhaps more frequently, lack of skilled application of the learning principles that are already known.

In the rehabilitation setting, one or more behavioral deficits of a sensory, motor, or discriminative nature may be evident in handicapped persons when comparison is made with non-handicapped individuals of similar age. There is presently no alternative to treating such deficits one by one, and the outcome, in terms of the total person or total behavior, depends on how many and how severe the deficits are and the degree to which generalization of newly learned behavior may be possible. As progress is made in over- coming behavioral deficits that are presently beyond rehabilitative knowledge, and as increased behavioral engineering skill is gained in reducing or removing other deficits, we may expect that the behavioral deficits that are presently associated with some physical disabilities will disappear, and some kinds of so-called mental retardation will be remediable.

REFERENCES

MEYERSON, L., and KERR, NANCY, *Learning theory and rehabilitation*, New York: Random House (in press).
MEYERSON, L., MICHAEL, J. L. MOWRER, O. H., OSGOOD, C. E. and STAATS, A. W. (1963) 'Learning behavior, and rehabilitation', in *Psychological research and rehabilitation*. Washington D.C.: American Psychological Association.
MICHAEL, J. L. (1964) 'Guidance and counseling as the control of behavior', in *Guidance in American education: backgrounds and prospects*. Cambridge: Harvard Graduate School of Education, (distributed by Harvard University Press).

45. Geriatric behavioural prosthetics*

OGDEN R. LINDSLEY
Behaviour Research Laboratory, Department of Psychiatry,
Harvard Medical School, Boston, U.S.A.

Human behavior is a functional relationship between a person and a specific social or mechanical environment. If the behavior is deficient, we can alter either the individual or the environment in order to produce effective behavior. Most previous attempts to restore behavioral efficiency by retraining, punishment, or physiological treatment have focused on only one side of this relation, the deficient individual. This approach implies that normal individuals can function in all currently existing social environments, that deficient individuals can be normalized, and that there are ordinarily no deficient environments. Scientists have only recently directly focused on the environmental side of deficient behavior functions and on the design of specialized or *prosthetic environments* to restore competent performance. [. . .]

In this chapter, I will offer suggestions, developed from the methods and discoveries of free-operant conditioning, for developing geriatric prosthetic environments.[1]

In *free-operant conditioning* the frequency of performance of an act is altered by locating and arranging suitable consequences (reinforcement). The person being conditioned is at all times free to make the response and receive the arranged consequences, or to make other responses. By isolating the individual within an appropriate enclosure, the behavior specialist can empirically — rather than merely statistically — control all environmental events which can affect the behavior he is studying. The behavioral response and any environmental manipulations whose effects on the response are being studied can be automatically and continuously recorded. This environmental control and automatic, continuous recording mark the method as a laboratory natural science, comparable to modern chemistry, physics and biology.

Free-operant methods are suited to behavioral geriatrics for several reasons. Concentrating on *motivational aspects*, or consequences, of behavior, free-operant conditioning alters the *immediate environment* to generate and maintain behavior. The sensitivity of the methods to subtle changes in such aspects of the person's performance as response rate, efficiency and perseverance makes these methods appropriate to the study of *single individuals*. Because the sensitivity does not decrease with very long periods of application with the same individual, reliable *longitudinal studies* are possible. Free-operant conditioning methods for the analysis of functional and dynamic relationships between individuals and both their *social and nonsocial environments* can produce separate measures of mechanical dexterity, intellectual functioning, and social adjustment.

Free-operant principles and techniques may provide behavioral geriatrics with (1) a fresh theoretical approach; (2) laboratory description, prognosis, and evaluation; (3) design of prosthetic environments; and (4) individualized prosthetic prescriptions. Although I know of no free-operant experiments on the aged, and research in our laboratory with senile psychotics has not been extensive, preliminary suggestions can be well supported by the results of extensive experiments

*From Robert T. Kaustenbaum (ed.) (1964), *New Thoughts on Old Age*, New York, Springer Publishing Company, Chapter 3, pp. 41–69.

on the behavior of psychotic, neurotic, and mentally retarded individuals, whose behavioral deficits are usually as debilitating and challenging as those of aged persons.[2]

A fresh theoretical approach

Free-operant conditioning principles can provide a highly relevant approach for increasing the efficiency of ward management and patient care routines. In this new approach, ward attendants do not perform custodial tasks. They are instead trained to act as behavioral engineers in arranging appropriate behavioral programs and reinforcements, so that the patients themselves maintain their ward and their persons. Most important in this application of free-operant methods are (1) precise behavioral description; (2) functional definition of stimulus, response, and reinforcement; and (3) attention to behavioral processes.

Precise behavioral description facilitates communication between behavioral engineer and ward supervisor. It not only focuses attention on the actual behavioral movement which is occurring at either too high or too low a rate, but also permits observing and counting the response and directly reinforcing it with suitable consequences.

Functional definition of stimulus, response, and reinforcement focuses the attention of the nurse or attendant on the relationship between the behavior she is attempting to manage and her management procedures. When she realizes that an event may be a stimulus for one patient but not for another, and that a second event may be reinforcing to one patient but punishing to still another, then she recognizes the full complexity of human behavior, and in behavioral management no longer makes errors based upon misplaced empathy and generalization. For example, the socially deprived patients found in large hospitals may be rewarded by any attention from the nurse, even scolding for misbehavior. Consequently, a patient will continue to do the thing for which he was scolded in attempts to obtain the social contacts from the nurse, even though the nurse designed the topography of these contacts as punishment for what the patient was doing.

Attention to the behavioral processes of positive reinforcement, extinction, satiation, and mild punishment has proven extremely useful in engineering a ward for maximal behavioral accomplishment. Ayllon and Michael successfully trained ward nurses to increase patients' self-feeding by talking to patients only when they fed themselves (Allyon and Michael 1959). Allyon also trained nurses to satiate a towel hoarder by filling her room with towels, and to punish the wearing of extra clothing by letting a patient eat only when she was below a certain weight with her clothes on (Allyon in press).

Important for generating maximal behavior on a geriatric ward is the early establishment of a conditioned general reinforcer, or token, which must be used to purchase all items and opportunities of importance and reinforcing value to the patients. The ward tokens are used by the attendants and the nurses to reinforce appropriate behavior. The patients can then use the tokens to purchase personal articles, cigarettes, afternoon naps, television and record playing time, talks with chaplains and volunteers, and all other events of value and importance to them. The patients will readily perform custodial duties on their ward in order to earn the tokens. Ayllon has successfully used tokens in this way in managing a ward of chronic psychotic patients.[3]

High on the list of types of behavior that it is desirable to generate in a geriatric patient are very mild physical exercise and sun-bathing. The patient is immediately reinforced with a token for each exercise period and for small daily gains in his exercise achievement. Such exercise, shaped very gradually and watched carefully by the ward physician, can do much to restore physical health and well-being to a geriatric patient. [. . .]

Design of prosthetic environments

There is little hope of retarding the aging process at this time, but we can reduce its behavioral debilitation by designing environments which compensate for or support the specific behavioral deficits of each aged person.[4] Because we will not actually alter the deficits, but merely provide an environment in which the deficits are less debilitating, these environments cannot be considered purely therapeutic. [. . .] Prosthetic environments, must operate continually in order to decrease the debilitation resulting from the behavioral deficit. Eyeglasses are prosthetic devices for deficient vision, hearing aids for deficient hearing, and crutches and wheel chairs for deficient locomotion.

To describe suggestions for geriatric prosthetic

environments as accurately as possible, I will use the analytical categories of the laboratory behavioral scientist: (1) discriminative stimuli; (2) response devices; (3) reinforcers; and (4) reinforcement schedules. The number of different types of special stimuli and devices required for prosthesis in each of these categories must be determined by the analysis of each aged individual. The types of environmental alteration required to support aged behavior cannot be determined until the number, degree, and range of behavioral deficits are determined. It may be that a given prosthetic device can be used to prosthetize more than one type of behavioral deficit. Adequately detailed analysis may also show that a single behavioral deficit can be prosthetized by more than one device. In these cases, the most economic and most general devices would be selected first. [. . .]

GERIATRIC DISCRIMINATIVE STIMULI

The environmental events which signal when a response is appropriate and when it should not be made are extremely important in controlling behavior. Traffic lights are a familiar example. These colored lights are useful discriminative stimuli to a person with normal color vision, much less useful to a color-blind person, and of no use to a totally blind person. The geriatric patient may well have behavioral deficits which, like blindness, limit the range of discriminative stimuli in the normal environment which can control his behavior. The full and exact nature of geriatric behavioral deficits has not yet been determined.

The *intensity and size of discriminative stimuli* for the aged has received some prosthetic attention. Eyeglasses have been developed for amplifying and correcting visual responses. Hearing aids have been developed for amplifying sounds to serve as discriminative stimuli for people whose hearing is deficient. Touch, smell, and taste amplifiers have not yet been developed, probably because our basic knowledge of these senses is more limited.

Simple and dramatic patterns, long durations and higher intensities of stimulation should be investigated, for we can increase the intensity of the environmental stimulus when prosthetic amplifiers are not available. It is amazing, for example, that although we give children books with large type, we force elderly people with deficient vision to use heavy eyeglasses or hand magnifying lenses

to read normal-size type. We might find that even with large type, certain aged persons with deficient vision develop headaches or become nervous while reading. If we provided Braille or 'talking books' for these individuals, we might find an increase in their usefulness to us and to themselves.

Multiple sense displays should be investigated in attempts to design geriatric discriminative stimuli. While an older person might not respond appropriately to a loud sound alone or to a bright light alone, he might respond appropriately to a simultaneous combination of loud sound and bright light. A normal person under the high control of a small portion of his environment is much more likely to respond to a multiple sense display than to a single sense display in the rest of his environment. Similarly, an aged person with generally weakened attention might respond more appropriately to a multiple sense display.

Expanded auditory and visual narrative stimuli should also be investigated. Melrose has found that many aged persons who cannot hear normal speech can hear expanded speech (Melrose 1962). Expanded speech does not differ in intensity or tone from normal speech. It is just spread out more in time, being truly slower. [. . .] By using video tape recording systems to expand visual materials, we might restore understanding of and interest in visual narration to many aged people. [. . .]

Response-controlled discriminative stimulation should be tried as a prosthetic device for geriatric patients who appear to have intermittent attention. If a patient is periodically unresponsive to stimulation, the stimuli which occur during these 'dead' periods in his attention may as well not be presented. To him the world has missing portions, as if a normal person were watching a movie and periodically the projector lens was covered for brief periods of time while the narration continued. There would be many important portions of the movie narration to which he would have no opportunity to respond.

Response-controlled stimulation permits the narration to move along in time only when the patient is responding to it. If the patient does not respond to a given stimulus, the next stimulus is not presented. Rather, it is stored until the patient responds again. [. . .]

GERIATRIC RESPONSE DEVICES

The design of prosthetic response devices for

geriatric patients is a wide-open field. Innumerable response force amplifiers are available for normal persons. Most hand tools, for example, amplify response force. Hammers increase the force of manual pounding by extending the leverage of the arm; wrenches, the force of finger grip. In a sense, most modern machinery is designed to increase the force or accuracy of normal human action.

Response force amplifiers should be provided for old people with extremely weak motor responses. Geriatric environments should contain a much wider range of response force amplifiers than the fully automated factory or fully electrified home. Why, for example, must the aged open their own doors in hospitals when supermarket and garage doors are opened electronically? [...]

Wide response topographies should be provided so that palsied move-tracts and inaccurate placement of hands and fingers would not be disabling. An individual with extreme palsy, for example, could operate a telephone with push buttons, instead of the normal dial arrangement, if the buttons were far enough apart and required enough pressure so they could not be accidentally pushed by a shaking hand. The voice-operated telephones in the Bell system design will, of course, completely prosthetize dialing deficits. [...]

Rate switches, which operate only when repeatedly pressed above a certain rate, would be useful in maintaining high constant attention from aged persons with intermittent or weak attention. [...] A switch that must be continually pressed should reduce the accident hazards of machine operation for many older persons with mild attention disorders. When their attention drifted so that they failed to press the switch at the required rate, the machine would automatically stop.

Response feedback systems should be developed so that response location errors can be corrected before they actually occur. [...] In effect, they would substitute for the deficient afferent input from the aged limbs which once guided the hands so accurately. [...]

GERIATRIC REINFORCERS

The generally low interest or motivation of the aged is very familiar. The elderly person appears capable of behaving but has lost his 'will to live.' We assume that he is able to respond, because on occasional brief instants he 'lights up' and behaves

appropriately. Rather than interpreting brief periods of appropriate behavior as normal episodes or phases in the aging process, we usually attribute them to special circumstances which temporarily increase motivation.

In precise behavioral terms, this means either that the reinforcers currently programmed in his immediate environment are no longer adequate or that the old person has simply lost the ability to be reinforced. The difference is of great importance and should be tested experimentally by attempting to reinforce his behavior with a wide range of events.

Individualized historical reinforcers. We should look closely at a geriatric patient's rare moments of high behavioral rate. Is some unusual, more appropriate reinforcer operating — something from the past — an old song, an old food, an old friend? If parts of such individualized historical reinforcers were recorded and presented on audio tape or closed-circuit television, an old person might perform regularly at high rates to hear and see them.

Expanded narrative reinforcers. Melrose's recent research suggests another possibility (Melrose 1962). If an aged person can comprehend expanded speech but not speech presented at a normal rate, he might be reinforced by expanded music and narrative themes, when the same themes presented at the normal rates would not be reinforcing. In seeking more adequate reinforcers for aged persons, we should explore music, movies, and video tapes expanded in both the audio and visual dimensions; for example, video tapes could be used to expand visits from family and friends. [...] By gradual shaping and conditioning, an old person could be given a new interest in contemporary life.

Long-range personal reinforcers, such as education, development of a skill, or the building of a reputation, would have little value for an old person. Each step in the development of skill or reputation would have little conditioned reinforcement value, since it would merely be a step on a stairway which an old person could hardly hope to scale completely. He might reasonably ask, 'Build a skill for what? To die tomorrow?' [...]

Long-range social reinforcers which would be of value to society no matter when the older person died might be more useful with the aged. The conditioned reinforcement would be the contribution to the next generation. However, the development of this type of reinforcer would be extremely complicated, would require the participation of the members of society at large, and would still have to be conditioned to immediate personal reinforcers. [...]

GERIATRIC REINFORCEMENT SCHEDULES
In most social situations, reinforcement occurs intermittently (Ferster 1958). Not all responses are immediately reinforced; only a small portion are followed by a reinforcing episode. Nevertheless, in normal individuals, responding continues at high, predictable rates which are presumably maintained by conditional reinforcement from the occasionally reinforced responses. In our long-term experiments with psychotic children and adults, however, we have found many patients who are unable to maintain high rates of responding on intermittent schedules of reinforcement, even when adequate reinforcers are used (Lindsley 1960). These deficits in responding for intermittent reinforcement are probably attributable to deficits in recent memory and in formation of conditioned reinforcement.

It is very possible that many geriatric patients will also prove unable to maintain high rates of responding on intermittent schedules and will have to be kept on regular reinforcement contingencies in which every response is immediately followed with a reinforcing episode. Other patients may have to be reinforced on conjugate programs in which the intensity of a continuously available reinforcer is a direct function of the response rate. Conjugate reinforcement permits the use of narrative social reinforcers and appears to go deeper into sleep, anesthesia, infancy and psychosis than does episodic reinforcement (Lindsley 1957, 1961, Lindsley *et al.* 1961). Conjugate reinforcement may also go deeper into aging and generate behavior in geriatric patients who would not behave on any episodic schedule of reinforcement. [...]

Continuity of aging
Even though the severe deficits characteristic of aging do not show up until very late in life, the process of aging might develop much earlier. The behavioral debilities produced by this continuous process of aging may not appear because there are ample devices available for middle-aged persons to use in prosthetizing their milder behavioral deficits. For example, our recent memory may

become poorer either because our ability to remember simply decreases with age or because our storage system becomes filled or overloaded. The older we become, however, the more we use prosthetic devices such as notebooks, address books, the telephone information operator and mnemonic devices. The young executive relies on his accurate recent memory, but the older and still highly productive executive relies heavily on his young secretary. It may be that it is only when he loses his secretary that he loses his 'recent memory'.

In other words, the age at which we see marked, severe behavioral deficits in older persons may only be the point at which appropriate prosthetic devices are no longer available. In this sense, forced retirement or 'disengagement' may not only deprive a man of necessary reinforcement, but rob him of his prosthetic devices at the time they are most needed. A justification of retirement by comparing his productive efficiency before and after retirement would therefore erroneously self-validate itself unless reinforcement and prosthetic devices were equated in each condition.

Social neglect of the aged
The problem of the aged has only recently become a major one. This is not only because more people are living to an older age because of the marked success of organic medicine, but because our more urban and complicated society provides situations in which the deficits of the aged are more debilitating. The increased complexity of the behavioral tasks required of modern society members is displacing not only the less skilful aged, but also the less skilful middle-aged person.

Since our aged citizens are less able to produce in this more complicated society, they have fewer reinforcers for the rest of society and will suffer greater social neglect. They have nothing with which to reinforce social attention from either their peers or the rest of society.

Even patients with organic illnesses may have social responses with which to reinforce their attendants, nurses, physicians and family visitors. The plucky words and weak smile of the organically ill patient are extremely strong reinforcement to a nurse or visitor.

An infant has little behavior with which to acquire reinforcing objects to distribute among his family, but people are so constituted that the gurgle, smile and primitive movements of an infant are strong social reinforcers for adults. The infant also promises genetic and cultural immortality to the adults who contribute to his genetic constitution or cultural education and training. These genetic and cultural immortality factors are also strong social reinforcers.

The retarded individual, although he has little future and does not promise much genetic or cultural immortality, has much behavior which is very similar to the infant's and therefore provides society with social reinforcers to satisfy what might be called 'maternal instinct.' The smile or caress of a retarded child is a strong social reinforcer for those who attend him or visit him. This is probably why the retarded have always been fairly well treated by society and considered the 'children of God' or the 'holy innocents.'

The psychotic, of course, has fared less well. And this may be because his behavior is not only less rewarding to normal adults, but in many cases is socially aversive. It is a strong attendant who can withstand the verbal onslaught of a sensitive paranoid who criticizes and verbally attacks the attendant's weakest spot. This aversive behavior of the psychotic, coupled with his inability to be a productive member of society, may be why the psychotic has been for centuries maligned, rejected, and considered 'possessed by the devil.' Family visits to chronic psychotics are much less frequent than visits to the mentally retarded. It is much more difficult to maintain volunteer groups to assist in the care of psychotics than it is to maintain those to care for the retarded. And again, among a group of chronic psychotics it is the laughing, joking, pleasant patient — the classic hebephrenic — who receives the most attention on the ward and is the most welcome at hospital parties and home visits.

And so with the aged, the patient with laugh wrinkles, a full head of white hair, and clean white dentures receives more attention and is more reinforcing to attendants and family than the tragic oldster with a scowl, vertical worry wrinkles, a toothless smile and skin lesions. The aged person whose countenance and behavior present aversive stimuli to other individuals is bound to be avoided and neglected. When he also has behavioral deficiencies, so that he no longer can produce in society or reinforce us with pleasant conversation, he becomes extremely aversive and subject to severe social neglect.

A realistic approach to the social neglect of the psychotic and the aged would accept the fact that they are just too aversive for us to expect highly motivated social response to them from normal middle-aged individuals. Rather than spend a great deal of time and money trying to talk people into overcoming this aversion in charitable attempts to help the psychotic and aged, it may be more economical to remove the source of aversion.

Psychotic and aged patients could be made much less aversive by cosmetic attention. Also, if prosthetic devices were developed which would permit them to communicate with normal people and produce positive, though limited, products for the use of society, they would become much more reinforcing to normal individuals and suffer much less neglect. By permanently removing the aversive causes of social neglect, this approach would be more lasting than the current attempts to reduce social neglect by repeated compensatory verbal appeals and the generation of guilt in others.

Conclusion

[...] Until we can halt the process of aging, we owe our grandparents, our parents, and eventually ourselves, the right not only to live, but to behave happily and maximally. Until behavioral medicine catches up with organic medicine, terminal boredom will fall to those unfortunates who live beyond their environment.

NOTES

1. Suggestions for designing prosthetic environments for the behavior of retarded persons have also been made recently (Lindsley 1963).
2. For an excellent review of these experiments see Rachman (1962).

3. Personal communication from T. Ayllon, State Hospital, Anna, Illinois, 1963.
4. The American Psychiatric Association (1959) conducted a survey on the care of patients over 65 in public mental hospitals and gleaned the following suggestions for improving the design of geriatric facilities: tiled bathroom mirrors for wheelchair patients; better lighting with no glare: ramps and short stair risers; guardrails, hold-bars, and non-skid floors; draft-free radiant heat; higher chairs to eliminate stooping to sit; facilities for daytime naps; and work, recreational, and social activities geared to the physical abilities of the patients.

REFERENCES

AMERICAN PSYCHIATRIC ASSOCIATION, 1959, *Report on patients over 65 in public mental hospitals.*

AYLLON, T., Intensive treatment of psychotic behavior by stimulus satiation and food reinforcement,

AYLLON, T., and MICHAEL, J., 1959, 'The psychiatric nurse as a behavioral engineer', *Journal of the Experimental Analysis of Behavior*, 2, pp. 323–34.

FERSTER, C. B. 1958, 'Reinforcement and punishment in the control of human behavior by social agencies', *Psychiatric Research Reports*, 10, pp. 101–18.

LINDSLEY, O. R., 1957, 'Operant behavior during sleep: A measure of depth of sleep', *Science* 126, pp. 1290–1.

LINDSLEY, O. R., 1960, 'Characteristics of the behaviour of chronic psychotics as revealed by free-operant conditioning methods', *Diseases of the Nervous System* Monograph Supplement, 21, pp. 66–78.

LINDSLEY, O. R., 1961, 'Conjugate Reinforcement', Paper read at American Psychological Association. New York, September.

LINDSLEY, O. R., 1963, 'Direct measurement and prosthesis or retarded behavior', Paper read at Boston University, Department of Special Education, March.

LINDSLEY, O. R., HOBIKA, J. H., and ETSTEN, B. E., 1961, 'Operant behaviour during anesthesia recovery: A continuous and objective method', *Anesthesiology*, 22 pp. 937–46.

MELROSE, J., 1962, 'Research in the hearing of the aged', Paper read at National Association Music Therapists, Cambridge, Mass., October.

ORLANDO, R. and BIJOU, S. W., 1960, 'Single and multiple schedules of reinforcement in developmentally retarded children', *Journal of the Experimental Analysis of Behaviour* 3, pp. 339–48.

RACHMAN, S. 1962, 'Learning theory and child psychology: Therapeutic possibilities', *Journal of Child Psychology and Psychiatry* 3, pp. 149–63.

SPRADLIN, J. E., 1962, 'Effects of reinforcement schedules on extinction in severely mentally retarded children', *American Journal of Mental Deficiency* 66, pp. 34–40.

PART NINE
Policy, practice and community involvement in the social services

Introduction

Items in Part Nine are grouped under related headings. Policy and Practice are concerned with organizational analysis, research, and political issues. The more fragmentary nature of the available literature under the final heading dictates a different approach and takes for its emphasis, practical situations in which voluntary workers participate. Readers may find it useful to consider this section in the light of questions raised and objectives postulated in the first two parts of this book.

Policy and practice

Gedye and Bermingham share common ground in considering the practice of planning for the disabled. Their approaches to this concept are, however, at different levels. For Bermingham a systems analysis of the services for handicapped people offers an operational solution. Gedye's concern is that obsolete modes of thought should not be applied to an environmental situation which is essentially dynamic. An example of this non-compartmentalization of thought might be to rewrite the contract implicitly drawn up between employers and employees in such a way as to enable a handicapped person to achieve success rather than failure.

Rehabilitation, variously described in these two items, is brought into sharp focus in the third article. The high proportion of paraplegic patients requiring readmission to the Liverpool Regional Centre precipitated the research described by Forder, Reti and Silver. The evidence presented demonstrates a need for professional care-groups to create, not only an effective system of communication, but also to have a realistic concept of their roles. The article by Johnson and Johnson in Part 8 is of direct relevance to this, in providing even wider information on the rehabilitation of paraplegic ex-patients in Scotland.

There is a tendency when considering policies and strategies for community care to think in terms of formal organizational structures established outside hospital and usually provided by local authority services. Many handicapped people are, however, for long or short periods taken into residential care. In Part 6 we have considered the aims and most appropriate forms of residential care for mentally handicapped children and adults, and referred readers to Miller and Gwynne's book. But it is essential to emphasize the demands that are made in face-to-face relationships, particularly when staff are operating within highly hierarchial organizational structures. In her article on the nursing service, Isabel Menzies analyses a situation, which has many parallels in other organizations with similar roles and regimes, in which one finds social systems acting as a defence against anxiety.

Improving social services is important enough, but of still greater significance is the establishment of an appropriate policy and the means by which it may be implemented. In his discussion of the state of the services for mentally handicapped people, Townsend describes some of the reasons why less than was hoped for has come out of the furore surrounding the disclosure of major scandals and relative deprivation in the geriatric, psychiatric and mental subnormality services from 1968–71. In particular one can see how priorities were altered and developments disjointed by the desire to tinker with an outmoded form of hospital service rather than finance the recommended alternatives to it.

With similar aims Jaehnig, in 'Seeking out the disabled', succinctly describes the rapid progress of the 1970 Morris Bill through Parliament. The effects of the bill's emasculation by amendment at committee stage, from 'requiring' local authorities to register the handicapped to taking 'such steps as are reasonably practicable to inform themselves,' are explored in the bill's subsequent interpretation and implementation by central and local government. Significant among the many issues it raises are the failure of various survey methods to provide a clear picture of the presence of handicap and the inability of many social service departments to meet an increased demand on their resources.

Rosalind Brooke presents a number of questions which stem from the recommendations in the Seebohm Committee Report. Clearly arguments for obtaining civic rights can be applied to the situation of handicapped people and their families. Exposure to constricting and inflexible procedures, benefit by discretion, lack of information, and invasion of privacy are not restricted to the non-handicapped user of the social services. A useful guide to the social services in general and entitlement to benefit in particular is provided by Phyllis Willmott (1971).

Community involvement

Apart from the statutory bodies and the charitable organizations, a wide range of voluntary bodies influence the situation of the handicapped person in the community. Much of the available literature on this work describes particular projects of which there are two examples in this final section. There is, however, less material evaluating the role of volunteers, which is why we have included part of the report on the voluntary worker. A combined committee from the National Council of Social Service and the National Institute for Social Work was asked '. . . to enquire into the role of voluntary workers in the social services and in particular to consider their need for preparation or training and their relationship with professional social workers. . .'. The excerpt given here initially considers the motivation and work experience of voluntary workers based on evidence from a specially commissioned study and a survey by the

King Edward's Hospital Fund. Both studies emphasized the reciprocal benefits of voluntary work and established that a voluntary worker's personal needs require close attention. 'The voluntary worker gives a service without seeking reward. The paid worker fulfills an obligation' is an implicitly pejorative judgement which is taken up in the Aves Committee's examination of relations between professionals and voluntary workers. Whether the explicit criticism of professional social workers is sufficiently answered by the committee's possible explanations is for the reader to decide. There has been considerable criticism of the way in which professionals often see volunteers as filling what the professionals insist on defining as gaps in their own services, which may not appear as priorities or as appropriate work to the volunteers who may define new needs and requirements. Can volunteers be catalysts for community action, leading to demands for services as well as a task-force meeting individual needs?

The motivation of youthful volunteers as outlined in the Aves report is exemplified by Butlin's description of the Wanstead High School Project. This is the first of two articles describing particular schemes and is significant for its analysis of both the individual and the group gains resulting from community involvement. Underlying the description of 'Aids for the Disabled' is the concept of a project linking the school community with a wider, and educative, community. In 'Handicapped Adventure' a charitable body, the Invalid Childrens' Aid Association, was the enabling agent in a project taken up and extended by parents of handicapped children under the direction of a professional social worker. One can discern a pattern of growth in the early stages and it is worth noting the range of statutory functionaries who were introduced to support the volunteers in a flexible way. Finally, we have included part of the National Council of Social Services' advice to those wishing to establish good neighbour schemes, which provides an interesting model for this form of voluntary domiciliary service. The check-list under 'Evaluation' is applicable to a variety of different situations and could appropriately be extended to alleviate the conditions of families discussed in Part Four, and the sort of work commissioned from Task Force volunteers.

REFERENCES

WILLMOTT, P. (1971) *The Consumer's Guide to the British Social Services*, London, Penguin Books.

46. The 'university contribution' to the definition of objectives for the disabled*

J. L. GEDYE
Senior Lecturer, Department of Electrical Engineering Science, University of Essex.

I have chosen to talk about the 'university contribution' to the definition of objectives for the disabled for two main reasons:

1. In order to emphasise the *multidisciplinary* nature of the 'university contribution', and the fact that although psychology is, without doubt, one of the most important of the relevant disciplines, its contribution must be evaluated in relation to the 'university contribution' as a whole.

2. To draw attention to the need to find ways of representing, more explicitly than we have been able to in the past, the ways in which universities contribute to the communities they serve. [. . .]

Each of the 'reasons' I have given for choosing my title relates to a key characteristic of contemporary life — of living in what has recently been referred to as an 'Age of Transience' (Toffler 1970). [. . .]

The first characteristic of an 'Age of Transience' is, therefore, that it brings problems of personal identity insofar as it requires us to work in multidisciplinary situations — problems which would seem to be soluble if we can learn to judge ourselves and others by what we can each contribute, rather than by what we each happen to be called. [. . .]

The second characteristic of an 'Age of Transience' is that it creates a need for up-to-date explicit representations of human organizations accessible, as appropriate, to members of the organization. The creation of such representations is, of course, a multidisciplinary task and it might even be possible to start to think of the 'university contribution' to the community being in essence the nuture, on behalf of the community at large, of the disciplines necessary for the construction of such 'representations' over the whole range of human activities.

To speak of our contemporary situation as an 'Age of Transience' is to mark our growing awareness of developments which have been apparent to those with foresight for some time. In a lecture given at Harvard Business School in the late twenties, A. N. Whitehead drew attention to the fact that our thinking on social issues was, and by and large still is, derived from an unbroken tradition stretching back over nearly 2,500 years. He went on to say 'The whole of this tradition is warped by the vicious assumption that each generation will substantially live amid the conditions governing the lives of its fathers and will transmit those conditions to mould with equal force the lives of its children. We are living in the first period of human history for which this assumption is false.' [. . .]

Many of us are beginning to feel that we may be witnessing the beginnings of epistemological revolution, the fruits of which will, hopefully, equip us to think successfully in circumstances of rapid change. Interestingly enough, this epistemological revolution seems to be linked with a growing emphasis on the need for understanding our present situation in terms of the processes which have led to it — in other words, in terms of its history, so that far from denigrating studies of the past it places a greater emphasis on them — as aids to discovering the points at which our

*Paper presented at a symposium on 'Defining objectives in the field of handicap', British Psychological Society Annual Conference, April (1973) pp. 1–12.

404

inherited tradition took directions that, although understandable in context, we now feel to be mistaken.

What is the significance of all this for disabled people? If we accept that the community has a responsibility to do what it can to ensure that disabled people suffer from as few handicaps as possible, then one of the first things to be done is to make sure that obsolete ways of thinking do not create avoidable obstacles that will prevent disabled people sharing aspirations with the rest of the community. Specific concepts of disability and handicap acquire their meaning in a particular historical context and will change as this changes. A spastic baby born today will reach the age of adulthood in 1990; in assessing his handicap we must somehow avoid the pitfall of assuming that what is today a handicap for a baby born in 1954 will necessarily be so in 1990, with all the implications this has for the child's education. In other words we could easily 'create' handicaps by thinking statically. An important part of the 'university contribution' is therefore, to subject specific concepts of disability and handicap to very careful scrutiny on a *continuing basis*. If this is done, I have a feeling that we will all turn out to be disabled (and handicapped) to some extent, that there will no longer be any rational grounds for discrimination against disabled people as such, and the way will be open for us to work out rational ways of setting reasonable individual levels of aspiration.

In order to be able to take the first steps in such a program, we need to produce working definitions of certain fundamental concepts — such as what we mean by 'living' — a task we might rather avoid, justifying our action perhaps on the grounds that it is no part of our job to tell other people how to run their lives, but this is to overlook the fact that whether we are willing to admit it or not, some such definition is implicit in our concepts of disability and handicap. Surely it is better to accept this as a fact, and make our definition of 'living' explicit so that we can discuss it openly, than to leave it as an unacknowledged influence on our thinking.

As a start, I would like to suggest that we think of 'living' as the *'art of the reachable'* — the art, that is, of setting and reaching objectives. One of the merits of the definition is that it reflects two important aspects of 'living.' These are, on the one

hand, that we do not, by and large admire people who fail to reach their objectives, however near they might come to success; and, on the other hand, that we do not, by and large, admire people who fail to set themselves objectives that we feel to be within their reach — we are, perhaps, even more critical of under-aspiration than we are of underachievement.

The process by which we learn to set and reach objectives is *habilitation*. It is this which earns us our place in the community, so that when, for one reason or another, our personal resources change for better or worse, we have to learn how to set and reach objectives in the light of our changed circumstances, that is we have to undergo a process of *rehabilitation*. By defining 'habilitation' and 'rehabilitation' in this way we provide ourselves with a basis for the development of an approach to the subject which concentrates on the problems faced by the individual who is required to adjust to changed personal circumstances — whether these be for 'better' or for 'worse'; and so it allows us to see the problems of disabled people as ones of a kind which, in an Age of Transience, faces us all at one time or another, to a greater or lesser extent. Dissatisfaction with current approaches to the subject has recently led to the suggestion that the words 'habilitation' and 'rehabilitation' should be abandoned; but it seems to me that it would be preferable to counter the debasement of these and related words by launching a program of etymologically-based semantic rehabilitation!

We could well start with the words 'disability' and 'handicap.' If we refer to someone as *disabled* we wish to imply that they lack the ability to succeed in the performance of some set of tasks: we are, in other words, making a forecast of their future performance based on a study of their past performance — either from typical instances of the set of tasks in question (as when, for example, we say on the basis of observations in an experimental kitchen, that a housewife who has 'had a stroke' cannot cut bread) or from observations of performance of some other set of tasks which we believe gives us a warrant to forecast what would happen if the individual were to attempt the set of tasks in question. A psychologist's 'test' is, from this point of view, a forecasting procedure based on observation of performance on a standard set of tasks, chosen to meet various practical requirements, and it is, of course, always open to challenge (Gedye 1971a).

One of the features of most everyday tasks (and laboratory tasks for that matter) is that, whilst it may not be difficult to judge whether or not they have been performed adequately, that is whether or not the objective has been reached, the *explicit representation of this judicial procedure* may be far from easy. I have suggested (Gedye 1964, Gedye 1971b) that it may be necessary to think in terms of an implicit (or explicit) contract of employment existing between an 'employer' (experimenter) and an 'employee' (subject) (allowing, of course, for self-employment) if one is to be able to represent the process of investigation of failure to achieve an objective at all realistically.

If our only aim is to judge 'success' or 'failure', this problem need not concern us unduly, but if, however, our aim is to assess degree of failure, which is tantamount to asking whether there are any ways in which the employer-employee contract could, in principle, have been rewritten to allow the employee to reach the objective specified by the contract, it is clearly of considerable concern to us. This is what we are, or *should*, be doing when we are assessing *dis*ability — specifying in what way, or ways, such an implicit contract between 'employer' and 'employee' would need to be rewritten to allow 'success' rather than 'failure' — If such modifications are *realisable*, then we have, at least, a *possible* solution to the rehabilitation problem posed by the disability.

We referred above to a specific everyday task — 'slicing bread,' however, when we speak of 'disability' in everyday life we usually have in mind a set of tasks — those involved in the activities of 'dressing' or 'shopping', for example. It is clear, therefore, that if our representational technique is to have any practical use, it must allow us to think 'hierarchically' to talk meaningfully both about such activities as 'shopping' and the activities into which they can be decomposed. In other words it must provide us with a 'language' in which we can describe — to whatever degree of resolution we find necessary — the *structure* of an individual's abilities. In this connection it is of interest to note that R. H. Atkin and his colleagues have recognised a similar requirement in their work on the development of a 'language' for describing the structure of urban communities (Atkin 1972—4, 1974).

It follows from what has been said above that we can each of us think of ourselves as having an *ability structure* in relation to a given set of tasks, and I have no doubt that it would not be too difficult to find sets of tasks in relation to which a comparison of the ability structures of any pair of us would show each of us to be at a disadvantage with respect to the other, with the consequence that we could each of us be said to be relatively disabled in some respect. Looking at things in this way helps to highlight the fact that our everyday concepts of disability imply a set or sets of tasks, or 'employment contracts' in relationship to which we assess an individual's ability structure, and to point to the urgent need to study the mechanisms by which these sets of tasks are chosen both by the community at large and by those who regard themselves as 'disabled.' Such a study would undoubtedly expose many important problems, such as the distinction between 'overt' and 'covert' disability (a distinction based on the ease with which individuals with similar disability structures can recognise each other), and would seem to be an essential part of any attempt to define the concept of disability. We might anticipate, for example, that it would show that certain configurations of specific disabilities result either in an individual being regarded or regarding himself as 'disabled', or both.

The concept of 'handicap' presupposes, at least figuratively, some kind of competitive situation — a contest between two individuals which one is expected to win and the other to lose. 'Handicapping' is the name we give to procedures by which, in recognition of the consequences of differing ability structures, an attempt is made to *equalise* the initial probabilities of the outcomes, or, one might say, the initial 'reachabilities' of the objectives, by altering the 'contract of employment' of one of the contestants — by, for example, requiring a runner in a race to carry an additional load.

This way of thinking enables us, by extension, to speak of contestants who differ in ability structure with respect to some sets of tasks as naturally, as opposed to artificially, handicapped: and allows us to go on to consider ways in which 'contracts of employment' might be rewritten to increase rather than decrease the reachability of objectives. It is perhaps worth noting here that one of the characteristics of an objective is that there may be many equally acceptable ways in which it can be reached, and specific 'contracts of employment' may handicap by unnecessarily failing to allow for some of these. At the same time it is not uncommon to have 'contracts of employment' which only specify the objective in terms of the desired end state, and say nothing about how it is to be reached — a situation familiar to research workers!

This approach allows us to think, therefore, of the problem of the disabled individual as one of learning to assess his or her natural handicaps in relation to specific sets of tasks with a view to determining the reachability of various objectives, so that 'contracts of employment' are only entered into if success is highly probable and failure is thus avoided. One can think of it as a problem of learning to navigate across a difficult terrain, hard enough at the best of times, but made harder, if one is disabled, by the fact that the experience of others who have made similar journeys in the past is in any case likely to be less relevant than if one is 'able-bodied', and by the additional fact that, in an 'Age of Transience', the terrain itself is changing.

I referred earlier to the need to learn to live in a 'world of change', and it may, by now, have occurred to you to ask what, exactly, is meant by this exhortation — for surely we, as human beings, have always lived in a 'world of change'? Yes, of course we have, but we are now concerned with a different kind of change. Consider the account we might give of the experience of watching a play — we produce a description in terms of foreground change taking place against a fixed background provided by the stage and scenery. When the background changes — say between scenes — it is to indicate a change of time or place which is too great to be contained within the action of the scene itself. However, the very fact that it is frequently necessary, in a play about human affairs, to change the background in this way indicates that our habit of partitioning our experience into dynamic foreground and static background components reflects a relative rather than an absolute distinction. The point that the 'futurologists' are trying to draw attention to when they talk about 'change' can, I think, be made by saying that we are moving into an age in which our ability to partition our experience in this way is breaking down, and changes of background are obtruding into the action of the play itself, which is, of course, exactly what happens when someone suddenly becomes 'disabled' — the 'set changes in the middle of the scene.' [. . .]

I believe that the solution to these problems will be found by pursuing the idea that the 'university contribution' to the problems of the disabled is to nurture the disciplines required to represent our day-to-day situation sufficiently faithfully to show us how we 'fit in' to the communities in which we live.

REFERENCES

ATKIN, R. H., 1972–74, *Urban Structure Research Project: Research Reports I–IV*, Department of Mathematics, University of Essex.

GEDYE, J. L., 1964, *Transient Changes in the Ability to Reproduce a Sequential Operation following Rapid Decompression, Report No. 271*, Institute of Aviation Medicine, Farnborough.

GEDYE, J. L., 1969, 'Problems in the Design of Interactive Terminals for Direct Use by Patients', in Abrams, M. E. (ed.), *Medical Computing — Progress and Problems*, London, Chatto & Windus for the British Computer Society.

GEDYE, J. L., 1971, 'The Use of an Interactive Computer Terminal to Assess the Effect of Cyclandelate on the Mental Ability of Geriatric Patients', in *Assessment in Cerebrovascular Insufficiency*, Stuttgart: Georg Thieme Verlag.

GEDYE, J. L., 1973, 'The Use of an Interactive Computer Terminal to Simulate Decision-Making Situations', Proceedings of NATO Conference on Computer simulation of Human Thought Processes.

Southend Project, 1972, Southend-on-Sea Hospital Management Committee, *Experimental Computer Project: Systems Study Report*, NE Metropolitan RHB Management Services Report No. 324.

TOFFLER, A., 1970, *Future Shock*, London, Bodley Head; Pan.

WHITEHEAD, A. N., 1933, 'Foresight' in *Adventures of Ideas*, Harmondsworth, Penguin Books (Pelican), reprinted 1942.

47. Organisation and development: systems analysis and planning for the intellectually handicapped *

IRENE H. BERMINGHAM
Psychologist and Australian Capital Territory Advisor
for the Intellectually Handicapped, Canberra, Australia

Introduction

The object of this paper is to show that the rehabilitation of the 'intellectually handicapped' — a better term than 'mentally retarded', 'sub-normal' or 'mentally defective', if only because of its more positive connotations — is an effort capable of successful realization. As such, it is the proper concern of all disciplines.

As an international community, we need to pool our resources to make the attainment of this goal easier. What needs to be demonstrated is our conviction that an intellectually handicapped person has the same right to enjoy habilitative and rehabilitative services as any other person in our community. The aim of the scientist should be to define the methods by which this can be done. The work of medical services and associated disciplines is to apply such methods, and the job of the planner is to demonstrate that this can be done efficiently and economically.

There is little point in evading the fact that those who allocate scarce national resources must be shown clearly the benefits that can be derived from the cost outlayed. So far, those who work with the handicapped have had insufficient time to demonstrate the usefulness of their efforts. The difficulty is to show in tangible terms that social and mental health benefits are as real as others. The contention is made here that the majority of people categorized as handicapped can be rehabilitated. Their rehabilitation may initially be more costly, but in the long term it produces financial savings and social benefits that far outstrip the apparently high initial outlay. (See 'Systems Thinking and Current Issues' p. 413.)

Concepts and methods exist that can effectively help in attaining our goal, by being used to produce effective rehabilitative systems. Services for the 'handicapped' have characteristically evolved in response to specific, urgent needs, and as such are often 'stop-gap' in nature. Concepts that allow a handicapped person to participate in the rehabilitative process in a gradually escalating degree, and lead to such persons having a normal working and recreational life in society, demand close attention. One conceptual approach found to be useful is 'systems analysis'.

Systems technology

'Systems analysis', together with 'operations research' and 'computer simulation', is one of the more important techniques of systems technology.

Advances made in systems technology, and the related fields of cybernetics, information and communication theory, deserve attention because they lead away from the concern for 'inherent substance, qualities and properties to a central focus on the principles of organisation per se, regardless of what it is that is organised' (Buckley, 1967).

'Systems analysis' is simply an examination of systems of organisation. Its technical definition is:

A specialized method of sub-dividing an integrated complex into its more basic parts in order to examine each component's use, and the functional relationship to other components' (Eicker *et al.*, 1967, p. 67).

*From *Rehabilitation International,* 1972. Report of a conference held in Australia 27 August– 1 September 1969.

Systems technology has been used with outstanding success to design, develop and evaluate the effectiveness of massive and highly complex aerospace mission problems. 'The power of the tools of operations research, systems analysis and computer simulation lies in their insistence on the primacy of conceptualizing any large operation as a necessarily dynamic configuration of inter-dependent components, that is a "system". Although single components of a system may be improved, best results are obtained by viewing a system in the broadest perspective including its surrounding social and economic environment and the information network binding the interacting components of a system together,' (Eicker *et al.*, 1967, p. 1).

AEROSPACE MISSIONS

A frequent objection is that although this may be an appropriate approach for aerospace missions, it cannot be applied to human beings and society. Indeed, the interaction of human beings and society is multiple and complex, and it is difficult to isolate and evaluate the variables of this interaction. However, interactions do occur within an 'integrated complex' (society), which has already been defined, non-rigorously, as a 'system'. Moreover, human beings are essentially distinguishable from other species by their ability to organise and systemize. To suggest the application of 'systems analysis' to the study of the service needs of a handicapped community is to utilize this unique quality of organisation.

FEASIBILITY

The feasibility of applying systems technology to social problems has been demonstrated. 'In 1964 California invited aerospace industries to submit research proposals for a feasibility study of the application of systems engineering on the evaluation and design of a new system for the control and prevention of crime and mental illness,' (op. cit, p. 3). Systems technology has been applied to a community mental health programme, by Eicker *et al.*, (op. cit.) in a research project designed to develop an optimal mental health operation in one region. This attempt was in their view 'unprecedented', and the applications of systems technology continue to be limited, perhaps because of the conceptual leap that 'systems' thinking

demands. The crucial point is that the technical problems of aerospace missions and a community mental health service are essentially the same. The complexity arises from the fact that 'mental health systems, like most social systems, have evolved through historical custom, and trial and error modifications rather than by deliberate design.' (op. cit., p. 5). It is this very lack of deliberate design, the disorganisation and reduced efficacy that they produce in our field of work, that has prompted the writing of this paper.

'HABILITATION' AND 'REHABILITATION'

In broad terms the author subscribes to Whitehead's concept of rehabilitation as being the 'cultivation, restoration and conservation of human resources' (Whitehouse, 1956). A distinction needs to be made, it is agreed, between the concepts of 'habilitation' and 'rehabilitation'. 'Habilitation' here refers to the 'cultivation of human resources', or an affirmation of life processes. 'Rehabilitation' is the restoration or conservation of human resources, which have been diminished, or the re-affirmation of life processes. The term 'rehabilitation will be used throughout to denote both aspects. Although there is likely to be consensus regarding broad aims of 'rehabilitation', disagreement occurs in the specification of particular goals.

APPLICABILITY

In most instances the rehabilitative process is carried out by specific acts in the context of a physical care institution or a mental health authority. For example, a clinic is set up for a specific purpose. The need is great and there is little time for planning. Soon the clinic is 'flooded' with cases and the main concern becomes surviving the clinical caseload. Stress, reduced efficiency through 'overload' of the system, follow, as do demands for more staff or a new clinic.

This one learns through experience. Had a systems approach been used from the outset, these difficulties could have been predicted, as could the stress points. Available resources would have determined the limits of the clinic system, and growth could be controlled. This is an example of a simple, though effective, way in which 'systems analysis' works and serves simply as an introduction to 'systems analysis' itself. Other examples will be given later.

SYSTEMS ANALYSIS

This process involves:

1. **Statement of objectives:** Objectives or 'end-points' have to be stated unequivocally. Then, working backwards, all necessary activities that should ultimately attain these objectives are outlined. Let us assume that the general aim is the 'affirmation of the life process'. As this is much too vague, a specific aim needs to be put forward, e.g. the achievement of independence.

What is meant by 'independence'? Can the problem be approached by defining its opposite dependence? Could a dependency scale be developed and related to a classification of handicap? This brings us to the next step.

2. **Information** — here a somewhat WHO—HEBER classification is used to illustrate the point:

of the way in demonstrating a relationship between variables, and it highlights problems. What is lacking is information — information about ways in which dependency can be measured, ways in which like things can be classified and ways in which one can scale a variable like dependency. A certain portion of resources have to be allocated to the seeking out of further information — i.e. research. Research will provide one with information that will enable goals to be reformulated.

Lack of information about one end-point does not exclude the possibility that there are other end-points that can be stated unequivocally, e.g. one 'known end-point' could be 'equality of educational opportunity' with others in the community, i.e. access to pre-schools, schools and post-school education. Specification of end-points

Table 47.1 The relationship between dependency and handicap

Degree of handicap	Degree of dependency	Percentage of dependence
Borderline handicapped	lack of dependency	0
Mildly handicapped	minimal dependency	20
Moderately handicapped	certain dependency	35
	some dependency	50
Severely handicapped	considerable dependency	65
Profoundly handicapped	great dependency	80
	total dependency	100

The foregoing model is an attempt to relate the degree of dependency to the degree of handicap, to scale dependency in terms of degree and even to express it in terms of percentages of dependency, and to describe 'dependency' in terms which could be meaningful.

The attempt reveals just how difficult it is to arrive at categories that are mutually exclusive. It also shows that within one category there can be varying degrees of dependency and vice versa. It becomes clear that categorizations that are used for convenience, can distort the fact that there are as many differences in individuals falling within certain degrees of handicap, as there are within the range of the 'normal'.

Such a model has many faults, but it goes part

also helps to formulate the general concept of rehabilitation, so that rather than saying 'rehabilitation is . . .' one says 'x, y and z acts constitute rehabilitation'.

3. Model building. This involves the creation of mathematical or symbolic models to show a system in its entirety. Information regarding the technical steps involved can be found in references to model construction. Below, is the classic model of 'systems analysis'.

The outside boundary shows the limit of the system. The left hand boundary in this instance shows the interaction of the system and the community. Within the boundaries, are outlined the necessary steps in the establishment of a system, showing its functional steps.

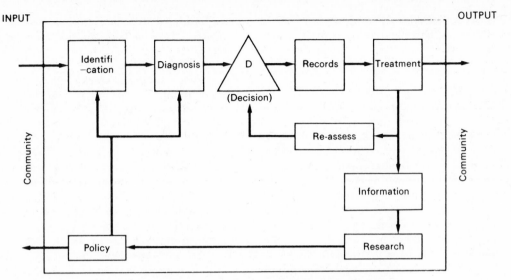

Figure 47.2   The classic model of systems analysis

When one has established structures that provide for each step to take place, one can say a comprehensive system of operation has been established.

4. Simulation — this concept refers to the step which involves simulated flow of a plan. For example, one intends to establish a diagnostic clinic and has obtained information and constructed a model. The progress of the patient through the clinic is simulated, the specific steps involved are investigated and the model is modified according to the 'feedback' provided.

5. Programme Formulation: Specific parts of the programme (sub-systems) are detailed, e.g. the follow-up of patients seen at the diagnostic clinic.

6. Trial: The clinic begins operation for a trial period of 3 months, during which parts of the system that show stress are identified, and modified.

7. Reassessment: With the information gained so far, end-points are reformulated. This is a continuing process.

The outline of the steps just given must not be considered as an exhaustive statement of all that is involved in 'systems analysis'. It is a description of the essential components of a simple open system. An agency or department responsible for the provision of services for handicapped persons, will perforce operate within a much more complex system, and is likely to be only one of the many sub-systems of such an authority.

Sub-optimization

As a sub-system, a service for the handicapped can endanger or 'sub-optimize' the total system. 'Sub-optimization', an important concept, refers to the 'development of a system component or activity which ideally satisfies its particular narrow objectives, but which detracts from the ideal operation of a system as a whole' (Eicker *et al.*, 1967, p. 67).

Sub-optimization is a problem relevant to Australian experience. Here, services for the handicapped, if not provided by a voluntary association, are part of the separate departments of Health, Education and Welfare. As such, these services stress the resources of individual departments. The last ten years have seen increasing co-ordination between departments, where the alternative of establishing a separate authority for 'handicapped services' has not already been chosen.

The choices, when planning new services or re-structuring old ones, really seem to range between:

(1) the development of an autonomous authority;

(2) the development of services within an existing authority (e.g. a health or mental health structure), and fully integrated with it.

Theoretically at least, if the aims of such services are rehabilitative, the latter approach, though more difficult to implement and operate because of its dependency on co-ordination and co-operation (dependency on other parts of the system), seem desirable. The difficulty, of course, remains that one never has the opportunity when building a social care system, to build from the group up.

Further applicability

The choice one makes will continue to be based on conjecture until a careful study can be made of the comparative benefits of each alternative. It is here that systems technology can play a part. It offers the conceptual tools to undertake such an analysis. This analysis would involve an operations research analysis to evaluate existing systems of administration; a 'systems analysis' and a computer simulation. The last is the most advanced development in systems technology and involves the development of alternative systems models which are computer programmed to establish 'optimal design parameters in terms of minimal cost in time and money for an effectively operating system' (Eicker *et al.*, 1967).

In this respect systems technology seems to have great potential for applicability to our field of work.

Systems – the handicapped – Canberra

A rare opportunity to test the feasibility of a systems approach to services for the handicapped has presented itself in Canberra.

This opportunity has arisen with the establishment of a mental health service (part of the general Health Service), one of the roles of which is to assist in the development of a comprehensive service for the intellectually handicapped.

Services for the handicapped in Canberra have existed for some time. They were developed by the combined efforts of voluntary associations, dedicated individuals and government departments. The role of the new 'agency' was to supplement existing services and to plan the eventual development of a coordinated comprehensive service in the ACT. As part of a mental health service it is dependent on the general staff resources available, and only has a very small staff. This in fact has turned out to be something of an advantage, as other members of the service have become deeply involved in providing services and planning future ones.

One of the problems facing the administration now, the very one touched on earlier, is whether to continue development of the section as one

fully integrated with the rest of the service, or to separate it into an 'independent' section with a perforce large staff establishment and better control of development. This decision has been deliberately postponed for a couple of years. Present feeling is that it is best to take the opportunity of testing the effectiveness of being integrated – (i.e. simulating a programme). However, integration involves careful analysis of existing systems and carefully planned development of future ones. It perhaps can be successful only if a systems approach is implemented in full.

This may be in part the reason that staff has become interested in the systems approach. An additional reason has been that stresses of a rapidly developing mental health service have demanded adaptation, and new ways of thinking. Research suggests that 'systems analysis' is one conceptual model that may assist this process.

How in fact, it may be asked, has the systems approach been used? The answer is that consciously it has been used only in very recent months, although the initial steps that were carried out, in fact, were those of operations research analysis. Recent developments and projects have been conceptualized in 'systems' thinking.

The initial steps included:

1. Identification of services already being provided in the district. Apart from special facilities for the handicapped such as pre-schools, schools, residential workshops and a residential hostel, many different departments and agencies provided services for the handicapped within their general services to the public, e.g. vocational guidance, infant health and social welfare.

2. Determination of Prevalence – Crude statistics exist, arrived at largely by a 'head count' method. A comprehensive survey has been planned for the near future.

3. Identification of Needs – and the ordering of needs in the most effective priority.

4. Determination of Needs – Services Relationship.

5. Researching the hidden needs of the population.

6. Proposing methods to meet above.

Familiar problems existed in the field generally: poor communication, lack of co-ordinated planning, limited consensus regarding aims, limited funds and staff resources. At about this time the benefits of a 'systems' approach were realised and this approach began to be tested. The emphasis began to shift from personalities, inter-personal relations, inter-disciplinary rivalries, to concern with organisation of structure which would be self-sustaining, self-monitoring, involving a more economic utilization of energy. One of the problems was how to retain the innovative enthusiasm that is so essential to a new and developing service and yet to channel this enthusiasm to producing benefits that would continue.

The practical methods used were basically the following:

1. Establishing frequent and varied exchanges of information with all agencies and departments concerned. The existence of an inter-departmental committee, established much earlier for just this purpose, facilitated this.

2. Finding and choosing projects with a potentially high interest level to facilitate involvement.

3. Creating opportunities for feedback once a project was initiated.

4. Providing the opportunity for many people to get personal 'kudos' from their involvement.

Community projects undertaken were conceptualized as 'systems' and were developed in the steps of 'systems analysis'. These projects include:

1. The establishment of multi-purpose evening classes under the auspices of the Evening College System. Their successful operation depends almost entirely on a high degree of co-ordination between agencies.

2. Formation of a group for parents of children who are placed away from the ACT in residential care establishments. This has provided the parents with support and planners with information.

3. Formation of a 'baby-sitting' service, run by Red Cross volunteers and providing a much needed relief for parents of handicapped children.

4. Several training courses have been run for various groups — Red Cross Volunteers, staffs of the Sheltered Workshops and the Training Centre.

5. A work assessment programme for handicapped persons has been established. It is run by the occupational therapist of the mental health service in conjunction with another government department.

Immediate plans include an extension of assessment and diagnostic services, establishment of three hostels, and the formation of a 'How to Manage' Clinic for mothers and children, to be run by physiotherapists and the domiciliary support staff.

A common characteristic of these developments is the fact that they rely on the staff of different establishments and a conscious effort is made to utilize community resources. The small section (staff of 3) within the mental health service, that works exclusively for the handicapped, can provide a very limited range of services. Services will expand rapidly in the next few years. Our basic aim is to help create structures that will continue to function effectively when the present staff has gone. An effort is made to ensure that structures set up are not dependent on the charismatic qualities of key personnel, that are likely to diminish in effectiveness with their passing.

The outline of developments in Canberra is not presented as an example of a fully operational 'systems approach'. At this stage it can only be said that we are thinking systems and are finding that this approach works! We offer the suggestion that others may find it useful. In any case, there is an invitation for others to help us with time to evaluate its effectiveness.

Systems thinking and some current issues

1. Relation of Government to Voluntary Associations: If the aim of provision is the 'habilitation' or 'rehabilitation' of the intellectually handicapped, remembering that these terms have been defined as 'affirmation or re-affirmation of life processes', rather than as a categorization of persons as disabled, handicapped or the like, there surely can be little question that the entire community, (including government and voluntary associations) should be involved in this process.

If this premise is accepted, then the relative contribution of each party becomes the issue. If the 'end-points' have been defined specifically, and the entire system of care has been accurately analysed, the provision of a particular service will be made by the sub-system that can most appropriately carry it. In Canberra, it was not feasible to have residential care for the severely handicapped provided by a voluntary association. However, a voluntary association, by its very community nature, is eminently suited to providing community hostels or holiday homes.

The view presented here is that the roles of the voluntary associations and governments in any community are complementary.

2. Shortage of Staff: This is a common problem, of great magnitude. A high degree of staff

specialization, customary in rehabilitation services, and the implicit demand it makes for more staff, is a trend not peculiar to the Australian Capital Territory.

Have the implications of increasing specialization and differentiation, one wonders, really been considered in the field of rehabilitative services? For instance, it is more than possible, even now, for one patient to be treated by 10 people simultaneously, for different aspects of the same condition. Is there commital to a 'system', that of itself demands greater and greater differentiation? Analysis of any system can suggest possible alternatives. Should we be aiming to produce a trained generalist to carry out the actual rehabilitative act?

3. Funds: It is difficult to persuade many that there can be returns for money invested in services for the handicapped. Is it, perhaps, because of the aims that have been communicated to society and the authorities? For long, the primary aim of care for the handicapped, was their containment in a 'niche', preferably isolated from the rest of society. Society's attitudes are changing — is the 'feed back' to society still the policy of 'containment'? Would more funds become available if the philosophy communicated was one of rehabilitation together with a clear demonstration of the social benefits that will accrue?

Conclusion

An effective rehabilitative system should include the sub-systems of identification; assessment; treatment; recording; data collection; research and policy formation. 'Feed-back' loops operating between all these components, are of course, essential.

Material benefits accruing from such an approach should include: reduction of national expenditure on social service benefits; lower capital spending on residential care facilities, as better community support systems develop; considerable range of savings gradually generated by a more efficient system of operation. Finally, major social and economic benefits for the community as a whole should result from the improvement in the mental health of 'handicapped' persons and their families.

Surely this is why it is imperative to devote close attention to the creation of an effective modern rehabilitative 'system' on moral, social, scientific, economic and political grounds.

REFERENCES

BOWMAN, E. H. and FELTER, R. B., 1961, *Analysis for Production and Operations Management*, Homewood, Illinois, Richard D. Irwin, (3rd ed.).

BUCKLEY, W., 1967, *Sociology and Modern Systems Theory*, Englewood Cliffs, N.J., Prentice Hall.

EICKER, W. F. *et at.*, 1967, *Application of Systems Technology to Community Mental Health*, Florence Heller, Graduate School for Advanced Studies, Brandeis University, (Waltham, Mass.).

HARE, V. C. JR., 1967, *Systems Analysis: A Diagnostic Approach*, New York, Harcourt Brace & World.

McMILLAN, C. and GONZALES, F., 1968, *Systems Analysis*, Homewood, Illinois, Richard D. Irwin.

MILLER JAMES G., 1965, 'Living Systems: Basic Concepts', *Behavioural Science*, Vol. 10, pp. 193–217.

WHITEHOUSE, F. A., 1956, 'The Utilization of Human Resources. A philosophical Approach to Rehabilitation', *Diseases of the Chest*, 30, p. 606.

48. Communication in the health service: a case study of the rehabilitation of paraplegic patients.*

ANTHONY FORDER, T. RETI AND J. R. SILVER
University of Liverpool and
Liverpool Regional Paraplegic Centre

The problems of co-ordination, and hence of communication, within the National Health Service, have long been recognised, and some studies have shown the effect of poor co-ordination both within the service and between it and other services (Ferguson and McPhail 1954). Yet there have been very few studies of the methods of communication used. Shaw made a study of communications and relationships between hospitals and general practitioners. He made a number of practical proposals about the arrangements for making appointments, and the transmission of reports. He also found that teachers in medical schools tended to stress the defects of general practitioners, rather than their virtues, to the detriment of relationships between them. Revans (1964) has examined communications inside hospitals. Rodgers and Dixon (1960) and Jefferys (1965) showed the lack of contact between general practitioners and other social services. But none of these studies has been based on the concepts of communication theory, and little reference has been made to studies of other large organisations. As a result, there has been a tendency to attribute breakdown in communication to the idiosyncracies of the National Health Service when factors common to other

organisations might be involved. For example, Leavitt and Mueller's studies showing the importance of feedback in the transmission of complex information are clearly of relevance to the medical field (Leavitt and Mueller 1951); so too are studies of the effectiveness of different communication networks, (Leavitt 1952) and of the effects on communication of cognitive similarity, i.e. similarity in the concepts used in describing a situation (Triandis 1960). This is the theoretical background implicit in the study described here.

Early in 1967, the authors became concerned about the large proportion of paraplegic patients needing to be re-admitted with pressure sores, contractures and urinary infections after discharge from the Liverpool Regional Paraplegic Centre at Southport. This involved three out of every eight patients discharged. The consultant's preliminary examination of the cases suggested that the likelihood of re-admission was not closely related to the severity of the disability, the most severely disabled, the tetraplegics, being somewhat less likely than other paraplegics to be re-admitted. The likelihood of re-admission is probably related to a variety of factors including particularly the attitude and social situation of the patient and his responsible relatives. But since the successful rehabilitation of paraplegics depends on co-operation between personnel in all the three branches of the National Health Service, it seemed to be worthwhile to make a preliminary study of factors that might affect this co-operation, particularly of communication between personnel and of their expectations of each other.

Paraplegia is a condition of partial or complete paralysis due to injury or disease in the spinal

*From *Social and Economic Administration* (1969) *3*, pp. 3–16.
The study on which this article is based was financed by the Research Committee of the United Liverpool Hospital Board and the Liverpool Regional Hospital Board.
A fuller report of the study by T. Reti is available from the Social Science Department, University of Liverpool, Liverpool, 7, and Liverpool Regional Paraplegic Centre, Promenade Hospital, Southport.

cord. If the arms as well as the legs are paralysed, this is known as tetraplegia. Paraplegia is a relatively rare condition. The Centre at Southport, although it comes under the Liverpool Regional Hospital Board, draws its patients from a much wider area, since there are no units in adjacent areas. Patients come from as far afield as Newcastle-on-Tyne, Lancaster and North Wales, yet there are only about 60 new admissions annually.

Until the introduction of modern methods of treatment by Munro in 1936, and by Guttman at Stoke Mandeville in 1944, the majority of patients with traumatic paraplegia died within a year of injury. Modern methods, which involve the segregation of paralysed patients in centres, where staff with special training can devote themselves to their care, have changed the picture entirely. Guttman's latest figures show that of 2,500 patients treated between 1944 and the end of March 1962, 1,681 are alive and living at home; 447 are in hospitals or hostels; and only 371 have died. Of the survivors, 66 per cent are gainfully employed, the majority full-time.

However, the maintenance of the fitness of paraplegic patients demands constant attention from the patients themselves and from those responsible for their care, to prevent the development of the conditions that used to be fatal for them. For example, if the patient remains resting on the same spot without being moved for as short a time as three hours, a blister may develop which could quickly become a pressure sore. This means that the patient must turn himself, or be turned, every two hours, throughout the day and night, to prevent deterioration in his condition.

The management of paraplegia in the community requires the use of a number of different community services. These may include in addition to the services of the general practitioners, rehousing and adaptation of housing; the provision of special equipment such as beds with lifting gear; home nursing; occupational therapy; home help; employment services; legal and other assistance with financial matters; and the assistance of social casework with the social and psychological problems of adjustment to the limitations created by the disability. At the same time, the comparative rareness of paraplegia makes it likely that few general practitioners or other workers in the community services will have had experience of treating the condition during or after training, so

that they may have difficulty in understanding the patients' needs.

These problems of co-ordination and understanding are shared with many other conditions involving physical and mental handicap, including old age. Often, the situation is further complicated by the speed of changes in the treatment of certain conditions under the specialist system which operates in the hospitals but not in the community services.

In examining the problems of communication in the social services that might be affecting the rehabilitation of paraplegics, it was decided to use a small number of case studies. Ten cases of traumatic paraplegia were selected from patients recently discharged from the Centre for the first time. The basis of selection was the area of residence, the primary consideration being to ensure that different types of local authority were represented. The ten patients came from one large and two smaller county boroughs, and from two county council areas. Eight of them were discharged home and two to local hospitals near their homes.

Initially, the research worker spent a good deal of time at the Centre seeing patients in the hospital and interviewing staff, to get an understanding of paraplegia and its treatment, and of the functions of the various staff involved. Particular attention was paid to their contacts with community services. The actual follow up involved interviews with the patients, their relatives, the general practitioners and local authority staff.

The patients were on average interviewed twice, usually in their own homes. The interviews lasted from 1½ to 2 hours and were unstructured. The patient and his closest relative, if present, were encouraged to recount their experience of the Paraplegic Centre, general practitioners, and the local authority and employment services. Particular attention was paid to the nature, purpose and timing of all contacts with these services. A close relative of each patient was seen, either spouse or parent, generally at the same time as the patient. It was felt that since the focus of the interviews was on the services, rather than on the personal adjustment and relationships of the patient and his family, the disadvantages of a joint interview would be outweighed by the support the patient and his relative would gain from being seen together. With the patients' consent, the general practitioners of the eight patients who were discharged home were also seen. These interviews took place in the surgeries, were structured and lasted about an hour. The questions were designed to elicit from the general practitioners their understanding of their patients' needs; their perception of their own role in treatment, and of the function of the Paraplegic Centre and the local authority services; and the extent of communication with them.

With local authority staff interviews were first sought with the medical officers of health, and where appropriate, the Chief Welfare Officers. These interviews were followed by group meetings attended by senior officers of health departments, welfare departments, and, at two meetings, housing departments, together with some field staff, including district nurses, welfare officers, a health visitor and an occupational therapist. There were altogether eighteen interviews in the five authorities, involving thirty-four people. These interviews were unstructured and were designed to elicit information about the type of services provided, their organisation, the method of communication between them and the way decisions were taken that affected the patients.

The Liverpool Regional Paraplegic Centre is situated in the Promenade Hospital at Southport. It has thirty-four beds under the supervision of a full-time consultant, assisted by a registrar. Responsibility for the nursing care of the patients is in the hands of the charge nurse. Auxiliary medical services are provided by the hospital. Of particular importance in this study were the occupational therapy and physiotherapy departments of the hospital. At the time of discharge of the patients studied, the medical social worker also had responsibilities outside the Centre but spent a large proportion of her time working for the Centre.

The hospital is not large and communication between the staff of the Centre and some of the other departments was good. This was not unfortunately true of all the departments in the hospital. Formal communication centred upon the weekly ward round at which the charge nurse, medical social worker, senior physiotherapist attached to the Spinal Centre and the senior occupational therapist were generally present with the consultant and the registrar. A good deal of information was also exchanged informally as the

consultant, being full-time, made daily rounds of the patients in the Centre, and encouraged the staff and patients to consult him on the problems of the patients. Treatment was initiated and co-ordinated by the consultant who was naturally in close touch with each patient.

The consultant's view of the function of the Centre was that once the patient had been restored to the maximum level of fitness and discharged, primary responsibility for the care and treatment of the patient should be with the community health services while the Centre adopted an advisory and supportive role. The patient himself would have been taught the techniques of management of the condition, and would be expected to co-operate actively with these services. To ensure for him and his relatives an easy transition from the dependence of the hospital situation to the relative independence of life at home, a system of preparatory week-end leaves was developed. Within the community services, the consultant saw the general practitioner as having a rôle like the one he himself had in the hospital, that is to say, the general practitioner had primary responsibility for maintaining the health of the patient, and would call on and co-ordinate the work of a similar range of skilled personnel from the other social services. Thus, it seemed reasonable to the consultant that his only direct communication with the community services was with the patient's general practitioner.

The general practitioner

In communicating with general practitioners, the consultant found himself in a dilemma. Since they are very unlikely to have had previous experience of paraplegics, they may well need some guidance on treatment. On the other hand, general practitioners are colleagues of equal standing to that of the consultant and he felt that they were often sensitive about communication from consultants that might appear patronising. The procedure adopted by the consultant was, therefore, to send a formal notification when the patient was admitted to the Centre, and then at the time of his discharge to send a detailed account of his medical condition. No instructions were given about treatment except perhaps to recommend the continuation of physiotherapy or similar treatment, and it was left to the general practitioner to get in touch with the consultant if he needed further advice.

The consultant also assumed that the patient and his family would be known personally to the general practitioner, and he, therefore, transmitted no information about the personal attitude of the patient or the family background.

Table 48.1
The general practitioners, summary of information

Total number of general practitioners interviewed:	8
General practitioners regarding themselves as 'family doctors':	5
General practitioners regarding themselves as 'medical advisors':	3
General practitioners informed of admission to Centre by relatives:	6
General practitioner informed of admission by Centre (telephone):	1
General practitioner taking over care of patient after discharge:	1
Previous experience of paraplegia:	1
No previous experience of paraplegia:	7
Some anxiety about demands of patient's care:	4
Requests for local authority services by general practitioners:	4
Requests for help from Centre by general practitioners:	
Information about physiotherapy:	1
Requests for re-admission:	3
Total local authority staff visiting 8 families:	20
L.A. staff known individually to general practitioners:	2
General practitioners with health visitors attached to practice:	3
General practitioners using health visitor in paraplegic case:	1

Eight of the patients were discharged home, and their general practitioners were all interviewed. They had been in practice for from five to twenty years. The number of patients on their panels varied from 1,800 to 3,500. Some of the facts gathered about their activities and attitudes in relation to the treatment of their paraplegic patients are summarised in the table. The general practitioners who regarded themselves as 'family doctors', in contrast to those who saw themselves as 'medical advisors' only, said they were interested in the social as well as the medical problems of their patients. An example of this concern was provided by one general practitioner who had arranged with a local authority that his patient should have a taxi service to school. Another had arranged for the patient to be re-admitted to the Centre temporarily to give relief to the patient's wife. But only one of these general practitioners saw himself as having a co-ordinating function and therefore needing to be informed about the social services.

For all these general practitioners, contact with the Centre and with the local authority services was minimal. Particularly striking is the fact that the general practitioners had direct contact with only two of the twenty local authority staff visiting the families, and this included none of the district nurses. One of the contacts was with the Mental Welfare Officer where the patient was mentally ill. This was also the only case in which the Centre got in touch with the general practitioner before the patient's discharge. None of the general practitioners had any record of receiving the consultant's notification of the patient's admission to the Centre, so in most cases the first effective communication from the Centre was the letter about the discharge of the patient. This was received between two and eleven days after the actual discharge. The general practitioners would have been satisfied with this arrangement had the letters arrived shortly before discharge.

All the general practitioners were satisfied with the medical information they received about the patient's condition but five of them said they would have liked more information about the personality and adjustment of the patient, and about such medical needs as occupational therapy and physiotherapy and arrangements for the supply of disposable surgical goods. All of them said they would have welcomed a leaflet on the home nursing care of these patients. Three of the general practitioners had known their patients for less than a year, and so did not know them very well.

In view of the fact that only one of the general practitioners had had previous experience of a paraplegic case, it is not perhaps surprising that they had little idea of the level of adjustment they could expect for paraplegic patients, and judged this from their current experience. Thus, a general practitioner whose patient was re-admitted with bedsores said that the community services could not be expected to keep the paraplegic patient healthy and free from bedsores all the time, while two general practitioners whose patients had an unusually high level of adjustment, were correspondingly optimistic about paraplegic patients generally.

The local authorities

Because the consultant saw the general practitioner as the main co-ordinator of the services for the patient, his communications with the local authorities were left to the medical social worker, and were largely limited to requests for home nursing equipment, and, where appropriate, house adaptations or rehousing. After discussing the home situation with the patient and his relative, the medical social worker wrote to the medical officer of health of the appropriate authority requesting help with these items. These requests were then passed by the medical officer of health to the appropriate officer or department. For example, the request for home nursing equipment, which is required in every case, was passed to the district nurse through the district nurse supervisor. The district nurse then visited the family and requisitioned the appropriate equipment, sometimes modifying, after discussion with the family, the list proposed by the medical social worker. One local authority indeed made a loan charge specifically because it was believed that items which were requisitioned were not in fact always used. When faced with a loan charge, patients often reduced their demands. In two cases, the request for home equipment stimulated the district nurse and her supervisor to visit the patient at the Centre and inquire about the nursing treatment of the patient and the equipment needed. Presumably, it was from this contact too that one patient was visited by the district nurse in each of his week-end leaves before discharge, since neither the local authorities nor the general practitioners were informed of these leaves beforehand.

Similarly, requests for rehousing and for housing adaptations were passed to an occupational therapist or to a welfare officer, or to a health visitor undertaking welfare duties, for assessment of need. The actual procedures varied between the different authorities according to their organisation, but in general the procedure for rehousing was simpler than for getting housing adaptations because the latter involved specific expenditure which had to be costed and approved by the appropriate committee. The most complex procedure for house adaptation occurred in one county borough where separate assessments were made by the health and welfare departments and expenditure over £300 had to be approved by the full council. Apart from this one case, the separation of health and welfare departments in city boroughs does not seem to have made co-operation more difficult than it was in the county councils where welfare was a section of the health departments. Similarly, co-operation with housing departments does not seem to have been affected by the fact that in county council areas the housing departments come under rural district councils and are not under the county councils which are responsible for health and welfare departments.

Communication with other hospitals

Usually, patients are first admitted to the Centre from their homes or from a hospital near the place where they received the injury. Most patients are discharged from the Centre to their homes, but some of these may attend the out-patient department of their local hospital for such treatment as catheter change or physiotherapy. This is usually arranged by the general practitioner on the request of the consultant. A few patients may be transferred after rehabilitation at the Centre to their local hospital because of social factors.

In all the ten cases followed up, the consultant had written at the time of the patient's discharge to the orthopaedic consultant at the hospital from which they had been admitted to the Centre. This letter gave a brief medical report on the patient's condition on discharge.

Two of these patients were discharged to their local hospitals, one to await rehousing, and the other because of social problems at home. Each patient was sent with a copy of his case notes, and in one case there had been prior correspondence between the consultants. However, the information provided to the consultant may not have filtered through to junior staff, and one of the patients complained that the hospital did not seem to be equipped to cope with a paraplegic patient, and staff did not observe any of the routine precautions the patient had been taught were essential, such as being turned at night to prevent the development of bedsores. While this evidence must be treated with reserve, it fits in with an earlier finding of J.R.S. that patients admitted to the Centre from other hospitals were much more likely to have pressure sores than patients admitted from home, and these sores were frequently very severe.

Three of the patients in the present study had attended their local hospital as out-patients. In these cases, there was no direct contact between the Centre and the hospital since the arrangements were made by the general practitioner. In one case, confusion arose because the hospital thought that the catheter should be changed every six weeks instead of weekly.

The employment services

Communication with the employment services seems to have been reliable, perhaps more so than communications with other services. In each case, the disablement rehabilitation officer at Southport visited the patient in hospital. He discussed the patient's condition with the patient, the occupational therapist, and occasionally with other staff. He then communicated this information to the local disablement rehabilitation officer in a form that enabled the latter to make immediate use of it. Since only one other DRO was seen, it is impossible to say how effective this system was.

Assessment of the communication system

Having given this outline of the methods of communication used, it is now possible to analyse them more carefully. First of all, communication between the Centre and the community services was almost entirely one way with no feed-back except where the district nurses took the initative in contacting the Centre. Since the information to be conveyed was complex and involved the community workers learning about an unfamiliar situation, it would not be surprising if difficulties arose. Moreover, the consultant and other staff at the Centre were unlikely to receive information on the effectiveness of the arrangements they had made.

Secondly, the consultant's picture of the role of the general practitioner as a co-ordinator proved completely false. Some co-ordination was provided by the medical officer of health, but he had no direct contact with the patient and little with the Centre. Because the information received by the medical officer of health came through the medical social worker, he tended to lack precise information about the medical condition of the patient, and this affected what he passed on to the housing and other departments. Moreover, the medical officer of health received a letter related to specific needs of the patient and responded accordingly. For instance, although the medical officers of health believed that paraplegics were

likely to need casework help, no referral was made to the welfare department unless home adaptation or rehousing was required. Similarly, welfare officers who visited in connection with these needs did not necessarily follow up to see whether casework help was needed.

Within the local authorities, a concept of the rôle of the general practitioner was held similar to that of the consultant. No member of the local authority staff attempted to make a total assessment of the needs of the patient and his family. Since the general practitioners made very few requests for help with services, the services that were received by the patients and their families depended on the initiative shown by field staff, who were not necessarily clear about their responsibilities in this respect. Thus, the two cases that were re-admitted to hospital were among the three that did not receive home nursing and no request for this was made. Only one family received a home help although three of the cases involved married women and only one patient received meals on wheels.

In effect, the role of co-ordinator was left to the patient and his relatives, who received no support in this. This contrasts with the position of the patient in the hospital. Although in the hospital he is more subject to pressure to conform to instutional requirements than outside it, at least he has direct contact with the consultant who is leader and co-ordinator of the work of the Unit. Outside he is much more alone and his contacts are with people who are also relatively low in the hierarchy of the services.

The effect on the patients and their relatives

One result of the system of one way communication that was used by the consultant was that he often did not learn of problems that occurred once the patient was discharged, despite follow up sessions at the Centre. Although patients and relatives spoke very highly of the treatment received at the Centre, and patients were given considerable understanding of the management of their condition, several relatives had met problems in nursing the patients, and felt that some practical instruction from the nursing staff at the Centre would have been helpful. In particular, two patients had been tipped out of the wheelchair the first time their relatives had tried to negotiate a kerb, because of lack of knowledge of how to

ontrol the chair. Such instruction is provided at
ome other centres, but requires a higher than
normal complement of nursing and physiotherapy
taff. Four patients had met difficulties in the
supply of disposable items such as condoms, urine
bags, catheters and elastoplast. Two relatives expressed inhibitions about approaching the consult-
nt, and there appeared to be a case for making
arrangements for a discussion of medical problems
arising out of the patient's disability, including the
effect on sexual relations. It is often assumed that
sexual intercourse is impossible for paraplegic
patients. This assumption is frequently mistaken.

A number of difficulties arose in relation to the
supply of home nursing equipment. The lists
normally supplied did not include a commode
although this was needed in every case; some of
he items, perhaps included on a routine basis,
were not always needed. In all but two cases, all
the equipment requested was delivered before
discharge, but in only two cases was this early
enough for it to be tried out at the weekend
eaves. In the worst case delivery of the equipment
before discharge was refused. It arrived on the day
of the patient's return home. The bed was too
high, and the chain attachment of the wrong
kind – it was replaced two weeks later. The
mattress was also delivered two weeks later. A
solid instead of an inflatable rubber toilet seat was
delivered and this had not been replaced after
eight weeks. Only one of the six pillows ordered
was delivered. A polythene sheet was provided
instead of a rubber one, and this proved completely unsuitable.

Most complaints about equipment centred
upon the beds provided. These were generally
standard hospital beds and were too high for
convenient use in the home. In one case, for
example, where the man weighed fourteen stone
and his wife was frail, the strain of pulling himself
into bed frequently caused an inadvertent bowel
movement. Eventually, the bed collapsed. One
young couple stressed the desirability of maintaining as normal a married life as possible which
they felt was difficult if a single hospital-type bed
was used. The beds provided were always single,
although seven of the patients were married.

Home nursing was never directly requested by
the Centre, since a decision about this was left to
the general practitioner. In only one case did the
general practitioner arrange this. In four other

cases, the provision of home nursing seems to have
been one of the fruits of the visit of the district
nurse in connection with the provision of equipment. In one case, the patient asked the district
nurse not to call after the first visit because she
gave him advice which conflicted with the instructions of the hospital staff. As has previously been
pointed out, the two cases re-admitted to the
Centre were among those who did not receive
home nursing.

One owner occupier required adaptations to his
house. Five other patients required rehousing and
adaptation of the new house. In all these five
cases, it took rather over a year, and in one case
almost a year and a half after admission before the
rehousing and the adaptations were completed. In
every case, more than six months of this time
occurred after the patient had been discharged,
with resulting inconvenience to the patient and his
relatives. One patient had to be admitted to a local
hospital to await completion of housing. A great
part of this delay was probably unavoidable, but
some of it seemed to be due to poor communications.

In four cases, the request for rehousing was
made by the Centre about a month after the
patient's admission; in one case, it was after nine
weeks. Earlier notification was impossible in the
view of the consultant because of the difficulty of
knowing sooner the degree of rehabilitation that
could be expected. A decision about rehousing
normally has to be made before adaptations can be
considered. It appeared that the information received by the housing departments was often not
as detailed as would have been desirable, and this
was one factor in producing a very high number of
unsuitable offers. There were altogether ten unsuitable offers made to the five families, but four
of these offers were rejected because the family
regarded them as too far from their present homes.
In one case, rehousing took place twenty weeks
after admission, but the house was in such poor
physical condition that eight months later the
family had to be rehoused again.

In arranging adaptations, there also seemed to
be difficulty in appreciating the needs of the
patients. In one case, a lavatory and bedroom had
to be built on the ground floor, but there was
delay first because the local authority was reluctant to build the bedroom, and then because the
first plan proposed only a single bedroom to which

the patient and her husband objected. In another case, it was not recognised that adaptation of a ground floor flat involved removing the dividing wall between bathroom and toilet to make the latter accessible. As a result the district nurse had to attend three times a week to perform manual evacuation of the bowels. In a third case, the welfare department's assessment omitted a hand basin in the patient's room although it was pointed out that he had no access to a bathroom and the only alternative was the kitchen sink.

All of the five patients requiring rehousing became very distressed at some stage during the process due to misunderstanding arising from lack of information. Some of this anxiety could have been relieved by more efficient liaison between the family and the local authority.

The five welfare officers, two occupational therapists and two health visitors who visited the patients were almost entirely limited in their responsibilities to the assessment of rehousing and adaptations. Apart from the services described above, one family received home help — although the patients included three housewives — one patient received meals on wheels, two patients were put in touch with voluntary associations and one schoolboy was provided with a taxi service to school. It is difficult to believe that if the total needs of these families had been assessed, more of them would not have benefited from these and other services.

General implications
The failures in communication revealed in this study did not appear to be attributable to any great extent to administrative divisions in the health and social services except insofar as these contributed to the isolation of the general practitioners. Thus failures occurred in communication between the Paraplegic Centre and other hospitals under the same Regional Hospital Board as well as between the Centre and the community services. Similarly, difficulties in co-operation between health and welfare workers appeared to be no greater where welfare services were administered in a separate department than where they were administered as a section of the health department. The one exception to this occurred where a recent separation of responsibilities resulted in a duplication of assessment procedures. Again, co-operation with housing departments seemed to be

just as easy in county areas where housing and health departments were in separate local authorities as in county borough areas in which both departments operated under the same council.

This does not of course mean that the way responsibilities are allocated, and the absence of any body with overall planning responsibility does not affect the situation. For example, the delay in getting discharged patients into properly adapted accommodation was partly due to the fact that very few authorities have given any priority to the building of special housing for handicapped persons,[1] while one patient appears to have been occupying a bed in a hospital because of lack of suitable hostel accommodation which is a local authority responsibility.[2] Priorities might be different if responsibilities were divided differently. Nevertheless, even if there was a substantial change in the organisation of the social services, problems of communication would still need much greater attention than they are given at present.

These problems of communication are related first to the size and geographical coverage of the National Health Service; secondly, to the complexity of the problems being dealt with; and thirdly, to the need of professional workers for a measure of independence in the practice of their professional skills.

The National Health Service has to be organised on a large scale in order to provide the necessary specialisation in skills. The Paraplegic Centre illustrates this. Its effectiveness in the rehabilitation of patients depends on the specialisation of its staff, which in turn requires a large catchment area to ensure an economical size of unit. Inevitably, this means contact with a large number of local authorities and an even larger number of department and staff members. No conceivable rationalisation of local authority boundaries could materially affect this position. Similarly, the Centre must deal with a large number of general practitioners. The grouping of general practitioners in health centres might improve this situation somewhat, if it allowed one general practitioner in a group to direct special attention to the problems of disabled patients, but it could not change the situation fundamentally.

The size of the National Health Service would present fewer problems if there was greater standardisation of the knowledge, experience and behaviour of individual workers within it; for instance, if the consultant could know exactly what information was required by each district nurse or general practitioner, or could be assured of a consistent response to any particular request for a service. However, such standardisation would involve an inflexibility of procedures which is neither desirable nor possible in a situation so much subject to change. Part of the difficulty moreover in this study appeared to be not so much because of actual differences in behaviour of members of the same professional group, as because of a discrepancy between the expectation of professional workers and their actual behaviour. This is most obvious in the case of the general practitioners. Although they had differing views of their own functions, all the general practitioners acted in very similar ways in the treatment of their patients. None of them actually co-ordinated the social services in the interests of their patients, which was the expectation of the consultant and the medical officers of health. This can be seen in the fact that only four contacts were made with the local authority services by the eight practitioners. Once again, the size of the organisation contributes to such misunderstanding.

There is then a need to develop communication procedures that take account of the real complexities of the situation. The complexity of much of the information to be conveyed and of the services involved require the encouragement of dialogue between the personnel concerned with different types of care, and the development of a variety of channels of communication, involving some redundancy, to insure against breakdown. These needs were reflected in the various recommendations on procedure in the rehabilitation of paraplegic patients discharged from the Centre made as a result of this study. They included the use of case conferences before and after discharge; more definite invitations to general practitioners, district nurses and other community workers to visit the Centre in connection with particular patients; the preparation of a simple leaflet on the nursing care of paraplegia; and the direct transmission from the Centre of information on particular patients to the departments of local hospitals which they have to attend, and to welfare departments of local authorities. It was also felt to be desirable that appropriate Centre staff should give more atten-

tion to relations with outside services, and that in each case, local authorities should make one member of their staff responsible for liaison between the patient and the social services. While the Medical Social Worker and Welfare Officer were in some ways the most obvious choice for these responsibilities, other staff such as occupational therapists, the charge nurse or district nurses, might also be used according to the circumstances.

As a direct result of this study, a number of changes have in fact been made in the procedures of the Centre. In particular, hospital staff are communicating directly with their opposite numbers in the community. Information is also being collected systematically about new patients to throw light on the relative importance of different factors which may affect the need for re-admission.

Summary

Concern about the high rates of re-admission of paraplegic patients to the Liverpool Regional Paraplegic Centre, suggested a study of the community services available to them and the methods of communication used in mobilising them. The study was based on the concepts of communication theory. Ten recently discharged patients were selected in a way that would ensure that different types of local authority were covered. The cases were followed up by interviews with the patients and their relatives, with their general practitioners, and with the chief officers and members of the staff of the local authority services.

The study revealed many failures in communication which resulted in frustration and hazards for the patients and their relatives. These failures did not appear to be due to administrative divisions within the service, so much as to the size of the organisation involved and lack of consideration of the problems of communication that this presents. Among the limitations of the communication system were the restricted channels used; lack of feedback in conveying complex information; mistaken assumptions about the rôles that people would play within the services; and the failure to provide in reports the information needed by the recipients.

NOTES

1. This is particularly serious for patients with a poor prognosis since local authorities are reluctant to incur the expense of adapting a house in these cases.
2. Dr J. R. Silver used the hospital accounts to cost the in-patient service to paraplegics. Taking into account hospital overheads, the cost was £34 per week. No comparable figure is available for community services.

REFERENCES

FERGUSON, T. & McPHAIL, A. N., 1954, *Hospital and Community*, London, Nuffield Provincial Hospitals Trust, Oxford University Press.

JEFFERYS, MARGOT, 1965, *An anatomy of social welfare services*, London, Michael Joseph, pp. 117—31 & table 17.

LEAVITT, HAROLD, J. and MUELLER, R. A. H., 1951, 'Some effects of feedback on communications', *Human Relations*, 4(4) pp. 401—10.

LEAVITT, HAROLD J., (1952), 'Some effects of certain communication patterns in group performance' in Swanson, Newcomb & Hartley (eds.), *Readings in Social Psychology*, New York, Holt.

REVANS, R. W., 1964, *Standards for morale: cause and effect in hospitals*, London, Oxford University Press.

RODGERS, BARBARA N., & DIXON, JULIA, 1960, *Portrait of social work*, chapter 10, London, Oxford University Press.

SHAW, MAURICE, *Report on Communications and Relationships between general practitioners and Hospital Medical Staff*, King Edward's Hospital Fund for London.

TRIANDIS, MARY C., 1960, 'Some determinants of interpersonal communication', *Human Relations*, 13 (3) pp. 279—287.

TRIANDIS, MARY C., 1960, 'Cognitive similarity and communication in a dyad', *Human Relations*, 13 (2), pp. 175—183.

49. Nurses under stress: a social system functioning as a defence against anxiety*

ISABEL E. P. MENZIES
Centre for Applied Social Research, Tavistock
Institute for Human Relations, London.

Nurses experience a great deal of stress in their work. This may seem so obvious as hardly to merit comment. For nurses confront suffering and death as few other people do. They work with ill people also under stress. They face heavy demands for pity, compassion and sympathy. They are often expected to do the impossible in the way of providing comfort or cure. Many nursing tasks are, by ordinary standards, disgusting, distasteful and frightening. Patients are sometimes difficult and nurses find themselves getting irritable or resentful. Such feelings seem unworthy of their profession and arouse guilt and anxiety. Indeed, there is no scarcity of situations which expose nurses to stress.

However, the fact that nurses are in a stressful situation is not a sufficient explanation of why they actually experience so much stress.

[When acting as consultants on organizational problems to the nursing service] We have noticed stress among nurses with whom we have worked in hospitals and elsewhere. They have made frequent references, when they have talked to us, to such feelings as worry, fear, guilt, depression, shame, embarrassment, strain, distrust, disappointment. In addition they have behaved in ways which were familiar to us in situations where people experience stress. Further, wastage among student nurses is heavy, many do not complete their training. Sickness rates among nurses are high, mostly through minor illnesses requiring only short spells of absence from duty. Social and medical research strongly suggests that such phenomena are an expression of a disturbed relationship between people and the organization in which they work, and are connected with stress. Such feelings may arise even when people have a good deal of satisfaction in their work, as nurses do.

Stress seemed to us, therefore, to be a problem of the profession arising from the professional situation, rather than a matter of the individual nurse's personality. We were recently in a position to study the professional problem in some detail and set ourselves the task of trying to account for the stress, in the hope that this might indicate steps which could be taken to change the professional situation and so relieve stress.

One must consider how nurses deal with stress. Readers will be familiar with the concept of psychic defence-mechanisms which people use to protect themselves against disturbing emotional experiences. A nurse, like everyone else, has her personal defences, but these were not our concern. However, social organizations as such also develop defence mechanisms, that is, established methods of helping their members deal with disturbing emotional experiences, methods which are built into the way the organization works. This is an extension of the familiar idea that a social organization must work in such a way as to provide adequate psychological satisfactions for its members as well as performing its tasks with a reasonable efficiency. We could presume, therefore, that a hospital nursing service would have set up social defences to protect its members against the stress arising from their work, although this would not have been the result of an explicit decision.

*From *International Nursing Review,* (1960), 7, 6, pp. 9–16

Since we were studying professional stress, we felt that the investigation of these social defences was our legitimate concern. We examined the way the service worked with a view to evaluating the protection it gave against stress, while facilitating also the performance of the tasks of patient-care and nurse-training. This involved considering such questions as how the service was organized, how the task of patient-care was actually carried out; what sort of behaviour was prescribed for nurses; traditional attitudes to work, patients or colleagues; and inter-personal relationships.

Examples of social defences

Selecting some of the more important and typical features, I will confine myself mainly to phenomena within the nursing service, although I am aware that there are other important relationships, notably with doctors.

NURSE–PATIENT RELATIONSHIPS

The core of the anxiety lies in patient-care and in the relationship with the patient. An examination of the ways in which the nursing service mediates the relation between patient and nurse, formally and informally, shows that they reduce the impact of patient on nurse and offer some protection from the subsequent anxiety. In general, the organization of the nursing service militates against close and prolonged contact between the individual patient and nurse, although nurses often want such contact and teaching emphasizes its importance. In a typical ward a group of about eight to ten student nurses with a sister and staff nurse look after about thirty patients. Consequently, the student nurses, and indeed the qualified nurses also, perform a few tasks for each of a fairly large number of patients and it is difficult to establish close personal contact. The service also reduces in various ways the direct impact of person on person. This amounts to a sort of de-personalizing of both nurse and patient. Patients tend to be described by bed numbers or illnesses. Nurses deprecate this practice and senior nurses teach emphatically against it, but the practice continues by custom because it alleviates stress. Nor is it easy to learn the names of patients, especially on large wards with rapid patient and nurse turnover.

A common attitude among nurses shown in behaviour rather than words is that any patient is the same as any other patient. On the positive side,

this implies that all must receive the same careful nursing. As a corollary, it implies that personalities should not matter, nor be taken overmuch into account. This implication is being fought, but persists. Preferences for particular patients or even types of patient are discouraged and nurses find it hard to admit them.

Much the same 'de-personalization' is true about nurses. They are treated as 'categories', *e.g.*, second year, rather than as individuals. Duties, responsibilities and privileges are, on the whole, accorded to categories rather than to individuals with their own capacities and needs. If all patients are the same, and all nurses are the same, at least by seniority, it follows that it should not matter to the patient which nurse or how many nurses nurse him, or to the nurse which patient she nurses. The nursing service functions as though this were true, although both patients and nurses know it is not. Patients are nursed by many nurses at one time, and even more over a period of time. The nurses' uniforms, besides having practical functions, emphasize role over person and are a symbol of an expected inner and behavioural uniformity; the expression of the nurse's individuality in work is discouraged. *The nurse tends to be an agglomeration of nursing skills of a certain level depending on her phase of training, rather than a person doing a job according to her own practice and skills.*

The nursing service also helps in achieving detachment from patients, a necessary objective for all professions working with people. Thus, student nurses were constantly being literally 'detached' from one work-situation, their colleagues and patients, and sent to another, as though these should not matter. In time, one could say they learned by bitter experience not to become too 'attached' because that made the distress of constant parting too severe. The nursing service, as such, seemed to act as though that kind of 'detachment' was helpful, although most individuals were well aware of its painful effects and disliked it.

The nursing service tried, therefore, to protect nurses from stress by fostering nurse-patient relationships which are often short and always rather tenuous. This does not prevent nurses from suffering great distress on occasion. Warm personal feelings still develop between nurses and patients; nurses care deeply about the welfare of their patients. They can be very upset by what happens to patients, by deaths, doctors' or nurses' mistakes, pain and emotional stress. Such feelings are hard to bear. There are certain accepted attitudes and behaviour in relation to such distress, at least while the nurse is on duty and in a working relationship with close colleagues. The emotional disturbance is denied as far as possible, and dealt with by brisk, though kindly, remonstrances of the 'pull yourself together' variety. Expressions of strong feelings are discouraged. Comfort, reassurance or help from an understanding colleague or superior in the work-situation are not usual, although nurses give each other much support in off-duty friendships. This learned attitude of denial of stress offers some protection against its conscious experience. Further, the restraint on expressing feelings offers some protection against spread of the distress among nurses who work closely together.

DECISION MAKING

Making decisions is always stressful because it implies making a choice between alternative courses of action and committing oneself to one without full knowledge of the outcome. The resultant stress is likely to be particularly acute when decisions directly or indirectly affect the well-being, health or even life of patients as many nursing decisions do. The nursing service seems to offer some protection against such stress by reducing the number of theoretically possible decisions that must actually be made, and substituting precise instructions. *Nurses are implicitly or explicitly forbidden to make decisions about certain things.*

The reduction of decisions has been carried farthest in the work of the student nurse. Very precise instructions are given about the order and timing of her tasks, and the way they must be performed. The service expects her to follow these instructions exactly: she must not, for example, decide that a change in the work-load of the ward merits a change in the order of her tasks or even the omission of some less necessary tasks. Similar attempts have been made to eliminate decisions made by senior staff, although this has inevitably not been carried so far, since their roles are more complex and precise instructions less possible. For example, they are not expected to decide what each student can and should do. This is deter-

mined by her category except in unusual circumstances.

When decision making cannot be avoided several techniques are used, both formally and informally to minimize their impact on any one person. Decisions are checked and counter-checked as are the executive actions consequent on decisions. Consultation about decisions is a deeply engrained habit. This is not only true of certain obviously dangerous procedures such as the administration of dangerous drugs. It affects all kinds of decisions, including many that are neither important nor dangerous.

RESPONSIBILITY

Taking responsibility may be satisfying and rewarding but always involves some conflict. Nurses experience this conflict acutely. The responsibilities of the nursing profession are heavy and nurses usually have a strong sense of personal responsibility. They often discharge their responsibilities at considerable personal cost. However, the very weight of the responsibility makes it difficult to bear consistently over long periods and nurses are sometimes tempted to escape from it, and to behave irresponsibly.

We have observed a customary but implicit technique through which nurses handle the painful conflict over responsibility, a technique learned by new nurses as they fit into the context of the hospital, its expected attitudes and behaviour. Briefly, this amounts to turning the personal conflict into an inter-personal one: nurses tend to refer to nurses junior to themselves as 'irresponsible', and they treat them as though this were true. On the the other hand, most nurses refer to themselves and their seniors as 'responsible', the implication being not only that they are more responsible than their juniors now, but always have been. In addition, they tend to regard seniors as unduly harsh disciplinarians, an accusation against senior staff which is familiar from many nursing investigations.

What happens seems to be a kind of psychological 'tidying-up' through which one's own irresponsible impulses and those of one's equals and superiors are not perceived where they really are, but are attributed to juniors. Thus, one need not feel unduly guilty or critical of oneself, but can take action to discipline the 'irresponsible' juniors. Likewise, one's own burdensome sense of responsibility and often harsh self-criticism are attributed to seniors. One thus expects to be criticized harshly by seniors and may behave so as to provoke their criticism, but one avoids some painful self-criticism. This makes for rather tense relations between categories of nurses, but spares each individual a good deal of her personal conflict.

In a more formal sense, the burden of responsibility is avoided by a considerable vagueness in the definition of responsibilities throughout the nursing hierarchy. The student nurses' task-lists look very specific, but students often exchange task-lists and not infrequently have two in the course of a single day, since nurses come on and go off duty at different times. So it becomes difficult to find out who has done or even who should have done what, and who is responsible for its being well or badly done. It is possible to be increasingly less specific about responsibility as the roles become more complex, and as the actual responsibilities become heavier. This prevents responsibility from falling fully and clearly on one person and protects nurses against the resultant conflict.

There also seemed to be a tendency to force responsibilities upwards through the nursing hierarchy, to try to hand over responsibility to people who are older or more experienced, and who, because of the customary attitudes to seniors, are regarded as 'more responsible'. This seems to result in senior nurses having actually less responsibility than would be expected from comparing their hierarchical positions with similar positions in other organizations, and from an estimate of their personal capacities. Many nurses are better than their jobs.

RESISTANCE TO CHANGE

Like decision-making change arouses stress, since it implies giving up a familiar present for a relatively unknown future. The nursing service seems to deal with this by avoiding change wherever possible and clinging to familiar ways of doing things, even when they are becoming demonstrably inappropriate. The case of student allocation is an example: the old method has long been a source of stress. The introduction of the National Health Service and radical changes in medical practice have greatly changed the demands on the nursing service. It is surprising to an outsider how little the service has changed to meet them. Indeed, if anything, the service has tended to stick more firmly to existing practices whenever possible, almost one feels, as a counterbalance to changes which could not be avoided.

Comment on the social defences

I will now consider why the social defences described above were inadequate as shown by the persisting unduly high level of stress. It is characteristic of this social defence-system to protect the individual against stress by helping her to avoid situations, events, tasks, and relationships which are likely to cause stress.

It has long been known that the individual whose psychic defences are based on evasion remains a prey to emotional disturbances and is vulnerable to stress. He cannot experience painful feelings fully enough and cannot, therefore, discharge them. On the other hand, the person who can face painful feelings and difficult situations more fully, grows in psychic strength. He can understand better the nature of the stress and of the situations which evoke it. He can reduce the degree of stress by developing greater capacity to deal with stressful situations.

A member of an organization which relies heavily on evasive social defences is in much the same plight as an individual who uses evasive psychic defences. This is the situation of the nurse. While on duty, she has little choice but to accept protection against stress by evasion, since her attitudes and behaviour while on duty must conform closely to those required by the service, implicitly or explicitly, formally or informally, *i.e.*, she must accept the social defences and use them as her own. For example, she is not free to decide that she will nurse only a few patients and abandon her task-list in order to deal more directly with stress in patient-relationships. The evasive social defence-system actually inhibits the development of the nurse's capacity to deal with her stress and to experience it less acutely. An example may make the point clear. A student nurse is 'protected' against the stress arising from decision-making by having the decisions she is allowed to make reduced to a minimum. This deprives her of many opportunities to learn how to make decisions effectively, to test them out and to experience their consequences. This slows down the development of her skill in making decisions and inhibits reduction of stress through the reassurance of decisions well-made and growing confidence in the skill to make them. Instead, since decisions cannot always be eliminated, especially at more senior levels, nurses come to face them without sufficient assurance from experience that they can make effective decisions and stress continues. One has the impression that few nurses are really secure about their ability to make wise decisions. In other words, one may say that the social defence-system protects nurses, to some extent, from current experiences of stress, but only at the expense of its more permanent reduction.

OVER-PROTECTION

One may indeed postulate that in some ways the social defence-system is over-protective. For example, there seems little doubt that many student nurses could take and enjoy more responsibility than the service now allows. To give point to this it may be necessary to clarify what is meant by responsibility. It seems that in nursing circles a 'responsible' student nurse is one who loyally and faithfully carries out her prescribed tasks. This is a departure from ordinary usage where responsibility is closely linked with using *discretion*, *i.e.*, a 'responsible' person is one who is capable of using direction wisely in doing his job, 'discretion' being just what the student nurse may not use. Many student nurses are capable, given appropriate help, of making, maintaining and enjoying continuous relationships with patients. They want to do this and are taught it is desirable, but the system of work organization prevents their doing it.

People do not always like being spared difficulties. Rather it is true to say that people enjoy facing them and enjoy and need the challenge they present, provided the difficulties are not beyond their capacities. Success can be a great reassurance. The over-protection makes it impossible for many nurses to deploy fully in their jobs their personal capacities and professional skills, and experience real success. Indeed, the more mature and capable the nurse, the greater the problem. Nurses feel guilty and anxious about it. Thus, the 'over-protection' built into the social defence-system itself evokes stress.

SERVICE-DETERMINED INEFFICIENCY

There are other ways in which the service itself gives rise to stress. For example, it is not very efficient as a method of organizing work. Similar phenomena are to be observed in other kinds of social organizations. They stem from the fact that in establishing a way of operating, a social organization cannot be concerned only with efficiency, *i.e.*, with finding the best way technically of doing its task, but must take into account, if only implicitly, the psychological needs of its members. Because of the high element of real danger in the nursing situation, care for the psychological needs of nurses tends to play a relatively large part *vis-à-vis* technical efficiency in determining the structure and method of functioning of the service. Some efficiency has had to be sacrificed, though not by conscious decision, to evasion of anxiety. Inefficiency in this sense is determined by the organization and is not a matter of an individual behaving inefficiently. Indeed, people who are behaving in one sense 'efficiently', *i.e.*, carrying out instructions carefully and well, feel 'inefficient' because they feel they are violating the general principles of good nursing or of common sense. Student nurses are on occasion not fully occupied. This arises from the rather rigid system of work-organization which makes it difficult to adjust to changing demands on a ward by re-organizing their work. Ward establishments tend to be aimed at peak rather than average work-loads and wards seem somewhat over-staffed. Nurses feel guilty about being under-employed, whether in respect of time or capacity and this increases stress. The system is also cumbersome and inflexible in a situation which increasingly demands flexibility, *e.g.*, decision-making tends to be slow. This makes nurses anxious lest decisions are not made in time and irritable about delays in important matters.

Counter-balancing factors

This account would be incomplete without referring to the satisfactions which nurses experience in their work, such satisfactions being in themselves a very important counter-balancing factor to stress, and helping to make work worth while in spite of difficulties. The potential rewards of a career in nursing are great, in terms of such things as the recovery of patients, suffering relieved, and satisfying relationships with patients and colleagues. The nurses in this hospital clearly experienced their work as rewarding. However, they did not seem to be experiencing the full potential reward because of certain features of the social system.

For example, while the nursing service had considerable success in nursing patients, it was difficult for any one nurse to experience this in a personal way. The task-list system makes the contribution of one nurse to the nursing of one patient rather small. The reward is dissipated as well as the stress. Patients are grateful to 'the hospital' or 'the nurses', *i.e.*, rather impersonally, and the individual nurse misses the personal gratitude which is part of her reward.

For student nurses an important satisfaction is the development of their knowledge and skill in nursing patients. The training and work-situations quite definitely slow down this development. The better the student the less satisfaction she finds in the rate of development of her nursing skills. Indeed, our feeling was that the better students suffered a good deal in this respect and a significant number of them could not tolerate it and gave up training. Further, the 'de-personalization' of nurses reduces the satisfactions of contributing in a personal way to work which tends to have a very personal meaning and of feeling that one's personal contribution is valued.

Nor is it possible under present conditions to realize at all fully the potential satisfactions in working with colleagues. Student nurses feel this particularly. The traditional relationship between juniors and seniors described above means that the student nurse feels herself singled out more for blame than praise. This she finds very distressing, as she has a particular need for encouragement in settling down to her difficult profession. The student nurse tends to feel she does not matter as a person. They complain 'nobody cares what happens to you', 'nobody helps you', 'you have no individuality'. They say the senior staff neither understand nor help them when they are in trouble, indeed, when they are worried and guilty about a mistake they are reprimanded instead of being comforted. The lack of such help is a serious deprivation for student nurses, the more bitterly felt as they watch the care lavished on patients with whom they cannot help implicitly comparing themselves.

It has not, however, been our experience that the senior staff do not understand or care. They understand only too well, many of them having vivid and still agonizing memories of their own training. They express their understanding and sympathy to us, but feel unable to do so with

operational relationships. They are often uncertain about the wisdom of entering into a close emotional relationship with their students, and uncertain of their skill in handling it. Their training has not prepared them for this. In the circumstances, they tend to fall back on the only behaviour they know, the discipline and severity they experienced in their own training. In any case, it is not easy for student nurses to approach their seniors for that sort of help since by tradition they expect seniors to be disciplinarians. However, as a result of this situation, many senior staff feel they are not helping their colleagues and juniors enough and, in turn, miss the satisfaction which comes from really helping colleagues in need.

Conclusion

We have little doubt that some action about the situation described is desirable. One would like to feel that something can be done since the present organization not only causes unnecessary stress but contributes to such phenomena as shortcomings in patient-care and wastage of good student nurses. It is clear that there is no simple solution; if there were, it would have been introduced long ago.

The ultimate solution must be a re-structuring of the system of work-organization and nurse-training, so that it incorporates a different kind of social defence-system less based on evasion. For example, one might try systems of ward-organization which give nurses more continuous and intensive contact with patients; this would require new techniques for dealing with the stress that would arise initially, especially among the junior student nurses. Together these would mean an earlier confrontation of stressful situations and, if successfully handled, would lead to an ultimate alleviation of stress. In our opinion, blue-prints for change are not possible although one has a general idea of direction. The most hopeful approach to the problem of change at this stage would seem to be to tackle it in a concrete rather than an abstract way, *e.g.*, to work in one hospital or even a part of a hospital and try to build a working model. Complete success would probably not attend the first attempt but one would learn a great deal from the attempt about how it could be done. This approach, through model-building and progressive modification followed by dissemination of successful models, has proved successful in building and re-building other kinds of social organizations. It is our hope that we have been able to contribute to the understanding of the nursing situation and so to the design of such new models.

Since we began our study four years ago a number of important developments have taken place in one hospital, partly as a result of the study. These can be regarded as attempts at partial new models. For example, a new system for allocation of student nurses is now in operation, which gives longer continuous duty tours, new training has been introduced for the post-graduate student to give more experience of administration and more real responsibility, an attempt is being made to develop a closer and more supportive relationship between the teaching staff and the student. We are very grateful to the hospital which gave us the opportunity to carry out the study and permission to publish this paper.[1] Particularly we are grateful to the nurses for their serious and courageous co-operation with us in what proved to be a long and arduous investigation, and for their sincere efforts to use the research findings.

NOTE

1. The hospital has, of course, no responsibility for the views we here express.

REFERENCES

BION, W. R., 1955, 'Group dynamics: a review', in Melanie Klein, Paula Heimann and R. E. Money-Kyrle. *New Directions in Psycho-Analysis*. Tavistock Publications, London; Basic Books, New York.

FENICHEL, O., 1946, *The Psychoanalytic Theory of the Neuroses*. Norton, New York.

FREUD, S. 1948 *Inhibitions, Symptoms and Anxiety*. Hogarth Press & Institute of Psycho-analysis.

FREUD, S. 1949, *Mourning and Melancholia. Collected Papers, Vol IV*, pp. 152—170 (Hogarth Press & Institute of Psycho-analysis, London).

FREUD, S., 1955, '*Studies on Hysteria*', Standard Edition Vol II, pp. 1—251, Hogarth Press & Institute of Psycho-analysis, London.

HEIMANN, P., 1952, 'Certain functions of introjection and projection in earliest infancy', in *Developments in Psycho-Analysis*, Hogarth Press & Institute of Psycho-Analysis, London.

JAQUES, E., 1955, 'Social systems as a defence against persecutory and depressive anxiety' in Melanie Klein, Paula Heimann and R. E. Money-Kyrle, *New Directories in Psycho-Analysis*, Tavistock Publications, London; Basic Books, New York.

KLEIN, MELANIE, 1948, *The importance of symbol formation in the development of the ego; in Contributions to Psycho-Analysis* (1921—1945). Hogarth Press & Institute of Psycho-anaylsis, London.

KLEIN, MELANIE, 1952, '*Some theoretical conclusions regarding the emotional life of the infant; in Developments in Psycho-Analysis*', Hogarth Press & Institute of Psycho-analysis, London.

KLEIN, MELANIE, 1959, 'Our adult world and its roots in infancy', *Human Relations*, 12, pp. 291—303. Also reprinted as Tavistock Pamphlet No. 2 Tavistock Publications London 1960.

MENZIES, ISABEL E. P., 1960, 'A case study in the functioning of social systems as a defence against anxiety', *Human Relations*, 13, pp. 95—120. Also reprinted as Tavistock Pamphlet No. 3, Tavistock Publications, London, 1961.

MENZIES, ISABEL E. P., 1965, 'Some mutual interactions between organisations and their members', in Pines, M. and Spoerri, T., (eds.) *Proceedings of the 6th International Congress of Psychotherapy*, 13, pp. 194—200.

RICE, A. K., 1958, *Productivity and Social Organisation: The Abmedabad Experiment*, Tavistock Publications, London.

SEGAL, H., 1957, 'Notes on symbol formation', *International Journal of Psychoanalysis*, 38, pp. 391—397.

TRISTE, I. and BANFORTH, K., W., 1951, 'Some social and psychological consequences of the longwall method of coal-getting', *Human Relations*, 4, pp. 3—38.

50. The political sociology of mental handicap: a case–study of policy failure[*]

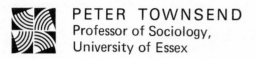

PETER TOWNSEND
Professor of Sociology,
University of Essex

It is commonly agreed that there is a crisis in Britain in the services for the mentally handicapped. Instances of bad treatment of patients in hospital, poor conditions, and understaffing in many wards have been revealed and have attracted wide publicity. Different solutions to the problems have been canvassed. None has yet been put into effect. This may be surprising to some people in view of the seriousness of the problems, the concern of the public and of medical, nursing and other staff, and the avowed intentions of Ministers in successive governments to put things right. How can our failure to do more in the last two years and to adopt an unambiguously specific policy be explained? My purpose is to analyse some of the structural and political factors standing in the way of a swift improvement of services and of the quality of life enjoyed by the handicapped. Political sociology has come to be differentiated from political science principally because of the sociologist's emphasis on the social aspects, both informal and formal, of political behavior and political institutions. Political acts are those which determine the fate of men other than the actors. They are sanctioned not only by law but by custom and structural situation. The fate of the mentally handicapped is determined not just by Parliament, Ministers of State and local councils,

but by the powers entrusted in or assumed by all those caring for them. The sociologist's interest in 'bureaucracy' and 'organization' leads him to investigate special problems like those of rough treatment in hospitals. But he tends to review social control in terms both of internal structure and external relationships.

The problem of understanding the gap between aims and performance is not, of course, peculiar to Britain. The deprivation which many of the handicapped experience, relative to the living standards in the societies to which they belong, is an international phenomenon. This continues to be so, even when powerful lobbies gradually arise to press for improvements. At the same time it is important to understand that conditions may not be uniformly bad. There is considerable variation in quality in many different systems, whether of firms, schools or hospitals. There are new hospitals as at Northgate in England as well as those 50 or 100 years old. Similarly, there are new hospitals in Denmark, such as Vangede and Lillemosegard, with high standards of material provision, but other hospitals like Ebborodgard, in North Zeeland, which are 75 years old.[1] In any national system there are elements which tend to become showpieces for international display or placatory gestures to the best elements among the professional staff, rather than models of what can be and are designed to become standard practice within a very short span of time. Variation in conditions is perhaps wider in Britain than in some countries. For instance, more buildings seem to have been adapted from other uses and embellished with annexes and architects' follies. This gives the

[*]From Peter Townsend, (1973) *The Social Minority*, London, Allen Lane, Chapter 12, pp. 196–207.

Paper presented to an international conference organized by the World Federation for Mental Health in association with the National Society for Mentally Handicapped Children, University College, Dublin, March 1971.

sub-communities who live in them a certain distinctiveness from the rest of the hospital population. I have been in hospitals and other institutions in the United States and on the Continent with worse living quarters and stricter custodial regimes than any I have seen in Britain.

Ministerial initiative to deal with a scandal

Britain's experience in the last two years, then, is an instructive example to study in order to understand why the problems of the mentally handicapped are so difficult to solve in any society. For it was two years ago this month that the report of an independent committee of inquiry into allegations of ill-treatment of patients in a Welsh hospital was published, and provoked immediate public anxiety (Cmnd. 3957). Official inquiries are conducted from time to time but rarely made public. After allegations had been published in a Sunday newspaper in 1967 a committee was set up under Sir Geoffrey Howe, QC ([later] Solicitor General in the Conservative Government) towards the end of that year. The committee completed its hearing early in 1968 and though the date of submission of the report for the Minister of Health is not specified there is internal evidence which makes it likely that it went to the Ministry in the middle of 1968.[2] While there it must clearly have become the subject of acute controversy. To his credit, Mr R. H. S. Crossman, the Secretary of State for Social Services, who became responsible for the amalgamated Department of Health and Social Security in the late summer of 1968, decided that the report should be published. It appeared in March 1969. The nature of the report should be clearly understood. It did not just find certain members of staff at fault in their treatment of patients but traced responsibility through the senior nursing staff to the chief male nurse, the physician superintendent, the Hospital Management Committee and its officers, the Regional Hospital Board and, finally, the administrative structure of the National Health Service itself, including the authority exercised by the Minister. Junior staff were to some extent the victims of an inadequate system and of inadequate resources provided by the Government, the Boards and local authorities to that system.

The present tripartite administrative structure of the National Health Service has failed, so far

as Ely is concerned, to produce a sufficiently integrated service and pattern of care for the mentally subnormal. The concept of community care has been insufficiently developed. (Cmnd. 3957 p. 128).

The Secretary of State then began to develop this theme with great energy. Recently I have studied afresh many of the press reports for 1969, 1970 and 1971. I would be surprised if there is any period in the history of Britain or any other country, even in the United States during President Kennedy's patronage of the issue, when the needs of the mentally handicapped have attracted greater public attention and sympathy. Having established a public bridgehead why was this advance not then consolidated?

It would, of course, be possible to give a narrative history at length. Mr Crossman visited hospitals, gave speeches and held press conferences throughout the country. He was applauded in Parliament for demonstrating in detail what he called the 'underprivilege' of the mentally handicapped inside and outside hospitals.[3] In April 1969 he set up a working party to advise him on policy. By coincidence, soon afterwards Dr Pauline Morris's national survey of hospitals, which had been financed by the National Society for Mentally Handicapped Children, was published. It reinforced with a wealth of factual evidence the case for reorganization of services (Morris 1969). Valuable information was becoming available also from Professor Tizard's and Dr Kushlick's research studies (Tizard 1964, Tizard *et al.* 1966, Kushlick and Cox 1967). Instances of ill-treatment at other hospitals came to light and were the subject of court cases, It will, of course, be many years before the full history of this period can be written. The Official Secrets Act prevents part of the story from being given. However, it is evident that the momentum was not sustained. A detailed statement of policy was delayed, first during the final six months of the Labour Goverment and then for the first nine months (so far) of the new Tory Government.[4]

Early contradiction in policy

In retrospect I think it can be shown that under both Governments, and very early in the crisis, a fundamental contradiction in policy emerged. Both Mr Crossman and Sir Keith Joseph have pursued simultaneously two policies, on the one hand diminishing and on the other increasing the already large role played by hospitals in the total system of services for the handicapped. On 18 June 1969, for example, Mr Crossman said, 'My own top priority in the hospital service at present is to divert more resources to the long-stay hospitals which, I fear, have in the past often been a deprived sector of the hospital service.[5] However on 25 September 1969, for example, he said, 'The basic policy will have to be that never again do we pile up human rejects behind these high walls' (*Guardian* 25 September 1969), and on other occasions added that there were thousands of the 60,000 long-stay patients who could live outside if there were places for them (*Guardian* 16 April 1970). Although no doubt Mr Crossman, Sir Keith Joseph and others would argue that it is possible to reconcile both objectives I do not believe they have insisted on spelling out the implications in full. Had they done so the contradiction would have become more apparent.

This contradiction has its roots in the structural contradictions of the management of the health and welfare services and in society itself. We have to draw on both political sociology and the sociology of communities for aid in constructing explanations. There are formal limitations on the powers of the Secretary of State which can largely obstruct him from putting into effect certain policies. To these can be added informal limitations as well — in terms of personnel, procedures and communications. There is a long chain of command down through the Regional Boards, Hospital Management Committees and hospitals, buttressed by Exchequer control of finance. The length of the chain and the weaknesses in some of its links make difficult the adoption and implementation in hospitals of new policies. The management committees badly need strengthening. Resolute policies can evaporate halfway down the hierarchy.[6] Moreover, a country which sets considerable store in the principles of local democracy and family self-determination is bound to find it difficult to accommodate a hierarchical system of this kind.

Secondly, control over the local authorities is indirect. Ministers can enforce statutory regulations, exhort and tempt in a variety of ways. But their powers are emasculated in part by the lack of authority over staff, by lack of forms of specific

grant and subsidy (especially since the percentage grant system was withdrawn) and by the cultural convention that local councils are supposed to have a very large measure of independence. Moreover, when all or nearly all local services can be shown to be starved of resources a Minister is likely to be inhibited from pressing his own particular claim too strongly. It would not have been surprising if Mr Crossman had been forced to conclude that the most important part of any new policy needing to be developed was ruled out because he was powerless to put it into execution. Even exhortation may have seemed impossible. During the campaign Mr Crossman was reported to have called all the Regional Hospital Board chairmen to meetings. To call together the representatives of nearly 200 local authorities in England and Wales must have seemed much less manageable. In any analysis of the distribution of power to determine the fate of men the cumulative effect of leaving out a key element at many stages of discussion and policy-making has to be remembered. Throughout 1969 and 1970 neither of the successive Secretaries of State could have been fully appraised of the importance of the community care services in any strategy. Even in the Department of Health itself the Secretary of State cannot be said to have an administrative staff which includes powerful representation in numbers and expertise of their interests. The same might be said of research. Those conducting research for the Hospital Boards are bound to have a different orientation to the mentally handicapped than if they had been working for the local authorities.

Thirdly, any proposed change of policy which appears to threaten the interests of bodies holding considerable power is likely to be resisted and to be diverted to those interests. The Secretary of State was indicating changes which might weaken the far-ranging authority of the nursing and medical professions, particularly those branches of the professions concerned with the long-stay hospitals for the mentally handicapped. Politicians and others called attention to the social and occupational needs of patients and therefore to the appointment of far more specialist staff, such as social workers, and occupational therapists, the introduction of volunteers from the community and the encouragement of patients to visit and work in the outside community. The call to reduce hospital numbers came not only from the Government benches but also from the Opposition.[7] There was a classical reaction on the part of nursing staff and medical superintendents. They closed ranks. All that was required, they said, was better resources and an end to the hurtful smears which sapped morale and endangered staff recruitment. Far from being run down the hospitals should be re-created and developed as centres of excellence, upon which the services for the community as well as the inmates could be based. Because so few staff work for the handicapped outside hospital and are also poorly organized, and because the nursing and medical staffs are dominant inside these hospitals and can bring pressure to bear on the Department of Health through a range of committees, it is not surprising that they were so successful in opposing the announcement of a new kind of policy.

Fourthly, the act of isolating mentally handicapped people, usually in large institutions, is also a political act. It confers greater power than perhaps we suspect on certain people but also on certain ideas and values. The staff determine every detail of life of patients to an extent which is unrivalled in, say, the most paternalistic firm. This creates special problems for staff as well as patients. But this conferment of power has other effects. Physically we create populations which are fundamentally different from any local community. In structure they do not consist of three or four generations, with very small family units, and complex social and occupational networks, which are in personal contact with a wide range of different public services. It would be misleading to suggest that they are 'communities' in any ordinary sense of that term. Scientifically they do not satisfy certain conditions which might be laid down for rural or urban communities.[8] As a consequence the system of political authority is much more oppressive for the patients. Compared with members of rural and urban communities they have fewer alternative groups to which to escape if the one in which they spend most of their time makes them feel unwanted or uncomfortable. There are fewer alternative channels of complaint, fewer alternative political agents to proselytize their interests and fewer possessions and less space in which to manoeuvre to show personal authority and independence. The individual patient is politically weak and vulnerable. It is important for us to understand that the very existence of the long-stay hospital shapes our concepts of mental handicap itself, our values, our fears and even our willingness to assume that the problem is one primarily for medicine and nursing.[9]

The structural factors obstructing reform

These four structural factors in the distribution of power over the fates of the mentally handicapped – the despotic but also fragile chain of command from Government and Secretary of State to individual hospital and ward; the restricted powers of the central Government over the local authority; the concentration of real power over the handicapped upon hospital medical and nursing staffs, and the separation in space of ghettoes for the mentally handicapped, seem to me to be the crucial factors in explaining the failure of policy to match needs. For nothing effective to alter them was introduced during 1969–70. They are the fundamental political obstacles to improvement of services. These four factors in the political sociology of mental handicap help to explain why the radical policy which might have emerged in 1969 shows even less signs of emerging now. A more subtle and powerfully planned strategy to overcome each obstacle would be required. Instead, they were reinforced. At the end of 1969, for example, the Government announced certain stop-gap measures to spend money on food and furnishings in hospitals and build prefabricated units. The sums committed were not large by national standards[10] and do not seem to have resulted in other than minor improvements.[11] The statement unfortunately weakened the demand for major measures to meet the crisis, and the pre-fabricated units have clearly been a mixed blessing. The need to reduce the hospital service in scale by rapidly building up local authority services and change its nature, by developing occupational and social therapy and introducing a new system of staffing, was quietly forgotten or at least postponed. As a consequence, policy was distorted into something almost the opposite of what was intended and radical reforms became much harder to introduce. This was a strategic mistake of the first order.

Nor should we ignore the impact that these changes might have wrought on the images of mental handicap held by first the medical and associated professions and secondly by other key groups in society – politicians, senior civil servants in the Department of Health and Social Security and organizations representing the interests of the mentally handicapped. By excluding mental handicap from having any substantial part in the medical curriculum the teaching hospitals have done notable disservice to the interest of the handicapped. The lack of adequate study and research has helped to perpetuate images of the mentally handicapped as incomplete persons and hence exposed them to custodial and authoritarian attitudes. All this can only gradually be undermined and replaced. Action on the four structural factors can accelerate the process.

Three solutions

Various attempts to rationalize the crisis are still being made. I shall refer briefly to three – the fake 'normalization' solution, the Central Board solution and the hostel solution. In Britain, as in other countries, great emphasis has been placed in recent years on policies which allow the mentally handicapped to lead a normal life. Thus 'normalization' has been defined as 'making available to the mentally retarded patterns and conditions of everyday life which are as close as possible to the norms and patterns of the mainstream of society'. This would allow them to sleep in a private bedroom, mix easily with people of both sexes, eat breakfast in a small group, have considerable choice in clothing and leisure-time pursuits and leave home each day for a place of work where they earned wages (Nirje 1969, and 1970 p. 62). The Government has broadly supported this thesis.[1][2] But much depends on how it is interpreted and worked out. It can, of course, be distorted.

Dr H. C. Gunzberg and others have seized on the concept of 'normalization' and invested it with a peculiar meaning partly, it would seem, to justify power being left with the hospitals. The term is, of course, a dreadful piece of jargon used to express an idea almost as old as man himself, namely that he should lead as normal a life as possible. But the elaboration of the concept seems to bear little relationship to our knowledge of human relationships. For example, no attempt is made to discuss the kinds of group within which individuals learn and practise the ordinary skills of living and whether the hospital can even in principle create

the conditions necessary to offer the same opportunities. The family and the private household are, after all, very intimate units in social and emotional terms and their complex qualities are not easy to reproduce. If we were to attempt to investigate how to do so we would have to draw extensively upon social psychology and sociology. But the huge literature on family relationships, community behaviour and the socialization of the child is almost ignored by latter-day adherents of the view that the hospital is omnipotent. Dr Gunzberg argues that the hospital 'should be reorganized to become a preparatory stage before placement in normal conditions'. He asserts that it can 'normalize' people although he admits that it is 'not normal in itself' (Gunzberg 1970 pp. 71–2). This seems to me to be a very damaging admission. It is rather like suggesting that if you want to teach a child what it is to follow a normal family life you cannot do better than commit him to the care of parents who are far from being normal. One wonders why it is necessary in the first place to remove many handicapped people from the family and the community if the hospital would find it so difficult to reproduce their benefits. Dr Gunzberg does not pursue the implications of introducing more training, employment and social education for a 'hospital', its staffing and staff training, nor does he analyse numbers of patients involved in the different activities. This is especially important since he admits that there will continue to be many patients who will have to be protected from 'the mainstream of society'. Throughout history the rehabilitation ward, the therapeutic community, and similar experiments have in part served as distractions from the fact that most long-stay institutions have essentially negative functions. The study by Julius Roth and Elizabeth Eddy of the myth of rehabilitation in the institution on Welfare Island in New York stands as a warning to all who suppose that a form of institutional service fulfils a laudable function when in reality that function applies to a tiny minority of patients and amounts to an elaborate deceit not properly grasped by the public or even by all the staff. Unless words are to be drained of all meaning, 'normalization' can only mean the gradual abandonment of the hospital as the principal agent of caring for the handicapped. This is in fact the central idea of some experts overseas whose conception of 'normalization' is very different from that discussed by Dr Gunzberg.[13]

A Central Board for the mentally handicapped on the model of those in Denmark and Sweden is currently regarded by some people in Britain as offering an alternative solution to all problems. They believe it would help to release much bigger resources for the mentally handicapped. But similar administrative forms play different functions in different countries. There are arguments from principle against such a change – for example that this would almost automatically give too much reliance on institutions in the overall system of care, make more difficult the sharing of responsibility with parents and the community, strengthen the already considerable powers of the professions, and reduce efficiency by hiving off certain kinds of services which are needed as much for the physically handicapped and elderly as the mentally handicapped. Some problems would therefore be solved at the expense of creating others. There are also arguments from history. Britain had a Central Board of Control which was would up by stages in 1948 and 1959 – although with the benefit of hindsight it might have been preferable to place the service, like residential and welfare services for old people and the disabled, under the entire jurisdiction of local authorities. Moreover, the Kilbrandon and Seebohm Reports have led to acts of Parliament integrating the local personal social services. No country would easily contemplate the dismantling of legislation so soon after enacting it.

The argument for hostels as a substitute for hospitals has to be developed carefully and questioned critically at each stage. If hostels are remote from urban centres, unintegrated with any local community and managed in an authoritarian way they can suffer from most of the disadvantages of existing hospitals together with other disadvantages as well. It is social structure and organization that is important. Private households, sheltered housing, local authority hostels, hospital hostels and large hospitals form a continuum of domestic and social organization. Measures of intelligence and other abilities among the mentally handicapped show that the majority do not fall far short of the mean in the normal distribution. My implication is that the domestic unit in which they live should also be close to the private household. The development of small children's homes, with six or seven children and houseparents, is a model which comes close to the ordinary family household. It is this which Dr Grunewald has in mind for the mentally handicapped,.[14] In British cultural terms this would be an extension to the mental handicap services of practice not only in large parts of the children's service but the services for old people and the disabled. In recent years local authorities have rapidly developed sheltered housing for small groups of elderly and disabled people. They can be placed in localities with which they are familiar and within easy distance of family and friends. Adapted or new flatlets or converted houses could be developed on the same model for mentally handicapped adults. The danger of the hostel of say 25 or 50 places, from a strictly sociological or social psychological point of view, is that it is not a household, a hospital, a family or a community.

This is not the place to elaborate alternative policy. If we were to confront the major obstacles which I have tried to identify we would need to adopt a programme of reducing overcrowding in hospitals, rapidly increasing sheltered housing, day centres and workshops in the community, by introducing a new percentage grant, or a five-year centrally financed community care programme to balance the reduction of the subnormality hospitals' share of the total costs of the National Health Service. Many other strategies would have to be pursued – such as the association of parents and local representatives with management of hospitals and hostels, and the training of new types of community work staff to support and advise the family. This amounts to a complicated redistribution of power. I have argued that the forces accounting for the present impasse lie deep. But the Government is now exhibiting moral cowardice. Only by putting its considerable weight unambiguously behind this central policy can the nation begin to resolve the crisis of the last two years.

POSTSCRIPT[15]

A White Paper published last week affords a decisive test of the Government's ability to comprehend a major human and social problem and do something effective about it. In 1969 the scandal of the ill-treatment of many patients in hospitals for the mentally-handicapped broke upon an unsuspecting public. The report of a Committee of Inquiry, headed by a Q.C. who is now the Solicitor-General, revealed desperate overcrowding, primitive institutional amenities, insufficient occupation, lack of clothing and furniture and 'old-fashioned, unduly rough and undesirably low standards of nursing care' in one large hospital in Wales. Similar revelations about hospitals in Somerset, Essex and elsewhere were also made in the press, on television and in the courts.

The then Secretary of State for Social Services, Mr. R. H. S. Crossman, deliberately fostered public concern. But when Labour lost the election in June 1970 it had taken only a few ill-considered interim measures and a White Paper was stuck in the pipeline.

The Tory Government has taken a whole year to ruminate over its predecessor's unpublished proposals and the decisions that have now been reached are tragically disappointing in nature and scale. The Government proposes a reduction of hospital numbers and a shift to a more balanced division of services between community care and hospitals but does so in a half-hearted and confused fashion which may result in a pattern of services little better than they are now.

For example, the question whether hospitals are an appropriate form of care for people who are not ill, but whose intelligence is limited, is not coolly and logically pursued. After all, it was only as a result of the administrative reorganization of the National Health Service in 1948 that many existing institutions were called hospitals.

That seems in retrospect to have been the wrong decision. All the statistical evidence (including some in the White Paper collected on behalf of the D.H.S.S.) shows that the great majority of people in such hospitals are not in need of continuous medical or nursing care, do not need 'assistance to feed, wash or dress' and even have 'no physical handicap or severe behaviour difficulties'.

This carries the inescapable conclusion that the basic forms of care required are social, occupational and educational and that, except for very handicapped people who are also physically or mentally ill, and who might be cared for in general hospitals or units attached to general hospitals, these hospitals should be phased out. A date could have been worked out with hospital and local authorities, say 1981—2. The numbers are not so large and financial resources so restricted as to make such a programme unrealistic. Instead the Government has decided not only to spend money

on improving old hospitals for temporary period (how long will they last?) but erect new, smal hospitals.

It carries the conclusion that priority should b given to the build-up of community over th hospital services. Instead the Government ha chosen to allocate most of the proposed increase in revenue and capital expenditures in the nex few years to the hospitals.

It also carries the conclusion that much more money should be devoted in the immediate future to community services — family support services such as home helps, workshops, day centres and group housing. A special rate support grant woulc be quite feasible as an emergency measure for a few years. Instead the Government accepts rates o growtn of expenditure over 15—20 years which are only a little higher, and in some cases lower, than for other types of public expenditure.

Finally, it carries the conclusion that the alternative forms of residential care for the ment ally handicapped should be worked out carefully particularly in relation to the responsibilities o housing and social service departments for the elderly and physically disabled. Instead, the Government offers no sustained analysis of the social and residential needs of the mentally handicapped, although it asks hospitals and local authorities to fix dates 'after which the hospitals will not be expected to admit any more people needing residential rather than hospital care'.

The need for residential care is left undefined. Yet any dispassionate examination of the 'care and attention' clauses in the National Assistance Act about residential care in relation to the capacities of the mentally handicapped suggests that the need for sheltered housing (like children's homes for six children with houseparents, and group housing for elderly and disabled) will be substantial.

Although the Government suggests that the hospital population might eventually diminish to 56 per cent of its present size, the difference is more than made up by a proposed increase of residential Homes, with up to 25 people per Home. Much depends on whether or not this resembles private housing in urban localities. What the nation does not want is a system of minor isolated barracks put up by local authorities in pale imitation of the larger Victorian barracks which are at present run by the hospital authorities. Yet the White Paper makes this an all too likely possibility.

Britain can do a lot better, and more quickly, for this underprivileged minority. Living conditions in hospitals must of course be improved temporarily while the alternative in the community is created. But the real drive must be to build up opportunities for the mentally handi-capped to lead an ordinary life like other people, go to work and school, attend day centres and physiotherapy sessions, and live in conditions of decency and privacy. That can be done only with the help of the new local social service departments, a sensitive appreciation of the needs of the family and imaginative leadership from Government.

NOTES

1. See Shearer 1971. Whether there are similar variations in, say, the USSR, is problematical. Certainly there are first-hand international accounts of very good standards of treatment and staffing in 'chidren's houses' for the severely subnormal. See Boom 1966.
2. The proceedings were clearly treated as a matter of urgency and evidence was last heard on 23 February 1968 (Cmnd. 3597, p. 8), Reference is made (Cmnd. 3597, p. 105) to the fact that 'the recommendations of a Special Sub-Committee have been adopted (*to come* into effect on 1 April 1968)' [my italics], which suggests that the report was completed in the spring. I also understand that the Department of Health requested the committee more than once to shorten its report.
3. For example, on 11 February 1970: 'In 1968 43 per cent of patients in hospitals for the mentally handicapped were in wards of more than 50 beds and 58 per cent had less than 58 square feet of bedspace. Thirty-one per cent had no lockers . . . The minimum standard is far below the minimum standard we set ourselves long before I was Minister . . .' The difference in costs for acute and mentally handicapped patients was 'inexplicable except on grounds of underprivilege'. *The Times*, 12 February 1970.
4. [A Government White Paper was published in June 1971. For a comment see the Postscript, pp. 437—9
5. In a speech (in the event read for him) to the Annual Conference of the Asociation of Hospital Management Comittees at Weston-Super-Mare.
6. The Ely Report gives instances of the local HMC failing even to *see* major Government circulars about policy, Cmnd. 3597, p. 106.
7. For example, Lord Balniel, the Opposition spokesman on health and social security, stated in Parliament on 11 February that 'At least half of the 60,000 patients in subnormality hospitals are not in need of constant nursing care at all although they need some kind of residential care. The emphasis should be on development of domiciliary services.'
8. See the review of meanings of 'community' by Stacey 1969.
9. The point has not escaped research workers. For example. 'Treating the institution as if it were primarily a hospital introduces at the outset an obstacle to thinking about how it may be best used to serve the inmates', Roth and Eddy 1967, p. 205.
10. In the financial year 1969-70 Regional Hospital Boards were believed to have been persuaded to re-allocate £2 million to long-stay hospitals from other uses. For the financial year 1970-71 the Government announced a further £3 million for these hospitals (or 7.3 per cent) but more than half of this would have been allocated in any case, since health service expenditure increases regularly each year, and current expenditure on all kinds of hospitals was planned to increase by 3.7 per cent at 1969 prices anyway. See Serota 1970, Cmnd. 4234, December 1969, p. 52.
11. For example, press reports on the first pre-fabricated units to relieve overcrowding have called attention to the relatively ungenerous space and facilities. See also the reservation by Kushlick 1970, pp. 260—61.
12. Most recently in the White Paper, *Better Services for the Mentally Handicapped* Cmnd. 4683, 1971. For example, the White Paper asks for help and understanding to give the mentally handicapped person 'as nearly normal a life as his handicap or handicaps permit' as one of the principles on which services should be based (para. 40).

13. See, for example, the work of Dr Grunewald from Sweden. In particular, he stresses the small group home for an average of seven people. Grunewald, K., 'The Guiding Environment: The Dynamic of Residential Living', in Schuman, V. (ed.) 1972, *Action for the Retarded*, London, World Federation of Mental Health and National Society for Mentally Handicapped Children, pp. 27–33.
14. Conditions in Sweden are in any case much more favourable to the handicapped than in Britain. For example, only 11 per cent of those in any form of residential care are in hospitals. Practically half of the mentally handicapped sleep in single rooms and altogether 97 per cent are in bedrooms with four beds or fewer.
15. Published originally in the *Sunday Times*, 27 June 1971.

REFERENCES

Better Services for the Mentally Handicapped, 1971, White Paper. Cmnd. 4683, London, HMSO.
BOOM, A. B., 1966, 'Children's House No. 15 for Severely Subnormal Children', in Segal, S. S. (ed.), *Backward Children in the USSR*, London, Arnold.
GUNZBERG, H. C., 1970, 'The Hospital as a Normalizing Training Environment', *Journal of Mental Subnormality*, 31 (December) pp. 71–83.
KUSHLICK, A., 1970, 'Residential Care for Mentally Subnormal', *Journal of the Royal Society of Health*, 90, No. 5 (September/October), pp. 255–61.
KUSHLICK, A. and COX, G. M., 1967, 'The Ascertained Prevalence of the Mental Subnormality in the Wessex Region on 1 July 1963', *Proceedings of the First Congress of the International Association for the Scientific Study of Mental Deficiency*, Montpellier, Surrey, Michael Jackson.
MORRIS, P., 1969, *Put Away*, London, Routledge & Kegan Paul.
NIRJE, B., 1969, 'The Normalization Principle and its Human Management Implications', in Kugel, R., and Wolfersberger, W. (eds.), *Changing Patterns in Residential Services for the Mentally Retarded*, Presidential Commission on Mental Retardation, Washington.
NIRJE, B., 1970, 'Normalization', *Journal of Mental Subnormality*, 31 (December), pp. 62–70.
Public Expenditure 1968–9 to 1973–4, Cmnd. 4234, December 1969, London, HMSO.
Report of the Committee of Inquiry into Allegations of Ill-Treatment of Patients and Other Irregularities at the Ely Hospital, Cardiff, March, 1969, Cmnd. 3957, London, HMSO.
ROTH, J. A., and EDDY, E. M., 1967, *Rehabilitation for the Unwanted*, New York, Atherton.
SEROTA, BARONESS, 1970, in *Subnormality in the Seventies, The Road to Community Care*, London, National Society for Mentally Handicapped Children.
SHEARER, A., 1971, *The Quality of Care, Report of a Study Tour in Denmark*, London, National Society for Mentally Handicapped Children.
STACEY, M., 1969, 'The Myth of Community Studies', *British Journal of Sociology*, 20, (June), pp. 137–47.
TIZARD, J., 1964, *Community Services for the Mentally Handicapped*, London, Oxford University Press.
TIZARD, J., KING, R. D., RAYNES, N. V., and YULE, W., 1966, 'The Care and Treatment of Subnormal Children in Residential Institutions', *Proceedings of the Association for Special Education*.

51. Seeking out the disabled*

WALTER JAEHNIG
Research Officer, Department of Sociology,
University of Essex

In those euphoric days of 1969—70, when a flood of mutual congratulation propelled the Chronically Sick and Disabled Persons Act through Parliament without a division in either House, the legislation was seen not only as a 'civilised and compassionate charter' for the handicapped, but also a setter of precedent in the social welfare field. As Alf Morris, MP, the sponsor of the Act, and Arthur Butler wrote (1972, p. 112):

It aimed . . . to add a new dimension to the welfare state.
No longer was it to be good enough for authorities to provide aid for the needy who came knocking at the town hall door.
A new obligation was being put on local councils: to go out and find all the chronically sick and disabled who could benefit from the support of the welfare services. This was an entirely new concept and a dramatic change in the law.

The spark meant to set off this revolution, Section 1 of the Act, was put into operation in October 1971 by Sir Keith Joseph, Secretary of State for the Social Services. This clause for the first time placed a statutory obligation upon Local Authorities to collect systematic information about the needs and numbers of persons eligible for and desiring assistance, and one of the major activities performed in Social Services Departments in 1972 was the implementation of Section 1. Had, however, the revolution envisaged by optimistic

backers of the Act been consummated this year, undoubtedly more than a single chapter of this volume would be devoted to it.

The result instead was confusion and caution: confusion flowing from the Act's curious parliamentary background and emphasised by ambiguous instructions issued by the Department of Health and Social Security, and caution in the way authorities acted in response. Was Section 1 meant essentially as a planning exercise, a firm but gentle method of requiring local authorities to use hard data in making long-term projections of the demand for welfare services? or did it contain a more urgent message, as claimed by Morris and its other supporters: that chronically sick and disabled individuals must be *identified* by Social Services Departments so that a start might be made in lending aid to lives contorted by injury, disease and incapacity?

Left a liberty to choose between these dichotomous views, Local Authorities used a wide range of methods in implementing the Act. Their common factor was a cautious unwillingness to perpetrate the 'Morris revolution'; it would not be too great an exaggeration to say that 'search parties' charged with seeking out the disabled were only reconnaissance missions. Yet the episode is worthy of reconsideration, if only for the flavour it gave to social policy in 1972. The story begins at the end of 1969 when Alf Morris's name came first in the annual Commons ballot for Private Members' Bills.

Parliamentary goodwill

Morris introduced his Bill in a spirit of parliamentary goodwill: a significant point because no one in

*From Kathleen Jones (ed.) (1972), *Year Book of Social Policy in Britain*, London, Routledge and Kegan Paul, Chapter 13, pp. 168—84

441

the three-year history of the Act has outwardly opposed his proposals. That the wide-ranging Bill was ready for its Commons debut was something of a minor miracle. Morris and other members of the disability lobby had less than three weeks to prepare it, and when he approached Richard Crossman (Secretary of State for the Social Services in the Labour government) for assistance, Crossman is said to have suggested instead a Bill on organ transplants (Morris and Butler, 1972). Morris needed little assistance on Section 1, however; he hoped to sweep away the remnant of Poor Law ideology that puts the onus on the handicapped person to 'go to Welfare' and apply for assistance. Instead, the authorities should be the initiators in identifying the handicapped and making their services known to them.

The mechanism he chose to do this was uniform registration of the chronically sick and disabled. Under the National Assistance Act 1948, registers were kept only of the blind and partially-sighted, and general classes of disabled persons applying for assistance. 'If the authority is not anxious to assist the disabled, it can obviously fail to advertise its services, and this inevitably limits the number of persons who apply for assistance,' Morris said in debate (Hansard 5, December 1969). Section 1 in his Bill would have made it a statutory requirement that authorities and hospitals identify and compile registers of chronically sick and disabled persons living in their areas or institutions, and every six months inform registrants of services available, such as domestic help, financial benefits and aids and appliances.

Opposition lurked not far away, however — most noticeably at the Elephant and Castle headquarters of the DHSS — and surfaced during Committee hearings. David Ennals, Minister of State at the DHSS 'was surprised at the scope of the Bill . . . and promised that for everything he had to take out of the Bill, for whatever reason, he would put something else in' (Morris and Butler, 1972, p. 22). One clause under pressure was Section 1 and, at the Committee's fourth sitting, Morris himself introduced the crucial amendment that markedly changed the scope and character of the legislation. From requiring authorities to register the handicapped, Section 1 was modified to making it a duty of every Local Authority 'to take such steps as are reasonably practicable to inform themselves of the number of persons . . . within their areas

and of the need for the making by the authority of arrangements for such persons'. Despite this obvious weakening of Section 1, Morris spoke positively of its merits and called it 'a more satisfactory form'. And while not saying that pressure from the DHSS forced him to climb down, he pointedly remarked that he was 'grateful to the Joint Under-Secretary of State [Dr John Dunwoody] and his staff for assistance in redrafting Clauses 1 and 2' (*Hansard* 4 February, 1970).

It would be misleading to give the impression that Section 1 was the only casualty of the Committee room. A number of important clauses, particularly those involving substantial financial expenditure on the part of the government or encouraging Local Authorities to take into account expenses incurred by handicapped people in assessing charges for services, were also lopped off. In return Morris received a Money Resolution which gave authority for money to be spent to implement the Act, a necessity because his legislation was a Private Member's Bill. The Money Resolution was introduced the day before Section 1 was amended in Committee — reinforcing the cynical view that the government's support of the Bill was a way of buying off the disability lobby until the country's economic problems could be put right.

The amended Bill swiftly received its third reading and moved into the Lords, now racing against time because of rumours of the approaching General Election. A number of Lords objected to the emasculation of the Bill in the Commons,[1] and presented amendments seeking to restore the registration element to Section 1. These were opposed by Baroness Serota for the government and withdrawn, though a third amendment to remove the words 'to take such steps as are reasonably practicable' from Section 1 was approved. In this state the Morris Act was given the Royal Assent on the last day of the old Parliament — along with the Seebohm reform of the personal social services.

The letter of the law
Alf Morris and the other supporters of the Act have always contended (and still do) that the legislative intent of Section 1 is that authorities are required to identify or register handicapped people in their areas. Following the Tory victory in the General Election, however, Conservative ministers

served notice that Local Authorities were bound only to observe the letter of the law regarding Section 1: to estimate the needs and numbers of chronically sick and disabled persons in their areas. In a joint circular issued by four government departments in August 1970, this was made abundantly clear (*Joint Circular*, para. 5): 'It is *not* a requirement of the Section that authorities should attempt 100 per cent identification and registration of the handicapped'. (Emphasis in circular). The joint circular was described in the Commons as 'a shabby document' and in the Lords as 'shocking' (*Hansard*, 23 February, 1971 and *House of Lords Debates*, 26 May, 1971). But not only did it reject the identification principle; it also understated the importance of the Act. For example, it said that criteria of need should be determined by authorities in light of resources available (and not the needs of the handicapped themselves), though the circular contained no exhortation for authorities to make more resources available to the handicapped and their families. The circular also offered a different version of the purpose of the Act from that suggested by Morris during the Commons debates:

> Morris: '. . . the Bill has a single intention. This intention is to increase the welfare, improve the status, and enhance the dignity of the chronically sick and disabled persons' (*Hansard* 5 December, 1969).

> *Joint circular:* 'Its underlying purposes are to draw attention to the problems . . . of people who are handicapped; to express concern that these problems should be more widely known and studied and to urge that when priorities are settled, full weight is given to finding solutions' (*Joint Circular*, para. 3).

In a historical progression this circular might be seen as an attempt by the government to buy time: to give the Seebohm re-organisation a moment to be carried out relatively unencumbered by new responsibilities, and to give the DHSS time to draft more specific instructions for local authorities under Section 1, which even in its denuded form constituted the key to the Act. While the majority of provisions came into force in August and November of 1970, Section 1 was delayed until October 1971 — nearly 17 months after receiving the Royal Assent. During this time Sir

Keith was under heavy pressure from the disability lobby in the Commons and other disablement groups to move on Section 1, and just as heavy pressure from local government associations to postpone it as long as possible.

The instructions finally issued by the DHSS (*Circular 45/71*) two weeks before Section 1 came into operation contributed to the ambiguity surrounding the Act. Where only 13 months previously Local Authorities were advised that 100 per cent registration was not required, they were now told that this should be their ultimate aim. While need was to be determined by resources available, they were now encouraged to be both generous and imaginative in expanding services for the handicapped. But while 100 per cent identification and registration should be their goal, authorities in the meantime might fulfil their obligations by carrying out sample surveys of the handicapped in their own areas — a strategy justifiable as a planning exercise, but hardly acceptable as a method of finding more than a fraction of the chronically sick and disabled. The carefully-worded circular did not in fact directly recommend sample surveys, but seemed to carry this intent in this key paragraph (DHSS, *Circular 45/71*, para. 11):

> One way of obtaining this information would be through local sample surveys. This would still leave Local Authorities with the ultimate task of identifying everyone who both needs and *wants* a service. The completion of this task should in any case be the authority's aim . . . But in many areas .. it appears to the Secretary of State that the cost and effort of making enquiries of each household in the authority's whole area may result in so great a diversion of resources that the whole purpose of the task would be nullified. There is also the danger of arousing expectations of service on the part of disabled persons which the resources of the authority will not be able to provide for some time to come. In these circumstances it may be desirable to begin by sample surveys . . . (Emphasis in circular.)

Why the government' and DHSS chose to recommend the sample survey is another question. It would appear that three choices were available: first, 100 per cent identification; second, leaving it to the Local Authorities to make their own response to the Act; third, the 'middle ground' solution, the sample survey.

Ministers of both governments opposed 100 per cent identification on strikingly similar grounds: it would be time-consuming and expensive, difficult to carry out (since a completed identification exercise would require continuous updating); it would in effect constitute registration, and many handicapped people were said not to want to be registered. What is undoubtedly the most pertinent reason for opposing full identification was never mentioned in ministerial statements: the enormous need uncovered by Amelia Harris's national survey of disability, carried out by the Office of Population Censuses and Surveys for the DHSS (Harris 1971). The survey found that more than three million people aged sixteen and over had some degree of physical, mental or sensory impairment, and more than one-third of them needed some form of social support:

Very severely handicapped, needing special care	157,000
Severely handicapped, needing considerable support	356,000
Appreciably handicapped, needing some support	616,000
Total	1,129,000

Even more important, only 12 per cent of the survey respondents were registered with their Local Authorities and only 40 per cent were using one or more of the health or welfare services available to them. Further, large though these figures were, they left room for substantial under-estimation of the number of chronically sick and disabled people in Britain. The survey did not for example include children under the age of sixteen, or people in residential accommodation or hospitals – though presumably one of the functions of a system of aid for handicapped people would be to make it possible for those in institutions to return to their own homes. Due to the methodology of the survey, people not on the electoral registers were excluded and those with certain handicaps, such as blindness, deafness, mental disorders and diabetes, were probably underestimated as well.[2]

While all handicapped people were not in need of welfare services or using services available to them, it was evident that 100 per cent identification would expose vast unmet needs, demanding a massive injection of financial support in community services. This in turn did not match the Conservatives' priorities in the health and welfare field, which placed the emphasis on upgrading institutional provision and the shifting of responsibilities for certain services from taxation to local rates, and were focused on the coming reorganisation of the National Health Service. The Tories were not alone in this attitude; successive governments have treated domiciliary welfare services as the poor sister in many respects, and as pointed out by Michael Brill in last year's [social policy yearbook], welfare services were often neglected in comparison with child care, education and other more glamorous Local Authority services as well (Brill, 1972).

The second choice available to the government – leaving it to Local Authorities to interpret and implement Section 1 – apparently was rejected out of hand. While a Social Services Department would be fulfilling its obligation under the Act by merely extrapolating figures from the national disability survey to its own locale and publicising its services, this would not satisfy the disability lobby and what Opposition MPs were now claiming to be the intent of the Act. To the DHSS, its instructions needed a stronger 'cutting edge': something that would impress authorities of the urgency to develop services and defer a sudden increase in demand for the services.

This left the sample survey. It had the virtue of settling the post-Seebohm debate as to where Local Authority research or intelligence units should be located by encouraging Social Services Departments to hire research workers and generate their own data. Establishment of this research function also fitted neatly into Sir Keith's plan to call for ten-year plans for the development of local services, due early in 1973. Collection of needs-data at the local level would supply ammunition for departments urging members of their Social Services Committee to demand a larger share of the local rates, and encourage committees to make decisions on welfare priorities based upon concrete information.[3] On the other hand, apparently little consideration was given to this diversion of resources for research into repetitive and unco-ordinated local surveys.

For a number of reasons, therefore, the sample survey slipped smoothly into the government's need for a progressive-sounding deferrent. An added bonus was that the national survey found considerable variations in the number of handicapped living in different geographical regions, and this was emphasised strongly in *Circular 45/71* as a reason why local authorities should carry out their own surveys.[4]

Local authority responses

Given the continuing debate over the meaning of Section 1, the ambiguity contained in the two circulars, and the local differences in terms of research resources available and effectiveness in completing the Seebohm re-organisation, it might be expected that Social Services Departments would not implement the Act in a uniform manner. This is certainly true, and a tendency to treat the Act with varying degrees of urgency was intensified by Section 1 itself. Not only are departments required to determine the needs and numbers of handicapped people in their areas; Section 1(2) also makes it a duty to publicise services made available under the National Asistance Act 1948, and to inform all users of these services of other forms of assistance available to them. In practice, collection of data and dissemination of information became confused, and a few authorities launched only publicity campaigns, or only sample surveys, thinking the one would also do the job of the other.

In August Sir Keith gave Parliament a report on the methods used by authorities to implement Section 1 (*Hansard*, 8 August, 1972). Six authorities did not reply to the DHSS's query and nine replied but did not provide any information; 15 of 158 English authorities therefore apparently had little progress to report.

	Method of implementation	Number of authorities
1	House-to-house distribution of leaflets	46
2	Sample survey in accordance with Office of Population Censuses and Surveys guidance	33
3	Other sample surveys	29
4	Other methods of implementation	21
5	Combination of two of above methods	14
6	No information given	9
	Total replies received	152

More than 60 of the remaining 143 English authorities carried out some form of sample survey, and another 46 distributed leaflets in households in their areas. The table is remarkable in what it does not say: no breakdown is given on authorities carrying out identification programmes, and authorities distributing leaflets are not divided into those calling back to pick up the completed form (a census operation) and those merely leaving the leaflet behind (a publicity campaign). The figures also seem to under-estimate the number of authorities carrying out sample surveys, as returns were due at the DHSS on 1 May, and a number of authorities initiated sample surveys after this date.

Later in the year Social Policy Research completed a survey of forty-two randomly-selected authorities in England and Wales (including the ten largest counties) for the National Fund for Research into Crippling Diseases, and found that fourteen had carried out sample surveys, two had performed household censuses, five house-to-house leafleting (publicity) exercises, and six had done nothing (Social Policy Research, 1972). Five were planning to carry out sample surveys or census operations of their entire areas, and another ten were planning partial censuses or surveys in selected localities. In short, it would appear that nearly half of the authorities carried out sample surveys, though sometimes in conjunction with other methods listed in the above table such as leafleting campaigns.

SAMPLE SURVEYS

About half of the authorities carrying out surveys followed a 'do-it-yourself' guide prepared by Amelia Harris and Elizabeth Head of the Office of Population Censuses and Surveys for the DHSS (1971). Three stages were recommended: first, a postal sift of a random sample of households in which the householder returned a form indicating the presence of an impaired or elderly person at the address; second, a follow-up interview at the impaired person's home to determine the degree of his handicap, and third, a personal call on the handicapped person to discover his need for assistance. Many of the eighteen authorities contacted directly for this paper followed this procedure, while others telescoped stages 2 and 3, or used volunteers to deliver the stage 1 forms instead of the post, or deleted specific parts of the interview schedule, such as the vision test, and added others.

However, variations in practices in carrying out the surveys are so great as to prohibit the comparison of results. Size of samples for example varied at least from less than 1 per cent of households in one authority to 20 per cent in another. Some authorities included children, while others did not. Some used the national survey's definitions of impairment, handicap and disablement, while others developed their own, or borrowed the general definitions from the National Assistance Act 1948 and the Mental Health Act 1959. Some authorities studied 'need' as defined by present policies in the Social Services Department, while others studied the needs of the handicapped people without reference to constraints caused by the local shortage of financial resources.

Further, some authorities had access to experienced social research workers, either on their own staff or at nearby universities. Others bought skilled help from market research or social research firms. Some made do with unskilled research personnel – who often made the usual beginner's mistake of collecting too much data and under-estimating the time involved in such a survey – or had to rely heavily upon volunteers drawn from schools or community groups.

In view of this, it is somewhat surprising to learn that preliminary returns in many authorities are finding a fairly uniform level, slightly under-shooting the extrapolations made from the national survey figures. One exception is Lancashire, which found slightly more disabled people than the national survey's estimate. But overall, either the national figures were very accurate for most authorities and the DHSS exaggerated the geographical variations, or the extrapolated figures were a magnetic target seeming to exert a strong influence on the surveys themselves. In either case, it seems likely that the local surveys also under-estimated the incidence of disability.

As a result, questions are being asked in a number of Local Authorities if the survey exercise was worth carrying out. In most cases it proved to be an elaborate, time-consuming and expensive project that yielded only an approximate confirmation of figures already available, and improved data regarding the needs of the handicapped. Most final reports are still not completed at the time of writing, some fifteen months after Section 1 was put into operation; the clerical work involved in

the survey and other demands upon the departments were the main roadblocks encountered, especially in smaller departments. One authority paid a social research firm £5,000 to carry out 1,100 interviews and process the data. Another department estimated its direct costs of the survey as £10,000, with indirect charges that size again. And most important (especially in the eyes of the disability lobby), the surveys produced preciously few names of handicapped people.

On the other hand, there can be little question that the survey process added to the prestige and importance of the research unit in many departments, and the prettily-packaged final reports could be influential in impressing Social Services Committee members of the need for greater resources for the handicapped. While the survey figures may in time prove to be under-estimates (because the process excluded people not living at home and may have missed a substantial proportion of people with 'socially-unacceptable' conditions, such as mental disorders or incontinence), the estimates are better planning tools than what was available in the past. Yet this experience also indicates that a handful of systematic surveys in different kinds of localities is a more effective research strategy than seventy poorly-controlled local surveys and is less expensive as well.

CENSUSES OF THE DISABLED
Census canvassing of the handicapped, in which leaflets are distributed on a house-to-house basis and someone calls back to pick up the completed form to ensure that no handicapped person in the household was missed, is a more satisfactory procedure to the disability lobby and apparently is the ultimate aim of the government as well (*Hansard*, 21 May, 1971). Few authorities, however, were bold enough to carry out complete census operations in 1972 for the obvious reason that full identification would unleash a sharp demand for services. One exception was the Isle of Wight, which carried out a complete census (contacting 91.5 per cent of 39,000 households) with the assistance of 600 volunteers and the Institute of Local Government Studies at the University of Birmingham (Inlogov, vol. 3). Less than half the number of households on the island than the national figures would have suggested were found to contain a chronically sick or disabled person.

Many other authorities carried out censuses in

particular wards, towns or other divisions of their areas, and plan to extend these exercises to other areas as services are developed. Lancashire County Council, for example, in 1972 performed a sample survey of 12,000 households and canvassed several areas of the county as well. The first is intended to provide planning estimates; the second to obtain names of people actually needing the services.

The major problems encountered in carrying out censuses were first, finding a method of contacting twice all households in the area being surveyed, and second, controlling the process to keep errors to a minimum. Some authorities approached the local elections officer to see if his staff would carry this out while updating the electoral register, but were refused. In the end, they fell back upon volunteers, with mixed success.

LEAFLETING CAMPAIGNS

These depend even more upon the support of persons outside the Social Services Department than censuses. There are two types: those which use 'middle men' such as general practitioners, health clinics, voluntary societies, post offices, libraries and other community institutions to distribute leaflets to the handicapped and their families, and those involving house-to-house distribution.

Campaigns using middle men often were highly unsuccessful: one county council, for example, distributed 70,000 leaflets with detachable forms and received less than 400 replies. Several departments reported poor results in using the local NHS executive council and family doctors: one authority sent 2,500 leaflets to general practitioners and received only eleven replies – all patients from one surgery. These experiences would seem to contradict the DHSS's suggestion in *Circular 45/71* that GPs are increasingly in contact with Social Services Departments and able to help (DHSS *Circular 45/71*, paras. 21 and 25).

Bursts of local publicity often accompanied house-to-house campaigns, with Jimmy Saville riding through town in an open car waving leaflets, and school children parading through shopping centres, singing songs like this (to the tune of 'The Blaydon Races') (Outset):

We're going to help disabled folk right here in Sunderland,

And everyone who lives in town can lend a helping hand . . .

While these efforts generated enough noise in some areas to bring the Act to the public's attention, they were primarily publicity ventures and not systematic attempts to find handicapped people. Accordingly, relatively few names came to the attention of departments solely through publicity campaigns.

One of the more active groups in this field was Outset, a charity which organised house-to-house campaigns for Local Authorities at a rate of £10 per thousand leaflets. Using Community Service Volunteers as organisers and school children to do the legwork, Outset ran campaigns in Ealing, Reading, Worcester, Coventry, Wandsworth, Enfield, Derby, West Suffolk, Northamptonshire, Surrey, Sunderland, Kensington & Chelsea and Newham. These were one-shot affairs, aimed at hitting all households in a short time-period, but in some areas, departments asked the organisers to pick up completed forms as well. The results were often disappointing from the standpoint of adding new names to the register; in Ealing, 97,000 households were covered and only 1,900 returns came in, 1,200 of them already known to the department. Most authorities found as many new names while doing sample surveys. However, Outset organisers also found that some departments were ill-equipped to deal with the referrals which did turn up in the campaign.

Volunteers did prove useful in many areas, under the proper circumstances. One rural authority for example used school children in a leafleting campaign in an area of 120,000 people. In another part of the county it co-operated with the Red Cross in doing a census, using contacts in villages to ensure that all households were covered. The census found three times as many handicapped people as the leafleting campaigning, in an area with only half the population. Other authorities found that Christmas holidays, rainy weekends and school examinations could be potent factors in limiting their success in seeking out the disabled.[5]

The experience of Newcastle upon Tyne is deserving of special mention because this authority carried out both a house-to-house leafleting campaign *and* a sample survey. Using a commercial firm experienced in house-to-house distribution, the authority delivered self-return leaflets to some 86,000 households and found 5,119 chronically sick or disabled people: 5.9 per cent of the households containing a disabled person. Then a 6 per cent random sample was drawn, and interviews were carried out in 3,507 households. A total of 627 disabled people were located in this process, but more important, the sample survey indicated that 18 per cent of the households contained a disabled person. Interestingly, of the 627 persons located in the sample survey, less than one in every four had returned the postal questionnaire in the leafleting campaign.

The Newcastle Social Services Department now estimates that 19 per cent of households contain a disabled person (including children) — about 16,500 people, or more than three times the number located in the leafleting campaign. In the past year the department's disablement register has grown from less than 2,000 to about 7,000. This seems to indicate that while some disabled people may be known to Local Authority departments without being registered, the country's most elaborate implementation of Section 1 has located only a fraction of those eligible for assistance.

Postscript and conclusion

The story of 1972 would not be complete without mention of an incident which occurred at 5.04 on the morning of 13 June in the House of Lords. At this bleak hour, the government was facing defeat on its 'fair rents' Bill because of the pressure being orchestrated by three disabled peers: Lord Crawshaw, Lady Masham and Lady Darcy de Knayth. Unless the government amended the Bill to allow the chronically sick and disabled to claim larger rent rebates and allowances — a right already accorded the blind — this important piece of legislation would suffer a crushing setback. Reluctantly the government agreed, and the 'wheelchair lobby' had successfully flexed its parliamentary muscles once again.[6]

In fact, relatively few handicapped people will benefit from this amendment to Schedule 3, paragraph 8(2), of the Housing Finance Act. It does not include those on supplementary benefits (who have their own rebate scheme), families in which the handicapped person is other than the tenant or his wife, or handicapped people who are owner-occupiers. But where the handicapped person is registered with the Social Services Department, it

can have a cash value of up to £16 a year and up to £26 if his wife is disabled as well.

The significance of this is that, for the first time, a direct cash value is placed upon registering as disabled. This incentive to register is already having an effect in some Local Authorities. One department for example conducted a publicity campaign under Section 1, distributing 16,000 leaflets through middle men, and received only 260 referrals — half of them already known to the department. Since the Housing Act went into operation, more than 600 handicapped people have applied for the increased rent rebate, many of them previously unknown to this department!

One lesson that might be drawn from this is that the chronically sick and disabled — and other 'missing' groups in need — will be located and identified where there is a positive benefit offered that makes it advantageous for them to be found. It might be hypothesised for example that the establishment of a disability income would locate more handicapped people than all this year's sample surveys lumped together. The same might be true on the local level. Yet in many cases, Local Authorities were not ready even for the fraction of handicapped people identified this year. A London borough carried out a sample survey of one in every five households and defined need as if there were no constraints on services: the survey generated more referrals than the social workers could handle, and new referrals no longer receive a visit because of the extent of the backlog and shortage of professional workers. As the assistant director in another area described the situation in this authority (*Inlogov*, vol. 2, p. 200):

> It would be pointless to embark upon large-scale excursions into unmet need even if we had the resources, since we are having difficulty meeting the increased demands made upon our services, due to recent legislation . . . we are in contact with less than a quarter of the total problem. Since a 25 per cent increase in referrals leads to considerable disruption, I would suggest that it would be extremely irresponsible to impose a 75 per cent increase on staff who are already overstretched.

Considering the magnitude of unmet need, the accomplishments of the Chronically Sick and Disabled Persons Act in 1972 were very modest ones. The government is now committed to seeking full identification ... eventually. Local Authorities are much better informed as to the extent of existing need and some have taken the first steps in expanding services to meet it, though this has tended to accentuate old disparities existing between authorities. Local Authority registers of the general classes of handicapped people grew by 30 per cent between the end of 1970 and 31 March 1972 (*Hansard*, 8 August, 1972). Registers in cities such as Liverpool and Newcastle grew by more than 200 per cent.

Perhaps even more important though is the climate of interest and opinion surrounding the Act that is making a political issue of disability; critical here is not so much what the Act says, but what people think it says. What changes occurred happened not because governments were concerned about the disabled, but because a Private Member's Bill and a growth in public demand for services succeeded in focusing attention upon the inadequacies of present provisions.

But the lesson that must be drawn from this episode is that in an atmosphere conducive to change, those seeking reform must not be too ready to settle for small concessions. The revolution planned by Alf Morris has not taken place because one cannot change traditions, institutions and values merely by fiddling with the wording of the law. No one, politician or civil servant, can openly oppose the extension of services for the handicapped and this underlines the importance of stating the scale and nature of reform desired in unambiguously clear terms. Because in this case the disability lobby did not adopt a strong enough

negotiating line, the Act did not disturb the government's order of priorities in the health and welfare field, and this is crucial as it thereby failed to acquire the financial support needed to make it work.[7] Nor did it change the basic orientation of Local Authority welfare services as they pertain to the disabled. Because of this the DHSS could and did internalise the Act and use it to suit its own purposes; the sample survey 'solution' not only took pressure off the Department by deferring activity under the Act, but also deflected the pressure on to Local Authorities to deal with their own disabled. One Member of Parliament observed this recently when he described the Act as 'a time bomb ... ticking away in our town halls' (*Hansard*, 21 May, 1971).

This little bomb did not go off in 1972. But it is still ticking.

Acknowledgments

Much of the data presented in this chapter was obtained in interviews and correspondence with officers of eighteen Local Authority Social Services Departments and the Department of Health and Social Security. As these interviews were not for attribution the officers remain nameless, but I would like to acknowledge their ready assistance. I would also like to thank Alfred Morris, M.P., George Wilson of the Central Council for the Disabled, Stanley J. Orwell of Social Policy Research, John Kingsbury of Outset, Adrian Sinfield, Timothy Booth and Peter Townsend for their help in preparing this paper.

NOTES

1. For example, Lord Fraser of Lonsdale replied to a speech by Lord Longford, the Bill's sponsor in the Lords, by saying, 'But I did not myself see any power compelling anything to be done in many fields, and I would ask the noble Earl [Longford] to have a look to see whether the Bill is as mandatory as many of us could have wished to see it and as, indeed, the original Bill was when it came to another place.' *House of Lords Debates*, 9 April 1970.
2. Harris, 1971, p. 9. Further evidence that the survey undershot the mark is provided by the attendance allowance. By 1 April 1972, 72,000 allowances had been granted, but the survey found only 25,000 in the categories eligible for assistance (1 and 2).
3. On the other hand, if this was really the DHSS's strategy, the question can be raised as to what the Department would have done to encourage Local Authority research if the Morris Act had not been available.

4. However, these disparities were not so great if the national survey's figures were examined in conjunction with census data. See *Inlogov*, vol. 4, pp. 45—6.
5. See, for example, the *Guardian*, Volunteer 'hazard' in surveys on handicapped, 5 May 1972, p. 9.
6. For a more complete account of this incident, see Tony Lynes, 'Wheelchair power', *New Society*, 10 August 1972, p. 290.
7. Following negotiations with Local Authorities, the government has increased the rate support grants to authorities in each of the last two years by 12 per cent to develop Local Authority welfare services. However, these funds are not specifically earmarked, and there is no guarantee that they will be spent on the disabled as opposed to highways, building projects or holding down the rates. Alf Morris said in a personal interview that he hoped that Local Authorities would continue to come back to the government requesting funds fully to implement the Act. [In 1974 he was appointed Minister with Special Responsibilities for the Disabled under the Secretary of State for Social Services.]

REFERENCES

BRILL, MICHAEL, 1972, 'The local authority social worker', in *The Year Book of Social Policy in Britain 1971*, London, Routledge & Kegan Paul, pp. 88—90.

Department of Health and Social Security, Ministry of Housing and Local Government, Department of Education and Science, and Ministry of Transport, *Joint Circular* (DHSS) 17/70, London.

Hansard, 5 December 1969, vol. 792, col. 1854.

Hansard, Standing Committee C Reports, 4 February 1970, col. 148.

Hansard 23 February 1971, vol. 812, col. 285.

Hansard, 5 December 1969, vol. 792, col. 1851.

Hansard, 8 August 1972, vol. 842, cols. 338—40.

Hansard, 21 May 1971, vol. 817, col. 1754.

Hansard, 8 August 1972, vol. 842, col. 339.

Hansard, 21 May 1971, vol. 817, col. 1663.

HARRIS, AMELIA I., 1971, *Handicapped and Impaired in Great Britain Part 1*, Office of Population Censuses and Surveys, London, HMSO.

HARRIS, AMELIA I., and HEAD, ELIZABETH, 1971, Sample surveys in local authority areas, *Office of Population Censuses and Surveys*, London, Department of Health and Social Security, September.

House of Lords Debates, 26 May 1971, vol. 319, col. 1175.

Clearing House for Local Authority Social Services Research, (periodic) *Ingolov* vols. 2, 3 and 4, Institute of Local Government Studies, University of Birmingham.

MORRIS, ALFRED and BUTLER, ARTHUR, 1972, *No Feet to Drag*, London, Sidgwick and Jackson.

OUTSET, *Operation Discovery: The Sunderland Project*, undated, p. 10.

SOCIAL POLICY RESEARCH, 1972, *The Implementation of the Chronically Sick and Disabled Persons Act 1970*, a report to the National Fund for Research into Crippling Diseases, RJ/5001, London, December.

52. Civic rights and social services[*]

ROSALIND BROOKE
Lecturer in Social Administration, London School of Economics and
Legal Advisor to the Child Poverty Action Group.

The Seebohm Committee has recommended that a new family service be established to take over work at present done by five or six separate local authority departments. The new service will be concerned with the 'prevention of social distress' (Cmnd. 3703 para. 427). Preventive aids will include casework and material help through better and improved services like, for example, home-help services, special laundry services and sheltered housing. The Committee, having analysed some of the causes of distress, significantly leave local authorities to review their own needs and services in order to determine current priorities. For this could only be done, they say, 'in relation to the needs and circumstances of specific areas, including their previous investment in particular services' (op. cit. para. 4).

The Committee was not asked to go into the possible implications for users and potential users of this new service, although they did point out that their recommendations were designed to prevent people falling between two departmental stools. One department would help establish a clear system of accountability (op. cit. para 157). Citizen participation in the social services was seen by the Committee as being one way to identify needs and expose defects (op. cit. para. 491). Ultimate responsibility for users of services whose needs were neglected or abused was placed on the elected representatives, the councillors (op. cit. para. 624). The special need for advice on housing

could be met either by citizens' advice bureaux or by local authority housing departments.

Will these recommendations succeed in alleviating all forms of social distress, some of which may be caused by the very social services designed to prevent such distress? Some problems face users and potential users of the social services which the Seebohm Committee was not able to consider at all, given its limited terms of reference. Furthermore, what problems may develop in the future from this new family service? So many questions are simply never discussed about the relationship between the citizen as user (as opposed to taxpayer or ratepayer) of the social services and the providers of those services, whether central government or local authorities. How does a user of services make his present needs felt? Who makes representations on his behalf to the providers and planners of services? How can the user influence the way a service develops? What rights has he if he is refused, or not even informed of, services? What avenues are there for complaints about the services he has been given? Are there different procedural standards in some services compared to others? If there are two standards, should there be? How do social workers decide whether to give material help to a client? Should so much help to users of some services be given under discretionary powers? Why should help from some social services be based on discretion rather than entitlement, and what effect does this have on administrative and complaint procedures? In what circumstances should there be entitlement? Should there be so many different means of testing when a potential user will be granted help? Does a lawyer have any role to play in the social services?

*From William A. Robson and Bernard Crick (eds.) (1970) *The Future of the social services*, London, Penguin Books, pp. 36–51.

451

What is the intended role of lay members on supplementary benefit advisory committees, regional hospital boards, and what is their actual role? Who acts as spokesman or advocate for users of services when refused an explanation, or refused help?

These are only some of the questions which could be asked about the relationships between the users and the social services. The major issue is perhaps the extent to which users of these social services should be subjected to many forms of procedure and control not imposed on other citizens (Reich 1965, p. 1245). Cohabitation which necessarily results in a higher moral standard for female as opposed to male recipients of supplementary benefit can be sufficient to justify the cutting off of benefit. But is it just that benefit can be withdrawn when the allegation is made, rather than after a hearing of the evidence? Another important issue is whether so much of the provision of help in individual cases should be governed by discretionary powers rather than based on entitlement to services in given circumstances. If it is decided that entitlement rather than discretion is the order of the day, then surely we need to put this into practice. The recent Ministry of Social Security Act 1966, by section 4(1), entitles those over sixteen to a supplementary allowance or, if of pensionable age, to a supplementary pension. But it is difficult to find out what a person is entitled to if the way to assess it is based on rules in the 'A Code', available only to Ministry officials.[1] This raises the third major issue: what information could and should be made available to users of services? Is it right that people are not told how council houses are allocated, or that the waiting lists have 5,000 families on them? How can people know their rights and entitlements if information is not given to them? Here it is important to point out that the SBC continued using supplementary allowance books with out-of-date earnings limit rules in them (Harvey 1968a p. 38.) A fourth issue is raised by the question to what extent social workers and social security officials should be allowed to make inroads on personal privacy. Should an old lady have to show her ragged underwear to a young male SBC officer before he will grant a special allowance for clothing? Should a welfare worker be allowed to tell a woman that she should get married or get an affiliation order before she and

her children are admitted to temporary accommodation for the homeless? The fifth major issue is whether local authorities should have a different standing at law, council tenants, for example, have a different legal status to tenants of private landlords.

The Seebohm proposals, particularly if coupled with recommendations from the Royal Commission on Local Government for much larger local authorities, will mean a far greater concentration of power in the hands of officials and social workers of the family service. What happens if an individual or family is labelled 'undeserving' or 'non-cooperative' by this new and powerful department, so perhaps being placed further down the housing list or denied other help asked for? What happens if the new department tries to reduce the number of families taken into temporary accommodation (Harvey 1966 p. 820) under Part III of the 1948 National Assistance Act by, for example, demanding a 'settlement'? (Skinner 1967 p. 16). (Relics of the Poor Law still remain as some boroughs will not take homeless families who have been resident in the borough for only a short time.) Welfare departments have been known to suggest to a homeless mother that her expected child should be adopted. Another local authority will not take families into Part III accommodation if through their 'own irresponsibility' (defined as getting into rent arrears, however caused) they become homeless (ibid). Children's departments differ in the amount of financial or other material help they are prepared to give under section 1 of the 1963 Children and Young Persons Act: some give help only when a child is taken into care, others beforehand.

Not only do local authorities vary in the interpretation and use of their many discretionary powers; they vary in the extent to which they are prepared to give information to the public. [...] One housing authority refers inquirers about rent rebates to the SBC, omitting to tell them that supplementary benefit rent allowances are based on a different means test which may be less generous (Harvey 1968 p. 778). This failure to give consumers information about a similar service (rent rebates) prevents them from making a wise choice about the 'best buy', and incidentally the housing authority's accounts are less likely to go into the red. Similarly, lack of information or explanation about the functions of rent tribunals and rent officers may lead somebody to make the wrong choice and as a result he may lose his home.

The social services in some areas appear to have evolved separate procedures, to the extent of establishing a more favoured position for themselves in the legal system. Some major housing authorities may be dilatory, if not reluctant, to carry out repairs on their own property. The public health inspector cannot take his own authority to court as he could a private landlord. Housing authorities sometimes obtain eviction orders against tenants and then hold them over their heads like a sword of Damocles — sometimes for years. It is most unsatisfactory for tenants that they should have to be given a formal notice to quit before their rents can be raised (Cmnd. 3604 para. 81). Some councils will refuse to have the wife as the tenant or to have husband and wife as joint tenants, so if the family breaks up, the housing authority may well not grant the tenancy to the wife until she has gone to court and got a separation order or a divorce (yet the tenancy was probably given to the family because there were children). The 1967 Matrimonial Homes Act does not apply to council tenancies (Stone 1968 p. 309).

The decision-making process by social workers and other social service officials has seldom been investigated. How does a child-care officer decide to give material help (if at all) by paying an electricity bill or the rent arrears? In some circumstances material aid is used as a lever to obtain a more 'cooperative' response from the family (Handler 1968 p. 486). Or a family might be refused aid if it were thought the parents were smoking unduly expensive cigarettes. Decisions based on inadequate evidence appear to be made by social security officials. A woman thought to be cohabiting may have her supplementary benefit cut off from the moment the official alleges this (Child Poverty Action Group 1968 p. 11). By contrast, of course, her husband would not be able to stop paying under his maintenance order until he had gone to the magistrates' court and proved his wife's adultery under section 8(2) of the 1960 Matrimonial Proceedings (Magistrates' Courts) Act. Unreal decisions are made about, for example, the possibility of employment for a severely disabled man. As long as he is thought to be capable of ordinary employment, he and his family will be wage-stopped.[2] [. . .]

Users of social services need, above all, adequate information about what is available, what their rights are and how to get them. The Seebohm Committee stressed the need for adequate information about housing. But people need advice about many other problems — this is borne out in a survey in which the author was recently involved.[3] People need information in a simple form, preferably verbal since many official explanatory leaflets are comprehensible only to the people who wrote them. Not only do they need information, but the more inarticulate and timid clients of the social services need spokesmen, negotiators and sometimes advocates. In some areas this function is admirably filled by the citizens' advice bureaux; in many neighbourhoods there is no bureau (there are at present just under 490 in the UK). Many of these open only part-time and often at times convenient to the workers rather than the users. Outside central London (where some 19 bureaux are run full time by the Family Welfare Association) the standards of service in bureaux vary considerably. The National CAB Council stress that CABs are neutral and unselective — they will advise landlords or tenants. Some individual CABs are most powerful advocates for their clients, but national policy is that CABs do not campaign or act as pressure groups. CABs are independent of central and local government (though local authorities often provide eighty per cent or more of their finance) and are admirably suited to provide the base for an expanded service for people to be told their rights, and to be helped to obtain them. They could also be powerful enough to stand up to the new proposed family service. People who come to CABs often have no professional pressure groups or trade unions to represent them, unlike the doctors, lawyers, social workers, electricians and dockers. The CAB movement will have to decide whether to retain the present emphasis on voluntary workers (there are some 5,000 of them). If the need for CABs were more widely recognized, then more money might be available so that standards and training of bureau workers could be improved and the considerable variation in service diminished. National CAB policy, which places such emphasis on impartiality and non-campaigning, may inhibit the recognition of the need for CABs and also makes for less sensitivity to the needs of their clients, because such needs may only perhaps be successfully met by making representations on their behalf nationally and by publishing the evidence of those needs.

The Seebohm Report is based on the assumption that social workers help people. Little attention was paid to whether this is a valid assumption at all or the actual role played by social workers, let alone how they are trained for it, and how their role may (or should) change if the new family service is introduced. How do social workers *help* people? Is what is seen by social workers as 'help' also seen as 'help' by their clients? Do clients want (or need) casework help which can sometimes be akin to psychotherapy, before practical help? Some senior social workers appear to regard attempts by younger colleagues to obtain an explanation about how a supplementary benefit has been computed as too militant (Child Poverty Action Group 1967b). Present social work training generally places far more emphasis on developing casework skills rather than encouraging social workers to discover what rights and benefits are available to their clients. Training does not usually involve studies of decision-making in power situations where material aid can be withheld.

Training for social work is not alone in being deficient in this respect. Legal education in this country in most universities (and certainly for the professional Law Society and Bar exams) is generally concentrated on those areas of law which affect the wealthy and big property and mercantile interests. A course on land law for undergraduates may well not mention post-1925 legislation except for the 1964 Perpetuities and Accumulations Act, let alone the Rent Acts. Many of the difficulties enumerated above might have been avoided had lawyers been involved in social welfare procedures. One American has written that because 'welfare clients seldom have legal assistance, statutory interpretations by administrators have generally gone unchallenged. But when a challenge is made, a significant change in prevailing practice may result' (Reich 1965 p. 1252). The presence of lawyers in tribunals will probably change the pattern at the hearings so that much more emphasis is placed upon the rights and entitlements of the client, rather than whether a fair hearing has been conducted.

Lawyers do not generally involve themselves in these areas of law for two principal reasons. Firstly, their training did not cover housing legis-

lation, social security law (except possibly for something on industrial injuries) or the functions of local authorities in relation to the allocation of council houses and temporary accommodation. Secondly, statutory legal aid is not available in the tribunals set up to hear disputes under social welfare legislation. The Lord Chancellor's Advisory Committee on Legal Aid, which has assumed the difficult and conflicting role of guardian for the Treasury and representative of the users of legal aid, has recommended the extension of statutory legal aid only to the Lands Tribunal because that Tribunal is most akin to the High Court (Lord Chancellor's Office 1968 p. 55). It is true that legal advice[4] can be obtained under the statutory legal aid and advice scheme on any point of English law, but the difficulty for some people is to find a solicitor in the locality (Brooke 1966 p. 13) and one sufficiently knowledgeable on, say, the intricacies of the Rent Acts from the point of view of the tenants, or supplementary benefits and allowances. Another major deficiency of the legal-aid scheme is that it covers advice or litigation (and tribunals are excluded) but does not cover letter-writing or making representations to, say, a local authority or social security office on the client's behalf, although the Law Society's proposals for the £25 scheme goes some of the way to meet this deficiency — assuming that it is implemented.

Formal procedures for resolving disputes have not been set up for many areas of social welfare legislation (Justice p. xi). No formal machinery exists for disputes about council house allocation, non-admission to an old people's home, temporary accommodation or the school of parental choice. There are, of course, arguments on both sides about setting up formal machinery of this kind, but in how much of this area of decision-making could the three virtues of the Franks Report on Administrative Tribunals — openness, fairness and impartiality — be said to operate?

It might be said that the English judges can ultimately review cases involving these areas of administrative law. Apart from whether English judges are best qualified to be arbiters of social policy,[5] one of the fundamental weaknesses in our present 'system' of judicial review is the court's inability to control wide discretionary power. Another important characteristic of English judicial review is that it is so seldom invoked (de

Smith p. 24). Remedies available are in urgent need of rationalization and at the same time greater emphasis should be placed on substantive due process instead of merely procedural due process.[6]

The Parliamentary Commissioner was set up with limited powers to review actions by central departments responsible to the Crown, so excluding local authorities, nationalized industries and the National Health Service. He has rejected over 50 per cent of complaints so far referred to him (Parliamentary Commissioner for Administration 1967 p. 3) — nearly half of these being rejected because they involved departments outside his jurisdiction. The Select Committee recently recommended that he should be able to investigate maladministration caused by a bad decision or a bad rule. The present government has announced the intention of setting up an ombudsman system for local government, while the Secretary of the Department of Health and Social Security has stated that there is a substantial case for a Health Commissioner (Hansard 22 July 1969). Even so, it is probable that the only solution for these problems raised by governmental power, administrative procedures and possible arbitrary decisions is to set up a proper administrative court, either as a separate court or as an administrative law section of the High Court, comparable to the French Conseil d'Etat and with similar powers of review, of remedies, and above all of judicial personnel.[7]

An alternative, or indeed supplementary, method of improving administrative procedures and decisions in the social services might be by increasing the central inspectorate and giving wider powers to inspectors. But central government in its turn needs to be clear about its relationship with local authorities. Professor Griffith (p. 515 *et. seq.*) has described certain Ministries as being regulatory (for example, the Home Office in relation to children's services); others as being promotional (the Department of Education and Science in relation to schools), and some completely *laissez faire* (the then Ministry of Health in relation to welfare departments).

The Seebohm Committee recommended that greater participation by users would uncover needs, defects and abuses. This is no doubt true, but at present we have little knowledge about what such participation has achieved or can

achieve. The Skeffington Report, which is post-Seebohm, considers that 'the success of participation depends largely upon the local authority member', while the main recommendation to promote participation in planning was that community forums should be set up by local authorities (People and Planning 1969 paras. 43 and 60). But this does not go anything like far enough because this degree of participation would probably achieve only a two-way flow of information, if that. Neither of the Reports tackled the central question of who should participate, in what way and with what powers. Should user-participants be allowed to be an efficient part (in Bagehot's phrase) of the social services or merely a Gothic facade behind which the officials continue to operate as they have always done? Who should act as user-participants? Is it really intended that senile old people, homeless West Indians and the mentally subnormal will be on the committees? If not, who is suitable to represent their interests? How do we define a user-participant or a lay member?[8] In 1952, eighty-five per cent of members of regional hospital boards had previous hospital experience, three per cent of members were manual workers, fifteen per cent of members were women (Eckstein p. 188). If we believe in user-participation (however we decide to define this), how many committees should there be, and should they be compulsory? In the field of education, only a small minority of local education authorities make specific provision for parent representation, while the grouping of schools makes nonsense of the notion of school managers as friends and neighbours of particular schools (Central Advisory Council for Education 1967 p. 414). If we do have user-participants or lay members, what powers should they be given and how effective have they been in the past? One member of a DHSS (supplementary benefits) advisory committee was told at a recent meeting that that was not the place to raise the question whether under-sixteen year olds should be entitled as of right to supplementary benefit. The recent investigations into the allegations about mistreatment of elderly patients in mental hospitals would appear to show that some lay members of hospital boards and committees were completely unaware of the difficulties experienced by some of the patients.[9]

The Seebohm Committee pointed out that if

the recommendations of the Maud Committee (Ministry of Housing and Local Government 1967) for fewer local government committees and for a board of management were implemented, then local councillors could be helped to play their role of being ultimately responsible for local government services. But if, at the same time, the number of local authorities is reduced, then councillors will become even more remote as they represent thousands of people. Furthermore, councillors represent so many types of constituents; which group will be dominant in their minds – the ratepayers or the users of Part III temporary accommodation? The Plowden Committee pointed out that as local authorities get bigger, local representative bodies of consumers become even more important (see *Children and their primary schools* p. 416).

No doubt it may be said that M.P.s and Parliament are the final resort for help. This may be true and certainly M.P.s are seen as the most powerful advocates and go-betweens in the attempt to obtain council housing. But some M.P.s hold infrequent surgeries while a survey in 1963 showed that one fifth of those replying held no surgery at all (see Dowse 1964 p. 73). And it is now more difficult for M.P.s to exert a check on Ministers and to raise local matters because parliamentary time is limited and parliamentary questions are often purely formal while the doctrine of ministerial responsibility can be exposed as a myth (see Crossman 1963 pp. 43–5).

The numbers involved in these areas of local and central government activities are not small. Local authorities own over four million houses and flats which represent a quarter of the nation's housing stock (Seebohm Report Appendix F p. 272). There were just under 70,000 children in care in 1967 (op. cit. p. 257). It is not known how many more applications for help of all kinds were made to children's departments. Over one hundred thousand people were living in residential, Part III accommodation, (op. cit. p. 277) while there are apparently conflicting figures about the numbers of people or families living in accommodation for the homeless. The Seebohm Committee thought there were 3,000 families (of which 1,860 had more than three children in the family), (op. cit. p. 279) while the Milner Holland Committee estimated that in 1965 there were 7,000 people homeless in the Greater London area alone (Re-port of the Committee on Housing in Greater London p. 1). It is not known how many families have been homeless during the year and applied for admission to homeless accommodation and been refused. Over one and a quarter million supplementary pensions (nearly seven million receiving retirement pensions) and three quarters of a million supplementary allowances were being paid (Ministry of Social Security 1968 p. 9).

Even as the problems are diverse, so the solutions must be numerous. But the problem of discretionary powers must be tackled. Why should not more benefits of both cash and kind be given as of right? Once this has been decided, then information about entitlement should be made more freely available (e.g. the Supplementary Benefits Commission 'A Code' should be published, and council housing points systems made known). There could well be a legal charter for council tenants and certainly the legal status of such tenancies needs to be clarified, and brought in line with private tenancies. Administrative decision-making should be made more open and fair, not only by bringing in the concept of entitlement and the right to information and reasons for refusal, but also by evolving procedures whereby would-be recipients and users can dispute what they have (or have not) been allocated. Social workers' training should be better designed to fit them to give material help. Lawyers should be educated in these legislative fields instead of going to what they regard as more delectable (and more profitable) pastures. We should be clear about the extent to which users of these social services should be subject to different sets of procedures; and if we retain such different procedures, then we should be clear about the philosophical reasons for distinguishing between classes of users and different standards of morals. Is there a right to privacy in these areas and what does this really mean? More consumer and lay participation is desirable, but again we need to be clear about what this means and what powers (if any) such participants should be given. If the CABs do not change their policy against 'campaigning', there will be even greater need for legal advice centres on the principle of the American neighbourhood law firms or a chain of national consumer shops housing both lawyers and social workers (Syson and Brooke 1968; Society of Labour Lawyers). There is a need for more information about services which are available, and more services to enable people to obtain such help. It is significant that the proposals published in the summer of 1969 for the Government's community development projects contained little on this subject, while lawyers and CAB workers were not even listed as important people to involve in the projects.* The powers of the Parliamentary Commissioner should be extended to cover local authorities and the NHS or, alternatively, separate commissioners should be set up to cover these services. Ideally, however, the more effective means of redress in cases of injustice where no satisfaction could be obtained, would be by resort to the courts, but courts which should be rationalized and strengthened by creating a new jurisdiction of administrative law and remedies similar to the Conseil d'Etat.

No doubt it will be said that we have not got

*Six months later CDP research projects were looking at information and legal-advice services.

enough of the right lawyers/administrators to staff a new court. It will also be said, no doubt, that unless we keep SBC discretionary rules secret, every decision will be disputed in countless appeals; that there is no money to strengthen CABs or set up neighbourhood law firms; and that if there was not an acute housing shortage in some areas, then there would be no problem about the powers of local authorities. But these are non-arguments. If there are not enough lawyers, then let us start teaching and inspiring them now. If discretionary rules were disputed on a grandiose scale, surely this is more fair and just than the present secretive processes. Why should not the CABs have money from the legal aid fund to strengthen their own service and employ lawyers on a consultancy basis if few solicitors are prepared to provide preliminary legal advice? Above all, let us try to answer the question whether social workers do help people and whether greater numbers of social workers will alleviate social distress.

NOTES

1. The Supplementary Benefits Commission is publishing a shortened version of part of the 'A Code'.
2. Child Poverty Action Group 1967. But see *The Administration of the Wage Stop*, 1967, para 36.
3. The Law and Poverty Survey, financed by the Ford Foundation, directed by Professor Abel-Smith and Mr Michael Zander; a book is to be published shortly by B. Adel-Smith, Rosalind Brooke and M. Zander.
4. It has, too, to be borne in mind that the income and capital limits are far lower for advice than for legal aid. But see the proposals by the Law Society in *Legal Advice and Assistance: Second Memorandum of the Council of the Law Society*, July 1969.
5. For example, the Popular Guardians case: see B. Keith-Lucas, 1962, p. 52.
6. *Public Law*, 1967, p. 185. Summary of Working Paper on Administrative Law by the Law Commission, and see Law Commission, *Administrative Law*, Cmnd 4059.
7. See Mitchell, 1967, p. 360.
8. See *Findings and Recommendations Following Enquiries into Allegations Concerning the Care of Elderly Patients in Certain Hospitals*. Cmnd 3687, p 1, where it is pointed out that the Minister of Health considered a member to be a lay member provided he was unconnected with that particular hospital board.
9. B. Robb, *Sans Everything*, and see Cmnd 3975, HMSO, 1969, Chapter XI.

REFERENCES

Administrative Law, Report of the Law Commission, 1967, Cmnd. 4059, London, HMSO.
BROOKE, ROSALIND, 1966, 'Why not more legal help?' *New Society*, 31 March.
Central Advisory Council for Education, 1967, *Children and their Primary Schools* (Plowden Report), London, HMSO.

Child Poverty Action Group, 1967, *Poverty* (spring).

Child Poverty Action Group, 1968, 'Tribunal Reports: Cohabitation', *Poverty*, no. 8 (autumn), p. 11.

CROSSMAN, R. H. S., 1963, 'Introduction' to W. Bagehot, *The English Constitution*, London, Fontana.

DOWSE, R. E., 1964, 'The M.P. and his Surgery', *Political Studies*, 11, pp. 333–41.

ECKSTEIN, H. H., 1958, *The English Health Service: Its Origins, Structure and Achievements*, Cambridge, Mass., Harvard University Press.

Findings and Recommendations following Enquiries into Allegations concerning the Care of Elderly Patients in Certain Hospitals, 1968, Cmnd. 3687, London, HMSO.

Fourth Report of the Parliamentary Commissioner for Administration, 1967, 1968, London, HMSO, p. 3.

GRIFFITH, J. A. G., 1966, *Central Departments and Local Authorities*, London, Allen & Unwin.

HANDLER, JOEL C., 1968, 'The Coercive Children's Officer', *New Society*, 3 October.

HARVEY, AUDREY, 1966, 'The Scandal of the Homeless', *New Statesman*, 2 December.

HARVEY, AUDREY, 1968a, 'Defrauding the Poor', *New Statesman*, 12 January.

HARVEY, AUDREY, 1968b, 'The Mockery of Rent Rebates', *New Statesman*, 6 December.

House of Commons, *Hansard*, 22 July 1969, col. 1520.

Justice (Sponsors), 1961, *The Citizen and the Administration*, Foreword by Sir Oliver Franks, London, Stevens.

KEITH-LUCAS, B., 1962, 'Popularism', Public Law.

Lord Chancellor's Office, 1968, *Report of the Law Society and Comments and Recommendations of the Lord Chancellor's Advisory Committee, 1966–7*, London, HMSO.

Ministry of Housing and Local Government, 1967, *Management of Local Government*, vol. 1, London, HMSO.

Ministry of Housing and Local Government, 1969, *People and Planning, Report of the Committee on Public Participation in Planning* (Skeffington Report), HMSO.

Ministry of Social Security, 1967, *The Administration of the Wage Stop*, Supplementary Benefits Administration Paper No. 1, London, HMSO.

Ministry of Social Security, 1968, *Annual Report, 1967*, Cmnd. 3693, London, HMSO.

MITCHELL, J. D. B., 1967, 'Administrative Law and Parliamentary Control', *Political Quarterly*, 38, pp. 360–74.

National Board for Prices and Incomes, *Increases in Rents of Local Authority Housing*, Cmnd. 3604, London, HMSO.

Report of the Committee on Housing in Greater London, Cmnd. 2605 (Milner–Holland Report), London, HMSO.

Report of the Committee on Local Authority and Allied Personal Social Services, 1968 (Seebohm Report), Cmnd. 3703, London, HMSO.

53. The volunteer*

From THE AVES REPORT

How people become volunteers

Volunteers were asked how and why they had originally taken up voluntary work, and their reasons for continuing it.

Their answers showed that many enter voluntary work in the first instance almost by chance, through hearing of it from some friend or relative who is already involved, as a result of a radio or television programme or a written article, or through their church or some other organization. Young people often hear of opportunities for service through their schools or colleges. A minority of the volunteers who were questioned had taken the initiative themselves, and made their own enquiries. We found no evidence of active recruiting methods having been used to any significant extent by individual organizations as a means of bringing in volunteers. The information given by volunteers interviewed in the studies carried out by the Institute of Community Studies and King Edward's Hospital Fund is given in Table 53.1.[...]

In short, voluntary work at present seems to have an infectious quality and to be something which people catch rather than something which they deliberately seek or which sets out to find them.

The motives of voluntary workers

Questions to volunteers about their motives for doing voluntary work were answered generously

*From Geraldine M. Aves (Chairman) (1969) *The Voluntary Worker in the Social Services*, London, George Allen and Unwin, Chapter 3, pp. 39–52.

and frankly. Most commonly the reasons given included an element of altruism, of wanting to help others, but there was also very general recognition of what the volunteer himself was getting from his work: personal benefit, interest, enjoyment, and social contacts. A group of Community Service Volunteers, all of pre-university age, were anxious at first to stress that they were not working from altruistic motives, were not 'do-gooding', and they were not alone in their pejorative use of this term 'do-gooding'. It was not always clear at first what was meant by it, but it clearly indicates a revulsion from the idea of patronizing benevolence. [...] The young volunteers seemed to see their work primarily as a way of gaining knowledge and experience, a step towards maturity, often a break from what they saw as the confines of an over-sheltered home or school background. In discussion, they admitted at a later stage that there was attraction in the idea of helping other people. Indeed, having disposed of any suggestion of 'do-gooding' they were able to admit to a genuine desire to be of service to society.[...]

Only a few mentioned religious beliefs as their motive for doing voluntary work, but it cannot be assumed from this that such beliefs play only a small part in the motivation of volunteers. Another motive which became evident in the course of these studies was the attraction of belonging to a nationally recognized organization. For some people loyalty to their organization appeared to be a stronger influence than their interest in the particular work which they were doing.[...]

Table 53.1   Methods of introduction to voluntary work (percentage distribution)

Method of introduction

Survey	Personal contact	Through an organization	Through publicity	Own initiative	Through work or school	Total	Number
Institute of Community Studies	42	25	24	9	0	100	114
King Edward's Hospital Fund	29	31	12	15	13	100	86

Satisfactions and frustrations

If voluntary workers are to make their maximum contribution, in terms both of continuity of service and quality of work, they must be helped to enjoy what they are doing, and to see that it is of value. They need to, and for the most part do, find satisfaction in their work, but some inevitably experience some dissatisfaction and frustration. Those whose views were obtained made it clear that on the whole satisfactions out-weighed frustrations. The great majority found that the work was rewarding in itself both from the feeling that they were being useful, helping less fortunate people, and contributing to the provision of a beneficial service, and from what they gained in the way of interest, activity, variety of occupation, and social contacts and companionship. Many stressed the sheer enjoyment which they found in their work. The attitude of a group of workers in clubs for psychiatric patients was that if a club went particularly well they did not think of themselves as having done a good job, but as having had a pleasant and enjoyable evening. A member of the same group said that the personal reward of the workers was a sense of fulfilment, of being a better person: 'Everyone wants to give, and when they give they get something back.' A worker on a London school care committee said at the end of a long discussion about her work, 'I may not have given enough the idea that it is fun. I am grateful to have met the people in the field, and my fellow workers.' A volunteer working with old people said that she had learned a great deal from them; she had been inclined to regret that she had lacked certain advantages, but found that these old people, lacking even more, had acquired wisdom and given it to her. She said 'People should know this about voluntary work, that it is a great compensation and reward.'

For some people the main attraction of their voluntary work was its contrast to their normal full-time job or domestic occupation. Work in Citizens' Advice Bureaux, or other services requiring specific knowledge, was appreciated for its mental stimulus; the interest and variety of work with people could compensate for a routine full-time job. The young Community Service Volunteers mentioned the thrill and the surprises which they experienced in learning about people, gaining insight into their ways of life, their problems and how they face them. One said that for a long time he had wondered 'what you were around for at all', but now, for the first time, he felt that he had done something that really mattered. For these young people, as for many other volunteers, spontaneous expressions of appreciation and gratitude from their clients, or the realization that in some particular instance their work had been of real benefit to someone in difficulties were, when they occurred, a great source of satisfaction. Most volunteers, however, regarded this kind of reward as a special bonus and did not depend on it or expect it as a general rule.[. . .]

The question of personal involvement was discussed with workers in various services. They were interested in talking about this, and there was a good deal of variety in the views which they expressed. Some thought that some involvement was inevitable where there was any sort of personal relationship, and that a volunteer must give something of himself. Others disagreed, and some went so far as to identify emotional involvement with unsuitability for the work.

The frustrations and difficulties which volunteers had experienced in their work fell into three broad categories, concerned with their relationships with professional and other full-time staff, relationships with their clients, and the type of work which they were given to do. Some had found that there were tensions between professional and voluntary workers, particularly in services where their respective roles had not been clearly defined. Of the eighty-six volunteers in hospitals who replied to the questionnaire of King Edward's Hospital Fund, one-fifth expressed some degree of dissatisfaction, and among their comments were 'some staff do not know what a volunteer is for', 'they seem uninterested in me as a person', and 'at first all the staff resented my presence but after a while the barriers broke down'. Only 20 per cent of the volunteers interviewed by the Institute of Community Studies said that they had no frustrations: 13 per cent criticized the inefficiency, inadequacy, or lack of resources of their organizations. Some workers in psychiatric clubs felt that they were not always appreciated by professional staff and some of the Red Cross workers spoke of difficult relationships within hospitals, and lack of liaison between the professionals generally. Some young volunteers working alone regretted their lack of communication with their own headquarters, and their sense of isolation.

In relationships with their clients, just as response and appreciation gave great satisfaction, so their absence sometimes caused distress or disappointment. Volunteers working in community care services found that people whom they visited were at times rude or disagreeable, others that their clients were occasionally inconsiderate or took too much for granted. Workers in psychiatric clubs, not surprisingly, found some of their clients 'disturbing': workers for the Simon Community referred to the tragedy of seeing people go down again after they had been helped. Ten per cent of the volunteers interviewed by the Institute of Community Services were reported to have found that 'personality difficulties of clients' caused them to feel frustrated.

Frustrations arising from the work which volunteers were given to do were of two kinds. There were those who found the problems which they faced too difficult for them; and others who felt that not enough was asked of them and that they had skills to offer which were not being used. In the study carried out by the Institute of Community Studies, 20 per cent of the volunteers said that they found some of the problems which they met to be insoluble, or too difficult. These were, for the most part, people working in services dealing with personal problems or with the giving of advice or information, and it seemed clear that

they did not know how to obtain the help which they needed when difficulties came their way. On the other hand there were volunteers in some services who complained that they were never allowed to deal with real difficulties, and that their potential was not being utilized. A volunteer quoted in the Manchester survey said, 'If you have given up half a day it is soul-destroying just to pass files or arrange the flowers.' It would be unrealistic to expect that frustrations and difficulties in the work of volunteers could be completely eliminated. It does seem, however, that they might be appreciably reduced if more care were given to the selection, preparation and guidance of voluntary workers, if their roles were more clearly defined, and better understood by paid staff, and if all organizations which use them showed more concern for individual volunteers. [. . .]

Attitudes to their work and to paid workers

Volunteers were found to be consistent on the whole in their views about their own work and the special contribution which they could make as volunteers, and also in their somewhat unflattering opinions of professional workers. They stressed the freedom, spontaneity, flexibility, and friendliness of volunteers, and contrasted themselves with social workers, whom they tended to see as rigid, inhuman, 'official' in their attitude, and doing their work 'simply as a job'. Only 15 of the 114 volunteers interviewed by the Institute of Community Studies thought that voluntary workers had no advantages over paid workers: 40 per cent saw volunteers as being more flexible, willing, and interested than paid workers; 37 per cent as being more friendly and understanding, and less 'official', and 17 per cent as having more freedom and working under less pressure. Some people gave more than one answer to this question. Their attitudes are expressed in the following examples, taken from many comments of a similar kind on the advantages of voluntary work:

> Quite a number of people regard the paid worker as government appointed. There is a superstitious fear of the professional among lay people.

> People [helped by volunteers] don't think they are treated like furniture: they like to feel people are doing things because they want to and not because they are paid. [. . .]

Some of the most illuminating comments were made by volunteers who were interviewed individually on behalf of the Committee. This is how they were quoted by the interviewer:

> He had expected professional social workers to be idealistic and care about what they were doing and be eager to talk about it. He was struck (and so were his friends) by their apathy. They didn't seem to know much about what they were doing. He wondered why they did social work; it just seemed to be a job. [. . .]

> Volunteers can cut off corners — go on and do things without having to go through channels. Professionals are bound to answer to someone else: I only answer to myself and my conscience. If financial help is needed, by the time the professional does it it is too late: the volunteer can give it and no one else will know about it: there is no record. The old people feel she is an ordinary person, one of them, not someone they are in awe of. [. . .]

The Institute of Community Studies asked volunteers what they thought were the disadvantages of using volunteers as compared with paid workers. In reply, 34 per cent said there were no disadvantages, 32 per cent that volunteers were less efficient, or had less skill, experience or training, 13 per cent that volunteers were less reliable, 10 per cent that they had less authority or power to help clients, and 9 per cent that they provided less continuity.

It will be apparent that the people with whom these volunteers are comparing themselves do not constitute one defined group. [. . .] The Institute of Community Studies enquired about the professional social workers with whom the volunteers had contact in their work. Respondents mentioned a great variety of 'professionals', including clergy, doctors, nurses, housing managers, legal advisers, matron of an old people's home, officials of the Ministries of Labour and Social Security, psychiatrists and members of the Women's Royal Voluntary Service. Nearly a fifth of these volunteers said that they had no contact with professional social workers, and about the same number said that they could not answer the question because they did not know enough about the matter to be able to judge.

Volunteers who had more to do with professional workers, particularly in services where their work supplemented that of social workers, sometimes took a rather different view from that of the majority. Members of a group working with disabled people said that they had been pleasantly surprised to find that social workers were human. Workers in clubs for psychiatric patients said that they needed the support of social workers and that it was dangerous for amateurs to attempt professional jobs, though they had found that social workers were not readily available, and were often too busy to give them the guidance they needed. A school care committee worker said that she thought that volunteers and social workers had basically the same approach to their work, but that a volunteer could not get near the job a social worker can do in intensive case work, for example with problem families.

Nevertheless, the Committee felt that thought must be given to the reasons for the very widespread denigration of officials. One possible explanation is that because, up to the present, so little has been done to clarify the role of voluntary workers, and to recognize their special place in the social services, they have to identify their own contribution and do this by endeavouring to show that paid workers, unlike themselves, have no real feeling for, or interest in their clients. The volunteer who over-identifies himself with his clients may see the social worker, who has to keep statutory boundaries in view, as rigid, tied up in red tape, and as one of 'them', at least partly responsible for his client's difficulties. Other volunteers, in order to convince themselves that their work is worth while, may need to see their clients as 'good' people, and will therefore be critical of the social worker who, while accepting the client for what he is, and as a person in need of help, does not ignore his inadequacies. The attitudes of social workers and others to volunteers [. . .] may, too, have contributed to their own unsatisfactory image. It is possible that the volunteers' idea of the way in which paid workers treat their clients has been coloured by ways in which they themselves feel that they have been regarded and treated by paid workers. It certainly seemed to us, from our discussions with volunteers, that with few exceptions they were getting little help in understanding their reactions and their relationships with clients and officials.

It is possible that the way in which training for

social work has developed has some bearing on the apparent difficulties in relationships between social workers and volunteers. [...] We suggest that the influence of psycho-analytic theory on the training of social workers, the emphasis on understanding how personality develops and the effect of earlier experiences on attitudes and behaviour, tended for a time to overshadow the need of some clients for help related to their present environmental difficulties. Problems were defined in such a way that only professional help would be adequate. The struggle for the recognition of social work as a profession has been another factor in the tendency to deny that any effective help could be given by non-professionals. More recent developments in the behavioural sciences, and growing interest in community involvement, are helping to modify these attitudes. [...]

It is suggested in the report of the Institute of Community Studies that volunteers are likely to be as much under an illusion in thinking that paid workers are just doing a job in which they have no real interest as social workers are who consider that voluntary workers are essentially undependable. We agree with this, and with the further comment: 'Could it be that both views are mainly symptoms of the gulf between the "volunteer" and the 'paid worker', and that both will diminish if and when the gulf becomes narrower and each side begins to perceive more realistically the contribution which the other makes?'

54. Aid for the disabled[*]

JONATHAN BUTLIN
English Department,
Wanstead High School, London

While visiting the Observation Centre, I noticed how frequently the children wrote their letters back to front. The teacher agreed that this was a common problem and suggested a special stencil whereby the child would be guided into forming the right shape.

Deidre Stock of the upper sixth brought this problem back to Wanstead High School. Several complicated and impractical ideas were abandoned before Marian Waskett and Elizabeth Pavitt proved that if the stencils were made narrow enough, the children would not be able to back-track on one groove.

The stencils were large, with the type of letters that the children were used to reading from elementary books. We left gaps between the beginning and end of the letters so that the children would not draw round them indefinitely. The vowels we picked out in one particular colour to be easily recognisable, and under each letter we drew a line so that they could be placed neatly alongside one another.

This serves as a reasonable example of Wanstead's 'Aid for Disabled' project. The stencils, fulfilling a special need, were supplied free to Woodman Path Observation Unit at nearby Chigwell, with the cost being met by funds raised by the school. Their design was original; for we make a deliberate point of not suppling aids that can be bought on the open market.

That would in part defeat the aim of the project. For just as important as the provision of individual tailor-made aids (probably more important to us) is the incentive that each problem we are confronted with brings to the pupils here to apply their native intelligence or their acquired skills to a practical solution.

Inventiveness and initiative – so often urged upon students by their mentors – gain meaning only through such application. Each problem is a challenge rather than an exercise; its solution offers greater reward than a correct text-book answer.

This incentive, together perhaps with the jolt to preoccupied teenagers from seeing at first hand a young child suffering from cerebral palsy, has fostered a desire in the school to become involved – personally involved – in social and community service; and in the case of many of the seniors it has encouraged a sense of responsibility of a deeper nature than the confines of a school can usually afford.

Douglas Selway, a prefect who has helped considerably in the administration of the scheme recently said 'Because of the immediacy of the problems presented to us, the whole project, quite simply, has captured our imagination.'

A particular case was Pete Finlay's, one of the earliest and one of the best workers on the project. He will, I hope, forgive my saying that by the end of the fifth form he had not distinguished himself and had not particularly endeared himself to the staff. But quite early in his sixth form career he became fascinated by one of the more difficult problems, and, after a brainwave, stayed on at school very late one night to come up with a beautifully simple answer.

It concerned the adaptation of tricycles. At the

[*]From *School Technology*, (1971) 2, pp. 78–82.

464

Ethel Davis School for handicapped children, about five miles distant, the pedalling of tricycles provided enjoyable therapeutic exercise — except that, with limited control of their leg muscles, the children's feet kept slipping from the pedals or their leg action became distorted and uncoordinated. What was wanted was a device to keep the child's foot horizontal to the ground throughout the circular motion. (It would then be safe to add straps.)

The illustration of his 'piston' solution serves better than a description. The spindle holding the pedal in position runs up and down a metal tube which in turn pivots on the rod fixed just below the handle bar. We have now adapted quite a number of tricycles in this way, and have added Velcro straps so that the foot can be secured and released quickly.

Anyway, after solving this problem in mechanics, Pete went on from strength to strength, his school work improved, and by the time that he required a testimonial to be written, he merited all-round praise from members of staff.

The 'Aid for Disabled' project started in the Christmas term of 1966. An article in *The Times* that year caught the eye of the headmaster, Dr Stanley Gardner: it stated that by 1970 one in six people in England would be suffering from some sort of disability. He felt that the school could help locally those people who needed aids that could not be provided through the regular channels and that at the same time an educational benefit would accrue.

Dr Gardner's vision and enthusiasm gave the project its initial drive, but even he could not have envisaged its rapid development. Indeed it grew so quickly that at one point it almost got out of control.

Dr Gardner left us at the end of last term for the Royal Colchester Grammar School, where he says he hopes to introduce a similar venture. But before he left he was largely instrumental in obtaining a £20,000 grant from the Good Neighbours' Trust of Bristol for the erection of a prototype workshop and design centre for the project.

At the start he contacted the Schools' Medical Officer. Redbridge's Dr Toms put us in touch with the Welfare Department and with two schools for the handicapped in the area, of which the Ethel

One of the prototypes for Pete Finlay's adaptation of tricycles

An exercising frame

Davis School is one. Faircross Special School at Barking, a neighbouring borough, heard of our work and enlisted our assistance too. These are our principal sources of problems and work, though we have also answered a few private pleas. Indeed, we once had the ironical situation where the son of one of the governors made an aid for the wife of another.

Most of the jobs we do for Redbridge Welfare Department concern the elderly:

> The old lady looked somewhat more spry than her budgerigar, but with severe arthritis in her hands she couldn't manipulate the switch on her gas fire. Result: she had to leave it on all day and night and it consumed most of her weekly pension. On a reasonably warm day we removed the Gas Board control, copied the fitting, which demanded considerable precision, in aluminium, and attached it to a lever handle, so that she could turn the fire on or off and adjust the heat merely by the pressure of the flat of her hand. The Gas Board just don't seem to think of things like that.

Jonathan Warwicker and Bernard Davies worked together on that problem from the Welfare Department. Peter Coppendale and Mark Roberts designed and made a typical Faircross job:

> Many of the children there with irons on their legs found it difficult to stand fully upright or to raise themselves from a sitting position. Stools placed on either side for support was not a very happy improvisation, especially as they were not always the right height. The most practical solution seemed to be two tubular steel frames like hurdles with supporting struts on both sides, adjustable in both height and width so that they could be adapted for any child.

The work we do for Woodman Path Observation Unit provides ample opportunity for the junior part of the school to exercise their ingenuity. The children there are mostly psychotic and autistic and they need elementary games with a built-in reward factor to encourage concentration, which they find difficult to maintain for more than a minute or two. Variations on jigsaws or 'matching shapes' are designed by eleven or twelve year-olds: when the correct 'fit' is made the puzzle is lighted up by means of a simple electrical circuit.

A modified art table top

However, our most intriguing work has emanated from requests from the Ethel Davis School, where groups of boys and girls repair throughout the week. Some of them are prospective teachers and they do some elementary teaching there; others simply help in the liaison between the schools.

David Clark, who won an open scholarship to Cambridge, probably executed the most complex task we have yet undertaken at the Ethel Davis School. Again, I quote from the school magazine:

> L . . . . appeared very intelligent, but she was completely unable to communicate. However, we adapted a television tube to produce a spot on the screen, adjustable to any one out of 32 positions by using a simple lever swithch. Each of these positions represented simple communication words or numbers from a grid placed over the screen so that L . . . . could attempt basic responses by visual means.

The child was so intelligent that she quickly outgrew this ingenious device, but it started her off very successfully.

A more recent problem was the walking frame. Previously, children at the Ethel Davis School used a small variation on the parallel bar principle. The trouble was that a nurse had to be in constant attendance to turn the children round at either end. John Gardiner and Kevin Sullivan produced a continuous walking frame in which the children

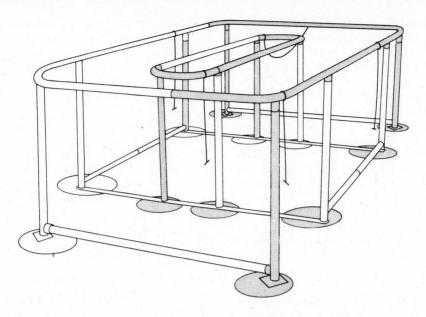

The walking frame made for the Ethel Davis School

could walk round and round. Very simple but no one had thought of it before. Some of the girls painted it in bright colours so that the children would be encouraged to progress from the red to the yellow to the blue. A film taken soon after its delivery shows one of the handicapped children most reluctant to come out of the frame — we hope he will be able to walk on his own without the supporting bars shortly.

Another of the jobs shows clearly how useful schools can be in aiding the disabled. John Gardiner again reports on the boy who could not walk:

> . . . he had no real legs or pelvis. The NHS had supplied him with artificial legs, but they couldn't get any crutches small enough for him to use. Seventeen engineering firms had been contacted but none of them would make the

The latest design for lightweight Canadian Crutches

necessary crutches, simply because it wasn't profitable for them. Then we were contacted. Alain Head designed a prototype and we had a pair of crutches out within a week. . . . We've made four more pairs of these 'Canadian Crutches' since then for similar cases.

Surely there must be hundreds of others required throughout the country. But at present they are not produced, even though they are cheap to manufacture. As with several other jobs that have come our way, only a school can provide the three essentials of labour, equipment and time needed to execute them. While this is still the case it alone argues for the spread of similar projects in other schools.

Work for the Ethel Davis School also makes demands upon feminine skills and ingenuity:

> This little girl had what is called a lazy hand; she was rather inhibited about opening and closing it and the teachers found it difficult to encourage her to exercise it. We made her a special pair of gloves with felt 'teeth' and a floppy felt 'tongue' sewn into the palm. By opening and closing her hand she could make this comic 'mouth' gape and champ; and it fascinated her.

Lots of glove puppets of a similar nature have been made, and a host of rag dolls too, with button-up clothes so that the children are given the initial confidence to attempt dressing themselves.

Fund-raising requires special mention. Fares for pupils to and from the schools for the handicapped or the private houses of the disabled amount, on average, to about £2 per week; little bills for nails, screws, wood, metal, paint, batteries, flex, perspex and all the various materials we need quickly add up to horrifying sums; even a 10/- parking fine once (justifiably) found its way into the 'expense account'.

The pupils raise all the necessary money themselves. In this way those unable or uninclined to design or manufacture aids can really help, and so become involved in the overall project. Again here, the pupils are encouraged to use their imagination in finding ways to raise money. Last summer the sixth form put on a revue and held a silver collection after it (profit: £23 6s and two French francs); last winter one of the girls designed a Christmas card, which we had printed and which swelled the kitty; and last Easter, in a form competition, one of the fourth forms raised nearly £70 towards the total of over £175.

These efforts prove far more stimulating to the pupils (and far more profitable to the funds) than a regular small weekly contribution to charity.

The organisation of the project within the school is complex and has undergone change after change as it has expanded. Details would probably be confusing, and though we hope that other schools will take up similar projects, they will have to adapt their ideas to the structure of their timetables and the general nature of their educational aims.

The basis of our organisation at present is a committee comprising about eight members of staff and about ten pupils. The staff representatives include members from the handicraft, art, physics and needlework departments, and the author of this article from the English department, chosen as co-ordinator principally because it seemed best that the position be taken by someone not immediately involved with the production line.

The pupils' section of the committee also has a co-ordinator, this year, Geoff Russell:

Some of the committee I chose myself, some on recommendation from other members, from the sixth forms. Two or three are the keenest workers for the project – the actual manufacturers; two or three are chosen from the groups that go regularly to the Ethel Davis School; two or three simply share a general interest in the project. On matters of overall policy we sometimes canvass a wider cross-section of the school or hold more general ad hoc open meetings. Some of the committee work involves a lively thrashing out of a compromise between what is ideal and what is practical.

We hope that soon the pupils will be able to run the project almost entirely on their own, especially now that we feel committed to the work we are doing. The ambiguity is deliberate. The idea of committal entails a sense of duty, and I think we do owe it to the schools for the handicapped to continue our work. However, we do not want our project to be marred by strict duty and routine. 'It's got to be done' is a different concept altogether from 'We must do it.'

The students themselves know best how to keep the project alive for their fellows, how to maintain their enthusiasm. If the staff remain in a purely advisory capacity then the pupils can feel more free and responsible at the same time.

The central student committee then can encourage their fellows to feel a desire to tackle the problems rather than feel it a forced necessity – a case of compulsion rather than coercion, to draw a fine distinction.

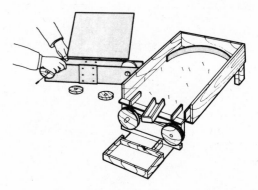

A pin table, designed to exercise wrist movements, in the process of construction

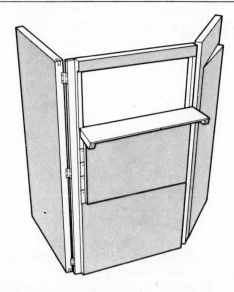

Children's play shop (Wendy-house principle)

The case for putting the responsibility for the project squarely upon the pupils' shoulders becomes most important in the context of the prototype workshop and design centre, which I mentioned earlier.

After the project had been in operation for a little over a year, a reporter from *The Times* visited the school and wrote up a feature article on the project (7 August 1967).

The momentous result of this article was a letter of inquiry from The Good Neighbours' Trust of Bristol. Their representatives came to visit us too. They saw that the expansion of the project was causing the woodwork, metalwork, needlework and art departments to burst at the seams; and they appreciated our case that a far closer liaison among all those involved was obviously necessary. For example, a complex problem involving, say, metalwork, physics and an overall design pleasing to the eye should not have to be shifted from department to department. The machinist, the physicist and the artist in such a case should try to understand each other's problems; for only through such liaison and coherence can real craftsmanship evolve. The integration of the various disciplines within one building would fulfil both the requirements of the project and an educational need.

For the erection in the school grounds of a workshop and design centre of the kind we envisaged, the Good Neighbours' Trust was prepared to make us a grant of £20,000

Perhaps our new building will serve as a prototype for new schools. Basically, we propose to erect a two-storey building, each floor having an area of about 1250 square feet. The ground floor will accommodate a small office for administrative purposes and a large workshop on an open-plan principle with bays for welding and spraying. On the upper storey, the open-plan idea will continue, with space given over to a discussion area (the committee will meet here), an electronics bench, a paint and glue corner, a model-making space, a needlework group and a central design area.

In working out the details of the allotting of space we have been fortunate in having the expert advice and assistance of a member of the Borough's Architect Department, as well as the Art Adviser and the Handicraft Adviser. They have attended meetings with members of staff involved where ways and means of correlating all our requirements have been thoroughly discussed.

We had hoped that work would begin on the building this term, but the prospect of seeing any concrete progress before the new year is rather remote. However, we are all eagerly awaiting news that the Council is sending men to clear and prepare the site.

When the new building is finally erected pupils engaged on the 'Aid for Disabled' project will, we hope, find it a reward for their past efforts and a stimulus for further invention.

55. Handicapped Adventure

DOROTHY E. S. HODGES
Director, Association for Spina Bifida and Hydrocephalus
Playgroups Project, Guildford.

A description of an experimental playgroups project developed in Surrey and Hampshire under the auspices of the North Hampshire, South Berkshire and West Surrey Association for Spina Bifida and Hydrocephalus.

Origins

This experiment was initiated in February 1968 by the Principal Social Worker for the Surrey branch of the Invalid Children's Aid Association as part of its casework service for handicapped children and their parents. Its purpose was two-fold — first to offer a serice in the shape of a playgroup for the children and an opportunity for their mothers to meet socially and to discuss their problems with a trained social worker; and secondly to demonstrate to those officially concerned for the children and responsible for their education something of the nature and extent of their predicament and their latent abilities as well as their more obvious disabilities.

Because spastic and mentally handicapped children were already well catered for and because very few children have been referred from sources other than parents and friends, the majority have always been those suffering from spina bifida whose parents' association ASBAH was well organised in the area. These children form a new group surviving in greatly increasing numbers in recent years because of dramatic advances in surgery and capable by virtue of intelligence and personality of profiting from normal education.

There were three basic hypotheses:

1. That all children should have the opportunity to mix freely with other children and adults and need organised play facilities to grow emotionally as well as physically, and that this is harder for physically handicapped children who are usually protected from their environment by their own fears and the fears of adults concerned with them.

Therefore play material must be presented under conditions acceptable to them and to their parents so that all may gain confidence.

2. That parents of physically handicapped children suffer from emotional stress caused by the hard reality of their children's condition and show this in different ways.

Therefore those dealing with the children must be aware of this stress and prepared and able to recognise and accept it, giving help as skilfully as possible.

3. That it is expedient when an enterprise is to be undertaken and personnel and money are limited, to start however imperfectly with the facilities to hand, so that it may be seen to be operating and can then attract help from those who might not be convinced of its value in the abstract.

Therefore a start was made in Woking, Surrey, with six children and a group of volunteer helpers in the belief that if the enterprise was sound it would develop with the quiet inevitability of natural growth.

Development

In effect this did happen. By August 1969 the numbers had risen from six to 16 and there was a growing demand from parents for another group in Farnborough, Hampshire, where there was a nucleus of children with spina bifida. The Invalid Children's Aid Association however did not wish to develop the idea further and in September 1969 handed it over to the parents of the North Hampshire, South Berkshire and West Surrey

*From Social Work Today, (1972) 13, 10, pp.7—10

470

branch of the Association for Spina Bifida and Hydrocephalus, who were prepared to take it on for as long as finances would allow – to Easter 1970. The social worker who had initiated the project was appointed as project director, an office was rented in Guildford, a part-time secretary found, and in April 1970 another group was opened in Cove, Farnborough.

Present position
The financial situation was improved by the fund-raising efforts of the newly-formed Friends of ASBAH, by parents, and by a temporary grant from the Spina Bifida Trust, so that there are now two playgroups, one in Woking, and one in Farnborough. Each operates for two sessions per week, each has two paid sessional staff two of whom are trained nursery nurses, and this staff is augmented by about 62 volunteers in all who help directly in the groups, or with transport or swimming. Surrey County Council pays the salary of a sessional teacher at Woking and the cost of a minibus to transport some of the children. The number on the roll at each playgroup stands at about 15.

Functions of the groups
In order to understand the work done it is necessary first to consider the effects of the condition of spina bifida as observed on the children attending these groups.

Briefly they are paralysed in varying degrees from the waist down and are usually doubly incontinent, though the hydrocephalus which can accompany the condition is now normally arrested before damage is done to the brain. The result is a child who as he grows older will probably be able to walk with calipers or use a wheelchair, have intelligence within the normal range and eventually learn to deal with the problem of incontinence. There appear to be no obvious difficulties of co-ordination, or of sight, hearing or speech, so provided the child and his family can be helped to overcome the emotional, social and practical effects of the condition he should be able to lead a reasonably normal life within the community.

In order to give this help these effects should be recognised. The child, having some loss of sensation and mobility, is limited in exploring his environment and in experimenting with whatever material comes to hand, nor can he release his feelings by running, jumping or other energetic movements. Long periods in hospital and the anxious care of adults on whom he must depend also control his freedom in this respect. In his attempts to deal with his experience he generally learns to inhibit emotions he considers dangerous or painful, particularly anger and anxiety, and so tends to become passive, apathetic, obedient and 'good'. His parents' problems are similar. They too are restricted in their social activities to some extent and also learn to control their normal feelings of grief, anxiety, and anger, particularly towards people in authority, since it seems better to remain quiet and 'co-operative' than to risk being considered troublesome and so alienate the help they so badly need.

The first function of the group therefore is to create conditions under which both children and parents can express their feelings in order to use them constructively and so gain the confidence necessary in the struggle with their very real difficulties. The children are given the normal playgroup setting, but within this framework encouraged by non-directive adults to behave exactly as they like, to move freely round the large room and use the standard equipment and materials, particularly water, sand, paint and pastry in any way they wish. Initially they are reluctant to involve themselves, or to make contact with each other, but they gradually let themselves go and become free enough to make noise, mess and demands, with consequent development of liveliness and initiative.

Simultaneously and on the same premises, though in another room, their mothers meet, can observe the children's response to this new experience and learn to accept their more normal behaviour. If they wish they may also attend a weekly discussion group with a visiting psychiatric social worker in which they are encouraged to talk as they like in a safe and understanding atmosphere. The result is an ascending spiral of improvement in the confidence of both children and parents. In addition fathers are encouraged to come to the playgroup whenever they can and there is a meeting every term with both fathers and mothers.

The second function of the playgroup is to act as preparation for attendance at other playgroups for non-handicapped children which the children attend when they have gained enough confidence to become part of a larger and more active group, thereby giving the leaders of these other groups the opportunity to visit and get to know the children and their capabilities before accepting them. This extension into other playgroups enlarges the social outlook of the children and makes transition into normal school easier. The playgroup in fact is not a reservoir but a channel outwards and onwards into the future.

A possible third function is beginning to emerge. Nine of the children are now attending infant school, most of them full-time but their mothers have said they wish to continue to attend the weekly meetings – and when the children come back on occasional visits they show quite clearly they enjoy meeting their friends again. This may indicate that some form of continuing contact acceptable to parents, children and schools needs to be found and much thought is now being given to the matter.

Public reactions

Individuals have responded enthusiastically to an invitation to contribute in their several ways, and it has always been possible to find people with a genuine interest which, whether it is expressed in creating a sympathetic atmosphere or in some form of action, is equally essential. Ideas and methods are first discussed, then the volunteer visits the group and is given time to think things over before deciding what she can offer, so selection is always two-way. The children themselves are the best recruiting agents, attracting and keeping by their charm those who have the ability to respond with sensitivity to their needs.

Groups have also responded in many and various ways – churches, youth clubs, secondary schools, women's organizations, councils of social service, the Confederation for Advancement of State Education, the Pre-school Playgroups Association, and particularly the Woking and District Society for Mentally Handicapped Children and the Royal Engineers who help with premises, and the Spastics Society and Fleet Swimming Club who offer swimming facilities at their respective pools. The Friends of ASBAH spontaneously arose when the funds needed by the new project in 1969 could not be raised by parents alone and they continue to provide essential support. There is always a steady demand for speakers and film showings.

Professional reactions

The Farnborough playgroup has developed on the same lines as the group in Woking and has had the same warm response from the general public. There are also indications that those professionally and officially concerned for the children may be friendly and cooperative, though the playgroup has not been in existence long enough for the reactions to have been gauged as fully as in Surrey where they are as follows:

Teachers have so far proved the largest interested group, many of whom when they have visited the playgroup and seen the children behaving so normally think they could be taught in the usual classroom situation, given the necessary support by the education department to overcome practical difficulties. Two teachers' training colleges have shown interest.

Psychologist The local educational psychologist is spontaneously interested and involved in the playgroup as far as his commitments allow. Given more time and a widening of his terms of reference his contribution both in assessing the children's educational potential and in maintaining useful contact with them and their teachers when they reach school could be of enormous value.

Social workers Those in the local authority service have not shown interest so far, but perhaps when the new department of social services is fully functional more contact may be possible. Psychiatric social workers in local child guidance clinics have always been particularly responsive and supportive, one giving a weekly session as a volunteer to hold the vitally important mothers' discussion group. Medical social workers appear to be mainly concerned with the children while they are in hospital.

Local authority reactions

Health department This was the first to be approached through the medical officers of health and the health visitors but has remained uninvolved. Only a few health visitors have referred children (six out of the 34 children who had used the group up to December, 1971). Nor has it proved possible to obtain from the medical officer of health information on the geographical distribution of the children so that the work could be intelligently developed in the area. This reaction has had a very significant effect in that the project has perforce developed on entirely non-medical lines, concentrating on the educational and social needs of the children which are rarely given parity with the medical needs. It has therefore been possible to demonstrate the case of working with the children in a normal environment to visiting teachers and playgroup leaders who then realise they could do likewise.

Education department This department has responded practically by paying the salary of a teacher to attend the playgroup, but though this is appreciated it has not, as originally hoped, led to the development of a working relationship in which plans for the children's education could be discussed informally with administrators, parents, teachers, psychologists, and playgroup staff so that new approaches to the problems involved might be explored. An attempt was made by the project director a year ago to initiate such discussions when the playgroup staff and parents felt a group placement of three children in one suitable school might be easier on the children and parents and administratively simpler and more effective than the current procedure. However, the department preferred to continue to place in its traditional way – one child per school – relying solely on the opinion of a medical officer of health. This attitude was supported by a visiting inspector from the Department of Education and Science who made clear to the parents that each should negotiate independently and directly with the education officer about his child's education, and abide by his decision.

Nine of the children are now attending normal schools, with welfare aides for part of the day and transport where necessary. Wherever possible friendly contact is made and maintained with the individual schools both before and after placement.

Future

Although the project has managed to exist precariously for two years longer than originally anticipated it has now become clear that if the service is to continue indefinitely on a firm basis the playgroups must be given an organisation which can be managed comfortably and with less financial strain by a small parent's group.

By July this year the overall direction of the project will cease with the withdrawal of the director, and the playgroups will be consolidated each with a small paid staff, supported by a volunteer group, the whole responsible to a parents' committee. The part-time secretary will remain, and the committee hopes to appoint a part-time social worker through the scheme organised by the National Association for Spina Bifida and Hydrocephalus. In this way the committee can keep the groups going for the younger children and also provide a service for other members of their Association with different needs.

This project has attempted, in however limited and inadequate a manner, to respond to needs already observed and commented upon in recent reports (see references), particularly *Living with Handicap*. These agree in stressing the fact that all handicapped children need pre-school education even more than non-handicapped children, that their parents need support on all levels, and that there should be a drastic reappraisal of assessment procedures in which medical opinion should form part only of a total process in which equal weight is given to the opinions of parents, psychologists, social workers, teachers, playgroup leaders and anyone else who knows and understands the children. Indeed according to *Living with Handicap* (chapter 3) some local authorities are already beginning to dispense with formal procedures of ascertainment of handicap, which many parents find so irritating and even distressing.

Findings

The findings of this project might be summarised as follows:

1. That the children respond physically, intellectually, and emotionally to the stimulus offered by the playgroup.

2. That parents show that they can accept help if it is offered freely and as part of a total plan for the children to which they can actively contribute.

3. That the community can accept the children when they are known personally, and this knowledge can begin to loosen prejudice based on ignorance or fear, so that the children are recognised primarily as children, secondarily as disabled.

4. That the groups could cater for a much wider range of handicaps, judging by the response of the few children included who were suffering from other conditions such as severe heart trouble or dislocated hips.

5. That a social service can be effectively organised in a practical and democratic way with each person concerned contributing to the whole,

so that decisions arise naturally from interaction and discussion rather than being mechanically formed and autocratically imposed.

Potential

These findings however only indicate what could be further explored, initially perhaps in the following ways:

1. By extending the terms of reference to include children with other disabilities.

2. By developing downwards into studying more closely the play needs of the birth to three age group, and upwards into the possibilities of offering a continuing service to the children after they have gone to school.

3. By making assessments over a period of observation to determine the educational needs of each child, whether for normal or special school, and by developing imaginative and realistic ways of working with teachers, parents and children throughout their schooldays. The careful concern thus established could accompany each child into the areas of further education, training and employment, open or sheltered.

4. By considering the contribution adult disabled people might make towards helping the children.

5. By encouraging and implementing the philosophy of planning dynamically rather than statically, thus allowing the social services to grow to fit the needs rather than struggle to fit the needs into the services.

Suggestions for future development

For this a strong organization would be needed, such as the National Pre-school Playgroups Association, working closely with the departments of social service and education in one of the more progressive local authorities. The former, still with a strong growth potential of its own, could comfortably incorporate a smaller developing organism and as it is concerned with developing playgroups for all kinds of children, integration of those with varying kinds of disabilities could follow naturally. The latter could use to the full the opportunities and powers afforded to them under recent legislation for experimental work, for training personnel, and for developing closer liaison with voluntary services.

Such a collaboration between voluntary and statutory bodies might have among its aims:

1. The establishment of a centre to serve as a base for all kinds of community involvement focused on the children and their parents in the pre-school years, and also to provide out-of-school activities in the form of a club or association to help the children explore their environment further, and to which they could invite their non-handicapped friends.

2. The provision of a service for the many people who wish to set up similar playgroups, or learn about integrating handicapped children into existing groups. This could incorporate practical experience in a playgroup and short training courses directed towards showing people how to make the best use of local facilities and personnel, rather than imposing a rigid pattern of action. On their return to their own areas the centre staff could visit if requested to give moral and practical support till the new groups were firmly established and in turn able to act as new centres themselves.

Conclusion

This undertaking has always had the quality of adventure, starting on its voyage of exploration from where it happened to be, and allowing the gaiety, courage and resilience of the children and their parents to magnetise for its support all the positive elements freely available in the community. It asks no great thing, no complicated structure, no elaborate gifts, simply a willing suspension of preconceived ideas and an ability to respond with sincerity and imagination to an observed need.

Action of this kind, while it appeals unerringly to the stifled romanticism in many people, can seem foolish or superfluous to the architects and operators of the statutory services, so that the adventure, like the children, has also been handicapped by its condition. Like them too it has clung to life against heavy odds, surviving equally the inward assaults of doubt and despondency and the outward constriction of circumstances, and it is symbolic that it was a parents' association which rescued it at the point of death in 1969 and has sustained it since. But it is now old enough to venture from the immediate family circle into the larger world of school and community where it can develop its full potential in association with people of like mind but with more knowledge and experience of this developing area of concern for all handicapped people.

REFERENCES

Handicapped Children & their Families. Reports to the Carnegie UK Trust on the problems of 600 Handicapped Children and their Families, 1964, Comely Park House, Dunfermline, Carnegie UK Trust.

Children and their Primary Schools (Plowden), 1967, Report of the Central Advisory Council for Education (England), London, HMSO.

Report of the Committee on Local Authority and Allied Personal Social Services (Seebohm), 1968, London, HMSO.

HEWITT, SHEILA and NEWSON, J. & E., 1970, *The Family and the Handicapped Child. A study of cerebral palsied children in their houses,* London, Allen & Unwin.

YOUNGHUSBAND, E. *et al.* (eds.), *Living with Handicap. Report of a working party on children with special needs,* 1970, London, National Bureau for Co-operation in Child Care.

56. Setting up a good neighbour scheme *

NATIONAL COUNCIL OF SOCIAL SERVICE

How to begin
The schemes most likely to succeed are those which have arisen naturally in response to community need: this need provides an in-built motive force, without which the project may well fail. An essential first stage, therefore, is a close and objective examination of what, if any, are the needs of the community and how these can most realistically be met.

Setting up any form of good neighbour scheme involves an immense amount of work. Unless there is someone available who can give a great deal of time and thought to the scheme, it is better not to embark upon it.

Administrative backing to this system includes a central organiser, responsible to an executive committee, and supported in some cases by area organisers. The central organiser is responsible for liaising with the professional social services, for organising the provision of the help reservoir and street wardens, for maintaining a recording system and for maintaining a supply of administrative and publicity material. In large schemes some of these functions will be delegated.

A diagram of the structure as outlined above is given below:

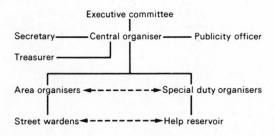

Note: *This is a formal pattern; in practice, schemes will evolve their own structures, and some will not have as many officers as this.*

First steps
An ad hoc consultative committee or group should be set up to examine the needs, objectives, type of scheme and how it might be operated.

A central organiser should be appointed as early as possible. The organiser's personality and ability will be of great importance to the scheme.

A sponsoring body should be found. This may be a council of churches, the local council of social service, the social services department, a community association or any other recognised body. It may be such a body which has initiated the project, but in any case some moral support and money will be needed to launch such a scheme so it is best sponsored by a body with some authority and standing in the area.

All local voluntary organisations and the social services department should be approached for discussions on the support services needed in the community. In this way duplication of work can be avoided, and these discussions may also be a valuable means of collecting information.

Is it necessary to set up a new organisation?
The consultative committee's examination may show that all the services which it had been hoped to provide through a good neighbour scheme

*From National Council of Social Service, (1972) *Time to Care: a handbook on good neighbour schemes*, London, pp. 7—15

could in fact be better provided by the existing organisations, possibly with the help of more volunteers. In these circumstances it might be more valuable to establish a volunteer bureau rather than a good neighbour scheme.

The main function of volunteer bureaux is to collect information about the needs and opportunities for voluntary services in their areas, to provide a centre to which volunteers may come for advice and information and to refer them to appropriate organisations in which their help can be used. A promotional leaflet is available for organisations in this field from the Community Work Division of the National Council of Social Service.

First public meeting
Assuming that the consultative committee feels that a good neighbour scheme is necessary, a public meeting should be called. Personal invitations should be sent to representatives of all the local welfare agencies, both statutory and voluntary; ward councillors; local press and radio; the police, clergy, probation service, district nurses, doctors, school teachers and any individuals who are known or likely to be interested.

At the meeting an outline of the proposed scheme should be given by a member of the consultative committee or the organiser-designate. This would be followed by a general discussion, and then by an invitation to those present to indicate their approval in principle of the action proposed.

A steering committee should then be set up and honorary officers elected. Its terms of reference should be to formalise the work and consultation which will already have taken place, by working out a detailed scheme to suit the area, discovering the financial requirements, sounding out local support and drafting a constitution.

General organisation of schemes
Where a large-scale scheme is planned it is advisable:

to start with a pilot scheme project covering a small area only;

to divide the district into manageable areas, each with its own street wardens and area organiser, responsible to the central organiser, who will act as co-ordinator and adviser.

A smaller scheme may have street wardens and a central organiser only.

The role of a street warden: knowing the people in his street, or part of a street; welcoming newcomers and informing them of the scheme; being ready at all times to match need with appropriate help.

Allocation of duties
Policy will have to be established on this; in the main, schemes fall into two patterns; either all calls are referred to and dealt with by the central or area organiser; or most calls are dealt with by street wardens and only passed on to central or area organisers if no helper can be found locally or if the case is beyond the competence of a street warden.

Where cases are to be passed on to the statutory welfare authorities or other voluntary agencies, this should be done through the central or area organiser. Only in this way can a clear line of communication be established, and from this exchange of information the organisers will soon learn what facts it is important to know and what questions to ask.

In a large scheme a system of delegation may have to be developed; in any case there should be a very close co-operation between a good neighbour scheme, the other voluntary agencies and the social services department.

Recruiting volunteers
Church congregations and existing local organisations may provide an effective reservoir of voluntary help, but recruitment could be developed by the distribution of questionnaires and explanatory leaflets to all whom it is felt might be able to help, including those at the first public meeting. Subsequently, recruitment may well become self-generative.

Regenerative area and street wardens: From these sources it should be possible to find street wardens and potential area organisers.

The training of volunteers will provide a necessary and useful supplement to these methods of recruitment by identifying the talents of volunteers.

General administration
Card indexes or files will be required, cross-referenced under the following headings:

skills and services offered: giving names of volunteers;

streets: volunteers available in each street;

names of volunteers: giving full details of services offered.

A large scheme may require the cards to be printed with headings indicating essential information, but it would be as well not to embark on printing until a pilot scheme has been completed.

A record of cases handled (cards or files) will be needed for the following reasons:

to have on record a measure of the success of methods used in previous cases;

to prevent abuse of the scheme;

to provide statistics to substantiate a case for the scheme, when applying for grant-aid, etc.

Files may be required for general information circulated by local authority and any correspondence with other organisations.

Final stages: public meeting

The final 'blast-off' will be a public meeting to which should be invited:

all who were invited to the first meeting; and

all who have volunteered to help.

The programme should include:

a description of the scheme by a member of the steering committee or the organiser-designate;

an explanation of how the scheme will fit in with the statutory and existing voluntary services, by the director of social services or his deputy; and

a description of an existing scheme elsewhere by its organiser.

Preparation for this meeting should include publicity:

the display of posters about two weeks before the date of the meeting;

the distribution of leaflets and personal invitations about seven to ten days before the meeting;

publicity in local press: a letter to the editor announcing the meeting and its intention may be an acceptable way of getting prior publicity, especially if advertising space is taken as well. The editor should also be invited to the meeting and sent a report of it;

publicity through local radio, parish magazines, sermons, newsletters, stall in local market.

The scheme is then launched and should be in operation the next day.

General comments

a. Be prepared for, but do not expect, immediate calls or dramatic results. It may take time for people to realise how the scheme can help them.

b. Close contact should be kept with welfare officers: they may ask for help with cases, and the scheme will also sometimes have to refer cases to them. This is important in order to ensure that the local authority is not already involved in a case, or to bring pressure to bear on the authority to take action. It is also necessary to watch against unscrupulous individuals who play off one agency against another.

c. Do not hesitate to ask for professional advice and help. It is better to discuss a doubtful case with the local social service office than to struggle on alone and fail to take advantage of other services available.

d. The central organiser should ensure that no part of the scheme or individual within the scheme, is overburdened. Individuals who abuse the services offered should be refused help, or passed on to the local authority. Equally a proper balance should be established between the statutory and voluntary services to prevent the scheme being overused by either.

e. The volunteer should resist the temptation to regard himself as an unpaid amateur 'ombudsman'. Mutual confidence must at all times be maintained between voluntary and statutory workers. Complaints should be heard without comment until facts have been checked, and social workers should be ready to listen with patience and understanding.

f. The giving of aid should be seen in terms of service rather than money.

g. At all costs avoid creating separate categories for the helpers and the helped. Those who have been helped one week may become the helpers the following week. No one should lose his self-respect from receiving aid or become patronising from giving it.

Evaluation

An essential part of any scheme must be an assessment of its effectiveness: it is only by an on-going and integrated evaluation system that the value of any project may be established and unnecessary work avoided.

In a small scheme this may be done on the informal basis that each individual will be sufficiently aware of the situation for complications to come to light spontaneously and in day-to-day discussion; but even under these conditions, and more particularly in a larger and less personal environment there are various questions which must be asked regularly in order to avoid inefficiency and ineffectiveness:

a. Does the method of recording information allow for all relevant details to be noted, while not recording useless information?

b. Are street wardens and volunteers given adequate opportunity to report back, and to discuss particular cases, methods of approach, etc.?

c. Is a high standard of confidentiality kept, so that individual privacy is protected?

d. Is the briefing and training of volunteers satisfactory?

e. Is the method of allocation of duties to volunteers satisfactory, and is a constant check kept on the suitability of volunteers to the tasks they are undertaking?

f. Is publicity as wide and as effective as it could be?

g. Does the communications network function efficiently?

h. Are relations with other organisations satisfactory?

i. Are the needs of the community being met in every respect? If not, is this through a fault in policy, in planning or in method of administration? It might be helpful to re-examine the papers of the first meeting, on a regular basis, so that organisers are reminded of the needs which were identified in the first stages.

Answers to the above questions should be obtained by asking all interested people, helped as well as helpers.

APPENDIX 1
Surveys: simple fact-finding

In most cases informal consultations with existing organisations operating in the neighbourhood will provide all the information that is required.

However, where there is doubt about the extent of the services required in the community, a simple approach to voluntary organisations and the social services may be undertaken to discover:

(i) the services already provided by each organisation;

(ii) the additional services needed; and

(iii) the best method of providing these services: either—existing organisations may be strengthened; or—a youth club, old people's club or other specific activity may be set up; or—a good neighbour scheme may be set up.

Door-to-door surveys: it is sometimes felt necessary to approach local people to see whether they would use the services offered. In planning a survey of this kind, the following should be remembered:

(i) questions need to be carefully worded so that the answer is 'yes' or 'no'. They should be as few as possible.

(ii) volunteer canvassers must be well briefed so that they understand the purpose of the questions.

(iii) it is often easier to get down name, address and simple answers on a note pad than to carry around a sheaf of questionnaires.

(iv) the public are more likely to be co-operative if warned in advance, through the press, of the impending survey. Those who do not wish to take part should not be pressed to do so.

(v) having recruited volunteers, the survey should be conducted quickly, in a period not longer than three weeks, while interest is high.

(vi) the patience of the public is limited: a survey should not be carried out unless there is a real need.

This method inevitably gives an incomplete result. People may not be aware of the needs they are likely to have or may be only concerned with their own short-term crises. Long established experts and professional workers have a broader view and can assess the recurring needs of the community more accurately.

APPENDICES

57. The Chronically Sick and Disabled Persons' Act, 1970

18 AND 19 ELIZ. II CAP. 44

An Act to make further provision with respect to the welfare of chronically sick and disabled persons; and for connected purposes. [29th May 1970]

Be it enacted by the Queen's most Excellent Majesty, by and with the advice and consent of the Lords Spiritual and Temporal, and Commons, in this present Parliament assembled, and by the authority of the same, as follows:—

Welfare and housing

1. (1) It shall be the duty of every local authority having functions under section 29 of the National Assistance Act 1948 to inform themselves of the number of persons to whom that section applies within their area and of the need for the making by the authority of arrangements under that section for such persons.

Information as to need for and existence of welfare services.
1948 c. 29.

483

(2) Every such local authority

(*a*) shall cause to be published from time to time at such times and in such manner as they consider appropriate general information as to the services provided under arrangements made by the authority under the said section 29 which are for the time being available in their area; and

(*b*) shall ensure that any such person as aforesaid who uses any of those services is informed of any other of those services which in the opinion of the authority is relevant to his needs.

(3) This section shall come into operation on such date as the Secretary of State may by order made by statutory instrument appoint.

Provision of welfare services. 1948 c. 29.

2. (1) Where a local authority having functions under section 29 of the National Assistance Act 1948 are satisfied in the case of any person to whom that section applies who is ordinarily resident in their area that it is necessary in order to meet the needs of that person for that authority to make arrangements for all or any of the following matters, namely—

(*a*) the provision of practical assistance for that person in his home;

(*b*) the provision for that person of, or assistance to that person in obtaining, wireless, television, library or similar recreational facilities;

(*c*) the provision for that person of lectures, games, outings or other recreational facilities outside his home or assistance to that person in taking advantage of educational facilities available to him;

(*d*) the provision for that person of facilities for, or assistance in, travelling to and from his home for the purpose of participating in any services provided under arrangements made by the authority under the said section 29 or, with the approval of the authority, in any services provided otherwise than as aforesaid which are similar to services which could be provided under such arrangements;

(*e*) the provision of assistance for that person in arranging for the carrying out of any works of adaptation in his home or the provision of any additional facilities designed to secure his greater safety, comfort or convenience;

(*f*) facilitating the taking of holidays by that person, whether at holiday homes or otherwise and whether provided under arrangements made by the authority or otherwise;

(*g*) the provision of meals for that person whether in his home or elsewhere;

(*h*) the provision for that person of, or assistance to that person in obtaining, a telephone and any special equipment necessary to enable him to use a telephone,

then, notwithstanding anything in any scheme made by the authority under the said section 29, but subject to the provisions of section 35(2) of that Act (which requires local authorities to exercise their functions under Part III of that Act under the general guidance of the Secretary of State and in accordance with the provisions of any regulations made for the purpose), it shall be the duty of that authority to make those arrangements in exercise of their functions under the said section 29.

(2) Without prejudice to the said section 35(2), subsection (3) of the said section 29 (which requires any arrangements made by a local authority under that section to be carried into effect in accordance with a scheme made thereunder) shall not apply—

(*a*) to any arrangements made in pursuance of subsection (1) of this section; or

(*b*) in the case of a local authority who have made such a scheme, to any arrangements made by virtue of subsection (1) of the said section 29 in addition to those required or authorised by the scheme which are so made with the approval of the Secretary of State.

Duties of housing authorities. 1957 c. 56.

3. (1) Every local authority for the purposes of Part V of the Housing Act 1957 in discharging their duty under section 91 of that Act to consider housing conditions in their district and the needs of the district with respect to the provision of further housing accommodation shall have regard to the special needs of chronically sick or disabled

persons; and any proposals prepared and submitted to the Minister by the authority under that section for the provision of new houses shall distinguish any houses which the authority propose to provide which make special provision for the needs of such persons.

(2) In the application of this section to Scotland for the words 'Part,V of the Housing Act 1957', '91' and 'Minister' there shall be substituted respectively the words 'Part VII of the Housing (Scotland) Act 1966','137' and 'Secretary of State'. *1966 c. 49.*

Premises open to public

4. (1) Any person undertaking the provision of any building or premises to which the public are to be admitted, whether on payment or otherwise, shall, in the means of access both to and within the building or premises, and in the parking facilities and sanitary conveniences to be available (if any), make provision, in so far as it is in the circumstances both practicable and reasonable, for the needs of members of the public visiting the building or premises who are disabled. *Access to, and facilities at, premises open to the public.*

(2) This section shall not apply to any building or premises intended for purposes mentioned in subsection (2) of section 8 of this Act.

5. (1) Where any local authority undertake the provision of a public sanitary convenience, it shall be the duty of the authority, in doing so, to make provision, in so far as it is in the circumstances both practicable and reasonable, for the needs of disabled persons. *Provision of public sanitary conveniences.*

(2) Any local authority which in any public sanitary convenience provided by them make or have made provision for the needs of disabled persons shall take such steps as may be reasonable, by sign-posts or similar notices, to indicate the whereabouts of the convenience.

(3) In this section 'local authority' means a local authority within the meaning of the Local Government Act 1933 or the Local Government (Scotland) Act 1947 and any joint board or joint committee of which all the constituent authorities are local authorities within the meaning of either of those Acts. *1933 c. 51.*
1947 c. 43.

6. (1) Any person upon whom a notice is served with respect to any premises under section 89 of the Public Health Act 1936 (which empowers local authorities by notice to make requirements as to the provision and maintenance of sanitary conveniences for the use of persons frequenting certain premises used for the accommodation, refreshment or entertainment of members of the public) shall in complying with that notice make provision, in so far as it is in the circumstances both practicable and reasonable, for the needs of persons frequenting those premises who are disabled. *Provision of sanitary conveniences at certain premises open to the public.*
1936 c. 49.

(2) The owner of a building, who has been ordered under section 11(4) of the Building (Scotland) Act 1959 to make the building conform to a provision of building standards regulations made under section 3 of that Act requiring the provision of suitable and sufficient sanitary conveniences therein, shall in complying with that order make provision, in so far as it is in the circumstances both practicable and reasonable, for the needs of persons frequenting that building who are disabled. *1959 c. 24.*

7. (1) Where any provision required by or under section 4, 5 or 6 of this Act is made at a building in compliance with that section, a notice or sign indicating that provision is made for the disabled shall be displayed outside the building or so as to be visible from outside it. *Signs at buildings complying with ss. 4–6.*

(2) This section applies to a sanitary convenience provided elsewhere than in a building, and not itself being a building, as it applies to a building.

University and school buildings *Access to, and facilities at, university and school buildings.*

8. (1) Any person undertaking the provision of a building intended for purposes mentioned in subsection (2) below shall, in the means of access both to and within the

building, and in the parking facilities and sanitary conveniences to be available (if any), make provision, in so far as it is in the circumstances both practicable and reasonable, for the needs of persons using the building who are disabled.

(2) The purposes referred to in subsection (1) above are the purposes of any of the following: —

(a) universities, university colleges and colleges, schools and halls of universities;

1944 c. 31.

(b) schools within the meaning of the Education Act 1944, teacher training colleges maintained by local education authorities in England or Wales and other institutions providing further education pursuant to a scheme under section 42 of that Act;

1962 c. 37.

(c) educational establishments within the meaning of the Education (Scotland) Act 1962.

Advisory committees, etc.

Central advisory committee on war pensions. 1921 c. 49.

9. (1) The Secretary of State shall ensure that the central advisory committee constituted under section 3 of the War Pensions Act 1921 includes the chairmen of not less than twelve of the committees established by schemes under section 1 of that Act and includes at least one war disabled pensioner, and shall cause that central advisory committee to be convened at least once in every year.

(2) This section extends to Northern Ireland.

Housing Advisory Committees. 1957 c. 56. 1966 c. 49

10. In the appointment of persons to be members of the Central Housing Advisory Committee set up under section 143 of the Housing Act 1957 or of the Scottish Housing Advisory Committee set up under section 167 of the Housing (Scotland) Act 1966, regard shall be had to the desirability of that Committee's including one or more persons with knowledge of the problems involved in housing the chronically sick and disabled and to the person or persons with that knowledge being or including a chronically sick or disabled person or persons.

National Insurance Advisory Committee.

11. The National Insurance Advisory Committee shall include at least one person with experience of work among and of the needs of the chronically sick and disabled and in selecting any such person regard shall be had to the desirability of having a chronically sick or disabled person.

Industrial Injuries Advisory Council.

12. The Industrial Injuries Advisory Council shall include at least one person with experience of work among and of the needs of the chronically sick and disabled and in selecting any such person regard shall be had to the desirability of having a chronically sick or disabled person.

Youth employment service.

13. (1) Without prejudice to any other arrangements that may be made by the Secretary of State, the Central Youth Employment Executive shall include at least one person with special responsibility for the employment of young disabled persons.

1948 c. 46.

(2) In the appointment of persons to be members of any of the bodies constituted in pursuance of section 8(1) of the Employment and Training Act 1948 (that is to say, the National Youth Employment Council and the Advisory Committees on Youth Employment for Scotland and Wales respectively) regard shall be had to the desirability of the body in question including one or more persons with experience of work among, and the special needs of, young disabled persons and to the person or persons with that experience being or including a disabled person or persons.

Miscellaneous advisory committees.

14. (1) In the appointment of persons to be members of any of the following advisory committees or councils, that is to say, the Transport Users' Consultative Committees, the Gas Consultative Councils, the Electricity Consultative Councils, the Post Office Users' Councils and the Domestic Coal Consumers' Council, regard shall be had to the desirability of the committee or council in question including one or more persons with

experience of work among, and the special needs of, disabled persons and to the person or persons with that experience being or including a disabled person or persons.

(2) In this section the reference to the Post Office Users' Councils is a reference to the Councils established under section 14 of the Post Office Act 1969, and in relation to those Councils this section shall extend to Northern Ireland.

1969 c. 48.

15. Where a local authority within the meaning of the Local Government Act 1933 or the Local Government (Scotland) Act 1947 appoint a committee of the authority under any enactment, and the members of the committee include or may include persons who are not members of the authority, then in considering the appointment to the committee of such persons regard shall be had, if the committee is concerned with matters in which the chronically sick or disabled have special needs, to the desirability of appointing to the committee persons with experience of work among and of the needs of the chronically sick and disabled, and to the person or persons with that experience being or including a chronically sick or disabled person or persons.

Co-option of chronically sick or disabled persons to local authority committees. 1933 c. 51. 1947 c. 43.

16. The duties of the national advisory council established under section 17(1)(*a*) of the Disabled Persons (Employment) Act 1944 shall include in particular the duty of giving to the Secretary of State such advice as appears to the council to be necessary on the training of persons concerned with—
(*a*) placing disabled persons in employment; or
(*b*) training disabled persons for employment.

Duties of national advisory council under Disabled Persons (Employment) Act 1944. 1944 c. 10.

Provisions with respect to persons under 65

17. (1) Every Board constituted under section 11 of the National Health Service Act 1946 (that is to say, every Regional Hospital Board and every Board of Governors of a teaching hospital) and every Regional Hospital Board constituted under section 11 of the National Health Service (Scotland) Act 1947 shall use their best endeavours to secure that, so far as practicable, in any hospital for which they are responsible a person who is suffering from a condition of chronic illness or disability and who—
(*a*) is in the hospital for the purpose of long-term care for that condition; or
(*b*) normally resides elsewhere but is being cared for in the hospital because—
(i) that condition is such as to preclude him from residing elsewhere without the assistance of some other person; and
(ii) such assistance is for the time being not available,
is not cared for in the hospital as an in-patient in any part of the hospital which is normally used wholly or mainly for the care of elderly persons, unless he is himself an elderly person.

Separation of younger from older patients. 1946 c. 81.

1947 c. 27

(2) Each such Board as aforesaid shall provide the Secretry of State in such form and at such times as he may direct with such information as he may from time to time require as to any persons to whom subsection (1) of this section applied who, not being elderly persons, have been cared for in any hospital for which that Board are responsible in such a part of the hospital as is mentioned in that subsection; and the Secretary of State shall in each year lay before each House of Parliament such statement in such form as he considers appropriate of the information obtained by him under this subsection.

(3) In this section 'elderly person' means a person who is aged sixty-five or more or is suffering from the effects of premature ageing.

Information
as to accom-
modation
of younger
with older
persons under
Part III of
National
Asistance
Act 1948.
1948 c. 29.

1968 c. 49.
1960 c. 61

18. (1) The Secretary of State shall take steps to obtain from local authorities having functions under Part III of the National Assistance Act 1948 information as to the number of persons under the age of 65 appearing to the local authority in question to be persons to whom section 29 of that Act applies for whom residential accommodation is from time to time provided under section 21(1)(*a*) or 26(1)(*a*) of that Act at any premises in a part of those premises in which such accommodation is so provided for persons over that age.

(2) The Secretary of State shall take steps to obtain from local authorities having functions under the Social Work (Scotland) Act 1968 information as to the number of persons under the age of 65 who suffer from illness or mental disorder within the meaning of section 6 of the Mental Health (Scotland) Act 1960 or are substantially handicapped by any deformity or disability and for whom residential accommodation is from time to time provided under section 59 of the said Act of 1968 at any premises in a part of those premises in which such accommodation is so provided for persons over that age.

(3) Every local authority referred to in this section shall provide the Secretary of State in such form and at such times as he may direct with such information as he may from time to time require for the purpose of this section; and the Secretary of State shall in each year lay before each House of Parliament such statement in such form as he considers appropriate of the information obtained by him under this section.

Provision of
information
relating to
chiropody
services.
1968 c. 46.
1947 c. 27.

19. Every local health authority empowered to provide chiropody services under section 12 of the Health Services and Public Health Act 1968, or under section 27 of the National Health Service (Scotland) Act 1947, shall provide the Secretary of State in such form and at such times as he may direct with information as to the extent to which those services are available and used for the benefit of disabled persons under the age of sixty-five.

Miscellaneous provisions

Use of invalid
carriages on
highways.

20. (1) In the case of vehicle which is an invalid carriage complying with the prescribed requirements and which is being used in accordance with the prescribed conditions—

(*a*) no statutory provision prohibiting or restricting the use of footways shall prohibit or restrict the use of that vehicle on a footway;

1960 c. 16.
1962 c. 59.
1967 c. 76.
1967 c. 30.
1957 c. 51.

(*b*) if the vehicle is mechanically propelled, it shall be treated for the purposes of the Road Traffic Act 1960, the Road Traffic Act 1962, the Road Traffic Regulation Act 1967 and Part I of the Road Safety Act 1967 as not being a motor vehicle; and

(*c*) whether or not the vehicle is mechanically propelled, it shall be exempted from the requirements of the Road Transport Lighting Act 1957.

(2) In this section—

1959 c. 25.

'footway' means a way which is a footway, footpath or bridleway within the meaning of the Highways Act 1959; and its application to Scotland means a way over which the public has a right of passage on foot only or a bridleway within the meaning of

1967 c. 86.

section 47 of the Countryside (Scotland) Act 1967;

'invalid carriage' means a vehicle, whether mechanically propelled or not, constructed or adapted for use for the carriage of one person, being a person suffering from some physical defect or disability;

'prescribed' means prescribed by regulations made by the Minister of Transport;

'statutory provision' means a provision contained in, or having effect under, any enactment.

(3) Any regulations made under this section shall be made by statutory instrument, may make different provision for different circumstances and shall be subject to annulment in pursuance of a resolution of either House of Parliament.

21. (1) There shall be a badge of a prescribed form to be issued by local authorities for motor vehicles driven by, or used for the carriage of, disabled persons; and—

(*a*) subject to the provisions of this section, the badge so issued for any vehicle or vehicles may be displayed on it or on any of them either inside or outside the area of the issuing authority; and

(*b*) any power under section 84C of the Road Traffic Regulation Act 1967 (which was inserted by the Transport Act 1968) to make regulations requiring that orders under the Act shall include exemptions shall be taken to extend to requiring that an exemption given with references to badges issued by one authority shall be given also with reference to badges issued by other authorities.

(2) A badge may be issued to a disabled person of any prescribed description resident in the area of the issuing authority for one or more vehicles which he drives and, if so issued, may be displayed on it or any of them at times when he is the driver.

(3) In such cases as may be prescribed, a badge may be issued to a disabled person of any prescribed description so resident for one or more vehicles used by him as a passenger and, if so issued, may be displayed on it or any of them at times when the vehicle is being used to carry him.

A badge may be issued to the same person both under this subsection and under subsection (2) above.

(4) A badge may be issued to an institution concerned with the care of the disabled for any motor vehicle or, as the case may be, for each motor vehicle kept in the area of the issuing authority and used by or on behalf of the institution to carry disabled persons of any prescribed description; and any badge so issued may be displayed on the vehicle for which it is issued at times when the vehicle is being so used.

(5) A local authority shall maintain a register showing the holders of badges issued by the authority under this section, and the vehicle or vehicles for which each of the badges is held; and in the case of badges issued to disabled persons the register shall show whether they were, for any motor vehicle, issued under subsection (2) or under subsection (3) or both.

(6) A badge issued under this section shall remain the property of the issuing authority, shall be issued for such period as may be prescribed, and shall be returned to the issuing authority in such circumstances as may be prescribed.

(7) Anything which is under this section to be prescribed shall be prescribed by regulations made by the Minister of Transport and Secretary of State by statutory instrument, which shall be subject to annulment in pursuance of a resolution of either House of Parliament; and regulations so made may make provision—

(*a*) as to the cases in which authorities may refuse to issue badges, and as to the fee (if any) which an authority may charge for the issue or re-issue of a badge; and

(*b*) as to the continuing validity or effect of badges issued before the coming into force of this section in pursuance of any scheme having effect under section 29 of the National Asistance Act 1948 or any similar scheme having effect in Scotland; and

(*c*) as to any transitional matters, and in particular the application to badges issued under this section of orders made before it comes into force and operating with reference to any such badges as are referred to in paragraph (*b*) above (being orders made, or having effect as if made, under the Road Traffic Regulation Act 1967).

(8) The local authorities for purposes of this section shall be the common council of the City of London, the council of a county or county borough in England or Wales or of a London borough and the council of a county or large burgh in Scotland; and in this section 'motor vehicle' has the same meaning as in the Road Traffic Regulation Act 1967.

(9) This section shall come into operation on such date as the Minister of Transport and Secretary of State may by order made by statutory instrument appoint.

Badges for
display on
motor vehicles
used by dis-
abled persons

1967 c. 76.
1968 c. 73.

1948 c. 29.

1967 c. 76.

Annual
report on
research and
development
work.

22. The Secretary of State shall as respects each year lay before Parliament a report on the progress made during that year in research and development work carried out by or on behalf of any Minister of the Crown in relation to equipment that might increase the range of activities and independence or well-being of disabled persons, and in particular such equipment that might improve the indoor and outdoor mobility of such persons.

War pensions
appeals.
1943 c. 39.

23. (1) The Pensions Appeal Tribunals Act 1943 shall have effect with the amendments specified in the subsequent provisions of this section.

(2) In section 5

(*a*) so much of subsection (1) as prevents the making of an appeal from an interim assessment of the degree of a disablement before the expiration of two years from the first notification of the making of an interim assessment (that is to say, the words from 'if' to 'subsection' where first occurring, and the words 'in force at the expiration of the said period of two years') is hereby repealed except in relation to a claim in the case of which the said first notification was given before the commencement of this Act;

(*b*) in the second paragraph of subsection (1) (which defines 'interim assessment' for the purposes of that subsection), for the words 'this subsection' there shall be substituted the words 'this section'.

(*c*) in subsection (2) (which provides for an appeal to a tribunal from a Ministerial decision or assessment purporting to be a final settlement of a claim) at the end there shall be added the words 'and if the Tribunal so set aside the Minister's decision or assessment they may, if they think fit, make such interim assessment of the degree of nature of the disablement, to be in force until such date not later than two years after the making of the Tribunal's assessment, as they think proper';

(*d*) subsection (3) (which makes provision as to the coming into operation of section 5) is hereby repealed.

(3) In section 6, after subsection (2) there shall be inserted the following subsection—

'(2A) Where, in the case of such a claim as is referred to in section 1, 2, 3 or 4 of this Act—

(*a*) an appeal has been made under that section to the Tribunal and that appeal has been decided (whether with or without an appeal under subsection (2) of this section from the Tribunal's decision); but

(*b*) subsequently, on an application for the purpose made (in like manner as an application for leave to appeal under the said subsection (2)) jointly by the appellant and the Minister, it appears to the appropriate authority (that is to say, the person to whom under rules made under the Schedule to this Act any application for directions on any matter arising in connection with the appeal to the Tribunal fell to be made) to be proper so to do—

(i) by reason of the availability of additional evidence; or

(ii) (except where an appeal from the Tribunal's decision has been made under the said subsection (2)), on the ground of the Tribunal's decision being erroneous in point of law,

the appropriate authority may, if he thinks fit, direct that the decision of the appeal to the Tribunal be treated as set aside and the appeal from the Minister's decision be heard again by the Tribunal'.

(4) In subsection (3) of section 6 (under which, subject to subsection (2) of that section, a tribunal's decision is final and conclusive) for the words 'subject to the last foregoing subsection' there shall be substituted the words 'subject to subsections (2) and (2A) of this section'.

S.I 1968/1699.

(5) In consequence of the Secretary of State for Social Services Order 1968, in section 12(1), for the definition of 'the Minister' there shall be substituted the following:—

' "the Minister" means the Secretary of State for Social Services'.

(6) This section extends to Northern Ireland.

24. The Secretary of State shall collate and present evidence to the Medical Research Council on the need for an institute for hearing research, such institute to have the general function of co-ordinating and promoting research on hearing and assistance to the deaf and hard of hearing.

Institute of hearing research.

25. (1) It shall be the duty of every local education authority to provide the Secretary of State at such times as he may direct with information on the provision made by that local education authority of special educational facilities for children who suffer the dual handicap of blindness and deafness.

Special educational treatment for the deaf-blind.

(2) The arrangements made by a local education authority for the special educational treatment of the deaf-blind shall, so far as is practicable, provide for the giving of such education in any school maintained or assisted by the local education authority.

(3) In the application of this section to Scotland for any reference to a local education authority there shall be substituted a reference to an education authority within the meaning of section 145 of the Education (Scotland) Act 1962.

1962 c. 47.

26. (1) It shall be the duty of every local education authority to provide the Secretary of State at such times as he may direct with information on the provision made by that local education authority of special educational facilities for children who suffer from autism or other forms of early childhood psychosis.

Special educational treatment for children suffering from autism, &c.

(2) The arrangements made by a local education authority for the special educational treatment of children suffering from autism and other forms of early childhood psychosis shall, so far as is practicable, provide for the giving of such education in any school maintained or assisted by the local education authority.

(3) In the application of this section to Scotland for any reference to a local education authority there shall be substituted a reference to an education authority within the meaning of section 145 of the Education (Scotland) Act 1962.

27. (1) It shall be the duty of every local education authority to provide the Secretary of State at such times as he may direct with information on the provision made by that local education authority of special educational facilities for children who suffer from acute dyslexia.

Special educational treatment for children suffering from acute dyslexia.

(2) The arrangements made by a local education authority for the special educational treatment of children suffering from acute dyslexia shall, so far as is practicable, provide for the giving of such education in any school maintained or assisted by the local education authority.

(3) In the application of this section to Scotland for any reference to a local education authority there shall be substituted a reference to an education authority within the meaning of section 145 of the Education (Scotland) Act 1962.

28. Where it appears to the Secretary of State to be necessary or expedient to do so for the proper operation of any provision of this Act, he may by regulations made by statutory instrument, which shall be subject to annulment in pursuance of a resolution of either House of Parliament, make provision as to the interpretation for the purposes of that provision of any of the following expressions appearing therein, that is to say, 'chronically sick', 'chronic illness', 'disabled' and 'disability'.

Power to define certain expressions.

29. (1) This Act may be cited as the Chronically Sick and Disabled Persons Act 1970.

Short title, extent and commencement.

(2) Sections 1 and 2 of this Act do not extend to Scotland.¹

(3) Save as otherwise expressly provided by sections 9, 14 and 23, this Act does not extend to Northern Ireland.

(4) This Act shall come into force as follows:—

(*a*) sections 1 and 21 shall come into force on the day appointed thereunder;

(*b*) sections 4, 5, 6, 7 and 8 shall come into force at the expiration of six months beginning with the date this Act is passed;

(*c*) the remainder shall come into force at the expiration of three months beginning with that date.

NOTE

1. On 27 July 1972 these sections of the Act were extended to Scotland, this being the day upon which the Royal Assent was given to the Private Member's Bill introduced by Dr Dickson Mabon (M.P. for Greenock).

58. Resolution A.P. (72) 5: On the planning and equipment of buildings with a view to making them more accessible to the physically handicapped[*]

 COUNCIL OF EUROPE,
COUNCIL OF MINISTERS

The Representatives on the Committee of Ministers of Belgium. France, the Federal Republic of Germany, Italy, Luxembourg, the Netherlands, the United Kingdom of Great Britain and Northern Ireland, whose governments are parties to the Partial Agreement in the social and public health field, and the Representative of Austria, whose government has participated in the activities of the Joint Committee on the Rehabilitation and Resettlement of the Disabled of the above-mentioned Partial Agreement since 11 September 1962,

1. Having regard to the recommendation on the planning and equipment of buildings with a view to making them more accessible to the physically handicapped, adopted by the Joint Committee on the Rehabilitation and Resettlement of the Disabled on 30 June 1972;

2. Considering that, under the terms of its Statute, the aim of the Council of Europe is to achieve greater unity between its Members for the purpose of safeguarding and realising the ideals and principles which are their common heritage and facilitating their economic and social progress;

3. Having regard to the provisions of the Brussels Treaty signed 17 March 1948, by virtue of which Belgium, France, Luxembourg, the Netherlands and the United Kingdom of Great Britain and Northern Ireland declared themselves resolved to strengthen the social ties by which they are already united;

4. Having regard to the Protocol modifying and completing the Brussels Treaty, signed on 23 October 1954 by the signatory States of the Brussels Treaty, on the one hand, and the Federal Republic of Germany and Italy, on the other hand;

5. Observing that the seven governments parties to the Partial Agreement, which have resumed, within the Council of Europe, the social work hitherto undertaken by the Brussels Treaty Organisation and then by Western European Union, which derived from the Brussels Treaty as modified by the Protocol mentioned at paragraph 4 above, as well as the Government of Austria, which participates in the activities of the Joint Committee of the Rehabilitation and Resettlement of the Disabled, have always endeavoured to be in the forefront of progress in social matters and also in the associated field of public health and have for many years undertaken action towards harmonisation of their legislation;

6. Having regard to Recommendation XX adopted by the Joint Committee on the Rehabilitation and Resettlement of the Disabled in April 1959;

7. Believing that the rapid and continuing expansion of modern cities makes it necessary to build new residential centres according to modern planning principles;

8. Considering it desirable to make buildings more accessible to physically handicapped persons, who constitute an appreciable proportion of the population in each country,

I. Draw attention to measures which can be taken to construct or adapt new buildings in such a way as to facilitate access to and use of such buildings;

*Adopted by the Committee of Ministers on 16 October 1972 at the 214th meeting of the Ministers' Deputies

II. Recommend that governments of the seven States parties to the Partial Agreement and that of Austria should take all necessary measures, in particular those referred to in the appendix to this resolution, to ensure that public buildings, including privately-owned buildings to which the public has access. should be constructed and fitted out in such a way as to make them more accessible to the physically handicapped;

III. Invite the said governments to inform faculties of architecture and town planning and schools of building of the measures referred to in the appendix to this resolution.

Appendix to Resolution AP (72) 5
MEASURES TO BE TAKEN

I. Measures common to all buildings and installations used by the public

1. Entrance at road level, adequately wide, to permit the passage of wheel-chairs.

2. All communicating doors between different parts should be adequately wide (minimum width 0.90 m).

3. Straight staircases with broad steps to allow the use of crutches. No 'open' staircases.

4. Hand-rails wherever possible: on wide staircases a hand-rail in the middle. The hand-rails should be designed in such a way as to offer real support and an easy grip (maximum height 0.90 m).

5. For blind people, who usually find their way by means of hand-rails, these should, without interruption, stretch the whole length of the steps, on floors or landings.

6. Lifts wherever possible: doors and cages should be adequately wide (the cage should have a minimum length of 1.50 m and a minimum width of 1.20 m the door of the cabin should be at least 0.90 m wide; at stops on each floor there should be an automatic levelling system so that the cabin is on a level with the floor; the inside and outside doors should slide sideways automatically; the outside and inside control panels should have the highest button at a maximum height of 1.20 m from the ground; an interphone system should be installed in the cabin in addition to the alarm bell and placed at a maximum height of 1.20 m).

7. Level entrances and non-slip covering for staircases, ramps and corridors.

8. Rooms including toilets accessible to wheel-chair users should have a minimum free area of 1.40 m x 1.40 m so that wheel-chairs may be moved around. Entrance halls and corridors should have a minimum width of 1.40 m.

9. At least one lavatory of sufficient size on each floor, with a handgrip at a convenient height on the wall.

10. Telephone booths in all buildings and installations accessible to the public should be adequately wide (minimum 1.20 m x 1.20 m) and the telephone should be on the wall opposite the entrance at an appropriate height (a maximum of 0.90 m above the ground).

II. Specific measures for certain buildings

11. In post offices, theatres, banks, stations etc. there should be outside or inside counters at an appropriate height for handicapped persons in wheel-chairs.

12. There should be an adequate space between ticket offices and barriers: in stations, at sports grounds etc.; there should also be adequate space at the exits.

13. In cinemas, theatres etc. room for visitors sitting in wheel-chairs.

14. In public baths there should be facilities specially designed to meet the needs of handicapped persons.

15. Provision should be made in primary and secondary schools on staircases and in the corridors for a second hand-rail at a lower height proportionate to the average age of the users, in addition to the normal rail at the standard height of 0.90 m.

III. Provisions for parking

16. In public car parks areas should be set aside for vehicles designed for use by handicapped persons. There should be an adequately wide space for the vehicle (wheel-chairs etc.) to be got out of the car (minimum width 3 m divided into two functional areas: the first with a minimum width of 1.70 m for the space taken up by the car and the second with a minimum width of 1.30 m to permit the handicapped person to move freely when leaving or entering the car).

The area of the car park set aside should display the appropriate international sign, which should also be attached to handicapped persons' vehicles.

Index